STUDIES IN EVANGELICAL HISTORY

John Wesley's Preachers

A Social and Statistical Analysis of the British and Irish Preachers Who Entered the Methodist Itinerancy before 1791

STUDIES IN EVANGELICAL HISTORY AND THOUGHT

A full listing of titles in this series
appears at the end of this book

STUDIES IN EVANGELICAL HISTORY AND THOUGHT

Commendations

'John Lenton is to be highly commended for this most comprehensive and exhaustive examination of the early Methodist preachers to date. No serious scholar of early Methodism should be without this encyclopedic work that is of critical importance for many years to come.'
Paul W. Chilcote, Professor of Historical Theology & Wesleyan Studies, Director, Center for Applied Wesleyan Studies, Ashland Theological Seminary OH

'John Lenton knows more about Wesley's lay preachers than anyone else and this book is the fruit of many years' research. Lenton examines the 'life cycle' of the early preachers, from their background, their education and training, their marriage and family lives, to their work on the circuits, their role at Conference, their task in North America and their efforts as missionaries. Moving the historical analysis away from the study of Wesley himself to a proper appreciation of the crucial role of the lay preachers, this will be a vital resource for those interested in the spread of early Methodism.'
Jeremy Gregory, Senior Lecturer, The University of Manchester

'An important work that needs to be made available to scholars.'
Richard P. Heitzenrater, Divinity School, Duke University NC

'I enjoyed reading this. An amazing amount of useful information, simply unavailable anywhere else. A real service to scholarship.'
David Hempton, Harvard University

STUDIES IN EVANGELICAL HISTORY AND THOUGHT

'A thoroughly scholarly work which frequently added to my knowledge and challenged my assumptions. He has placed his subject in a solid historical context. On the preachers he draws on a mass of primary material and this and his systematic analysis produces a work which renders all previous (and imperfect) treatments obsolete. It sets a standard which one cannot imagine being superseded or even revised for years to come. He casts much fresh light on early Methodism generally. Too much early Methodist history has depended on treatment of Wesley seen through his extensive writings. Here, much that we now learn about the preachers throws light on the nature and variety of rank and file Methodism. This is a really major contribution to the understanding of early Methodism generally.'
Henry Rack, Manchester University

'This book offers a fresh approach to the study of early Methodism. Through a detailed analysis of the 800 mainly lay men who served Methodism within the lifetime of John Wesley, Lenton goes beyond the leader on horseback, whose exploits are so well chronicled in his celebrated *Journal* as he circulated round the country, to do justice to the officers in the field who sustained and developed Wesley's work week by week as they proceeded on horse or on foot around the smaller circuits marked out for their preaching tours. Who these men were, where they came from, how and where they operated, how they married, worked, retired and died, are questions tackled systematically and quantitatively. These preachers were the circulating life blood of early Methodism and their story is here told in a manner which both does justice to their labours and opens up for the reader a new understanding of what Methodism was and how it was spread.'
Edward Royle, Emeritus Professor of History, University of York

'The lay preachers employed by John Wesley played a vital part in the growth of early Methodism. Treatment of them has been largely anecdotal. Their varied social, educational and religious background have not hitherto been analysed in the way in which John Lenton has examined them in this detailed study.'
John A. Vickers, Editor, *Dictionary of Methodism*

John Wesley, supported by the Edinburgh Assistant Joseph Cole and the Local Preacher Dr James Hamilton. 'Drawn as they were walking in the Street at Edinburgh in the year 1790 by an eminent Artist. Originally engraved and published by Chas. Seymour 131, Digbeth Birmingham.'

Images from the Wesley Historical Society Library, Oxford Brookes University. Used with permission from the Wesley Historical Society, with thanks to Peter Forsaith.

STUDIES IN EVANGELICAL HISTORY AND THOUGHT

John Wesley's Preachers

A Social and Statistical Analysis of the British and Irish Preachers Who Entered the Methodist Itinerancy before 1791

John Lenton

Foreword by Richard P. Heitzenrater

Paternoster:
thinking faith

MILTON KEYNES · COLORADO SPRINGS · HYDERABAD

Copyright © John Lenton 2009

First published 2009 by Paternoster

Paternoster is an imprint of Authentic Media
9 Holdom Avenue, Bletchley, Milton Keynes, MK1 1QR
1820 Jet Stream Drive, Colorado Springs, CO 80921, USA
OM Authentic Media, Medchal Road, Jeedimetla Village
Secunderabad 500 055, India

www.authenticmedia.co.uk
Authentic Media is a Division of IBS-STL UK, a company limited by guarantee
(registered charity no. 270162)

15 14 13 12 11 10 09   7 6 5 4 3 2 1

The right of John Lenton to be identified as the Author of this Work
has been asserted by him in accordance with the Copyright, Designs
and Patents Act 1988.

All rights reserved. No part of this publication may be reproduced, stored in a retrieval system, or transmitted, in any form or by any means, electronic, mechanical, photocopying, recording or otherwise, without the prior permission of the publisher or a license permitting restricted copying. In the UK such licenses are issued by the Copyright Licensing Agency, 90 Tottenham Court Road, London W1P 9HE.

British Library Cataloguing in Publication Data
A catalogue record for this book is available from the British Library

ISBN 978-1-84227-625-9

Typeset by J. H. Lenton and E. J. Ibbotson
Printed and bound in Great Britain
by AlphaGraphics Nottingham

STUDIES IN EVANGELICAL HISTORY AND THOUGHT

Series Preface

The Evangelical movement has been marked by its union of four emphases: on the Bible, on the cross of Christ, on conversion as the entry to the Christian life and on the responsibility of the believer to be active. The present series is designed to publish scholarly studies of any aspect of this movement in Britain or overseas. Its volumes include social analysis as well as exploration of Evangelical ideas. The books in the series consider aspects of the movement shaped by the Evangelical Revival of the eighteenth century, when the impetus to mission began to turn the popular Protestantism of the British Isles and North America into a global phenomenon. The series aims to reap some of the rich harvest of academic research about those who, over the centuries, have believed that they had a gospel to tell to the nations.

Series Editors

David Bebbington, Professor of History, University of Stirling, Stirling, Scotland, UK

John H. Y. Briggs, Senior Research Fellow in Ecclesiastical History and Director of the Centre for Baptist History and Heritage, Regent's Park College, Oxford, UK

Timothy Larsen, McManis Professor Christian Thought, Wheaton College, Illinois, USA

Mark A. Noll, McAnaney Professor of History, University of Notre Dame, Notre Dame, Indiana, USA

Ian M. Randall, Senior Research Fellow, International Baptist Theological Seminary, Prague, Czech Republic

To my dear wife Chris, who has for a long time lived with 'John Wesley's Preachers' and read many different versions.

Contents

List of Maps, Charts, Timelines and Tables	xviii
Foreword by Richard P. Heitzenrater	xxi
Acknowledgements	xxiii
Abbreviations	xxv
Chapter 1 Introduction	**1**
Great Britain and her Empire	2
Reasons for the Lay Preachers	3
Focus of the Book	9
Sources	11
Chapter 2 Definitions	**21**
The Evangelical Revival	21
Spirituality	26
'Methodist'	29
Cohorts	31
Who was the First Lay Preacher?	32
Women Preachers	33
Titles	35
'Church Methodists'	37
Chapter 3 Origins	**39**
Countries	39
Counties	40
Religious Upbringing	44
Origins by Class	46
Illegitimacy	49
Where were They Converted?	50
Foreign Descent	52
Stories of Origin	54
Conclusion	55

Chapter 4 Education — 57
Standard of Education — 57
Levels of Earlier Education and Age at Leaving School — 59
Need for Education? — 61
Wesley's Policy — 62

Chapter 5 Probation — 73
'On Trial' to 'Full Connexion' — 73
Age at Entry — 77
Probation and Marriage — 80
Becoming an Assistant Young — 81
Probation in their *own* Circuit — 83
Starting Probation during the Year — 85

Chapter 6 Marriage — 87
Marriage in the Eighteenth Century — 87
Preachers Married at Entry — 89
Proportions Married — 90
Wesley's Rules on Marriage — 94
Allowances for Wives — 95
Wife 'Desertion' — 97
Age at Marriage — 99
'Wealthy Wives' and Motives for Marrying — 101
Remarriages — 105
Wives' Roles in Methodism — 106
Place of Marriage — 107
Remaining Unmarried — 107

Chapter 7 Family — 109
Allowances — 109
The Wesleys — 110
Childbirth and Infant Mortality — 111
Education and Training for the Children — 113
Parental Control — 115
Daughters — 118
Size of Families — 119
Care for Families — 119
Other Family Relationships — 123

Chapter 8 Circuits — 127
Travel — 127
Preachers and Circuits — 127
Duties of the Preacher — 129
Wesley's Organization — 136

Contents

The Preacher in his Circuit	142
Portraits and Appearance	149
Conclusion	151

Chapter 9 Conference — 153
Introduction	153
What Happened at Conference	158
Later Developments	164

Chapter 10 Wales, Scotland, Isle of Man, Channel Islands — 173
Wales	173
Scotland	180
Isle of Man	185
Channel Islands	190
Conclusion	193

Chapter 11 Ireland — 195
Introduction	195
Wesley's Policy in Ireland: John Smith	196
Origins of the Preachers	198
Entry, Education and Marriage	206
Development of Methodism	208
Richard Bourke and Charles Graham	212
After Wesley	213
Conclusion	218

Chapter 12 America to 1778 — 219
Introduction	219
Pilmore and Boardman	222
Asbury, Rankin and Shadford	230
British Preachers and the War	235

Chapter 13 America from 1778 — 243
Asbury, the American Preachers and the War	243
Coke, Asbury and the New British Preachers	247
Growth and Changes in American Methodism	254
Asbury's Later Years	259

Chapter 14 Missionaries — 265
Introduction	265
Selection of Missionaries	269
Training and Formation	274
Why Were There so Many from Ireland?	275
The West Indies	276

xvi   *Contents*

The Maritimes	280
Marriage and Family	283
Death, Leaving or Return	284
Finance, Organization and Thomas Coke	286
Conclusion	288
Chapter 15 Why Did Men Leave?	**291**
Introduction	291
Reasons for Leaving	292
Conclusion	308
Chapter 16 Numbers and Destinations of Leavers	**311**
Numbers of Leavers over Time	311
The Leaving Process	312
Destinations of Leavers	315
Common Patterns	329
Chapter 17 Preachers Returning to the Itinerancy	**331**
Introduction	331
Charles and John	332
Early 1750s	335
Preachers Administering Communion	338
Examples of Leniency	339
Wesley's Leniency	344
After Wesley	347
Conclusion	348
Chapter 18 Ordination	**349**
Introduction	349
Wesley's Change of Mind	350
Ordinations under Wesley	355
After Wesley	359
Ordination by Conference 1836	361
Conclusion	364
Chapter 19 Retirement	**367**
The Problem	367
Preachers' Fund	368
Being a Supernumerary	372
Superannuation	374
Individual Preachers in Retirement	375
Wesley and the Preachers' Fund	378
Reasons for and against Retirement	378
Where Retired Preachers Lived	380

After Wesley	381

Chapter 20 Death — **385**
Introduction	385
Death while on Circuit	386
Age at Death	387
Reasons for Death	388
Deathbeds	394
Wills	397
Burials and Ceremonies Following Death	397
Obituaries	400
Conclusion	401

Chapter 21 Conclusion — **403**
Introduction	403
Jesuits?	404
Mission Preaching and Methods	405
The Preachers and Wesley	408
Methodism After Wesley	412
Standards	419
Rewriting Methodist History	420
History of Methodism and the Preachers	420
Wesley's Preachers: Wesley's Memorial	421

Appendix One: Tables — **423**

Appendix Two: Total Numbers — **441**
Early Preachers and Differences between the Cohorts	441
Numbers who Entered Each Year	448
Wesley's Empirical World View	449
Length of Service	450

Appendix Three: List of Preachers in the Database — **453**

Bibliography — **461**

General Index — **485**

LIST OF MAPS, CHARTS, TIMELINES AND TABLES

LIST OF MAPS

Map 1:	Birthplaces of Wesley's Preachers	41
Map 2:	Yarm Circuit 1768	138
Map 3:	West Tyrone	201

LIST OF CHARTS

Chart 1:	Wesley's Preachers by Cohort	31
Chart 2:	Wesley's Preachers by Country of Birth	39
Chart 3:	Preachers by Religious Upbringing	45
Chart 4:	Wesley's Preachers by Class	46
Chart 5:	Education Where Known of Wesley's Preachers	60
Chart 6:	Wesley's Preachers: Age at Leaving Education	61
Chart 7:	Age at Entry	78
Chart 8:	Percentage Married by Cohort	90
Chart 9:	Legal Hundred by Cohort	167
Chart 10:	Numbers of Preachers Who Left Each Year	311
Chart 11:	Percentages Leaving by Cohort	312
Chart 12:	Number of Preachers Who Returned	331
Chart 13:	Preachers' Fund	369
Chart 14:	Wesley's Preachers: Number of Deaths at Any Age	388
Chart 15:	Numbers of Years Travelled on Circuit	450

LIST OF TIMELINES

Timeline 1:	Conference	154
Timeline 2:	Britain's Periphery	179
Timeline 3:	Methodist Preachers in America	225
Timeline 4:	Missionaries	268
Timeline 5:	Ordinations	351

LIST OF TABLES

Table 1:	Wesley's Preachers by Cohort	423
Table 2:	Wesley's Preachers by Countries of Birth	423
Table 3:	Wesley's Preachers by English Counties of Birth	424
Table 4:	Wesley's Preachers by Region of Origin	425
Table 5:	Wesley's Preachers by Religious Upbringing	425
Table 6:	Wesley's Preachers by Class	426
Table 7:	Standard of Education of Wesley's Preachers	426
Table 8:	Wesley's Preachers' Age at Leaving School	426
Table 9:	Age of Wesley's Preachers on Entry	427
Table 10:	Marriage Totals by Cohort	427
Table 11:	Age at Marriage of Preachers and Their Wives	428
Table 12:	County of Birth for Wesley's Preachers: British Isles outside England	429
Table 13:	Irish Membership Growth by Circuit 1799-1802	430
Table 14:	Irish Preachers' Fund Payments Recorded in the British *Minutes*	431
Table 15:	Reasons Why Wesley's Preachers Left (by Cohort)	432
Table 16:	English Preachers Leaving by Area	433
Table 17:	Wesley's Preachers: Numbers Left	434
Table 18:	Destination of Leavers among Wesley's Preachers	435
Table 19:	Wesley's Preachers: Returners by Cohort	435
Table 20:	Dates of Return of Wesley's Preachers	436
Table 21:	Wesley's Preachers: Number of Deaths at Any Age	437
Table 22:	Wesley's Preachers: Numbers Received On Trial and Total Number of Preachers	438
Table 23:	Wesley's Preachers: Length of Service/Number of Years Travelled on Circuit	439

Foreword

Many stories about early Methodism focus on the characters who formed the living matrix of the movement — the preachers. Many of these 'circuit riders' followed Wesley's pattern of riding tens of thousands of miles and preaching thousands of times in their lifetime. Others persisted as preachers in the Methodist connexion for only a short time. Many of the former became well known in the connexion; others have met a less illustrious fate. Some are remembered for their unique contributions to the movement; a few have been nearly forgotten or lost in a maze of misinformation and confusion.

In the world of Wesley studies scholars rely on a growing supply of research materials that are beginning to provide the sort of information that is necessary to do first-rate historical scholarship. The last generation relied heavily on Frank Baker for accurate information about a host of topics in early Wesleyan history, including the preachers. John Lenton has benefited from that legacy and has taken the topic into the next level of usefulness. In this work he presents the latest and best information possible on the itinerant preachers.

Those who have tried to trace grass-roots Methodism in the eighteenth century, or perhaps have tried to trace genealogical information about their own elusive relatives, can appreciate the difficulties entailed in such a task as this. Lack of documentation, similarities in names, ambiguities about locations, and many similar problems confound the task. The appearance of this volume will make the writing of reliable Methodist history much easier for all and will help focus the spotlight on those who represent the heart of the Wesleyan movement — the preachers called Methodists.

Richard P. Heitzenrater
Duke University, NC
August 2008

Acknowledgements

The author's acknowledgements are mostly at the appropriate part in the text. However, special mention needs to be made of the late Frank Baker who created and worked on a great folder about the preachers over a fifty year period and handed it on to me, of Dick Heitzenrater who has continued to encourage me to publish, of Henry Rack and John Vickers who have read the book and suggested improvements (John also supplied the index), of Peter Forsaith who supplied the images for cover and frontispiece and of many other friends who have discussed preachers with me. I have benefited from the help of all my family, but special mention should be made of my daughter Esther Ibbotson who has advised on presentation, produced the maps and managed the pre-press, and of my son-in-law Tom Ibbotson who has improved both charts and tables. None of them have any responsibility for any errors. I am grateful to the publishers Paternoster and especially to Anthony R. Cross for his guidance on consistency of presentation.

John Lenton
Wellington, Telford, Shropshire, UK
August 2008

Abbreviations

AC	*Alumni Cantabrigienses.*
AO	*Alumni Oxonienses.*
AM	*Arminian Magazine.*
Asbury Jol	E. T. Clark, J. M. Payton and J. S. Potts eds. *F. Asbury, Journals and Letters* (London: Epworth, 1958).
Atmore	C. Atmore, *The Methodist Memorial* (London: Hamilton Adams, rev. ed. 1871).
Bennet MSS	John Bennet MSS at MARC BNNJ Colman box.
Church 1948	L. F. Church, *Early Methodist People* (London: Epworth, 1948).
Church 1949	*More About The Early Methodist People* (London: Epworth, 1949).
CJ	MS Conference Journal at MARC.
CMHA	*Cornish Methodist Historical Association Journal* (1960-).
CMHS	Canadian Methodist Historical Society.
CWJ	T. Jackson, ed, *Charles Wesley's Journal* (repr. Kansas City: Beacon Hill Press, 1980).
CWP	G. Lloyd, ed, *Charles Wesley Papers* (Manchester: MARC, 1994).
Crk	C. H. Crookshank, *Days of Revival: History of Methodism in Ireland* (Clonmel: Tentmaker, 1994).
Crk (1882)	*Memorable Women of Irish Methodism* (London: W.M. Bookroom, 1882).
Crowther	J. Crowther, *A True and Complete Portraiture of Methodism.* (London: Edwards, 2nd ed. 1815).
DEB	D. Lewis ed, *Blackwell Dictionary of Evangelical Biography 1730-1860* (Oxford: Blackwell, 1995).
DNB	*Dictionary of National Biography* (Oxford: OUP, 1886).
DOMBI	J. A. Vickers ed, *A Dictionary of Methodism in Britain and Ireland* (Peterborough: MPH, 2000).
DWB	*Dictionary of Welsh Biography* (London: Honourable Society of Cymmrodorion, 1959).
Dyson (1865)	J. B. Dyson, *Methodism in the Isle of Wight* (Ventnor: Burt, 1865).
EMP	T. Jackson ed, *Early Methodist Preachers* (London: WCO, 1865).

e.m.	entered ministry
Ev. Mag.	*Evangelical Magazine.*
FB 'Origins'	F. Baker, 'The Origins of Methodism in the West Indies: The Story of the Gilbert Family' *LQ & HR* Jan 1960 8-17.
FB 'Polity'	F. Baker, 'Polity' in *HMGB* 1: 213-255.
FHS	Family History Society.
Gallagher *JB*	R. H. Gallagher, *John Bredin: Roman Catholic Schoolmaster and Methodist Preacher* (Belfast: WHS(I), 1960).
GHR	J. W. Laycock, *Methodist Heroes of the Great Haworth Round 1734-1784* (Keighley: Rydal Press, 1909).
Hayman	J. G. Hayman, *A History of the .Methodist Revival of the Last Century in...North Devon* (London: WCO, 1881).
Heitzenrater	R. P. Heitzenrater, *Wesley and the People Called Methodists* (Nashville: Abingdon, 1995).
HMGB	R. E. Davies, A. R. George and E. G. Rupp eds, *History of Methodism in Great Britain* (London: Epworth, 1965-88).
ICA	*Irish Christian Advocate* (1883-1971).
IGI	*International Genealogical Index* (accessed 4/5/1996) http://www.familysearch.org/Eng/Search/
Ives	A. G. Ives, *Kingswood School in Wesley's Day and Since* (London: Epworth, 1969).
JEH	*Journal of Ecclesiastical History.*
JB's Minutes	*John Bennet's Copy of the Minutes of the Conferences of 1744, 1745, 1746, 1747 and 1748; with Wesley's copy of those for 1746* (London WHS 1896) WHS Occasional Publication No. 1.
JICH	*Journal of Imperial and Commonwealth History.*
JRULMB	*John Rylands University Library of Manchester Bulletin.*
JWJ(C)	N. Curnock ed., *John Wesley's Journal* (London: Epworth, 1938).
JWL	J. Telford ed., *John Wesley's Letters* (London: Epworth, 1931).
KBG	K. B. Garlick, *Mr Wesley's Preachers* (London: Pinhorns, 1977).
KOGU	Kingswood and Old Grovians Union.
KS Reg	*Kingswood Register* (Frome: KOGU, 1910).
Lednum	J. Lednum, *A History of the Rise of Methodism in America* (Philadelphia: the author, 1859).
LQ & HR	*London Quarterly and Holborn Review.*
Lyth	J. Lyth, *Glimpses of Early Methodism in York* (York: Sessions, 1885).
MARC	Methodist Archives and Research Centre.
MH	*Methodist History.*
MHB	*Methodist Hymn Book* (London: Methodist Conference Office, 1933).
MM	*Methodist Magazine.*
MM(I)	*Methodist Magazine* (Irish edition) (1804-22).
MNC Mag.	*Methodist New Connexion Magazine.*

Minutes MCA	Minutes of the Methodist Conferences Annually held in America 1773 to 1813 Inclusive (New York: Hitt and Ward, 1813)
Moore CI	R. D. Moore, *Methodism in the Channel Isles* (London: Epworth, 1952).
MPH	Methodist Publishing House
MRWN	*Methodist Recorder Winter Number*
Myles	W. Myles, *A Chronological History of the People called Methodists,* (London: Cordeux, 4th ed. 1813).
Pawson L	J. Bowmer and J. A. Vickers eds, *The Letters of John Pawson,* (Peterborough: WMHS, 1996).
PMM	*Primitive Methodist Magazine.*
PPIM	R. H. Gallagher, *Pioneer Preachers in Irish Methodism,* (Belfast: WHS (I), 1965).
PWMM	*Primitive Wesleyan Methodist Magazine*
PWHS	*Proceedings of the Wesley Historical Society*
Rack	H. D. Rack, *Reasonable Enthusiast* (Peterborough: Epworth, 2nd ed. 2002).
Seymour	A. C. H. Seymour, *The Life and Times of Selina, Countess of Huntingdon* 2 vols (London: Painter, 1839-40).
Sidelights	B. Gregory, *Sidelights on the Conflicts in Wesleyan Methodism* (London: Cassell, 1898).
Simon	J. S. Simon, *John Wesley* (London: Epworth, 1921-8).
SJR	S. J. Rogal, *A Biographical Dictionary of 18th Century Methodism* (Metuchen: Scarecrow, 1997-99).
Smith Meth	G. Smith, *History of Wesleyan Methodism* (London: Longmans, 1857-61).
Smith *Raithby*	Mary Smith, *Raithby Hall* (London: Wertheim, 1859).
Smith *Ireland*	W. Smith, *History of Wesleyan Methodism in Ireland* (Dublin: Doolittle, 1830).
SMU	Southern Methodist University.
Smyth	David Smyth, MSS 'Short Account of the Life of the Late John Smyth Methodist Preacher' in MARC (C 319 Diaries box STS).
SOAS	School of Oriental and African Studies.
Sprague *Annals*	W. B. Sprague, *Annals of the American Pulpit* vol VII (Methodist) (New York: Carter, 1970).
Taft Diary	MSS Diary of Mrs Mary Taft in Birmingham University Library (copy at MARC).
Taft Memoirs	*Memoirs of the Life of Mrs Mary Taft: formerly Miss Barritt, Written by Herself* (London: the author, 1827).
TRHS	*Transactions of the Royal Historical Society.*
Turner HBA	J. H. Turner, *Halifax Books and Authors* (Halifax 1906).
Tyerman	L. Tyerman, *Life of John Wesley* London: Hodder, 1870-71).
Tyerman BMM	L. Tyerman, MSS Biographies of Methodist Ministers 'A-D' in MARC, MAB B 1234 onwards.
Wakeley	J. B. Wakeley, *Lost Chapters Recovered From The Early History of American Methodism* (New York: Carlton, 1858).

W. Banner	Wesley Banner.
WCO	Wesleyan Conference Office
WHS	Wesley Historical Society.
WHS Br	Bulletin of the Bristol Branch of the WHS.
WHS Cul	Wesley Historical Society Cumbria Journal.
WHS (I)	Bulletin of the Irish Branch of the WHS.
WHS (LC)	Journal of the Lancashire and Cheshire Branch.
WHS (Lond)	Bulletin of the London and Home Counties Branch.
WHS NE	Wesley Historical Society North East Branch Bulletin.
WHS N. Lancs	North Lancashire WHS Branch Bulletin.
WHS Scotland	WHS Scotland Journal.
WHS Shropshire	WHS Shropshire Branch Bulletin
WJW	F. Baker ed, *The Works of John Wesley* (Oxford and Nashville: OUP and Abingdon, Bicentennial Edition 1965-).
WMM	Wesleyan Methodist Magazine.
WMHS	World Methodist Historical Society.
WMMS	Wesleyan Methodist Missionary Society.
WMMS (RJ)	Wesleyan Methodist Missionary Society, The Report of the Jubilee Fund of the Wesleyan Missionary Society 1863-8 (London: WMMS, 1869).

Chapter 1

Introduction

> 'Jesus, the Truth, and Power Divine,
> Send forth this Messenger of Thine,
> His Hands confirm, his Heart inspire,
> And touch his Lips with hallow'd Fire.'
> Charles Wesley: 'for a Minister, going forth to preach.'[1]

In 1761, when the Sheffield Methodist Mary Midgeley lay dying in her home, 'The Mr. Wesleys & the Preachers were much laid upon her Mind.'[2] For her and the ordinary Methodist a mere twenty years after the genesis of Methodism, the Wesley brothers and their preachers were important and inextricably linked. As time went on the preachers became more important, as first Charles and then John ceased to travel.

This book is about those preachers whom John Wesley called his 'Sons in the Gospel,' their lives, their importance in the Methodist movement and their wider significance. It concentrates on those who entered in Wesley's lifetime; they had begun their work by 1791. The book is arranged in a chronological fashion so far as the preachers' lives are concerned. After introductory and defining chapters there is a chapter on their origins from birth to conversion, then ones on their probation in the itinerancy, their marriage and their families. There are two central sections on circuits and Conference, the life of the itinerant and the consequent organization which has supplied much of the evidence about that life. Four chapters deal with the widening nature of the itinerants' task as they fanned out from their original base, England, to Wales, Scotland, Ireland and then outside the British Isles to America, the other colonies and beyond. There are several sections on those who left the itinerancy and later returned to it. A chapter follows on ordination, after which there are two on retirement and death, and a conclusion. Statistical tables are in Appendix One, details on total numbers in Appendix Two and a list of all the preachers in Appendix Three.

---

[1] The verse is from C. Wesley, *Hymns and Sacred Poems* (Bristol: Farley, 1749) vol 1 pt 2, 302, a reference I owe to Dick Watson.
[2] Mary Midgeley's story is in MS Letter of Francis Gilbert London to Charles Wesley 7th November 1761 at MARC JRULM DDPr 1/32, 2-3.

Great Britain and her Empire

Great Britain from 1714 was under the rule of the Hanoverian Kings and their Whig governments. The term 'Great Britain,' invented in 1707, was merely a name for 'greater England.' No eighteenth century monarch went to Wales, Scotland or Ireland, though George I and George II frequently visited their native Hanover.[3] Britain was the entrepot for a large, flourishing and diverse empire. Her ships brought home raw materials from the empire and much of these, like sugar, were refined or otherwise processed and re-shipped to other European countries. In return finished goods were sent back to the colonies. The population was growing steadily, with the chief development being the growth of cities and urban areas. The British Isles were not united. In the important matter of religion, divisions reigned. A majority of the inhabitants of England were Anglican, belonging to the official Established Church, but there were Roman Catholic and Dissenting minorities including Independents, Presbyterians, Baptists, and Quakers, though these were in decline. What strength they had lay particularly in the remoter areas from London where the government lacked effective methods of enforcing its laws about religion and religious practice. When it came to religion these areas could be neglected. Cornwall, for example, had no local Bishop but was run ecclesiastically from distant Exeter. In the Pennine Dales there were large parishes such as Halifax and Whalley, unaltered since the Reformation, and unable to cope with the growth of the population. Huguenots and other foreign Protestants formed significant minorities in some parts of London, port towns and elsewhere. All but Anglicans were excluded from local and national government and the two English universities.

However, in comparison with most of Europe, Britain was a tolerant society as Voltaire had noted in the early eighteenth century, and this tolerance was to contribute to the rise of Methodism. Outside the British Isles the haphazard empire which had been developing for more than a century, especially the growing colonies on the American eastern seaboard, was also religiously diverse. It lacked religious provision in most areas which was the reason why the Wesley brothers went to America briefly, if ingloriously, in the 1730s.[4]

---

[3] The last English king to set foot in Ireland was William III in 1690 to reconquer it.

[4] For Britain and the Empire in the eighteenth century see the classic work which has altered perceptions, L. Colley, *Britons: Forging the Nation 1707-1837* (New Haven: Yale UP, 1992). Also valuable is R. B. Winks, ed, *The Oxford History of the British Empire. Vol 4: Historiography* (Oxford: OUP, 1999). See also M. A. Noll, *The Rise of Evangelicalism* (Manchester: IVP, 2004), Chapter 1 'Landscapes.' For religion in Europe see R. Remond, *Religion and Society in Modern Europe* (Oxford: Blackwell, 1999) 36, 131-2. Bill Gibson comments that the numbers of foreign Protestants were never significant, but see Chapter 3 below.

Scotland, Wales, Ireland

In Scotland and Ireland the Gaelic language was declining and English was used by the ruling classes except in the Scottish Highlands. In Wales Welsh was still the majority tongue, though again the ruling classes used English. Only Ireland had a parliament after 1707 and that was usually very much under English control. Scotland rejoiced in its clearly separate legal and educational systems. Scots universities were so good that they attracted English students, especially for key subjects such as medicine.

But in religion, again diversity was the rule. Strength lay in the divisions rather than any unity. Scotland had an established Presbyterian national Church, but there were significant pockets of Catholicism in the Highlands and of the Episcopal Church in the North East. In Ireland 75-80% were Roman Catholic. In the Protestant minority half were Scots Presbyterians, mostly in the north. The established 'Anglican' church had the livings and the church buildings, but in most places not the people. Only in Wales was there a majority for the established (Anglican) Church. The anglicizing pressure of the early eighteenth century led to the great reaction and revival which made Wales literate and (by 1850) Nonconformist. As Hempton said 'In 1750 the Established Churches in Britain accounted for over 90% of all churchgoers. The proportions had altered dramatically by the time of the census on public worship in 1851.' Nowhere by 1851 had the established churches more than 50%. In Ireland barely 10% were in the Church of Ireland. Diversity was increasing throughout this period, partly because of increased mobility in the population as transport improved.[5]

Reasons for the Lay Preachers

The Church of England

At the time and since Evangelicals have concentrated on explaining the failings of the Church. Recent research has centred on defending the eighteenth century Church and showing that it should be compared favourably to the seventeenth century rather than (as in the past) unflatteringly to the nineteenth. Fewer than 10% in England were Roman Catholics or Dissenters. Historians today are both pessimistic and optimistic about the eighteenth century Church of England.

Pessimists point out that it was a Church that would find it almost impossible to change quickly to meet the new needs of a faster changing society. Bishops were independent of each other. Many were elderly as were

---

[5] S. Gilley and W. J. Shiels, eds, *A History of Religion in Britain: Practice and Belief from Pre-Roman Times to the Present* (Oxford: Blackwell, 1994); D. N. Hempton, *Religion and Political Culture in Britain and Ireland* (Cambridge: CUP, 1996); Noll, *Rise* 35-37. For Ireland see Chapter 11, for Scotland Wales and the Islands see Chapter 10 below.

their clergy in an age when nobody retired. Some Bishops concentrated on their political concerns. Half the livings in England in 1736 were below the clerical poverty line of £50 per year. Because the Church was poor, pluralism and non-residence were rife and increasing, and so common that they were hardly complained about. Many parishes, especially in the north and west, were parishes of scattered settlement which created problems for the incumbents of two or more chapelries. In these areas there were fewer churches and clergy per head of the growing population. In the large parish of Whalley in Lancashire, for example, the Church was progressively withdrawing from several long-established areas of its pastoral work. Tithes were perennial causes of conflict making clergy 'appear more like wolves than shepherds of the flock.' The Church had lost its Convocations for acting together, and found it difficult to decide on a united front to meet the developing Evangelical Revival. There were reforms and improvements like Queen Anne's Bounty, but they were uneven in effect and often late. The church courts, still effective in mid-century, suffered a decline of authority later. There were fewer diocesan visitations compared to the seventeenth century. Sacramental practice, seen as a sign of spiritual life, varied widely from diocese to diocese and even within dioceses.

Later in the century the clergy gained from the agricultural changes which increased their glebe and income from tithes, but this separated them more from their parishioners as their social status rose and they became tax men not pastors. Their learning improved as a higher proportion had attended the universities, but this also separated them from their parishioners. The clergy defined themselves as a closed calling, to which it became more difficult to gain access without the right qualifications. Clergy were unable to relinquish any control over worship to the laity. They were often suspicious of change and inflexible in resisting lay involvement in religious initiatives. They refused to countenance the idea of lay preachers. Their view of the Methodist preachers in this book can be summarized as one of contempt.

The Church of England was perhaps at its lowest ebb around 1750. In addition to differences between north and south and town and countryside there were areas which were so remote that they had all but been forgotten. This applied not only to the colonies, theoretically under the charge of the Bishop of London, but to islands and other remote areas (like Cornwall or Cumbria) which were also neglected by the Church. The Church regarded them as backwaters neither deserving nor needing any help. Even the active Bishop Thomas Wilson in the Isle of Man made little impression on the fact that clergymen did not want to go there, because the money was less than elsewhere. Such places were thus liable to suffer from a shortage of trained men to serve the Church. Whether it was the new rapidly-growing industrial areas or rural backwaters, the Church was in no position to care properly for the religious needs of many communities.[6]

However, optimists emphasize that the Church was trying to improve, and in many respects succeeding. Its chief rival from the previous century, Dissent, was in decline for most of the century. Compared to the church in 1660 the eighteenth century church was certainly improving. Its own spirituality did not decline. Christian beliefs were almost universal and strongly influenced folk religion. An individual such as that notorious borough monger and leading politician the first Duke of Newcastle prepared as carefully for the sacrament as for parliamentary elections. The Church's concern for those in need and for mission, expressed through the religious societies and groups, like the Society for Promoting Christian Knowledge and the Society for the Propagation of the Gospel, can be shown to be stronger and more effective than in the previous century. Most people, even among those forced to leave it, wanted to remain within the national church. It was seen as, and indeed was, the foundation of the State and a leading instrument of government. There was much loyalty towards the local parish. Hence Wesley and the early Methodists were often attacked by local clergy and others as Jacobites, opposed to the political establishment. By 1791 Methodists were to be accused of supporting the French Revolution.

The Church's diocesan Bishops were usually men who cared about their charges and worked hard to improve the church's services within their dioceses, as evidenced by regular confirmations, ordinations and visitations. They set clear objectives for themselves and their clergy. The clergy served even remote parishes when they were unable to reside. There was much clerical fraternity, consensus and cooperation. Many new churches were built and more were enlarged; galleries were installed, true of most Lancashire churches, for example. The Church was, in Cobbett's phrase, everywhere. There was a strand of local clerically directed reforms aimed at improving the Church's structures, admittedly sporadic in the eighteenth century. Towns and northern parishes were likely to have more services. Some recent studies have shown the Church in some areas of Lancashire to be particularly prosperous and improving. There is evidence of much significant lay activity. It was a Church which remained more united than it had been in the previous century, or was to be afterwards. Wesley himself deliberately insisted that Methodists remain within the Church.

---

[6] See especially the sources quoted in J. Gregory and J. S. Chamberlain, eds, *The National Church in Local Perspective* (Woodbridge: Boydell, 2003) 1-27, 263. Particularly useful also are J. D. Walsh, 'The Church and Anglicanism in the long Eighteenth Century' in J. D. Walsh, C. Haydon, and S. Taylor, eds, *The Church of England c1689-c1833* (Cambridge: CUP, 1993) 1-64; P. Virgin, *The Church in an Age of Negligence: Ecclesiastical Structure and Problems of Church Reform 1700-1840* (Cambridge: Clark, 1989); D. Rosman, *The Evolution of the English Churches 1500-2000* (Cambridge: CUP, 2002), especially 136-146; D. A. Spaeth, *The Church in an Age of Danger* (Cambridge: CUP, 2000) 6-11, 56-7, 59-82, 133-4. The quotation on tithes is from Spaeth, *Church in Danger* 134, see 149 for taxmen and pastors. Queen Anne's Bounty improved the poorer clergy's living standards from 1704.

Optimists suggest that the growth of Methodism was itself a sign of the new life within the Church.[7]

Growth of Methodism

By 1815 Britain had emerged from her longest period of wars as the unchallenged ruler of the seas and strongest commercial country in the world. Methodism was still relatively weak with 181,709 members in Britain who amounted to only 2.2 % of the total population.[8] But it had become a major influence in the large parts of the empire that remained after 1776, and it was poised in America to become the largest denomination as the newly independent nation expanded across the continent. At this period and on into the twentieth century historians believe that Methodist adherents were something like four or five to every one member. Joseph Entwisle in 1797 wrote that 'In the 3 Kingdoms upwards of 90,000 persons have united in Christian fellowship, and perhaps, more than four times that number constantly attend preaching & approve of the doctrines they hear.' Solid evidence is available, in studies based on the 1851 Religious Census, which shows that between three and four times the number of Methodist members were actually worshipping on Census day. Those worshipping occasionally and those ill and unable to attend mean that the total number of adherents was likely to be more than five times the number of members. At Sampford Peverell in Devon, for example, there were forty Wesleyan Methodist members in 1850. The 1851 Census shows 140 seated there in the morning and 170 at night. Some of the morning and evening attenders would have been the same, but five times the number of members would seem to be a low estimate.[9] The number influenced by Methodism, therefore, was far larger than the number of members reported.

---

[7] For parish activity see J. Gregory, 'The Eighteenth Century Reformation' in Walsh, *Church* 67-85. For diocesan activity see J. Gregory, *Restoration, Reformation and Reform 1660-1828* (Oxford: Clarendon, 2001), and J. Jago, *Visitation Studies in the Diocese of York* (London: Chapman, 1999) for Archbishop Drummond. For unity and the objectives of the episcopate see W. Gibson, *The Church of England 1688-1832* (London: Routledge, 2001). I am grateful to Bill Gibson for his comments on these sections, which have improved them, though he would not agree with all my views.

[8] R. Currie, A. Gilbert and L. Horsley, *Churches and Churchgoers: Patterns of Church Growth in the British Isles since 1700* (Oxford: Clarendon, 1977) 65, 75, 188 and discussion in Chapter 3.

[9] See, for example, a discussion of this in M. Watts, *The Dissenters* (Oxford: Clarendon, 1995) vol 2, Appendix 1, 671-5. Supporting and anecdotal evidence makes it likely in the eighteenth century as well. The Entwisle MS is at Duke University, NC, and printed *HMGB* 4: 290. The Devon case comes from M. J. L. Wickes, *The 1851 Census in Devon* (Devon: Wickes, 1990) and can be paralleled by many studies throughout the country. Numbers of members did not include all those who met in class. See Cooney, 'Dublin Methodist Society Membership 1788' in *WHS (I)* 10 (2004-5) 58.

A recent important study has shown that Wesley rarely stayed with Methodist members. His influence and that of the Methodist preachers went far beyond the lists of members and is therefore difficult to quantify.[10]

Importance of the Itinerant Preachers

The success of Methodism in the eighteenth and early nineteenth centuries should be put down to many factors. Among these the most important was not the preaching of Wesley, nor even his organizational expertise, but his building up of a successful cadre of preachers like Adam Clarke, Francis Asbury, John Nelson and Freeborn Garrettson. To these and to their successors should the spread of Methodism throughout Britain, her colonies and America be attributed. There are several reasons for this. After the early 1740s Wesley did not pioneer new areas. It was his preachers who did that. His first visit to Dublin in 1747 was only after several preachers had led the way. It was Pilmore and Boardman who pioneered in the American colonies in 1769, John Crook who was the first in the Isle of Man in the 1770s, and Robert Brackenbury and Adam Clarke in the Channel Isles in the 1780s. It is significant that the growth in numbers of members was steepest in the 1790s after Wesley's death, when the Connexion was freed from his control.[11] As Baker said 'neither the spread of the Methodist Societies nor their proliferation into a connected network of evangelical pockets throughout the land would have been possible without the itinerant lay preacher, Wesley's "helper," "assistant," other self.'[12] Baker's phrase 'other self' is not found elsewhere, but is most suggestive. His original 'other self' in Methodism had been his brother Charles, but Charles settled down and did not travel as John wanted. The preachers did travel.

Wesley saw clearly that because they were lay and untrained they must be itinerant. No society could grow if the preachers remained too long because they would become bored and stifled, as were many congregations with settled pastors. The variety of preaching as well as the reliability was important. Dr John Whitehead, Wesley's doctor, joint executor and one of his first biographers, wrote in the inscription on the memorial to Wesley at Wesley's

---

[10] J. Rodell, '"The best house by far in the town" John Wesley's personal circuit' in J. Gregory, ed, *John Wesley Tercentenary Essays* in *JRULMB* 85: 2 and 3 (Summer and Autumn 2003) 111-122.

[11] Wesley went first to Scotland with Hopper. But it was Hopper who remained and went much further North in Scotland. Hempton has cast doubts on Wesley's organisational expertise, see D. Hempton, *Methodism Empire of the Spirit* (New Haven: Yale UP, 2005) 16. For Wesley's leaving pioneering to others see Rack, 'John Wesley and Ireland' in *WHS (I)* 10 (2004-5) 5. For the preachers in America see Chapter 12 below.

[12] For a masterly modern summary of reasons for the rise of Methodism see Hempton, *Empire* 2-10. F. Baker, *John Wesley and the Church of England* (Nashville: Abingdon, 1970) 81.

Chapel that he was the 'patron and friend of the lay preachers.' By this he meant (as a former itinerant himself) that Wesley's chief claim to fame was the impressive lay preaching body he had created.[13] The three ideas of lay preachers, itinerant preachers, and preaching in the open air were not original,[14] but Wesley's creation of a sizeable, reliable and effective body of preachers was. British Methodism retains the lay and itinerant characteristics to this day.

After the two Wesleys' conversions in May 1738 religious societies in both Bristol and London were being formed, partly by Whitefield. These needed preachers. In 1739 the New Room was built in Bristol to be Wesley's base there. In the same year he took over Whitefield's base at Kingswood near Bristol after Whitefield had gone to Georgia. The Wesley brothers were preaching frequently to a society in Oxford. In London Wesley's main preaching services were at the Foundery, which was established in 1740. Religious societies were not new. However, over the next ten years the Wesley brothers made it their business to create a number of societies across the country, often taking over those of others. The class system within these societies aimed at filling the social life of the ordinary Methodist, providing everything which could be needed rather like the Roman Catholic voluntary system in late nineteenth century continental Europe. By the time of his separation from the Moravians over the 'stillness' question in July 1740 Wesley was already beginning to realize the need for lay helpers to preach to and care for these societies, because the number of clergy who would help the two Wesley brothers was so limited.[15]

Early Lay Preachers

Joseph Humphreys, John Cennick and Thomas Maxfield vie for the title of the first of the lay preachers, alongside the more doubtful John Hall of Bristol and David Taylor, the servant of Lady Huntingdon.[16] By 1744, when the first Conference was held, at least sixteen youngish men had come forward, been approved by both brothers and were moving regularly about the country at least

---

[13] It is usually forgotten that Whitehead had been an itinerant himself. Church noted it but not Heitzenrater or Rack. Jabez Bunting in 1823 altered the inscription to read 'the chief promoter and patron of the plan of itinerant preaching,' so removing the emphasis on layness while dramatising the itinerancy. Both were true and important. J. A. Vickers, *A Short Guide to the Memorials at Wesley's Chapel* (London: Wesley's Chapel, n.d, 1995).

[14] The Evangelical Revival's first lay itinerant was Howell Harris, exhorting in Wales since 1735 and recognised by Whitefield as his co-worker in 1740. Harris also often preached outside and had built up an itinerary of some thirty societies by 1740.

[15] The best description of Wesley's life is H. D. Rack, *Reasonable Enthusiast* (Peterborough: Epworth, 2nd ed. 2003). For the growth of mostly male nonreligious societies cf K. Wilson, *The Island Race* (London: Routledge, 2003) e.g. 37.

[16] See Chapter 2 below for detailed discussion of this point.

every quarter from one area to another.[17] These 'Assistants,' as they were then called, the travelling preachers as they became known and whose numbers soon grew, were the foundation of Wesley's success. When John and Charles were far away they were on the spot, only a week at the longest from riding into a village, meeting the class and society, preaching on a weeknight or Sunday and leading the faithful to parish communion or going with a brave band of helpers to take a stand outside in a village as yet unvisited. As the Connexion grew and the seven circuits of 1746 became the thirty nine of 1765, so the basic organization became three travelling preachers riding round the six weeks' circuit. This meant every society should be visited once a fortnight, and the more important weekly (on Sundays). More preachers were converted by other preachers than by John Wesley himself.

John had been at first against the idea of lay preachers. Very quickly his 'attitude changed to an eager use of the new method' and he gathered around him men, mostly lay, who would travel in the circuits he was forming. They were to preach to the societies and in the open air, to whomever would listen. They faced many problems and often gave up as a result. Each year from 1744 they met in a 'Conference' called by Wesley to discuss their practice and doctrine, provide training, report on their success or otherwise and discover where Mr Wesley would station them next.[18]

Focus of the Book

Purpose

The purpose of the Wesley's Preachers' Database[19] has been to try to analyse what can be found out about them: parentage and place of birth, age at various points, social class, education, religious upbringing, conversion and its circumstances, marriage and reasons for leaving if any, writings and cause of death. I am concerned about their relationships with the Wesleys and others, their children, the circuits they travelled in, offices held, length of service, ordination, their leaders, and common factors and experiences. Also significant is the range and variety of the preachers' lives, from birth to death. However, I do not wish to claim that this attempt to describe their lives can represent the final word. There is too much uncertainty about eighteenth century sources, not only the Methodist ones which are often lacking in vital information about many of the preachers, but also other sources such as parish registers, which were frequently defective. Because Methodism was only in the process of

---

[17] The question of total numbers of the itinerant preachers at any one time is a difficult one which I leave to Appendix Two.

[18] For the Methodist Conference see Chapter 9 below.

[19] See Appendix Three for the complete list, also Page 11 and J. H. Lenton, http://www.gcah.org/site/c.ghKJI0PHIoE/b.3945307/ (accessed 2/8/2008) 'Wesley's Preachers 1740-1791'.

beginning, our materials for it are poor. Circuits did not necessarily record their preachers. Many accounts come from hostile witnesses. Much of the evidence about the individual can not be corroborated.

Period

The main focus for this book is the period up to Wesley's death in 1791. However, most of Wesley's preachers (because so many entered in his final years) lived on until the nineteenth century. The last to survive, John Hickling, did not die until 1858 and spent a profitable period of his retirement lecturing around the Connexion about Wesley and his times (of which he can have remembered little, having entered in 1788). He did this to up to a fortnight before he died, so great was the demand. Hickling's Bible is still preserved in the Northwich circuit.[20]

As a result this book concentrates on the fifty years up to Wesley's death, but also deals with Wesley's preachers as they survived into the first half of the nineteenth century. The period covered, therefore, is from 1740 when the first lay preachers appeared, to Wesley's death in 1791, and beyond to 1858. However, after 1820 Wesley's preachers tended to lose their power in the Wesleyan Connexion to the younger post-Wesley generation, symbolized by Jabez Bunting. There will be little discussion of events much after 1820.

Place

The main concentration will be on Great Britain and Ireland. The latter country has often been omitted or passed over rapidly in studies of the rise of Methodism. This is wrong. Not only did most of the early British preachers travel to Ireland; from 1747 to at least the 1780s the two were worked by Wesley as a single unit. It was only a combination of growth in the north of Ireland from the 1760s, his own increasing age and the appearance of Thomas Coke as an alternative to Wesley as president of the Irish Conference that persuaded Wesley to alter this. In the 1780s he allowed the two to grow more separate which meant more autonomy for the Irish Conference (see below Chapter 11). A higher proportion of Wesley's preachers originated from Ireland than might be expected. In the thirty years after Wesley's death many of the leading British preachers had come from Ireland and their ideas had been formed there. It has been argued that Methodism's hostility to Catholicism in this period was the direct result of these links. In addition Irish Methodists were responsible for the origins of Methodism in America and were prominent among the leaders of Methodist missions in such varied areas as the West Indies, Canada and Gibraltar. The growth of Methodism in the thirteen

---

[20] *WMM* 1859: 837; *PWHS* 26 (1947-8) 15-6, 27 (1949-50) 47. For Hickling see also Chapter 19 below.

American colonies, in the Canadian Maritime provinces and the West Indies will also be dealt with, for the original personnel in each case came from the ranks of those who were Wesley's British and Irish preachers in his lifetime.

Sources

Chief Early Sources

Evidence about the preachers is sparse. This book is the latest result of compiling a database containing all Wesley's preachers, or at least 802 of them, many of whom must remain only doubtful. It began with a list of 677 prepared by the late Dr. Frank Baker, including all who entered up to and including the Conference of 1790 (the year before Wesley's death early in 1791).[21] This total number is based not only on the *Minutes of Conference*,[22] that is those accepted 'On Trial' or later 'Full Connexion' or found on the printed stations, but also includes those who from various references can be shown to have travelled as itinerant or travelling preachers. Only from 1765 is there a regular printed series of *Minutes* for each year's Conference and these were full of errors large and small, with preachers' names often (sometimes deliberately) omitted. From 1744 to 1764 we have some *Minutes* which give lists of preachers, assistants (those in charge of circuits, hence 'assisting' Wesley), and sometimes stations. These are rarely complete in terms of covering all the preachers and only cover some years. In the Bicentennial Edition of *Wesley's Works* the *Minutes* are in Volume 10, edited by Dr. Henry Rack, which is still awaiting publication. However, most years of this period have little evidence from the *Minutes*.

I have therefore used many other sources, not only for the period 1744-64 where the *Minutes* are clearly absent in their later form, but also the period from 1765, to supplement and correct the printed *Minutes*. The most significant of these other sources are the lists found in the historians Myles[23] and

---

[21] I am indebted to many friends for their help with this project. Most acknowledgment should go to the late Dr Frank Baker who nurtured it for many years and asked me to continue it for him. His kindness, deep knowledge and the accuracy of his references provided a model which few historians have matched.

[22] There are two main editions of the Collected *Minutes*, 1812 and 1862, though they were also published annually. Surviving copies of the Annual *Minutes* are very rare for the eighteenth century though common by the 1830s. I have used the 1862 corrected edition in general, and all citations refer to that unless otherwise indicated or where the material exists only in the 1812 edition. There are also *JB's Minutes*.

[23] W. Myles, *A Chronological History of the People Called Methodists* (London: Cordeux, 4th ed. 1813). Myles' dates of chapels have been suspect among historians, partly because each local historian can find errors in the dates Myles gave for the erection of chapels in his or her area. With regard to preachers, however, his dates are much more reliable because he was usually working from the published *Minutes*. He is also useful as he states if they were or became clergymen in the Church of England, also whether they were local preachers rather than itinerant and therefore did not travel.

Crowther.[24] Myles is important because he classified them as '3 races.' The first race (220 names) entered before 1765, the second (470) before Wesley's death. He then pointed out differences between them. Others have used his figures since. Both Myles and Crowther normally took the Conference *Minutes* as their main source. They therefore said someone entered or left at the time of the Conference when this was reported. So a man who actually started travelling in September 1777 was recorded by them as starting at the next Conference, 1778. Similarly a man, who left after the Conference of 1784 because his name was not in the Deed of Declaration, was not recorded as leaving until 1785 when it was recorded at Conference. Where possible I have used the actual date, which would have been in that case 1784. Manuscript letters and diaries, printed local histories and memoirs have also been used, as have manuscript accounts of early circuits and societies which often show payments to travelling preachers who were not otherwise known to have been in the circuit. Preachers who began travelling in a circuit after the 1790 Conference but before Wesley's death are included, since Wesley may be assumed to be responsible for sending them out to travel, as with Isaac Lilly in the Otley circuit in 1790.[25] So are clergymen who travelled with Wesley who were recorded as preaching, for example John Meriton, or those who preached regularly to Wesley's societies in their area in his lifetime, such as Walter Sellon in Leicestershire.[26] Also included are those from the British Isles sent by Wesley to serve abroad until 1784 for the American Church, for example John King and Robert Williams. Once the Christmas Conference of 1784 set up the Methodist Episcopal Church in America, that Church was independent. Americans who entered there before 1784 are not included unless they served in Nova Scotia or Britain, so appearing in the British *Minutes* after 1784.[27]

Myles's third race was those who entered between 1791 and 1813.

[24] J. Crowther, *A True and Complete Portraiture of Methodism*, (London: Edwards, 2nd ed. 1815). Crowther's listings were less complete than Myles' with fewer details, but fuller than J. Pawson, *A Chronological List of all the Travelling Preachers now in the Methodist Connexion* (Liverpool: J. M'Creery, 1795). His lists were slightly different from Myles.' There was also a list in Atmore.

[25] *WMM* 1852: 914 said Lilly 'began his ministerial career in Otley in the year 1790'. He did not appear in the *Minutes* until 1791.

[26] For Meriton see A. S. Wood, *Brothers in Arms: The Clerical Associates of John Wesley* (Nantwich: WHS, 1992) 18-22. For Sellon see *WJW* 20: 473 n. 13. This last, for which Baker was the overall editor, when completed will replace all earlier editions.

[27] *Minutes MCA*. As with the British *Minutes* these can also be consulted in the annual version. They show that 120 men had entered by 1784, which would be a significant proportion if incorporated within the existing overwhelmingly British database. See Chapter 9 below.

Introduction 13

Previous Books about the Preachers

There have been attempts to write about the preachers before. The most significant early work was Charles Atmore's *The Methodist Memorial* (1801).[28] He wanted to provide improving stories of dead preachers and concentrated on conversion, spiritual experience and deathbeds. His dating is vague, approximate and often wrong. Atmore can be shown to be sometimes prone to error almost as much as Myles has been judged to be in the past. Yet he remains a key source for information about many of the preachers, providing otherwise unobtainable detail. A typical short biography in Atmore is that of Robert Naylor:

> He was admitted on trial at the Conference in 1778, and was appointed to the Norwich circuit. He was a deeply pious, *zealous, active*, lively *young man*: and as a preacher, was both acceptable and useful. He travelled but a short time, for *he was caught away by a fever in the strength of his years: but it was in a good hour, for he returned to Him whom his soul loved, in the full assurance of faith*, and with the pleasing prospect of a glorious immortality, in the year 1783.

The words in italics represent the exact words in the obituary in the *Minutes*, which shows how little Atmore often added. In fact Naylor was an Englishman, probably from the West Riding, who married Sarah Harrison at All Saints, Wakefield, in July 1780 and went that year to Ireland where he served until his death, which took place between the Conferences of 1782 and 1783, so reported in 1783. His widow returned to England and was supported by the Preachers' Fund until at least 1813.[29] Atmore, who was Superintendent in the Wakefield Circuit from 1803 until 1805, could have spoken or written to her during those thirty years and asked for more information, such as where he came from and when he was born. He did not, because neither wife nor background were relevant to his purpose. A modern biographer would at least mention the wife. Most other early Methodist sources were like Atmore in their priorities, intending to supply spiritual enlightenment and concentrating on the death or at least the last years.

In the early nineteenth century Thomas Jackson edited *Early Methodist Preachers*,[30] a collection of mostly autobiographies of forty-one preachers,

---

[28] I have used the 1871 edition (London: Hamilton Adams). Charles Atmore was a close friend and protégé of John Pawson. Atmore arranged his biographies alphabetically with Naylor's on page 160. Atmore's major source for the older preachers was the letters from Pawson found in J. Bowmer and J. A. Vickers, eds, *The Letters of John Pawson*, (Peterborough: WMHS, 1996). Pawson's judgment was sometimes jaundiced, but Atmore often altered Pawson without good reason. Because his career covered such a long period and Pawson was relatively open in his letters, he has been a major source.

[29] The Preachers' Fund references are in the relevant *Minutes*. The marriage details are from the *International Genealogical Index*.

[30] All these were intended to improve the reader's spiritual life. Often this was spelt out

almost entirely reprinted from Wesley's *Arminian Magazine*. It was hugely and deservedly successful and went through many editions, eventually republished as *'Wesley's Veterans.'* The only common factor in their appearance was the publication of their memoirs in the *Arminian Magazine*.[31] Wesley as editor could not ask for memoirs from those who were dead, and so those who died earlier were automatically excluded; he did not want to publicize those who had left. Jackson's list has often been taken even to the present as definitive. Some historians have done much work on those preachers who appear in it. It is unfortunate that they assume that these forty-one preachers are representative when the first preachers are absent except for John Nelson. Furthermore, of the preachers Jackson included, Sampson Staniforth appears never to have travelled at all and was only a local preacher. Despite this Kent still cited him as a typical preacher, admittedly of the 'rank and file.'[32] Another, William Adams, travelled only in America and was perhaps included by Jackson to enlarge the sales across the Atlantic. Neither of them are in my Wesley's Preachers' database. As a sample, therefore, of the total number of preachers, Jackson's thirty nine out of 802 is both small and slanted. Nearly all those included were still alive in the 1780s, and *that* was the chief reason for their inclusion. Only three had left, very different from the percentage of leavers shown in Table 1 in Appendix One. *Early Methodist Preachers* is, contrary to popular view, not a typical cross-section of Wesley's preachers. However, as a detailed source for the preachers' subjective views of their long struggle against sin and then of their conversion, Jackson's work remains unrivalled. The admittedly edited words of some of the preachers themselves provide a primary source of great value.

At a slightly later date came *Wesleyan Takings*, an anonymous summary of two hundred preachers, mostly nineteenth century though some belonged to the eighteenth or had at least started under Wesley. Its anti-Conference colouring and its coyness about doing anything other than painting a superficial pen picture of the man concerned have removed much of whatever value it once had. West's *Sketches of Ministerial Character* is better, perhaps because it was not anonymous and is therefore more trustworthy, but it contains only a few preachers from the eighteenth century.[33]

In the twentieth century the first relevant book was by Pike, both unoriginal and disappointing. Bett, however, in an article for the *Proceedings* of 1925 and then in the first WHS Lecture in 1935 on 'Wesleys Preachers,' was more

---

first. *EMP*: later retitled as *Wesley's Veterans,* 6 vols (London: WCO, 1865-6).

[31] Not all the memoirs were regarded by Jackson as interesting enough to include.

[32] J. S. Wilder's 'The Early Methodist Preachers and their contribution to the 18th century Revival in England' New College, Edinburgh University PhD dissertation, 1948; J. H. S. Kent, *Wesley and the Wesleyans* (Cambridge: CUP, 2002) 91-98.

[33] Anon, *Wesleyan Takings* 2 vols (London: Hamilton Adams, 1845, 1851); R. A. West, *Sketches of Ministerial Character* (London: Simpkin and Marshall, 1849).

Introduction 15

interesting. Doughty looked at preachers and Conferences in his perceptive 1944 lecture.[34] Garlick tried in 1977 to list the preachers and their stations to fill the gap before *Hill's Arrangements*. He provided details of 300 preachers but he only covered those who died in the work and omitted most Irishmen. An important early preacher like John Downes was left out. He also included some who entered after Wesley's death, as his criterion was those who did not appear in the first edition of *Hill's Arrangements,* that is they had died in the work before 1819. All this meant he omitted more than half of Wesley's preachers.[35]

There have also been attempts to classify them sociologically. The pioneer here was Wilder's Edinburgh thesis of 1948 which discussed sixty-six of the early Methodist preachers, including nearly all those in Jackson's collection of forty-one.[36] An American, Shipley, wrote relatively briefly about the eighteenth century Methodist ministry in a collection of papers produced in the USA in 1960. Most significantly, Field in 1977 surveyed all Methodists not just the preachers for their social class origins.[37]

Recently my WHS Lecture of 2000 and other articles listed in the Bibliography have started to unravel some of the details about the preachers. This book brings them all together.[38] Hindmarsh, in his illuminating study of conversion, has compared the early Methodist preachers' accounts of their conversion with both women preachers and ordinary Methodist converts. However, he too only deals with those in Jackson's *Early Methodist Preachers* and only uses the evidence there or in the *Magazine*.[39] Burdon in 2005 studied

---

[34] G. H. Pike, *Wesley and his Preachers: Their Conquest of Britain* (London: Fisher Unwin, 1903); H. Bett in *PWHS* 15: (1926-7) 85-92 and *Early Methodist Preachers* (London: WHS Lecture no. 12, Epworth, 1935); W. L. Doughty, *John Wesley: His Conferences and His Preachers* (London: WHS Lecture no. 10, Epworth, 1944).

[35] *Hill's Arrangements* listed the Wesleyan preachers with former and existing circuits. They appeared every 5 years or so from 1819 to 1968. For a detailed analysis see *PWHS* 40 (1975-6) 2-5. K. B. Garlick, *Mr Wesley's Preachers* (London: Pinhorns, 1977) needs to be checked against the *Minutes*.

[36] Note 31 above. A similar work is the 1985 'Wesley's Preachers: An Analytical Study in Legible Longhand' by the Rev Roger Taylor, former Vicar of Felixstowe, mostly dependent on *John Wesley's Letters* (1938 edition), in the WHS Library at Oxford Brookes University Biographical Cuttings Files (B/WES/TAY).

[37] D. C. Shipley, 'The Ministry in Methodism in the 18th Century' in G. O. McCulloh, ed, *The Ministry in the Methodist Heritage* (Nashville: Abingdon, 1960) 11-31; C. D. Field, 'The Social Structure of English Methodism 18th-20th centuries' in *British Journal of Sociology* 28 (1977) 199-225.

[38] J. H. Lenton, *'My Sons in the Gospel': An Analysis of Wesley's Itinerant Preachers* (Wolverhampton: WHS Lecture, 2000).

[39] D. B. Hindmarsh, *The Evangelical Conversion Narrative* (Oxford: OUP, 2005) mentions Nicholas Manners' autobiography, but never used it. Examples from the *Magazine* such as the experience of John Kershaw (*MM* 1802: 177-83, 221-6) were not used, presumably because he was not in *Early Methodist Preachers*. MS sources such as correspondence are not mentioned for the preachers.

Wesley and his preachers, concentrating especially on their ordination and Wesley's ideas behind his ordination of laymen. His perceptive work is particularly aimed at Methodism's relationship with the eighteenth-century Church of England in order to provide lessons for the twenty-first century ecumenical Covenant.[40]

For the database I have tried to check all the references. I have relied on many sources available for modern genealogists, such as the *International Genealogical Index* which has enabled me to find many probable marriages and children, though not all are proved. Many local historians have been most helpful, as have descendants of Wesley's preachers, now scattered across the world.[41] Suzanne Schwarz provided information on Melville Horne. John Vickers kept asking me about those who left, quizzing me on definitions and providing useful references. None of them, however, are in any way responsible for what appears either in the database or this book. The manuscript letters, journals and diaries of the preachers and other Methodists also supplied much useful material. Letters exist in large quantities, not only at the Rylands but elsewhere in libraries over several continents and in private hands. Diaries and journals are rarer but have often survived, especially at the Rylands.[42]

Account books of circuits such as the Manchester Circuit Account Book, the Staffordshire Circuit, the Todmorden Book, and others have all been useful in tracing who was paid what and when, the mark of the travelling itinerant. The payment distinguished him from his local preacher brother. Especially important is the London Stewards' Book. These have often enabled me to say with firmness that a half itinerant like William Shent was sometimes travelling

---

[40] A. Burdon, *Authority and Order: John Wesley and his Preachers* (Aldershot: Ashgate, 2005) also only uses printed sources.

[41] Genealogists issue a warning about the *IGI* which should be checked against the relevant Parish Register. I have rarely been able to do this. Local historians include Norma Virgoe and Brian Hart in Norfolk, John Anderson in the Potteries, Robin Roddie in Ireland, Jeff Spittal in Somerset, John Hargreaves in Halifax, the late Geoff Milburn in Sunderland, Colin Dews in Leeds, Maurice Wright in Shropshire, Jonathan Rodell for several links in the South, Colin Short in Cornwall, Roger Thorne in Devon, Edward Royle in Yorkshire, Frank Whaling for Scotland, and Frances Coakley for the Isle of Man. Relatives include F. W. Adkin, the late Ida Johnson and Robert Higginson for their ancestor William Orpe, Andrew Hindmarsh for his Hindmarsh ancestry, Paul Booth on John Booth, Richard Blagborne for William Blagborne, Anne Dray about the Hitchens family and Captain Dick Williams of Gwennap, Brian Beanland on the two Beanlands, Thelma Woolf on Francis Woolf, John Carlill for Thomas Carlill, Janet Wright on George Baldwin, Charlotte Walker on John Stamp, Derek Olphert on James Rennick, Keith Sherwood on the Kershaws and Shirley Jackman about Blakeley Dowling.

[42] For Asbury, Coke and Pilmore see below Chapter 12. For Pawson see note 22 above. T. Bennis, *The Christian Correspondence of Mrs Elizabeth Bennis* (Philadelphia: Graves, 1807). Occasionally some of these have been printed as with Asbury, Coke, Pilmore, Pawson or Mrs Bennis.

in a circuit far from home.[43]

Problems

LACK OF INFORMATION

Even so for many there is little or no information. For the typical preacher who left, we do not know where or when he was born, when he was converted, from what circuit he entered, or even if he was preaching before he was recorded as appearing at Conference 'On Trial.' We do not know why he left, what he then did, or when he died. We do not know whether he was married or had children. This is most likely for common surnames, but can be so for less usual ones as well. There is one case where the surname is completely unknown, the preacher called only 'G--h' who helped Sarah Crosby in Derby on the 24th and 25th February 1761. The reference from the *Magazine* is to the Memoir of Mrs Crosby by Ann Tripp[44] which says 'Bro G preached' for the 25th February and 'Bro G-h came the evening before to Mrs Crosby.' This was at Derby where she had gone (to Mrs Dobinson's) on the 8th January. What circuit was Derby in or near in early 1761? Staffordshire? Leeds? Epworth? The Derbyshire circuit of 1765 came after Manchester and before Sheffield in the list in the *Minutes*. In 1763 there was no Derby circuit in the list. Closest circuits were Staffordshire, Chester, Sheffield or to the South, Bedford. Sheffield seems most likely. In 1748 the Yorkshire circuit included Derbyshire. Though in 1749 Chester had Derby and Nottingham, Sheffield is favourite. The two preachers known to have been in Sheffield that year (1760-61) were John Hampson senior and George Tizard. Was Mr G--h the third preacher that year, otherwise unknown? Chilcote mentioned Hampson as coming next to Derby to the group led by Sarah Crosby, which fits.[45]

This lack of information is also true for many who died in the work, especially the earliest. These problems were worst before 1765, twenty-five years of early Methodism when Myles' 'first race' entered and many preached but were often not recorded. *Minutes* including lists of preachers only survive for seven or eight years of this period. Even these often have more preachers omitted than listed. Further, the printed *Minutes* from 1765 to beyond 1791 are

---

[43] A MS of the Manchester Circuit Account Book, as copied by Marmaduke Riggall, is in the possession of the Rev. H. D. Rack. The MS Staffordshire Circuit Stewards Account Book 1768-93 MB/1/1 is at Birmingham City Library. The accounts of the Great Haworth Round are in the Todmorden MS Account Book 1748-1793 at Keighley Public Library, BK15/1/1/3a. The MS London Stewards Book 1760s-1804 is at MARC. Wesley used the London Stewards to support preachers elsewhere such as Nelson. Some superannuated preachers came to London for support.

[44] *AM* 1806: 519.

[45] P. W. Chilcote, *John Wesley and the Women Preachers of Early Methodism* (Metuchen: Scarecrow, 1991) 120-3, 135-6.

inaccurate and incomplete. The corrected 1862 edition still has mistakes and omissions. Obituaries, which are obviously most use to the modern historian, only began to appear in 1778. From then onwards for some time they were brief in the extreme, for example Jacob Rowell was described as 'a faithful old soldier fairly worn out in his Master's service.'[46] Until the early nineteenth century many preachers died without an obituary appearing. None had age at death before 1798 and not all had this as late as 1813. The general feeling of how 'our departed brother' should be recorded and celebrated had not been codified even in the early nineteenth century.

This can be compared with the American Conferences.[47] There the question 'What Preachers have died this year?' was not asked until the regular (not the Christmas) American Conference of 1784. The reply that year was simply the names of two brothers with no details at all. In 1785, with the influence of Coke and the British Conference there were not only the names but a little detail, comparable to Rowell eight years before 'George Mair, a man of affliction, but of great patience and resignation; and of excellent understanding.' By 1788 the American *Minutes* gave length of time as a travelling preacher. Date of death was usual by 1794 and age at death by 1796, so codification of what should appear, once it began, was much faster in America. Was this perhaps because they were further from the hand of Wesley? Asbury as a preacher himself was more sympathetic to their emotional needs and felt the obituary was worth doing properly. Time of travel was being measured by Conference.[48]

MISTAKES AND OMISSIONS IN THE *MINUTES*

In the British *Minutes* men in lists of 'On Trial,' 'Full Connexion' or on station were missed out, grossly misspelt ('Wiltam' in place of 'Miller'), their Christian names completely altered, or alternatively listed without ever arriving on any station, usually because they had not been consulted.[49] There is also the problem of separating those with the same or similar name, for example Samuel Wells, the father a local preacher, the son a travelling preacher, both resident in Cheltenham at the same time, and Thomas Eden of Broad Marston and his father of the same name.[50]

Part of the identification problem is that of the definition of local preachers.

---

[46] *Minutes* 1784 Question 5.
[47] *Minutes* MCA 1784. For more discussion see Chapter 20 below.
[48] R. Richey, *The Methodist Conference in America: A History* (Nashville: Kingswood, 1995) 32.
[49] See Chapter 5 Probation below. James 'Wiltam' appeared in the *Minutes* in 1769 in the Dales Circuit and nowhere else. No Wiltam was ever admitted on trial in that year or any other. However, A. Steele, *History of Methodism in Barnard Castle and the Principal Places in the Dales Circuit* (London: Vickers, 1857), based on local sources, stated James Miller was appointed to the Dales that year. A historian dependent on the *Minutes* alone would have invented a new preacher called Wiltam.
[50] See the two John Watsons as explained in Lenton, *My Sons* 7.

Introduction

In Wesley's day all preachers (except ordained Anglican clergymen) were lay in his view. Pawson, Thomas Hanby and others felt the effect of this in his last years. They were first ordained for Scotland to administer the sacraments and then returned to England where they were told they must refrain.[51] From an early stage there was a division in Wesley's mind between those who were local preachers, working during the day and usually only preaching on Sundays, and travelling preachers who preached on every day of the week and travelled much more; but one could easily become the other. Especially in the early days it is difficult to distinguish between the two. Individuals might be listed as one the first year and the other the next, the only certainty apparently coming from the *Minutes,* if these existed. Usually *Minutes* were absent in this period, or if not, then always incomplete. In between men could be found travelling and preaching at the opposite end of the country. The truth is firm divisions, so clear by the nineteenth century, were often inapplicable in Wesley's day, not least for Wesley himself to whom both local and itinerant preachers were lay. William Shent, who was travelling and local at different times, appeared on the stations in 1749, 1753 and 1755.[52]

Some even later were itinerant preachers but *never* appeared in the *Minutes,* the best example being John Holdsworth. According to his obituary he began to preach in 1772 and 'for many years took the work of a circuit as an itinerant preacher' but his name was not recorded in the *Minutes.* Sigston's *Bramwell* described Holdsworth in 1818 as living in Cleckheaton as 'an aged preacher in the Connexion' so an itinerant.[53] I doubted Holdsworth's obituary description at first, then found Sigston's confirmation and realized that others like John Cricket were preaching at this relatively late period without necessarily appearing on the stations in the *Minutes.* An eccentric preacher at any time, Cricket began as a local preacher in January 1774 in London and became a travelling preacher in April 1779. He appears to have been entirely supported for these five years by John Wesley and seems to have travelled, as there was a reference to Cornwall in 1776. In 1779 he went to Staffordshire and then to Birstall, neither in the *Minutes.* He first appeared in the *Minutes* in 1780 in Ireland.[54] The total number of travelling preachers who can be deduced from the *Minutes* must in the eighteenth century always be seen as an underestimate.

---

[51] *Pawson L.* 1: 45 *passim*; Hanby's letter 27th February 1789 in MARC PLP 48.55.11.
[52] *EMP* 5: 59; Myles 448; G. E. Milburn and M. Batty, eds, *Workaday Preachers* (Peterborough: Epworth, 1995) 20 n43. For more on Shent see pages 444-45 below.
[53] *WMM* 1828: 502; J. Sigston, *A Memoir of the Life and Ministry of Mr W. Bramwell* (London: Nichols, 2nd ed. 1820) 280; F. Peel, *Nonconformity in the Spen Valley* (London: Senior, 1891) 194.
[54] *WMM* 1830: 507; *City Road Magazine* 1874: 268, 1875: 401-5, 1876: 70. See also Appendix Two on total numbers.

Chapter 2

Definitions

> 'They think themselves inspired by God and are not.'
> John Wesley on enthusiasts 1762 in *Letter to the Bishop of Gloucester*.

The Evangelical Revival

Traditionally historians identified the Evangelical Revival as the recovery of England from the morass of immorality, which had been seen as typical of the country from the Restoration on into the eighteenth century. Whether immorality increased or decreased in this period is now considered impossible to quantify. However, this does not alter the significance of the Evangelical Revival in its own right. Men and women *felt* it was important, and so it was.[1]

Historians have agreed on Bebbington's four-fold definition of the Evangelical's characteristics: conversionism, the belief that lives could be changed; activism, the expression of the gospel in effort; biblicism, a particular regard for the Bible; and crucicentrism, a tendency to concentrate on the death of Christ on the Cross. Of these perhaps the most important is the first, the emphasis on the 'religion of the heart.'

Methodists have always realized the importance of this, Wesley wanting his preachers to be 'affectionate,' by which he meant directing their attention at the hearers' hearts and exciting their passions. Evangelicalism itself is a fluid subject with various emphases being more important at different times and places. There were many types of Evangelicals, just as there were many kinds of Methodists, but the personal religious experience remains vital when looking at the Methodist individual.[2]

There has been a tendency among historians, at least Methodist ones, to concentrate on John Wesley and England. The Eighteenth Century Revival, however, was much wider, not least trans-Atlantic. It started in Germany with the origins of Pietism in the early seventeenth century and spread in many

---

[1] See for example Rosman, *Churches 1500-2000* 147-8.
[2] D. Bebbington, *Evangelicalism in Modern Britain: A History from the 1730s to the 1980s* (London: Unwin, 1989) 2-3. For a more recent short, but well referenced, summary of the Revival see J. M. Turner, *John Wesley* (Peterborough: Epworth, 2003) Chapter one. See also Noll, *Rise* 13-18, 20-21 quoting Rawlyk, ed, *Aspects of the Canadian Evangelical Experience* (Kingston: McGill, 1997) xiv-xvii.

directions partly because of the migration of religious groups, of whom the Huguenots and the Moravians are the most famous but Salzburgers, Silesians and others were also influential. Most of these were refugees from Catholic persecution, which had had the opposite effect from that intended, so that Protestantism became stronger and more widely distributed. The writings of Arndt and Bengel were equally productive. As John Walsh wrote 'German Pietism cross-fertilized High Church Anglicanism' sparking off the Evangelical Revival. 'The Moravians were the catalysts.'[3] In America the 'Great Awakening,' which was associated with Jonathan Edwards in Northampton, New England, from 1734, is now seen as having links with Germany, Scotland and elsewhere. In Britain it began in Wales, with Griffith Jones itinerating in the first decade of the century and then installed in Llanddowror in Carmarthen in 1716. Daniel Rowland began his Welsh itineraries in 1736. In Scotland in the 1730s there was the Cambuslang revival, with the appearance of 'praying societies' among the Presbyterian Church of Scotland. The High Church Anglican societies in London and elsewhere from as early as the late 1670s helped to increase spiritual life. These societies were the first to respond to the new Evangelical preaching. In England the first generally known leader was not John Wesley but his friend George Whitefield. This great dramatic preacher began in London churches in 1736 and immediately created a large popular following; he gained many invitations to religious societies while the Wesleys were in Georgia. This led to preaching extempore. He used weeping, exclamations and body movements to affect his hearers. Large crowds gathered and many conversions were reported. The Wesley brothers were converted independently of each other in May 1738, partly as a result of travelling with Moravians to Georgia. Whitefield led the Wesleys in preaching outside in 1739, partly because of his exclusion from many churches previously open to him. Laymen like John Bennet, William Darney and David Taylor began their own smaller preaching itineraries. Thomas Lee was another layman who formed his own societies in Nidderdale to which he preached for a time and then took them into Wesley's Methodist connexion. Evangelical clergymen like Walker in Cornwall and later Venn in Huddersfield appeared completely separately from Wesley, though a few turned to him afterwards. The Wesley brothers were therefore comparative latecomers both on the worldwide and the British Evangelical scene.[4]

---

[3] For the world wide nature of the movement see W. R. Ward's writings, e.g. his essay 'Power and Piety: the Origins of Religious Revival' in *Faith and Faction* (London: Epworth, 1993). See also *idem, The Protestant Evangelical Awakening* (Cambridge: CUP, 1992) and J. D. Walsh, 'Origins of the Evangelical Revival' in G. V. Bennett and J. D. Walsh, eds, *Essays in Modern Church History* (London: Black, 1966) 157. The final quotation is from Hempton, *Empire* 13.

[4] For the Great Awakening in America see F. Lambert, *Inventing the 'Great Awakening'* (Princeton: Princeton UP, 1999). For Bennet, Darney and D. Taylor see S. R. Valentine,

The revival spread for many reasons. In England, Wales and Ireland the Latitudinarian nature of the leadership of the Anglican Church of England tended to inhibit attempts to crush any possible opposition, because of their own divergences from diocese to diocese and insistence on the value of a 'spirit of free enquiry.' The revival was partly a reaction against this and in any case many prominent Anglicans supported it. For some time the leaders of the Evangelical movement had been writing to each other, sharing strategies and exchanging signs that a world revival was indeed on the way. There was a large market for religious works and all the Methodist leaders sought to fill it with their letters and journals. Whitefield and others in the late 1730s held 'Letter Days' at which they read aloud to any who attended letters received from elsewhere. In 1738 Whitefield began publishing his Journal. In 1740 John Lewis's four page penny paper *'Christian's Amusement... containing letters concerning the progress of the Gospel'* was started. In seven months it was taken over by Whitefield, printing the letters already read publicly. Wesley's Journal (published by him from 1742 at various points for almost 50 years) was another influential work.

The revival's appeal to many different groups from high church Anglicans like Wesley to former Dissenters like Bennet was important. It provided a way out for Deists, who had speculated about theology, by supplying an experience which meant they could concentrate on what God had done in them and what they could now do for Him. Because much of the preaching was necessarily outside, it was novel and attracted those who would rarely come to church. The revival appealed to the widespread popular belief in the supernatural shared by Wesley and later illustrated in the *Arminian Magazine*. All the English and Welsh leaders of the revival wished to remain within the Church of England and reform it from within. This enabled them to say that they were loyal to it, even when their actions were flagrantly against its rules. Their loyalty was also

---

John Bennet and the Origins of Methodism and the Evangelical Revival in England (London: Scarecrow Press, 1997). For the Latitudinarians see Walsh, *Church* 35-43. For Whitefield see H. Stout, *The Divine Dramatist: George Whitefield and the Rise of Modern Evangelicalism* (Grand Rapids: Eerdmans, 1991). For Welsh Calvinistic Methodists see D. C. Jones, '*A Glorious Work in the World': Welsh Methodism and the International Evangelical Revival 1735-50* (Cardiff: Wales UP, 2004); G. Tudur, *Howell Harris: From Conversion to Separation 1735-50* (Cardiff: Wales UP, 2000). For other Evangelicals in the Church of England see L. E. Elliott-Binns, *The Early Evangelicals: A Religious and Social Study* (London: Lutterworth, 1953). For the Countess of Huntingdon's Connexion see A. Harding, *The Countess of Huntingdon's Connexion* (Oxford: OUP, 2003). Wesley had been the leader of the Holy Club in Oxford but this was neither known nor having any effect outside the Oxford area. Whitefield seems to have preached outside first to the colliers of Kingswood on the 21st February 1739. He had been preceded in preaching outside by Howell Harris in Wales. For Thomas Lee (1727-86) and William Darney see *GHR* 53, 98-101, 104-114, 179, 228-34. For more on other 'circuits' and leaders see Chapter 21 below.

politic, for most of those to whom they appealed were dedicated to the idea of a national church.[5]

The hymn-singing character of the revival mattered since, when the preacher reached a place where he wanted to preach, he announced his presence by singing a hymn. If he were accompanied by his friends, they sang with him. The hymns were a badge, a means of defence when opponents tried to shout the preacher down, and a source of spiritual strength. These hymns and their tunes came from many quarters and were largely collected by John Wesley, the inveterate translator and publisher. He often used folk-tunes, while other music was composed by local or even international musicians like Handel. Charles Wesley was the inspired writer of those hymns which were central to the revival, because they best expressed the spiritual progress of the new convert. Complex theological ideas were transmitted in accessible language, enabling Methodists to sing their faith.[6]

The dramatic success of Whitefield in Britain and during his visits to the American colonies from 1739 spurred on the revival. George Whitefield was the evangelist par excellence, the 'Grand Itinerant,' who attracted huge crowds on both sides of the Atlantic. Having tested out techniques like open air extempore preaching and daily itinerant preaching in a different place every day, these became standard for other itinerants in many areas. Suddenly what had been successful in a few scattered places seemed to be more general and sweepingly successful everywhere. Whitefield's 'print and preach' strategy was most successful. He used the newly expanding newspapers to publicize what he was doing.

Charles Wesley also proved as effective as a preacher and evangelist as much as a hymn-writer. It was difficult to see either brother as more active than the other in the 1740s. Charles was a pioneer in new areas as much as John. Charles was a much more rounded and humane personality than his brother John. A comparison of their letters immediately makes the reader realize they were very dissimilar. Where John's letters were brief and to the point, following the same format down to the abbreviated 'JWesley' signature, Charles's letters were often very different from each other. The historian might even describe them as chaotic, often without any place of writing, date, or even signature appearing. Some had 'Farewell' or 'Adieu' at the end; some lacked even that. Charles was not writing for the historian, whereas John often was. Charles was the poet, John the organizer. Charles stayed in bed when he felt

---

[5] For the increasing demand for printed works see J. Raven, 'The Book Trades' in I. Rivers, ed, *Books and Their Readers in 18th Century England: New Essays* (London: Leicester UP, 2001) 2; Rosman, *Churches 1500-2000* 148-154; M. Mascuch, 'John Wesley Superstar' in R. Dekker, ed, *Egodocuments and History* (Rotterdam: Verloren, 2002) especially 137-148. For Wesleyan Letter Days from Conference 1744 see Chapter 4 below.

[6] See for example Turner, *Wesley* 51-72 and Hempton, *Empire* 68-74.

like it, but John got up early always. If he did not, it was most unusual and he was ill. The two differing personalities complemented each other, for those whom Charles converted, John organized.[7]

John Wesley drew his ideas from a very broad spectrum. Though brought up a high church Anglican, interested in the Early Church and recovering the practices of primitive Christianity, he read widely and republished writers of all denominations. Catholics, particularly those of the Counter-Reformation, Puritans, Moravians, Pietists, Mystics, Dissenters and Non-Jurors were all grist to his mill. The practices he adopted, such as the key one of the small religious class-meeting, came from many quarters. The criterion was: did it work? Though an enthusiast, he adopted the logic of Locke and the Enlightenment. Also significant were the many areas which were favourable to Methodist growth. Its ability to expand where the Church of England was already important but not able to meet the new challenges, as a kind of parasite feeding on its mother church, has recently been pointed out by Hempton.[8]

The mark of the Revival was preaching for conversion, for change within an individual, convicting the sinner of sin and the need for change. Even noteworthy intellectuals like John Wesley and Jonathan Edwards preached to move the heart not just convince the mind. It was notable also for the power of prayer to move individuals. Take the description of the conversion of Samuel Handy by Paul Greenwood in Ireland in 1747. Handy had been taken to a Methodist meeting at Dolphin's Barn by his sister-in-law and began by securing his pockets against his mean looking fellow worshippers. Then

> A tall thin man in plain black clothes with dark hair entered and took possession of the pulpit. He was Paul Greenwood. Mr Handy regarded him with surprise, he being minus wig, gown and bands, which according to his ideas were essential to a minister of the gospel. He was still more astonished when the preacher having given out a hymn, the congregation united in singing it with one heart and voice. 'Wonderful,' he thought, 'that so despicable a people should be able to sing so delightfully!' The extempore prayer that followed... filled his heart and prepared him to follow... the preacher's discourse. This was accompanied by such light and power as produced a complete change in his views and feelings and led him to resolve 'This people shall be my people and their God my God.'[9]

Greenwood came from the small Pennine village of Stanbury, west of Keighley in the West Riding of Yorkshire. He was converted at 17 in 1740 in Ponden, a village close to his home later associated with the Brontës and *Wuthering Heights*. He may well have been in the Army with John Haime and preaching at Bruges in 1744. He began to travel in 1747 at the age of 24, probably in his

---

[7] For Charles Wesley see Chapter 17 below and K. G. Newport and T. Campbell, eds, *Charles Wesley: Life, Literature and Legacy* (Peterborough: Epworth, 2007).
[8] Hempton, *Empire* Chapter 1 'Competition and Symbiosis.'
[9] Noll, *America's God* 93; *GHR* 87.

own circuit of Haworth at first, and was then sent by Wesley to the new mission field of Ireland where this relatively young and unpractised preacher influenced Handy so completely. Greenwood was representative of the Yorkshiremen and women who were responsible for the extension of Methodism. Where he and John Nelson trod, Pilmore, Lumb and Warrener were to spread their wings even more widely. The early Irish dimension of Wesley's Methodism was also important. Irish preachers would be as influential across the world as Yorkshire ones. It was preachers like the 24 year-old Paul Greenwood who were to change the world because they changed people's lives.[10]

Spirituality

The word 'spiritual' has already been used and needs some definition and explanation. Spiritual experience was basic to the growth of Methodism and the life of Wesley's preachers. Though difficult for some secular historians to understand, it is vital if we are to build up a picture of what the preachers were like. Their conversion and subsequent sanctification, their Christian life, their reliance on the 'means of grace' through the class meeting, public worship, love-feasts, private prayer and Conference were all important, because spiritual experience mattered most to them. 'Spirituality,' in Gordon Wakefield's helpful definition, is the amalgam of 'attitudes, beliefs and practices which animate people's lives and help them reach out to supersensible realities.'[11] Methodism was essentially a spiritual movement, as Mark Noll put it 'constituted by its ardent gospel preaching and its personal networks of organization.'[12] Norman Goldhawk emphasized three factors: 'a strong personal urge towards holiness, an evangelistic missionary impulse and adherence to a distinctive church order and discipline.'[13]

Wesley's combination of reason and enthusiasm was both persuasive in the first instance, as with Greenwood and Handy above, and provided security on later reflection. Wesley was sometimes sceptical of this 'enthusiasm' with which he was sometimes surrounded, as the quotation at the head of this chapter illustrates. 'Fellowship,' that great Methodist institution, filled the time available with sympathetic companions. The early Methodist convert

---

[10] For Greenwood see *GHR* 85-93, 145-6, 348; *DOMBI* 140; *EMP* 1: 209, 247, 4: 27,35, 5: 12; Atmore; F. Baker, *William Grimshaw 1708-53* (London: Epworth, 1963) 98f, 148; MS Todmorden A/C Book 1748-1793 at Keighley Public Library. BK15/1/1/3a. 3, 9, 11, 25, 27. The reference to Bruges in 1744 from *AM* 1778: 277 says 'Mr Haime and Mr Greenwood.' The identification of Haime is clear. Greenwood is a more common name and there is no later reference to Paul Greenwood having been a soldier.
[11] G. S. Wakefield, ed, *A Dictionary of Christian Spirituality* (London: SCM, 1983) 539.
[12] Noll, *America's God* 330.
[13] N. Goldhawk in *HMGB* 2: 113-4.

immediately tapped into a continual round of helpful spiritual activity which consumed the mind and developed the soul. A glance at a later itinerant's biography makes the point. Jonathan Coussins who was born in 1757 disturbed Methodist services in Bristol. He went to the chapel of the Countess of Huntingdon there and

> thought the discourse was entirely directed to him. He returned home in great distress, *but having no-one to speak to,* concerning what then oppressed his mind, his convictions soon died away. In the nineteenth year of his age he and his (elder) sister went to Cheltenham in the service of a genteel family... Miss Coussins enquired if any of the preachers in Lady Huntingdon's interest came to that place and was answered in the negative... A member of the Methodist society (at Cheltenham) being informed of the enquiry... embraced the first opportunity of soliciting her to attend their meetings. The invitation was accepted and at this ...house she met Miss Newman... They entered upon the subject of Christian Experience, and, during the conversation, Miss Coussins wept much. They went to the meeting together; Mr Geo. Snowden preached, and under the sermon her mind was greatly affected. On their return they talked and wept together till they arrived at her lodgings. Mr Coussins let them in, but there appearing no opportunity for religious conversation, Miss Newman retired. He accompanied her home, and as they walked together, she asked him if he had ever heard the Methodists. He answered 'No.' She then told him the Gospel was there preached by them and that there was reason to hope his sister had felt the power of it. ...She proceeded to enquire, if he ever had been convinced of the wretchedness and misery of his state by nature. He replied that he had been made ...sensible of it under one sermon, but that the impressions were soon effaced. She ...admonished him of the danger consequent upon stifling conviction and the misery of losing the soul. His mind was much affected and he requested ...a further interview to renew the subject.... In a few days he called on Miss Newman in company with his sister... They were by her introduced to Mr Samuel Wells, then a Local Preacher and Class Leader in the Society... After some conversation he admitted them into his Class; they received his instruction with gratitude, renounced their former course of life, and were evidently only intent upon obtaining the pardoning love of God. One evening while Miss Newman was praying with them, the divine presence was very sensibly felt. When she was about to conclude, Mr Coussins cried out, 'pray on! For God is here!' His sister also repeated the request, saying 'Do pray! Do pray! God will give us the blessing. After they arose from their knees he said: '...while you were engaging in prayer, I saw Jesus Christ crucified for me.' ...Next morning he determined to pray and fast till he should attain a sense of pardon. 'For this he besought the Lord, with strong cries and tears, until eleven o'clock ...when ...God condescends to reveal to him his pardoning mercy. Immediately he repaired to Miss Newman's house and informed her what God had done for his soul and they rejoiced together...' This was on the 24th of October 1766...

Coussins then joined a Methodist society in Bath and looked for the moment of sanctification. Samuel Wells wrote to him

> I am glad you have already experienced redemption in the blood of Jesus, the forgiveness of your sins; and I hope you are continually seeking after that [perfect] love which casts out fear and expels the carnal mind. Indeed my dear brother you cannot expect it too soon... when you experience this degree of salvation, you will feel yourself calm in the presence of God; your soul will rejoice before him as a little child... While your heart dares not move... But with full submission to his will; then also you will feel that all your soul is open to his view...Let your mind be always stayed on God; do not leave his presence for any person or thing whatsoever... All your labour must be to walk with God now. Set the Lord always before you, and you shall never be moved. Do all the good you can to others. Persuade all you can to expect a present, entire deliverance...

In 1778 he heard John Fletcher preach at Bath and

> At that time felt power to give up his whole soul unto God, in a way he had never done before. His sacrifice was accepted: he felt a larger measure of the sanctifying influence of the Spirit. Jesus became more than ever precious to him, and he experienced the blessedness of being made pure in heart. 'I was happy, unspeakably happy, when justified in faith in the Lord Jesus Christ; but what do I now feel! What love to God and all mankind!' Many strong temptations ...followed... yet he was enabled to hold fast that which he had received These words of St James 'he giveth more Grace' were as an anchor to his soul; he lived on the promise and experienced its accomplishment.

By this time Coussins was already leading prayer meetings in different places. Next he became a local preacher and in 1780 was encouraged by the Assistant preacher John Valton to go out to preach, his first circuit being Norwich. Later he married Penelope Newman who had been the means of his conversion.[14]

This account was typical of many. Coussins was in his teens as were many new converts. There was the discussion of 'Christian Experience' as the foundation for what later occurred. He found the means of grace in the class meeting, the preaching and the individual concern of existing Methodists who here included his future wife and his former class leader with whom he corresponded. The two stages of conversion and sanctification were both important to him. Coussins celebrated his conversion and spiritual rebirth each year. He had felt real psychological distress and agonizing which kept him awake at night and included weeping and fasting. It was a highly charged emotional experience eventually leading to joy. His story would be told and retold in many different ways and situations. Sanctification took him several years to achieve; it was an ecstatic experience which provided him with peace and security, symbolized by the 'anchor to his soul,' and was then followed by immediate new service as a preacher. This search for peace and security recurred in so many of these stories, as did the immediate dedication to an active service of others and the determination to speak about his conversion

---

[14] *MM* 1806: 289-296, 337-8, with my italics.

come what may. Coussins was mobile as were many early Methodist converts. As he moved around he tapped into a strong network of supportive Methodists which contrasted with the decentralized Anglican parish system.

In Hindmarsh's terms these accounts were autobiographical with an apologetic for the individual. They were narrative with a structure which pointed to a moral meaning and had an identity in which the 'real' ego was partially revealed. They were about the conversion or change within the person and the evangelical gospel in the sense of good news relating to belief in their own salvation. Hindmarsh has identified the conversion process for Wesley's preachers as being influenced by the fact that the description was being made much later, looking back over what had often been long lives. Their lifespan was divided into 'different shades of unsatisfactory' before their conversion and a much happier existence afterwards. They were very influenced by this reflection and also by Wesley. Many accounts, because they appeared in the *Arminian Magazine,* were 'Arminian' in that they often explicitly included deliverance from Calvinism. They were also Arminian in their emphasis on how the perfection process continued after conversion.

Entire sanctification was another theme which was often present. John Kershaw's autobiography, having described how he had been convinced of his unworthiness in the Greenland fishery and converted after his return home, continued 'I was still a stranger to one of the glories of Methodism... Viz the Witness of the Spirit.. I could not say,- 'Jesus is the Lord, by the Holy Ghost.' I understood it was my Christian privilege and was determined not to rest short of it.' This insistence on claiming all the Methodist doctrine and continued progress in the Christian life was at the heart of so many conversion stories.[15]

'Methodist'

It is important to discuss the term 'Methodist.' In the eighteenth century it was applied to anyone who was seen as too Evangelical, all those who preached for conversion and all who were too 'enthusiastic,' the first two of Bebbington's characteristics. It was given to the Welsh Methodists surrounding Williams of Pantycelyn and Howell Harris, to Whitefield and those who supported him, later to the Countess of Huntingdon and her preachers, and to any within the church who were 'enthusiastic' or sympathetic to Wesley or any of the others. Other groups like the Inghamites, followers of Benjamin Ingham mostly in Yorkshire and in the Pennine Dales, were also called Methodists. So were the societies who gathered around the Wesleys, the Holy Club in Oxford earlier, the Society at Fetter Lane later. However, in this book it will generally be given

---

[15] Hempton, *Empire* Chapter 3 'the Medium and the Message.' The five concepts were explained more fully in Hindmarsh, *Conversion Narrative* 4-16. He summarised the testimonies of the preachers most usefully in 238-260. See Chapters 5 and 20 below for further characteristics identified by Hindmarsh. Kershaw's account is in *AM* 1802: 221.

only to those who supported Wesley since in the long term the Wesley brothers successfully appropriated the term.

Later, as Hempton pointed out, Methodism created rules, lists, conventions and the like, which became hallowed traditions because they suited the inventors. These 'Methodist' traditions could often be late in origin and growth, so the Legal Hundred did not begin until 1784 and the first camp meeting was held only in 1799.[16]

Quite often in their letters Methodists in the period 1740-1820 referred to 'our friends,' particularly at the end of the letter where regards or respects would be sent to 'all friends.' The reference was usually to Methodist members at whatever place. Frequently, however, it was to local people of influence, who might sometimes attend but were not members, though they were sympathetic. Such influential 'friends' might entertain Wesley or leading preachers like Coke. If a preacher were imprisoned or attacked they would use their influence on the local magistrate or Lord Lieutenant. If money were needed for building they might supply all or part, or at least the land needed. Such 'friends' were an important part of the late eighteenth century scene. Their influence protected and encouraged Methodism. Though they might generally worship at their local parish church, they should also be described as Methodists in this period.[17]

The Methodist denominations, looking back to Wesley as their founder, expanded far faster than any other part of the Evangelical Revival. From a base of zero in the late 1730s they had grown to 25 million adherents and members by 1900. Though in America and Britain this had declined by the twenty-first century, in Asia, Africa and Latin America the growth still continues, to the amazement of many who find it difficult to visualize that there might be far more Methodists in Brazil than Europe, or Korea than Britain. The fact that this has mirrored the changes in the distribution of Christians generally only makes the point that Methodism has been and has remained a main driver in the growth of World Christianity over the last three centuries. Methodists have had this world view from the outset.[18]

---

[16] For the use of the term Methodist see Heitzenrater 45-6 and Rack 84. Because of his apt and persuasive use of illustrations, maps and diagrams Heitzenrater's book is vital for understanding early Methodism. For Ingham see H. M. Pickles, *Benjamin Ingham, Preacher among the Dales, Forests and Hills* (Skipton: Pickles, 1995). For the origin of camp meetings see W. C. Barclay, *Early American Methodism 1769-1849* (New York: Board of Missions, 1949) 1: 145.

[17] Pawson's letter to William Eden in 1769 ended: 'Give my kindest respects to all the good family, to William and the shepherd and his wife and all friends' (*Pawson L.* 1: 7). The phrase was often repeated. Compare the definition of 'friend' in Shani D'Cruze, 'The Middling Sort in 18th Century Colchester: Independence, Social Relations and the Community Broker' in J. Barry and C. Brooks, eds, *The Middling Sort of People: Culture Society and Politics in England 1550-1800* (London: Macmillan, 1994) 189.

[18] Hempton, *Empire* Chapter Eight and Chapters 10-13 below.

Definitions 31

Cohorts

One of the ways I have analysed the Wesley's Preachers' Database is by cohorts, to enable changes to be detected over time. So the preachers have been divided into cohorts based on date of entry (see Chart 1 below based on Table 1 in Appendix One). This is refining Myles's idea of first, second and third races.

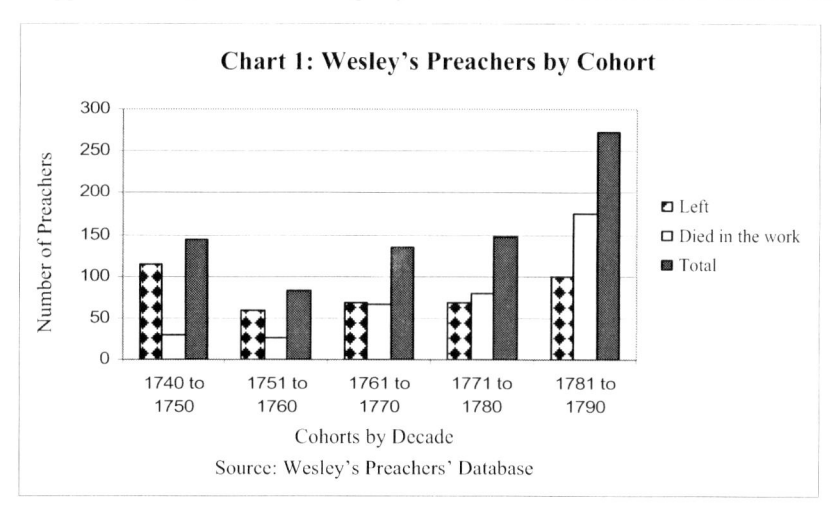

Chart 1: Wesley's Preachers by Cohort

Source: Wesley's Preachers' Database

144 entered before 1751; 84 between 1751 and 1760; 135 between 1761 and 1770; 149 between 1771 and 1780 and 273 came in during the final decade between 1781 and 1790. I refer to these as cohorts 1, 2, 3, 4, 5, so that cohort 1 entered in the 1740s, 2 in the 1750s, and so on.[19]

The reason for the relatively large number in the first cohort was because of the very fluid state of the connexion in the early years. I have included in this first cohort a number of Anglican clergy, such as R. T. Bateman, John Meriton, Henry Piers and John Simpson,[20] and others who had links originally, for example Thomas Crouch and David Taylor, but had cut them by 1750 or would do so soon after; there also remain some doubtfuls. The 1740s was a period of great flux in the evangelical field, one illustrated by Ward, Podmore, and Harding among others. William Holland, for example, was one of the 'Cambridge Methodist' circle. A devout Anglican with a painting business in Basinghall Street, London, he is thought to be the reader of Luther's Preface to Romans which John Wesley heard at Aldersgate Street on the 24th May 1738. Holland was a founding member of the Society at Fetter Lane, who in 1740 remained with the Moravians on their split with Wesley. On March 31st 1741 he married Elizabeth Delamotte, to whom Whitefield had recently proposed. Both William and Elizabeth Holland still appeared in Wesley's list of the

---

[19] 17 preachers have not been assigned a cohort because it is too difficult to decide when they entered.

[20] For these see Wood, *Brothers in Arms* an important pamphlet often overlooked.

Methodist London society in 1742/3. William had become an Elder of the London Moravian society, however, by August 1743. He gave up his business to be a full time preacher for the Moravians which included being in charge at Fulneck. He left them in 1747 because he wanted to retain more Anglican connections than they did. Wesley therefore suited him and he returned to work with John. Holland accompanied John Hodges' curate, Philip Thomas, in December 1746 to Neath on a tour of Hodges' Wesleyan societies in Glamorgan. He lived in Brentford and rode to Basingstoke with Wesley in November 1747 and was present at Wesley's Conference on the 6th June 1748. Eventually he left Wesley and died in 1761, still an evangelical Anglican.[21]

After the 1740s the numbers of preachers rose steadily with the expansion of Methodism. The large number in the final cohort should be noted. It links with the rapid expansion of the connexion after Wesley's death.[22]

Who was the First Lay Preacher?

There were several laymen who were preaching before John Wesley came on the scene. Howell Harris and others had been preaching in Wales since as early as 1736. Whitefield had several laymen assisting him. Thomas Adams and John Cennick were two examples among many. Cennick had assisted Wesley in Bristol in 1739; having been Whitefield's protégé first, he helped Wesley for a very short period.

Wesleyan Methodism, however, has always tended to regard Thomas Maxfield as the first lay preacher, partly because of his remaining with Wesley for over twenty years and partly because of the good story told later by Coke and Moore in their biography in 1792, claiming they had been told it by Wesley himself. Wesley had been away from London in Bristol, had appointed Maxfield 'to meet the Society (at the Foundery) at the usual times, to pray with them and give them such advice as might be needful.' Maxfield, encouraged by the increasing numbers, had begun to preach and 'the Lord so blessed the word that many were not only deeply awakened and brought to repentance, but were also made happy in a consciousness of pardon. The Scripture-marks of true conversion, inward peace and power to walk in all holiness, evinced the work to be of God.' But

> a complaint was put in form to Mr Wesley and he hastened to London in order to put a stop to it. His mother then lived in his house adjoining to the Foundery. When he arrived, she perceived that his countenance was expressive of

---

[21] *WJW* 18: 249 n75, 20: 130 n78, 197-8 n49, 26: 278; MS letter in the National Library of Wales; C. J. Podmore, *History of the Moravian Church in England 1728-60* (Oxford: Clarendon, 1998) 41, 86-7, 116-7, 126, 181-6; A. A. Dallimore, *George Whitefield: the Life and Times of the Great Evangelist of the 18th Century Revival,* 2 vols (Edinburgh: Banner of Truth, 1970) 1: 183, 186, 217, 357-68, 473-6, 492, 524, 581-98, 2: 49.

[22] See Appendix Two for my discussion of total numbers.

dissatisfaction, and enquired the cause. 'Thomas Maxfield' said he abruptly, 'has turned preacher, I find.' She looked attentively at him, and replied, 'John, you know what my sentiments have been. You cannot suspect me of favouring readily anything of this kind. But take care what you do with respect to that young man, for he is as surely called of God to preach, as you are. Examine what have been the fruits of his preaching: and hear him also yourself.'

Having listened and presumably calmed down, Wesley accepted that Maxfield was called and encouraged him and others. A nice story, but it was not told till long after it happened and after Wesley's death and is difficult to date.[23] A way out of the difficulty would be if it was all invented, but this is unlikely! What is probable is that others such as Cennick had preached in Bristol before this date.[24]

The other problem is that Wesley said different things about this at different periods. In 1763 he said Maxfield was 'employed by me not long after as a preacher in London,' that is not long after 1739. This does not fit with Baker's dating of the Maxfield story in January or March 1741. The 1766 Minutes say 'After a time a young man came, T. Maxfield and said he desired to help me as a son in the gospel. Soon after there came a second, Thomas Richards and a third, Thomas Westell...' Obviously none of these memories are close to the period. It may have happened as Wesley eventually told it. Wesley always remembered what it suited him to remember and suppressed what he would rather forget.

Women Preachers

In the eighteenth century it was assumed women would not preach, except among the Quakers where female 'ministers' had travelled extensively from the seventeenth century. From the first Wesley encouraged women to lead in prayer. He appointed them as class leaders and was rewarded by their support. More women consistently joined the early Methodists than men. This was true for hearers and for full members of society. Over the period 1750-1825 Clive Field has shown that, of a very large sample of 53,250 Methodist members,

---

[23] F. Baker, 'Thomas Maxfield's first sermon' *PWHS* 27 (1949-50), 7-15. The first printed version of the story was in T. Coke and H. Moore, *Life of the Rev. John Wesley* (London: Paramore, 1792) 219-20, when Wesley was dead and could not confirm it. Baker dated Maxfield's first preaching at the Foundery as January or March 1741.

[24] A. Clarke, *Memorials of the Wesley Family* had a slightly different version 353-4 (London: J. & T. Clarke, 1823). For another assessment of the whole story Burdon, *Authority* 22-3. Burdon is wrong, however, on Charles Delamotte where he suggests he did not 'arise from the Methodist revival.' Delamotte came from an Anglican, not Dissenting, background. He accompanied the Wesleys to Georgia, even if he did become a Moravian later. Moravians should be seen, as they were generally at the time, as 'Methodists,' even if opposed to Wesleyan Methodism.

57.5 % were women. In addition there were more women than men among such groups as band members.[25]

However, in general Wesley seemed at first to be opposed to women speaking. Recent evidence unearthed by Lloyd showed that Sarah Perrin spoke among early Methodists, mostly in the Leominster area where no male lay preachers were available in the 1740s and early 1750s. She and Grace Walton, a Northern woman preacher who travelled with Bennet briefly in 1746, appear to have been isolated examples in that period, though there is a reference to women preaching in Cornwall in May 1747.[26] However, from 1760 onwards a substantial number of Methodist women, notably Sarah Crosby, Sarah Ryan and others, spoke in religious services and preached over a wide area. In most cases they were class leaders of such power and influence that men and non-Methodists clamoured to hear them and insisted that their hearers were not confined to women or Methodists. This book does not deal with women preachers, except incidentally, as wives of the male preachers for instance. This is because they were not employed as full time itinerants, unlike the men, or later with the Primitive Methodists and Bible Christians.[27]

The differences between the two were real, apart from the gender. Male itinerants were under discipline, responsible to Wesley and the Conference. Nearly all were appointed to circuits and though they might easily be moved they were supposed to remain within those circuits, where they had a clear round as will be described in Chapter 8 below. Only when they stayed in one place for more than one night were they likely to be involved in prayer meetings. Women preachers, however, could choose themselves where they

---

[25] For gender proportions see C. D. Field, 'Adam and Eve: Gender in the English Free Church Constituency' *JEH* 44 (1993) 63. For the band member lists see G. J. Stevenson, *History of City Road Chapel* (London: Stevenson, 1872) 28-39.

[26] Valentine, *Bennet*. The first Methodist woman preacher, however, like the first lay preacher, would appear to be Welsh. Elizabeth Thomas of Blaen-porth in Cardiganshire had already begun to exhort a little in the private society when Howell Harris met her in 1741. According to Eryn White 'With a becoming modesty she questioned whether it was appropriate for her to continue to do so. In the absence of any other exhorter in the area, Harris gave his permission.' She was only speaking in the society and not in Church. (E. M. White 'Women in the Early Methodist Societies in Wales' *Journal of Welsh Religious History* 7 (1999) 106). See also the article by G. Lloyd on 'Sarah Perrin (1721-87): Early Methodist Exhorter' *MH* 41 (2003) 79-88. The Cornish reference comes from a hostile and vague reference in the Lavington Correspondence from Luney near St Ewe: 'and even women of the same (ignorant and wicked) stamp are adored Preachers.' No named example is given. (*PWHS* 42 (1979-80) 168-70).

[27] The best general account of Methodist women preachers in the 18th Century remains Chilcote, *Women Preachers*. The Appendices are most useful. Chilcote's view that they gave up after Wesley's death and the Conference prohibition of 1803 was answered by my '"Labouring for the Lord:" Women Preachers in the 19th century' in R. Sykes, ed, *Beyond the Boundaries* (Oxford: Applied Academic Press, 1996) 58-86.

went. They were subject to the whims of the male Assistant who might invite them or hinder them from preaching. If they preached they were more likely to stay in one place for some time, leading prayer meetings and classes as well as preaching. Male itinerants travelled together rarely, perhaps going to Conference or accompanying a leader like Wesley. Female preachers travelled together more frequently. There were fewer of them. Many remained in a particular area and rarely strayed outside it, though some made preaching tours often in different areas. Among the latter were Sarah Crosby in the north, especially in the 1770s, Betsy Hurrell in Yorkshire from 1775 to 1780, Ann Cutler in the north-west in 1793/4, and Mary Barritt throughout much of the north from 1794 on to her marriage in 1802. It can be seen that the north, particularly from Preston across to the Yorkshire coast, was their stronghold, though there were also groups in Cornwall, Norfolk, and at different times centring on Mary Bosanquet Fletcher at Madeley in the West Midlands or Leytonstone and Essex.

Titles

Travelling Preachers and Local Preachers

Wesley's lay preachers were originally called 'helpers' by him because of the practical support they gave him. They were authorized by him 'in the absence of a minister' (Wesley meant a Church of England clergyman) 'to feed and guide the flock.' Often they accompanied one of the Wesleys or they would be left behind in Newcastle, London, Bristol, Cornwall or Wednesbury to look after the society and its class meetings. The terms 'Helper' and 'Preacher' were used equally during the eighteenth century to describe Wesley's preachers. The term 'Assistant' was used to describe the chief preacher in each circuit who later became the Superintendent. The term 'minister' was not used of Wesleyan preachers before 1810. The chief distinction was between those preachers who were full time itinerants and local preachers who had an ordinary job and usually only preached on Sundays and to the smaller societies or when the travelling preacher was away, for example at Conference time.[28] In Wesley's day, especially in the period before 1765, it was easy to move from being local to itinerant and back again. Indeed there were many described as 'half itinerant' because they moved from one state to the other at different seasons. In the pre-industrial days of the eighteenth century this was easy. There were natural quiet periods in every occupation where other tasks could be undertaken. Just as most ceased their other jobs to concentrate on agriculture at harvest time, so those interested in a spiritual harvest turned to reap that at times they thought particularly hopeful. Neither group in Wesley's day was to administer the sacraments, for which all Methodists went to their local Anglican Church. It

---

[28] B. E. Beck in *DOMBI* 239. For more on probation, 'On Trial,' 'Full Connexion' and Assistants see Chapter 5 below.

was only late in Wesley's life, from 1784, that this began to change.[29]

Later Titles

In the nineteenth century the travelling preachers became generally called ministers. It was only in September 1821, after a discussion on this at Conference, that the official titles of the portraits in the *Magazine* changed from 'Mr. Willm. Dixon, Preacher of the Gospel' to the 'Revd. John Bell.' Even then they were not sure and retreated in October to 'William Hinson Preacher of the Gospel' before resuming in November with the 'Revd. John Lancaster'![30]

Wesley's 'Sons in the Gospel'

The phrase 'Son in the Gospel' was one frequently used by Wesley and others which expressed the relationship between the Wesley brothers and their preachers, remaining true both for Wesley's lifetime and beyond. There were many examples of Wesley using the phrase, the first being in relation to his brother Charles and John Cennick, writing to Cennick 'You came to Kingswood upon my brother's sending for you. You served under him as a son.' It was Charles who had begun the whole process, at least in this early example.[31] Nine letters of the early Yorkshire evangelist John Nelson to Charles Wesley survive. Each ended 'as a son to serve in the Gospel' before Nelson's signature.

It worked both ways, as in Asbury's famous reference to Wesley as his 'Old Daddy' in a letter to a British preacher in 1788. Even after Wesley's death he was thought of as the father of his preachers. So Samuel Bradburn, who entered in 1774, in his *Sketch of Mr Wesley's Character,* published soon after Wesley's death in 1791, wrote of how he thought it right 'as a son, to say something of my father in the Gospel.'[32] In 1791 Frances Pawson wrote of 'a very consoling letter from my husband (John) of the peace and union of the Conference. Surely this is of God, for the preachers were left as children without a father.'[33] The phrase expressed the personal relationship which existed.

---

[29] For more details on the half itinerant and some examples see Appendix Two.
[30] *MM* 1821; 1822.
[31] *WJW* 19: 186. Journal entry March 8th 1741, cf also *Minutes* 1766 as quoted above. The phrase is 'Son(s) *in* the Gospel' not 'Sons *of* the Gospel' as in the subheading in Burdon, *Authority* 22. I know no eighteenth century Methodist use of Burdon's variant.
[32] *Asbury Jol* 3: 62. The letter was to Winscom, a favourite of Wesley's and a quarrelsome character, not a good choice for confidences. T. Blanshard, *The Life of Samuel Bradburn, the Methodist Demosthenes* (London: Elliott Stock, 1870) 130-1.
[33] P. W. Chilcote, *Her Own Story: Autobiographical Portraits of Early Methodist Women* (Nashville: Kingswood, 2001) 98.

'Church Methodists'

Charles Wesley and many others expected the Methodists, led by most of the preachers, to leave the Church of England as soon as John Wesley's death was announced. It did not happen like that but more gradually over a long period of time. That period was longer than has sometimes been suggested. Gareth Lloyd has shown that pro-Anglican opinion, which was in the majority within Methodism in Wesley's lifetime, did not suddenly vanish in the 1790s or with the 'Plan of Pacification' of 1795. Indeed, the separation from the Church of England was neither assured nor present in many places for some time. 'Church Methodists,' as laypeople who attended both were described, were often wealthy with considerable local power as major employers like the Ryles and Roes in Macclesfield. In Madeley until the 1830s, in Bridgerule (Devon) till 1821, in York until the 1820s, in Wellington (Shropshire) till 1819, in Colne to after 1804, in Bradford, Macclesfield, Manchester, in Portsea, Methodists avoided meeting together in church hours in order to go in large numbers to the local parish churches. Ordinary Methodists, especially in the countryside, continued to do this into the twentieth century and beyond. The travelling preachers, though increasingly pulled by Conference in a different direction, were amenable to local custom and practice, at least while Evangelical clergy remained friendly.[34]

---

[34] G. Lloyd, 'Croakers and busybodies: The extent and influence of Church Methodism in the late 18th and early 19th Centuries,' *MH* 42 (2003) 20-32; (Madeley and Wellington) B. S. Trinder, *The Industrial Revolution in Shropshire* (Chichester: Phillimore, 2000); (York) Lyth 178-79; (Portsea) A. S. Wood, *Thomas Haweis 1734-1820* (London: SPCK, 1957) 210; (Bridgerule) A. Warne, *Church and Society in Eighteenth Century Devon* (Newton Abbot: David and Charles, 1969) 109; (Colne) M. F. Snape, 'The Church in a Lancashire Parish: Whalley 1689-1800' in Gregory and Chamberlain, *National Church* 246. The list could be much extended.

CHAPTER 3

Origins

'He that humbleth himself shall be exalted.'
Luke 14: 11.

Countries

Within the British Isles there tended to be more Methodists in the industrial and semi industrial areas, the miners of Kingswood or Tyneside, the nailers of the Black Country, the fishermen of West Cornwall. It is interesting to check the place of birth of Wesley's preachers in relation to the early distribution of Methodism. Though numbers in some areas in Chart 2 based on Table 2 in Appendix One are small and therefore statistically insignificant, some facts can be drawn from these statistics. Of the 507 of Wesley's preachers whose country

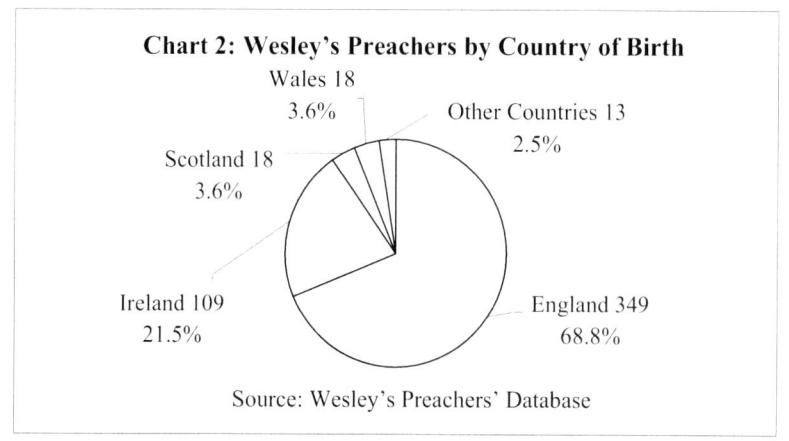

Chart 2: Wesley's Preachers by Country of Birth

- Wales 18 — 3.6%
- Other Countries 13 — 2.5%
- Scotland 18 — 3.6%
- Ireland 109 — 21.5%
- England 349 — 68.8%

Source: Wesley's Preachers' Database

of birth is established, 349 (68.8%) came from England, 109 (21.5%) from Ireland, 18 (3.6%) from Wales, 18 (3.6%) from Scotland and there were thirteen others. These thirteen were a mixture including those from the British colonies in America, the West Indies, Germany, the Channel Islands,[1]

---

[1] The two born in Germany were both preachers in Ireland, Guier and Miller. The three from the Channel Islands were William Dieuaide, William Mahy and John de

Switzerland (John Fletcher) and Samuel Bradburn who was born at sea off Gibraltar. These figures are not in general unexpected. Wesley never had much success in Wales or Scotland.

Counties

For counties I am using pre-1974 boundaries in Britain. The numbers from many counties are too small to be statistically significant (see Table 3 in the Appendix). For 339 of the English-born 349, we know the county from which they came. Map 1 is useful in seeing where there were concentrations within the counties. The old West Riding produced more of Wesley's preachers than any other county by a long way. 78 (23%) came from the West Riding, compared with 37 (10.9%) from Cornwall, the next highest. Again it is interesting to compare the different cohorts. The West Riding mirrored very well the overall percentages, having 12 in cohort 1, going down slightly to 10, and then relatively steadily increasing to 31 in the 5th cohort. Cornwall, which started with slightly more at 14, never reached that number again. Wesley went to Cornwall more than he did at first to Yorkshire. Cornwall was not short of Methodist members; 6% of all Methodists were Cornish in 1791. Indeed, as Nicholas Gilbert wrote from the county to Charles Wesley in 1760 'There is a great willingness in the inhabitants of this County to hear the preaching of the Gospel of Jesus Christ.'[2] Was there, however, a prejudice against Cornish candidates by the 1760s? Or do we just not know enough about origins?

To return to the West Riding, reasons for the large numbers are easy to determine. The majority came from what were to be the industrial areas from Sheffield north to the Wharfe valley. John Nelson, the stonemason of Birstall imprisoned in the cell below the butcher's shop in Ivegate, Bradford, is an early well known figure, invited to Wesley's 'Conference' in 1743. Many preachers came from the Birstall area because of Nelson.[3] William Darney was someone who already had his own group of societies on both sides of the Pennines. Methodist organization led by Grimshaw of Haworth and his preachers, supported by John Bennet and William Shent, made the whole of the Great Haworth Round strongly Methodist, especially the small communities remote from parish churches and growing in population thanks to the Industrial Revolution. In the South of the Riding preaching by David Taylor and Bennet gave a firm foundation to Methodism in the Sheffield area.[4]

Queteville. In the *Minutes* he was always 'Queteville.' Later writers often refer to him as 'Quetteville.' *WJW* 23: 376 n37; H. de Jersey, *Vie de Rev. Jean de Queteville et Vie de Madame de Queteville* (London: Mason, 1847). Discussion of these figures will be in later chapters under the countries concerned.

[2] *Minutes* 1791. Quotation from MARC DDPr 1/33. Gilbert was himself a Cornishman.
[3] For Nelson see *EMP* 1: 1-178.
[4] For Grimshaw see Baker, *Grimshaw*. For Bennet see Valentine, *Bennet*.

Origins

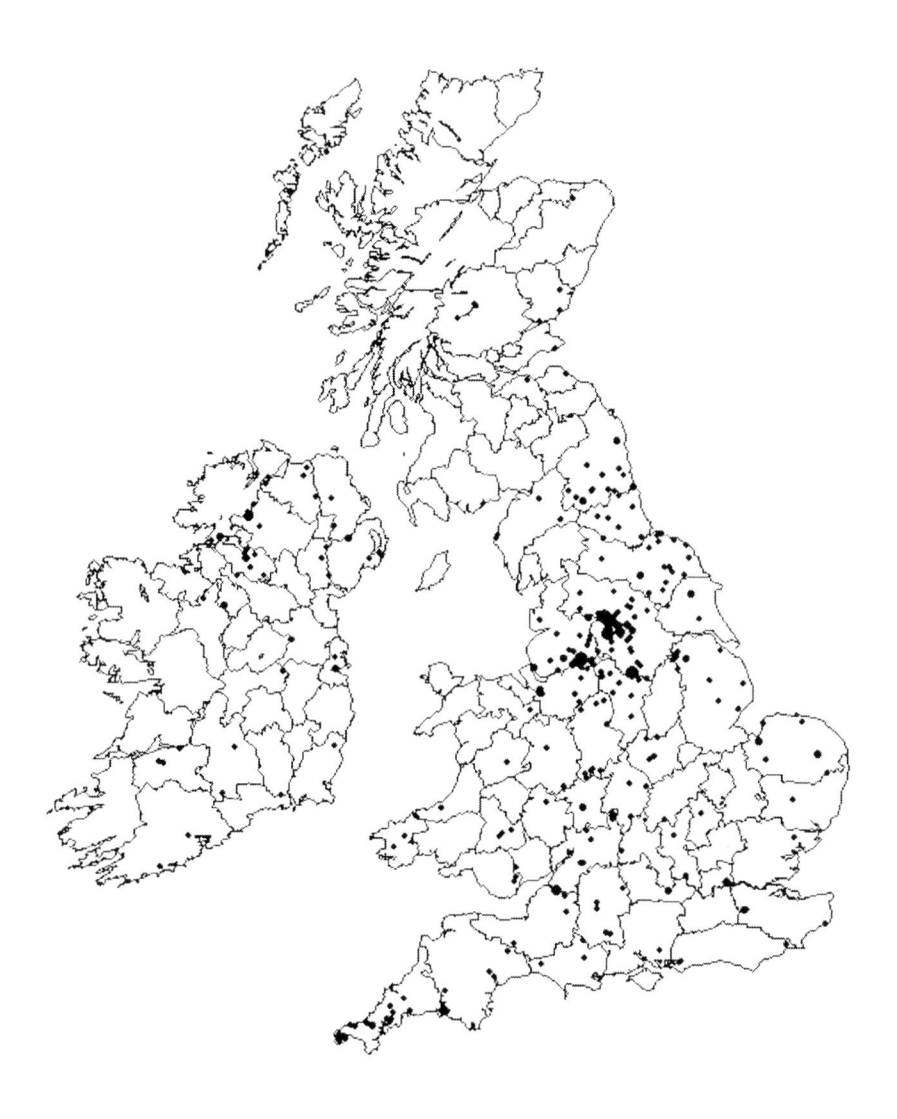

Map 1: Birthplaces of Wesley's Preachers

Particular areas in the West Riding were stronger such as Keighley, Halifax, Bradford, Birstall, and Wakefield. In contrast, Leeds and Huddersfield produced relatively few preachers. Huddersfield was a parish where Wesley tended to keep his preachers out till 1771 because of the Evangelical Vicar Henry Venn. Edward Royle also pointed out that it was a cul-de-sac in the eighteenth century, with no roads over the Pennines. While Wesley travelled down the Calder on his way to Birstall and Leeds, he did not come to Huddersfield till 1757, eleven years after his first visit to Halifax.[5] The reason for the weakness in Leeds in the eighteenth century is not clear but may be linked to the importance of William Hey, a leading citizen of Leeds and Circuit Steward since 1764 who left Methodism in 1784, and the lamentable history of William Shent, the first male Methodist in Leeds and a leading local preacher, who fell into drunken notoriety.[6]

In the West Riding by 1760 deep roots had already been put down in what were still very rural areas such as upper Airedale and Wharfedale. Certainly Methodism was strong in industrial towns like Halifax and Bradford and semi industrial villages like Bingley, Birstall, and Horbury, but it was also fast growing in the rural villages around Keighley, Addingham and Heptonstall, the heartland of the 'Old Haworth round.' Kent's recent view,[7] implying no rural Methodism existed at this early period outside Cornwall, may be true for much of the south and midlands but is wrong so far as the West Riding is concerned.

In the North Riding 22 preachers were born. Only three came from the neighbouring East Riding. Within the North Riding the majority came from Cleveland or from the plain immediately north of York and heading towards the North York Moors, rather than from the Vale of York and the Dales. There was a strong tendency for the whole of the north and the north midlands to produce itinerant preachers. This was especially true for three other areas within the 'greater north:' first, places within a 40 mile radius of Newcastle; secondly those within the same distance of Manchester; and finally Lincolnshire, John Wesley's old county to which he returned regularly, especially in his native north and in the villages around Epworth where many preachers appeared.

In contrast in the south of England there were few born (see Table 4 in Appendix One). This was not only the Methodist desert of Hampshire, Sussex, Surrey, Berkshire, but also London, East Anglia, the south west except for the

---

[5] For Henry Venn (1725-97) see Elliott-Binns, *Early Evangelicals*. E. Royle, *Queen Street Chapel and Mission, Huddersfield* (Huddersfield: Huddersfield Local History Society, 1994).

[6] For Hey and Shent see *DOMBI* sv Leeds and Shent. Industrial towns like Leeds grew from migration from surrounding areas, so this weakness was corrected by the early nineteenth century by migration of Methodists from the strongly Methodist villages to the rural north and east of Leeds.

[7] Kent, *Wesley and the Wesleyans* 64.

Origins

area around Bristol, and Cornwall, and vast swathes of the midlands and south in general. One gap was in the east midlands where the map shows no-one from Huntingdon, Cambridge and Rutland and none from southern Lincolnshire and most of Northamptonshire. All these areas produced fewer preachers than would be expected from the numbers of Methodist members in 1791. In Cornwall it was the west and to a lesser extent the centre which produced preachers. Few came from the east of Cornwall except near the south coast. Notable exceptions to this rule previously unnoticed were the dockyards, especially around Portsmouth and Plymouth. These were some of the most important concentrations of industrial workers in the eighteenth century, employing 9,000 men even in peacetime. Skilled workers here became preachers and class leaders and took Methodism to places like Antigua and Gibraltar as the navy expanded. Plymouth Dock was the name of an important society and circuit. Portsmouth was almost as significant and rather more isolated so far as Methodism was concerned.[8]

Long ago Edwards pointed out that Methodism was strongest in the industrial areas of the midlands and the north. Currie took this further and argued that Methodism did best in the thirteen counties in the north and midlands where the Established Church was weakest. Rack in 1989 argued that in addition it did well where nobody was strong like Cornwall. Gay illustrated all this in his maps in 1971 which have been improved by Watts' more detailed and precise maps.[9] In the midlands and south in general there was more competition from Dissent. The Countess of Huntingdon's Connexion was strongest in the midlands and south centre, areas like Birmingham and Berkshire where Wesleyan Methodism was always relatively weak. In contrast her Connexion had little in the north or the south west.[10] Recently a major study of the Anglican clergy in the long eighteenth century has shown that they also had an over-supply in the north and west and an under-supply in the south and east.[11]

---

[8] The 'Methodist desert' is a phrase from W. W. Pocock, *History of Wesleyan Methodism in Some of the Southern Counties of England* (London: WCO, 1885). For the dockyards see J. G. Coad, *The Royal Dockyards 1690-1850* (Aldershot: Scolar Press, 1989). Preachers linked to the dockyards included William Freemantle and Peter Price from Gosport, John Baxter of Chatham, Richard Condy, Thomas Janes, William Stevens and William Palmer from Plymouth Dock, e.g. *MM* 1816: 54-7.

[9] M. Edwards, *After Wesley* (London: Epworth, 1935) 142; R. Currie, 'A Micro-Theory of Methodist Growth' *PWHS* 36: (1967-8) 67; Rack 438; J. D. Gay, *The Geography of Religion in England* (London; Duckworth, 1971) 145-48, 271, 310; Watts, *Dissenters*.

[10] Harding, *Countess's Connexion* map and Annex B List of Chapels 1790.

[11] W. M. Jacob, *The Clerical Profession in the Long Eighteenth Century 1680-1840* (Oxford: OUP, 2007) 38-9.

Towns versus Countryside

It would be tempting to suggest that most of Wesley's preachers came from the countryside rather than the towns or cities. Where known this is true, at least to the extent of birthplace. However Rule[12] has suggested a three way division for population growth in the period: 1) Agricultural rural population rising slowly; 2) rural non agricultural; 3) Urban. In the last two, the population was increasing strongly in the eighteenth century. The reasons for Wesley's preachers having rural origins were complex. More people then lived in the countryside than in the towns. Rural areas tended to be more neglected than the towns by the Established Church and so were more likely to turn to Methodism. Methodism appealed more to the less sophisticated outside rather than the better educated in the towns. The Methodist itinerant system especially suited the sparsely populated or industrial settlements growing on the outskirts of parishes, rather than the established towns where there were many strong churches which were often Dissenters' as well as parish churches. Of Rule's three groups, Methodism was strongest among the rural non agricultural workers, the tinners, miners and fishermen of Cornwall, the colliers of Placey in Northumberland or of east Shropshire, the weavers and spinners of Lancashire and the West Riding. However, towns in the eighteenth century still preserved links with the surrounding countryside. The link between urban workers and seasonal agricultural work was strong even in large cities like London, where thousands would leave the capital for the Kentish hop-harvest. It remains true that no generalization is correct everywhere. On the one hand, Manchester had 3% of its population as Methodist members in 1801, around three times the national average,[13] average. On the other hand, there were some agricultural areas, such as most of Shropshire and Herefordshire, which Methodism never reached until the nineteenth century and the coming of the Primitive Methodists. There were some industrial towns where Methodism was always weak at best. And there were even semi industrial rural areas where they never penetrated, at least in the eighteenth century. There were many Methodisms and not all were successful.

Religious Upbringing

Mostly the preachers' religious upbringings are unknown. However, for 161 (see Chart 3 below based on Table 5 in Appendix One) it is known. Of these 65 (40%) were brought up in the Church of England or Church of Ireland. This included James Wood, born at West Buckland in Somerset in 1751, who had been baptized as a Dissenter but his parents switched to the Church of England before he was eight years old. 40 of them (25%) had been raised as Methodists.

---

[12] J. Rule, *Vital Century: England's Developing Economy 1714-1815* (London: Longmans, 1992) 96-7.
[13] Rack 437.

37 (23%) were brought up in the nonconformist sects, a large penumbra including Scots Presbyterians, Quakers, Moravians and Unitarians, but not in this period Methodism. John Bennet, one of the best known of the early preachers, was brought up a Dissenter at the chapel at Chinley End in Derbyshire. Of these most (seventeen) were Presbyterians. There were eight described as Dissenters, most of these probably the equivalent of the later Congregationalists though some may have been Presbyterian. Among these thirty-seven six were Quakers, one Unitarian, three Moravians and one Baptist.

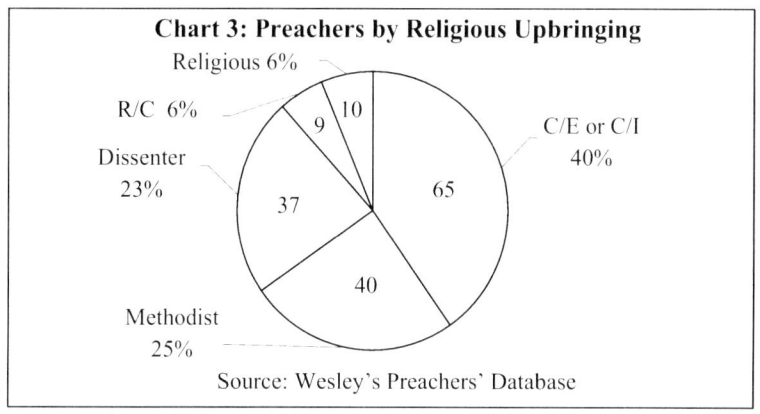

Chart 3: Preachers by Religious Upbringing

- Religious 6%
- R/C 6%
- Dissenter 23%
- Methodist 25%
- C/E or C/I 40%

Source: Wesley's Preachers' Database

There were nine Roman Catholics (6%). The best known of the Catholics was the Irishman Thomas Walsh.[14] There were another ten preachers where the upbringing was described as 'religious' but it is not clear in what context.

This is important because there has been much argument as to whether Wesley and Methodism owed more to Anglican or Dissenting influences. So far as his preachers were concerned it looks as though they had been more influenced by the Church of England. All good Methodists attended the Church in Wesley's day, so that over 65% of those known came from that background. In addition 68% of those brought up as Anglicans or Methodists died in the work, compared with only 51% of those raised as Dissenters. They were therefore more likely to stay. John Bennet is a good example of a preacher brought up as a Dissenter who left, a contrast with James Wood who died in the work as an aged Supernumerary in 1840. On the other hand Dissenters in the eighteenth century were a much smaller (and reducing) proportion of the population, and Anglicans were the majority of the population. This shows that Wesley did attract some of those who had been brought up as Dissenters and despite his high church links and ideas he was not prejudiced against them. All three of these examples were born in rural areas. Thomas Walsh was born in County Limerick at Ballylinn, twelve miles from the county town.

---

[14] For Wood see *WMM* 1842: 889-900, 977-85. For Bennet see Valentine, *Bennet*. For Walsh see *EMP* 3: 11-292 and R. O'Glaisne, 'Our Blessed Thomas Walsh.' *WHS (I)* 2; 7 (1994) 5-7.

Origins by Class

It was a class ridden-society where few questioned that there was a natural order of high and low. This was true of Wesley and the early Methodists. Sydney Smith later called Wesley's preachers a 'band of sanctified cobblers.' While it is easy to find a large number of other jobs apart from shoemaking that Wesley's preachers filled before they began to travel, it has been difficult to establish the classes from which they came. There was first the question as to what system to follow. With Clive Field I have used the 1760 work of Joseph Massie, whose estimates that year divided the population into six groups A-F (see Chart 4 based on Table 6 in Appendix One).[15] Massie was even more precise with his boundaries, dividing his groups into subgroups according to

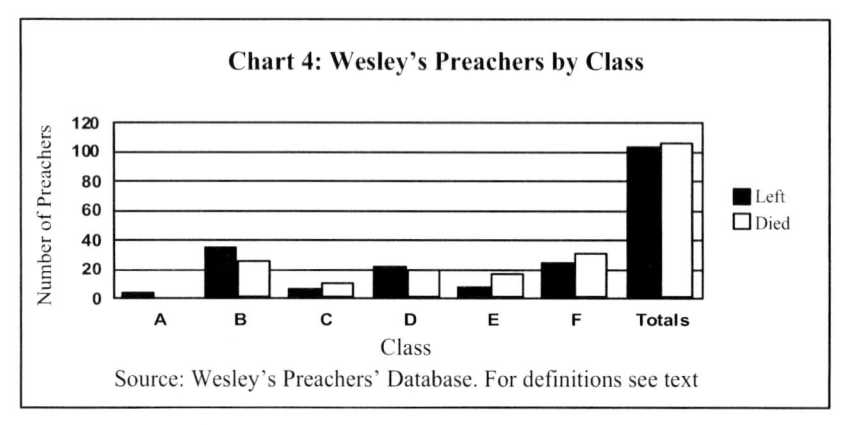

Chart 4: Wesley's Preachers by Class

Source: Wesley's Preachers' Database. For definitions see text

their income per year. For the preachers we have no such figures and therefore such precision is impossible. Then there is the question of which point in time is taken to establish class. William Bramwell's father was a fairly prosperous farmer at Elswick near Preston in Lancashire (Class C agriculture). Bramwell himself began as an apprentice currier in Preston (Class F labourer). However, by the time he entered the itinerancy he was running a successful business as a

---

[15] C. D. Field, 'The Social Structure of English Methodists 18th-20th Centuries' *British Journal of Sociology* 28 (1977) 2: 199-225. Field used six broad sub-headings as follows: A: Spiritual and temporal lords, baronets, knights, esquires, gentlemen. B: Clergy, lawyers, persons in the liberal arts, civil, naval and military officers. C: Freeholders, farmers. D: Merchants, tradesmen, innkeepers. E: manufacturers. F: Labourers, husbandmen, cottagers, seamen, fishermen, common soldiers. These are rather different from the more familiar Registrar-General later categories. P. Mathias, 'The Social Structure in the 18th century; A Calculation by Joseph Massie.' *Economic History Review* 2nd ser. 10 (1957-8) 30-45. See P. Earle, 'The Middling Sort in London' in Barry and Brooks, eds, *Middling Sort* 141-58 for a critique of Massie's formula as applied to 18th century London. So far as Methodism is concerned I have followed Rack's criticisms in *Reasonable Enthusiast* 439-442.

currier (Class E master manufacturer). He married Ellen Byrom, a daughter of a gentry family (A) or at least scientific (B), though at the time of the marriage she is described as a dressmaker in Preston (probably E). I have classified Bramwell as E and followed, where possible, the principle of what the preacher was employed in doing immediately before entry.[16]

The typical person in the eighteenth century worked at different pursuits at different times of year. This was well summarized in the 1851 census; 'The same person is... an innkeeper and a farmer, a maltster and a brewer, a fisherman in the season and a farmer or labourer for the rest of the year.'[17] If these seasonal occupations were true in 1851 they were truer in the eighteenth century when large numbers had dual employments, combining a small-holding or market garden with industrial work like spinning, or framework knitting. The term 'manufacturer' is itself ambiguous. Originally it meant someone who made things with his hands, that is an artisan. By this period it could mean someone like Matthew Boulton who employed 500 men, or someone who still worked with his hands and employed no-one outside his family circle. All these factors make it difficult to be certain that any individual is within one class or occupation group only.

In addition, the evidence for most preachers is lacking. For only a quarter (211) can an estimate be made. The results fit with Clive Field's wider sample except for three groups, the most notable being the larger numbers in the professions. This is not only caused by the inclusion of a number of Anglican clergy. It is also the recurrence of such jobs as excise officer, schoolmaster, and surveyor. These were what were sometimes described as the 'middling sort.' They were a very diverse group occupying a position between the gentry and the labouring classes. They stressed the importance of financial probity and the efficient use of time and resources. They were often mobile. It was their literacy which fuelled the explosion of printing which Wesley exploited.[18]

There were several servants (included in F). Some of these were well off; Benjamin Biggs, Sir James Lowther's butler, was left £59 per annum for life in Lowther's will. Richard Elliott, Richard Arkwright's coachman, was probably only marginally worse off. Henry Rack pointed out that preachers were going to be different from the much larger number of ordinary members, who were going to be different again from the even larger group of adherents.[19]

There were a number of skilled workers; there was a strong tendency for the preachers to come from those groups who were independent, not those either at the bottom or the top of the economic pyramid. They were joiners like Thomas

---

[16] For Bramwell see Sigston, *Bramwell* and N. Cunliffe, *The Beckoning of the West: A Lancashire Odyssey* (Blackpool: N. Lancs Methodist History Group, 1992) 43-7.

[17] B. Hill, *Women, Work and Sexual Politics in Eighteenth Century England* (Oxford: Blackwell, 1989) 40.

[18] D. C. Jones, *Glorious Work* 59-64.

[19] Rack 439-441.

Westell and Francis Scott, cobblers like Thomas Olivers or Samuel Bradburn, bakers like Alexander Mather. They had served their apprenticeships. Apprenticeships, as has been pointed out, were a way of placing children to try to secure their future. Though the system was declining in the eighteenth century, it was very common among Wesley's preachers for them to have been an apprentice. It was a system characteristic of the middling sort and involved much geographical mobility, again typical of early Methodism. Robert Dall (1745-1828), for example, was apprenticed at the age of 15 in 1760 for five years to the Dundee firm of Dicks and Son, mercers and manufacturers of thread. At least seven preachers had worked in a dockyard. These skilled men were also mobile and took their trades to the places of highest demand like Manchester or London. Alexander Mather came from Scotland, Thomas Olivers from Wales, Dall moved to Glasgow.[20]

It is true that many relatively lowly men and women in the eighteenth century 'deliberately chose to be Methodists, because it offered them tangible benefits of various kinds.' These benefits were spiritual, psychological and material. Within the Methodist society each member was expected to make a spiritual contribution to the whole, and so there was a feeling of equality present. The first Methodist preachers were often strong characters who rose from relatively humble origins to leading positions. When Wesley sent two preachers to America they were a former cobbler and a bastard-born ex-farm labourer. They began a church which would sweep the continent. In addition, the Methodist preachers came from similar backgrounds to those who made up a majority of their hearers. John Nelson and Alexander Mather knew how to appeal to men and women like themselves.[21]

However, Clive Field states that he would now want to refine the categories and add further material. I too am doubtful of the significance of the figures about Wesley's preachers' class as they stand.

It is interesting comparing Wesley's preachers with working class evangelists in the nineteenth century identified by Janice Holmes.[22] Admittedly the evangelists were a smaller self selecting group a century later and by definition 'working class.' Similar characteristics turn up in both groups.

---

[20] Barry and Brooks *Middling Sort* especially C. Brooks 'Apprenticeship, Social Mobility and the Middling Sort', 52-83. Dall's apprenticeship indenture is at MARC MA 3181.8. See also R. P. Heitzenrater ed, *The Poor and the People Called Methodists* (Nashville: Abingdon, 2002) especially 16-20, 27-30.

[21] For other examples see C. A. Bayly, *The Birth of the Modern World 1780-1914* (Oxford: Blackwell, 2004) 9. The quotation is from Hempton, *Empire* 9, but see also his Chapter on 'Boundaries and Margins'. For American Methodist preachers' class origins see J. Wigger, 'Fighting Bees: Methodist Itinerants and the Dynamics of Methodist Growth 1770-1820' in N. Hatch and J. Wigger, eds, *Methodism and the Shaping of American Culture* (Nashville: Kingswood, 2001) 88-90.

[22] J. Holmes, *Religious Revivals in Britain and Ireland 1859-1905* (Dublin: Irish Academic Press, 2000) Chapter 5, a book with many useful insights into revivals.

Several had fathers who were absent or alcoholics or both. Of Wesley's preachers, Thomas Johnson's father died when he was six, Charles Kyte's father when Charles was three or four, Thomas Vasey's before his first birthday and Matthew Lumb's when Matthew was four. John Leggett, father of Benjamin Leggett, died before Benjamin was two. Richard Whatcoat's father died when he was 'very young.' Paul Martindale, father of Miles Martindale, disappeared to the West Indies when Miles was very young and never returned, leaving his wife to look after the family. It is doubtful if this was restricted to Wesley's preachers. Because of the low expectation of life many children in the eighteenth century lost father or mother during childhood.

Several nineteenth century evangelists belonged to a group Janice Holmes described as 'sport and entertainment' such as Richard Weaver the prize fighter, known as 'Undaunted Dick,' or Henry Moorhouse, the 'prince among card players.'[23] Among Wesley's preachers of the eighteenth century there was a similar group, in an age when possibly fewer could make a living this way. They included John Beaumont, the Yorkshire child prodigy and itinerant musician, John Allen who also made his living in a group of itinerant singers, and Thomas Johnson the 'army drummer.' John Smith was the 'foremost cockfighter and bruiser of Newry,' who later for ten years led a major revival in south west Ulster. Charles Skelton had been an Irish dancing-master. John Peacock wrestled and boxed in Misterton in Nottinghamshire until he became converted. In America the young Benjamin Abbott was another street-fighter, while Henry Metcalfe, converted by Shadford, had been another dancing master. Many of these were used to an itinerant life.[24]

Illegitimacy

It was a society where there was an extraordinarily low rate of bastardy. The illegitimacy ratio was 1.779%, fewer than two in every hundred births.[25] It is not surprising that of the 802 Wesley's preachers, only four are known to be have been illegitimate. Others may have been, but as usual for the majority we do not know. Finding the evidence is a result of consulting the baptismal records. It does not appear in the biographical materials in Methodism or elsewhere. This was therefore a ratio lower than the average for the day. One was John Edwards, an early preacher, first for Whitefield. He was baptized as

---

[23] Holmes, *Revivals* 138.

[24] John Nelson was a boxer, but did not make his living that way. For Abbott see D. Andrews *The Methodists and Revolutionary America 1760-1800: The Shaping of an Evangelical Culture* (Princeton: Princeton UP, 2000) 157. For Metcalfe see P. P. Sandford, *Memoirs of Mr Wesley's Missionaries to America* (New York: Lane, 1843) 273. For Beaumont and Peacock see Chapter 5, Allen Chapter 6, both below, and for Smith *WMM* 1826: 73-84.

[25] T. Hitchcock, *English Sexualities 1700-1800* (London: Macmillan, 1997) 25 and n6.

John Edwards at St Alkmunds, Shrewsbury in May 1714, son of Edward Poyner and Anne (Edwards), so illegitimate. He had joined Wesley by 1749 and travelled widely, leaving to found his own congregation in Leeds and marry in 1754. He remained an Independent minister till his death in 1785. The next two were Joseph Pilmore and John Crosby (1754-1816), both of whom came from the North Riding of Yorkshire. Their early lives were similar in other ways, coming from the North York Moors area in the east of the Riding. Both were hired out as farm servants and converted some distance from where they were born. Their later history, however, was very different. Where Pilmore was sent by Wesley to America and was a pioneer preacher in the early years there, later returning to act as an Anglican clergyman in the newly independent country, Crosby was sent no further than Aberdeen and suffered nothing more exciting than his preacher's house collapsing as a result of mine-sinking in Whitehaven in 1791. The fourth and last was Thomas Bartholomew, an otherwise typical preacher from the West Riding. He was born in 1759 at Keighley, a strongly Methodist area, the son of Jeremiah Carrodus and Sarah Bartholomew. Baptized in October 1759, the son of Sarah Bartholomew at Keighley, he was presumably illegitimate. He was educated at a school, run by the early Methodist class leader Mary Denbigh, and converted in 1774 under Robert Costerdine. Bartholomew was a contemporary of the future preachers Jonathan Edmondson, Charles Bland (with whom he was in band) and John Sugden Smith who met in Thomas Colbeck's class in 1779. Colbeck had to come from Otley to lead it. Bartholomew became a local preacher around 1780. Brought up by his mother, he became friendly in his youth with several young Methodists and with them began to preach, being sent out as a travelling preacher in 1782. A good linguist, he died in 1819 of diabetes.[26]

Where were They Converted?

The early Methodist preachers regarded as vital two moments in their lives. There was the point when they realized their need for Christ and for conversion. Then the time of conversion arrived, when they became 'happy again' and accepted that Christ would indeed live with them. Preachers tended to be converted, that is the second of these 'moments,' in major centres of Methodism. This means that towns and cities show up more strongly in the list of conversion places than in the places of birth. So Sheffield, which had five preachers born there, had four converted of whom only one, Jonathan Parkin,

---

[26] For Edwards see *Ev. Mag.* 1793: 221-30 and *IGI*. For Pilmore see Chapter 12 below. Crosby was described as the illegitimate son of Sarah Crosby in the Whitby Parish Register at his baptism the 1st February 1755 aged 8 weeks. Bartholomew was baptized the 20th October 1759 according to the Keighley Parish Register, son of Sarah Bartholomew. His father was said to be Jeremiah Carrodus (Turner, *HBA* 239). See also *GHR* 307 and Bartholomew's MS Notebook at Keighley Library.

was born there. The others' places of birth are significant: George Story was born at Harthill, a village ten miles east south east of Sheffield, near the modern Woodhall Services on the M1. John Furness was born at Stony Middleton, Derbyshire, a village a little further, 12 miles west south west of Sheffield, Charles Tunnycliffe came into the world at Leek, 36 miles in the same direction. All were within 40 miles of Sheffield, with good connections via the carters. This kind of pattern was typical of many others. The four converted at Sheffield is a higher proportion of the total known than the five born there. This is because fewer conversion places are known, only 218 places of conversion being identified as opposed to 385 places of birth.[27]

Large cities like London were magnets for the whole British Isles and beyond. Twenty-three preachers at least were converted in London. Where they had come from previously is interesting; only four were born in London which, more than anywhere else, depended on labour coming from the country. Two were born abroad, the relatively well-connected John Fletcher and Francis Gilbert. Another four were born in Ireland, Wales and Scotland. Two came from coal mining areas in county Durham, presumably via the colliers bringing coal from Newcastle, an important trade in the eighteenth century. Eight of the rest came from the south or east, areas which produced few preachers, for example Suffolk and Leicestershire with two each. It was because they had been attracted to London that they fell into the Methodists' orbit. They included gentry and the wealthy, such as Gilbert and Fletcher, as well as early preachers important in Methodist history like Nelson and Mather. There were two tailors, a grocer, a physician, a shoemaker, a baker, a mason, a cotton dealer and a blacksmith.

Many of the early preachers were converted a long distance from their place of birth. This was especially true of the first cohort, but became less true as time went on. This was partly because Methodism was good at looking after strangers and making them welcome. Men were converted in centres of industry, to which population moved in large numbers in the eighteenth century and where death rates were higher than birth rates. The ports on the west coast, expanding because of the growing Atlantic trade, were also notable for their Methodism. They included such strongholds as London, Bristol, Liverpool, Dublin and Manchester. Early Methodist preachers born elsewhere but converted here included Thomas Dancer, John Nelson and Alexander Mather in London, Samuel Bardsley in Manchester, Joseph Cownley in Bristol and John Edwards in Dublin. Four men were born in Bristol, nine converted there. In Liverpool two were born and a different two converted.[28] The army was also an

---

[27] For Furness see *WMM* 1830: 446, 641, Story *EMP* 5: 218-41, Parkin *MM* 1818: 69, 560, 702, Tunnycliffe *WMM* 1828: 502, 643 and Myles.

[28] Those born in Bristol were Thomas Maxfield, Thomas Westell, Victory Purdy and Theophilus Lessey. The nine converted there were, in addition to Cownley, Maxfield and Lessey, John Appleton, Peard Dickinson, Simon Day, Joseph Jones, Thomas

important early centre for Methodism; men from anywhere might accept the call to preach to their fellow-soldiers, though they might not go on to become one of Wesley's travelling 'sons in the Gospel' in this country for some years like George Shadford. Others who later were itinerants included Duncan Wright, John Haime, Joseph Burgess, John Crook, William Smith and John Dillon. This army revival continued, so that the early missionaries were often called to army stations originally evangelized by Methodist soldiers. There were many reasons for this revival among the soldiers: the increased danger as in fishing and mining communities, the large concentrations of soldiers in wartime which brought like-minded individuals together, the Methodist appeal to Providence easily accepted by the fatalistic soldier, and the way Methodist preachers in Ireland concentrated on the soldiers.[29]

Foreign Descent

At all times there have been many immigrants in British and especially English society. They have rarely been popular. In the eighteenth century there were many Protestant immigrants such as the Huguenots from France, religious refugees escaping from persecution. It should be noted, however, that 'Huguenot' generically included Francophone émigré communities, some of whom had moved for reasons other than religion.[30] Others have noticed the number of those with continental links in early Methodism. It is worth looking at the proportions among Wesley's preachers. We have already noted those born in Europe, namely the two Germans and John Fletcher. Vincent Perronet and his two sons were also of Swiss descent. Then there was John Valton, son of a foreign-born courtier, and the Irish Palatine Philip Embury. Finally there were those of Huguenot descent, James Rouquet, Walter Sellon, the grandson of a refugee pastor, and James Massiot, a Huguenot from Cork. The total is eleven. The number might be small, but the influence of the individuals was

---

Olivers and Jonathan Reeves. The two born in Liverpool were John Ellis and George Highfield. The two converted were John Boyle and Miles Martindale.

[29] For Methodists in the army see. O. S. Watkins, *Soldiers and Preachers Too* (London: WCO, 1906). M. F. Snape, *The Redcoat and Religion* (Abingdon: Routledge, 2005) 1-68 provides a valuable summary of Methodism in the army and of the Flanders Revival of 1745-6. Snape stressed the importance of the Scots contingent though, of the list given, only Wright came from Scotland. He also suggested that John Mitchell was a Methodist preacher, but he may be confusing him with Thomas Mitchell who spent a year in the army 1745-1746, did not preach then, but was later converted and became an itinerant. Of the others he cited, Staniforth was only a local preacher and Nelson was a preacher before he was impressed.

[30] P. S. Forsaith, 'The Correspondence of the Rev. John W. Fletcher: Letters to the Rev. Charles Wesley considered in the context of the Evangelical Revival,' D Phil thesis at Oxford Brookes 2003, 299. John Valton is a good example of this point. For Rouquet see *PWHS* 54 (2003) 33.

immense. At least three, Perronet the elder, Valton and Fletcher, were men to whom John Wesley listened and Charles Wesley wrote as friends. James Rouquet, the much loved clergyman in Bristol, would probably have had a position within Methodism similar to Fletcher's if he had not died early. Embury was the co-founder of Wesleyan Methodism in America. The group must be seen as significant in effect if not in numbers. Of the twelve preachers born in London, Kent or Middlesex, six were from this group.[31]

If we add those with Huguenot connections, such as wives of Huguenot descent, the number is almost doubled. Joseph Cownley married the Huguenot Massiot's daughter. Thomas Taylor married Anne Dupuy, a Huguenot orphan, also from Cork. Benjamin Colley, an Anglican clergyman who helped Wesley in London in the 1760s, married Elizabeth la Croissette shortly before his own death in 1767. William Holland married Elizabeth Delamotte, sister of Wesley's friend Charles Delamotte. The Delamottes were probably descended from a Tournai Protestant of the sixteenth century who had escaped from Alva's persecution. William Briggs married Vincent Perronet's daughter and their daughter married Peard Dickinson. They were imitating their leaders. In marrying Mary Bosanquet John Fletcher joined one of the most famous Huguenot families, while John Wesley himself married the widow of a Huguenot, Molly Vazeille.[32] Part of the reason for this strong link was that both Wesleys by the 1760s were preaching at two former French churches in London, West Street and Spitalfields which, though considered Methodist for fifteen years by around 1759, retained a strong French element. The Palatine connection has been noted and written about in many places. The Huguenot connection has escaped most historians' notice. Rack pointed it out briefly, and Forsaith has written about it in his work on Fletcher.[33]

The Continental revival certainly had an influence on Methodism in the realms of ideas and methods and the links between the early Methodists and Moravians in the late 1730s, as has been shown especially by W. R. Ward. However, it is also important to note the contribution of outstanding individuals like Fletcher, Rouquet or the Perronets, who came from disparate continental

---

[31] For the Perronets see M. Batty, *Vincent Perronet 1693-1785: The Archbishop of the Methodists* (Emsworth: WMHS, 2002). For Valton see *DOMBI*. For Rouquet see P. Thomas, J. H. Lenton and R. P. Heitzenrater, 'John Wesley's 1770 Will' in *PWHS* 54 (2003) 32-3, a will which would have given him that kind of position if John had died.

[32] For the Delamottes see J. Nayler, *Charles Delamotte John Wesley's Companion* (Wesley Bicentenary Manuals no 10, London: Epworth, 1938). Rack 175-6 and note citing J. D. Walsh, 'Methodism and the Origins of English Speaking Evangelicalism' in Noll, *Evangelicalism* 157 and *PWHS* 4: (1903-4) 5, 67-79. P. S. Forsaith thesis 2003.

[33] For the Palatines see below Chapter 11. P. S. Forsaith, '"A dearer country" the Frenchness of the Rev Jean de la Flechere of Madeley: a Methodist Church of England Vicar' 519-526 in R. Vigne and C. Littleton eds, *From Strangers to Citizens: The Integration of Immigrant Communities in Britain, Ireland and Colonial America 1550-1750* (Brighton: Sussex Academic Press, 2001) 301-3.

traditions but found a home in Methodism. This was true at every level of Methodism, though it was particularly obvious in London and the south east where most immigrants had settled and also noticeable in southern Ireland.

Stories of Origin

Some stories about preachers' origins came up again and again, what might be described as the period's equivalent of the twenty-first century's 'urban myths.' One of these concerned disinheritance. The basic story was that the parents, relatives or guardians disinherited the young man when he became a Methodist or a Methodist preacher. This was told of at least six preachers and was not in itself unlikely. Methodism was regarded with suspicion by much of the nation. It was how the older generation thought it could influence and control the younger. The story about Thomas Vasey recounted how his rich uncle disinherited him and as an orphan he suffered the consequences. There is no particular reason to distrust this story.[34]

However, with regard to Lawrence Kane the story is less satisfactory. Kane was said to have been the younger son of an Irish peer who disinherited him.[35] This is much less plausible since no Irish peerage of 'Kane' ever existed. There was the Irish Viscountcy of Keane, pronounced 'Kane,' which might have been possible, except that it was not created until 1834, by which time Kane had left the ministry having served twenty years! A very similar story was told about John King, the later preacher in America who was supposed to have been born in Leicestershire, youngest of the three sons of Joel King.[36] Converted by Wesley, again his parents were said to have disowned and disinherited him when he joined the Methodists. He was also reported to have previously studied at Oxford and studied medicine in London.[37] Since he does not appear in *Alumni Oxonienses* this must be questioned, which in turn brings suspicion on the whole story. There was no medical college in London, but he could have studied with an existing practitioner as many did. But no doctor's name was given and so the whole story has to be unlikely. The same basic disinheritance tale with variations was told of George Sykes, Thomas Seccomb and Jonathan Parkin, without particular reason for doubting it.[38] However, when the same story was recounted of the West Yorkshireman Jonathan Maskew, again its

---

[34] *City Road Magazine* 1871: 529-30, *WMM* 1827: 644-5. For more on Vasey see Chapter 13 below.

[35] J. Wright, *Early Methodism in Yarm* (Billingham: Billingham Press, 1950) 15.

[36] Chapter 12 below; *Asbury Jol* 1: 29; M. H. Moore, *Sketches of the Pioneers of Methodism in North Carolina and Virginia* (Greenwood, SC: Attic, 1977) 51-6; *IGI*.

[37] Moore, *Sketches*.

[38] Sykes was threatened with disinheritance, but his father was later reconciled with him see W. Greenwood, *Memoir of the Life, Ministry and Correspondence of the late Rev George Sykes of Rillington* (Malton: G. Barnby, 1827). For Seccomb see Atmore, for Parkin where it was a 'rich relative' see *MM* 1818: 560, 702.

Origins 55

truth has to be questioned. Jonathan was supposedly turned out of his home by his father for supporting Methodism. The turning out may be true, but the reason cannot be, since it seems Jonathan's father died in 1728, long before Methodism was dreamt of![39]

John Miller was said to have been a German page to George II. However, it is not clear what he was doing after George's death (1760) until he appeared as a preacher in Ireland in 1780. This unexplained gap throws suspicion on the whole tale.[40]

Most of the accounts of the preachers' origins, however, can be accepted. Persecution was usual and in many cases is well documented. It is the extra dramatic bits of the stories, like the stately home for Kane or the Oxford education for King, which must remain very doubtful.

The access to courts claimed by Crookshank for Miller was perfectly possible. John Valton was the son of a gentleman from the Franche Comte in Eastern France who held the post of Page of the Presence under George II. In view of the clerkship Valton himself held through patronage, he was not claiming more illustrious ancestry than he in fact had. According to his autobiography in *Early Methodist Preachers*, Valton moved freely in society with the relatively well-born Wesley brothers, Fletcher, and Edward Smyth.[41] Whitehead, in his early biography of Wesley, was biased against the travelling preachers with whom he had quarrelled, yet he was prepared to admit the main reason for the growth of Methodism was 'the artless simplicity, the zeal and integrity of the Preachers at their setting out to travel.'[42]

Conclusion

The preachers' origins therefore were diverse, like the society from which they came and to which they ministered. Dominated numerically by men from the north, especially the West Riding of Yorkshire, they also had many from the Celtic fringe. They belonged to the full range of society, but included particularly the aspiring skilled artisan from the village or small town. There were itinerant entertainers like Beaumont. Their origins stretched from a courtier's son like Valton to a bastard like Pilmore. They were already mobile, often migrants from one part of the British Isles to another. The one thing they all had in common was their conversion experience, often in a large town or city, which led them to dedicate their lives to spreading the gospel wherever Mr. Wesley sent them. Over time that dedication might waver when faced with the difficulties they had to surmount, but their mobility was likely to remain.

---

[39] Baker, *Wesley and the Church* 98-9, 148-50, 170, 248-53; *GHR* 71-4.
[40] Crk 2: 181. Crookshank was not a contemporary and did not give sources.
[41] *EMP* 6: 1-136.
[42] J. Whitehead, *The Life of the Revd John Wesley, M.A, Sometime Fellow of Lincoln College, Oxford*. 2 vols. (London: Couchman, 1796) 2: 516.

CHAPTER 4

Education

> 'Vulgar, illiterate and obscure,
> And ignorant of all but Thee'.
> Charles Wesley on the early preachers 1786.

Standard of Education

Wesley did not include the word 'education' in his own *Dictionary* which he published in 1753.[1] However, to Wesley education was important. Education means both systematic training at home, in school or college or from a tutor, and also the more general 'education for life,' improvement in moral and intellectual character, what the twenty-first century describes as 'life-long learning'. This chapter investigates how far his preachers were educated already before they came to Wesley or became travelling preachers; also how Wesley tried to improve their education and ensure the life-long learning he certainly wanted and they needed.

In general their education, as expressed by Charles Wesley at the start of this chapter, was poor. At least one, the Irishman John Smith, is definitely known to have been unable to write, though he could read.[2] Another Irishman James Morris, a Palatine who Myles said began preaching in 1748, was received by the Irish Conference of 1752. Morris was described as one 'who could hardly spell his name' by the snobbish Toplady whom he converted in 1756, though Cooney denies this illiteracy.[3] Thomas Butts, the critical Bristol steward of

---

[1] This chapter, slightly altered, first appeared as 'The Education of John Wesley's Preachers' in J. H. Lenton, ed, *Vital Piety and Learning* (Oxford: Applied Theology Press, 2005) 25-37. W. T. Graham, 'Pupils in the Gospel' in P. Taylor, ed, *Wesley Papers* (Lutterworth: Wesley Fellowship, 2002) 15-70 is particularly useful in its summary of who were the travelling preachers. For the early American preachers' education see J. Wigger, 'Fighting Bees' 120-6.

[2] For John Smith see David Smyth, MS 'Short Account of the Life of the Late John Smyth Methodist Preacher' in MARC (C 319 Diaries box S TS) and below Chapter 11.

[3] D. A. L. Cooney, *The Methodists in Ireland: A Short History* (Dublin: Columba, 2001) 146. The Calvinist clergyman Toplady on Morris is quoted from Crk 1: 117. Cooney gave no source, but pointed to Toplady's prejudices against Methodist preachers.

1752 expressed this well

> I think Mr. W. [John Wesley] is highly to blame, in taking so many raw, young fellows from their trades to a work they are as utterly unqualified for, as for Minister of State![4] [He suggests also that they often did not try to improve, continuing:] Am clearly convinced the want of study ruins half our preachers. Perhaps one reason of their unwillingness to improve themselves may arise from a misunderstanding of St. John's words: 'Ye have an unction from the Holy one etc. And the same anointing teacheth you all things.' True, but not without the use of all other helps. No more than the Spirit sanctifies without prayer, or hearing the Word etc... Tis the grossest enthusiasm to think to attain the End without the Means. Whoever thus vainly dreams, is fitter for a place in Bedlam than to be a Preacher of the Gospel. Without making use of every improvement, a man is no ways qualified for the Ministry. The mere emanations of his own mind are no ways adequate to such a work. Be his natural talents ever so great, he will stand in need of all assistance. The want of this makes their discourses so jejune, trite, & sapless; the same dull round notwithstanding the many different Texts they speak from. A horse in a mill keeps going on, but tis in the same dull track. So the congregation may feed & feed, but it must be upon one dish still!

On the other hand, most comment at the time came from hostile sources who, like Lord Chesterfield, described anyone ignorant of Latin and Greek as 'illiterate.' Most of Wesley's preachers would be illiterate on this definition, though not all. Another hostile source was the Wiltshire 1784 Visitation used by Kent.[5] The incumbent of Broughton Gifford near Melksham described the Methodist preachers as 'ignorant itinerants.' In fact they were a group where at least twenty-four of those who were not already clergymen could read Hebrew. Seven of these were Irish (four from the North) and five Scots, reflecting the interest in education in Scotland and the North of Ireland. Many more than this had had a classical education. Those who came from Scotland had often had a good education, like John McGowan or Duncan McAllum. From Ireland came Thomas Walsh who would have been an exception in any age. Wesley said of him that if he were questioned as to any Hebrew word in the Old Testament or Greek in the New Testament, he would tell after a brief pause how often the word occurred and what it meant in each place. John Downes, as a boy at school learning algebra, was able to devise a proof for the proposition in a better way than the one demonstrated in the textbook. Later, having visited a clockmaker and observed what he did, he made himself tools and constructed his own clock to tell the time as accurately as any other.[6]

Those who were from higher social groups like Thomas Coke, Joseph

---

[4] Thomas Butts' MSS Diary in Baker Collection, Duke 190-4, partly printed in *HMGB* 4: 115. The Biblical quotation is an expanded version of I John 2: 20.

[5] B. Dobree ed, *The Letters of Philip Stanhope, Lord Chesterfield* (London: Eyre & Spottiswoode, 1932) 3: 1155, Kent, *Wesley and the Wesleyans* 69-75.

[6] For Downes see *WJW* 22: 435-6.

Benson, John Valton, Mosley Cheek or Edward Smyth had all had a good education for the period. John de Queteville, the 'Apostle of the Channel Islands,' had been a boarder at Winchester School. Miles Martindale, later Governor at Woodhouse Grove School, had studied the classics and learned French to read Voltaire and Rousseau. John Broadbent had a skill for learning languages, though we know nothing about his education. John Reynolds, who entered the ministry in 1785, was a 'hard student,' who Jackson said 'had a considerable knowledge both of Biblical and French literature.' The preachers also included many largely self-taught luminaries. James M'Quigg entered the Irish ministry in 1789 and translated the Bible into Irish. John Mason from Hampshire, who entered the itinerancy in 1764, made a large botanical collection. James Grant began travelling in 1790 from Lincolnshire and was nicknamed the 'Walking Bible' because of his knowledge; he gave the future founder of Primitive Methodism, Hugh Bourne, his lessons in Greek and Hebrew. Thomas Taylor was another who taught himself Greek and Hebrew and produced a *Concordance* in 1782.[7] Last but not least there was Adam Clarke, the Irish schoolmaster's son, whose eight volume *Commentary* pales beside his position as the Government's chosen expert on archival sources of all kinds, because of his linguistic abilities.

Levels of Earlier Education and Age at Leaving School

Statistically we know little about the preachers' education (see Chart 5 based on Table 7 in Appendix One). For only 112 (11% of the total) can the standard of their education be estimated. That estimate is somewhat rough and ready. They are in three categories, those typical of eighteenth century education. '1' represents what was seen as the 'best' education available, classical with a tutor or at a public or grammar school, preparing for university entrance. It would be typical of most clergy of the Church. '2' represents the education for trade available in the Dissenting Academies. Many considered it at least as good as '1,' and included in this category are all those who are known to have attended Kingswood, even though this was a more classical education, partly because Kingswood pupils mostly left much earlier than pupils at schools in class 1. '3' indicates those whom we know had some education, but either it is known to be below the level of the other two grades, or there is no evidence as to what was

---

[7] T. Jackson, *Recollections of My Own Life and Times* (London: WCO, 1873) 118. Benjamin Rhodes could even pass as a schoolmaster to a late twentieth century historian. J. Feather, *The Provincial Book Trade in Eighteenth Century England* (Cambridge: CUP, 1985) 110. For de Queteville see M. Lelievre, *Histoire du Methodisme dans les Isles de la Manche 1784-1884* (London: WCO 1885). Lenton, *My Sons* 18. H. Bett was very useful on this question in *PWHS* 15 (1926), 85-92. This tradition of 'sanctified scholarship' was common among preachers who were local also; see T. Shaw, *A History of Cornish Methodism* (Truro: Bradford Barton, 1967) 62.

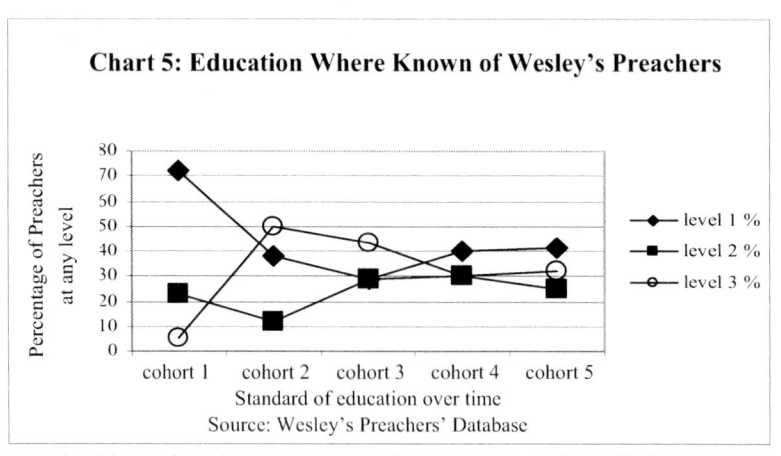

Chart 5: Education Where Known of Wesley's Preachers

Standard of education over time
Source: Wesley's Preachers' Database

the standard but education was received. Typically a '3' is likely to have left school by the age of 14.[8]

Of the preachers whose education is known, almost half, 49 out of 112 (45%), were at level 1. As the chart shows, cohort 1 had most whose education was at level 1, 16 (72%). This was because they contained many of John and Charles Wesley's university trained friends, like Henry Piers Vicar of Bexley, Vincent Perronet Vicar of Shoreham, and Richard Bateman Vicar of St Bartholomew's in London. However, the important point is that even in cohort 5 a substantial number, 13 of the 32 whose education is known, were educated at the highest level. Admittedly most of those whose education is unknown were likely to be at the lowest level, but these figures show that of those whose education is known, the standard was much higher than would have been expected. In general, after the exceptional first cohort, educational standards seem to have improved over time, as would be expected. After the first cohort those in category 3 remain a substantial minority, despite the general improvement. They were frequently the largest group.

Age of leaving school has also been investigated (see Chart 6 below, based on Table 8). This is less good in producing a large enough sample, only 63 of the original 802 preachers having evidence about this important point in their lives. The reason is straightforward. In most cases knowledge about them is based largely on their autobiographies as published in the *Magazine*. To them leaving school was not important, unlike their equivalents in the twenty-first century. The most important moments in their lives, they felt, were when they first recognized their sinfulness, became converted, joined the Methodist society and felt sanctified or began to preach. These were the key points which are much easier to date. Because of the paucity of the data it is difficult to prove anything from the table. When the unusual first cohort is taken away, then a

---

[8] J. Rule, *Albion's People* (London: Longmans, 1992) 140-146.

Education 61

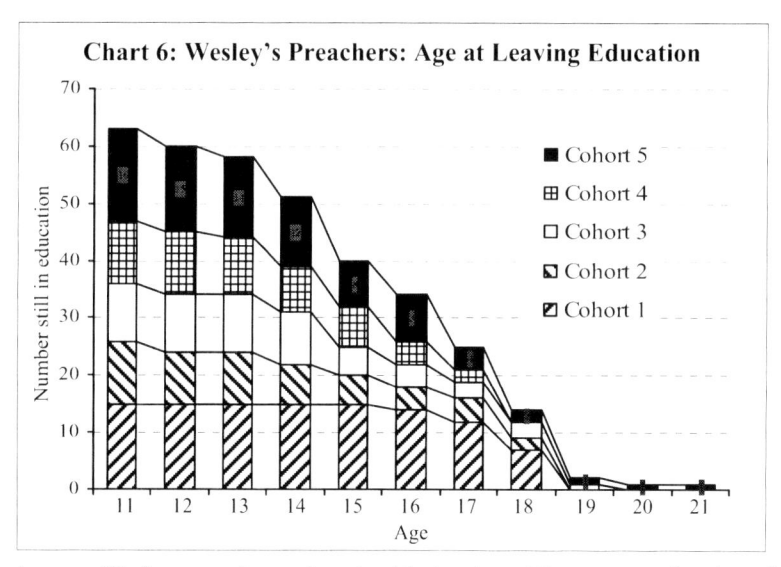

Chart 6: Wesley's Preachers: Age at Leaving Education

much more likely curve is produced with the data. The average for the other four cohorts then, the most common year to leave school, becomes just over 14, with a substantial proportion, 12 out of 48 (25%), leaving earlier and over half, 25 out of 48 (52%), leaving later.

In conclusion, the standards of education of Wesley's preachers can be said to have been much higher than their enemies have tried to convey. For the eighteenth century they were relatively well trained, eleven previously being teachers, with four of these coming from Ireland.[9] These can be assumed to have reached a higher standard of education than the average for the day.

Need for Education?

There was a major debate among the early Methodists about whether the travelling preachers really needed education. A common view well into the nineteenth century was that scholarship and training were dangerous in that the preachers would become less concerned about evangelism. Wesley defended them despite this view 'I trust there is not one of them who is not able to go through such an examination in..... practical, experimental Divinity as few of our candidates for holy orders, even in the University... are able to do.'[10]

The view was also expressed by an anonymous preacher poet, actually the returned missionary Joshua Marsden, on the Conference in 1816 about the candidates before it

---

[9] These include Christopher Hopper, John Bredin, Thomas Walsh, Titus Knight of Halifax, Samuel Wells of Cheltenham, Andrew Coleman, William Wilson, William Penington, Robert Wilkinson, Philip Guier and John Hoskins.
[10] E. Royle, 'Methodism and Education' in Lenton, *Vital Piety* 1-3; *WJW* 8: 219, 221.

> It is not whether he can logic chop,
> Define a broom, philosophize a mop;
> Truth, truth's the word! who barters bread for stones,
> Or meat, for metaphysical dry bones?
> Can famished sinners feed on Latin scraps?
> Who catches souls, must better bait his traps:
> The man who edifies an hungry flock,
> Should find a richer field than hic haec hoc.
> Will an encyclopedia, in his head,
> Convert a soul, to faith and morals dead:
> The aid of science no man should despise,
> But is our candidate divinely wise:
> Has he himself, the life he would impart,
> The truth-taught mind, the renovated heart;
> Or takes he, all his knowledge from a shelf,
> And preaches, what he never felt himself? [11]

Many Methodists in the eighteenth century were suspicious of those who 'took their knowledge from a shelf.' They expected their preachers to preach extempore from what they felt themselves.

Wesley was concerned about their training. The first Conference was held in 1744.[12] Under Friday June 29th there was 'Question 11. Can we have a Seminary for labourers? A. If God spare us to another Conference.' In 1745 under Saturday August 3rd was 'Question 6. Can we have a seminary for labourers [yet]? A. Not till God gives a proper tutor.' However, Wesley as a University teacher remained concerned about their education, though he was never able to found the seminary he suggested at the 1744 Conference. He always felt sensitive on this issue when he was attacked over it. At the 1746 Conference he wrote 'Q. In what light should your Assistants consider themselves? A. As learners rather than teachers: as young students at the University, for whom therefore a method of study is expedient in the highest degree.'

Wesley's Policy

Kingswood

Wesley's policy for teaching his preachers can be seen as having five strands: Some would-be preachers were sent to Wesley's school at Kingswood near Bristol. Whitefield had founded a school for the local colliers' sons there in 1739 which, since he was absent in America, was rapidly taken over by his

---

[11] J. Marsden (Anon), *The Conference or Sketches of Methodism* (London: Blanshard, 1816) 2: 60-61.
[12] *JB's Minutes* 17.

friend John Wesley.[13] Myles suggested that this school was already taking fee-payers and non locals before the traditional re-founding by Wesley in 1748 'for the sons of our principal friends.' This suggestion has been re-emphasized recently by Bishop.

Certainly Wesley, the Oxford don who wanted all his Methodist geese to be swans, saw this establishment as a place where preachers could be trained in large numbers on what we would call 'short courses,' or 'refresher courses.' So in February 1749 he wrote in his Journal 'My design was to have as many as possible of our preachers here (at Kingswood) during Lent as could possibly be spared and to read lectures to them every day as I did to my pupils at Oxford. I had 17 in all divided into 2 classes, and read to one Bishop Pearson on the Creed, to the other Aldrich's *Logic* and to both *Rules for Action and Utterance.*' We don't know who the seventeen were. I reckon there were something like 50 preachers in late 1748 who might have been included, of whom Grimshaw was a clergyman already 'trained' and therefore not at Kingswood. These 17, therefore, would have been a high proportion of the total number of preachers at that time. His course (which must reflect only one day's work?) is an interesting one based on theology, logic and preaching.[14]

He also saw Kingswood as a place where they could be trained over a longer period before they actually began to travel as itinerant preachers. This was true of John Catermole, Joseph Pilmore, Adam Clarke (in 1782), Jeremiah Brettell, William Baynes and John Pritchard (September 1760) among others. John Floyd spent four quarters in 1769-70 before entering[15] and Thomas Cooper 15 months there, from May 1780 to August 1781, before he entered. When the masters included John Jones, Walter Sellon, Thomas Richards, James Rouquet and later Cornelius Bayley and Thomas McGeary (from 1783), preachers could learn much. In the 1780s Wesley promised the young William Black in faraway Nova Scotia that there would be a place for him at Kingswood. In 1790 he told McGeary that Mr. Bradiley, a pious young man from Antigua, 'earnestly desires' to be a boarder at Kingswood.[16] In the 1770 *Minutes* Wesley explained the use of Kingswood as a place of reserve for preachers. Benson proposed in his plan of 1775 that Kingswood should be turned into a college for the preachers who were in need of extra help. It was not, however, until 1834 that the Wesleyans founded a seminary at Abney House.[17]

---

[13] Ives; M. Bishop, 'Wesley and his Schools at Kingswood' in Lenton, *Vital Piety* 16-24; G. M. Best, *Continuity and Change: A History of Kingswood School 1748-1998* (Bath: Kingswood School, 1998); Myles.

[14] *WJW* 20: 263 and notes which make it clear that the third part, the 'preaching' was his own treatise. For estimates of total numbers see Appendix Two below.

[15] *EMP* 6: 249-72 for Pritchard in September 1760; Kingswood MS Account Book 1766-70 at the Wesley Centre, Kingswood School, Bath for Floyd.

[16] *JWL* 7: 183; Ives; *JWL* 8: 196.

[17] Large Minutes 1770 in *Minutes* (1862) vol 1; Heitzenrater 256; K. B. Garlick in *PWHS* 39 (1973-4) 104-6.

Reading

Wesley corresponded with the preachers at length, encouraging their reading and giving them books, this being partly a result of his publishing enterprise. He produced a large number of books partly aimed directly at them. Many were paperbound duodecimo pamphlets for mass distribution, at the inviting price of 4d each. The publishing machine that was John Wesley has received some attention in recent years,[18] but not yet enough. The reference in a letter to Bardsley in 1771 to the need to read one of his books 'several times' can be replicated in many other letters to his preachers.[19] As early as 1744 there was a list of 'what an Assistant may read.' The list is worth quoting in full to give a flavour of what Wesley expected: 'Sallust, Caesar, Tully (sc Cicero), Castellio, Terence, Virgil, Horace, Vida, Buchanan, Greek Testament, Epictetus, Plato, Ignatius, Ephrem Syrus, Homer, Greek Epigrams, Duport, Bishop Usher's Sermons, Arndt, Boehm, Nalson, Pascal, Frank, R Gell, our tracts.' This is an astonishingly wide list. (Arndt was a noted early seventeenth century Lutheran theologian, while Buchanan was a Calvinist Scots reformer of James I's period). So the list covered ancient and modern, not surprising from the Oxford don that he still was, but probably a shock to the men who had to read them over the next few years. Next year he doubled the size, including English poetry, such as Spenser, Milton, and Sir John Davies. How many persevered to the end we do not know, since their time for reading was limited. In 1745 Wesley suggested that all Assistants should spend the six hours of the morning in 'reading, writing and prayer.' In 1746 a new shorter list emerges, including Law's Tracts, Beveridge's Private Thoughts, Heylin's Devotional Tracts, the Lives of Mr. Halyburton and M. de Renty, Bishop Pearson on the Creed, Bishop Fell on the Epistles, Mr. Boehm's and Mr. Nalson's Sermons, Mr. Pascal's Thoughts, Milton's Paradise Lost and Cave and Fleury's Primitive Christianity. However, the time for reading grew to seven hours of each day. He made clear the way they should read, pausing to think back over what had been read to see how it fitted with their own experience and to consider how to put it into practice in their own lives.[20]

The publishing enterprise was also a significant help. Preachers were expected to carry copies to sell, and to read them until they were sold! 'Selling' was not entirely what it seemed. At the 1767 Conference there was the following Minute: 'How may the books be spread more? Let every Assistant give them away prudently and beg money of the rich to buy books for the

---

[18] F. Cumbers, *The Book Room* (London: Epworth, 1956); I. Rivers, 'Dissenting and Methodist Books of Practical Divinity' in I. Rivers, ed, *Books and Their Readers in Eighteenth Century England* (Leicester: St Martins,1982) 128, 145-164; F. Baker, *John Wesley, London Publisher 1733-91* (London: Wesley's Chapel, 1984); R. L. Maddox in *MH* 41 (2003) 2, 3: 42 (2004) 2; Graham in *Wesley Papers*.

[19] *JWL* 5: 290.

[20] *JB's Minutes* 17 (1744).

poor.'[21] Wesley's work on abridging tracts and volumes of the *Christian Library* was particularly important. This had only a limited circulation at first, and so in 1748 Wesley said he would only print 100 copies, a little more than the total number of itinerants at that point. Much later Joseph Cownley's library, as described in his will, showed many Methodist works including the whole of the *Christian Library*. Rankin's will demonstrated his wide reading, such as Dr Johnson's *Lives of the Poets* (4 vols) and his *Beauties* (2 vols). Wesley's *Thoughts on Marriage and the Single Life,* published in 1743, was aimed particularly at Methodist itinerants, as was his *Directions Concerning Pronunciation and Gesture* of 1749. In this he told them never to clap their hands or thump the pulpit and 'Your hands are not to be in perpetual motion'![22]

Other works aimed at the preachers included Charles Wesley's seven *Hymns for the Use of Methodist Preachers,* published in 1758. Graham aptly quoted the first two verses of Hymn IV

> Master at thy command we rise
> No prophets we or prophets' sons
> Or mighty, or well born or wise;
> But quickened clods, but breathing stones
> Urged to cry out, constrained to call,
> And tell mankind – He died for all!
>
> We speak, because they hold their peace,
> Who should thy dying love proclaim:
> We must declare thy righteousness,
> Thy truth and power and saving name,
> Though the dumb ass with accent clear
> Rebuke the silence of the seer.

In 1748, in a letter to his friend Ebenezer Blackwell, Wesley explained his idea for *The Christian Library*, suggesting that it might be as much as 80 volumes. The eventual 50 volumes, reissued by Jackson in the nineteenth century using Wesley's revised text as 30 volumes, were an attempt to include all Christian

---

[21] *Minutes* 1767.

[22] J. Wesley, *The Christian Library* 50 vols (Bristol: Farley, 1749-55); *WJW* 26: 322, 'I should print only a hundred copies of each.' Heitzenrater 154-7. Cownley was a senior preacher and former solicitor's clerk who at his death in 1792 left over 539 books. The list, which has several etceteras, does not include his Latin, Greek and French books which were all left to his grandson. The estate was valued at less than £100, so books must have been the chief item. *WHS NE* (1998) 16-22 where the text of Cownley's will is printed (the MS is in the Tyne and Wear Archives). A copy of the will of Thomas Rankin is in the UMC Archives at Drew University, Madison NJ. R. Green, *The Works of John and Charles Wesley: A Bibliography* (London: Kelly, 1896) 59-60 said the Directions also appeared as Rules for Action and Utterance.

writings which would be of value to his preachers. They were, without permission, abridged and edited by Wesley from the originals. They included early church fathers and writers on spirituality from every background including key Catholic writers, modern (that is eighteenth century) writers, theologians, and church history. With a range from Pascal to Bunyan via Polycarp, a Kempis and Alleine, Wesley was generous in what he borrowed. There was a boom in religious publishing and Wesley was determined to take advantage of it. Libraries were established at major centres like London, Bristol, Newcastle and in Ireland for preachers based there to use.

Despite all this, Wesley often felt his preachers did not take their opportunities to read as much as he did himself. So in 1766 at the Leeds Conference Wesley castigated the preachers for not reading religion 'because we are idle.'[23] He softened the criticism by including himself. Few of his hearers would have accepted this view, knowing very well the breadth and depth of *his* reading. In the *Minutes* of 1765 he had added 'if you stay above an hour at any place, take out a book and read.' To the new preacher Zachariah Yewdall in 1779 he wrote 'Read every morning a chapter of the New Testament with the Notes,' his own *Notes upon the New Testament*. Yewdall having just entered into his first circuit of Pembrokeshire on September 5th wrote in his diary of being 'much emploid (sic) in the reading of Magazin,' presumably the *Arminian Magazine* which had begun the year before. Later reading recorded by him includes 'a little pamphlit wrote by Miss Bosanquit of Cross Hall,' and the life of Thomas Walsh,[24] though there was no mention of Wesley's letter!

John Bredin, an Irish preacher who possessed a good library, was given books by Wesley. So was Richard Watkinson, a 46 year old local preacher from Leeds who had probably entered the itinerant ministry in 1778 in Scotland, where Benson seems to have acted as the channel for delivery. In actual fact Wesley was successful in persuading his preachers to read. This can be seen in the number of books they possessed. The story of Thomas Jackson in the next generation, and his desire to read and possess books, is typical of many who went before him. A former agricultural labourer from Sancton in the East Riding, each year he recorded the books he purchased or read. When Jackson spent a year in Horncastle he was able to use Brackenbury's library at Raithby, a real eye-opening and mouth watering experience. He ended his life among the volumes of Richmond College. In 1789 Samuel Bradburn was forced to record in his diary he had 'sold above 100 volumes of excellent books towards paying

---

[23] Doughty, *Wesley: His Preachers* 10, quoting the *Minutes*.
[24] *JWL* 6: 157-8, letter of the 9th October 1779; MS Diary of Zachariah Yewdall in MARC Diaries Box vol 1; D. Eastwood 'The Yewdalls of Eccleshill and Calverley' typescript privately published Timperley 1997 (copy in MARC), provides a careful assessment of Yewdall's diaries, showing their usefulness and reliability; J. Morgan, *The Life and Death of Mr Thomas Walsh* (London: Cock, 1762) is in *EMP* 3: 1-292.

my debts.'[25] Those numbers were typical for one of Mr Wesley's preachers.

One result of this wide reading from Wesley's *Christian Library* and elsewhere can be seen in the fact that many preachers began to write for publication. It has often been said that the active life of the Methodist itinerant was not favourable to authorship. Early Methodist preachers travelled every day. If they had a home they were rarely there and because of the incessant travel they had few books. Yet at least 150 out of the 802 were authors, 18.7%, rather higher than might be expected, especially when it is considered that so little is known about many. Joseph Benson or Adam Clarke were major authors, producing many books and pamphlets especially in the period after Wesley's death. Wesley himself had boasted that 'It is the glory of the Methodists to have few authors'. In Wesley's lifetime his bar on publication by his preachers without his permission certainly reduced the amount produced, and was a cause for leaving the ministry on occasion. His basic reason for this was that he did not trust the preachers on this point. This was based on his experience of a man like William Darney whose poetic doggerel he deplored. Another example which is said to have dismayed Wesley was James Kershaw, who entered the ministry in 1750 and was the author of some considerable polemic and some memorably bad verse (*The Methodist* (1780)). Some preachers even published attacks on Wesley, such as Michael Moorhouse. After Wesley's death the Conference relaxed the rule somewhat and encouraged men to use the Book Room to publish books and not go elsewhere where they would get more money. Even a leading preacher like Samuel Bradburn, who entered the ministry in 1774 and in the period after 1783 only travelled in leading circuits, did not publish until after Wesley died.[26]

Travel

Wesley encouraged his preachers to travel with himself (or his brother Charles) to watch and learn. Just as local preachers 'On Note' went out with a more

---

[25] *PPIM* 66; *AM* 1780: 512. Watkinson, who may have acted as a travelling preacher earlier, judging from his early use as an Assistant as soon as he made the stations, received books according to *JWL* 6: 131. For Jackson see his *Recollections*. Wesley began the *Arminian Magazine* in 1778 and it remains a largely untapped vital source for his practice, at least as compared to the use made of his published *Journal* and *Letters*. For the kind of use which could be made see V. T. Collins, "'Walking in Light, Walking in Darkness:' The Story of Women's Changing Rhetorical Space in Early Methodism' in *Rhetoric Review* (1996) 336-354; M. P. Jones, "'Her Claim to Public Notice' The Historiography of Women in British Methodism' in R. Sykes, ed, *God's Own Story* (Oxford: Applied Theology Press, 2003). Blanshard, *Bradburn* 129.

[26] M. Simpson, ed, *The Cyclopedia of Methodism* (Philadelphia: Everts, 1887) 73. For Benson, Bradburn, Clarke, Darney, and James Kershaw see the relevant entries in *DOMBI. PWHS* 3 (1901) 23; Cumbers, *Book Room*. For Methodist authors of the period see G. Osborn, *Outlines of Wesleyan Bibliography* (London: WCO, 1869).

experienced local preacher who was on 'Full Plan,' so possible travelling preachers went with the great itinerant himself. In the early twenty-first century British Methodist local preachers On Note still go out with a full local preacher. Perhaps some British ministers 'in formation of ministry' should travel with the President each year or American student ministers with a Bishop of the United Methodist Church?

Richard Moss, who was born in 1718 in Cheshire, was with John Wesley for long periods during 1744 to 1746, first as servant and later as preacher. He preached around Newcastle, in Sykehouse, Epworth, Sheffield, Bristol, London and in Cornwall. He finished his preaching career as an ordained clergyman for the Society for the Propagation of the Gospel in the Bahamas from 1767 to 1791. In March/April 1752 the otherwise unknown William Crane travelled with Wesley from at least Hereford to Shrewsbury and on to Dublin.[27] John Hampson senior, brought up in a Unitarian congregation at Chowbent in Lancashire and previously the steward of the Shackerley society in the Manchester round, was with Wesley in the large Newcastle circuit at Cockermouth in March 1753. The Yorkshire mason Thomas Mitchell was riding with Wesley in May 1753 in his home county. Richard Lucas was travelling with John Wesley in the Manchester circuit in April 1757. William Ley, who seems to have entered the itinerancy aged 19 in 1758, was with Wesley in Ireland in 1760 and again, apparently, in 1762.[28]

The eighteen year old Joseph Benson travelled with Wesley to Bristol in 1766 before becoming tutor at Kingswood at the start of his Methodist career. He twice served as president and was Editor of the *Magazine*. Duncan Wright, the former soldier and new preacher in the itinerancy, began by travelling with Wesley in June 1765, 'but... the exercise was too much' for Wright! Thomas Tennant rode with Wesley from March to August 1769. In Tennant's case Wesley was bent on persuading this twenty-seven year old local preacher that he should become a travelling preacher. Despite the six months training on the job Wesley did not succeed immediately. Tennant did not enter until the Conference of 1770, when he was sent to the important Manchester circuit. Richard Bourke, an Irishman already married with a family and three years into his itinerancy, toured with Wesley in Ireland in 1769. Later Wesley encouraged him to come to England.[29] Thomas Rankin and John Helton travelled with Wesley northwards from Birmingham in the spring of 1770. Again it was too much, at least for Helton who was left behind. In 1775 Thomas Halliday rode

---

[27] For Moss see *WJW* 20: 53 n25, 84-5, 252; Atmore 155-6; C. Williams, *The Methodist Contribution to Education in the Bahamas* (Gloucester: Sutton, 1982), for Crane see *WJW* 21: 353 n7.

[28] For Hampson see *WJW* 20: 451 n7, *WMM* 1840: 813, for Mitchell *EMP* 1: 240-59, for Lucas see *PWHS* 27 (1949), 61. For Ley see Crk 1; 130; *WJW* 21: 363 n24.

[29] For Benson see *DOMBI*, for Wright, from whom the quotation comes, see *EMP* 2: 107-30, for Tennant see Atmore; *AM* 1779: 469-74. For Bourke see Chapter 11 below.

with Wesley in Ireland. This was probably because Wesley was concerned about this English born preacher who had travelled in difficult circumstances in Ireland for nearly ten years. In 1780/81 the young Samuel Bradburn, later to become a great favourite of Wesley's and a president of the Conference, was riding with Wesley in several circuits. When Wesley took him with him again in March 1786 this was to take Bradburn's mind off the loss of his wife. John Barritt, a young farmer from Foulridge near Colne, is known to have travelled briefly with Wesley in 1784, before he entered the itinerancy. In June 1785 James Byron, a young Irishman, was introduced to Wesley as a candidate. Wesley clearly thought he was worth persevering with and had him ride with him through much of England and Ireland until November 1785 when he was sent to Norwich as a travelling preacher in his own right.[30] Often they were left behind when Wesley had to travel on, but it was intended as instruction by example for them. It seems likely that many more travelled with him, but it was not recorded or at least, as with much else, was edited out of his *Journal*.

All this includes well known preachers and those about whom little is known like Lucas. It was usual for someone to be travelling with Wesley and for them to find it difficult to keep up with their urgent and active leader even in his old age. The Cornish Methodist excise officer James Chubb, well used to riding in Wales, found it impossible to match Wesley's rapid riding 'He left Pembroke a little before me and altho' I rode at the rate of seven miles an hour I could not get up with him. It is almost nine miles and Mr W(esley) 76 years old!'[31] These preacher companions had one thing in common. Usually they were towards the beginning of their itinerancy.

Each year as Wesley travelled round the circuits the Assistants' duty was to travel with him for short stages round their own circuit. This was in the *Minutes* as early as 1749. In practice frequently the other preachers would do it for sections of the circuit. In America also this was enshrined in the *Minutes* in 1782. These said 'every assistant preacher shall so order his Circuit, that either himself or one of his helpers may travel with Mr Asbury, Wesley's deputy there, in the circuit.'[32] The modern equivalent of this in twenty-first century British Methodism is the minister who is the Chair of the District accompanying the President on his District visits. This was so that Wesley was guided by the most knowledgeable person. It was also for their benefit as well

---

[30] For Helton see *JWL* 6: 284-8. For Halliday with Wesley see Crk 2: 55, 160 and *PWHS* 10 (1910) 157. Halliday was expelled for drunkenness in 1786. For Bradburn see Blanshard, *Bradburn* 85, 110-1. For Barritt see E. Thompson, *'This Remarkable Family:' The Barritts of Foulridge* (Barnoldswick: The Author, 1981). For Byron see *WMM* 1829: 577-91.

[31] J. Chubb, *The Bristol Journal of James Chubb* (Bristol: New Room Booklets No. 8, 1988).

[32] 'Let the Assistant… Travel with me through all the Societies,' *Minutes* (1862 ed) 709. *Minutes MCA* 37. Later Asbury and Whatcoat determined that when they were not travelling together each should have the local elder travelling with him.

as his, and they certainly saw it that way, as did the young Zachariah Yewdall.[33]

Letters

Wesley corresponded with his preachers to an extent which, pre-email, few can have achieved. It was an apostolic tradition. One reason for the size of the correspondence was the improvement in the postal service earlier, particularly the merger of the systems of England, Scotland, Wales and Ireland in 1711. This enabled safe delivery and reception and a reduction of expense. It was assisted by the improvement of the roads throughout the century. To assess this correspondence it is necessary to read through the eight volumes of John Wesley's printed letters, read the unpublished letters, and remember that the number we know he wrote, but are lost, is also substantial. Heitzenrater stated that 'he (Wesley) wrote (to) each preacher at least annually.'[34] This is a statement which can not be proved, but is likely, at least until Wesley's old age. Wesley certainly began in 1744 intending to write to each Assistant (and some other person in each society) once a month on the Letter Days.[35] Of the 802 preachers in the Database, 417 have a reference in a letter, 234 are known to have either received or sent a letter or both. It may well be argued that Wesley wrote to the others, but the letters have been lost. If Heitzenrater's estimate is correct, then Wesley wrote over 5,000 letters just to his preachers! Like other evangelical leaders he must have had a stack of unanswered letters with him at any time, ready for him to seize a moment and reply. Certainly he spent much time and energy writing to his preachers, usually briefly, to guide, warn, encourage and advise. This was a significant 'correspondence course'.[36]

For some, like William Black in Nova Scotia, it was the only training they ever had, and so Wesley wrote fatherly letters giving doctrinal and practical advice in even measure. Thus in 1786 he wrote 'The same thing (revival) I am in hopes you will now see in America likewise. See that you expect it, and that you seek it in His appointed ways- namely with fasting and unintermittent prayer. And take care that you be not at all discouraged, though you should know that you should not always have an immediate answer.'[37] Black took it to

---

[33] Note 24 above.

[34] For the postal service in the 18th century and its importance for Methodism see Heitzenrater 237; *WJW* 25: 20-23. As well as the Standard Letters cited above there have been two more recent letter collections, some otherwise unpublished. P. Thomas, ed, *I am Your Affectionate Brother J Wesley* (Dallas: Bridwell Library, 1994) and M. Bendall, ed, *Yours Affectionately John Wesley The Rev. John Wesley and his Correspondents ... Letters... at Wesley's Chapel London* (London: Wesley's Chapel, 2003). We need Baker's masterly collection in the Bicentennial Edition to be completed.

[35] *JB's Minutes*; W. J. Townsend, H. B. Workman, and G. A. Eayrs, eds, *A New History of Methodism* 2 vols (London: Hodder, 1909) 1: 299-300.

[36] Hindmarsh, *Conversion Narrative* 74-5 writing about Whitefield and Newton.

[37] *JWL* 7: 352. For Black's letters and epistolary style see his 25 MS letters at Drew

heart and like many others modelled himself on Wesley as to his writing, his signature and his exhortations. Wesley was seeking to form his preachers' character, their habits, their prayers and their sermons. The further they were away from him, the more he demanded regular letters so he could support them better. So in 1771 Wesley wrote to Joseph Pilmore in America

> Dear Joseph, I cannot find your letter.., so at present I can only answer it by guess. There are some of our friends here who bitterly condemn both you and Richard Boardman. This they do in consequence of a letter from one of their correspondents in New York who asserts 'That the preaching houses there and at Philadelphia were settled in the manner of the Methodists; but that one or both of you destroyed the first writings and procured others to be drawn, wherein the houses are made over to yourselves.' I could not tell how to answer the charge. Send me the plain state of the case that I may know what to say... I complain of you for writing too seldom. Surely it would not hurt if you were to write once a month. O, beware of every degree of sloth or indolence. Be good soldiers of Jesus Christ and send a circumstantial account of your proceedings to, dear Joseph, Your affectionate friend and brother, John Wesley.

The request for monthly letters goes back to the 1744 Minutes 'Question 12. With whom should we correspond and when? A. Once a month with each Assistant and with some other person in each society.'[38] The Minute was also a warning that he would be regularly writing to ordinary members of each society, so he would receive their views as well. To Bardsley he wrote

> It is a great blessing that your fellow labourers and you are all of one mind. When that is so then the work of the Lord will prosper in your hands. It will go on widening as well as deepening while you draw in one yoke. If you desire it should deepen in believers, continually exhort them to go on unto perfection, steadily to use all the grace they have received and every moment to expect full salvation. The *Plain Account of Christian Perfection* you should read yourself more than once and recommend it to all who are groaning for full redemption.[39]

His preachers appreciated his letters and the way this method of training worked in with the other methods. As John Haime put it 'after I had continued some time as a travelling preacher, Mr Wesley took me to travel with him. He knew I was fallen from my steadfastness, but he knew how to bear with me. And when I was absent he comforted me with his letters.'[40] It was the leaders like Cownley, Pawson, Hopper and Mather with whom he corresponded most,

---

University NJ 1646-5, many to his fellow preacher Daniel Fidler. One to Fidler at Shelburne from Halifax NS on September 14th 1796 closed 'NB Study the Bible,- Study your E(nglish) Grammar.'
[38] *JWL* 5: 232; *JB's Minutes* 17.
[39] *JWL* 5: 290.
[40] *EMP* 1: 302.

and sometimes with those who caused him problems like Thomas Wride. But those who stayed in the itinerancy received a letter at some time or other, and all who sent him a letter seem to have had a reply. Wesley wrote to the young Adam Clarke in 1785 'I do not remember ever to have seen that letter from Norwich, else I should certainly have answered it.'[41] The other notable point about his letters is his consistent use of the familiar diminutive, even preachers he hardly knew were addressed as 'Sammy,' 'Billy' or 'Franky.' The high rate of preservation of his letters is witness to his influence upon the preachers. They certainly valued them and were parted from them with difficulty.

Conference

Further education for the preachers was at the Annual Conference where Wesley laid down a fraternal discipline for them. These were important spiritual gatherings at which men and women were converted. Here the preachers could see their 'father' Wesley, be admitted to the Connexion, meet their brother preachers, learn their stories and encourage each other. They were monitored, trained and at the end of Conference deployed. They would also discuss problems, agree a common policy, share the sacrament, sing old hymns and learn new ones. It was how the 'Order of Travelling Preachers' developed. The Question and Answer method of procedure allowed Wesley both to consult and teach. The early *Minutes* were mostly doctrinal. From the beginning itinerants, whether new or not, might be examined and would have to testify to their spiritual experience.[42] They learned what to teach, how to teach, and how to regulate doctrine, discipline and practice. It was a source of energy for the Methodist movement and also self definition. Conference provided a chance to learn from each other and from the Wesleys and to listen to sermons at all hours of the day. Both preachers and lay folk yearned to go to Conference.

These methods, education at Kingswood, reading the books of the *Christian Library* and the other works he printed, travelling with him, correspondence, and a common collegial discipline at Conference, were Wesley's education for his preachers.

---

[41] *EMP* 7: 255.
[42] See Richey, *Conference in America*, especially the first three chapters, for a wide ranging survey of the various uses to which Wesley put the early Conference, not merely educational. For Conference as 'fraternal' Richey quoted the early American itinerant William Watters 'We were of one heart and mind and took sweet counsel together, not how we should get riches and honors or anything this poor world could afford us; but how we should make the surest work for heaven, and be the instruments for others' (P.24). See also below Chapter 5 on Probation and Chapter 9 on the Conference.

Chapter 5

Probation

> 'Qu 1 What preachers are admitted this year? Qu 2 Who remains on trial?
> Qu 3 Who are admitted on trial?'
> Conference *Minutes* first three questions.

'On Trial' to 'Full Connexion'

All Wesley's preachers had a period of probation at the beginning of their ministry. This period was short but important, a significance highlighted by the fact that the questions about it were the first business for the Conference. At the start of their probation, or soon after starting, they would at Conference go through a ceremony in which they were accepted on probation or as it became known 'On Trial.' At the end of their probation there was another Conference at which there were many questions which enabled them to testify to their call. This was followed by what became known as 'Reception into Full Connexion,' an even more solemn moment, the equivalent of ordination in the twenty-first century Methodist Church. They had become fully-fledged Wesley's preachers. During the period of probation they received some of the training discussed in the last chapter. The candidate found his feet as a full time preacher in collaboration with the more experienced men in his circuit, who counselled him, prayed with him and advised him in his actions. When he offered to serve as 'a son in the gospel' Wesley asked him for a 'written account of his early life, including the time and circumstance of the conversion, and the manner in which he was led to preach the Gospel.' These were based on their oral testimonies, honed over many class meetings and love feasts. When Wesley's preachers reflected on their lives in these letters to Wesley, which were often later reprinted in the magazine, their entry bulked large. It was a turning point like their conversion, something which would determine their future lives and actions. The 22 year-old Samuel Bradburn had in 1774 been preaching for some time in his local Chester circuit and next door in Liverpool, the last bit filling in for the itinerants there

> When the preachers returned from Conference, Mr. Mather gave me the Minutes; and I was exceedingly affected to find myself appointed for the Liverpool

Circuit... The importance of the work made so deep an impression on my mind, and I had a sense of my own weakness, that I was greatly cast down for some time... However, as I was stationed with a people whose love had already been proved, and among whom I had seen some fruit of my feeble endeavours to save souls, and knowing Mr Morgan to be a judicious, honest, tender-hearted man, I was rather comforted and I found a willingness, though with fear and trembling, to begin the vast and important work of a regular travelling preacher.[1]

Wesley in the early *Minutes* and elsewhere clearly had his preachers on probation, as 'on trial' became known in the nineteenth century. These stages of apprenticeship were part of the Methodist discipline which provided structure to the lives of men and women shaken by the emotional changes through which they were going. It had some similarities to the system of apprenticeship already mentioned under 'Origins.' Though for a shorter period than the seven years then standard for the young apprentice, there was an agreement under which the new preacher promised to go where he was sent, do as he was told and not to marry during his probation. In return the local circuit tried to find him food and accommodation, and replace and mend his clothes as needed.

After some hesitation at first, in 1749 at Conference Wesley drew up rules for 'receiving a new Helper' which from then on changed relatively little

> 1. Let him be recommended by the Assistant to whose Society he belongs.
> 2. Let him read and carefully weigh the Conferences, and see whether he can agree with them or no.
> 3. Let him be received as a Probationer by having a book given to him inscribed thus: You think it your Duty to call Sinners to Repentance. Make full proof that God has called you hereto and we shall then be glad to act in concert with you.
> 4. Let him come to the next Conference and after examination fasting and Prayer be received as a Helper by having a book given him being inscribed thus: 'So long as you freely consent and earnestly endeavour to walk according to the following rules we shall rejoice to go on with you hand in hand. We are yours affectionately,'
> 5. Let a new Book be given at every Conference and the former returned.[2]

Regulation 5 did not last in that the original book tended to be retained, not replaced each Conference; otherwise these regulations remained virtually unchanged long into the nineteenth century. The Assistant, who was Wesley's representative within the circuit, must recommend the new itinerant from the

---

[1] Jackson in Introduction to *EMP* 1: 11. Blanshard, *Bradburn* 39. John Morgan, entered 1761, died 1782, was the more experienced colleague with the tender heart. The *Minutes* are the main source for this chapter. Hindmarsh, *Conversion Narrative* 228 pointed out that Wesley was moulding by this request the stories which would be written and published. See also Burdon, *Authority* 24-7.
[2] *JB's Minutes* 66, cf. *Minutes* 1: 556-71.

Probation

ranks of the local preachers of that circuit. A good example of this is from the testimony of Thomas Mitchell. This Yorkshireman, who entered in 1748 and was travelling in the late summer of 1753 in the Wiltshire circuit, wrote 'While I was in this Circuit I went to see a young man (Mr Thomas Olivers) who had given an exhortation at times among the people. I found him working hard for his bread. He seemed to me to have much sense and to be very sincere. I wrote to Mr Wesley and told him that I and many more thought he might be very useful. Mr Wesley desired he might go with me into Cornwall (Mitchell's next circuit) ...the Lord made us a blessing to that people.' Olivers described it without mentioning Mitchell 'Mr Wesley desired that I would give it (his business) up and go immediately (to preach) in Cornwall. With my boots on my legs, my great coat on my back, and my saddle-bags with my books and linen across my shoulder, I set out on foot, October 24th, 1753.'[3]

The preachers must have shown 'gifts, graces and fruit.' In other words they must have been approved by the local societies, have ability for the work, which included health, and have converts to show for their preaching already. This was the ideal, though the memoirs of many itinerants show that in their own eyes at least it did not always happen like that. The rules and doctrine in the *Large Minutes* of the Conference had to be agreed by the new preacher.

Both at the beginning of the period of probation and at its end when the probationer was received into Full Connexion there was a ceremony at which a book was presented to the preacher. This practice was a very early one. When Joseph Cownley was admitted as a preacher at the Conference of 1747, he 'kneeled down and Mr Wesley putting the New Testament into his hand said: 'Take thou authority to preach the Gospel.' He then gave him his benediction.' The book given with an inscription was the *Disciplinary Minutes* of 1749, under a procedure outlined in the 1749 *Minutes* and largely kept to later. From 1753 it was the *Large Minutes*, adapted slightly as time went on. The inscription in this first book, having said the new preacher was claiming God's call to preach, was aimed at encouraging him to follow the regulations. It held the attractions of being accepted in Full Connexion before him. Until around 1780 the sentence was added 'Observe, you are not to ramble up and down, but to go where the Assistant directs and there only.' This was to prevent the new itinerant straying out of the usual paths without help and instruction. It is interesting that by 1780 Wesley thought he could omit it, presumably because it was no longer needed. Some historians, knowing what some preachers did have wished it had remained!

The preacher had been given one book as a Probationer. Then at first at the next Conference, after examination, fasting and prayer, he would be received as a 'Helper,' so into Full Connexion. In 1790 Joseph Sutcliffe received the *Large Minutes* 1744-1789, the descendant of the *Disciplinary Minutes* of 1749. Such books survive today, showing how much they were cherished by the individual

---

[3] *EMP* 1: 252-3, 2: 73.

preacher or minister.[4] The inscription in the second book reminded the preacher in Full Connexion of the rules under which he must work. From 1765 the preacher in Full Connexion was given a copy of the current *Minutes* with this book, both with the same inscription.

In the eighteenth century this probationary period was often expressed as 'On Trial' and George Story claimed to be the first to be admitted on trial in 1762 at the Conference that year.[5] It is quite possible that it was indeed in 1762 that the phrase 'On Trial' was first used for being on probation. Certainly, as the 1749 regulations show, probation went back to the 1740s. The length of time spent 'On Trial' increased over the years. In 1765 it was still clearly one year, as it had been probably since the beginning. Those admitted on trial then were all admitted into full connexion in 1766. In 1767 the probation had been increased to two years for some, but more commonly it varied. William Thom, for example, in 1774 was received into Full Connexion having been only on trial for one year. Adam Clarke has been claimed to have had an 'unique probation' of less than one year in 1782-3.[6] It would be better described as 'possibly unique' as earlier preachers may have had less, but we do not know. Certainly no preacher after Clarke had less than this and Clarke was certainly very unusual at ten months. Clarke illustrates the point that the length of time on probation varied, some were shorter, some longer. Discipline problems might well lead to probation being lengthened. Thomas Tennant who was received on trial in 1770 and James Thom in 1783 found themselves on probation for three years each, being received into the full itinerancy in 1773 and 1786 respectively. Tennant at least probably took longer because of his fragile health. Poor health meant a man might not survive the tough life of an itinerant; therefore full acceptance was delayed until he was shown to be well.

In 1784 the usual period of probation was increased to four years. Of the 25 British preachers who appear in the list as 'received On Trial' in 1786, for example, eleven were received into Full Connexion four years later in 1790.[7] Of the others one, James Gore, had died in 1790, five left, three were received into Full Connexion a year late in 1791, and five a year early in 1789. Those accepted early had all done a year or much of a year in circuit before they were officially received On Trial in 1786. The three accepted late had all had problems such as illness or weakness of some kind which justified their deferral. This illustrates the fact that though Conference was important in the movement from one stage to the next, it could happen without Conference and

---

[4] *HMGB* 1: 234, 250; *PWHS* 15 (1926) 57.
[5] Chilcote, *Her Own Story* 254.
[6] Chilcote, *Her Own Story* 275. This is based on the assertion in J. B. B. Clarke, ed, *Account of the Life of Adam Clarke, Partly Written by Himself* (London: T. S. Clarke, 1833) vol 1 162 that when he was admitted into Full Connexion, it 'was perhaps the earliest admission.' Clarke himself was rightly cautious, hence the 'perhaps.'
[7] See on probation *DOMBI* and for reasons for leaving Chapter 15 below.

men could be travelling as itinerants for some time before they were formally received at a Conference. The rules surrounding the period of probation were flexible and pragmatic in this period and were frequently bent to suit the individual situation. Charles Wesley urged further regulations on John in 1751

> With regard to the Preachers, we agree:
> 1 That none be permitted to preach in any of our societies, till he be examined, both as to his grace and gifts, at least by the assistant, who sending word to us, may by our answer admit him a local Preacher.
> 2 That such preacher be not immediately taken from his trade, but be exhorted to follow it with all diligence.
> 3 That no person shall be received as a Travelling Preacher, or be taken from his trade, by either of us alone, but by both of us conjointly, giving him a note under both our hands.[8]

Charles was unable to maintain this insistence on his veto on the preachers, as many whom he purged were soon allowed to return by John. As the numbers grew it became impossible for the centre to keep track of the admission of local preachers. Itinerants were much more important and had to be agreed to by John or later the Conference as his successor.

There were other regulations surrounding the new itinerant during his probation. The Limerick Conference in Ireland of 1752 stated that if the man were unable to preach more than twice a day he must not enter. In other words, there was a demand for physical fitness, the forerunner of the later medical reports. It also made it clear that new preachers were 'given the right hand of fellowship,' another symbol which has continued down to the present day.

Age at Entry

Historians and others have tended to assume that Wesley's preachers were young at entry, like the twenty-two year old Bradburn.[9] This was partly put about by Wesley himself to indicate the contrast between 'the whole body of aged, established, learned clergy' opposed to Methodism and the 'handful of raw young men without name, learning or eminent sense' that were its chief support.[10] Many were young, particularly at that relatively early point of 1753 (see below Chart 7). Their ages are not always known nor necessarily accurate. Jonathan Catlow of Keighley is said to have entered at sixteen in 1748. This age depends upon Atmore's assertion; the actual evidence is that he was only a

---

[8] *HMGB* 1: 237, quoting J. Whitehead, *The Life of the Revd. John Wesley, MA, Sometime Fellow of Lincoln College, Oxford,* 2 vols (London: Couchman, 1793-6) 2: 269. See also Chapter 17 below.

[9] E.g. J. G. McEllhenney, 'Itinerancy Is Dead But It Can Live Again' in *Quarterly Review* 23 (2003) 60. 'They (Wesley's itinerants) were young.'

[10] Whitehead, *Wesley* 2: 272 quoting John Wesley February 1753.

Chart 7: Age at Entry

Source: Wesley's Preachers' Database

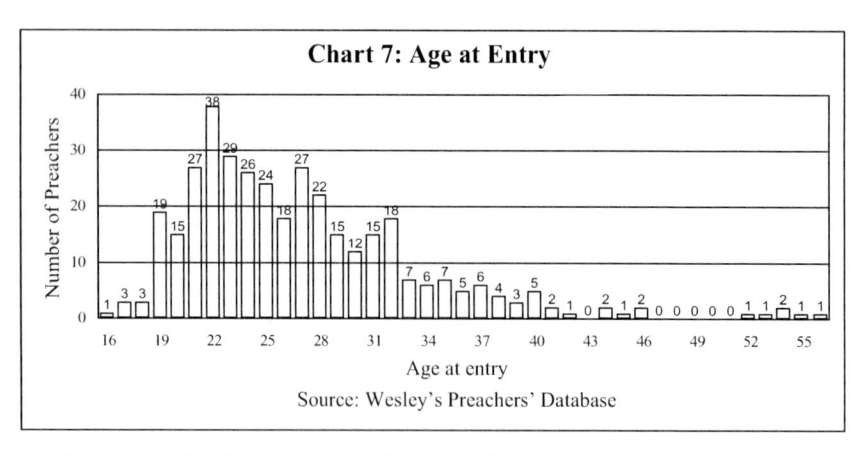

local preacher in that year and for several years to come. Catlow was an interesting and not untypical early preacher, in that the stories about him sometimes conflict with each other. He was the son of Jonathan Catlow, farmer of Twolands, Scartop, near Oxenhope, Keighley, with at least one sister (Sarah, later the mother of the preacher Jonathan Edmondson). He certainly began preaching at sixteen; his first sermon was preached in a house called Lough on the edge of the moors to a few old women, his mother as the better reader giving out the hymns. Scartop is close to the moors dividing Lancashire and Yorkshire and close also to where Paul Greenwood's original home was at Stanbury. Catlow was one of William Grimshaw's preachers in the Haworth Round. The evidence, apart from that much later from Myles and Atmore, is that he remained a local preacher until around 1753, by which time he was twenty-one. I therefore doubt his entry at sixteen. He was preaching at Todmorden in August 1751, then aged around nineteen, but that was within his own large Haworth circuit. In May 1753 we find in Wesley's Journal the fascinating story of him preaching in his sleep, 'somniloquist' being the technical term. Catlow appeared at the Leeds Conference in 1753 definitely a travelling preacher. In 1759 he argued with a Baptist preacher to such good effect that a number of local Methodists were dissuaded from turning Baptist. He left Methodism and the itinerancy in 1762. This is supported by his appearance as 'Jon. Catlow' 'Teacher at the Independent Society at Arncotes, Luddington, Lincs. 1762' (cited by Baker). There are at least three different accounts of when he died.[11]

There were three preachers who entered as seventeen year olds, two early,

---

[11] For Catlow see *WMM* 1826: 286; 1833: 382; 1850: 1; *MRWN* 1904: 86; Baker, *Grimshaw* 148, 244; Myles; Atmore 42; *GHR* 223-25; *WJW* 20: 460-1 and note; 21: 416; Crowther; Turner *HBA* 103-4; J. W. Laycock's MS Notebook Keighley Library 138. For preaching while asleep see S. Juster, *Doomsayers: Anglo-American Prophecy in an Age of Revolution* (Philadelphia: Pennsylvania UP, 2003) 111-4.

James Glassbrook and Thomas Greaves, and the third being Adam Clarke's friend, Andrew Coleman, in 1785, the only seventeen year old after 1760. Of these Thomas Greaves' date of entry, 1756, depends on Myles who was writing more than forty years later, and may have meant when Greaves began to preach, as with Catlow, rather than when he began to travel. We only know of Greaves actually preaching in the Haworth Circuit in 1760 at the age of twenty-one, and even then he could still be a local preacher. My view is that his age at entry must be doubtful.[12] Of the three seventeen year olds, therefore, only Andrew Coleman, whose friend Adam Clarke vouched for his age, is definite.

On the other hand, the average age for entry was twenty-seven, old by nineteenth century standards, with the oldest known entrant in England being John Whitley, a farmer of Toils Farm at Eldwick Cragg near Bingley, entering in 1777 at the age of 55. Again Whitley is an interesting character, of similar origins to Catlow. He was born at Hawshaw in Nidderdale around 1723. He was led 'by providence to take' Toils Farm at Eldwick Cragg, east of Bingley in Airedale as a tenant farmer. The farmhouse still stands there on the right hand side of the road from Beck to Cragg. Finding the house not ready for occupation he and his wife Martha lodged at a neighbour's house where there was regular preaching. Here they heard the local preacher John Skirrow preach in 1759 and were converted. Preachers stayed in Whitley's farmhouse and one travelling preacher, Samuel Smith, inscribed leaded panes in it. Whitley became a local preacher himself. His wife Martha died in February 1776 aged 58. In 1777 Wesley called the widower to become an itinerant. Whitley declined, saying 'I have only two sermons, sir, what am I to do?' Wesley, as he often did, (probably wrongly) did not accept Whitley's refusal, saying 'God that has enabled you to preach two, can give you ability to preach two thousand.' John Whitley did as he was told, went to the Staffordshire circuit in 1777 and came back to his native Yorkshire at Thirsk in 1778. He did not last as an itinerant and had given up by 1779. At home he had left his son Francis, already a local preacher, in charge of the farm. John Whitley died in London in 1813 aged 90, but his body was buried with his wife and son at Bingley parish church.[13]

---

[12] For Glassbrook see J. H. Lenton, 'James Glazebrook: A Protégé of Fletcher and his Double' *WHS Shropshire* NS 4 (1998) 4-5. For Coleman see Atmore; J. Everett, ed, *The Miscellaneous Works of Adam Clarke* (London: Tegg, 1836-7) 12 348; No 65 in *Wesleyan Takings*; *PPIM* 17-19; W. Smith, *History of Wesleyan Methodism in Ireland* (Dublin: Doolittle, 1830) 259-60. For Thomas Greaves see Ives 51; *KS Reg* 228; *GHR* 217; *WJW* 22; 27; *AO*; and Myles.

[13] The main source for Whitley is J. Ward, *Historical Sketches of the Rise and Progress of Methodism in Bingley* (Bingley: Harrison, 1863) 30-32. Myles and others have sometimes confused this John Whitley with the Irishman John Whitley from Monaghan who was accepted in 1774, sent to Charlemont Circuit (Armagh in the *Minutes*) but 'married a gay young lady' and did not go. There were two window panes of early Methodist inscriptions at Eldwick, one with a Wesley portrait (*GHR* 353-5).

These two stories of Catlow and of Whitley, the one perhaps the oldest known, the other perhaps the youngest entrant, illustrate the importance of the probationary period. Many like Whitley did not last through it.

At least 102 are known to have entered at thirty years of age or over. Out of the 369 whose ages are known this is substantial (36%), and an substantially increased percentage. In 2000 the figure I gave was 26% but much more has been discovered about the preachers. So, in other words, the well known tended to be younger and the more we learn about the preachers, the older at entry they appear to be. So far as cohorts are concerned age of entry did not change much in Wesley's lifetime. Nor was there much change at first after Wesley's death in 1791. As late as 1803 Conference accepted a 48 year old local preacher, Philip Rawlins, a tradesman of London, into the ministry.[14]

Probation and Marriage

There were a number of Wesley's preachers, possibly as many as fourteen, certainly eleven, who entered when their wife died. These included Timothy Crowther, Richard Boardman, probably James Lyons senior and possibly Richard Whatcoat.[15] Many had children still surviving who would need to be supported, for example William Hainsworth. Admittedly often they married again, as soon as they could. Some historians have suggested that it was impossible to marry while on probation. This again is reading the nineteenth century situation back into the eighteenth century. In Wesley's day several men married while still 'On Trial.'

An example of one preacher like this was John Beaumont. Born near Huddersfield in 1761 he entered in 1786 after the death of his first wife. Left off the stations, apparently because his Assistant spoke against him to John Wesley in 1788 at Conference, he was then sent to Huddersfield (his home circuit!) in place of a sick preacher. There, though still 'On Trial,' he married his second wife. There was no accommodation problem as they lived at home. Next year at Conference he was 'received back' though now married. As an irony his wife died in the next circuit (Burton) and he was eventually received into Full Connexion in 1791 after Wesley's death, again without a wife. Another example was William Butterfield who entered 'On Trial' in 1784. He was admitted to Full Connexion in 1788. That same year before his probation had ended he had married in January Jane Allen at Topcliffe. Presumably she would be no burden for that Methodist year since no-one objected to his marrying early. Another who married early was William Bramwell, whose

---

[14] *Minutes* 2: 166, MSS list of preachers On Trial 1803-31 MARC. There are many other instances of relatively late entry, for example John Crook in Chapter 10. For the slightly different pattern for Irish-born preachers see Chapter 11.

[15] For Crowther see Chapter 7, Boardman Chapter 12 and for Whatcoat Chapter 13. Others were Thomas Longley, Thomas Eden, John Johnson and William Hainsworth.

marriage was certainly inconvenient for the Connexion. He was coming to the end of his first year on probation but still had two to do. He had been in Kent and was being sent to King's Lynn in Norfolk, not untypical for journeys expected of probationers. He refused to go. Since Bramwell had had Coke's promise that he could marry on his return from Kent, Wesley was in this case prepared to compromise and eventually sent him to Blackburn, followed by a year at Colne. Meanwhile Bramwell's wife Ellen, a dressmaker at neighbouring Preston in the Blackburn circuit, remained at home, running her business and receiving monthly visits from Bramwell.[16]

Becoming an Assistant Young

An Assistant was 'that preacher in each circuit who is appointed... to take charge of the societies and *the other preachers*' in the circuit, that is to act for Wesley in his absence. There is a letter in which Wesley referred to Hampson in Dublin as 'the assistant (or Superior Preacher for the time being).' In America the title soon became 'preacher in charge.'[17] Most of the evidence about Assistants (who after Wesley were called Superintendents) and how Wesley saw them is in the *Minutes* which were only regularly printed from 1765. Before then we are dependent on very sparse information. In the 1740s there seem to have been two groups, 'helpers' and 'Assistants.' It is not clear whether Assistants then were in charge of circuits or simply his more trusted helpers. The helpers included those fully itinerant, partial itinerants and those who were later known as local preachers. In 1749 he restricted the title of Assistant to those responsible for the oversight of each circuit.[18]

Yet as late as 1765 Wesley was not clear whether Assistant was a status that some preacher in the circuit must have, or whether it was attached to the person. Thus in the late 1760s some preachers were 'Assistants,' but not even on the stations at all, such as James Morgan in 1765. Others, who included James Morgan and Thomas Brisco, had their names appearing second, or in the case of William Thompson at Athlone fourth in the list of preachers for the circuit. Circuits which were single man stations found that their preacher was not listed as an Assistant in the *Minutes* because his status did not need to be differentiated from his colleague (for example Canterbury and Colchester). All these were from 1766. Some circuits appeared to be without an Assistant. So clear status for the Assistant as the preacher responsible for the circuit was not

---

[16] Sigston, *Bramwell* 60-71. Others who married early were Thomas Hutton, John Booth and William Church.

[17] Unpublished copy letter of JW 10 October 1777 at Craigavon Museum. The capitals for 'Superior Preacher' were Wesley's. For 'preacher in charge' see Simpson *Cyclopaedia of Methodism* under Assistant. This section on the Assistant is based on a detailed study of the eighteenth century *Minutes*.

[18] FB 'Polity' 230-1 and n.

there until the early 1770s.

Wesley regarded Assistants as important people to whom he gave much responsibility. From the earliest days the names of those who were Assistants were recorded, at first more often than their stations. In the early *Minutes* other travelling preachers were often not recorded at all, since they were less significant. In 1796 the *Minutes* changed the title 'Assistant' to that of 'Superintendent,' following Conference's decision to this effect. In the nineteenth century becoming a Superintendent was similarly important, but reserved for those who had been twenty years in the ministry. In the twenty-first century it is rare in British Methodism for even a senior candidate to be a 'Super' until his or her second station. It would be usual to wait until the third or even fourth. However, Wesley was concerned that Assistants should be energetic, devoted and *not* elderly. The pattern would seem to have been five years' travel and most would have become Assistants at least on one occasion. At the other end, those who did twenty or thirty years would often find themselves under the authority of a younger Assistant. George Snowden entered the itinerancy in February 1769 aged 31. At Conference in 1769 he was received 'On Trial' and sent to Enniskillen as Assistant there, with only six months experience as an itinerant! Admittedly as an older candidate he might have had other useful experience and been senior to his colleagues. James Thom, a Scotsman from Aberdeen, was received 'On Trial' at the Conference of 1783 and sent immediately as Assistant to the large circuit of East Cornwall. John Cowmeadow, also received that year, was responsible to him and so was Joseph Algar, having entered in 1782. Thus three very recent entrants were responsible for 496 members. Wesley must have been tempted to repeat the experiment when they reported 650 members at the end of the year! Richard Drew was in his first year according the *Minutes* in 1788, when he was sent to be Assistant of the new circuit of Bideford in Devon with William Sandoe to help him, a local man of one year's experience. It must have been a success since the next year he was moved to be Assistant at Tiverton, this time over John Poole who had entered forty years before in 1759.[19] These were all examples of Probationers (to use a later title) acting as Assistants in their first year, in each case over more senior colleagues.

John Crook was an Assistant in his second year. Known as 'the Apostle of the Isle of Man' and first 'On Trial' in 1775, he became an Assistant in 1776. Certainly Crook was a man of exceptional ability. But this pattern of early promotion was true of most of Wesley's preachers. In 1787 the 26 year old John Reynolds, who entered in 1785 but was only found in the *Minutes* in 1786, was Assistant in Sussex over the much more senior Robert Empringham, who had entered in 1771 and was 48 years old. By the next year Reynolds was

---

[19] Another example was William Jenkins who first appeared in the *Minutes* as being received On Trial in 1789 (aged about 25, though he was probably travelling in Bedford during the previous year), and in the same year was sent back to Bedford as Assistant.

still Assistant, but in a different circuit, Lynn, over two other more senior preachers, the 51 year old John Cricket who had entered in 1778 and the 49 year old William Green who had begun in 1780. Both Cricket and Green had been Assistants already, Green for five of the previous six years, but they both had to defer to the much younger and junior Reynolds. Andrew Blair, a relatively junior Irish born preacher, found himself in the late 1780s acting as Assistant over senior preachers like John Murlin, William Eels and Duncan Wright in large and important English circuits such as Birmingham and Leeds.[20] Most of the older men had previously been Assistants under Wesley and usually he had given them the chief post in any circuit. But not when Andrew Blair was around!

On the other hand, Thomas Mitchell, a senior and most successful preacher from the first cohort, was an Assistant at least three times in the 1760s but never in the 1770s and 80s. Wesley apparently thought he had become too old.[21] There were exceptions to this pattern. There were those who were never an Assistant such as David Evans, Michael Fenwick after 1750, or Robert Hayward after 1769, having entered in 1768. There were also those who after the first two or three years were always the Assistant, such as John Mason who entered as early as 1764, first held the post in 1766 aged 33 and then, except for 1768, held it every year to Wesley's death. However, the most common pattern under Wesley was to be Assistant after four or five years from entry until middle age and then not again. The number of men appointed as Assistants while still on probation is also interesting and shows Wesley's flexibility and the importance he laid on youth right up to his death. Later, after 1791, age and years travelled became major qualifications without which 'promotion' such as being Assistant or Superintendent could not be gained.

Assistants were the vital people in the administration of the circuit and responsible to Wesley for it. This might lead to business considerations being more decisive in Wesley's choice. Pawson disgustedly reported that when 'old John Hampson was proposed to act as an Assistant and I urged this to Mr Wesley, his answer was he will not sell a shillingsworth of books in a year! A wonderful reason was it not?'[22] It was one of the motives for Wesley wanting younger, more energetic men as Assistants.

Probation in their *own* Circuit

Many itinerant preachers, particularly in the early years, began to travel in their own circuit. This was a logical development. In circuits in the Channel Islands or in Ireland or northern Scotland they would know the local language, be it

---

[20] Other senior preachers over whom he was imposed were Robert Costerdine, George Story and Jeremiah Brettell. Blair entered in 1778, Murlin in 1754 and Wright in 1764.
[21] Mitchell entered in 1748 and was around 40 in the later 1760s.
[22] Lenton, *My Sons* 24-5; *Pawson L* 3: 106, in 1804, rather after the event.

Gaelic or French, or at least the dialect. It was a circuit where they were already known. It would ease the difficulty, particularly if there was a wife and family, in that for the first year they would not have to move. On the 10th October 1768 the Cornishman Francis Woolf 'went out to preach the Gospel' in his own circuit, since he was born at Redruth in 1740. He married in 1760, became converted in 1767 and had a young family of five by 1768.[23]

In his own circuit the preacher would certainly be able to find the way. He should have been already approved by the members of the Quarterly Meeting and therefore welcome in all the societies. (As we shall see below, this did not necessarily happen in the early years of Methodism.) If he had to give up at the end of the first year, he would have lost less. Travel to a faraway area could be a problem. At least 107 preachers began as itinerants in their own circuit. This was a high proportion of those for whom we know their first circuit. They included Thomas Rutherford in Newcastle, Jasper Winscom in Wiltshire, Francis Asbury in Staffordshire and Thomas Walsh in Limerick.[24]

John Peacock, born at Scotter near Kirton in Lindsey, North Lincolnshire, in 1731, lost his mother at seven. As a young man he made a name for himself locally as a wrestler and boxer. In 1754 he heard George Whitefield at Misterton, was converted and joined the Methodists. He married and moved to Misterton where he became a local preacher. In 1767 he was called out by Wesley and travelled in the West Lincolnshire circuit. Next year he was in East Lincolnshire and had to leave his wife and two children behind in Misterton, presumably supported by her father's family. It was not surprising that he then desisted for a year. By being a travelling preacher in his own circuit for the first year, he had cushioned the blow to his family.[25]

Very often the call out was in an emergency. In the Manchester circuit in 1776 the Assistant Robert Roberts asked the local preacher James Hall from Boaredge to 'supply his circuit,' in other words to travel in his place as one of the two itinerant preachers, which he did for a few weeks. At the next Conference Hall was accepted and sent to a neighbouring circuit, Macclesfield, to break him in gently.[26] This tended to happen more with the early cohorts and less often with later entrants, though sometimes it was the neighbouring circuit in which later entrants began. It was not necessarily a success. Peter Mill from Arbroath found great hostility when he became a travelling preacher in his own Dundee circuit in 1774. Neither of his two young Assistants, Thomas

---

[23] T. and G. Woolf, *'dear Franky:' the Life and Times of Francis Woolf 1740-1807* (Southampton: n. p. 1995).

[24] Others included John Pawson in York, Jonathan Maskew in Haworth, Jacob Rowell in the Dales, John Whitford and John Murlin 'the Weeping Prophet' in Cornwall and Charles Atmore in Norfolk.

[25] *MM* 1803: 383-8; J. J. Hastings, *Misterton Methodism Past and Present* (Gainsborough: Newbold and Humphries, 1928) 9.

[26] *AM* 1793: 288-9.

Rutherford and Robert Wilkinson, could persuade the local Methodists to accept him. In the end he gave up and went to Aberdeen to be under the care of the veteran Duncan Wright. Mill later paid tribute to Wright as the man who saved his ministry. Jasper Winscom was a similar kind of failure. An irascible and elderly leading layman and haberdasher in Winchester, he refused to be stationed too far away from his business interests. The even older Wesley was prepared to accept this, but not his itinerant preachers. When Wesley died, they promptly stationed Winscom in faraway Norfolk at Wells, censured him for not deferring to his Assistant, and when he refused to accept their stationing, were pleased to see him go back to his local preaching, another example of Conference inflexibility and Wesley's lenience.[27]

Starting Probation during the Year

Another important difference from modern practice was the large number who began as travelling preachers during the Methodist year as James Hall had done, rather than being stationed by the Conference at the beginning of the Methodist year starting at Conference time. One of the problems about this from the historian's point of view was that it often was not mentioned. Clearly it would leave no impact on the *Minutes* and historians have tended not to notice it. If Wesley felt there was a need for an extra preacher in any circuit, he was likely to send a suitable existing local preacher to serve, from the circuit if possible or from elsewhere if necessary. It was similar to the later practice of the 1790s onwards of having preachers 'in reserve,' who could be called out during the year by the president of the Conference. These were recorded in the *Minutes* from the 1790s and there were many instances. In 1794, for example, there were eleven such preachers listed. Later the President could call men from the Colleges, and this happened through most of the twentieth century as well as the nineteenth, much to the disgust of their College Tutors who repeatedly deplored the practice. On the other hand, from the point of view of the circuits, their needs became suddenly worse during the year because of illness, death or a man leaving. They did not want to wait for Conference, which might be eleven months away, nor did Wesley or his successors in Conference think they should. Admittedly many of them went because of the work increasing, rather than someone being ill.

The point to be made here is that this practice not only goes back to Wesley, but seems to have been even more common then than it was later. The numbers and the proportions seem higher. Thus at least five seem to have served for up to a year before they were put On Trial in 1786 (25% of the total that year).

Alan Harding, in his admirable *Countess of Huntingdon's Connexion* showed that, within that other Methodist denomination in England in the

---

[27] Compare Joseph Bradford's letter to Winscom of the 6th April 1791 Drew 1647-3-1: 56 with the August letters between the two in Dyson (1865) 170-1.

eighteenth century, there were three groups among the preachers. Those who were clergymen, those who were already active as preachers, and those trained at Trevecca, the last being the largest number.[28] A similar pattern can be seen among Wesley's preachers. A sizable number, higher at first and smaller later but always present, were Anglican clergyman, usually after the first few years unbeneficed. Once they had shown Methodist convictions they were most unlikely ever to receive any church living. There were exceptions who held livings like Fletcher, Walter Sellon or Cornelius Bayley, but these after the death of Grimshaw were always few in number. A smaller but still important group of men were already preachers, like Bennet or Thomas Lee already referred to. The vast majority, however, and increasingly so as time went on, were neither. Their training has been described in Chapter 4 above.

The completion of the preacher's period of probation took place at an impressive ceremony at Conference. In the 1766 Minutes the otherwise unimportant preacher William Ellis is recorded as being asked various questions, designed to produce his public testimony

> Have you faith in Christ? Are you going on to perfection? Do you expect to be perfected in love, in this life? Are you groaning after it? Are you resolved to devote yourself wholly to God and his work? Do you know the Methodist Doctrine? Have you read the Sermons? The Notes on the New Testament? Do you know the Methodist Plan? Have you read the Plain Account? The Appeals? Do you know the Rules of the Society? Of the Bands? Do you keep them? Do you take no snuff? Tobacco? Drams? Do you constantly attend the Church and Sacraments? Have you read the Minutes? Are you willing to conform to them? Have you considered the twelve rules of a Helper: especially the first, tenth and twelfth? Will you keep them for conscience sake? Are you determined to employ all your time in the work of God? ... Will you meet the Society, the Bands, the Select Society, the leaders..? In every place? Will you diligently and earnestly instruct the children and visit from house to house? Will you recommend fasting, both by precept and example?[29]

William Ellis was probably from Cornwall and the Mr Ellis responsible for a revival in Dundee around 1768. He left in 1773.[30] These questions were asked of each and every travelling preacher. The ceremony ended with the presentation of the book. This was a symbol of the public testimony and fraternal acceptance by the body of itinerants which was long remembered.

---

[28] Harding, *Countess's Connexion* 78.
[29] *Minutes* (1812 ed) vol 1 Qu 2 (52-3).
[30] MARC MS Dall papers autobiography MA 3181 13; *JWL* 7: 273.

CHAPTER 6

Marriage

'A Preacher's wife should be a pattern of Cleanliness, in her person, clothes and habitation. Let nothing slatternly be seen about her; no rags, no dirt; no litter. And she should be always at work, either for herself, her husband, or the poor.'
Large Minutes 1780.

Marriage in the Eighteenth Century

The importance of women in the Methodist societies in the eighteenth century has already been discussed. Wesley's preachers had to appeal particularly to women. It is not surprising therefore that many were married. This chapter is about those marriages, when, where and to whom they were married; also how often and why those marriages took place.

Before Hardwicke's Marriage Act of 1753 marriage in England was a legal minefield. Both before and after the Act it is very difficult to trace the wives of the preachers. Many remain nameless and even where there is a name little else is known. However, the existence and availability of other sources, often via the internet, enables us to know more for some wives. From 1753 only the church wedding was binding. No-one under 21 could be married without the consent of a parent or guardian. Delaying marriage was common in post-Reformation Europe, unique to Western Europe and the period 1500-1760. One result was the high proportion of celibacy, so that in one small sample of people aged 40 to 45, 22.9 % still remained unmarried; but this delaying of marriage was beginning to break down.[1] The mean age of marriage was falling. For men in 1700-49 it was 27.5 and in 1750-99 26.4. For women the equivalent figures were 26.2 and 24.9.

The duration of marriage was often short because of the high mortality rate, which was especially high in childbirth. Marriage in the eighteenth century could be a transient institution. If a Wesley's preacher married a woman of childbearing age, she frequently died young, leaving him with a young family.

---

[1] Hitchcock, *English Sexualities* 25-6 n5, quoting A. MacFarlane, *Marriage and Love in England 1300-1840* (Oxford: Blackwells, 1986) 25. The rate of celibacy fell to less than 10% in the early nineteenth century.

Almost invariably he married again. Nationally remarriages for one or other partner were one quarter of all marriages. For Wesley's preachers we usually don't know whether the wife was married before. Sometimes this was true for the preacher as well. Because marriage often did not last, less was expected of it than in twenty-first century British society.[2]

Courtship

Church had always been a favourite place for meeting one's betrothed for the first time and the Methodist meeting-house or chapel was to be no different. The courtship could be lengthy. For example, Joseph Cownley is known to have been the object of the love of Martha Massiot, a Methodist in Cork in September 1750. Cownley had first come to Ireland as a preacher in 1748. He did not marry Martha until October 1755. Once married, Wesley, who had himself reported her love to Cownley and promised to 'do all that lies in my power to remove every hindrance out of the way' allowed the happy couple to be based in Newcastle for the next thirty years. Thomas Rankin had an understanding with Mrs Bradshaw before he went to America in 1773. He did not marry her until after his return in 1779. More usually the courtship was relatively brief, the six months which was the usual minimum in ordinary society.[3] Itinerants knew they might move soon and were ready to marry quickly. John M'Kersey left Pembroke in 1791 and went to Hexham. By April 1792 he had married Jane Bell at Hexham. Alexander Kilham, the future founder of the Methodist New Connexion, went to the Scarborough circuit in 1787. By April 1788 he had married Sarah Grey of Pickering. It is interesting that the examples of longer courtship are early and shorter courtship late. Wesley's preachers did tend to delay marriage more at first and less later, as with the wider society around them. However, Methodist ministers after this period continued to delay marriage more than happened on average outside the ministry.[4]

---

[2] L. Stone, *The Family, Sex and Marriage in England 1500-1800* (London: Penguin: 1979), a classic work which set the agenda for a generation of historians. Figures should be corrected from E. A. Wrigley and R. S. Schofield, *The Population History of England 1541-1871* (Cambridge: CUP, 1989) 255. See also C. A. Heywood, *A History of Childhood: Children and Childhood in the West from Medieval to Modern Times* (Oxford: Polity Press, 2001) 46-8. The source for most of the preachers' marriages is the *IGI*. I am indebted to Henry Rack's important article, '"But Lord, let it be Betsy:" Love and Marriage in Early Methodism' in *PWHS* 53 (2001) 1-13.

[3] Wesley wrote this to Cownley in a letter of the 18th September 1750, printed Bendall, *Yours Affectionately* 79. For Rankin see *PWHS* 9 (1914) 92-3; *EMP* 5: 135-217. MacFarlane, *Marriage* 295-6.

[4] For Kilham see W. J. Townsend, *Alexander Kilham the First Methodist Reformer* (London: J. C. Watts, 1889); J. Blackwell, *Life of the Rev. Alexander Kilham* (London: Groombridge, 1838). Another short courtship was that of Mrs Jane McTarget by

Preachers Married at Entry

It has often been assumed that Wesley's preachers were unmarried when they entered, and sometimes that they remained unmarried.[5] In the nineteenth century hardly anyone entered the ministry already married. This continued right up to and beyond the relaxation of marriage rules of 1956. However, of Wesley's preachers entering before 1791 at least 93 (12%) preachers were already married when they entered. This was a much higher proportion than the nineteenth century. It was partly because they were often older, as discussed in the last chapter. Also, because of the larger number of candidates available in the nineteenth century, the supply was greater and so they could be refused if they were already married. Wesley needed travelling preachers so badly that, though he preferred single young men as candidates, since he could not get them he often settled for older men bringing with them wife and family. Examples included many of the most famous early stalwarts, John Nelson, Christopher Hopper, William Shent, and John Haime. Leaders of the middle years like Alexander Mather, Robert Costerdine, John Hampson senior, Thomas Lee, Richard Rodda, and later entrants such as Lawrence Kane (1783), Mathias Joyce (1787), Miles Martindale (1786) and William Smith (1789) were also married. William Stephenson, born about 1759 in Eccleshill, a township in Bradford, and a local preacher in the Bradford Circuit by 1781, was married before he entered in 1789.[6] Again there was a contrast with America where Asbury refused to accept men already married. Richey aptly sums up Asbury as having 'viewed marriage as inimical to Methodist ministry.' While American Conferences rejected most married candidates and were a largely single fraternity (only three out of the 84 Virginia preachers in 1804 were married), Wesley was accepting a high proportion of married men in Britain.[7]

The percentages of those known to be married are shown in Chart 8 below, based on Table 10 in Appendix One. The highest percentages of those known to be married at entry are in the first four cohorts, with a peak coming in the third. As time went on Wesley was more able to insist that men should be single if they wanted to be itinerants. It is interesting that his need for preachers

---

Thomas Warwick in Edinburgh 1797. On March 22nd Coke arrived at Glasgow and found Warwick 'had lost his excellent wife a few days before.' In September Braithwaite carried out Warwick's second marriage. J. A. Vickers, ed, *The Journals of Thomas Coke* (Nashville: Kingswood, 2005) 233-4; Dickinson, *Braithwaite* 299-300.

[5] For example McEllheney in *Quarterly Review* (Spring 2003) 60, 'They (Wesley's itinerants) were... unmarried.'

[6] *Minutes*; W. W. Stamp, *Wesleyan Methodism in Bradford* (London: Mason, 1841) 64-5; Dickinson, *Braithwaite* 138.

[7] Richey, *Conference in America* 58. However, even Asbury could not hold the line for ever. By 1811 he was grumbling to Coke that most Conferences had nearly 50 married out of 85 or 90 preachers, *Asbury Jol* 3: 450. Coke advocated provision for married preachers in America at a time when he was not yet married himself.

Chart 8: Percentage Married by Cohort

Source: Wesley's Preachers' Database

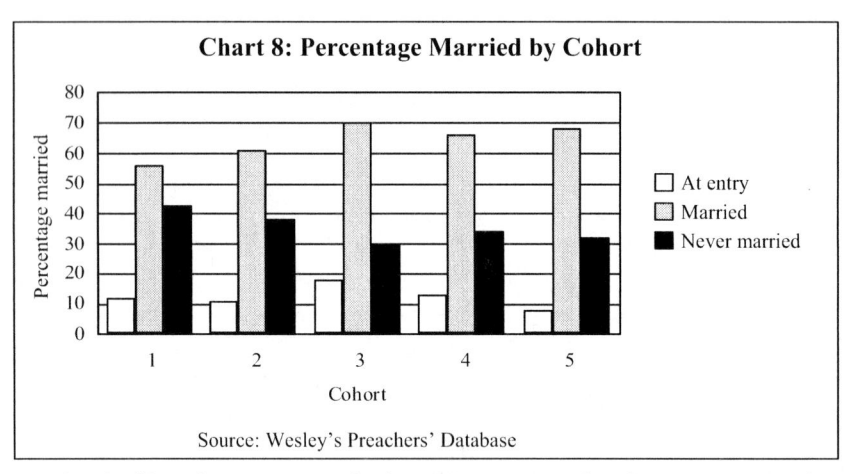

remained still so desperate even in the 1760s. For Wesley the 1760s were a key period when he had more needs than men to send to deal with them and had therefore to receive more already married and older men. By the fifth cohort the percentage of those married on entry had fallen to 8% from the high of 18% for the third cohort. This shows Wesley became more able to find single men. By the 1780s he could afford to demand increasingly that preachers only marry after they had entered and then wait several years. This was presumably because more young unmarried men were offering to travel. Thus he wrote to Duncan Wright about James Bogie in 1781 'if he is still single, let him travel' (!).[8] In addition it is noticeable that in the last two cohorts there are several doubtfuls, such as Richard Steel, and the Irish percentage of already married rose, as though Wesley could keep the line against married men more easily in England than in Ireland where there was more shortage. There were also several from missionary areas, the right men in the right place such as John Baxter, John Mann or William Mahy. More of these in the last cohort were known to have been able to support their wives, not only the first two of the three mentioned but also men like the prosperous tradesman Jasper Winscom; or they were already clergymen like the Irishmen Edward Smyth or James Creighton.[9]

Proportions Married

As Methodism and the number of itinerant preachers grew, so many of Wesley's preachers in England married. What were the **proportions** of this? Heitzenrater said at least 25% of the then active preachers had married by 1775.

---

[8] *JWL* 7: 94.
[9] Richard Steel's existence depends on the *Minutes* entry for Armagh in 1768. He appeared nowhere else and was never admitted on trial. *MM (I)* 1805: 1-24 said the preacher for Armagh that year was Richard Seed, so Steel was probably a misprint.

It should be noted that simply to add up the wives supported in the *Minutes* is not enough, which is why he makes the careful statement 'at least.' The current figures are shown in Chart 8. A number of wives are known for whom their husbands did not claim financial assistance, as with Thomas Cooper, either for his first wife in 1787 or his second in 1790, or Barnabas Thomas who entered the ministry in 1764 and superannuated in 1788. Barnabas Thomas's wife, née Helen Clark, is referred to in letters between 1767 and 1787, but never appeared in the list of preachers' wives in the *Minutes*. This may relate to Wesley's view of Barnabas Thomas, which was not high, but is more likely to be due to Helen's wealth, since she was described by Pawson[10] as 'a woman of considerable property in Scotland.' In each case the wives had money and so count as 'wealthy wives.' Some preachers did claim later, presumably when families had begun to appear and their wives had become poorer, or they themselves had become more established in the ministry, or the Connexion was better off and could afford the payments. William Thom, the future co-founder of the New Connexion, married his first wife, Hannah Spensley from Low Row in Swaledale in 1776, when he had been travelling for three years and in full connexion for one. She did not get support until 1778, when he had been travelling for five years. Similarly Alexander Suter, a preacher who had originally entered in 1779 though not received into full connexion until 1786, married Hannah Grills at St Just in Cornwall in April 1790. 'Sister Suter' was not given support until Conference 1794.[11]

Bates stated that Wesley's memory was at fault when he said that the early preachers were unmarried. Though the proportion of married men then was not large, the chief point is that they behaved as though they were not married even if they were![12]

Care has to be taken over when the marriages took place. Some were married before they entered, but the wife died and the man entered the ministry. Others married after they left, often on the point of leaving, or at least just after. William Orpe married and left at the same time. Others married when they retired, or at least during their retirement. Figures therefore have to be carefully constructed to allow for all these. Of those 376 who died in the work, at least 305 married at some time which is 81%; at least three of these married soon after or at the point of becoming a supernumerary.[13]

---

[10] Heitzenrater 275. For Barnabas Thomas' wife see *Pawson L* 1: 44, 3: 57, 141-142. Another example was George Sargent.

[11] For 'wealthy wives' see below. For Thom's first marriage see M. Batty, *Bygone Reeth... Methodism in Reeth* (Reeth: Reeth Methodist Church, 1985) 51, 54; MS letter of Mary Thom in MARC PLP 106-2-54 and *WHS Yorks* 72 (1998), 14-8. I am indebted to Richard Grylls for information on the Suter family. Joseph Sutcliffe (entered 1786) married in 1792, but his wife did not appear in the *Minutes* until 1796, four years later.

[12] E. R. Bates, 'The Wives of Wesley's Preachers' *WHS Br* 15 (1975) 1-3.

[13] The three were John Downes, John Brettell and John Valton.

The relatively high number of marriages differed from their brethren both in America and Ireland. In Ireland wives were difficult to afford into the 1770s and beyond, so that one of the factors encouraging Irish preachers to come to England was the lack of support for wives in Ireland. Richard Bourke had difficulty in supporting his wife and children in 1770. John Wesley felt he had to give him an extra £5 himself, and in 1771 transferred him to England where Bourke remained with his family until his death.[14] Irish wives did not appear at all in the lists in the early 1770s.

In America the example of Asbury meant that eighteenth century American preachers rarely married or, if they did, they 'located' first. Of the 811 American preachers who entered up to 1799, 364 located and another 243 left or were expelled, a much larger proportion than in Britain. 'It was impossible to remain in the American itinerancy unless one remained celibate.' This was partly because of the distances and extra travelling involved and partly because of Asbury who 'preferred it this way. When it was called to his attention that the low and precarious financial support resulted in an involuntary celibacy he responded "All the better." (!) The American circuits were equally hostile to the idea of paying for wives and families.' The American itinerants wrote to each other about the threat of marriage to their travelling.[15]

One reason for the frequency of marriage in Britain was the example set them by their leaders. While Charles and John Wesley, George Whitefield, William Grimshaw and John Fletcher all married, it was difficult for John Wesley to hold any line against it. He often preached about no marriage, but he had to allow it, though he insisted (usually successfully) on his agreement being obtained. Another reason for frequency was the high death rate among the wives, often caused by childbirth.[16]

It is possible to follow the question of marriage through the cohorts and see what happened over time. In the first cohort there were 82 who were married at some point (57%), but some of these married after they left. This compares with 62 others, those not known to have married. Only 51 were married during their itinerancy (36%). Two thirds of these are known to have had families. Ten of them married a second time when their wives died, usually within two or three years and often to a friend of the first wife, for example James Rogers, John Pawson and Thomas Roberts. Seventeen or more were married at their entry, 12% of the total entry, though at least one wife was not dependent, that of Richard Moss. Twelve were 'wealthy wives,' 15% of those who married. The 62 not known probably included some who married, but we do not know about it. These unmarried or unknown were 43% of the total. In the next cohorts the proportion of unmarrieds and unknown gradually decreased, while

---

[14] For Orpe see Myles. For Bourke see *JWL* 5: 189. Bourke died early in 1778. His widow, Lucia, was supported for almost twenty years afterwards.

[15] Wigger, 'Fighting Bees' 110-111, 112-120.

[16] For the difficulties of childbirth in this period see the next Chapter.

that of married preachers increased. So in the 2nd cohort there were 52 married (62%), while 32 (38%) were unmarried or unknown. In the third cohort marrieds were 95 (70%) and in the 4th 99 (66%). Unmarrieds or unknown went down to 40 (30%) in the third cohort, and to 32% in the final cohort.

Marriages while Travelling

Among those who married later, that is after entry, three categories can be detected. The first category was those who went back to their home area and married someone from their locality. John Atlay was a good example of this. He came from Sheriff Hutton in Yorkshire and entered in 1761. In 1772 he married Jane Spencer, who was a year younger and whom he would have known before he left the village. This was when he was made Book Steward by Wesley and could look forward to being less itinerant, so his wife would travel little if at all.[17] One advantage was that, like Jane, the partners were often known to each other previously. The new wife might also continue to live in the village even after children began to arrive. The young David Barrowclough was another example. Born in 1767 at Sowerby in the large Halifax parish, he entered in 1787. In 1792, the year after being accepted into full connexion, he went back to Halifax to marry Mary Hirst.[18] There were at least 21 marriages in this first category.

The second category was a wife from a circuit in which the preacher travelled, frequently an early one. Often the preacher married a daughter from a family where he stayed. Charles Wesley and Sarah Gwynne were an example of this process. Marmaduke Gwynne supported and hosted the preachers; their leader married his daughter. Examples of marriages to someone from the circuit to which they were appointed include Algar and Allwood. Joseph Algar probably began to travel in 1781 and was sent to Wiltshire in 1782 where he met Elizabeth Emblem of Keevil and married her there in 1786. William Allwood, who entered in 1755 from Rotherham, was in the Cheshire Circuit in 1757. There he met the widow Mary Davison whom he married at Acton in Cheshire in 1760. The two Young sisters of Coleraine in Ulster, Anne and Isabella, married two preachers who were sent there, Henry Moore and Thomas Rutherford. At least 82 marriages of preachers fit in to this most popular category, even more common in the next century.[19] One of the most famous of

---

[17] *AM* 1778: 578-81.

[18] Baptised as David son of John Barraclough at Sowerby near Halifax on the 13th December 1767. Both this and his marriage are in the *IGI*. His wife is first mentioned in the *Minutes* in 1792.

[19] Joseph Algar married Elizabeth Emblem on the 22nd July 1786 at Keevil (*IGI*). For Allwood see MS Notes by J. Thackray and W. J. Dutton in Biographical Cuttings files in WHS Library. For the Young sisters see M. A. Smith, *The Life of the Rev. Henry Moore...* (London: Simpkin and Marshall, 1844).

these marriages was that of John Bennet and Grace Murray, who met at the Orphan House, Newcastle, while she was working there as matron.[20]

The third category was those who fit into neither of these; they had met somewhere else. Often it was Methodism that brought them together. Thomas Bartholomew married a daughter of a trustee of City Road London whom he had met there, though he was never stationed in London. Thomas Richards met Mary Davie when she was working as housekeeper at Kingswood and he was the schoolmaster. Joseph Bradford, a widower in the late 1780s, travelled with the aged Wesley to look after him. In 1789 he married Elizabeth Edwards, then the housekeeper of Wesley's House at City Road.[21] Sometimes it was through mutual friends. Joseph Benson had pursued Elizabeth Ritchie of Otley with a view to matrimony. She refused him, but introduced him to her friend Sarah Thompson of Leeds, whom he married on the 28th January 1780. Wesley favoured the newly married couple by sending them to Leeds for the next two years.[22]

Wesley's Rules on Marriage

Until Hardwicke's Marriage Act both men or boys over fourteen and women or girls over twelve could marry without their parents' or guardians' permission. 1753 marked the point when parents' permission became necessary for all those under twenty-one. Wesley went further than the law and demanded that no itinerant preacher get married without gaining the permission of the parent or guardian, whatever the age of the woman concerned. Widows, seen as independent, did not need this. This was certainly one motive for marrying a widow. No permission need be sought except Wesley's and her own.[23] In addition the intended bride should be 'awakened' and preferably a Methodist. This could often be a major barrier. The young Christopher Hopper, before he had been converted, had been courting Jane Richardson. In his words

> She had every accomplishment I wanted, but religion! Alas! She was unacquainted with God.. This was a bar indeed. I found a desire to break off correspondence with her, but was afraid she could not bear it. I was greatly troubled, and prayed for Divine direction. God was pleased to hear and grant my request. She was soon awakened and found peace with God.

---

[20] Valentine, *Bennet* 206-9, which has provided the first full account of the life of Grace Norman, best known as Grace Murray, who was for most of her life Grace Bennet.
[21] Another Kingswood housekeeper, Molly Francis, in 1751 married the Cornish preacher John Maddern. Wesley approved and John was the English master at Kingswood for the next 6 years or so, while his wife remained housekeeper.
[22] M. M. Jemison, ed, *A Methodist Courtship: Love Letters of Joseph Benson & Sarah Thompson* (Atlanta: Emory, 1945).
[23] MacFarlane, *Marriage* 127.

The now well matched pair were soon married.[24] Methodist preachers, however, sometimes married those who were 'unawakened,' (not converted) against the regulations. Wesley accused Methodists in general of doing this in the *Minutes* of 1766. Certainly later, when marriage for preachers was more common and Wesley much older, this happened among preachers as well. 'Hence worldly prudence, maxims, customs crept back upon us, producing more and more conformity to the world.' As Wesley rightly said 'this is not cured by the Preachers. Either they have not light or not weight enough.'[25]

The rules might well mean that the preacher was unable to marry as with John Prickard, whose sweetheart's parents refused permission. Robert Lindsay, who married Jane Lawder of Leitrim against her father Frederick Lawder's wishes, was expelled. Admittedly in his case Wesley allowed him back 'On Trial' after a year. Wesley helped those whom he favoured like Bradburn and his 'dear Betsy.' A missionary preacher like John Mageary, who married a settler's daughter in Nova Scotia despite not having his father-in-law's consent, might be able to break the rules in a place like Nova Scotia and get away with it, partly by immediately leaving that country.[26]

The quotation from the *Large Minutes* at the head of this chapter shows that standards among preachers' wives were not always what Wesley would have wanted. Not all wives of preachers won immediate or even later approval. Some were seen as offending against the Methodist rules on dress. In 1786 Miss Paton of Edinburgh was about to marry the young Robert Johnson, but Pawson thought she was 'dressing far beyond the Band Rules,' which stated 'to wear no needless ornaments, such as rings, ear-rings, necklaces, lace, ruffles.'[27]

Allowances for Wives

Originally most of Wesley's preachers were not married. Those in the first or second cohorts, who were already married or became married, either dropped out (the majority) or were able to support their wives by other means. There was no stipend for the wives. Sometimes there could be payments as in the 1749 Conference *Minutes* '1. Let the Assistant enquire at the Quarterly meeting

---

[24] *EMP* 1: 196.

[25] *Minutes* 1766; Kent, *Wesley and the Wesleyans* 66.

[26] For Prickard see *JWL* 7: 120. Robert Lindsay on the 6th May 1784 married Jane (or Jenny) Lawder daughter of Frederick Lawder of Leitrim with a fortune of £40 per annum but without the consent of her parents (Letter to Dromgoole 18th May printed in W. W. Sweet, *Religion on the American Frontier. vol 4: The Methodists* (Chicago: University of Chicago Press, 1946). Presumably this was the reason why he desisted that year, so he was only five months in the Legal Hundred see *PWHS* 13 (1922) 15. The Irish *Minutes* of 1784 (Coke was in the chair) said '"What shall we do with R.L.?" A(nswer) "We suspend him and refer him to Mr Wesley."' He was allowed to return as On Trial in 1785. For Mageary see *PWHS* 32 (1960) 186-7.

[27] *Pawson L* 1: 40 and note. Johnson was born in 1762 and entered the ministry in 1783.

what each Preacher's wife will want for the coming quarter. 2. Let this be supplied first of all out of the common stock.' This, however, was a rule for the circuits, like many, which was often not kept. At the first Irish Conference at Limerick in 1752 it was recorded that Sister Edwards should receive £21, Sister Kead and Sister Morris £10 each and John Fisher's wife ten guineas. This was from central funds, not the local circuits which could not pay.[28]

The earlier pattern was broken with the entrance of the London baker Alexander Mather in 1761 with a wife and family. He would only enter if there was an allowance for her. The London Stewards guaranteed it, whether he was in London or not. From then on allowances were more usually paid, as Wesley said in 1769 'If he is married he has ten pounds a year for his wife.' Throughout his lifetime Wesley wanted to restrict the number of wives and families on the stations, if only to put fewer demands on the circuits.

The *Minutes* do not show this connexional support of wives until 1770 when the allocation was first officially made by the Conference and the backup to this circuit provision fell on connexional funds. Each year from then on the circuits were expected to give allowances for most named wives, and the remainder were found allowances out of connexional funds. The naming in the *Minutes* of wives who needed to be supported enables the counting of most wives from 1770 onwards, though even then some wealthy wives were not mentioned or supported. The numbers of wives who were to be supported increased dramatically over the next forty years to a state where preachers seriously doubted whether the system could be sustained. Like much else, it was reformed and established on a sounder footing by Jabez Bunting in the early nineteenth century. It was only one of the ways in which he became indispensable to his brethren.[29]

Because of this financial problem no preacher was allowed to marry 'without consulting his brethren.' Reasons for turning the marriage down included the fact that the preacher was still 'On Trial,' that the woman was unsuitable, or she was refused permission by her parents and guardians. The first reason meant that the couple usually had to wait. There were exceptions. In 1791 George Sargent, who entered in 1790, wanted to marry a widow with seven children, Mrs Elizabeth Chafer widow of a captain, presumably from his home circuit. Because she had money and support for her and the family would not fall on the stations, he was allowed to do this, though he remained on trial till 1794. No support was given to her until 1798, four years after he had ceased to be on trial.[30]

If the woman was unsuitable, or the parents' permission was not given, this

---

[28] *Minutes* (1862 ed) 45, 716.

[29] The *Minutes* from this point are the major source for all the marriages in this chapter. Wives received an allowance of 16 guineas from 1806.

[30] *JWL* 5: 155. For Sargent's marriage see *WMM* 1842: 353-66. They had a further ten sons and one daughter, so certainly became expensive.

usually meant that the marriage would never take place. However, Wesley was in several cases prepared to intervene on behalf of his preachers when he felt parents were behaving unreasonably in refusing permission. Wesley was particularly lenient towards some of his preachers over parents' permission and marriage, perhaps (especially in his old age) recognizing his own failings over marriage.[31]

The wife sometimes supported herself and her children after marriage. Elizabeth Bennis had a useful description of this in 1771 'Brother Hern and his family leave town (Limerick) tomorrow... His wife... refused subsistence... supported herself by working at her trade... though a young child at the breast.' Many wives acted as teachers, often with their daughters' aid. An example of this was the wife of Benjamin Rhodes, who with her daughters kept a school at Union Crescent in Margate after her husband superannuated there in 1810. Some ran a shop as did Jane Rowell near the Market Cross in Barnard Castle from 1757 to 1761. William Bramwell's wife was a dressmaker. Many kept animals, worked in the fields, had a garden where produce was grown and sold or bartered some of their produce. Many were spinners, or did other work in the textile industry. All in addition performed the usual domestic tasks. They obtained and prepared food, cleaned rooms, laid fires, hauled water, darned, washed and dried clothes. Those who had children, or who married husbands with young children from a previous marriage, spent much time over their upbringing. The idea of 'separate spheres,' the woman at home, the man out at work, was not important for most of the population in the eighteenth century. For Methodist preachers' wives it was in any case modified both by financial necessity and by the acceptance of the idea that women's souls were as important as men's and that each should, as far as possible, contribute to the partnership both spiritually and materially. Most of the surviving evidence about the wives comes from the husbands rather than from the wives themselves. It is therefore from a male perspective that we see the wives and their marriages.[32]

Wife 'Desertion'

Kingsley Lloyd had a fine chapter on the marriage of Wesley's preachers in which he made clear the early Methodist preacher before 1757 was usually not married. Mather was wrongly described by Myles as the first to be received 'with a wife,'[33] but he was the first for whose wife the financial care was

---

[31] More on this lenience over marriage and other issues is found in Chapter 17 below.

[32] Bennis, *Correspondence* letter of 15th October 1771. For Rowell see *MRWN* 1905: 47-9. Hill, *Women, Work* especially Chapter 3; L. Davidoff and C. Hall, *Family Fortunes: Men and Women of the English Middle Class 1780-1850* (London: Routledge, 2002) xv-xxxix. Few letters of preachers' wives survive and these are usually brief.

[33] A. K. Lloyd, *The Labourers Hire: The Payment and Deployment of the Early*

accepted. Until then men like John Nelson and Christopher Hopper simply accepted that their wives would have to cope when they were away and that even when they returned, their husbands might be too busy on the Lord's business to spend time on their own family. It put a premium on wives being able to manage for themselves and their children and was only possible in a close knit society where strong kinship and affinity groups existed. Nelson and Hopper had their new converts around them as a small group of family and friends, on whom their families could depend for help while the husbands were away. Supporting families was a major reason for men giving up full time preaching and for the phenomenon of 'wealthy wives' explored below. Wives were usually left behind for long periods with their children. As late as 1785 Simon Day's wife Grace was still living in Cornwall, though he had been travelling in circuits outside Cornwall since 1783. Most early preachers who were married could be said to have deserted their wives. John Brown, who entered the ministry in 1743 from his farm at Tanfield Lea, was later criticized by his family for leaving the farm, in other words leaving his wife to do all the work on it and support the family for critical periods. John Furz's story was typical of many

> When I set out on my travels as a travelling preacher, leaving *my* children in her care, she never once asked me when I should come home: but in all her letters said, 'I find difficulties, but let not that distress you. I am content. Go straightforward in the work that God has called you to'. When (c 1755) I was informed that she was very ill, I rode seventy miles in one of the shortest days to see her. I found two young women with her who came to see her at the beginning of her illness and never left her after..... (after her death) I found her clothes had been sold, to procure her necessaries in time of affliction. So that naked as she came into the world, naked did she return.[34]

This is a harrowing account of desertion to the twenty-first century mind, though admittedly such behaviour by either party was not unusual in this period. Sarah Crosby was deserted by her husband in 1757. William Allwood was deserted by his second wife after a mere six weeks in 1775. John S. Pipe's father deserted his mother. Richard Moss, a journeyman tailor in Cheshire who became a travelling preacher in 1745 and left around 1762, deserted his wife shortly after their marriage in 1741, well before he became a Methodist. His story that she had blackmailed him, threatening to commit suicide if he did not

---

Methodist Preachers. 1744-1813 (Cheshire: WHS Lecture, 1968) 19-27; Myles 81.

[34] For Simon Day's wife see *JWL* 7: 179. For John Brown see T. Blanshard, *Methodism in the Shotley Bridge Circuit* (Consett: Jackson, 1872). The story of Furz is in *EMP* 5: 108-134, the quoted passage at 131-2. He set out from Wilton near Salisbury to travel in Cornwall around 1750. The emphasis on *my* children is mine and to the modern reader deeply ironic. We do not know whether they survived. The reference to one of the shortest days shows he returned in midwinter, when they would be most in need.

marry her, turned out to be false, as we learn from Charles's irate letter to him later still. She then went to live with another man in Dublin.[35] Sarah Ryan was another whose marriages were unsuccessful. William Minethorpe was described as being 'uncomfortably married.' When John Wesley could be described by his own wife as 'running after strange women' as he travelled the connexion rather than stay with her, it is not surprising that the ordinary preacher might be seen as behaving similarly. Since in the eighteenth century the only way (for most) of dissolving marriage was by death, running away or desertion was relatively common.[36]

Age at Marriage

Godwin wrote of the choice to be made between marrying early and marrying late 'everyone, possessed of the most ordinary degree of foresight deliberates long before he engages in so momentous a transaction. He asks himself again and again, how he shall be able to subsist the offspring of his union. I am persuaded it rarely happens in England that a marriage takes place, without this question having first undergone a repeated examination.' Wesley's preachers in general married late, having thought very hard about the whole question.[37]

Age at first marriage for preachers is known for 226 of them. The average age (31.3) was higher than the average for the population, which was going down for men from 27.5 in the first half of the century to 26.4 in the second half. Often the age is not known, but it could be higher still, such as John King born in 1752, who married after 1809 and so was at least 57 years old on marriage. Quite possibly he like others married at his moment of superannuation, in his case 1811. In addition, at least 31 had married before entry, often young. For those who entered unmarried, the average age of marriage was higher still.[38]

Age at marriage for wives is also often not known. Only 112 of the ages of the first wives are known. The youngest was Agnes Higginson, the fifteen year old Irish heiress who married the well-connected Irish clergyman Edward Smyth well before his conversion. He became one of Wesley's London curates in 1782 at £60 per annum. She died the next year and he returned to Ireland.

---

[35] Chilcote, *JW and Women Preachers* 255; Thackray and Dutton Notes in WHS Library, *AM* 1797: 365-70, 417-22, 477-82; 1785: 489-90. The MS Charles Wesley letter is late 1769 in MARC ref W4/46.

[36] For Sarah Ryan see Chilcote *JW and Women Preachers* especially 124-30 and 278-80. For Minethorp see Atmore 148 'his life for many years was one continued scene of suffering.' Lloyd in *PWHS* 53 (2002), 169-74 writes about Wesley. Hill, *Women, Work* 211 explains the prevalence of the desertion of wives in the 18th Century. Divorce was much more possible in Scotland, where the legal position of women was better.

[37] F. Place, *Illustrations and Proofs of the Principle of Population* (London: Allen and Unwin, 1930) 162. MacFarlane, *Marriage* 5-19.

[38] Table 11 in the Appendix. The oldest known was John Cricket, who was sixty.

The oldest was Francis Wrigley's wife Elizabeth, whom he married when she was 64 in 1802 and he was 55. Unhappily she died less than two years later in 1804.[39] The average age for the first wife was 29.2, two years younger than the preachers. Where age is known, it was often considerably different from the husband's in either direction. In the preacher's eyes the most important qualification was religious suitability. Age, in comparison, seen as important in the twenty-first century, was then of little importance. Again comparison with the general population is instructive. Age at marriage for women fell from 26.2 in the first part of the century to 24.9 in the second half[40] so Wesley's preachers tended to be marrying wives older than the average, partly because the men were also older than the average. In addition, the women who married Wesley's preachers tended to wait considerably longer than the general population before they married. Frequently we do not know whether they had married earlier or not.

Difference of age at marriage is of interest: while there were many of similar age (within five years of each other) there were a large number who were either considerably older or younger than their wives. At least 47 were older, the largest known difference being the 49 years between Thomas Olivers, the former Book Corrector for Wesley, and his twenty year old second wife Mary Ellis, whom he married in 1796 (significantly, after Wesley's death). He was the exception and his ministerial brethren were so disgusted with him that he was suspended. When a year later his wife was pregnant, Pawson was prepared to say that she 'had been playing the harlot.' He thought it preyed on Olivers' mind and caused his sudden death in 1799.[41] A more typical example was Duncan Wright, the soldier preacher then 42, and his convert Dorothy Gibbon, then 21, the niece of Wright's brother preacher George Gibbon. What is more unexpected was the number who married those noticeably older than themselves. There were 23 in this position. Certainly some were only five years younger than their wives. That applied to Joseph Pescod, William Black and John Crosby. On the other hand, nine men were nine or more years younger, the biggest difference being that of James Oddie (30) marrying Sarah Thompson (45). This was also mirrored among the early Evangelical leaders. Benjamin Ingham at 29 married Lady Margaret Hastings at 41 in 1741. There was no trace here of Titow's rural medieval pattern of remarriage, where the younger man when widowed of his older wife remarried a wife considerably younger than himself. Indeed Oddie, when later he was a widower, remarried a widow of similar age.[42]

---

[39] For Elizabeth Wrigley see the Laycock MS at Keighley Library.
[40] For John King see *WMM* 1824: 1-8. Rule, *Vital Century* 15.
[41] *Pawson L* 2: 101, 148.
[42] Other examples were John Murlin (39) and Elizabeth Berrisford (52) and Zachariah Yewdall (32) and Agnes Mackrill (44). B. S. Schlenther, *Queen of the Methodists: The Countess of Huntingdon and the 18th Century Crisis of Faith and Society* (Bishop

'Wealthy Wives' and Motives for Marrying

One result of the preachers' problems over marriage and money was the fact that many, at least 93, married 'wealthy wives.' My definition of a wealthy wife is one with an income or property or a wealthy father. The last may not have meant money in practice. As with most other fields, lack of information is most common. However, where there is information, wives tended to have had wealth more often than their husbands. Was this deliberate? I would argue that usually it was and again they followed the example of their leaders. John Wesley and George Whitefield married wealthy widows. Grimshaw also married a widow as his first wife. John Fletcher married a wealthy wife, while Charles Wesley's wife was well-connected. Even in America Devereux Jarratt, the Methodist-favouring Anglican clergyman in Virginia, married a wealthy wife, Martha Claiborne, with a 640 acre plantation and 24 slaves.[43] Unlike the others he did his best to disguise this fact, succeeding in concealing it from most historians. Eighteenth century clergymen often married wealthy wives.[44]

The leading preachers set a similar example. Both John Pawson's wives were well-off, his second inheriting £200 when her brother died in 1794. Samuel Bradburn's 'Betsy' was the step daughter of a wealthy Dublin jeweller, Mr Karr. His second wife was Sophia Cooke of Gloucester who had helped Robert Raikes set up his Sunday school there. Bradburn was hastier then most, Betsy having died on the 1st February 1786. On the 14th March he had gone with Wesley to Gloucester where he met Sophia. Left behind by Wesley (had Bradburn consulted him?), Bradburn proposed on the 21st March and was accepted.[45]

This was true in general for eighteenth century practice, summed up for the middle class by Matthew Boulton's dictum 'Don't marry for money, but marry where money is.' Hill suggested that evidence for this period is often one sided and tends not to exist for the labouring classes. Courtship below the upper classes was something where both sides retained the liberty of choice and where the question of monetary support was the chief limiting factor.[46] Methodist travelling preachers might well find it difficult to marry unless the bride had some money of her own. Often their chief link with the bride was their common religious beliefs. John Allen was appointed to the Bristol circuit

---

Auckland: Durham Academic Press, 1997) 21; MacFarlane, *Marriage* 236.

[43] 105 'wealthy wives' so far found. Widowers often remarried a 'wealthy wife'. D. Jarratt, *The Life of Devereux Jarratt: An Autobiography* (Cleveland: Pilgrim Press, 1995) xvii-xx.

[44] J. S. Chamberlain,"'A regular and well affected diocese" Chichester in the eighteenth century' in Gregory and Chamberlain, *National Church* 82-3; Jacob, *Clerical Profession* 158.

[45] Rack, 'Betsy'; Blanshard, *Bradburn* 107-115. Other leading preachers who married wealthy wives included Thomas Coke (twice), Thomas Maxfield and John Jones.

[46] Cited in Hill, *Women, Work* 174, 179.

in 1772 as a Supernumerary because he was ill as a result of his travels. By June 1772 he was corresponding with Jane Westell, related to the travelling preacher Thomas Westell. In 1773 Wesley at Conference told him to go back to Bristol as an itinerant (Wesley surely knew of his interest!); in September they were engaged, marrying in January 1774 at Bristol.[47]

The preachers' letters even contained advice where they told younger preachers how they should wait for 'a good woman with money.' One example was William Fish's letter to Alexander Kilham in 1788, two North Lincolnshire men who went on trial together at the 1785 Conference. In it Fish, a future missionary in Jamaica, listed *sixteen* points a preacher's wife should have, the last being 'as much fortune as will maintain herself, her husband and children if need be.' Fish never married! Kilham, who was about to marry, married twice.[48] Thomas Olivers, a member of the second cohort, in his autobiography written around 1780 about his life as a preacher in 1758, was admirably candid about his first marriage. Having answered the question 'Am I called to marry at this time?' in the affirmative, he went on to ask 'what sort of person ought I to marry?' He listed four qualifications, the last being 'since I was connected with a poor people, the will of God was that whoever I married should have a small competency, to prevent my making the Gospel chargeable to any.'[49] He described Miss Green of Leeds whom he married then as 'a person of good family,' that is possessing such a competency.[50]

The reasons for this tendency among the preachers were the lack of support from the circuits and the preachers' need for someone to look after them, particularly in old age which was when John Valton married a wealthy Bristol widow. The most notable example of marrying wealthy wives, however, was Thomas Roberts. Born in Cornwall in 1765, he entered the ministry in 1786. In Ireland in December 1787 he wanted to marry Christian Davenport, but her parents opposed and Wesley supported them. He still had two and a half years to do on trial! With Wesley dead there was no stopping Roberts. In 1793 he married Miss Wogan, heiress of the Weston estate in Pembroke. She died in 1795 after childbirth. Roberts became ill and was allowed to superannuate in 1795. Next year (1796) he married his second wife, Mary, the daughter of W. Randolph Esq. of Bristol. He then settled in Bristol and acted as an extra preacher for neighbouring circuits, not being paid by them since he was supported by his wife's money. Meanwhile Roberts was influential, helping to found the Annuitant Society in 1798 and preaching special sermons. His second wife died in 1804, having borne seven children. He was friendly with Thomas

---

[47] Tyerman BMM 1. Allen was born in 1737. The rest of the story is less happy. Jane died in June 1779 leaving two young daughters, while Allen remarried by 1785.
[48] *PWHS* 21 (1937-8) 32-3. Kilham's first wife had some money see above note 4. For more on Kilham see Chapter 16.
[49] *EMP* 2: 80. Olivers was born in 1725.
[50] *Pawson L* 2: 101, 148-50. Olivers was less careful about his second wife.

Coke, whose executor he was, with Samuel Bradburn and with Adam Clarke, all highly influential after Wesley's death. His third wife, Jane Lee whom he married in 1805, was the coheiress of Benjamin Lee, goldsmith of Dublin, the other coheiress having married a Guinness. In the next generation there was a Benjamin Lee Roberts to match his first cousin, the better known Benjamin Lee Guinness. Thomas Roberts became a supernumerary again in 1811 when he visited Ireland, but did not die till 1832. The speed of his remarriages is also noticeable, though in each case there were young children to be cared for.

Many preachers married women with some money. John Baxter married a lady with an estate in Antigua 'The house we now have is a life estate of my wife's.' It happened in America as well, often with the preacher locating on the wife's estate, as with John King. The American preacher Thomas Haskins married wealthy wives in Philadelphia on two occasions while remaining an itinerant; both Martha Potts and Elizabeth Richards belonged to local iron-founding families.[51]

Prospective wives could, of course, be too wealthy. John Fletcher was reported as saying after his marriage to Mary Bosanquet 'Five and twenty years ago when I first saw my dear wife, I thought that if I ever married, she would be the person of my choice; but her large fortune was in the way, she was too rich for me, and I therefore strove to banish every thought of the kind.' By 1780 when he did marry her she had spent much of her inheritance. He was not to know that her brothers would so highly approve the marriage that they would make it their business to see that her inheritance was replenished.[52]

There were many other motives for marriage apart from the need for money emphasized above. One was to produce children. Another was what Malthus in 1803 was to describe as the 'passion between the sexes being constant.' This was generally unstated among Wesley's preachers but should be assumed to be usually present. Joseph Bradford writing to his wife in 1789 addressed her as 'My truly precious Eliza.'[53]

In the eighteenth century the idea of companionate marriage where 'love' or at least 'friendship' should be present had overcome the ideas of previous centuries, at least outside the nobility. Vickery suggests that genteel marriage in the later eighteenth century was governed by both prudence and affection. Wesley's preachers would add religious conviction to those two.[54] 'Love' or at

---

[51] For Thomas Roberts see *WMM* 1837: 1-15, 81-95, 161-76; *MM* 1807: 29-42; *JWL* 8: 232. The quotation from Baxter comes from Tyerman BMM 1237. Many of these wives were annuitants belonging to the 'middling group' in society discussed in Chapter 3 above. For the American marriages see Andrews, *Methodists and America* 116.

[52] A. Bulmer, *Memoirs of Mrs Elizabeth Mortimer (Miss Ritchie)* (London: Mason, 1859) 95.

[53] For children as a motive see the next chapter. Bradford's letter is at Duke, Durham NC, Baker Collection, Box 14, Presidential book Sept 1st n. d. n. pl. but probably 1789.

[54] Stone, *Family* title of Chapter 8. He cited Catherine Banks writing to her husband as late as 1732 'Dear Mr Banks…' A. Vickery, *The Gentleman's Daughter: Women's*

least affection was usually present. Preachers and their wives when they corresponded addressed each other as 'My Dear' or 'My Dear Love,' rather than the stilted 'Dear Mr(s)' which had been usual earlier in the century. Henry Moore had not yet married Anne Young when he addressed her as 'My dear Nancy' in 1778. Similarly Mary Taft, when writing to her husband Zechariah in 1803, addressed him as 'My Dear Love' and 'My Dear Best Friend.'[55] Fish's letter to Kilham never mentioned 'love' yet the implication in many of the letters is that this existed and was important, if usually unstated. It is admitted occasionally, as by Joseph Cownley on the death of his wife in 1774 'None that have not my feelings can judge what spears and daggers went through my heart when I saw and kissed her in her shroud.' A later example came from Duncan Wright in 1789 at the death of his wife

> my Dolly went to rest about ten o clock in the morning of the 14th of May, and was sensible (feeling) to the last, her last words were 'Lord have mercy on me' and believe me, notwithstanding I looked for (expected) it so long, I found it no easy matter to part with her who has been my pleasant companion for 12 years.[56]

The 'companionate marriage' for the Methodist travelling preacher's wife was one of little actual companionship while he was active, because of the number of nights and, even larger, days that the preacher spent away from her. However, absence often provoked a flow of letters, like those between Adam Clarke and his wife Mary or Henry Moore and his wife Ann, some of which have survived. These letters show the strength of love between the pairs. Both partners assumed that the wives' purpose in life was to put the interests of God first and the husbands' next. As Joseph Pescod's wife Sarah put it in a letter to a friend in 1797 'what makes my situation not so agreeable to my feeling is, my husband, being so much from home as he is, (only) three nights in every three weeks in Malton, but as he is employed in the Lord's work I am though enabled to give up my will.' If the husband was out on the circuit, and the wife's accommodation was poor, this was seen by both as the wife's being unselfish for the good of God's Kingdom, just as the husband was. She should support him in his labours. She should try to manage the household with 'prudent

---

Lives in Georgian England (London: Yale UP, 1998) 82.

[55] It is difficult to date this letter of Moore's. However, it is clear that though not yet married, he still had no hesitation in addressing Anne as 'his dear.' MARC Folio Letters of the Methodist Preachers Vol 5 Second half 25 Letter of Henry Moore from Ballymena Monday morning to Anne Young Coleraine n.d. but c March-July 1780; MSS letter in MARC Rylands MAM PLP 104/4/14 19 June 1803 to Z. Taft.

[56] MS letter of Cownley to CW 9/5/1774 MARC DDPr1/104. MS letter of Wright to C. Hopper 8th June 1789 MARC PLP 115.823. Cf. Isaac Lilly who 'suffered from melancholy as the result of the loss of his beloved wife' of 40 years (*WMM* 1852: 914) and the story of John Allen's wife's death in Chapter 20. More examples are given by Rack in his article cited above.

economy.' This last task can most easily be seen in the way Wesley organized his preachers' wives to look after himself (as well as the husband) in his declining years. Several letters are full of the skills of different women in managing his household, either for a short period when he visited or his main establishment at City Road. Mary Clarke, Adam's wife, found the strain of even a short visit from Wesley difficult. Hester Ann Rogers was brought back from Dublin to City Road, partly because Wesley knew he could rely upon her skills, so James Rogers had to be appointed to London, much to the chagrin of some other preachers. Such management put severe stresses upon the wife, like Mrs Andrew Blair who confided to her diary in Chester in 1787 'Our quarter day. I was a little hurried at the preparation of the dinner, yet I experienced the language of the poet "Far above all earthly things" etc.'[57]

Remarriages

At least 92 of the preachers married twice; of these at least fourteen married three times. Four married four times, one of whom being John Johnson, married five times, at least two being to widows. All the preachers who married four times were long lived. Often the second marriage was soon after the death of the previous wife, sometimes to a friend of the previous wife who had specifically directed the widower to do this, thinking of her young children left motherless. James Rogers, for example, married in December 1778 Martha Knowlden who was then 23, daughter of a Baptist draper of Loose, near Maidstone at Shoreham, Kent. He had first met her in Edinburgh in 1775. Had he asked Wesley to send him to Kent at Conference that year? His first wife died of consumption on the 15th February 1784 aged 29, having asked her friend who was standing beside her deathbed to marry Rogers. His youngest son died at the same time, leaving Rogers with two other young sons, Joseph and Benjamin. He married secondly on the 19th August 1784 six months later at Prestbury, Cheshire, his first wife's friend Hester Ann Roe, a long term correspondent of Wesley and daughter of Rev. James Roe of Macclesfield. Pawson was shocked when told a mere three months after the first wife's death about the impending marriage in May 1784. After marriage they served what Vickers described as 'a judicious six year exile' in Ireland until 1790, presumably as expiation for marrying too soon. Hester Ann Rogers died in childbirth in Birmingham on October 10th 1794. Though there was still a large young family, this time James Rogers waited for nearly four years before he married the third Mrs Rogers at Bradford, Wiltshire, in August 1798. This was despite pressure from others to marry again, described in a letter to Mary

---

[57] MS Letter of Joseph and Sarah Pescod in MARC PLP 83.32.3 to Mr Simons 16 December 1797. For women and household management see Vickery, *Gentleman's Daughter* chapter 4 'Prudent Economy'. Extracts from the unpublished diary of Mrs Blair are at the WHS Library in the Biographical Cuttings files, B/Blai/Mrs.

Fletcher in 1796, where he said several of his friends had expressed surprise that he had not 'changed his station.'[58] A similar case of rapid remarriage was that of Richard Rodda in 1794. Rodda was married by 1768 and had a sizable family though several died young. In May 1794 his wife and two children embarked at Bristol to join Richard at Pembroke. The ship was lost. By December 1794 he married a widow, a 'high church woman with a fortune of £1,500 from Bristol.' Questions were raised because the body of his first wife had not been found. In February 1795 there was even a rumour she had turned up alive, though this proved not to be the case. Rodda died in 1815 in London and the second Mrs Rodda, who was a correspondent of many of the preachers in her second widowhood, died in 1835.[59]

At least forty preachers married widows, who were free to choose their own partners and often had money which they controlled themselves. They were older and sometimes wiser. John Bennet married the widow Grace Murray. John Wesley married the widow Molly Vazeille. The lack of possibly hostile male relatives who might have objected could be an advantage. Thomas Richards married the widow Mary Davie, who had been housekeeper at Kingswood. John Pawson married Mrs Frances Wren in 1785, a marriage almost as celebrated as that of Fletcher and Bosanquet, and more long lived.[60] Often these widows were already significant leaders within Methodism, such as Mrs Ann Haddock in Rye or Mrs Dorothea King in Dublin.[61]

Wives' Roles in Methodism

At least twelve preachers married women who were either already preachers or began to preach after their marriage. Together they were able to provide for the spiritual needs of the circuits in which they travelled. Despite the work done by Chilcote and others, we still do not know about all the women preachers of this period. However, there were a number of male preachers who married women preachers, including leading Methodists like John Jones, Francis Gilbert or John Fletcher, Irish preachers like George Brown, or English preachers like Jonathan Coussins, George Sykes, or George Holder. Most preachers who married women preachers came from the north, like the women preachers themselves. Some women only preached outside Wesleyan Methodism, like

---

[58] *Pawson L* 1; 23-4; see *EMP* 4: 274-329; MARC MAM Fl 6/1/15 MS letter Rogers to Mary Fletcher, printed Fletcher/Tooth Papers Vol 7: 51-3.

[59] For Rodda see *Pawson's L* 1: 168; 2: 22.

[60] Others included John Stamp and Mrs Ward, John Murlin who twice married a widow, Francis Gilbert, John Dean, Owen Davies, Robert Crowther, John Crook's 2nd wife, Thomas Rankin's 2nd wife and John Nelson jr. Widows usually inherited one third of their late husband's estate.

[61] Ann Haddock married John Holmes in 1801. He then settled down in her home, Rye. Dorothea King married John Johnson as his fourth wife. They eventually settled in Lisburn where they became leaders of the Methodist community in north east Ireland.

Kilham's second wife and most of them married preachers of the later cohorts. This is partly because women preachers were very unusual before the 1760s, but also because we know less about the first two cohorts.[62]

Those wives who were not preachers were often band or class leaders or became class leaders. The domestic nature of Methodism meant many women played a leading part within it. Women, like men, would testify at the Lovefeast, which was a significant happening in early Methodism. Women provided a majority of the members and of the adherents. Women were attracted by a movement in which they could play several important roles, not only class leader but prayer leader, letter-writer, host and carer for the preacher and in small societies even steward. The preacher's wife often had more knowledge than the preacher about many of his flock, certainly the society where she lived and was a member. John Pawson was like others much impressed by his wife's labours in Leeds in 1788 'My wife meets Bands (as their leader) and meets in other people's Bands almost every day, and seems to be never weary of those good people with whom she is quite delighted. Religion and the heights and depths of it seem to be her whole delight.'[63]

Place of Marriage

Up to 1753 marriage could take place in any building and without any religious ceremony. However, for Wesley's preachers the place was usually the local parish church and the service conducted by the local clergyman. George Holder, who had entered the ministry in 1782 from Robin Hood's Bay, in August 1788 married the woman preacher Mary ('Polly') Woodhouse, a friend of Mary Fletcher, at St Mary's Whitby, her home town. Many of the preachers were married at St Luke's, Old Street, near the Foundery and Wesley's Chapel in London. It is very difficult to find any who were married before 1800 outside the Anglican Church if they were resident in England, Wales or Ireland. Scotland was another matter, but there again it was the Established (Presbyterian) Church of Scotland which was used.

Remaining Unmarried

Before leaving the subject of marriage, it should be said that many remained unmarried. Celibacy, as pointed out above, was relatively common in the eighteenth century. Rack, quoting Sutcliffe, reported that many of the leading preachers remained unmarried until they were old and infirm; this was most likely to have been for financial reasons or to retain a degree of Christian

---

[62] Chilcote, *JW and Women Preachers* especially Appendix A which details their marriages. Other preachers who married women preachers included William Hainsworth, John Wiltshaw, James Ridall and William Stevens.

[63] *Pawson L* 1: 60. 17th March 1788.

freedom. Rack suggested that the practical arguments against marriage had weight, both the economic one and the fact that the man's life was one of service to God and humanity, with little room for anyone else. The example of Asbury, the American Bishop who travelled incessantly and had no home, was followed on an admittedly lesser scale by British preachers. William Fish, a former pioneer missionary in the West Indies, on his death at a friend's house where he had been living some time, had no known relatives. Thomas Carlill, a Lincolnshire pipemaker who entered the ministry aged 27 and remained single, having travelled 36 years, was in old age offered half a guinea by a young Methodist who took pity on him. 'I have everything I need' the veteran replied, refusing it.[64]

Nor did all marriages last. Mrs Sarah Sharp of Otley (née Flesher), born in 1738, had married Thomas Colbeck successfully in January 1765. The marriage, her second, lasted more than fourteen years to his death in 1779. However, when she married another preacher, James Oddie, in March 1784 at Keighley, this third marriage was not a success. After six weeks she went back to Otley.[65] Charles Wesley summed up the centrality of God for the ideal Methodist marriage thus

> Author, Prince of lasting Peace,
> Us thy ransom'd spirits bless,
> Make us thro thy grace alone
> One of twain for ever One.
>
> One in will, and heart, and mind,
> Each for each by heaven design'd
> One with perfect harmony,
> Spiritually one in Thee.[66]

---

[64] Rack, 'Betsy', 6-8. J. N. Clarke and M. S. Anderson, *Methodism in the Countryside: Horncastle Circuit 1786-1986* (Horncastle: Cupit, 1986) 114.

[65] Otley Parish Register. Divorce in this period was almost impossible (MacFarlane, *Marriage* 225).

[66] Vv 1 & 2 of six stanzas, Hymn for a Husband and a Wife in S. T. Kimbrough and O. A. Beckerlegge, eds, *The Unpublished Poetry of Charles Wesley* 3 vols (Nashville: Abingdon, 1992) 281-82 (MS Misc Hymns 169).

Chapter 7

Family

> 'When Shepherds are Single
> they're active and nimble
> And their hearts above.
> But when they're double
> They meet with much trouble
> and pay for their love.
> Young babies require
> both Clothing and fire
> And their Mama's Tea.
> But when you have none,
> You may up and be gone
> and run the Good way.'

So wrote the Rev Alexander Crumlin to the thirty-one year old Robert Dall, an unmarried Scots travelling preacher for Wesley at Belturbet in Ireland in 1776. Dall kept the ditty among his papers, so presumably agreed with it. When he married in the Isle of Man three years later he ceased to travel for eight years.[1]

For Wesley in the ideal situation the travelling preacher would have no family to hold him back. In reality the situation was different. The preacher had parents who might be against his travelling or who might need his support. He usually had brothers or sisters who might help or hinder. Most of all, if he had a wife, then he might well have children who would require feeding as well as Crumlin's suggestion of money for clothes and heat. The mothers would breast-feed for the first few months, but money and food for the children were necessities,[2] hence the need for allowances.

Allowances

Allowances paid by circuits for children of the preachers dated from 1770. In 1769 the problems of families had again been discussed at Conference 'If married preachers are sent, the people look at them with an evil eye, because they cannot bear the burden of their families.' In 1770 it was agreed that

---

[1] This is no 2 of Dall's papers at the MARC, MA 3181, see also the end of this Chapter.
[2] See note 32 in the last chapter to the quotation from Mrs Bennis about Jonathan Hern's wife working at Limerick in 1771 'though a child at the breast.'

preachers should receive £4 for each child per quarter from the circuit in addition to the £24 allowance for the wife. The payments for the boys ceased usually when they reached the age of eight, as most would be sent to Kingswood. At the school they would be fed, clothed, and given books and pocket money as well as education. For girls the allowances were to be until the age of fourteen. By 1780 it was £6 for each girl paid out of the Kingswood Collection, and so the equivalent of the education received there by the boys. The circuits often found it difficult to raise the money which could vary enormously according to the size of the families, and these child allowances had more and more to be paid from central funds. Lloyd estimated the allowances were mostly coming from the Preachers' Fund by 1781 rather than the circuits. By 1795 £12 was allowed for boys who were not admitted to Kingswood; £6 was allocated for the girls, though in 1796 that rose to eight guineas but was limited to a four year period from the age of nine. By 1799 £18 was considered necessary for the boys, £12 of which was for their education and £6 for their maintenance. This did not alter the basic problem. Jonathan Crowther wrote in his memoirs in 1816 'I travelled 11 years before I married. During those years I cared very little how far I travelled, and it was no concern of mine what sort of home I should have to live in, or what allowances the preachers had for board etc… But I find myself (now) in very different circumstances. A large family and a poor Circuit (York!) with scant allowances, and uncomfortable house, must inevitably be discouraging…'

The Children's Fund was eventually set up in 1819, with a complex plan devised by Jabez Bunting under which each circuit and district paid according to their membership and all children of the relevant ages were listed. Large families would inevitably still cause problems. As with wives this enables the tracing of most of the children from 1770 for both boys and girls. Again there was a catch in that they needed to survive to the age of eight and the parents had to claim the allowance. Many died young and some did not claim. Using the *Minutes* in this way gives a realistic number for the preachers' families allowing for these drawbacks.[3]

The Wesleys

For Wesley himself family relationships were important. He and Charles were brothers, disagreeing about many things but always united over what they felt was most significant. His mother had come to live with him at the Foundery after his father's death. His relationship with his parents always remained vital to understanding him, long after their deaths. His sisters and their children were

---

[3] MS Volume 'Life and Travels of a Methodist preacher…Jonathan Crowther written by himself' vol 2 only, 56-7, Baker Collection, Duke NC, F. Box 4; Lloyd, *Labourers Hire* 25; W. Peirce, *The Ecclesiastical Principles and Polity of the Wesleyan Methodists* (London: WCO, 1873) 517.

close to him in thought, and one sister Martha (Patty), who had married and been deserted by Westley Hall, lived in London with John until his death. She has been described as very much like John Wesley, both physically and in feelings. She died in 1791, the last of John's siblings.[4]

John Wesley had no children. But he adopted his step daughters, the two daughters of his wife, the former Molly Vazeille, and delighted later to see his step grandchildren about whom he was concerned and for whom he felt much love. Wesley's preachers also loved their children and (usually) had that love returned. In Walsh's phrase 'the most characteristic image of the English (Methodist) movement is... Wesley as he is described in John Barritt's diary, standing in a barn with a knot of shabby people around him, explaining the love of God in the process of regeneration. Would they recognize God's love? Yes they would. For how did husbands and wives recognize the love they bore each other, or children know they were loved by their parents? They felt it in their hearts. And so too it would be with God's grace.'[5]

It was a male dominated age and it would be foolish to expect anything else. Boys generally were regarded as more important than the girls. This is why we know of more sons than daughters for the preachers. Both, however, were usually welcomed in contemporary society. This was also true among Wesley's preachers where Alexander Mather could write to a fellow preacher 'May the increase of your family also be for His Glory.'[6] Olleson has pointed out we know much about what Charles Wesley did in regard to his gifted sons, Charles junior and Samuel, but little about what his wife Sarah did or about the upbringing of their daughter Sally.[7]

Childbirth and Infant Mortality

Childbirth was a trying time for women. The early London Moravian Mrs Elizabeth Claggett feared her inability to withstand the pains of childbirth would lead to the sins of abortion and cursing God. 'I had uncommon Sufferings in Childbearing' she wrote to Charles Wesley in 1738.[8] Most babies entered the world with the help of female relatives and friends of the mother

---

[4] For Mrs Hall see Clarke, *Wesley Family* 511-537. Clarke knew her from 1783.

[5] J. D. Walsh, 'Methodism and the Origins of English Speaking Evangelicalism' in M. A. Noll, D.W. Bebbington and G. A. Rawlyk, eds, *Evangelism: Comparative Studies of Popular Protestantism in North America, The British Isles, and Beyond 1700-1990* (Oxford: OUP, 1994) 34

[6] MacFarlane, *Marriage* Chapter 4 The Benefits and Costs of Children. The quotation is in a MS letter in the Museum of Methodism at Lake Junaluska in the British Presidential file from Mather at Hull January 29th 1794 to Lancelot Harrison at Colne.

[7] P. Olleson, *Samuel Wesley: The Man and his Music* (Woodbridge: Boydell and Brewer, 2003).

[8] P. Mack, 'Religious Dissenters in Enlightenment England' in *History Workshop Journal* 49 (2000), 9-10, quoting MS letter from Mrs Claggett to CW 24 July 1738, EMV 2: 48 in MARC.

only. Doctors were regarded with suspicion, often abundantly justified. The policy of letting nature take its course had much to commend it. Complications might cause the death of the child or mother or both.[9] Condamine in France in 1760 said that of sixty women in childbirth one would die.[10]

Among Wesley's preachers' wives many died in childbirth. Hester Ann Rogers was the most famous. A preacher's wife who had long corresponded with Wesley before her marriage, she nursed Wesley in his last illness. A mere three years later she died in childbirth. Thomas Bartholomew suffered twice. His first wife died at Blackburn aged thirty-nine in November 1810 'never having recovered (from) her lying in.' His second wife died in childbirth in 1816 producing twins. Thomas Longley's wife Martha died in 1792 in childbirth, bearing a still-born child. Fear of the perils of childbirth must have encouraged some women to put off marriage until later, when conception would not occur. Some who survived childbirth found that they were unable ever to recover and remained in a state of semi-invalidism.[11]

Most of Wesley's preachers who had children lost some in infancy. Nationally infant mortality rates, that is up to the age of five years, were as high as at least 150 per 1000 births. In certain areas the figures were much higher. In London in 1800 Heberden found that of every 400 deaths recorded 147 were of children under the age of two and another 35 between two and five.[12] Most preachers did not dwell in London. Many lived, however, in industrial towns like Bradford, Sheffield, Liverpool, Manchester and Leeds where conditions were similarly unhealthy. An example of the influence of infant mortality on a family can be found in the story of Thomas Rutherford. In 1780 he married Isabella Young of Coleraine, sister of Anne Young, Henry Moore's wife. Thomas and Isabella had a relatively large family of fourteen. After an operation Rutherford retired around 1804 to London and died there. Eight of the fourteen children were dead by 1813. His widow died in October 1817 at

---

[9] Mack, 'Religious Dissenters' 18-19 suggested that Mary Taft may well have had nobody present when giving birth in 1811. Heywood, *Childhood* 58 cited a maternal death rate of 10 per 1000 births in the first half of the eighteenth century in England. For infant mortality itself see Heywood, *Childhood* 148-9 and 151-3. Vickery, *Gentleman's Daughter* 96-8 suggested that perinatal mortality for women was as much as 1 in 5 for deaths of women between 25 and 34.

[10] Rusnock, *Vital Accounts* 79.

[11] *MM* 1811: 74; G. Lloyd, ed, *Catalogue of Early Methodist Personal Papers* (Manchester: MARC, 2000) 1: 39. The WHS 2005 Conference on Women in Methodism at York had several papers on Hester Ann Rogers, which showed how the Wesleyan Methodist leadership encouraged her virtual canonization in the 1790s. Was this because she was safely dead unlike Sarah Crosby, Mary Fletcher or Mary Taft? For women's attitude to childbirth see MacFarlane, *Marriage* 148-9. For Longley see C. Appleby, *Thomas Longley in Cornwall 1798-1801* (Redruth: CMHA, 1983) 1.

[12] W. Heberden, *Observations on the Increase and Decrease of Different Diseases and the Plague* (London: Payne, 1801) 47, cited by Rusnock, *Vital Accounts* 167-70.

Leeds, with at that point four daughters and one son surviving, her obituary being written by her daughter Isabella.[13] This is quite typical. The known deaths occurred in 1799, 1800, 1802 and 1809, the years the family was living in Sheffield and London. That high number of deaths was most distressing for the parents. Some of Thomas and Isabella's letters have survived. The Stone/Aries idea of parents being indifferent to their offspring because they knew they might well die young is not borne out by Wesley's preachers and is now discounted by sociologists. There are many examples of preachers and their wives mourning their losses deeply.[14]

Education and Training for the Children

Children were expected, at an early age by modern eyes, to support themselves. Before the nineteenth century 'the age of seven was an informal turning point when the offspring of peasants and craftsmen were generally expected to start helping their parents with little tasks about the home, the farm or the workshop. By their early teens they were likely to be working beside adults or established in an apprenticeship. They might well have left home by this stage to become a servant or an apprentice of some sort.'[15] 'There was what has been described as the peculiar English tradition of sending young children away from home to earn their separate keep.' 'The majority of families sought work for their children as a matter of routine.'[16] For Wesley's preachers' sons, after the 1760s at least, this was replaced by going away to board at Kingswood at the age of eight or even earlier. Having spent around three years there they would be apprenticed, often to a fellow Methodist, perhaps even a former itinerant. So John Tregortha, the Cornish-born itinerant who located in Burslem in 1790 as druggist, later printer and bookseller, had Theophilus Lessey the younger apprenticed to him by his preacher father in 1801.[17]

The preachers' children tended to have more education than the majority of the population. Their parents laid more stress on it and as a result they were better qualified. John Henderson has already been mentioned. Three of John Beaumont's sons qualified as doctors, while two of William Jenkins' sons were

---

[13] Rutherford was the fourth child of seven, and the eldest son of Presbyterian parents, baptized on the 15th March 1752. He lived in lower Redesdale in Northumberland and in 1767 first heard the Methodists. Converted in December 1768 by William Hunter, he was a class leader by autumn in 1769. He began preaching in May 1770 and on the 1st January 1772 was asked to supply as itinerant in his own circuit. *AM* 1808: 337-46, 385-94, 433-42, 481-94, 529-44, 577-82; 1813: 444, 451, 1819: 762-4.

[14] P. Mack, 'Does gender matter? Suffering and salvation in eighteenth-century Methodism' *JRULMB* 85 (2003) 173; Stone, *Family* 81-89.

[15] Heywood, *Childhood* 37.

[16] MacFarlane, *Marriage* 82; Heywood, *Childhood* 121.

[17] *PWHS* 22 (1939) 15-20. The younger Lessey had been at Kingswood since 1795 (*KS Reg* 122). The two Lesseys had the same names.

architects. Two of Alexander Suter's sons were chemists, as was William Aver's son. Both the sons of Thomas Colbeck and Joseph Benson became surgeons. Lawyers included a son of William Bramwell. John Ogylvie's son was a Fellow of Balliol College, Oxford. Three of Thomas Bartholomew's sons were engineers.[18]

In 1746 Wesley founded a school at Kingswood, partly to provide education for the sons of the itinerant preachers. In eighteenth century society, as boys moved from the care of their mothers, usual up to eight, towards adulthood and apprenticeship, the father would take more part. As they travelled and were away from home so much, the preachers could not give this care to their sons. Wesley wanted the preacher to give less thought to his family since he was ensuring that some of the family at least were being well educated there. It is difficult to discover how many sons of preachers were at Kingswood in the early years. As preachers began to marry and have children, so it became a more prized and used privilege that the sons of Wesley's preachers were given free education at Kingswood, or money in lieu. Most Kingswood pupils at first were 'the sons of our friends,' not those of preachers. The numbers of preachers' sons at Kingswood may well have increased after the first annual appeal to the Connexion in 1756 on its behalf. It should be seen as an important act by John Wesley, well in advance of his age, that girls as well as boys were admitted at that early stage. Later, when girls were no longer taken by Kingswood in 1774, Wesley suggested they should be sent to Miss Owen's school at Publow. Next year he seems to have agreed that the Connexion should pay for at least some of these girls, and by 1780 it was clear that any daughters of preachers of the right age (around eight to eleven) should receive money towards their education. These allowances, already referred to above, were a valuable assistance to the families of the preachers. They were an interesting early example of Methodism being very conscious of equal rights. It was remarkable in an age when daughters were rarely given education and even more rarely sent away to school.[19]

We know of few early names for the children at Kingswood. William Grimshaw of Haworth sent both his son John and his daughter Jane. The latter died at the school in January 1750, aged just under thirteen. Other relatively early sons of preachers include John Henderson from 1760, son of the Irish preacher Richard Henderson, Walter Sellon's son Walter who drowned in 1752, two sons of Cornelius Bastable by the early 1750s and three sons of John Hampson in the 1760s. Total numbers were small, and so in 1763 there were

---

[18] *KS Reg*, which also covered boys educated at Woodhouse Grove.

[19] More boys (559) have been recorded than girls (411) in preachers' families, partly because of the existence of records at Kingswood, though the listing of grants for girls' education mitigated this. 1798 provides an example of how the records show this in practice. There were 34 girls who received grants that year and a total of 48 boys, 32 at Kingswood and 16 others who received grants. Ives 108; *Minutes* 1: 433-34.

'thirteen or fourteen' pupils. From 1770 at least one son of a preacher was admitted every year, often more, and this was then (but not earlier) recorded in the Minutes. This led to a rise in numbers and in 1776 Thomas Simpson reported over fifty pupils.[20]

Ages of pupils at Kingswood varied. Most were sent at seven or eight years old. They might stay for only one year, or two or three. A five year stay was unusual, so there was a relatively swift turnover of pupils. Often a pupil would not see his family again for a whole year and maybe not then, because transport was difficult to arrange. John Henderson, later described as a genius, went at four. He began to teach Latin in the school at the age of eight and at twelve moved to Trevecka to teach there, having thus stayed eight years at Kingswood. Later he went to Pembroke College Oxford and attracted Dr. Samuel Johnson's notice. 'Scarcely a book could be mentioned, but he would give some account of it; nor any subject started but he could engage in the discussion of it.'[21]

Often the parents wrote many letters to their sons away from home for the first time. A few letters and diaries have survived and help to show the love and concern Wesley's preachers had for their children.[22] Life for the children at Kingswood was ruled by work, for Wesley forbad play. However, there were changes of activity, and singing, prayer, work in the garden, music, reading, worship and walking played a regular part in the daily pattern of life. Wesley was reacting against the too common half holidays of the so-called 'best' schools of the age. Part of the problem at Kingswood was that he was not there enough and in his absence the system sometimes slipped. From 1788 the character of Kingswood changed, as preachers' sons became the majority. From 1796 it was exclusively for them. It was not until the foundation of Woodhouse Grove in 1812 that most preachers began to send their sons to one of the two schools, because preachers living in the north found Kingswood too far away. Food was usually sufficient. Boys wore caps, long coats of fine wool, breeches to below the knee of corduroy or doeskin, long stockings and flimsy shoes needing constant repair. They had linen shirts and carried handkerchiefs. There were no underclothes. Hair was long and cut twice a year.

Parental Control

Children were expected to behave well and usually did. It was an age of autocratic fathers. Children of Wesley's preachers expected no different

---

[20] Joseph Cownley and William Darney, eponymous sons of the preacher fathers were there in 1766, and John and William Maddern sons of John Maddern late 1760s. MS letter at Duke University of Thomas Simpson 27 February 1776 from Kingswood to Joseph Benson, Newcastle.

[21] For Kingswood the main source is Ives Chapters 2 and 3. The quotation is from L. Tyerman, *Wesley's Designated Successor* (London: Hodder, 1882) 146.

[22] L. F. Church, *Early Methodist People* (London: Epworth, 1948) 224-26.

behaviour. Mothers might find it more difficult to bring up their children, especially if the husband were dead. So the reference to John Wesley sending home from Kingswood 'that bad boy Isaac Barry to his mother' could be blamed on the early death in 1783 of his father, the preacher James Barry, who left a large family including six boys. On the other hand, there could be provocation. The son of the Irish-born preacher James M. Byron, having run away from Kingswood three times, was chained by the leg.[23] Misbehaviour was not limited to boys. Mary Payne, daughter of the preacher Thomas Payne, had to be sent home from her school at Publow in 1780. In her case separation from her father at an early age, because the East India Company had sent him away from St Helena where the family had lived, could be partly responsible for the later problems. Children's misbehaviour, however, tended to be reported only after they had grown up. Joseph Bradford's son of the same name was described as being flogged and thrown out of the army in 1806. Sometimes the misbehaviour was because the children had been 'dressed up' beyond their means and spoilt, as Pawson complained to Benson in 1802.[24]

Wesley's preachers usually blended affection and discipline successfully in bringing up their families. Adam Clarke, while at the Liverpool Conference in 1793, wrote at the end of the letter to his wife that he had 'bought a wooden thing for John (aged four), called *Noah's Ark*, there are 18 different figures of men, women, birds and insects in it.' Like others they played with their children and bought toys for them. In general the children were not spiritually manipulated but absorbed their parents' spirituality, partly through family observances such as prayers and the reading of suitable texts. The pattern of the Epworth Rectory children's upbringing with individual love and care was frequently repeated, though the absent father was away on the circuit rather than in a debtor's jail![25]

Some sons became preachers like their fathers. The existence of Kingswood and later Woodhouse Grove helped to encourage this. It was only after Wesley's death that this became common. In the nineteenth century the Wesleyan ministry was known for its relatively high proportion of ministers with ministerial fathers, which Brown has shown was increasing to as high as

---

[23] Ives e.g. 110-11. The story about Byron is 115-16 and relates to 1812. For Woodhouse Grove food see F. C. Pritchard, *The Story of Woodhouse Grove School* (Bradford: Woodhouse Grove, 1978) 61-63.

[24] *PWHS* 31 (1958) 180 quoting a 1785 letter. The widow settled in Chester and was being given money. The story about Bradford comes from Crowther's MS Memoirs at Duke University 62. For Payne see *EMP* 2: 285-89 and *Minutes* for 1780 (146) 'consider how to dispose of Mary Payne' showing that she was a problem for the school. Pawson wrote 'We dress up our wives and children in such a wise as ninety-nine of every hundred of those who support us cannot afford to do.' (*Pawson L* 3: 74).

[25] MS Letter from Adam Clarke to his wife Mary, 4th August 1793 Bridwell Library, SMU, Dallas. The emphasis was by Clarke who was pleased with his purchase.

over 12% of the total ministry in the later part of the century.[26] Before 1791 the two known and certain examples of two father and son ministers entering were the John Hampsons, senior and junior, both of whom left in 1784, and James Kershaw, who left and became a quack doctor, and his son John Kershaw, later Book Steward. John was not proud of James and did not mention his father's name in his autobiography, though praising his parental training.[27] There were others probable or possible: very probable were William Collins senior and junior and John Watson senior and junior, and also Lancelot Harrison and his son Thomas Harrison. Possible but less likely were the William Hunters, the James Lyons and the William M'Cornocks all senior and junior. There may have been as many as eight who entered in Wesley's lifetime, which is only 1%. After Wesley's death it became much more common, partly because of the expansion of the Methodist itinerancy. So in the next generation 37 of Wesley's preachers had a total of 39 sons who entered the ministry. This included two sons who entered the Methodist Episcopal ministry in the United States of America. In most cases the son entered the British ministry after 1791. George Mowat had two sons who entered, William in 1812 and James in 1819. Some started ministerial dynasties with a son and grandson in the ranks. The most famous of these dynasties were the Macdonalds. The Irishman from Enniskillen James M'Donald (1761-1835), Assistant Editor to Joseph Benson from 1811 to 1817, was followed by his son George Browne Macdonald (1805-68) and grandson Frederic William Macdonald (1842-1928). They were matched by Thomas Trethewey, his son Humphrey Trethewey and grandson Thomas Trethewey, and by John Simpson, his son and grandson both Samuel Simpson. Fourteen sons became clergymen in the Church of England. This was particularly true of the leaders in the generation who succeeded Wesley. Joseph Benson had two sons who did this and Adam Clarke one. There were many others in the generation who entered after Wesley's death.[28]

It is interesting to make a comparison between the children of those who left and those who died in the work. This shows that, among the children of those who left, there were three who entered the ministry of the other Nonconformist churches. Those who died in the work had only one child who did this. This is because those who left sometimes became Dissenting ministers. When they did,

---

[26] K. D. Brown, *A Social History of the Nonconformist Ministry in England and Wales 1800-1930* (Oxford: Clarendon Press, 1988) 3 and table 3.3 on 95.

[27] For John Kershaw see *MM* 1802: 177-183, 221-29. I am indebted to a descendant, Keith Sherwood of Cambridge, for pointing out a relationship I had discounted.

[28] For the Macdonalds see I. Taylor, *The Macdonald Sisters* (London: Weidenfeld, 1987). The simplest way of finding out about the sons of most preachers in the early nineteenth century is through the Kingswood Register, which provided most of the information about sons. The two entrants to the Methodist Episcopal Church were the sons of Charles Atmore and James Dempster, Dempster having settled in America already. William Atherton and Thomas Jackson were other Presidents of Conference in the early nineteenth century whose sons who entered the Anglican ministry.

like John Bennet, it was natural for a son to follow his father's calling. So John Thorpe's son and John Gilbert's son followed John Bennet's son into the Nonconformist ministry. The only case of a son of a Wesley's preacher who died in the work entering the Baptist ministry was a son of George Sargent, who had had six sons. Perhaps John Sargent felt the need to be different from his numerous siblings, perhaps he doubted that he would be accepted by his own Methodism.

Daughters

Some preachers' daughters married other preachers, for example Robert Miller married Thomas Taylor's daughter Anne. Daughters of preachers were likely to meet young preachers because the latter would live, when not out on circuit, in the preachers' accommodation under the eye of the Assistant, later Superintendent. William Simpson was in the Chester circuit in 1781 under Jonathan Hern as Assistant. Two years later he married Hern's daughter in Manchester's Collegiate Church. This process tended to increase over time as the ministry grew, the families became larger, and there were more opportunities for this to happen. At least thirty preachers had daughters who went on to marry younger preachers.[29]

Some daughters married the sons of other Methodist preachers. James Rogers' daughter married Samuel Bradburn's son, both preachers of some weight in the connexion. The daughter of Joseph Burgess married the son of Francis Truscott, both preachers with strong links to Devon and Cornwall.[30]

Many of the daughters, if single, entered the world of small schools and governesses, the society made familiar by the Brontë sisters whose father inhabited a very similar social circle to the preachers. Benjamin Rhodes's daughters helped his wife keep a boarding school for young ladies at Union Crescent, Margate, where he retired as Supernumerary in 1810. On her death they ran it themselves. When Samuel Taylor died suddenly in 1821, his widow and daughters went to Madeley, invited by Mary Tooth with the idea of setting up a similar school. After the death of William Stevens, his widow and her daughters continued a girls' school at Kingswood where he had taught.[31]

Some daughters had the literary ambition of the Brontës. Eliza Weaver

---

[29] A. Lawrence, 'The Question of Celibacy' in *JRULMB* 85 (2003) 192. Daughters are much more difficult to trace than sons, because of no Kingswood Register for them. For Robert Miller see Chapter 8 below. William Simpson's marriage is in the *IGI* as are most of the others mentioned. Others who married older preachers' daughters included Joseph Cownley, Joseph Burgess and Peard Dickinson. The practice was common among Anglican clergy as well see Jacob, *Clerical Profession* 158.

[30] *WMM* 1874: 857. Robert Harrison's son married George Morley's daughter.

[31] For the Rhodes family see E. Rhodes, *Memoir of Mrs Elizabeth Rhodes, Widow* (London: Mason, 1829), for Taylor's family see Fletcher/Tooth Papers 3/1/31, for Stevens see *MM* 1814: 73, 801-15.

Family

Bradburn, Samuel's governess daughter, wrote regularly for the Wesleyan magazines *Youth's Instructor* and *Early Days* as well as being her father's biographer. Daughters especially, but also sons, had their aged parents living with them. Unmarried daughters living at home were expected to care for their elderly parents and usually did. So the unnamed daughter of the dying diabetic preacher Thomas Bartholomew 'constantly waited on (took care of) him.' Harriot Atmore cared for her parents Charles Atmore and his second wife.[32]

Size of Families

The families of the preachers were not generally as large as those in the remainder of the population since usually the preachers started having children later. This was because of the period of probation and the fact that they were not usually allowed to marry until they had been received into Full Connexion. The largest number known of children of a preacher were those of Thomas Roberts. With three wives at different times he had an advantage and fathered at least sixteen children. The largest known family by one wife was that of Thomas and Isabella Rutherford. The average number of children per preacher was 3.412, but the real figure would be larger, because often the children were unrecorded and many families were simply described as 'large.' These figures should be compared with those for the later nineteenth century when family size for the whole population as well as ministers was declining. The figure of about three children for marriages contracted by Methodist ministers before 1880 fits well with this, despite the time gap between the two.[33]

Another reason for the smaller size of preachers' families was the tendency of Wesley's preachers to marry wives who might be considerably older than themselves. The average couple in the late eighteenth century had delayed the woman's childbearing years by ten years and reduced the number of children by a third. Wesley's preachers did more than that by marrying later and choosing wives older than the average. Absence from home for many, perhaps most,[34] nights of the year reduced the opportunity for conception further. In addition many remained unmarried like Asbury, so decreasing the number of children more.

Care for Families

Baptism

Baptism for their children was important to Wesley's preachers partly because

---

[32] For Bartholomew see *MM* 1820: 563-5. For Harriot Atmore see *WMM* 1845: 921.
[33] Rule, *Albion's People* 5-6 argued that as marriage age fell in the late eighteenth century so family size increased. Brown, *Ministry* 181 and table 5.3.
[34] Title of chapter 3 in Vickery, *Gentleman's Daughter*. The figures are from Heywood, *Childhood* 46-48.

no other form of registration was available. William Percival's wife was typical of eighteenth century parents in taking her newborn child to the local parish church and asking the clergyman for baptism in 1787.[35] Parental use of names like John and Charles has already been discussed. Other names chosen tended to be from the close family of parents, grandparents, uncles and aunts. Particular names might well be given several times to try to keep them in the family because of the high rate of infant mortality. James Rogers had three sons baptized John, the first two having died within a year of their baptism. Relatively few used Biblical names not already in the family, though there were examples such as George Button's daughter, christened Hephzibah Beulah Button in 1807. There was a tendency to choose parental surnames as second or even first names. Quite often children had two or more given names where the parents only had one. Sometimes the child was called after a friend, godparent or fellow preacher. So Alexander Mather had his son christened Thomas Marriott after his friend and patron, the leading London Methodist of that name. There were preachers who disagreed with their brethren and wanted to baptize their children themselves. Thomas Cooper baptized his four surviving children from 1787 and recorded them in 1799 in the Wolverhampton Noah's Ark Baptismal Register. Such incidents had begun by 1758, at least in London. Wesley opposed the practice of baptism by preachers and expelled those who insisted on doing it publicly, but it was difficult for him to hold the line and by the late 1780s these baptisms were open, particularly by those preachers who were already looking for separation from the Church of England. Twenty-three preachers can be proved to have baptized during that period. Pawson continued to baptize despite Wesley's explicit command.[36]

Maternal Care

Mothers rather than fathers were expected to care for young children. The usually absent preachers wanted to be at home at the time of their child's arrival. Several times Wesley either sent his preachers to convenient places because their wives were about to give birth, or allowed them to stay on in their existing circuit for a month or so after Conference because they were concerned about their wives. The women were often by this time in the last months of pregnancy and because of the difficulties of travel in the eighteenth century immobile. In 1781 Thomas Rutherford, who had been put down for Lisburn in the *Minutes*, was allowed to change with Hugh Moore in November for a month or six weeks, so that his wife Isabella could give birth in the

---

[35] *JWL* 7: 369.
[36] B. G. Holland, *Baptism in Early Methodism* (London: Epworth, 1970) 106-116 had a detailed discussion, together with the Appendix 3 which lists the occasions and preachers. See also Chapter 15 below. Wolverhampton City Archives MSS Baptismal Register of the Noah's Ark Chapel 1793-1825 (under Darlington Street) 1.

Londonderry circuit where her family was. At other times the care of the children would devolve almost totally on the mother. 'For fertile women, motherhood could absorb almost all reserves of physical and emotional energy for at least a decade.'[37] It is not surprising that, while there are many letters surviving from Wesley's preachers, relatively few have survived from their wives. They were too busy.

Movement of Families

The existence of wives and families complicated movement from circuit to circuit. Husbands often went to Conference and, having discovered their new station, went there direct without returning to their family. Wives, having already done whatever packing was needed, often moved slightly later. The families placed an extra complication on the movement between circuits, which could delay it further. Journeying separately could result in tragedy, as when Richard Rodda's wife and children were lost in 1794 when travelling from Bristol by sea. Jonathan Crowther's Memoirs written in 1816 illustrate this 'On the 23rd July 1805 our Betsy was born. When she was three days old I set off for the Conference, and when she was 30 days old we all left Keighley, & went to Todmorden.' That was a relatively short and easy move to the neighbouring circuit, even if it was in the Pennines.[38] Most moves were much further. This was also where the poverty of the itinerants was an advantage, for there was relatively little to move, no furniture for example, since it was provided by the circuit well into the twentieth century. There would be the clothes they stood up in, spare clothes if they had any, some books and a few personal possessions. The gigantic farm wagon of 1825, described by Benjamin Gregory in his childhood recollections, was a later phenomenon for a longer journey than the average, and unusually large even then, for his preacher father had more books and extra shelves than the ordinary itinerant.[39]

Servants

Servants were part of the family. Society was such that servants were plentiful and cheap. Relatively poor tradesmen and smallholders would employ them. Even poor preachers might if they had children, because of the heavy load of physical labour in the household. Preachers, who were relatively wealthy like William Grimshaw or Robert Brackenbury, had several servants in their household, though most early ones would not. After Wesley's day the

---

[37] For Rutherford see *JWL* 7: 94; Vickery, *Gentleman's Daughter* 97.
[38] Crowther MS at Duke NC Vol 2: 5. Cf Mrs Blair 1787 in her diary 'August 4 preparing to go to Chester Circuit is a trial, my dear infant is greatly afflicted and his recovery doubtful'; Biographical Cuttings in WHS Library B/Blai/Mrs.
[39] B. Gregory, *Autobiographical Recollections* (London: Hodder, 1903) 22-26.

economic standing of his preachers improved and servants became more likely for married preachers with children, at least in wealthier circuits. A circuit like Colne in the north had '£2 for maid and washing' in the accounts as early as 1778. Pawson referred to taking a servant with him to Scotland in 1785, but he had just married a wealthy wife. The first mention in the *Minutes* is in 1802 where it stated 'No married preacher shall be allowed anything for a servant, unless he has two children or has one of the single preachers boarding with him or in case of affliction.' Clearly some circuits by then were allowing money for servants. Further, the next year the rule was repealed, so there was no limitation on allowances for servants being given to the preachers. Most preachers by the period after Wesley's death certainly had servants.[40]

Food and Drink

What did they eat and drink in their families? The question arises from the quotation at the beginning of this chapter and has also been recently been raised by Wallace. Crumlin the Presbyterian thought in terms of tea for drinking. Wesley himself had once famously opposed tea and in 1748 published a pamphlet suggesting alternatives such as infusions of English herbs or even cocoa. He argued against taking caffeine in any form, in favour of frugality and against over-eating. Wesley published his own version of Fleury's *Manners of the Ancient Christians* in which he recommended practices like abstaining from 'drinking wine or eating flesh.' Methodist preachers certainly imitated Wesley in their austerity, but there is no evidence that they refused to drink tea or eat meat. Wesley advocated water and plain food. His preachers were often forced to eat nothing else. In Scotland for the single Thomas Taylor in 1765 'a pennyworth of oatmeal furnished him with breakfast and supper, the half of that in carrots and bread his dinner, his drink being cold water.' Methodists bought teapots with copies of Wesley's bust on them. Most preachers, like the bachelor Samuel Bardsley, were abstemious. However, by the 1790s there were individuals like Charles Atmore who gained the reputation of liking a good meal too much. There are some stories about Wesley and food, like the bed of asparagus at Thirsk, some of which he ate while staying there and which was preserved long into the nineteenth century in his honour. Whether preachers and their families were also allowed asparagus we do not hear.[41] The evidence shows that the preachers' families ate little. Taylor said in twenty years travelling as a preacher with a family he never received enough to feed the family. This was common, which was why preachers' wives often worked and

---

[40] W. Jessop, *Methodism in Rossendale and. Neighbourhood* (London: WCO, 1880) 126; *Pawson L* 1: 31; *Minutes* 2: 140, Porter, *English Society* 143-4.

[41] C. Wallace, 'Eating and Drinking with John Wesley' *JRULMB* 85 (2003) 137-155. For Taylor see Jessop, *Rossendale* 95. For the asparagus see J. Ward, *Methodism in the Thirsk Circuit* (Thirsk: Peat, 1860) 20-21. The bed belonged to an Anglican, Mr Routh.

preachers tended to marry wives with money.

Fasting was recommended for all Methodists, originally for Band members every Friday but eventually quarterly on a Friday. It was something the preachers and other Methodists did, particularly when it was felt the country was suffering the wrath of God. At the public meeting of the 1781 Conference at 10-00 am James Chubb heard 'Mr W(esley) desired all to Remember every Friday as a Fast. (Be) particular not to breakfast, if weak take a little milk & water and a little bread.' So in 1799 with corn scarce, Pawson mentioned the 'day of prayer and fasting' he had kept on two different days at two local villages that week. Again in 1801 at a time of national danger he and others kept a day of prayer and fasting on a Friday.[42]

Other Family Relationships

Several sets of brothers entered the itinerancy in Wesley's lifetime, making a total for Britain of 17 preachers. The two Manners brothers, Nicholas and John, came from Sledmere in the East Riding of Yorkshire. The younger by a year, Nicholas Manners began to preach first as a local preacher. '3 months after me my brother began to preach.' Soon the older brother, John, began to travel. Nicholas 'continued a year longer at home,' starting travelling in 1758.[43] In Cornwall in Sancreed Nicholas and Honour Rodda allowed the preaching in their house from around 1750 and had at least ten children. Three sons became preachers including Richard Rodda, a leading preacher of the period who lived on after Wesley, and Martin Rodda who was sent to America.[44] Later there were the three Crowthers from Halifax. Of all these brothers the Crowthers were best known, providing a later president. In Ireland there were more Methodist itinerant brothers than would have been expected, almost half from West Tyrone.

Reasons for this plethora of brothers included similar upbringing and experience, the family nature of early Methodist groups which often met in the family home, and the influence of older brothers on their younger siblings. This was certainly true of the three Crowthers, the children of Timothy, a carter of coal, and Hannah Crowther who lived near Halifax at Jackson's Hill. The oldest son Timothy, his first wife, and the next brother Jonathan, were all

---

[42] MS Chubb Journals at the New Room Bristol Friday 6th August 1781 Vol II 35; Rack 443; *Pawson* L 3: 2, 43. Fasting is a subject which historians of Methodism have generally avoided. It lasted much longer than *DOMBI*, for example, suggested.

[43] For the Manners brothers see N. Manners, *Some Part of Life and Experience of... Nicholas Manners* (York: 1785). It sounded almost like a brotherly competition! There were also the three Hitchens from Cornwall, sons of the blacksmith at Busveal near Gwennap and the two Rowells from Allendale in Northumberland.

[44] For the Roddas see J. Pearce (a descendant), *The Wesleys in Cornwall* (Truro: Bradford Barton, 1964) 7, 20, 138, 144 and *EMP* 2: 295-323. Later there were also the two Brettells from Kingswinford near Dudley and two Saundersons from Wakefield.

converted by Brian Bury Collins in 1779. The third brother Robert, born in 1762, was converted later 'after this his brothers took him along to the weekly class meetings.' Jonathan and the other two brothers all began to preach locally in 1782. By 1784 Timothy's wife had died and he and Jonathan entered the itinerancy in 1784 and 1785. In 1789 the two older brothers were being received into Full Connexion at the Leeds Conference nearby and 'sent for their brother Robert to come to Leeds. After mature deliberation, he fully gave himself to the Conference, to do with him as they judged best.' Conference put Robert on the list of those On Trial, but did not station him. 'He then returned home, and in November following was instructed to get ready without delay and go to the Norwich Circuit.' Robert had already travelled as an itinerant in the Colne circuit for six weeks in 1787 and reckoned it was not for him, but was in the end reluctantly persuaded by his two older brothers.[45]

Often the preachers were financially supported by members of their families. Francis Isherwood from the Yorkshire village of Slingsby, who entered the ministry in 1761 from a comfortable home, was sent to Manchester where he died in 1762. The accounts of the Manchester circuit show a large payment sent by his father which covered everything he received.[46]

The preachers were often seeking to support aged members of their family, if only by visiting. The local preacher Richard Burdsall was a widower, had four children, and also an aged mother who was dependent on him. He filled in for an itinerant in the York circuit for a month in 1779. The circuit paid £6 for his mother and wanted to keep him. Having consulted Wesley he felt it his duty to return to his job. Adam Clarke was very concerned about his mother who lived in Ireland, and was pleased when in 1799 she went to live with his brother Tracy in Liverpool. Samuel Bardsley corresponded regularly with his widowed mother in Manchester and visited her whenever he could. Later we shall see that old preachers, especially when widowed, were often in the households of their children being looked after there, often for lengthy periods.[47]

There were also other relations of preachers in the ministry. John Nelson's grandson of the same name entered before Wesley's death. There were many uncles and nephews. There were paternal uncles like John Brown of Tanfield and his nephew Jonathan Brown. He had a nephew John Brown who entered in his turn. There were maternal uncles like Jonathan Catlow and his nephew Jonathan Edmondson, and John Allen and his nephew Robert Lomas. Others were related by marriage; James Anderson married Daniel Bumstead's niece. The former missionary William Warrener, when he returned from the West Indies in 1797, married the sister of the preacher Thomas Wood. All these were

---

[45] For Irish brothers see Chapter 11. The quotations are from *WMM* 1834: 881-4.

[46] Atmore; *Pawson L* 3; 25; MS Manchester Circuit Account Book at MARC which has payments to him for October 1761 to May 1762 and a large payment in from his father. Pawson said he died near Manchester 1762 and John Furz preached his funeral sermon.

[47] Lyth, *Methodism in York* 136-7, 303. See Chapter 19 Retirement.

Family

examples of the importance of kinship in eighteenth century society, in a period of dense and multiple relationships. Most people then lived in these intricate networks of close friends and families, which were important both in encouraging the spread of Methodism and then within Methodism and its later life.[48]

The quotation addressed to Robert Dall found at the beginning of this chapter came before he had a family. In July 1779 he married a thirty-two year old widow, Margaret Stevenson, who already had three daughters, aged twelve, eleven and five. He left the itinerancy and became a merchant in the Isle of Man, moving to Glasgow by 1785. By then the couple had four children of whom three, including twins, had died. On the 1st January 1785 another daughter, Susanna, was christened in Glasgow. Three more children, all boys, were born by 1790. Susanna and one son died in 1790, leaving the couple with a surviving family of six. In his 'Reminiscences' Dall wrote about Dumfries in 1787, where he was building a large chapel 'Dumfries kept me and my family still poor, but we were well satisfied with the most common fare and were comfortable...' Dall had a relatively 'wealthy wife,' which cushioned his family even in difficult circumstances.[49]

---

[48] See for example Davidoff and Hall, *Family Fortunes* xviii-xix and A. Turberfield, *John Scott Lidgett: Archbishop of British Methodism?* (London: Epworth, 2003) Appendix 2. For Warrener see Chapter 13 below.

[49] G. W. Davis, *The Robert Dall Story 1745-1828* (Arbroath: the author, 1995) 22.

CHAPTER 8

Circuits

*'O'er winter's bleak forests I roved
Or tried the impassable road:
With terrible dangers I strove
Then found a cold smokey abode.
A few hours there made my stay,
Then meeting the Tempest again
I weathered the cold winter's day
Exposed to the frost snow and rain.'
Benjamin Rhodes 'The Itinerants' Anthem.'*

Travel

John Wesley himself was celebrated as a ceaseless traveller. Travel was not easy. In Porter's words, the traveller shared his 'bed at the inn with strangers and fleas, and his roads with gibbeted corpses and highwaymen.' Porter also described livestock droves turning the roads into 'ribboned dung heaps.' Both Wesley and his preachers were helped by the development of roads in Britain in the eighteenth century, especially of turnpikes. Though the latter gradually improved travel in the later eighteenth century, in many country areas such as the Yarm circuit there was frequently little change away from the turnpike.[1]

A contemporary suggested that where Whitefield preferred the crowds, Wesley systematically visited little places. His people would flock to hear him. German Protestants frequently travelled large distances to preach or hear the word. In America and elsewhere itinerancy was the order of the day. Whitefield preached throughout the American colonies as well as Scotland, England and Wales. Zinzendorf travelled from the Baltic to Pennsylvania.[2]

Preachers and Circuits

Wesley's preachers were very different from most other ministers or clergy because of their unique sphere. A clergyman served his parish. The

---

[1] Porter, *English Society* 17, 191.
[2] Ward, *Faith and Faction* especially Chapter 13 John Wesley Traveller; Rosman, *Churches 1500-2000* 156.

Independent minister looked after his congregation in the chapel. Wesley's preacher rode round his circuit for a brief period, before going on to the next circuit. Only the Moravian pastors had a similar system and their circuits were different, with the pastor having to earn his own living, in at least one case as an itinerant tailor.[3]

The term 'circuit' described the practice of the preacher as well as a geographical area. From a very early stage Wesley asked his preachers to travel *round* circuits of the societies he had started. They were smaller versions of the 'national circuit' which he himself rode, including Cornwall, Bristol, London and Newcastle. In Baker's words, they 'covered in a series of smaller circles the same ground traversed by the larger circle of his own itinerancy.'[4] The circuit was Wesley's solution to maintaining the societies in between his visits. His lay helpers or 'Assistants' travelled round the societies at regular intervals of two weeks or more instead of him. In 1744 Wesley

> took some 15 or 20 Societies, more or less, which lay round some principal Society, in those parts and ...united them into what was called a Circuit. At the yearly Conference, he appointed two, three or four Preachers to one of these Circuits according to its extent, which was at first very considerable, sometimes taking in a part of three or four counties. Having received a list of the Societies forming his Circuit, (the Assistant) took his own station in it, gave to the other Preachers a Plan of it, and pointed out the day, when each should be at the place fixed for him, to begin a progressive motion round it, in such order as the plan directed... They now followed one another thro' all the Societies belonging to that Circuit, at stated distances of time.[5]

There might be the occasional unfilled day where the preacher could try a new place. Alternatively he might 'receive a sufficient call to a new place,' that is 'an invitation from a serious man, fearing God, who has a house to receive us.'[6] In January 1763 John Manners reported from the four man York circuit to John Wesley 'Since I was able, when I could be spared from the round I have laboured a good deal in fresh places; and in spring I shall think it my duty to do it more. The language of most places is; Come over and help us.'[7]

The first Methodist usage of the word 'circuit' in print seems to be in the *Minutes* of 1746 when seven circuits appeared. The word meant a group of societies and lay preachers were appointed to ride round them. In 1748 there

---

[3] F. Dreyer, *The Genesis of Methodism* (London: AUP, 1999) 65, suggested the first such was Johann Lange in Stuttgart and area 1739, a suggestive date in the rise of Methodism, but not early enough. For more on 'circuits' in Church history see page 405 below.
[4] FB Polity 230. Peter Howard has helped me clarify my ideas in this chapter.
[5] J. Benson, *An Apology for the Methodists* (London: Story, 1801) 201-2. *Minutes* 1763.
[6] *Minutes* 1: 452.
[7] *AM* 1782: 104.

were nine circuits and 71 societies which shows that then there were more like eight societies to a circuit rather than the fifteen or twenty of Benson's 1801 description.[8] During these early years the word 'round' was used as often as 'circuit.' However, 'circuit' became the established official term. Baker said that the term implied an ordered tour, so both societies and the other preachers knew where the individual preacher should be at any time.[9] In Bennet's Journal there is in 1744 an interesting example of how the organization was developing '10 (August) I came to Staley Hall where I met Mr Meyrick, not knowing of his coming. 11. After having given Mr Meyrick directions when to preach and where to be during his stay in Derbyshire...' Clearly Bennet was the expert on his own 'round' (neither word used here) and explained to the new itinerant the circuit and his role in it.[10] John Meyrick was one of John Wesley's friends from the south, new to the area.

Organization for these circuits soon began to develop and the first circuit quarterly meeting was held at a farmhouse on Todmorden Edge, presided over by the Rev. William Grimshaw in 1748. When Bennet described it he said it was a 'meeting of the leaders in the several societies belonging to William Darney, Etc.' Next, when a quarterly meeting at Woodley in October 1748 was held by him, he called it a meeting of the 'leaders in Derbyshire, Cheshire and Lancashire,' rather than of the circuit.[11] Wesley encouraged Bennet to introduce the quarterly meetings into other circuits.

Duties of the Preacher

Societies

In each society there were tasks for the preacher whose

> office is, in the absence of the minister:
> (1) To expound every morning and evening.
> (2) To meet the United Society, the Bands, the Select Society and the Penitents once a week.
> (3) To visit the Classes (London and Bristol excepted) once a month.
> (4) To hear and decide all differences.
> (5) To put the disorderly back on trial, and to receive on trial for the Bands or Society.
> (6) To see that the Stewards, the (Class) Leaders and the schoolmasters faithfully discharge their several offices.

---

[8] Peter Howard pointed out that both 'itinerant' and 'circuit' were used of the judiciary since at least the sixteenth century. For 1748 see K. B. Garlick, *Wesley's Chapel: An Illustrated History*. (London: Wesley's Chapel, n.d. c 1978) under the 1748 Conference.
[9] FB Polity 231.See also the description of the Yarm circuit later in this chapter.
[10] Valentine, *Mirror of the Soul* 87.
[11] Farmhouses were often used at first, such as Medrose for east Cornwall in the 1760s, T. Shaw, *A Methodist Guide to Cornwall* (Peterborough: MPH 2005) 37; *WJW* 26: 336.

(7) To meet the Leaders of the Bands and Classes weekly, and the Stewards and to overlook their accounts.

Wesley set this out in 1748 or 1749.[12] He was thinking of the large societies beginning in each of the new circuits. In fact the preacher rarely stayed long with most of the early societies because they were so small; to remain would be to overburden them. Much better for all was for the preacher to travel round the circuit and for another preacher to come in a fortnight's time. A typical Methodist itinerant was responsible for a largely rural circuit with several small towns. He was expected to complete this circuit every six weeks. His fellow preachers either followed or preceded him on the circuit. Hence, on a six week circuit, the people could expect preaching about every two weeks, but only rarely from an itinerant on a Sunday. The description in the quotation above was Wesley's ideal for the town society, the leading one in the circuit. There the preacher might stay for a whole weekend and later on for a whole week.

By 1763 there were a number of additional tasks laid down for the Assistant

(3) To keep watch-nights and love-feasts...
(5) To hold Quarterly meetings and therein diligently to inquire both into the spiritual and temporal state of each Society.
(6) To take care that every Society be supplied with books and that the money for them be constantly returned.
(7) To send from every quarterly meeting a circumstantial account to London of every remarkable conversion, and of everyone who dies in the triumph of faith.
(8) To take exact lists of the Societies every Easter, and bring them to the next Conference...
(10) To see that every Society have a private room and a set of the (Christian) Library for every helper.
(11) To write an account to Mr Wesley of all the defects of the helpers, which they themselves cannot cure...
(12) To travel with Mr Wesley if required, once a year through the Societies in his circuit.[13]

If there might be twenty or even forty societies in a circuit, this was no easy task Wesley was setting his preachers. Robert Costerdine was told in 1771 to 'meet the children and visit from house to house.' An explanation of the latter was given in a letter to Hannah Ball also in 1771 'I trust Mr Wells will be made a blessing to you and to many, especially if he visits from house to house; not only those with whom he eats or drinks, but all the Society from one end of the town to the other.' This brings out the additional point that meals were provided by the local Methodists. The burden was likely to fall on those better

---

[12] *WJW* 9: 270-1. It appeared first as a letter to Vincent Perronet possibly dated 1748, with the printed versions in 1749. The visiting the classes once a month had become the more possible once a quarter by the 1772 edition.
[13] *Myles* 91 quoting *Minutes* 1: 596-97. For more on the Assistant see pages 81-3 above.

off, because they had more from which to provide, and so Wesley was insisting his preachers should visit the poorer ones as well.[14]

Preaching

The preachers were required always to prepare carefully. Methodist itinerants were certainly expected not to read their sermons, but to be spontaneous, inspired in their preaching by the Holy Spirit. The leading ideas should be clear in their mind. They must have the Bible and should have some notes. They should pray extempore first for 'no more than eight or ten minutes (at most) without intermission.' Wesley instructed them to follow the three part form of the sermon: preamble, points of doctrine and application. They were to preach on the great and vital doctrines of redemption, free will, grace, justification and sanctification, and to identify the sinner in order to persuade him or her to change. They tended to preach on New Testament texts with practical application to the daily lives of their hearers, using examples like farming or craftsmanship, housewifery, travel and the temptations of daily life. They sought to preach 'with liberty,' by which they meant their oratory was powerful and affected their hearers. They expected results such as sinners crying out as they were affected, and these would be greeted as evidence of the necessity for their preaching and for their hearers to be 'convicted' of sin. Texts were often drawn from the millenarian books of the Bible such as Daniel and Revelation, and current events were frequently commented upon as being beyond ordinary expectations and showing God's intervention in the world. They would use recent occurrences, or even what was happening at the time like an attack on the itinerant as he preached, as examples in the sermons. The preaching services were often followed by love-feasts and prayer-meetings. At these the message could be made relevant to each individual who could share the preacher's experiences of conversion, sanctification and supernatural mercies, which could again be explained and accepted.[15]

At Conference Wesley was keen to question the preachers about what they did, just as he wanted to hear them preaching there rather than preach himself. What he demanded from them was clarity, so that they would be understood. He wished to prevent shouting, or 'screaming' as he called it, about which there are a number of references in his letters. He was concerned about this because of the effect on their health. He was even more interested in their success as preachers, which was partly why they had to bring the numbers in the society to Conference each year. Preachers with regular decreases of membership would

---

[14] *JWL* 5: 283 letter to Costerdine, 291 letter to Hannah Ball.
[15] Andrews, *Methodists and America* 78-92, quoting F. Asbury and T. Coke, eds, *Doctrine and Discipline* (Philadelphia: Tuckniss, 1798) 84-85; Wigger, 'Fighting Bees' 124-133; R. P. Heitzenrater, 'John Wesley's principles and practice in preaching' in Sykes, ed, *Beyond the Boundaries* 12-35.

be warned, or could even be dropped altogether.[16]

Many itinerants recorded the details of their preaching in terms of places preached at, texts used, date etc, following the example set by Wesley himself in his sermon registers. George Story's list of the societies and their membership in the Isle of Wight for 1783-85 also included a record of what sermons he preached at each society during those years. Most itinerants kept manuscript journals and many of these included details of sermons. Some kept their manuscript sermons and so two volumes of Adam Clarke's survive, dated as around 1808.[17] Because of Wesley's opposition to publishing by the preachers without his permission, they published few sermons in his lifetime. However, at least fifteen of those who left and were thus out of his control, made their sermons available to a wider public. After Wesley's death twenty-eight or more of those who died in the work, including some of the more important preachers, published some of their sermons. Sermons tended to be positive, about the blessedness of faith and hope for the believer, rather than negative and concentrating on hellfire and damnation. As Hempton suggests, they dealt with themes such as 'grace, godliness, repentance, temporal and eternal joy, perseverance, vigilance and assurance.'[18]

The problem of shouting continued after Wesley's death. Adam Clarke described his fellow preacher John S. Pipe in 1803: 'a pipe he is of the first bore and magnitude. He has decidedly adopted the shouting system and opens on the people in the most deep-mouthed manner. He is full of life and zeal.'[19] The 'life and zeal' was also typical of their preaching. Thomas Rutherford described his fellow preacher M'Nab as having 'the most copious flow of natural simple oratory of any man I ever heard.'[20] Zachary Macaulay in West Africa reported of the former Methodist preacher turned missionary Melville Horne that he was a fine preacher, who, with 'fire, perspicuity and simplicity,' was able to move the congregation.[21] In America in February 1780 the experienced Francis Asbury, not far from his lowest point during the American Revolution, testified to the preaching of the American Joseph Cromwell

---

[16] Heitzenrater, 'Wesley's preaching.'

[17] Wesley's sermon registers survive for 1747-61 and 1787-8. The Salisbury or Sarum book is in the Story papers, part of the Frank Baker Collection at Duke University. The Clarke sermons are in the Everett papers at MARC. Three of Thomas Wride's MS sermons are also there ref PLP 115/9/24/1-3.

[18] J. Wigger, 'Fighting Bees' 125-8; Hempton, *Empire* 74-78; Osborn, *Bibliography* is very useful for tracing these sermons.

[19] *JWL* 8: 27. Copy letter 1803 in Adam Clarke letter book at MARC MA 9888.

[20] D. P. Thomson, *Lady Glenorchy and her Churches-The Story of 200 Years* (Perth: Munro, 1967) 29.

[21] A. Porter, *Religion versus Empire? British Protestant Missionaries and Overseas Expansion 1700-1914* (Manchester: Manchester UP, 2002) 47.

At nine o'clock (a.m.) we had a love-feast-a time of great tenderness; after some time brother Cromwell spoke, his words went through me, as they have every time I have heard him-he is the only man I have heard in America with whose words I am never tired; I always admire his unaffected simplicity; he is a prodigy- a man who cannot write or read well, yet according to what I have heard, he is much like the English John Brown or the Irish John Smith... The power of God attends him in every place, he hardly ever opens his mouth in *vain*; some are generally cut to the heart.[22]

Preaching was important to the early Methodists. It was one of the major reasons why Methodism was so attractive and why it grew so rapidly. In England, in America and elsewhere, men and women flocked to hear them.

Worship

The first of all the preacher's tasks was to conduct worship and it was no accident this came first. Worship was the chief priority, his most important work. The early Methodists fed on it spiritually and it was one of the main reasons why they wanted to attend Conference, because there were so many services there. Not only the preaching, but also the prayers, the reading in public of the Christian Library, the singing of hymns, the feeling of being with and worshipping with others who had the same concerns built up the preachers as much as any other Methodist. Preachers must inspire others and as a result of the worship they were themselves also inspired. Because of its origin in field preaching, worship as conducted by the preachers took one of two forms. The first, in some town chapels, used the liturgy of the Book of Common Prayer, though some prayer would be extempore. The other, more common, was two or three hymns with extempore prayer and the sermon in between them. A Scripture reading was only introduced later. Hymns were sung without accompaniment, led by the preacher or a 'principal singer.' Worship tended to be judged by its immediate effect on the worshippers. It was this freedom of worship and emphasis on the sermon which led both to their success and their need to separate from the Church.[23] The hymns, used as a devotional exercise as well as for singing, provided a further spiritual experience. Methodism's growth and strength cannot be understood unless this spiritual dimension is grasped.[24]

The range of different worship services and where they were held needs to

---

[22] *Asbury Jol* 1: 333. For John Smith see Chapters 4 and 11. For John Brown see *WJW* 24/4/1747, 28/9/1749.

[23] *HMGB* 2: 123-132, 180; D. M. Chapman, *Born in Song: Methodist Worship in Britain* (Warrington: Church in the Market Place, 2006) 44-51. There are different descriptions of Methodist services in the eighteenth century and this has led to different views among modern historians, for example Burdon and Wallwork.

[24] Cf. Chapter 2 above.

be examined. There was preaching outside, usually in summer and in new areas, often each time in the same public space like the market cross or Gwennap Pit in Cornwall. At Alpraham in Cheshire John Nelson, who preached there first, stood under a pear tree in a friend's garden, and since Methodist preachers did that for some time, they became known as the 'pear tree preachers.' For preaching inside there were the house meeting, the barn, the hired room and later the preaching house, whether octagon or rectangle. This redefined sacred space. Society meetings and preaching services and the rest were also held in cottages, both front rooms and back rooms, farmhouse kitchens or outbuildings, lofts, taverns, shops, factories, and foundries, like the one at London made famous by Wesley himself. In many places these were where the society met for anything from ten to over a hundred years, sometimes in the same place for the whole of that time. In Cornwall, for example, they included 'William Chenhall's inn opposite the Church gate at St Just; James Dabbs' opposite the inn at Probus; Richard Wood's in Middle St, St Isaac; William Flamank's in Fore St, St Austell; John Rommet's house, and later Zebedee Minard's at Polperro; John Nance's at the top of Street an Garrow, St Ives; the humble cottage of the penurious Mally Short by the bridge at Stratton; and the more imposing homes of Medrose, in Luxulyan, and Cosawes, near Ponsanooth.' Wherever it was, the service would be notable both for the directness of the sermon and the personal nature of the hymns sung. Hymns would be lined out for what would be at first the illiterate majority. The love feast, the class meeting, the watch night service and the Covenant Service were all different mechanisms for varying the diet of worship and fellowship and providing the 'means of grace.' They offered meat for the spiritually hungry with testimony and fellowship. However, these services were not particularly orderly. On the one hand frequently there was opposition, and local youths might hurl curses or stones at the preacher, whether the preaching was inside or out. But, well into the nineteenth century there were stories of youths who came to mock and became converted. On the other hand, the worshippers were often carried away. Particularly in Cornwall there would be wild scenes of singing, clapping and shouting.[25]

Pastoral Care

It is also important to emphasize the pastoral tasks of the preacher. While the preaching and the conduct of worship came first, the looking after of the

---

[25] Church 1949 210-288; *WJW* 20: 486; *HMGB* 1: 257-75; J. R. Watson, *The English Hymn: A Critical and Historical Study* (Oxford: Clarendon, 1997). Turner, *Wesley.* 49-72, which includes an excellent clear summary of the 'instituted and prudential means of grace.' Alpraham is in F. F. Bretherton, *Early Methodism in and around Chester* (Chester: Phillipson, 1903) 9-10. For Cornwall see Hempton, *Empire* 25-6. The quotation comes from Shaw, *Cornish Methodism* 21-22.

people, both inside and outside of the societies, came not far behind. They met the Society, the class and the band; they spoke to the children, they cared for the sick and dying and visited from house to house. John Nelson wrote in 1755 in his report to Charles Wesley that

> the last time I was at Sunderland I took nine fresh members into the Society in one day and there hath hardly been one week this winter but someone hath stepped into the pool in the north rounds (*sic*)... (in Birstall) on Sunday his arm was bared amongst us in such a manner that some was struck to the ground, and one Magdalen that night was allowed to kiss the feet of Jesus. O Sir, join in prayer with us for her that she may stand, for such a brand was never plucked out of the burning in Birstall before... Br(other) Jones[26] is here. He is very weak so that he is to attend [be waited on] both day and night, and Williams[27] is but poorly yet, so that my wife is hurried beyond her strength, for we have not had the house free from sick preachers these fifteen months, and without death or a miracle healing I know not when it will be free. My wife hath lately had a pleuritic fever, but is much better, and our house is so taken up with sick preachers and nurses to wait on them that we have not room for the labouring preachers and our own family.[28]

The Methodist preacher led a very organized life of travel, preaching, visiting and a round of services. It was not all giving and doing. Often these services were times when others would contribute at such occasions as love-feasts and the preacher would *receive* the spiritual nourishment he needed. Alone at night, or like Asbury in the woods, he would reflect on his day, pray about his concerns and refresh himself for the business of tomorrow. He would add to his journal, receive letters from his brother itinerants and from hosts in previous circuits, and reply when he could, preferably when someone was travelling in their direction. The itinerant preachers lived the disciplined life of the Christian, in Charles Wesley's words 'twixt the mount and multitude, Doing or receiving good.'[29]

---

[26] A 'Magdalen' was a prostitute. 'Jones' was the former blacksmith Joseph Jones (1722-?), who was stationed that year in the Haworth circuit. He entered in 1744 and left in 1760 to settle as a farmer.

[27] This was either Enoch Williams entered 1742, in Yorkshire 1753-4, a half itinerant in London 1755 (the more likely), or Thomas Williams (1718/20-1787), the Welsh-born first preacher in Ireland, see below Chapter 11 note 2.

[28] MARC PLP 78-53-1 MS letter Nelson, Birstall 4/3/1755 to Charles Wesley, printed *GHR* 157-8.

[29] From the last verse of hymn 598 in *MHB*. The full version is: 'Vessels, instruments of grace, Pass we thus our happy days Twixt the mount and multitude, Doing or receiving good; Glad to pray and labour on, Till our earthly course is run, Till we, on the sacred tree, Bow the head and die like Thee.'

Wesley's Organization

Size

The circuits were at first enormous. Bennet described his circuit in 1749. 'My circuit is 150 miles in two weeks, during which time I preach publicly 34 times, besides meeting the Societies, visiting the sick, and transacting the temporal business.'[30] The early Staffordshire circuit included as far west as Shrewsbury and as far south as Stroud, while its centre was Wednesbury. In most of Britain circuits became a little smaller over time, but in Wesley's lifetime they remained large and long by twentieth or even nineteenth century British standards. Even as late as the early nineteenth century circuits in areas like Wales or the Pennines, or some rural areas, especially Cumbria, remained difficult and extensive.[31]

Early circuits were also unrelated to each other. The map of Methodist circuits in 1749-50 illustrates this well. There was a huge gap between Cornwall and Bristol and another between the Newcastle circuit and those to the south. In the vast area east of Lincoln and Oxford and north of London there was no Methodist society at all.[32] Very often, when a circuit was divided, the new circuits were expected to cover a much wider area than the old.

The Irish Castlebar circuit in 1769 included Ballyshannon (in County Donegal), Longford, Sligo and Galway, including parts of at least seven counties and most of the province of Connaught. An English circuit like Colne, as late as 1786, might be smaller, but it was still 231 miles to travel on a six week round in which 61 sermons would be preached. The six week round was completed eight times a year, making 1,808 miles, all to be done in Pennine weather on foot or horseback. The Salisbury circuit at the same time included the Isle of Wight and Swanage as well as much of Wiltshire, in other words parts of three counties. The preacher was to follow the pattern of travel in his circuit exactly, so everyone knew where he would be. Wesley described this as 'All our preachers should be as punctual as the sun, never standing still or moving out of their course.'[33] Not all preachers did this. Zachariah Yewdall in Scotland in 1787 complained that the senior preacher John Pawson, living in Edinburgh, never took his turn at Dalkeith but left it to others like Yewdall. Pawson, who himself often complained about the shortcomings of his brethren, should have known better.[34]

---

[30] MS Letter to John Wesley in MARC Bennet MSS BNNJ (25/04/1749) Colman box.

[31] Cf. the problems facing the Countess of Huntingdon's Connexion as explained in Harding, *Countess's Connexion* 88-91.

[32] Heitzenrater map on 180.

[33] *JWL* 4: 34. For Colne see Jessop, *Rossendale* 397; Map in E. A. Rose, 'Methodism in South Lancashire to 1800' in *Transactions of the Lancashire and Cheshire Antiquarian Society* 81 (1982) 81. For Castlebar see T. Dixon's report in Tyerman BMM. For Salisbury see Story MSS at Duke.

[34] *JWL* 7: 385.

Yarm Circuit

A typical circuit to be examined in detail was the Yarm circuit in 1768 (see Map 2). This had originally been formed from the York circuit, probably soon after 1759. Osmotherley was the oldest society, founded by Wesley as early as 1745. In 1768 Yarm was a three preacher circuit with 892 members in 36 different societies. The three preachers were the Assistant Jacob Rowell, whose records provide the evidence for this, James Brownfield and William Brammah. Even in southern County Durham there were no large industrial enterprises, but there were many thriving ports on the north-east coast where Methodism was already strong, like Whitby, Yarm itself, Hartlepool and Stockton. The main centres of the circuit were these and inland market towns like Thirsk, Stokesley and Northallerton. It was a six weeks' circuit, and so twice a quarter each preacher rode round the circuit which he would do eight times in the year. Each society on the map has the initial for the day of the week when a preacher would sleep there. The furthest distance between overnight stops was nine miles, and most societies were four or five miles from each other and it could be walked if need be. The major centres had a preacher every other week for the weekend. Village societies like Castleton or Fryup in Eskdale only saw the preacher on a week night for the class meeting and preaching. The exception to this was Hutton Rudby, a strong Methodist centre, which had travelling preachers every other Sunday. It was a semi-industrial village with many linen weavers. The parish church was at Rudby in the next village. Once a fortnight the three preachers would return close to the centre of the circuit so that they could meet if they needed to discuss anything. One preacher was always at Yarm that weekend, the other two were at Hutton Rudby and at Stokesley, the greatest distance being the eight miles from Stokesley to Yarm. Quarterly meetings would be held that weekend once a quarter, possibly at Hutton Rudby as the one closest to the other two. The circuit steward was George Merryweather, merchant of Yarm, a long time correspondent of Wesley. Yarm was a convenient stopping point for Wesley on his journeys to and fro to Newcastle and the northeast. Merryweather had first invited Wesley to Yarm in 1748.[35]

Change in Size of Circuits

The number of societies and members in the circuits varied; Devonshire circuit

---

[35] MS Jacob Rowell's pocket books in Durham Record Office M/BC 83-5 printed in *MRWN* 1905: 47. For Merryweather, Yarm and Osmotherley see *DOMBI*. Brownfield was the first preacher to preach in Glaisdale (J. Davison, *Chronicles of Lealholm and Glaisdale* (n. pl., Duck, n.d. c. 1991) 37) which was not in Rowell's list. This shows it must have been on a Wednesday, when travelling from Fryup to Castleton, probably next year in late 1769. I am indebted to Ted Royle for information on Hutton Rudby and to Peter Howard for suggestions about the circuit.

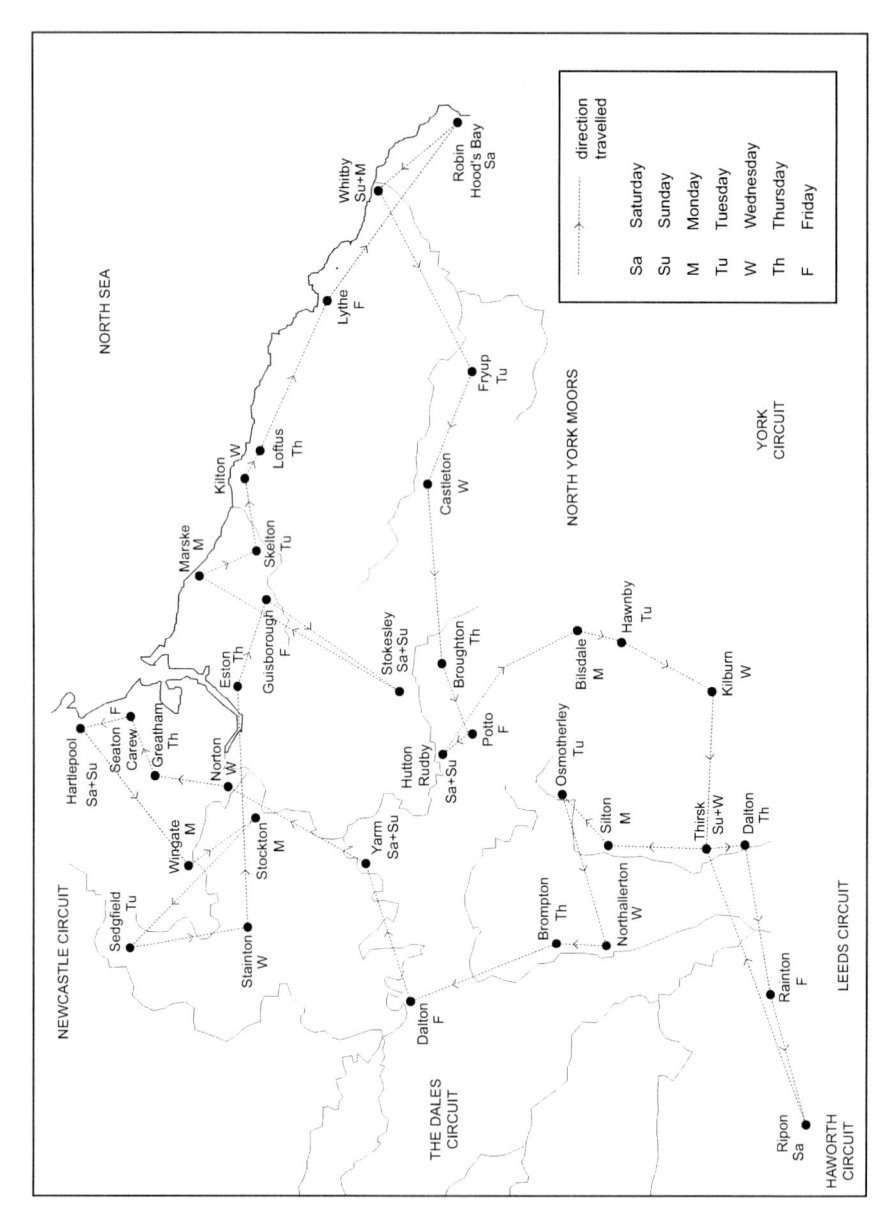

Map 2: Yarm Circuit 1768
The three preachers travelled round the 36 different societies

Circuits 139

in 1778 had 18 societies while Macclesfield in 1786 had 35. These were probably typical numbers for the south and north respectively. Devonshire had only 453 members, Macclesfield 972. Both circuits had two preachers.[36] Even before Wesley's death circuits tended to become smaller, at least in terms of the distance for the itinerant to cover. For example, the three preacher Manchester circuit of 1784 was a six week round, but for almost half the time the preacher stayed in Manchester itself. In between he made three 'mini' rounds, one south west including Davyhulme and Stockport, one north east to Middleton, Ashton and Oldham, and one south east to Stockport, New Mills and Oldham. The total travelled in the weeks 'out' was only 120 miles. The three preacher York circuit of 1798 had similar distances, a six week round, of which three separate Sundays were in York, alternating with three separate weeks out round the villages. These were all within ten miles of York, the furthest being Alne to the northwest and Westow to the south. Total distance outside York was about 165 miles. The only other town was Tadcaster which, like York itself, always had a travelling preacher on a Sunday. It was a circuit which could be walked.[37]

Movement between Circuits

At first Wesley moved the preachers from one circuit to another each month or quarter. Thus in the early 1750s new preachers came to the Cork circuit each quarter. Later it might be every six months. It was only from 1758 that most preachers might remain in a circuit for as long as a year, unless there was some good reason why they should be moved. Not until 1765 was it usual to stay for a whole year, hence the annually printed *Minutes*.[38]

Preachers were at first often asked to travel great distances to reach their next circuit. As they got older they tended to stay in a similar area, sometimes that from which they had come. The tendency always was to want to stay longer. In 1771 Wesley wrote to Christopher Hopper 'I see an evil growing among us; preachers *claim* to be two years together in the same round, because it has been suffered sometimes. If it be so I must suffer it no more. Every preacher shall change every year; unless they will leave it to *my* judgement to

---

[36] E. Chick, *Methodism in Exeter* (Exeter: Drayton, 1907) 48, Story MSS at Duke University. Notebook 7: 15-64.

[37] The Manchester circuit was described by Pawson in his letter to Atmore in the neighbouring Colne circuit. He was trying to organise a time when the two friends could meet. *Pawson L* 1: 25. The York circuit is in Lyth, *Methodism in York* 305. The Manchester circuit had slightly more members (1757 to York's 1600).

[38] For the Cork circuit see T. Whittemore, ed, *The Life of John Murray: Preacher of Universal Salvation* (Boston: Trumpet, 1833) 24; cf. Baker, *Wesley and the Church* 226. A good reason can be illustrated by James Jones remaining in Staffordshire. He was a wealthy man who built the first chapel at Tipton himself. *WJW* 20: 10-2; 26: 286, 485; *PWHS* 4 (1904) 116-7.

make an exception now and then when I may see sufficient cause.'[39] By the 1780s it was more possible to be allowed to stay for two years in the same circuit, but only the Assistant would do.[40] But even at the end of Wesley's life, two years was the maximum a preacher could expect to remain in a circuit and was still unusual. Wesley was here holding a line for what he believed strongly, against the wishes of both preachers and circuits. Circuits wanted to retain the better preachers for an extra year. Most preachers wished to stay longer. In 1776 Wesley wrote to Kitty Warren of Pembrokeshire, who asked for 'her' Assistant, Joshua Keighley, to stay another (third) year 'every year I have many applications for the continuance of profitable preachers more than two years in a circuit. I have had several such within these two or thee months... But I dare not comply.' It created problems because one exception meant everyone clamoured to be allowed a similar 'exception.' As Wesley told Sarah Crosby on the same subject in 1789 'When I broke my rule formerly in favour of Mr Pawson, by letting him stay a third year in Bristol, I did not hear the last of it for several years. I will not, cannot, dare not, break it again, only in favour of a wife near the time of lying-in.'[41] The Scot George Mowat, who entered in 1770, was still moving to a new circuit every year in the 1780s except for 1787, when having moved to Epworth from Gainsborough in February to pacify the local squabbles, he was allowed to remain for 18 months! After nearly twenty years of travel his first two year period in one circuit did not happen until 1789, when he spent two years in Horncastle.[42]

Range of Circuits Travelled

Thomas Simpson, who came from Scotland, was sent first to Wiltshire, then Devon. After that he returned to Scotland and did not venture further south than Newcastle. Thomas Tattershall, who entered in 1781 from Barnsley, had as his first three circuits Epworth, the Isle of Man and Londonderry. After 1785 he travelled in Norfolk, Lincolnshire, South Yorkshire and Derbyshire. Some went much further. James Watson began in 1771 in Aberdeen. In 1772 he was sent to the Dales, in 1773 to Newry, and then found himself the next year back in Aberdeen, about 250 miles each time he moved circuit. In 1775 he travelled to Cornwall, a distance of 700 miles! Another example is Edward Slater who entered from Settle in 1770. As Wesley's coachman previously he should have been used to the itinerant life. In 1770 he was sent to Sussex (50 miles from

---

[39] *JWL* 5: 279.
[40] Howard said that out of 1,517 appointments in the 1780s only 250 were for a second year, of which 187 were Assistants, see WHS Conference 1983 Report (typescript in WHS Library) 10.
[41] *JWL* 7: 330 (18th June 1786) and 8: 143; article on Circuits in *DOMBI*; FB Polity; Heitzenrater 162, 234.
[42] *WMM* 1850: 5.

London), next year to Athlone (450 miles for his journey), and the following year Limerick (75 miles). He returned to Haworth (280 miles), after which he had two relatively short moves to Staffordshire (120) and Derbyshire (40).

The early years of Methodism were worst. So John Fenwick, entering around 1750 probably from Sunderland, was first in Ireland, second back at Newcastle and then returned to Ireland. His next circuit was Cornwall. Such an itinerary was not unusual. Most preachers in the 1750s went to Ireland, and that did not just mean Dublin but travelling to places like Cork, Limerick and Athlone at least. In turn each of these circuits covered wide areas.[43]

Numbers per Circuit

Circuits were to be manned with three preachers wherever possible. Most had three after 1765. More than four and the circuit was too large and Wesley looked to divide it. In his old age, however, he was adamant that circuits should not be split unless there was no alternative. To William Horner he wrote in 1790 'I am determined there shall be no circuits in England with more than four preachers as long as I live. Four are too many, if I can help it.' In March 1790 he wrote to another preacher, Jasper Winscom 'I am... in no haste to multiply preachers or divide circuits. Most of our circuits are too small rather than too large. I wish we had no circuit with fewer than three preachers in it, or less than four hundred miles' riding in five weeks. Certainly no circuit shall be divided before Conference. If we do not care we shall degenerate into milksops.'[44] Laymen and preachers might want different kinds of circuits, smaller and easier to manage with the preacher remaining in one place. Wesley was determined to do what he thought best, however unpopular it might be with both preacher and people. So in 1786 he wrote to a layman in Hull 'We entirely disapprove of such a division of the Hull Circuit as has been sent to us. We totally reject the thought of a preacher staying a fortnight together in one place. There is no precedent of this in England, nor shall be as long as I live.'[45] The reference to

---

[43] *PWHS* 54 (2003) 29, 33-35 for Simpson and Slater. For Tattersall see *AM* 1784: 45-50, 103-7, Watson see Steele, *Barnard Castle*, and *WJW* 22: 333 n69, and Fenwick see *WJW* 22: 333 n70.

[44] *JWL* 8: 200, 206. Horner was the Assistant at Oxford with two preachers with him. Winscom was a prominent layman turned itinerant. Despite this letter Salisbury circuit was divided in 1790 into Sarum (Salisbury) with two preachers and Portsmouth with three preachers. It had been one of the largest English circuits. *Cirplan* 12 (2001) 4.

[45] *JWL* 7: 337 letter to Mr Torry or Terry of Hull. He went on to say that 'No one of my preachers must be still while I live' Telford printed the approved Plan. However, Hull *was* actually divided that year contrary to Wesley's apparent wishes with Pocklington, listed in the plan he approved being separated off. The two preachers left took it in turns to be in Hull, every other Sunday preaching at Beverley and Hull Bridge. If Conference, that is the preachers, wanted smaller circuits by this time, often they obtained them despite Wesley's protests. Cf W. H. Thompson, *Early Chapters in Hull Methodism*

England is interesting. It did happen in Scotland, where preachers often stayed in towns for long periods. After his death even English circuits became geographically smaller and urban preachers at least tended to remain in the towns, going home to their own beds each night, rather than making long journeys and only returning home after substantial intervals.

It is possible to study his circuits from 1765 to 1790, and to have snapshots of them before that. As early as 1746 when seven circuits were delimited and preachers changed each month, only one, Wales, had just one preacher assigned to it. Two circuits had two preachers each, but already the majority, four circuits, had three preachers each. Despite division and redivision of circuits, this pattern continued in England to the end of Wesley's life. In 1765, for instance, there were five circuits with four preachers (including London), eight with three, twenty-one with two and only nine with one. Of those nine, five were in Scotland and Ireland where distances were greater. By 1780 there were eight with four preachers, twenty-four with three, thirty-one with two and no circuit with only one preacher. If circuits became larger than four preachers, they were divided. The 400 miles he suggested to Winscom could often be fewer, as with the Colne circuit of 239 miles in six weeks.

The Preacher in his Circuit

Foot or Horseback?

As is well known Wesley rode and so did most of his preachers. Some walked, especially in the earlier years, and certainly needed strong legs. In 1786 the Colne circuit had three preachers but only two horses for them, so they had to walk at least a third of the time. Sometimes conditions were too bad for the horse. Matthew Lumb wrote later about the Dales circuit in the winter of 1783 'The winter was very hard, so that it was many times impossible to cross the mountains with a horse; therefore at three different times I walked in my boots and great coat, about one hundred and fifty miles.' Even as late as 1794, when the young John Braithwaite went home to Whitehaven from London, the last section was to be walked in four days from Ellel 'to Plumb Tree Bank 20 miles, on Thursday to Ambleside 18 miles, on Friday to Keswick sixteen, and on Saturday to Whitehaven about thirty, in all 84 miles.'[46] The 'all walked' of the Primitive Methodist early preachers was not the rule for the early Wesleyans. Most rode their own horses to their new appointment, even if it was as far away as Ireland. In August 1769 Wesley wrote to the newly accepted preacher Robert Wilkinson 'Your best way is to carry your own horse over from Whitehaven, or rather Portpatrick, where you have a short and sure passage; then ride on to the

---

1746-1800 (London: Kelly, 1895) 37,41.
[46] Lumb's quotation is in Steele, *Barnard Castle.* 148. The Itinerants' Anthem at the start of this chapter was probably written by Rhodes about the same Dales circuit in which he travelled in 1782, see Batty, *Bygone Reeth* 48-9; Dickinson, *Braithwaite* 206.

widow Cumberland's at Lisburn, and any of our Preachers whom you meet with will direct you to Charlemount or Augher.' Thomas Olivers rode the same horse for 25 years, for what has been estimated as 100,000 miles. It speaks volumes for the stamina of both horse and rider.[47]

Sometimes the preacher was given a horse. In March 1762 Wesley wrote to Rankin, the Assistant in Sussex 'Before eight weeks are ended, the Societies will be able to secure you an horse.'[48] Most early chapels like the New Room at Bristol were built with a stable for the horses, sometimes to be turned into a kitchen or toilet in the twentieth century.

The availability of the horse depended partly on funds and partly on how large the circuit was. Wesley wrote to John Bredin (probably in Coleraine) in Ireland in 1781 'It is hardly worthwhile to keep an horse for the sake of three or four little places. We have need to save all possible expense. Several of our preachers in England now walk their Circuits.' However, whether on foot or on horseback, the preacher was expected by Wesley to be constantly on the move. He was required to stand, not sit, when writing his letters to Wesley! Wesley wrote to John Valton in 1782 'You should take care never to write long at any one time, and always write standing; never on any account leaning on your stomach.'[49]

Troubles with horses were legion. On April 6th 1748 Wesley was at Philipstown in Ireland and 'As soon as I mounted my horse, he began to snort and run backward without any visible cause. One whipped him from behind and I before, but it profited nothing. He leaped to and fro, from side to side, till he came over against a gateway, into which he ran backward and tumbled head over heels. I rose unhurt. He then went on quietly.' In 1778 John Pritchard reported more prosaically that in the Northampton circuit 'In winter my horse fell ill; and I being poor (for a Methodist Preacher is likely to be poor for as long as he lives), and the people poor also, I travelled the winter and spring quarters on foot, about 12 hundred miles.'[50] As late as 1801 at Birstall, Pawson reported 'my poor mare struck a nail into her foot to the very bone; ...whether she will ever recover is very uncertain.' Preachers might later use the mail coach as these became established, particularly to travel longer distances, for example going to Conference.[51]

Wesley was most concerned about the care of horses. In 1765 he had the

---

[47] The quotation 'all walked' is from K. Lysons, *A Little Primitive* (Buxton: Church in the Market Place, 2001) 33. *JWL* 5: 145-6. Wilkinson was a Durham schoolteacher who had been dismissed from his job for his Methodist preaching by the Vicar of Stanhope. He knew Whitehaven well because Rowell had sent him into the Whitehaven circuit in the previous year.

[48] *JWL* 4: 180.

[49] *JWL* 7: 84-56, 101. Hindmarsh commented on this that the itinerant wrote his life 'in itinerant mode-in snatches' (*Conversion Narrative* 240).

[50] *WJW* 20: 217; *EMP* 6: 266.

[51] *Pawson L* 3: 51.

question added in the *Minutes* 'Are all the Preachers merciful to their beasts?' To this the Answer was 'perhaps not. Every one ought, 1 Never to ride hard. 2 To see with his own eyes his horse rubbed fed and bedded.' In 1770 this was added to the *Large Minutes*. In 1780 it was translated out of the question and answer format to the more positive 'Be merciful to your beast. Not only ride moderately but see with your own eyes that your horse be rubbed, fed and bedded.' It was a mark of the financial problems facing the Connexion when at the Leeds Conference Wesley warned preachers that they would have to support their own horses during Conference.[52]

Accommodation

Local Methodists at first and often long into the nineteenth century provided the preacher with a place to stay. Sometimes they would give him their bed while they slept on the floor. At others the only place was on the floor. Nanny Blake of Wadebridge in Cornwall gave the preacher her only room to sleep, while she passed the night in the old arm chair in the passage outside. Food would be short, but usually the preacher received the best they had. At Botternell, also in Cornwall, Molly Nile put aside some choice meat for Adam Clarke, but on at least one occasion, the cat found it first! At Stratton nearby, Mally Short, who could only afford barley bread for herself, somehow managed a wheaten loaf for the preacher. His clothes would be dried and mended and washed if he stayed long enough. The care shown for the early itinerant by the ordinary Methodist member should be remembered. In the literature the itinerant usually appears as the hero. Equally self-denying, persistent and heroic were the local members who hosted the preacher, but had to remain behind and face persecution later, often without leadership because the itinerant had left.

Next, accommodation might be hired, with the preacher still often staying with a local Methodist. In 1789 when Wesley wrote to the Assistant in Brecon, William Holmes, he addressed the letter 'to Mr W. Holmes, at Miss Williams, milliner, in Brecon.' The difference from the early days was that Miss Williams should have received regular payments from the circuit stewards to cover at least some of her costs. The hosts in the local societies would not usually receive payments because the preacher would only stay one night each time he came, or two at most. Each preacher would stay longer in the circuit town, though rarely with the other preachers.[53]

Sometimes preaching houses would be built with a 'prophet's chamber' beside for the preachers to stay in whenever they came. Such a one was the house at Trewint originally provided by Digory Isbell and his wife in 1742 for John Nelson on his first visit to Cornwall. This survives as a museum today, a

---

[52] *Minutes* 1862 ed vol 1: 529, 547; *WJW* 23: 218 n99.

[53] *CMHA* 8: 78; T. Shaw, *Methodism in the Camelford and Wadebridge Circuit 1743-1963* (Camelford: the author, 1963) 15; *JWL* 8: 37.

powerful memento of the Wesleyan itinerancy on the route into Cornwall, and an important jumping off point for the crossing of Bodmin Moor, the last major obstacle on the way to the distant Methodist haven of west Cornwall. Also preserved is the prophet's chamber at Mount Zion, Ogden, above Halifax. In York at first a room was rented for the preacher at a cost of 30 shillings a year to the circuit. By 1774 a larger dwelling was hired next to the chapel. There is a list of the furniture for that year. In 1780 a house was built costing £305, with a carpet to replace the preacher's previous piece of matting.[54]

When eventually houses for preachers were provided, often others would live there and act as hosts, but preachers were expected to have most of their meals out with local Methodists. At Rochester, according to George Osborn's description, the Chapel House was built in 1774

> For some years after the Chapel House was built, it was inhabited by John Baxter, Mr Ewings and Mr Bowles, and the preachers used to lodge with them as they came round the (Kent) Circuit, and go out to the Friends for their meals, breakfasting at one house, dining at another etc, according to a plan made out for the victualling of the preachers, and what meals were deficient in the plan they took at the Chapel House, for which a regular charge was made of 4d for breakfast, 6d for dinner, 4d for tea and 4d for supper, which was paid by the Society Stewards.[55]

Even when such a system was replaced by the preachers' families being the main occupants of the dwelling, the houses were often filled with non-paying guests. These were Methodists who were travelling from town to town who seemed to have thought it almost their right to stay in the preacher's house. Not all were young and poor like the twenty-year old James Mort from Newcastle-on-Tyne travelling to Burslem in 1790

> In Leeds I stopped a few days. Mr James Wood who was then in the Leeds Circuit and to whom I was known kindly entertained me. I was much refreshed in my mind among the pious friends in this favoured place. My next stage was to Manchester. Sleeping a night in a large town in a public house I much dreaded; I therefore repaired to the preacher's house to enquire if I could be recommended to private lodgings. After some fruitless inquiry, it was agreed I could sleep there. Mrs Rodda, after a little shyness treated me more like her own child than a stranger. After breakfast and praying with the family, I set off for Newcastle under Lyme.[56]

---

[54] To see Mount Zion and Trewint consult the annual publication of *Methodist Heritage www.methodist.org.uk* (Heritage) (accessed 12/12/2008). For York see Lyth, *Methodism in York* 110-1.

[55] M. F. Osborn, 'Some Notes on Early Methodism in Rochester' *WHS (Lond)* 21 (1980) 6. There were 12 pence (d) to the shilling and 20 shillings to the pound.

[56] *MNC Mag* 1829: 359. Richard Rodda was stationed at Manchester in 1790. James

Houses were to be equipped with books for the preacher, such as the Christian Library. One of the advantages of this was that he would not need to take them with him when he moved on. But books were often lost and not replaced and houses were rarely good. Frances Pawson described the flea-ridden house in Scotland in which she had to live. Zachariah Yewdall reported fleas in the beds in Earby which kept him awake all night. It was particularly difficult for the preacher in poor rural circuits, where stipends were often below the official minimum and any savings the preacher had were eaten up.[57] Furniture was often not provided or poor. Even as late as 1796 Thomas Taylor was writing in disgust to his son-in-law, the preacher Robert Miller, about the lack of furniture in the house Miller and his wife were to move into

> London Aug 12. 96.
> Dear Robert (Miller).
> I have just received a letter from Nancy (Miller's wife and Taylor's daughter) intimating a very great deficiency of Furniture in the dwelling house at Rochdale. Mr. Mather says, the Collection which Mr Gaulter made at Manchester was expressly made to furnish the house which you are now going to live in; but if that Collection was laid out in his house, our friends in the Circuit must exert themselves to put necessaries into your house. This circumstance you must lovingly speak of with Mr. Gaulter (the Superintendent), and he must contrive ways and means in the best manner he can. Every fund we have is exhausted, so that we have no money, and none can be had; and I hope the Circuit will do their best, and the sooner it is set about is the better before the beggars come into your Circuit for Chapels. A sum of money should immediately be borrowed, the better to obtain some necessaries of the best kind. If no other method can be found, lay down a sum of your own money, and I make no doubt but principal and interest will be refunded. This is Mr Mather's advice - who is now at my Elbow. He blames Mr Gaulter very much; but, I think if you help your friends you will get whatever is necessary -The Circuit must prepare for themselves or expect fewer Preachers; this is the determination of the Conference, and means that some Circuits have fewer Preachers sent them than they had the last year and I hope our Rochdale friends will not be satisfied with one Preacher... You need not put yourself in any hurry in taking Nancy to an empty house, you know she is welcome in my house until it is convenient for her to go to Rochdale.[58]

Preaching Outside

Most of their preaching, at least at first, could well be outside, subject not only to the weather but also the mob. However, many preachers and others often

---

Wood was that year officially at Blackburn, but had been at Newcastle in 1787, when he would know Mort.
[57] MS Diary of Zachariah Yewdall in MARC for 1807.
[58] MS at Duke University, Baker Collection Loose Presidential volume 35. Letter from Thomas Taylor London August 12th (1796) to Robert Miller Rochdale.

preferred to be inside, relatively safe. Wesley himself might attract more hearers than could be squeezed into the early places used for preaching. Other preachers would get fewer, but the real reason for going inside was the caution of the locals. In the 1765 *Minutes* Wesley asked 'Why is field-preaching often omitted' and replied 'To please the Stewards or Society.' In 1766 Wesley wrote to the preacher James Rea that 'Tis a shame to preach in a house before October, unless in a morning.'[59] Once larger preaching-houses were built, then the pressure to stay inside them became very strong, though still resisted by Wesley. In the 1767 *Minutes* he said 'The want (lack) of preaching abroad (outside), and of preaching in new places, has greatly damped the work of God.' He then went on 'Wherever we have a large preaching house at one end of a great town, let us preach abroad at the other end of it, every Sunday morning at least, if it be fair.' Even a keen preacher like the young Zachariah Yewdall in his first circuit, the poor and remote Pembrokeshire where there was a shortage of suitable buildings, did not preach outside until 25th April 1780 when the weather was a little better, though he had started there on the 27th August the previous year, some time before October. Outside preaching remained common in the summer at least, long after Wesley's death. For example, in 1796 Robert Miller going to Rochdale circuit wrote 'At Bacup I found a very affectionate people. I preached outdoors at Shaford, Heywood, Mill Row and other places.'[60]

As late as 1797 the *Large Minutes* read 'regard them not, neither Stewards, Leaders nor People. Whenever the weather will permit, go out in the name of the Lord into the most public places and call upon all to repent and believe the Gospel; every Sunday in particular; especially where there are old Societies, lest they should settle upon their lees. The Stewards will frequently oppose this lest they lose their usual collections. But this is not a sufficient reason against it. Shall we barter souls for money?'[61]

Selling Books

The preachers were expected to take Wesley's publications with them in their saddlebags wherever they went and sell them to the Methodist people. England in the eighteenth century had an explosion of book and tract reading. Where till 1695 printing was restricted and not available in the provinces outside Oxford,

---

[59] *JWL* 5: 23. Rea entered in 1765 in Ireland. At the time of the letter he was in the Newry Circuit. He desisted 1780. A morning to Wesley meant 5 am, which is why he would allow inside then!

[60] *Minutes* 1: 51, 74. MS Zachariah Yewdall Diaries 1780 at MARC. It is therefore wrong to say that it had died out even before Wesley's death as Gareth Lloyd has recently in *PWHS* 55: (2005) 103. For another example of preaching outside see *AM* 1797: 55, 161. The Miller example comes from Jessop, *Rossendale* 180, cf. 194.

[61] *Minutes* 1: 683.

Cambridge and York, by 1800 England was a well developed print society. Provincial booksellers mushroomed. Wesley's followers were mostly in the provinces where there was a huge untapped market, especially for religious works.[62] Wesley filled this gap with an unending stream of publications from the numerous Methodist presses. The profits he made from this supported not only himself, his brother and his family, but helped the whole itinerancy as well. By the early nineteenth century the Book Room was the one Methodist organization whose financial strength was able to support the whole Connexion.[63] Wesley therefore insisted to his preachers that they must carry and sell as much as possible. In 1760 he wrote to George Merryweather, his society steward and later circuit steward at Yarm, 'I wish you would everywhere recommend two books in particular ...*The Christian Pattern* and the *Primitive Physick.*'[64] To Matthew Lowes in 1761, about to go from Newcastle to his new circuit (Whitehaven), he wrote 'Do all you can to propagate the books in that circuit and to fulfill the office of an Assistant.'[65] William Penington, the young Yorkshireman who died in Ireland in 1767, was held up as a model to his surviving brethren much to Pawson's disgust, because he carried with him Wesley's works everywhere and sold them. 'Billy Penington in one year sold more of these (practical tracts) in Cornwall than had been sold for seven years before.'[66] One of the important transactions at Conference was settling up on the question of books. As late as 1780 Wesley wrote to Bradburn 'I fear the late Assistant (in Athlone) neglected many articles (in the *Minutes*) dispersing the books in particular.'[67]

Payment

The circuits had to pay the preachers a stipend. In 1751 John wrote to Charles 'The Societies both must and shall maintain the preachers we send among them.' The societies sent money with the society stewards to the circuit meeting, where the circuit stewards received the money and paid the preachers a quarter late. In 1769 Wesley described the situation 'each of these preachers has his food wherever he labours and twelve pounds a year for clothes and other expense.'[68] In fact, in addition to the actual monetary stipend, the stewards, with the societies, provided food and accommodation. The preachers

---

[62] Feather, *Book Trade* passim especially Chapters 2-4.
[63] F. Baker, *A Union Catalogue of the Publications of John and Charles Wesley.* (Stone Mountain GA: Zimmermann, 2nd ed. 1991); Cumbers, *Book Room.*
[64] Cumbers *Book Room*; *JWL* 4: 83.
[65] *JWL* 4: 164.
[66] *JWL* 4: 262 John Wesley to Thomas Rankin 1764. For Pawson and Penington see *Pawson L* 3: 105-6 where he described Wesley as a scheming intriguer trying to make money, and *WJW* 21: 500. Penington (1736-1767) died at the age of 30.
[67] *JWL* 7: 33.
[68] *JWL* 5: 155.

were also given help with new clothing, the horse, and such varied necessaries as boots, haircuts or washing and repair of clothes. However, the fact that the stipend was being paid a quarter in arrears caused problems which were exacerbated when circuits could not even afford the whole stipend and paid only some. In 1765 the York stewards went to Conference to protest that the proposed rise in stipends was unaffordable. Though overruled they did not pay, as Thomas Johnson, the preacher in the circuit, confessed next January. The preachers might be reimbursed a little from central funds, but this would be late and often less than what was owed.[69]

Portraits and Appearance

Many of Wesley's preachers were best recorded through their portraits. These were engraved and then reproduced each month at the front of the *Arminian Magazine* (this later became the *Methodist Magazine*). Four are shown on the front cover of this book. Wesley decided which portraits should be sat for and printed. Many nineteenth century albums were filled with them and the more famous, like Adam Clarke, Pawson and Coke appeared again and again. Wesley did not include portraits or engravings in the original first few monthly numbers of the *Arminian Magazine* from January 1778. Such engravings were very popular in the eighteenth century. An anonymous correspondent had written to Wesley in June 1778 with various criticisms, one of them being the lack of pictures. Wesley's answer at the beginning of the monthly issue in November was to include with Jaco's life a portrait of 'Mr Peter Jaco, aetatis 49' engraved by Bodlidge, King Street, Upper Moorfields. The first of many, this graphic image certainly attracted the reader's attention. The way in which Methodists have since collected portraits from the magazine shows this attraction, which was not always attached to the written word. The inclusion of such images could also be controversial. Hindmarsh details the story of the London printer Alexander Hogg and his *New Spiritual Magazine*, begun in July 1783. It included portraits of 'gospel ministers.' He ran into vitriolic opposition from one minister, Thomas Towle, and replied in kind.[70]

The original idea of printing the portrait opposite the printed account of the preacher's life was not long held to even under Wesley. In January 1781 John Mason's picture appeared, but no life with it. Instead Christopher Hopper's life was printed with no portrait. Was Hopper in the north while the engraver was in London? Hopper had presided at the previous Conference, and so his likeness could have been engraved there. The separation of the portrait from the story was also partly because the preachers' biographies were often too long for

---

[69] FB Polity 234-6.

[70] Hindmarsh, *Conversion Narrative* 230-3. He also makes the point that biographies of living preachers, rather than just dead ones which Wesley had concentrated on in the early issues of the *Arminian Magazine* were also controversial. *AM* 1778 opposite 541.

inclusion in one monthly number, so were spread over several months, but a portrait was needed each month. Later still there were simply portraits with no descriptions of the living preachers portrayed.

Early portraits showed older preachers like Thomas Olivers and John Murlin wearing wigs. The Manchester Circuit Accounts for the 1750s show several preachers having their wigs paid for by the circuit, so this was not new in 1778. In 1782 the *Minutes* suggested that preachers should abstain from both powdering their hair and wearing artificial curls! The slightly younger John Mason or Thomas Carlill[71] were wearing their own hair and in the 1780s this was already true for the younger preachers. In 1790 Sutcliffe's report of the Conference described how on each side of John Wesley sat 'about 20 venerable men on the benches, ten on each side, distinguished by bushy or cauliflower wigs, aged men that had borne the heat of the day.' However, by the 1790s judging from their portraits, most preachers wore their own hair, exceptions being seniors like John Pawson. The hair would normally be worn long and combed forward 'straight over his forehead.' 'It would have been considered out of order to have worn (one's hair) so as to exhibit a noble forehead.'[72]

Most wore plain serviceable clothes, black shoes with buckles for towns or boots for the country, black waistcoats and breeches, blue or black coats, white linen shirts and stocks and black three cornered hats. The portraits in the *Magazine* were usually without the hat, though the engraving of Wesley in Edinburgh had him supported by the former itinerant Dr. Hamilton on the near side and the current itinerant Joseph Cole on the far side, with all three men wearing the standard tricorne hat and shoes with buckles. The itinerants' clothes would be washed and mended by ordinary women members in the societies with whom they stayed, and replaced by the circuits as they wore out. Thus on the 20th April 1752 two items were recorded in the Haworth circuit accounts 'for William Darney: foreside of his waistcoat 7s. For trimming of his coat 9/1 1/2.'[73] As they rode round the circuits they had their wardrobe, medicines, journal, hymnbook and library in their saddlebags on a strictly as needed basis, rather like a long distance cyclist in the twenty-first century. Their appointments could be kept through careful attention to another vital component of the preacher's wardrobe, the pocket-watch.

Preachers usually sat for their portraits at Conference. For example, Samuel Taylor recorded in his notebook for the 1796 Conference that on Thursday the

---

[71] *PWHS* 13 (1922) 142; *Minutes* 1: 157. Was this 1782 comment on their hair provoked by the controversy about the portraits in the *Magazine*? *AM* 1781 for portraits for Mason and Carlill as frontispiece and opposite 121 (January and March). Hopper's portrait, with wig, was the 1782 frontispiece, some time after extracts from his life had ended.

[72] *PWHS* 14 (1924) 124-5, 15 (1926) 57; Andrews, *Methodists and America* 209.

[73] See this book's frontispiece. *GHR* 69. For more on dress see Chapter 20 below (items of particular value left to other preachers). E. Ehrman, *Dressed Neat and Plain: The Clothing of John Wesley and his Teaching on Dress* (London: Wesley's Chapel, 2003).

28th July he 'sat for his likeness in the Magazine.' His portrait only appeared there in September 1799, with his age described as twenty-eight which he had been in 1796, so the editor had built up a collection of 'back' portraits to put in as it suited him.[74] Portraits might be included in the *Magazine* some time after the preacher depicted was dead, with no apparent indication that he had already died. An example of this happening was James Gore, who died in Bristol about the 4th February 1790. However, his portrait did not appear in the *Magazine* until over a year after his death.[75]

Mistakes in the title on the portrait sometimes occurred. A 'Mr John Horne age 34' appeared in the *Magazine* in August 1788. Since there were no Hornes then travelling, apart from Melville who was rather well known (and rather younger), the simplest solution is that this was a mistake for John Howe, who had entered the itinerancy in Ireland twice and was just about to leave for the second time in 1789.[76] Some were better likenesses than others, but the general standard by the early nineteenth century was high, with many done by William Ridley or later John Jackson R.A.

Conclusion

The short length of time that any itinerant spent in one circuit had as many advantages for Wesley as for the circuits themselves. From the circuit point of view the continual turnover meant that weaker itinerants would be tolerated for a shorter period and then passed on elsewhere. From Wesley's point of view it meant that itinerants found it difficult to build up a personal following. If they left they might take some with them, but this was usually limited. When the relatively young James Brownfield left Methodism in Whitby in 1770 he was unable to get support outside the town. Even within it he was limited by the two years he had spent in the circuit, though strengthened by his marriage to the local property developer's daughter, Rebecca Skinner. (His new break-away, later Independent, chapel was built in the prestigious development on Silver Street on the top of the West Cliff, next to the eponymous Skinner Street.)[77] The fact that there were usually three itinerants in a circuit continually replacing each other with the societies again made it difficult for any one man to build up a personal following, and since itinerants did not usually go to the next circuit together, they were less likely to break away together.

Circuits were complex systems which emerged and changed over time. They

---

[74] *PWHS* 22 (1940) 123-26; *MM* 1799: 417.

[75] For Gore's death see *JWL* 8: 200-201. The portrait was in the March 1791 *AM* 113.

[76] *AM* 1788: 393. The *Magazine* that year until September had a high proportion of Irish preachers' portraits, no fewer than five being Irish born preachers even without Howe, so this makes this suggestion more plausible. The English printer would be more likely to make a mistake over an Irish preacher of whom he had not heard.

[77] Kent, *Wesley and the Wesleyans* 68.

provided the mechanisms through which Methodism grew. They were vital to its life and especially to the preachers who were stationed in them, cared for in them and knew them better even than Wesley himself. The preachers found every circuit different, but because they moved so frequently the circuits followed similar systems. If a Methodist travelled to Lands End, to Castlebar or to North Shields he would find a familiar pattern, with the same hymns sung to the same tunes in the same way. The eighteenth century was a time of faster and further travel. The Methodist preacher was there on his circuit, prepared to preach outside in a new community, one like Stourport which had become the centre of a circuit before the end of the century. He was an encourager of the religious revivals of the period, on his horse or on foot, and profited from the spiritual result. The 'ordered tour' of Baker's description gives an impression of leisure far from reality. The circuit was ordered, certainly, but continual journeys in all weathers, usually alone, where the preacher though often a stranger was welcomed at once as a fellow Methodist and a 'preacher of the gospel' among Wesley's people, were hardly a 'tour.' Jonathan Crowther put it dispassionately in 1810 'A *Circuit* consists of a number of places, at each of which there is generally a society... In these circuits the preachers go round in rotation according to a fixed plan.' There was a fixed plan, though it could easily be varied. What was not variable was the fundamental importance of the circuit both for the organization of Methodism and for the individual preacher.[78]

---

[78] For the industrial centre of Stourport, founded because of the new canal, see J. F. Wedley, *History of Methodism in the Stourport Circuit from AD 1781 to AD 1899* (Stourport: Stourport Printing Company, 1899) 8, 53. For the 1790s religious revivals see the MSS Diary of Mary Taft (then Barritt) in Birmingham University Library. Note the vital part played by Wesleyan Assistants in inviting her and travelling with her. The final quotation is from J. Crowther, *The Methodist Manual* (Halifax: Walker, 1810) 148.

Chapter 9

Conference

'In the Methodist lexicon "Conference" refers to a body of preachers... that exercises legislative, judicial and (to some extent) executive functions for the church... Established by John Wesley, the Conference remained his creature during his lifetime but on his death inherited much of his decision-making and policy setting authority. It became a central feature, perhaps *the* central feature of Methodist polity.'
Richey, 1995.[1]

Introduction

John Wesley laid down which preachers should be invited to Conference and decided who should be received 'On Trial,' a Methodist phrase without any legal connotations. He controlled how long each should spend in that probationary state and when they should be received into 'Full Connexion.' Originally it was only a year, but by the 1780s had become a norm of two years which could be lengthened if necessary. Exceptions could always be made, such as for Adam Clarke admitted by Wesley into Full Connexion in 1783 after being in the Bradford (Wiltshire) Circuit, though in the previous *Minutes* he was not even accepted on trial, so had actually done less than a year.[2] Wesley decided who should be expelled and who should cease to travel and under what circumstances. He allowed many preachers who had left to return.

Despite all this and Richey's assertion at the beginning of this chapter, Wesley was not in complete control of Conference. Conferences began with Wesley and several other clergymen present, each of whom needed to be heard. Later, when there were fewer clergy, there could be laymen present who were not preachers. But gradually it became a Conference made up almost entirely of the preachers, and he needed them. At any time Wesley depended on the preachers supporting him. This was particularly true when the preachers had means of their own, or were themselves the creators of their own rounds or societies. Thus, someone like Thomas Lee, who set up his own round in Nidderdale in the 1740s and itinerated for Wesley until his death in 1786, was

---

[1] Richey, *Conference in America* 13, emphasis and capitals added. Many of Richey's insights are basic to this chapter.
[2] Clarke, *Life.* For examinations of preachers see Chapter 5 above

Timeline 1: Conference

Year	Conference	First lists	Other
1740			Welsh Assembly
1743	John, Charles Wesley, and John Nelson		
1744	London June. 8 present		Doctrine and discipline
1749		Large Minutes	
1751	1st at Leeds		
1752			First Irish Conference
1763		Preachers' Fund	
1765	1st at Manchester 1st printed Minutes	Kingswood Fund	
1766		List of those leaving	
1767		Expenditure on chapels	
1769		wives	
1772		PF expenditure	
1773			1st American Conference
1779		Circuit plan to be brought	
1780	Hopper presided for JW		
1784	Deed of Declaration	Start of Conference Journal	Legal Hundred
1788	Annual Address to the Societies		Book Committee
1790			Building Committee
1791	William Thompson first president		Death of John Wesley
1792		Chairmen listed	
1797	District may ask president to visit		
1803	Committee of Privileges	Superannuated preachers	
1805	1st at Sheffield		
1807	1st at Liverpool		Camp meetings 'improper'

always a man of standing whose opinions needed to be considered.[3] John Bennet and John Nelson came into the same category. Wesley had to listen to his preachers and do something about their wishes, even if not necessarily granting them. There is the revealing story of Robert Roberts at the 1779 Conference. When the roll of preachers was read and their fitness queried, Roberts said Wesley should be questioned first. Wesley allowed this and Roberts complained about the supernatural stories which made up part of the (then relatively new) *Arminian Magazine*. Wesley asserted 'the man that does not believe that spirits may appear is an infidel.' Roberts replied 'Then I am an infidel.' Wesley smiled and said they would talk on this another time. By giving way to Roberts' request and listening to his views he was able to pacify him and yet continue to print what he wanted.[4]

Recompense for the preachers was obviously something Wesley needed to provide. Conference decided stipends for them; later they agreed allowances for wives and eventually for children. These were poor at best and often not paid in full. Conference limited the number of wives who could be supported. At any one time in the 1770s and 1780s there were up to twenty wives who were not being supported for a variety of reasons. Most of these were because they had their own property, being able to support themselves, their families and even their husbands. Some were because their husbands had married without asking the permission of their brethren, which meant they had not asked Wesley. Further rewards for the preachers came in approval from Wesley and recognition by their brother preachers especially at Conference. After 1778 some had their portraits engraved and printed in the *Arminian Magazine*.

The Annual Conference

The Annual Conference was a great moment for the preachers. During the rest of the year they looked forward to this period. At first for five days or fewer but later for longer, they could see their 'father' Wesley, meet their brother preachers, learn their stories and about the spread of the message into new areas, encourage each other, and welcome new preachers into the fold. They might also discuss major problems, perhaps celebrate a preacher who had died, or sympathize with one forced to retire through ill health. They would share the

---

[3] Baker, *Grimshaw* 148, MS Diary, etc of Thomas Lee at MARC, *EMP* 4: 152-169, 5: 158-160, *DEB*, *MM* 1800: 213, 1802: 397, 1811: 646-7, Crk 1: 143-146, 155, *JWL* 5: 92, 116, 120, 123, 6: 24, 50, 272, 380, 7: 187.

[4] The story is quoted by Rack in 'Wesley Portrayed: Character and Criticism in Some Early Biographies' *MH* 43 (2005) 113. It comes from the Everett scrapbook f 420 in MARC. Roberts was an experienced itinerant, born in 1731, entered in 1759, with independent resources, who travelled mostly in the north-west. By 1779 he had travelled twenty years and was forty eight years old. If he could challenge Wesley there were many others in a similar position.

sacrament together, listen to each other's sermons, stay in houses with old friends, sing old hymns and learn new ones, and find out from Wesley where they were all to be serving during the next year. This was when the 'order' of 'Travelling Preachers' could be seen to be developing, with a strong sense of their common identity and discipline. Hindmarsh described them as a craft guild: former apprentices who were moulded into a cohesive company of preachers with their own culture and Wesley as the master-preacher and itinerant.[5] Other Methodists, including women, wanted to be there to listen to the sermons. A layman like the later travelling preacher John Valton attended the London Conference of 1780 and wrote 'my soul was filled with humility, praise and love.'[6] The leading laymen were also admitted during the second half for the discussion of finance and administration, while the preachers alone were there for the business to do with their order such as doctrine, admission to the order and stationing. Some preachers who were not itinerant were often allowed into earlier meetings. At the 1767 Conference Whitefield, Harris and many stewards and local preachers were present during the last two days.[7] In 1781 the exciseman James Chubb rode all the way from Pembrokeshire to Leeds and back, just to share as much as he could in Conference. He described it simply as 'eleven of the best days I have ever spent.' This continued after Wesley's death. In the 1790s and early 1800s Mary Barritt went to several Conferences for the services and also to meet the preachers.[8]

Origins

Conference developed gradually during the fifty years of itinerancy under Wesley, though Rack pointed out there is little evidence apart from the *Minutes* about what really happened at Conference. The idea was there in 1740 proposed by the Oxford group.[9] It may have come from the Welsh Calvinistic Methodists who had been holding their Assemblies since 1740, though only for relatively small areas. The first step was when Wesley summoned his brother and Nelson in August 1743 to London. If Wesley had already 'effectively separated himself from the active life of the Church by late 1739,'[10] then this move seems a little slow in coming. Whitefield and the Moravians, who had also been invited, were not present so it was postponed for a year. The first Conference Wesley actually held was in 1744 at London for six days in late

---

[5] Hindmarsh, *Conversion Narrative* 241; FB Polity 242-55; Richey, *Conference in America.*
[6] *EMP* 6: 83.
[7] FB Polity 244.
[8] Chubb, *Journal* 23-4; Chilcote, *Her Own Story* e.g.162.
[9] Rack 246; Heitzenrater 112.
[10] W. M. Jacob, 'John Wesley and the Church of England 1736-40' in *JRULMB* 85 (2003) 71.

June, with four of his lay preachers and four 'friendly' clergymen there. Viney, a Moravian, was also invited but did not come. At this stage Wesley envisaged three Conferences a year, in his words 'if God permits, Nov 1st at Newcastle, Feb 1st at Bristol, May 1st London.' Heitzenrater pointed out that it was not till 1745 that the principle of an Annual Conference was established.[11] The 1744 Conference laid down a code of discipline and a scheme of doctrine, both often discussed and (less often) modified over the years. It also clarified the organization, especially the function of the preachers, and concentrated on relations with the Church of England. Again, the early Conferences of the later 1740s had much more on this and there were further modifications later. The sections on doctrine published as the *Large Minutes* by Wesley in 1749 were to be the doctrinal standard of Methodism. They were what was put into the hand of every new preacher. Early Conferences were often ad hoc, summoned by Wesley to bring together the preachers in an area rather than the whole country. So Charles summoned his own Conference of mostly northern preachers in Leeds in 1751. Conference was also something Wesley wanted because it enabled him to find out what was happening around the country. Each circuit had to send the Assistant to report the numbers of members. It was a way Wesley could keep a check on the preachers and the societies. They would also bring the circuit's money for connexional causes such as Kingswood or the Preachers' Fund. This had to be brought before Conference began in order to make sure the accounts could be completed. From 1779 they had to supply a circuit preaching plan as well.[12]

Benson looking back in 1801 said that Conference was set up because the preachers only had reference to Wesley previously and that it was to create a closer union with each other, so they would be aware of the 'utility of acting in concert and harmony.'[13] In 1760 Wesley was delayed in Ireland by contrary winds. His preachers waited for him in Bristol for much of a week before he arrived. Wesley kept the right to hold a conference with whomsoever he wished at any time, and did so. In early January 1765 he held an ad hoc Conference in London because of the ordination of some six preachers by Bishop Erasmus. Because it was so sudden not many were present, in fact only three preachers in addition to three clergymen and eight London stewards. So there was at least one Conference after the 1740s at which the travelling preachers were in a minority.[14]

---

[11] *JB's Minutes* 1744: 18. Heitzenrater 142-3, 152.
[12] *Minutes* 1: 106, 115, 140.
[13] Benson, *Apology* 200-201.
[14] *JWL* 4: 290-1.

What Happened at Conference

Introduction

In Conference he kept an equally tight hold on what happened. He decided that they should proceed by Question and Answer. *He* asked the questions and seems to have written the answers. When the *Minutes* were printed he organized what they should say. The form of Questions and Answers enabled individuals to feel they had a say in the discussion which followed, though the final answer was always what Wesley laid down, while Wesley remained in absolute control because he had chosen which questions were to be asked. Over the years, however, some of this control tended to pass to the Conference itself, because it became assumed that once the question was asked one year, then it would be asked the next and so on. Next year the answer might be slightly different or with more detail. Wesley always insisted on his right to invite, so all the preachers were never present. On discipline one recurring theme was relations with the Church of England. In 1744 Question 7 was 'Do we separate from the Church?' Answer: 'We conceive not. We hold communion therewith.' Another theme was about membership and how to receive members with solemnity (1746 Qu 3).

Worship

With regard to the services during Conference, by 1754 we have a plan of public services in which fifteen different preachers delivered 33 sermons at eight different locations in the immediate London area. Wesley himself preached frequently at Conference and expected his preachers to do the same at little notice. In 1775 John Valton went to the Leeds Conference to begin to travel. Once there he was told by Pawson, the Leeds Assistant, to preach.[15] Quite often individuals would arrive at Conference, sometimes very new and nervous like Valton, to be told 'you are preaching tomorrow!' It was also a major spiritual occasion, hence its attraction to non-preachers. It was expected that local Methodists and, more importantly, others interested who were then known as 'enquirers,' would be drawn in and there would be an effect on the locality. Local Methodists throughout a large region around the Conference centre looked forward to the Conference. After 1760 the numbers concerned made it difficult for all the preachers to attend. Pawson spent some time grumbling in the 1790s about colleagues who wanted to go to Conference and who would cost the connexion its goodwill with the laymen because of the preachers' failure to see that not everyone could go. It was a problem that

---

[15] The undated plan is in Wesley's Colman Collection MS notebook 20 in the MARC. Heitzenrater from internal evidence dated it as Conference 1754, see Heitzenrater 190, where one of the pages is illustrated. *EMP* 6: 95. Cf. E. Hoole in *WMM* 1855. The fifteen preachers included both Wesleys, though John only once.

Pawson and Wesley's other advisers had been wrestling with for some time.

Sessions began at six in the morning following preaching at five as instituted by Wesley. There was a break at 9 am for an hour and another at 12 noon for two hours. The Conference ended at 5 pm, a warning to twentieth century British Conferences which did not start till 10 am but might sit long into the evening. The eighteenth century total for Conference business was therefore eight hours each day, a comparable amount, but skewed to a much earlier period of the day which left time in the evenings for friendly conversation, services or other business meetings. After 1784 the first task was to fill up the Legal Hundred replacing those who had died or were supernumerary.

Place and Time

Conferences were held at the same or similar place. The Foundery chapel London was used for 1744, 1747, 1748 and 1749. The New Room Bristol (still there) was the place for 1745, 1746 and 1750. Conference met in 1751 at Leeds for the first time and in 1765 Manchester, in each case in the main preaching-house in the town, so creating a rotation among the four places. Some time after Wesley's death more towns in the north were added.[16]

The first Conference took place in late June, very close to the time of the modern British Methodist Conference. However, times have varied enormously over the next three centuries. Conferences were at first at different points in the year, for example 1751-55 each year in May, with 1754's beginning on the 22nd May. Then from 1756 it was held in August, but late August in 1760, early September in 1761 and late July in 1763. From there on it was always late July or early August, so in 1769 the next one was fixed for the 'first Tuesday in August;' later this became the last Monday in July.[17] Another piece of Conference had become fixed. It was only in the twentieth century that it moved earlier in Britain to the end of June, to allow more time before the annual move of stations.

In Ireland it was held at different times to suit Wesley, the first Conference being in August. Eventually it was usually two or three weeks or so before the one in Britain, and as soon as it was over Wesley or Coke and his companions would catch the boat to England to prepare for the Conference there. It is very similar today, though now the British President and his or her companions often travel by air. In America Conferences were held at whatever time was most suitable. The Christmas Conference took place then because it was as soon after Thomas Coke had arrived that the American preachers could be summoned together and also a convenient holiday. Later, with so many different Conferences, it became established that they were all the year round, with Bishop Asbury's chief task being to preside at each in turn. He took care to

---

[16] Sheffield joined the rota in 1805 and Liverpool in 1807.
[17] Crowther 249.

organize southern Conferences for the winter to reduce travelling problems.[18]

The first Conference lasted five days, and by the 1750s four days were common or even three on one occasion at Bristol. Conferences should, in Wesley's view, do spiritual rather than temporal business. By 1769 he noted in the Minutes that 'this year we have spent above two days on temporal business,' to which the answer was 'let the clerks do as much as they can by themselves.' However, from 1780 they became longer, even to nine or ten days, to allow the Conference more power and to learn how to use it, a deliberate decision by Wesley.[19] After Wesley's death it became longer still, the 1794 Conference, for example, beginning on July 28th and ending on August 8th. Wesley's successors were beset with far more problems than Wesley faced and lacked his ability always speedily to send away those who refused to accept direction. After 1747 doctrine was discussed less at Conferences, except in particular crises such as 1770.

Numbers Present

Wesley wanted at least one travelling preacher from each circuit, but there were times when, because of emergency such as the crisis over separation from the Church of England, he wanted more. The preachers all wished to be there. Usually Wesley was against this because of cost and the difficulty of putting everyone up for what could be an extended period, with some arriving early and others staying late. In 1755 there were 63 at Conference out of a minimum of 66. This contrasted with 1754 when apparently there were only 14 attending. In 1756 Charles Wesley wrote to Samuel Walker that 'between 40 and 50 or almost all of our itinerant preachers were present at our (Bristol) Conference.' By 1784 according to the formal lists shown by the Conference Journal there were 150 present out of around 200 who might have come.[20] Wesley also wanted at least one of the preachers (usually not the Assistant) to remain behind and run the circuit in his colleagues' absence. A preacher would not learn of his destination until after the Conference if he was not there and this was another reason why all preachers wanted to attend. This caused problems for Wesley each year, as can be seen in his correspondence. He spent much time assuring preachers they did not need to attend. Over time the number of clergymen

---

[18] Richey, *Conference in America.*

[19] London in 1754 *may* have been only three days. Baker, *Wesley and the Church* 220.

[20] The 1754 Conference was most unusual. The number given is reliant on T. Mitchell's memory in *EMP* 1: 252. It may well not be accurate. While thirteen preachers were preaching in London during Conference week, another five names appear preaching the week before and it is unlikely any went home first. MS London plans in Colman notebook 20. For 1755 and 1756 see Tyerman 2: 199, 252. For the 1765 Conference see *PWHS* 18 (1932) 130-35. The MS Conference Journal is at the MARC. For estimates of the total numbers of preachers see Appendices One and Two. Charles was being optimistic in his letter to Walker.

present stayed constant or declined, but the number of lay itinerant preachers increased. Wesley was the one who was vital. In 1771 Pawson predicted gloomily 'I know not what we shall be able to do at Conference without him.'[21]

We have for the 1765 Manchester Conference a list of sixty-six preachers, almost two thirds of the total then, and five of their wives who attended and their hosts. It is a list of hosts and guests, and so probably others who lived close enough, for example in the Manchester Circuit, may need to be added; but it gives a good idea of the requirement for extensive hospitality at such times, one which at any period was a problem for the organization and one of the reasons why Wesley did not want all the preachers to attend. For most Conferences before 1784 and the introduction of the Conference Journal we do not know which preachers were present. 1765 was the exception.

The five wives were Mrs Guilford, Mrs Murlin, Mrs Mary Brammah, Mrs Elizabeth Oliver and Mrs Rourke. Two of their husbands Joseph Guilford and Thomas Rourke had been in the circuit recently from 1762 to 1763. Their wives would have friends in the area and may even have come from there. Oliver was being stationed in Manchester that year, and so his wife had to arrive sometime. Murlin's wife was the widow of a London banker, who could and did pay her way wherever she wanted, and was soon to demand that her husband be stationed in London. Another strong character was Mary Brammah, who had walked from Sheffield to Cornwall to be with her travelling husband. Sheffield to Manchester, her journey in 1765, was nothing in comparison. Wives, like their husbands, wanted to attend again and again. Wesley preferred that they did not come, in order to reduce the accommodation problem and cost.[22]

Officers

It is not known who acted as secretary to the Conference for most of Wesley's lifetime. Notes which have survived from Conferences before 1765 tell us that John Bennet, Jacob Rowell and others made notes, but whether they were acting as secretary, or whether most preachers made notes, cannot be deduced. Thomas Johnson, the former carpenter from Wakefield, is said to have taken the Minutes at the 1761 Conference, along with John Jones, but both versions disappeared.[23] Certainly from 1765 at least one preacher acted as secretary or clerk. We know the relatively well-educated John Valton did this in 1784 and was still among the group of clerks in 1790 at Wesley's last Conference. The 1769 *Minutes* referred to asking the 'clerks to do the temporal business' by

---

[21] *Pawson L* 1: 14 letter to Bardsley of the 12th June, so six weeks beforehand.

[22] *PWHS* 18 (1931-32) 130-35. For Murlin's marriage to Mrs Elizabeth Berrisford see *AM* 1786; 422-26. We do not know the Christian names of Mrs Rourke or Mrs Guilford. The other two preachers were William Brammah, e(ntered) m(inistry) 1762, died 1780, see *PWHS* 36 (1968) 169-177 and John Oliver, e. m. 1759, left 1784.

[23] Simon 4: 106.

themselves, presumably beforehand, or perhaps, like the business committee today, meeting in the evenings when Conference was not in session, for 'it will save us half the time.'[24] One of the reasons for setting up districts after 1791 was to expedite Conference business by doing much of it at district level.

Stations

One of the most important points of Conference for the preachers was the reading of the stations for the next year. At the end some might approach Wesley requesting changes in the stations because they did not want to go to the circuit assigned. In America Asbury developed a system for avoiding this, by having his horse saddled and ready to ride brought to the door of the Conference. The American Conferences were at first at Baltimore and he would read the stations and immediately ride to his friend Mr Gough at Perry Hall to get away from the preachers.[25] Wesley did not involve himself in this kind of ruse, but could suffer similar pressures both before and after the stations were announced and occasionally he gave way.[26] Preparations for the stationing can be seen in his correspondence with many of the preachers from at least February each year. Many stations were already agreed with the preacher concerned before the Conference. However, an emergency could occur and the preacher be sent somewhere else. Early Conference Journals have several cases of preachers entered for one circuit during Conference and then, later but before the end of Conference, the name crossed out and another's entered. After Wesley's death this preoccupation with future stations became worse, partly because preachers tended to stay longer and the place was therefore more important. The ancestor of the Stationing Committee was to meet 'three days in the week preceding the Conference' in 1792 to draw up plans for the stations. From December on in this period the letters of Pawson, Atmore, and others were full of which circuits they would go to next. Pawson wrote to Atmore in March 1797 'Where do you intend to fix your staff after next Conference? Does John Pritchard wish to stay another year in Bristol? Do the people wish to have him? ...Is it the general wish of the people that A(dam) Clarke should (go there)? I hear that Thomas Taylor wants to come to Bristol...'[27] This kind of frenetic questioning had not happened under Wesley because there were fewer permutations possible and one relatively fixed will in control.

---

[24] *Minutes* 1: 86.

[25] Sprague, *Annals* 7: 20.

[26] Pawson (*EMP* 4: 54) recounted how in 1785 he expected to return to his Manchester circuit, having married his new wife in York. Instead they went to Scotland. Sutcliffe described Wesley publicly altering his original MS at Conference (*HMGB* 4: 232-3).

[27] *Minutes* 1791 1: 247; *Pawson L* 3: 113. Atmore was at Bristol. Pritchard did stay in Bristol. Clarke joined Atmore and Pawson at London. Taylor went to Halifax.

Lists

By 1765 there were lists of preachers admitted 'On Trial' and to 'Full Connexion,' Assistants and the stations. There were rules about the collections, details of how much money was received, what it was to be spent on, the Preachers' Fund in particular, which chapels could be built, how big their debts were and how they could be met. The date and place of the next Conference was another constant in the business. The Kingswood Fund was recorded from 1765. From it the connexion supported the school for the sons of the preachers. From 1781 it made grants towards the education of both girls and boys, including those who did not attend Kingswood. This has already been discussed as an enlightened view for the late eighteenth century.[28]

In 1766 came the first list of those 'laid aside,' protected that year by initials. 1766 also had the first (incomplete) list of numbers in the circuits. From 1767 the complete numbers of members in each circuit were printed. These came from what was brought to Conference by the Assistants from each circuit and depended on their carefulness. The 1767 *Minutes* summarized what was spent from the Annual Subscription for debt on the chapels etc, and this was first itemized in 1769. How wives were to be supported first appeared in 1769, when provision was made for 36 wives, the *Minutes* saying that there were only 32 in England and the surplus was to be used to help children. In 1770 the *Minutes* named the wives who were to be supported and which circuit should support which wife. 43 wives appeared that year. Details of payments from the Preachers' Fund first appeared in 1772. In 1769 the preachers at Conference pledged themselves to stay together after Wesley's death and preach the old Methodist doctrines. Similar more developed articles of agreement were signed at the Conferences of 1773, 1774 and 1775. The historian is thus enabled to tell who actually was at Conference for those years. However, not all the preachers present at the Conference would have signed. Some could have resisted the undoubted pressure to sign from Wesley and their brethren. These lists and rules mark the development of the separate organization.

Annual Printing of the Minutes of Conference

The 1760s are now seen as a turning point in the development of Methodism. This was expressed in many different ways.[29] 1765 should be seen as a key year. Historians have known that this was the year when Wesley first decided to print the *Minutes*, listing all the preachers and all their stations. The first few Conferences had *Minutes* taken, but these were mostly doctrinal and organizational, and the list of stations was incidental and rarely complete. Why did Wesley decide printed *Minutes* were necessary both in 1765 and from then on? The pattern of where and when individuals were in circuits before 1765 is

---

[28] *Minutes passim.* See also Chapter 7 above on Family.
[29] See for example Rack in *PWHS* 54 (2003) 54.

also still not completely clear, because of lack of information. However, it seems that in the 1740s nearly all preachers were moving from circuit to circuit each month or each quarter. In the 1750s it is difficult to pinpoint differences, but it looks more like every six months that they changed, though some still were moving each quarter or each month, especially for their first two years. After 1765 this became usually a minimum of one year. Reasons for this are fairly clear. The preachers, as they became more practised, both asked for more stability and were more capable of remaining longer in a circuit successfully. They were not all the unpractised laymen of the 1740s but had become experienced itinerants. There were more members locally and the distances between the societies were less.[30]

This is surely one reason for the beginning of the annual printing of the *Minutes*. While stations were only for six months or fewer, the cost of printing could not be justified. But from 1765 for a whole year the preachers would be remaining in their stations. It was useful for the preachers, perhaps the stewards and for Wesley himself, to have a list of who was where for that increased period. It was part of the building of the fraternity of the preachers that each should receive a copy of the *Minutes* with their name and circuit in it. It was a mark of the growing size of the Connexion as well. This is probably the *root* cause of the annual printing of the *Minutes* beginning in 1765. It is also a sign of the growing importance of Conference in that from 1765 it usually delimited the start and end of a preacher's assignment to a circuit. The preacher should not begin his year in the circuit until Conference had sent him. He would then be there, normally, for a year, until it sent him elsewhere. Earlier, preachers moved frequently at other times of the year, but after 1765 this became rarer.[31]

Later Developments

Growth of Business

As the numbers grew there was what the twenty-first century would call a business committee of the great and good, or at least those with most influence, to guide and plan the proceedings. On Monday the 6th August 1781 Wesley wrote 'I desired Mr Fletcher, Dr Coke and four more of our brethren, to meet every evening, that we consult together on any difficulty that occurred.' This was the day before the Leeds Conference began. This group met with Wesley and three of the seven were clergymen. As always it depended on whom he invited![32]

---

[30] Joseph Cownley's stations provide a good example of this kind of transition in practice. See *AM* 1794: 473-78, 523-29, 561-67, 617-27.

[31] Later in 1777 a rule was made that 'none but the travelling preachers' should have a copy of the *Minutes* see MS letter at MARC PLP 28/3/2 Thomas Coke from Brecon to Thomas Churchey 25th September 1777.

[32] *WJW* 23: 218. I presume the other four were lay preachers. Their names are unknown.

Finance

Conference was the key moment in the Methodist year for finance. The preachers were supposed to bring money to Conference for the different funds collected in the circuits, so that the Connexion remained solvent. There were many problems with finance and the preachers were expected to be prudent and to fund raise on occasion. Often it seemed difficult. Wesley wrote to the reluctant Joseph Benson 'You are no novice among the Methodists. You have frequently seen at the time of Conference how much every shilling brought in was wanted. Therefore you cannot omit the collection on any account. But you will consider which is the most proper time to make it.'[33]

After Wesley's death finance became more complex as the Connexion continued to grow, and Wesley's successors continued to find finance a difficult subject. Methodist finance depended on preachers accepting expenses from the circuit instead of a salary and this being essentially the same in any circuit. As the number of preachers grew fast, the number of their wives and children needing to be supported grew even faster. This was partly because the control Wesley had maintained over itinerants' marriages disappeared, to be replaced only by the rule that the itinerant could not marry until he entered into full connexion. The finances depended on a continual increase in membership, or an increase in the prosperity and ability of the members to give. If either faltered, as prosperity did in the economic crises of the French Wars, or membership did after 1815, then the financial credibility of the connexion was in jeopardy. As the preachers' expectations and the number of their dependants rose, and financial liabilities increased, so Methodism had to appeal to wealthy outsiders. They did this by stressing foreign missions, for which large sums could be and were raised. It was by organizing collections for foreign missions after 1813 that Jabez Bunting won the acclaim of his fellows, cemented by the support of Methodist lay worthies of Manchester and the industrial towns with whom he worked so closely.

Complaints of financial malpractice among the itinerants, caused partly by an increase in their aspirations, led to lay unrest. This was behind many of the splinter movements which afflicted Wesleyan Methodism after the death of Wesley, from Kilham in 1798 to the 'three expelled' of 1849.[34]

Committees and the Annual Address

In the 1780s Wesley set up Committees to run various concerns and report to Conference. The Book Committee was appointed in 1788, and a Building Committee, along with an Irish Building Committee and a 'Committee for the management of our affairs in the West Indies,' the ancestor of the powerful Overseas Missions Committee, were set up in 1790.

---

[33] *JWL* 7: 375, 9th March 1787.
[34] Hempton, *Empire* Chapter 5; Hempton, *Culture* 103-106.

Often there was a letter from Wesley to the societies which was included in the Conference *Minutes* and sent to the societies with the preachers when they returned from Conference. For example, in 1786 there was one (mostly written in 1785) on 'Separation from the Church' (of England). From 1788 this became an official 'Annual Address to the Societies,' though it did not become enshrined in the *Minutes* until 1819, long after Wesley's death. There developed the habit of sending 'Addresses' to the American Conference and the Irish Conference. The first Address to the Irish was sent in 1793. From then on annually each Conference usually addressed the other, though in 1795 in the 'multiplicity of business' it was forgotten by the British Conference, much to the chagrin of the Irish. In 1796 the first Address to the American Conference was sent via Thomas Coke. In the following years there were addresses in each direction annually, generally around the theme of who needed Thomas Coke's services most. However, with the General Conference in America being every four years, there gradually developed the system of only sending an address to America once in that period.[35]

Conference, though started by Wesley and dependent on him for invitations, nevertheless developed a life of its own. This was partly because the itinerants wanted to be more professional, to gain more status as the societies continued to develop. Kent recently suggested this was true for the 1770s. I would suggest this began as early as the 1750s and continued as the Connexion grew.[36]

Gerontocracy

The first Conferences were those of young men. The first cohort and their immediate successors tended to leave, but once provision for wives and children was introduced in 1761 those entering during the 1760s and 1770s tended to stay. This encouraged the existence of a body of senior preachers who came to dominate Conference. The feeling grew that those who had travelled less should defer to or even be silent beside those who had travelled twenty, thirty or even forty years. So in 1780, when Wesley was ill at Conference, the senior preacher Christopher Hopper, who had travelled for thirty-one years at that point, was then put into the chair as president. It is interesting that thirty-one years represented the longest any preacher present had done. Fifteen years later it would have been over forty. In 1781 Wesley shared the presidency with Coke and Fletcher on each side of him, at least for the public meeting at which James Chubb was present. In 1783 Wesley was unable to preside all the time and put the much younger clergyman Thomas Coke into the chair. When Wesley was unable to preside briefly in 1785, again he asked Hopper.[37] After Wesley's death it was senior preachers like the Irishman William Thompson

---

[35] Peirce, *Polity of the Methodists* 476.
[36] Kent, *Wesley and the Wesleyans* 27.
[37] Heitzenrater 294. For 1781 see Chubb, Journal 2: 32.

and the Scot Alexander Mather, or the even more senior Joseph Hanby, who were chosen at first. They were selected in preference to the upstart, bright, relative juniors who had been favourites of Wesley, such as Thomas Coke, not elected president until 1797 and Adam Clarke not elected till 1806.[38]

Similarly it was by seniority that the Legal Hundred was filled up after Wesley's death. This was not true of the original names in the Deed of 1784 when, consistent with Wesley's policy of encouraging youth, 'On Trials' and younger preachers were put in over the more senior Hampsons, Atlays and others. This is illustrated by Chart 9 below. There were more preachers from cohort four, none of whom had travelled more than fourteen years, than there were from any other cohort. Wesley's rule for filling up the Hundred was that they should have travelled one year, and he himself broke that rule!

Cohort	Number of preachers
1740s	2
1750s	10
1760s	29
1770s	47
1780s	10
Total preachers	98

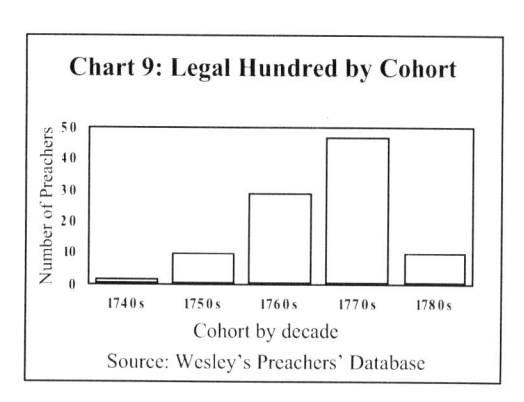

Chart 9: Legal Hundred by Cohort

Source: Wesley's Preachers' Database

Similarly it was only the Hundred who voted for president and secretary.[39] This contrast between Wesley and Conference over promoting youthful ability can be seen in much that Wesley did, especially with Conference's actions in the 1790s and early nineteenth century. Even in Wesley's final will of 1790 determining the disposition of the Book Room, Wesley put in the relatively

---

[38] Thompson and Mather had travelled 35 years when elected, Hanby 41. Coke and Clarke had done 20 and 24 years respectively when first elected. Others of the gerontocracy included John Pawson (travelled 31 years when elected 1793) and Thomas Taylor (travelled 35 years when elected 1796). Relative juniors included Henry Moore a man whom Wesley had wanted, (not elected until 1804 when he had travelled 25 years), an able preacher like Sammy Bradburn who waited for election as president until 1799 when he had travelled 25 years, or the scholar Joseph Benson who was not elected until 1798 when he had travelled 27 years. Even Wesley's faithful travelling companion Joseph Bradford had travelled 23 years before being elected in 1795.

[39] Crowther 249-50. J. S. Simon, 'Elections to the Legal Hundred' in *PWHS* 13 (1922) 14-21 for the full details to the twentieth century. Simon, a prescient senior himself, also worked out that 47% of the first Legal Hundred had travelled ten years or fewer and suggested reasons in *PWHS* 12 (1920) 85-87. Chart 9 is about the 98 preacher members of the first Legal Hundred, the Wesley brothers making up the 100.

young preachers Adam Clarke (aged 30), Joseph Taylor (38) and James Rogers (43) with three more senior preachers as the Trustees responsible.[40]

Later Bunting was to make his name as the champion of the younger preachers against the older, rewarded by being the first preacher to be voted into the Hundred not on grounds of seniority. The irony was that he then became the leader of the established gerontocracy of the next generation! Wesleyan Methodism tended to be dominated by the over-60s from then on in every generation. Young men like Hugh Price Hughes and Thomas Bowman Stephenson would be told to shut up and listen to their elders who knew better than they.[41] Even during Wesley's lifetime there was a tendency for junior preachers to go to less established new circuits, further away from the older circuits of the industrial north and midlands, London or Bristol, while these circuits were reserved for more senior preachers. In 1786 the original Methodist centre of Bristol had four preachers, the most junior having entered in 1768. Similarly Leeds circuit had three preachers, the most junior having entered in 1771. On the other hand, the new circuit of (King's) Lynn had three preachers of whom the senior had entered only two years earlier. The large Dales circuit, notorious for the distances to be travelled over mountains in all weathers, had James Thom, who entered in 1783, as Assistant with two preachers entered in 1785 and 1786 to help him. After Wesley's death this tendency increased in the early nineteenth century. As Ward aptly put it for the 1820s 'it was no accident that Bunting, John Stephens, Richard Reece and the other toughs of the Connexion migrated among the town circuits which were at the core of these districts.' Others never moved away from poor country circuits.[42]

Conference after Wesley was in charge, and behaved like it. They were determined that no one man should ever control them as Wesley had. The aged Cownley confided to the equally elderly Hopper in the summer of 1791 'No single man in the Church shall reign over me for the future.'[43] Because of this they had long and turgid debates over what seem two hundred years later to be issues of minor importance, debates which would never have happened under

---

[40] The other three were Coke (aged 43), Mather (57), and Valton (50). There was also the young clergyman Peard Dickinson (31). Peirce, *Polity of the Methodists* 692.

[41] Lunn, Hughes' friend, was forced out for questioning missionary policy. His description, while perhaps too colourful, illustrates the point 'George Osborn dominated the Conference and ... dropped or expelled every young minister who had not a clear and vivid sense of the reality of hell... Methodism had its Siberia, like Russia under the Tsar, which is found in the Shetland Isles. Thither turbulent young ministers ...were ruthlessly exiled to ponder on their misdeeds... The officials dreaded Hughes' Forward Movement and all the new ideas that he had introduced...' Sir Henry Lunn (founder of Lunn-Poly), *Chapters from My Life* (London: Cassell, 1918) 89-91.

[42] W. R. Ward, *Religion and Society in England 1790-1850* (London: Batsford, 1972) 104. The four districts were Liverpool, Manchester, Halifax and Leeds, wealthy districts at the heart of the Industrial Revolution since Wesley, see also Hempton, *Empire* 114.

[43] MS Letter of Cownley to Hopper 6th June 1791, printed *WHS NE* 8th October 1966.

Wesley and then took ages. Conference could take umbrage in a way Wesley never would and was far wordier than Wesley who knew how to make words count. Individual preachers behaved more independently there. Letters were written from Conference before 1791, but they were usually penned with the authority of Wesley or Conference to indicate a cessation of membership, or to explain a change of station. After 1790 these continue, but are joined by a stream of others. Such letters from Conference give the historian a participant's view of what happened, and were often written during the sessions of Conference 'in full Conference.' They include loving husbands to their wives and preachers to other preachers or lay folk, full especially of how the new stations will affect them in the coming year. Would Wesley have allowed such letters in his time during the Conference sessions? I think he would have insisted on attention to what he described as the '(necessary) business.'[44]

Conference Journal

1784, the year of the Deed of Declaration, was also the year when the Conference Journal began to be filled up. Until then the *Minutes* which were printed were not legally binding documents, merely published by Mr. Wesley. From 1784 the *Minutes* became secondary to the Journal which was the legally significant document under the Deed of Declaration of 1784. The Journals listed those preachers present, those with dispensations not to attend, and those of the Legal Hundred not present. Also from 1784 John Wesley signed as president and Thomas Coke as secretary. All this is important and enables us for the first time since the 1740s, apart from 1765, to clearly see which preachers were present. The Journal was also part of the building up of the authority of the Conference, giving it and the preachers who composed it, more status. The legal niceties surrounding its filling up and attestation remain to the present as a vital part of the ending of Conference, the last memory before all the preachers returned to their different circuits.[45]

Presidency

From 1791 the post of president of the Conference was of significance. But it was not the position it became later, for presidents did not travel as Wesley had or later presidents were to do. It could not be compared with the position of Asbury in America or even Coke in Ireland, because in each case there was continuity of office and much influence through regular travel in the country.

---

[44] '(Necessary) business' is a direct and revealing quotation which recurs very frequently in Wesley's Diary. Wesley knew very well what it was to be 'busy' but it had to be necessary as well. Not all 'busyness' was.

[45] The MS Conference Journals are kept in the MARC. The corrections are valuable and both often differ slightly from the printed *Minutes*.

No one in Britain had continuity. Instead presidents had their week or two of glory and then their post was not mentioned again until someone else held it. The president chaired Conference, an important function, as Wesley had done, but only at most once in eight years, and so he lacked any continuity. He possessed two votes, but voting only happened rarely. He did not have the influence on the agenda of Conference which Wesley had done. Nor had he Wesley's power over who made up the personnel of Conference, let alone the ability to sway or close debates in the way Wesley had. When Coke as president in 1797 moved from the chair that circuit stewards should be allowed to attend the District meeting, he lost the vote. When the *Minutes* of Conference were printed, the name and office of president did not appear anywhere except at the foot of a public letter sent by the Conference. It was not until 1813 that the stations actually included a statement as to who was president that year. He had little to do once the Conference was over and certainly did not travel.[46]

Mather, an ex-president, wrote in October 1798 to Benson, president that year, about the possibility of a preaching journey which Benson made soon after the letter, a successful tour of the north briefly described in Treffry's *Life of Benson*. It began on the 30th October, ten days after this letter was written concluding at the end of November, with Benson preaching at many of the places mentioned by Mather and concentrating particularly on Sunderland where he preached at least three times. What is interesting is that Benson, though president of the Conference that year, does not have that office mentioned. Benson was being asked to do this because of his 'own might,' not because of any office he held. Benson had in 1795 made a very effective tour in Cornwall, long before he was president. Mather thought it should be repeated elsewhere. Though clearly proposed before, it was still not certain and depended on Benson's choice. Such a tour was unusual. The idea of a 'presidential' journey was just not there.[47]

In fact the *Minutes* in 1792 of the second Conference after Wesley's death specifically resolved that 'The president's power shall cease as soon as the Conference breaks up.' His jealous brethren, determined that no person should wield the power that Wesley had, tended to be suspicious if he did do anything. In the 1790s the preachers' letters are full of the Conference or the preachers or (some times) the Trustees or even the people. They hardly ever mention the president. In 1797 Conference began the process of giving him power to sanction the change of a preacher's station or to visit a circuit, but only if the district committee asked him. Few did. It is interesting to note that this lack of power was symbolized by the absence of a capital letter in the minute as elsewhere. Conference must have a capital 'C' but the 'p' of president was not

---

[46] *Minutes passim*. Vickers, *Thomas Coke* 221. Walter Griffith was president in 1813.

[47] MS letter at the Bridwell Library, SMU, Dallas BPF 1/10-12, A. Mather to J. Benson 20th Oct 1798, Leete Collection; R. Treffry, *Memoirs of the Life of the Rev. Joseph Benson* (London: Mason, 1840) 235-6.

capitalized as late as 1873. Conference was what mattered. He did not.[48]

The most powerful group during the absence of Conference from one year to the next was the travelling preachers in London, led by their Superintendent. In Wesley's lifetime letters for advice and help had come to City Road, whether he was there or away travelling. This did not cease on his death. The London preachers were seen as particularly influential and their advice was sought on all sorts of varied topics well into the nineteenth century. In 1806 two trustees and a mob of opponents to the Superintendent, the aged if respected Thomas Taylor, broke into the chapel at Wigan. Taylor wrote to Adam Clarke at London 'As you are at the fountain head of knowledge, we wish to know what must be done. They (the local loyal Methodists) are certainly very much distressed for a place to preach in, having no other than a small dwelling house and debarred from their own chapel. I sincerely wish the Jaws of these oppressors to be broken, and this prey plucked from their Teeth. But I am no adept in law matters. Mr Hewett told me, -some time ago, that the only method would be to apply to the Lord Chancellor; but I thought the Conference had got more eligible advice. However, I beg you will make speedy enquiry...' In London they had access to the best legal help in the land and they would know what to do.[49]

Though the British Conference remained most important at least for Wesley, other Conferences were held. Conferences in Ireland and America developed and Conferences were also held by Coke in the West Indies (see those Chapters). The American Conference became independent to match the independent nation in 1784. The Irish Conference became independent, though still closely linked, after Wesley's death.

Conclusion

Conference was the keystone of Methodist organization, which differentiated it from Dissenters and Anglicans who were organized by local congregation or parish. It was a vital part of the way in which Wesley controlled his preachers, his societies and his circuits. Each year he decided which preachers went to what circuits. Methodism was hierarchical, managed by Wesley through the Conference. Preachers were expected to accept all that Wesley through

---

[48] *Minutes* 1792 1: 269, 1797: 1: 390. Peirce, *Polity of the Methodists passim*. The lack of capitals derives from the Deed of Declaration by which Wesley set up the legal Conference in 1784. Curnock and others capitalized them later, reading back their present into the past. Compare *HMGB* 4: 196 and Pierce on one side with no capitals as against the capitals in Curnock in *JWJ* 8: 339 and Rogal in *MH* 44 (2006) 111. In the original MS at MARC the 'p' is definitely lower case.

[49] MS at Bridwell Library, SMU, Dallas BPF 1/23-4 Thomas Taylor letter to Adam Clarke October 1806. Clarke was president that year, but it was his position in London which was mentioned as the reason for the letter. His presidency was not mentioned at all.

Conference said. Differences of opinion on doctrine, organization or anything else could only be allowed if the preachers kept quiet about them. After Wesley's death the Wesleyan gerontocracy wished that they had the same control. However, we should not imagine that because Wesley or Conference said or did something, that their instructions were necessarily followed to the letter. The existence of regulations proves only that there had been a problem beforehand, not that the regulations were always kept. At all periods there has been much local independence in Methodism. Local circuits and societies often did what they wanted or what their general practice had been, whatever Wesley or Conference might have said as, for example, with allowances for the preachers. Wesley, by travelling round the connexion and conducting his enormous correspondence, at least in his younger or middle period could keep in touch with what was happening and keep such fissiparous tendencies in check. Preachers who did not like it left, or in Wesley's last years remained silent waiting for his death. On his demise admittedly less power passed to the Conference. Both policy and practice changed. It is not surprising that the preachers in Conference, who were themselves often divided, found power more difficult to exercise, and that the influence of local power sources, whether wealthy trustees, earnest local preachers or class leaders, increased.[50]

There was no executive to govern while Conference was not sitting. Wesley had had various ideas for the succession but none worked properly. There was a gap which was never properly filled. The American expedient of Asbury and Bishops worked for a longer period, even if in the end this was not completely successful either.[51] The power of Conference, and hence that of the preachers, gradually increased during the eighteenth and early nineteenth centuries. This was for many reasons, not least because Wesley encouraged it and towards the end devolved some power to it. The main reason for its impact, however, was that it acted as the deciding force of the preachers when joined together. Whatever the preachers felt, that was what the Conference did. Its importance was that it was the preachers in action.

Conference represented the pinnacle of the itinerant's life. The next few chapters deal with widening the travelling preachers' tracks towards further expansion within the British Isles and overseas. After that we turn to the slope down from the peak to the problems of those who left and those who might return; we consider health problems, retirement, death and other episodes, often less praised but still significant, especially to the individuals concerned.

---

[50] J. C. Bowmer, *Pastor and People: A Study of Church and People in Wesleyan Methodism 1791-1858* (London: Epworth, 1975); M. Batty, *Stages in the Development and Control of Wesleyan Lay Leadership 1791-1878* (Peterborough: WMHS, 1988).

[51] The American system was unable to prevent the division between North and South, for example.

CHAPTER 10

Wales, Scotland, Isle of Man, Channel Islands

'I never saw in England so many stout well-looking preachers together.'
Wesley describing the Local Preachers of the Isle of Man.[1]

Methodism's Arminian theology meant that the message was always to be carried further from Wesley's original base in England. Methodism gradually expanded in other parts of the British Isles, then beyond to the Thirteen Colonies in America and on to the rest of the world. The next five chapters deal with this expansion. It was the individual preachers who played the major part in this. Since Wales, closest to the major Methodist centre of Bristol, was first, Wales, Scotland and two other dependent island areas form this next chapter. Ireland, where expansion came after Wales but before Scotland, had sufficient preachers to demand a chapter for itself. After that the book turns to America, where the most extra-ordinary success merits two chapters, followed by one on the other British colonies where Methodist missionaries preached.

Wales

Introduction

Wales was a backwater in this period with a pastoral economy and lacking even a capital. Compared with Scotland or Ireland it was dramatically under-urbanized, but like them it retained its own legal system up to 1830.[2] The majority of the population counted themselves as within the Church of England. There were many problems for the Church, some becoming worse after 1760. Livings in Wales had suffered from the widespread lay impropriation of tithes and were very poor by English standards, leading to multiple pluralism and non residence. Most people in Wales spoke only Welsh, with the exception of the gentry, border areas and the south coast fringe. The

---

[1] *WJW* 23: 208 and note.
[2] M. G. H. Pittock, *Inventing and Resisting Britain: Cultural Identities in Britain and Ireland 1685-1789* (Basingstoke: Macmillan, 1997) 13, 15. This was a common English feeling in the early eighteenth century. According to Ned Ward writing in 1701, Wales was 'the fag-end of Creation; the very rubbish of Noah's flood'. It was regarded as an utterly remote and backward corner of Britain, populated by (to use the words of Geraint Jenkins) 'rude, uncouth and dishonest people'. G. H. Jenkins, *The Foundations of Modern Wales 1642-1780* (Oxford: OUP, 1993) 213.

prevalence of the Welsh language in most of the country created difficulties for the Church, though many services were held in Welsh; for example, in the diocese of Bangor all-Welsh services were the norm, though that did not prevent non-Welsh-speaking clergy holding office. The language problem was to create difficulties for the Wesleys. It also created a growing linguistic divide between the Anglicized gentry and the common people. The clergy, who were appointed by the gentry, tended to be on the wrong side of the divide and after 1760 more English clergy were preferred to Welsh livings. They often excluded Welsh bibles and prayer books and also became magistrates. The Welsh clergy suffered more than in England from lack of leadership. Bishops would spend time in London as absentees. No Bishop of Llandaff, the poorest diocese, resided in the diocese from the 1680s to 1821. If the Bishops came to Wales they were seen as carpet-baggers hoping for further preferment out of Wales. No Bishop wanted to die in office there; they wanted promotion to a richer English see. The arch-Whig politician Hoadly probably never visited his diocese of Bangor. The last Welsh-born Bishop had been John Wynne of St Asaph, who died in 1727. The next was consecrated in 1870. Welsh-speaking clergy lacked preferment and were often stuck as impoverished curates at best.[3]

Growth of Methodism

John and Charles Wesley from their base in Bristol crossed the Severn estuary to visit Robert Jones of Fonmon Castle, a prominent landowner in the Vale of Glamorgan who had close links with Minehead, and so the Wesleys and their preachers frequently visited them on their way to and from Cornwall. A society met in the dining-room at Fonmon Castle for some years. Other societies were established at Cardiff and neighbouring villages. Cardiff was the first society, established in 1740, opting against the Calvinistic Methodists and for Wesley in 1741. Many societies in South Wales did not choose between Wesley (Arminian) and Harris (Calvinist) until much later. The first 'New Room' which was built in Cardiff between July 1742 and May 1743 was for some time part of the Bristol Circuit, dependent on preachers coming out from the Bristol New Room.[4]

In 1749 Charles Wesley married Sarah Gwynne at the church at Llanlleonfel in Brecknockshire. She was the daughter of a Welsh squire, Marmaduke

---

[3] P. Jenkins, 'Church, Nation and Language: The Welsh Church 1660-1800' in Gregory and Chamberlain, eds, *National Church* 265-284.

[4] D. G. Knighton, 'English-Speaking Methodism' in L. Madden, ed, *Methodism in Wales: A Short History of the Wesley Tradition* (Llandudno: Methodist Conference, 2003) 1-2; A. H. Williams, ed, *John Wesley in Wales 1739-90* (Cardiff: University of Wales Press, 1971) Introduction which points out that when Wesley preached in Wales he was usually at first preaching to those who were Calvinistic Methodists. D. Young, *Origins and History of Wesleyan Methodism in Wales* (London: Kelly, 1893) and A. H. Williams, *Welsh Wesleyan Methodism 1800-58* (Bangor: Methodist Press, 1935) have also been very useful for this section on Wales.

Gwynne of Garth, a prominent supporter of the revival in mid Wales for several decades. A circuit may have been established based on Brecon, with societies at Hay, later Rhayader, Builth, Llandrindod Wells and Newtown. Considerable doubt, however, falls on how long this lasted. A circuit called 'Wales' was certainly established for Glamorgan in 1749, which may have included Brecon and the area further north. Though travelling preachers were shown for this circuit in 1749, 1753, 1755 and 1758, the societies north of Glamorgan do not seem to have survived. No records survived either.

Expansion in South Wales 1760s to 1781

In 1761 that intrepid pioneer Thomas Taylor was appointed to Wales as his first circuit. He began at Chepstow, preached in the Glamorgan societies and reached the Gower in February 1762. There he settled for the rest of the winter and formed societies. In the summer he also visited Pembrokeshire, travelling to Brecon as well. He stayed until the summer of 1763 and was the real founder of the societies in Pembroke. He established a Pembrokeshire circuit among the English speaking villages of Pembroke with bases also at Carmarthen, Fishguard and Haverfordwest. It was a little like Cornwall, with a number of small societies, even to the extent that there were often Cornish miners there. Again there was prominent gentry support, the Bowens of Llwyn-gair and Admiral Vaughan at Trecwn. The homes of both of these were places where Wesley stayed several times when he visited from 1772. The Bowens, though the further away, contributed a large share to the cost of the building at Haverfordwest. A sister of Admiral Vaughan was a member there.[5]

In 1769 two circuits were formed, Pembroke and Glamorgan, the second of these including Brecon. In 1770 a 'North Wales' circuit was set up with Brecon as its centre and three preachers. Richard Rodda was appointed that year and spent part of his time in Pembroke and part in the new 'North Wales' circuit, much of it 'enlarging our borders,' in other words founding new societies.[6] A chapel was built at Watton in 1770 and another preaching house at Hay by 1771. Haverfordwest was the biggest centre in the Pembroke circuit. It had sixty members in 1781. The other societies in order of size that year were Carmarthen fifty-three, Pembroke twenty-two, Roch eighteen, Spittal ten, Warren eight, Houghton and Morlais four each. It was still a tiny circuit by English membership standards, if large by miles to be travelled.[7]

From these bases Wesley and his preachers made regular journeys to Ireland via Holyhead or Fishguard. Welsh-speaking Gwynedd, Powys and most of

---

[5] *EMP* 5: 18-24. For Cornish miners see the reference to Cornish colliers led by Martin Rodda in J. Pilmore, *Narrative of Labours in South Wales in the Years 1767 and 8* (Philadelphia: Staveley, 1825) 20. Williams, *Wesley in Wales* 87n2, 94n2.

[6] *EMP* 2: 310-4. Unfortunately his description here is of places on the English side of the border. It was written for an English audience.

[7] Young, *Origins* has the numbers from the MS Circuit Book.

Deheubarth were left virtually untouched. All these were the province of the Calvinistic Methodists led by Howell Harris and others. Wesley tried not to intervene. As these became more under attack by Anglican clerics, so they became more disaffected to the Welsh Church in which they had been nurtured.

North Wales

There was little early attempt to preach in the relatively small areas of English speaking north Wales. As early as 1750 Holywell was on the Circuit Plan of John Bennet in Cheshire. In 1762 there was a Methodist society in Mold; Wrexham had one by 1763. Another early Methodist society was started at Rackery Farm near Gresford around 1766, the home being that of the Williams family, who became prominent in Wesleyan Methodism. The influence of the Williams' drapers shop in Wrexham helped to start Welsh-speaking Methodism in North Wales. Three of Richard Williams' six daughters married probationers stationed at Chester. Wesley preached in Wrexham in 1781 where he said that 'a flame was kindled both in Chester and Wrexham which, I trust, will not soon be put out.' Industrial development in Denbigh and Flint led to English migration and the beginnings of societies in the area. Further south in Montgomery Thomas Carlill from the Brecon circuit preached at Pentre Farm in 1776. A society was founded at Pentre Llifior in May 1778. However, in general in north and central Wales there was little expansion before the Welsh Wesleyan Mission inspired by Thomas Coke and William Jenkins, headed by Jenkins' friend, the Welsh-speaking preacher Owen Davies.

Wales was similar to Scotland in the smallness of the societies and poverty of the circuits. Though the weather was worse in Scotland, both involved long distances to walk. Circuits often could not afford horses. Preachers who came from Wales tended to spend most of their time in England, again like the Scots. Methodism remained relatively weak in both countries.[8]

Numbers and Distribution of Travelling Preachers

Methodism in Wales under Wesley only flourished, therefore, where there was gentry support and leadership. So it was almost entirely from these more anglicized parts of South Wales that any of Wesley's preachers came. This can be seen from the map on page 41. A total of eighteen preachers were born in Wales, which at 3.6% was much higher than might be expected from the number of Methodist members. Three preachers came from Brecknock, led by Thomas Coke, the son of a well-to-do apothecary in Brecon. Another three came from Pembroke, while two came from each of Monmouth, Glamorgan and Cardigan. Here again most entered in the early years and many had been converted elsewhere, like Thomas Olivers at Bristol or William Holland in

---

[8] Knighton, 'Methodism' 5-6. Williams, *Welsh Methodism* 45-68.

London. The two from Glamorgan both came from the more Anglicized east close to Bristol. After 1753 only four preachers from individual Welsh counties are known to have entered.[9]

Welsh Preachers

In Brecon the local preacher John Watkins of Llanusk had been preaching since circa 1754. Even earlier Henry or Harry Lloyd, a property owner from Rhydri in Glamorgan had been converted in August 1743. From 1746 he was a local preacher, the first apparently who could preach in Welsh. He was described in the Minutes in 1747 as someone who 'assists us chiefly in one place,' but also travelled. Lloyd was on good terms with the Calvinistic Methodists and was a freelance exhorter who wrote elegies on Harris and Whitefield. He spent most of his time in South Wales but frequently acted as guide and interpreter for John Wesley in Wales, as in April 1749 at Llanwynno when in Wesley's words 'few could understand me, so Henry Lloyd, when I had done, repeated the substance of my sermon in Welsh.' He had a wife and family, though little is known about them. He travelled sometimes in English circuits such as Cornwall and Manchester as well as neighbouring Bristol and so was not permanently in Wales. He was still 'preaching up and down chiefly in Welsh at the discretion of the Assistant' in Wales, according to John Wesley in 1779. Lloyd translated some works of both Wesleys into Welsh. Myles described him as a travelling preacher who 'died in the work.' He remains an elusive figure about whom we know little, typical of Welsh Wesleyanism for most of the century.[10]

Owen Davies and the Welsh-language Mission

Owen Davies was typical of the later preachers in many ways. He was significant because he led the successful Welsh speaking mission. A twin born at Llanrhaiadr-ym-Mochnant in Welsh-speaking Powys, he was baptised there in March 1752. His father (also Owen Davies) worked as a tailor and moved when Owen was very young to nearby Wrexham, a town on the edge of Wales where there was growing industry and more money. Owen was therefore brought up to speak both languages. Owen heard the preaching of the local

---

[9] Appendix One Table 12.

[10] For Henry or Harry Lloyd (his names are spelt in many different ways) see Williams, *Welsh Methodism* 32-3; *JWL* 6: 359, 8: 134: *WJW* 20: 266 n40, 22: 200 n95; Young, *Origins* 94; Atmore; Williams, *Wesley in Wales* 40n2; *Bathafarn* 23 (1968) 11, 24 (1969) 36-40; Myles; G. Lloyd, ed, *Catalogue of the Early Preachers Collection* (Manchester: MARC, 1995) DDPr 2/20; *PWHS* 2 (1900) 67, 27 (1949-50) 74-5; *DOMBI*; *HMGB* 3: 257; Manchester Circuit Account Book at Manchester Central Library; *DWB*. Llanwynno is on the top of a mountain between Llantrisant and Aberdare in Glamorgan.

preacher Mr Gardner in Wrexham, which was part of the Chester circuit. His older brother John had moved to London and Owen followed, a tailor like his father in search of work. He became a Methodist and married Mrs Hemmings who kept a school in Ealing where the wedding took place in March 1778. She was a Cornishwoman, mother of Thomas Hemmings who entered the ministry in 1794 but left in 1795 unable to cope with itinerant life. Owen Davies moved to the East End of London and became a local preacher, first as part of a team who preached at the Mile End workhouse. In 1787 he was asked by Thomas Olivers to become a travelling preacher. He refused and Olivers rebuked him strongly. Davies regretted his refusal and offered his services to Henry Moore and may well have become an itinerant in 1788; certainly soon after the 1789 Conference he was sent to Manchester.[11] Although he was already married, Davies was one of the few who was allowed to become a preacher which suggests his preaching ability. He became Chairman of the Cornwall district early, in 1797, where he helped to lead a revival. He was the friend of William Jenkins, who had a similar history. Jenkins was another London Welshman who was better off than Davies since he had trained to be an architect. As trainee local preachers in London Methodism they would have known each other before they entered. In 1790 the 27 year old Jenkins was sent back to Bedford, where he had been the previous year. With him went his friend Davies, ten years older than Jenkins, and the friendship became deeper during the year. In that circuit Jenkins had already converted his future wife, whom he had 'brought out of the gay and fashionable world' of Northampton. In 1791 the friends spent the year in the relatively new King's Lynn circuit. Jenkins had ability and influence. He was stationed in important circuits from 1797 onwards, partly because he could and did use his architectural expertise to build significant chapels, like Hinde Street London and Carver Street Sheffield. Sensibly Conference had put him on the Connexional Building Committee, which gave permission to build, as early as 1790 when he was still on trial. A sign of his standing among the preachers was that they elected him in 1806 to become Secretary of the Itinerant Preachers' Fund.[12]

---

[11] For Owen Davies see *WMM* 1832: 159, 389-99, 469-81, 541-7; Williams, *Welsh Methodism* 72-81, 85-9; *PWHS* 18 (1931-32) 94-98, 21 (1938) 176, 27 (1950) 155-6; MSS at National Library of Wales at Aberystwyth e.g. MS Journal 1800-8 of John Hughes; Atmore 531; *DWB*. Mrs Hemmings also appears as Hemmons in the marriage at Ealing in the *IGI* and as Hemans. Hemmings served briefly in Chester circuit alongside his stepfather.

[12] For Jenkins see *MH* 41 (2000) 33-48; *WMM* 1838: 399; Atmore 533, MS London Stewards Book (at MARC), *WJW* 24: 197, 340. His MS Papers 1806-42 are at MARC. Jenkins superannuated because of ill health in 1810 and joined the family architectural firm based in Red Lion Square again. Jenkins' importance to the Welsh mission was such that it became the basis of a legend: see A. R. Williams, *Legends of the Severn Valley* (London: Folk Press, 1925) 11-20. The quotation about Northampton is from his wife's obituary.

Timeline 2: Britain's Periphery

Year	Wales	Scotland	Isle of Man	Channel Islands
1740	Cardiff 1st society			
1749	1st Welsh circuit			
1751		John Wesley's first visit		
1757		Dunbar society		
1759		Hopper explored to Peterhead		
1761		First Edinburgh building		
1762	Taylor in the Gower & Pembroke			
1765		Taylor in Glasgow 4 circuits		
1766	Rackery society			
1769	Pembroke circuit			
1770	Brecon circuit			
1774				1st society in Jersey
1775			John Crook as Missionary	
1778	Pentre Llifior Society	3 circuits	Separate circuit	
1781			JW visit. 2,000 members	
1784				Robert Brackenbury to Jersey
1785		Four preachers in Scotland ordained		Guernsey society
1786			Crook Assistant again	John De Queteville in Guernsey
1787				Alderney society
1791	3 circuits	7 circuits	2,500 members	3 circuits and French mission
1799			Revival	
1800	Owen Davies Miss'y 1,244 members	1,056 members	3,650 members	795 members
1803	Welsh District (Welsh-speaking)			
1810	5,649 Welsh & 2,451 English members	1,449 members	2,660 members	900 French & 286 English members

By April 1800 there was Welsh language work around Ruthin. Thomas Coke, who had been born in Wales and had frequently travelled through it to Ireland, bemoaned his inability to preach in the language. When he and Jenkins combined to persuade the London Conference of 1800 to support a mission in Welsh speaking north Wales, Coke had already sounded out Davies about it. Davies, born closest to north Wales of all the preachers accepted by Wesley, volunteered to head the Mission. He was sent to north Wales as missionary in 1800 with an 'unlimited commission to form a new Circuit.' In 1802 he was appointed Superintendent of the Welsh Missions and in 1803 a Welsh district was set up with him as Chairman. However, his stationing in Wales was not permanent, for in 1806 he was moved to the English work for a year and then again for the longer period 1808-15. Davies found it difficult to walk or ride a horse, being both large and corpulent. Because he had lived so long in England, he was never able to do more than exhort in Welsh. His Welsh writings were completed in English and translated by others. Like many of the period, he too often built chapels in Wales with no regard to the regulations on debt. The chapels depended upon being filled regularly and depressions at that time meant industrial growth faltered. Debts pursued the trustees for generations after his death. However, Davies was the real founder of Welsh Wesleyanism which produced 5,700 new members and nearly 50 ministers in ten years. He died in 1830 aged 77 at Liverpool, which acted as the capital of Wales in England in the nineteenth century with a strong Welsh community, and he was buried in the entrance of Brunswick Chapel. He had been a Supernumerary in the town from 1818. The retirement of Jenkins and the death of Coke, however, meant that the connexional financial support largely ceased after 1815. Welsh-speaking Methodism went into a period of retrenchment. Some of the best preachers were, like Davies, transferred to the English work.[13]

The striking growth of Methodism in Wales came with the rise of Welsh-speaking Methodism after 1800, and in the nineteenth century with the growth of industry in South Wales which brought in many English speakers, some of whom brought their Methodism with them.

Scotland

Introduction

The people of Scotland in the eighteenth century mostly spoke Scots, a language as far from English as Dutch is from German. This itself, though easier than Welsh, was a difficulty for Wesley and his English speaking preachers. Another problem for him was that Scotland, though becoming more British, was strongly anti-English. Wesley and most of his preachers in

---

[13] CJ. For the beginnings of Welsh-speaking Methodism see G. T. Hughes, 'Welsh-speaking Methodism' in Madden, *Methodism in Wales* 23-38. The other leaders of the movement entered after Wesley's death and so are excluded from this account.

Scotland were English, though many like Hopper came from the north of England. The country was divided between the largely Jacobite Highlands, where many clans were proscribed after Culloden in 1745 and many clansmen over the next eighty years emigrated, and the prosperous Lowlands, where trades of all kinds from cattle droving to metal-working thrived. The (Presbyterian) Church of Scotland, though beset by opposition from Anglican and Roman Catholic alike, did win its battle to Protestantise and gain for the English language the Highlands of Scotland, due partly to superior resolution but also to its successful use of lay agencies.[14] In the eighteenth century it remained overwhelmingly the religion of the people of Scotland, despite substantial challenges from Episcopalians in the north east, Catholics in the Highlands and Seceders in various places. However, economic and social changes were leading to a pluralization of religion away from the Established Church. Evangelicals were growing more rapidly than the dominant Moderates. It was the Evangelicals who later tended to break away.[15]

Numbers of Preachers and Distribution

In Scotland the number of Methodists and therefore of Scottish-born preachers was very small. Eighteen preachers came from Scotland (3.6%), rather better than Methodist membership which in 1791 was 1.6 % of the whole. As with the Welsh or Irish, therefore, more Scots became preachers than would be expected from the raw number of members and probably for very similar reasons. The small numbers mean than we are less certain about drawing any conclusions.[16]

Within Scotland Methodism did best further north on the east coast, where two preachers came from Aberdeenshire, two from Perthshire and three from Angus, Robert Dall, Alexander Mather and Peter Mill. 64% of those known were from those three counties in the north east. Numbers rose in the 1760s, with eight preachers entering; it stayed almost level in the 70s when six entered, but fell in the 1780s to a single preacher in the fifth and final cohort. This could well be due to the Erskine controversy, when John Erskine attacked Wesley's Arminian views in 1765 in the preface printed in Edinburgh to Hervey's *Aspasio*. After the 1760s Scottish Methodism failed to grow at either the pace of increase of the population or of the other churches in Scotland. From 1767 to 1784 the annual rate of growth was on average a mere 0.2% per annum compared to 55% in England, 65% in Wales or almost 85% in Ireland.[17]

---

[14] J. MacInnes, *The Evangelical Movement in the Highlands of Scotland 1698-1800* (Aberdeen: Aberdeen UP, 1951); Pittock, *Inventing Britain* 45, 57.

[15] C. G. Brown, *Religion and Society in Scotland since 1707* (Edinburgh: Edinburgh UP, 1997) 16-25. Pittock, *Inventing Britain* 10 for the Episcopalians having between a half and a third of the Synod lists as late as 1708.

[16] Appendix One Table 12 for this and the next paragraph. For possible reasons see Chapter 11 below.

[17] Brown, *Religion in Scotland* 36. Myles suggested this on 103. F. Whaling's article

Growth of Methodism

What success occurred was due to Wesley's preachers rather than his own efforts, as Wesley Swift said as long ago as 1947. Wesley's first visit to Scotland of two days was in 1751, against the advice of most of his friends. The invitation came from Colonel Gallatin who led a society among the soldiers in the garrison at Musselburgh. From the first Wesley tried to work with the Scots Presbyterian Kirk, usually without success. However, in 1753 Dr John Gillies of the College Church in Glasgow invited him to stay and this began a long friendship. Wesley planned his journeys to Scotland around visiting him, Gillies' home becoming his Glasgow base. The Newcastle preachers may have crossed the border a little, but it was not until 1759 when Christopher Hopper rode north as far as Peterhead, preaching en route, that the preachers began to make a serious effort. By 1763 prospects had improved and so Hopper spent the winter in Edinburgh, the equivalent of the first circuit, though we do not know that it was an official circuit at that point. When the circuits emerge from the mists in the printed *Minutes* of 1765 there were four Scottish circuits, Edinburgh, Glasgow, Aberdeen and Dundee. There were societies at Dunbar (meeting in a room in 1757), Edinburgh (with a building from 1761), Aberdeen (with a building from 1764), Dundee (with a resident preacher from 1764) and Glasgow (where the pioneer in Pembrokeshire, Thomas Taylor, was stationed in 1765 to found one). In other words, in Scotland fourteen years after Wesley had first visited Methodist members were still extremely scarce. In Wesley's later years he worked closely with various members of the Scots aristocracy such as Lady Glenorchy and Lady Maxwell. However, though the second of these actually became a Methodist member, in general the support was from a distance and without lasting effect. Noble families, as elsewhere, rarely became Methodist for more than a single generation.[18]

Early Preachers who went to England

Whereas in Wales very few Methodist preachers were born, in Scotland the number was larger, though still much smaller than Ireland. As in Ireland the most important went to England and stayed there, often before they became Methodists. This applied to William Darney, the itinerant who raised his own societies on the Lancashire/Yorkshire border and was difficult for Wesley to control. It was also true of Alexander Mather, the baker born in Angus, who went to London young, eventually became a travelling preacher and became Wesley's right hand man in the final fifteen years of Wesley's life. Similarly

---

'The development of Methodism in Scotland pt 1 to 1791' in *WHS Cul* 45 (2000) 12-14 pointed to the striking decline in Scots membership from 735 in 1774 to 439 in 1782.

[18] W. F. Swift, *Methodism in Scotland: the First Hundred Years* (London: WHS lecture no 13, Epworth, 1947) 12, 18, 42; W. R. Ward, 'The Evangelical Revival in Eighteenth Century Britain' in Gilley and Sheils, eds, *Religion* 268.

Thomas Rankin, who was born in Dunbar and was a preacher from 1761, was sent by Wesley to America to run that operation more forcefully. When he returned from America he married and settled down in London, but remained Wesley's close adviser until his death. Others who only preached in England included Alexander Coates, who, though born in Scotland, was converted in England and travelled for twenty years but never in Scotland. All four of these played key parts in the development of Methodism under Wesley. They were as significant as the Irish preachers, though far fewer in number.

Later Preachers

There was later a small group of Scots-born preachers who remained mostly in Scotland. The most important of these was Duncan M'Allum, the Highlander son of a clansman of the Whig leader the Duke of Argyll, who was fluent in Gaelic. He was born in Arrochar in Argyll in 1755, becoming a Methodist preacher at nineteen and travelled for fifty-one years. Nineteen of those years he spent in the far north of Scotland, either in Inverness or Aberdeen. Though he crossed the border he never went further south than Newcastle. Wesley called M'Allum the 'North Star.' For most of his Scots ministry he preached four times on Sunday, twice in English and twice in Gaelic. In 1786 Coke wanted him to be the Scots missionary to the Highlands. Nothing came of it.[19]

There were others the majority of whom, though they travelled in Scotland for some periods, spent more time further south, mostly in Yorkshire. This applied to James Dempster (who went to Ireland and America as well), Alexander Suter, Robert Dall, the soldier Duncan Wright, and Alexander M'Nab. Most of these married English wives. Two of them, M'Allum and Suter were ordained for Scotland.[20] This is a relatively low proportion both of those born in Scotland and those ordained for Scotland, and shows that Wesley depended on English preachers for Scotland and had no compunction about sending Scots preachers outside their own country. His attitude was a British solution to the problem, not a Scots nor English one. It was one of the reasons why Methodism did less well in Scotland, both under Wesley and afterwards.

The north of Scotland was particularly hard in terms of weather for the Methodist preacher. Matthew Lumb arrived in the Inverness circuit in 1784. He found 'everything disagreeable to flesh and blood, except the kindness of the people'. Travel was difficult, with the winter longer and harsher and the circuits

---

[19] For M'Allum see W. F. Swift, *The Romance of Banffshire Methodism* (Banff: Banffshire Journal, 1927) 28-9; *City Road Magazine* 1875: 560-9. For Coke's plan and its failure see Vickers, *Thomas Coke* 136-141. When M'Allum superannuated in 1827 he spent the next five years at Aberdeen, before dying at North Shields.

[20] For the ordinations see Chapter 18. For Suter and Wright see Chapter 6, Dall Chapter 7 above, Dempster Chapter 12 and M'Nab Chapter 15 below. Others like these who went south included Duncan Kay, Andrew Inglis, Peter Mill, George Mowat, Thomas Simpson, Robert Swan, and William and James Thom.

more extensive than England. Journeys were done on foot because circuits could not afford a horse. Aberdeen and Inverness were in the same circuit until 1784.[21]

Why did Methodism do less well in Scotland?

The question as to why Methodism registered a relative failure in Scotland in this period and later is an interesting one. Brown defined it as 'the general and seemingly unique failure of Methodism amongst an English-speaking Protestant manufacturing population.' He suggested a possible reason in the Scots' desire for fully ordained clergy rather than lay preachers. Wesley gave way to that pressure in 1785 and this resulted in a doubling of membership in four years. After his death Conference partly reversed this with consequential losses (below, Chapter 18). Scots felt that the power of elders in the Presbyterian system was more than that of stewards or local preachers in Methodism, not that there were many calls for local preachers in Scotland. There were so few societies that most of the preaching was done by the travelling preachers. Some circuits consisted of one or two societies only. As a result a smaller proportion became local preachers in Scotland, which in turn led to fewer travelling preachers coming from Scotland. It is also clear that the dominant note of Methodism's call to conversion was already being preached by others in Scotland and therefore Scots simply saw Methodists as unnecessary. The system of one minister one church was working more successfully in the Church of Scotland than in the Church of England in the eighteenth century. Methodists found it difficult to provide the same. Their preachers, when restricted to one or two societies in the towns and cities, struggled to preach every Sunday to the same congregations who were in any case used to a higher standard of learning from their ministers. Scotland in the eighteenth century was strongly Presbyterian and the national church was just that, Scottish, proud of it and representative of Scotland. Most Calvinists were in principle opposed to the Methodists who were keen Arminians and seen as English. Perhaps the other reason was the one Brown did not rate: that in fact the linguistic difference was so great that it was not a true 'English-speaking population.'[22]

After Wesley Scotland gradually lost the input which Wesley had provided. He had sent there some of the best preachers (Hopper, Benson, Pawson, Bardsley, Atmore and others). By the nineteenth century many Scots appointments were filled by probationers, who were less experienced. Most seized the first opportunity to head south again and never returned. Swift suggested that the number of preachers did not grow sufficiently to match the number of members. Distance proved difficult for societies widely separated

---

[21] *AM* 1791: 609-10.
[22] Brown, *Religion in Scotland* 36-7.

from each other, like those in the Borders or in the far north. The only areas where Methodism was relatively strong were Glasgow and Paisley, which provided almost half the membership in 1810.[23]

Isle of Man

Introduction: Islands

Islands have always been fertile ground for Methodism. In addition to the examples considered here, there has been the work in the West Indies to be described in Chapter 14 and later, in places like Tonga, Fiji, or, closer to home, the Shetlands. These all maintain a strong Methodist witness into the twenty-first century. Sociologists say it was because they were cut off and isolated. Methodists say it was because Methodism gave them help from outside in the form of one of Wesley's preachers and later the trained and experienced minister, while encouraging local community life and development. It was a partnership where benefits were gained by both parties.

The Isle of Man, despite the good work of the long lived Bishop Wilson in the early eighteenth century, was in many ways a deprived area with Manx still the language of the majority. Porter described both it and Guernsey, where Methodism was also to be very effective, as 'smugglers' lairs.'[24] John Crook was the first successful Methodist missionary here, a layman sent by the Liverpool society in 1775. Wesley swiftly took the mission up, sent Crook back several times as a travelling preacher and visited twice himself.

John Crook

John Crook (1742-1805) was famous as 'the Apostle of the Isle of Man' and should be better and more widely known. He was a Lancastrian whose father lost his estate through debt and went to sea and died. His mother remarried. John was apprenticed to a trade but wanted to get away and so he joined the army, serving mostly in Ireland. At the age of 24 he married in Cork and at 28 while in Limerick he was converted and joined the Methodists. His uncle helped to buy his discharge from the army and he became a local preacher in Liverpool. By March 1775 Crook had gone to the Isle of Man as a missionary. He saw little prospect of doing good when he went over. His Journal for March 1st 1775 says 'not a happy time; they think I turn preacher for what I can get.' Coming out of church in Peel he caught the regular congregation and gave them another sermon; 'many were converted' of the four hundred he said listened to him. He had some impact on Peel and, when his first six months were over, there were requests for Crook to return. He concentrated on Castletown but

---

[23] Swift, *Scotland* 64-7. The 1810 *Minutes* showed 650 members in Glasgow and Paisley.
[24] Porter, *English Society* 34.

raised a class in Peel and another in Douglas. Ramsey appeared somewhat more hostile towards him but he was obviously extremely popular, possibly because of his singing. Meanwhile the island societies had been placed under Whitehaven from where the three travelling preachers in the circuit each spent one month in turn on the island. For the two years of 1774 and 1775 Wesley sent Crook back as an itinerant to the Isle of Man, unheard of for one who was still a probationer. Or rather, he was sent to the Whitehaven circuit but spent most of his time on Man. During 1776 he met with strong opposition. His meetings were broken up and Bishop Richmond sent his clergy a letter warning against 'unqualified and unordained persons who presume to preach and set up conventicles.' Crook instituted the Manx Conference based on Peel, which unlike elsewhere in Methodism was a meeting of the local preachers and which personally examined all candidates for the local preachers' plan. The local preachers were important because part of their task was to accompany the English speaking travelling preacher and 'improve' on his message in the vernacular.[25] Crook encouraged the Manx language despite Wesley's opposition. He did three more years there, 1778-1781, and then two more, 1786-1788. By 1785 there were almost as many Methodist members on the Isle as in the whole London circuit in which Wesley had preached for over forty years, something like one in fifteen of the then Manx adult population. Meanwhile Wesley had also sent Crook to Ireland where he stayed after Wesley's death, alone among British-born preachers.

In 1797 Crook's wife died in Ireland and in 1798 he came back to England to Whitehaven where he was Superintendent and Chairman of the Whitehaven District, one which included the Isle of Man. He suffered from a scorbutic complaint after 1798 which made him unable to stand. In 1799 this meant he had to be a Supernumerary and he was supposed to be sent back to Dungannon in Ireland, but went instead first to Leeds and then to Liverpool. In 1800 he became an effective minister again at Birmingham despite his illness and continued working in various circuits. He married a second time at Rochester in the connexional year of 1802-3 and died at Scarborough. His active ministry was thirty years.[26]

Manx Language

Methodism in the Isle of Man gained 2,500 members in the short period up to Wesley's death, though no island-born travelling preachers were produced.

---

[25] The major source for this section is F. Coakley, 'The Rise of Manx Methodism' http://www.isle-of-man.com/manxnotebook/methdism/rise/rise.htm (accessed 5/3/2006).
[26] Crook was only put On Trial in 1775 and entered into Full Connexion in 1776. For his singing see *WJW* 23: 51, 208. See also for him *AM* 1781: 537; *MM* 1808: 3-10, 49-57, 97-105, 145-51, 193-204; *JWL* 6: 177-8, 228, 7: 144, 8: 3, 77, 120; *HMGB* 1: 238; *Pawson L* 2: 112, 3: 35, 43, 129; MS letter to JW 1776 in MARC DDPr 2/17, and 1801 at New Room; Tyerman BMM MAB B1245.

This success was largely because of the use of the Manx language. Even by 1809 two thirds of the population read, spoke and understood Manx much better than English, and one third of the population spoke only Manx. Although Castletown and Douglas would be expected to have relatively large English-speaking populations, Peel was always considered the most Manx of the towns, and so it is surprising that the English-speaking Crook achieved so much there. A small Manx hymnbook of translations from Wesley and Watts was produced early and much sung.

John Boyle

The closest the island came to producing a travelling preacher in this period was the half Manx John Boyle. Baptised at Whitehaven in 1767 his father was a Scot and his mother Manx. In 1774 he went to live with his maternal grandfather in the Isle of Man. He returned aged 14 to Whitehaven to live with his father as his mother was already dead. Boyle became a seaman to the Isle of Man and Liverpool and, after conversion about 1787, became a local preacher, entering the itinerancy in 1790. He was sent to Cornwall and married Elizabeth Magor, daughter of a leading Methodist in Kea near Truro. In 1799 he wrote a letter about the revival at Penzance to another preacher, John Braithwaite, who also came from Whitehaven. Boyle never travelled in the Isle of Man but left in 1802 and settled as a teacher among his wife's relations. He conducted preaching campaigns in the area and formed a breakaway connexion, the Boylites. After he retired in 1817 his followers joined the Bible Christians with the rest of the circuit. The Boylites were typical of many small Methodist breakaways in the early nineteenth century. Did Boyle's Manxness enable him to flourish in equally Celtic Cornwall?[27]

Polly Holder on Manx Methodism

A description of Methodism in the island showing some of the problems for preachers came from Polly Holder, the woman preacher married to the itinerant George Holder. She arrived with her husband in 1788

> We soon had many friends to welcome us. But everything was new and strange to me. The people,-their manners,-language; I neither knew yes nor no in their tongue. In the evening we went to hear a Manx preacher, and I was struck with surprise at seeing the people flock to chapel. The strangeness of their dress, with the unknown language of the preacher, seemed to put me in a maze; but while I sat, and reflected upon the goodness of God in causing the Gospel to be sent

---

[27] Shaw, *Cornish Methodism* 79; *PWHS* 26 (1948) 138; Dickinson, *Braithwaite* 322; J. C. Edwards, 'Memoir of John Blewett of Truro' in *Bible Christian Magazine* 1844: 227-36, 251-57, 274-80; *Arminian (Bible Christian) Magazine* 1824: 330. I am indebted to Colin Short for much help with Boyle.

amongst the people, through the means of a missionary sent from England, my heart and my eyes were much affected with gratitude and love to God and His servant Mr Crook who was the instrument of so much good here. Our first Sabbath was spent in Douglas, the public and private means were a blessing to many; their hearty singing, -their Amens, and serious countenances, affected me much. I was pleasingly disappointed to meet with so many agreeable pious persons in Douglas, and the place appeared to be far more pleasant than I expected. But as there was no house for a preacher and his wife, Mr. Smith, who was going to stay a second year, advised my husband to take me into the country with him, and one of the friends would prepare a furnished room for us upon our return. Our first ride was ten miles to Castletown, we had a pleasant view both of land and sea, the fields clad with corn, and a number of boats on the sea, with the men casting their nets for the fruit of the great deep. We had a blessed season in the evening. After preaching, the body band met and a sweet spirit of simplicity ran through the people; they freely told of the Lords dealings with their souls. We then had a short ride to Bellafeason; here we met with a few of our Lords children, and had a refreshing time together. From thence up the mountain to a place called How, here we could hardly understand one another, as they conversed chiefly in Manx. The next day we rode to Colby, where the word was precious and prayer powerful. The day after to Ballasalla, where are 22 in Society. My husband preached in the morning, and returned to Castletown to preach, noon and night. It was a day, I believe of general spiritual profit. On Sept. 9th we had a pleasant ride to Ballaclague and had a good meeting. A young woman was restored who had lost her evidence. To the Lord be the praise. The 10th we came to Ballacharry. We everywhere met with kind friends, and what makes all things more agreeable, our spiritual strength was renewed, in waiting upon God. The 11th we crossed the Moor and had a pleasant ride between the mountains to Berrol (Barrule) and had a view of the lead mines, and were blessed with divine favour.[28]

This passage illustrates important features of Manx Methodism such as its wide variety and the already very strong village societies. Despite the poverty of the entire community, the faith of the fishermen, the miners, and the Manx local preachers shone through in the vitality of their worship.

Crook and the Local Preachers

Crook's Manx Conference was criticised in the early nineteenth century by John Mercer

> He established good order in all the Societies; and had everything among them as regular as clockwork. However he set up one rule, which in my opinion has been, and still is, a great evil. I mean his giving so much power into the hands of the Local Preachers. He began by meeting them regular every Quarter, but instead of giving it the simple and proper name of Local Preachers' Meeting he gave it the

---

[28] G. Holder, *A Short Account of the Life of Mrs Mary Holder* (Whitby: Horne, 1836).

high sounding name of Manks Conference, and adopted most of the phraseology used in the Minutes of the English Conference. But the evil did not consist so much in the name, as in the nature of that meeting. For instead of attending to the simple business of a Local Preachers' Meeting, they also transacted the business of the Quarterly Meeting too, and I may say almost everything which belongs to the Leaders Meeting. And at last grew to such a height of despotism, that no man, however well qualified, must be a Circuit Steward but a local preacher. The above particulars have been a source of much grief to many of the travelling preachers, and of much contention between them and the Local Preachers. Mr. Lumb was the first who attacked their mixed system with any degree of success; for which daring attempt he brought on a paper war between himself and the Local Preachers, which was carried on with great spirit by both parties and ended in an appeal to the Conference.[29]

Mercer's criticism shows some of the reasons for later squabbles. Crook's use of the local preachers, however, was clearly the main reason for Methodism's success.

After Wesley

After Wesley's death Manx Methodism remained much the same. There was a large increase in membership as a result of revivals in 1799, but this was lost in the immediately following years. Strains arose in the early nineteenth century between the local preachers and the 'English preachers', as the travelling preachers were known. This was partly caused by the majority of the itinerants being probationers, as in Scotland. Their lack of experience meant they were often unable to stand up to the local preachers. It was also the result of Crook's creation of the Manx Conference which gave local preachers more power. The growth of Primitive Methodism in the Isle of Man from 1823 was largely a result of this strain. The Primitive Methodist Robert Faragher wrote in 1848

> What has Methodism done in the Isle of Man? Go ask our Sunday Scholars and their teachers, who and what they had been without it. Ask our benevolent and charitable institutions whence they sprung; or our friendly societies who gave them the first impulse. Methodism we say, with the greatest propriety, has changed the moral condition on Man; it has laid the foundation of many useful institutions; and is blessing thousands of our present population.[30]

---

[29] Mercer was a Yorkshireman who married a wife from the Isle of Man, had a farm there and travelled there several times. Matthew Lumb, a former missionary whom we met in Scotland, went in 1805. The letter of 1820 is in the MARC PLP 74-17-1; an edited version (leaving out the personal or entirely Manx comments) is available in W. R. Ward, ed, *The Early Correspondence of Jabez Bunting* (London: Royal Historical Society, 1972) 2: 29-36.

[30] The travelling preachers were called 'English preachers' because they preached in

The Channel Islands

Beginnings

The French-speaking Channel Islands in the late eighteenth century were as poor as the Isle of Man, dependent on smuggling and fishing. Methodism came late; two Jersey men in the Newfoundland fishery were influenced by Lawrence Coughlan's ministry there and on their return home formed the first Methodist society in 1774. This was unknown to Wesley. News only came to Britain when the army was drafted in at a time of war, when the islands were threatened by the French. The soldiers had served recently in America and been converted by Captain Webb. Corporal Miller, having joined the society led by Peter le Sueur and Jean Tentin, urged them to write to Wesley for a travelling preacher.[31] So in 1783 there was an appeal for a bilingual preacher to which the Lincolnshire squire Robert Carr Brackenbury responded. He arrived in 1784, lodging with Philip Perchard in La Place du Vieux Marche. On Sunday mornings he preached there inside, in the afternoons going to preach on a local hill overlooking the sea, La Chapelle de Notre Dame de Pas which belonged to Peter le Sueur. Meanwhile in Guernsey Pierre Arrivé heard in 1785 that his sisters in Jersey had become Methodists and wished to convert him. Arrivé was determined to stop them attending services and went to Jersey to reason with them. First he met Peter le Sueur who persuaded him to listen to the Methodist preaching. He was then converted and invited Brackenbury to Guernsey. Le Sueur's wife decided to leave him and take their child with her, but she was charmed by the genteel Brackenbury and became converted, much to the husband's relief. Brackenbury preached not only outside in Guernsey, but also in the drawing-rooms of some of the wealthier inhabitants. His ability to preach in French was the key advantage.[32]

De Queteville

Brackenbury had to return to Jersey and the pressing need for a preacher for Guernsey led to the first native Channel Islander preacher. Coke came immediately to discuss with Brackenbury how an itinerant who would preach in French could be found. He knew there was no suitable English itinerant for this work and asked whether de Queteville, a Jersey man already converted who had been preaching as a local preacher for a year, would serve. Coke promptly asked de Queteville. 'Yes,' came the reply, 'provided you can give me four or five weeks to prepare for it.' Coke decided to go himself to Guernsey to pave the way for the young missionary and spent a fortnight there in January 1786

English only. Faragher was a former Wesleyan local preacher reviewing Rosser's *History of Methodism in the Isle of Man*. I owe the quotation to Frances Coakley.

[31] E. R. Bates, *Captain Thomas Webb* (London: WMHS, 1975) 26-7.
[32] *MRWN* 1903: 61-2.

receiving eighteen names of those who wanted to form a class.[33]

Jean de Queteville, later known as 'The Apostle of the Norman Isles,' was the son of a local farmer, Elie de Queteville and his wife Marthe, nee Perchard. Born in 1761, he had been a boarder at Winchester School until 1777. He was therefore almost twenty-three when converted by Brackenbury in the spring of 1784. He began to preach on Christmas Day 1784, choosing I John 3:1 as his first text. In February 1786 he went as an itinerant preacher to Guernsey where he formed the first class. He suffered persecution.

In 1786 Wesley sent the young Irish-born preacher Adam Clarke to the islands since he could read French. Early in 1787 Clarke visited the much smaller neighbouring island of Alderney on hearing they could understand English; he was welcomed in the house of the Barbensons in Marais Square. A Jurat of the island, Jean Olivier, listened to Clarke and ensured he was heard out despite more hostility. De Queteville was the next to visit Alderney later in 1787. He and other French preachers raised the first society there and built a chapel. At the end of April 1788 he married the 20 year-old eldest daughter of Henry de Jersey of Mon Plaisir in Guernsey. She had been converted in 1786 by Thomas Coke and died in 1843 having borne several children.[34]

With the departure of Adam Clarke in 1789 and Brackenbury in 1790, de Queteville was left alone of the founders of Methodism in the Islands. He was seen by John Wesley as over strict, a not uncommon problem among new converts. He offered to serve in Nova Scotia despite having children by then, and went to London where he preached to the French refugees. However, his offer was accepted for the French mission in the 1790s, when the French Revolution seemed to give Thomas Coke and Methodism new and previously undreamt-of horizons. De Queteville was ordained at St Helier on the 22nd September 1791 by Coke to be a missionary in France. He travelled mostly in Normandy and suffered persecution, especially from the Jacobin regime. Eventually he returned to the Channel Islands where his father-in-law built a home for him and his family in Guernsey. He became a supernumerary in 1816. In his retirement on the island De Queteville wrote extensively and was much involved in children's Christian education. He was the author of many French Methodist hymnbooks and translated Wesley's *Sermons* into French. From 1817 to 1841 he was the editor of *Le Magasin Methodiste*, the magazine of the French Methodist Church and of Methodism in the Channel Islands. De Queteville died at St Jacques in Guernsey at the age of 81. By the time of his death, and thanks largely to his educative and translating work, Methodism in the Channel Islands had continued to grow and develop. There were then over 3,000 members, more than two thirds of whom were French-speaking.[35]

---

[33] Moore, *CI* 25-6.

[34] *WMM* 1843: 248, 769, 1035, 1854: 1-11, 1906: 340-4; H. De Jersey, *Vie Du Rev. Jean De Queteville* (London: Mason, 1847); *DOMBI*; Atmore 535; *AM* 1792: 104-8.

[35] M. Lelievre, *Histoire du Methodisme dans les Iles de la Manche 1784-1884* (London: WCO, 1885) *passim* esp. 385-94, 449-67, 545; Vickers, *Thomas Coke* 142-44, 312-14; *PWHS* 1 (1898) 53-4, 21 (1937-38) 81-7, 28 (1951-2) 68-72, 32 (1959) 75, 36 (1967)

Other Channel Island Preachers

Two other Channel Islanders entered in Wesley's lifetime, both less important but interesting in different ways. The first was a Jersey man William Dieuaide who was born in 1757, probably a nephew of Pierre Arrivé. In 1788 Dieuaide was in Alderney preaching and so he was already a local preacher prepared to travel for a short period. He was the first Channel Islander after de Queteville to be recognized as a travelling preacher, being accepted at the age of 32 in 1789. That year he was in Jersey, the next year in Guernsey. In 1791 he made four new members in Alderney. In 1793 he and his wife bought the building known as Les Calvins in Rue des Trois Pigeons, St Helier, Jersey, which had been used as a meeting room. They turned it into a dwelling house, living there until 1813 when the government took it over. In 1797 Dieuaide left the ministry under a cloud and apart from the fact he continued to live in the same house we know no more about him.[36]

The second preacher was the first Guernsey man to travel, William Mahy. He was born in 1763, his father a farmer. He himself was converted by John de Queteville. His family became strongly Methodist and produced several other preachers, including his younger brother local preacher Jean and his cousins Henry, who entered in 1791, and Pierre. By 1788 he was a local preacher living at Annesville, described by Adam Clarke as so poor he had to put his four or five children to bed to keep them warm. In 1790 he was employed as a travelling preacher in Jersey and Alderney, being in danger of losing his life in Alderney through persecution. He then went to France where he worked for several weeks before his ordination. Mahy was ordained in September 1791 by Coke at Courselles, Normandy for the French Mission. He itinerated in France for some time, but then became ill in 1806 and had to return first to Guernsey in 1810 and then to England. His mind became unbalanced with melancholia and he died in a mental home near Manchester where he had been since 1812. His widow was living at Periers in Normandy in 1814, but had moved to Guernsey where she was receiving some money from the Auxiliary Fund at least from 1824 to 1834.[37]

These three home-grown preachers give a hint of some of the factors which

---

37; *JWL* 7: 313, 377, 8: 19, 22: 26-8, 124; Moore, *CI* 22-59, 66-70.

[36] Dieuaide's age is given on his portrait. Myles; *JWL* 8: 68; E. T. Nicolle, *The Town of St Helier* (Jersey: Bigwood, 1931); Lelievre, *Methodisme* 322, 394; De Jersey, *Queteville* 235-6, 252; Clarke, *Adam Clarke* 1; 204; Smith, M. A. (Mrs R.), *The Life and Correspondence of Mrs Adam Clarke* (London: Partridge and Oakey, 1851) 65. Myles described him as expelled; Lelievre said he had committed 'reprehensible acts.' No details have survived.

[37] *MM* 1810: 126-7, 1814: 705; Lelievre, *Methodisme* 402-26, 502-3, 512; Moore *CI* 67-72; T. Roux, *Le Methodisme en France* (Paris: Librairie Protestante, 1940) 6-13; *Pawson L* 1: 166n; Vickers, *Thomas Coke* 372; *PWHS* 36 (1967) 37; *Magazin Methodiste des Iles de la Manche* October 1891 343-385; Atmore 534; De Jersey, *Queteville* 78-82.

helped Methodism in the Channel Islands, including the strong family ties typical of Methodism everywhere and the importance to them of the French language. They displayed missionary zeal by going first to other islands in the group and then the larger, more dangerous mission to France with which they had so many links. France was a different society, dominated by the revolutionaries and then by Napoleon who would tend to regard these Channel Islanders as foreign spies. In the longer term Methodist missionaries from these islands would come to play an important part in other French-speaking societies such as Haiti and the Ivory Coast.

Conclusion

In the 1801 census the population of Scotland was 1,599,068 and that of Wales 541,546. In comparison estimates for the Channel Islands are about 40,000 and the Isle of Man a mere 31,000. In 1800 the Channel Islands reported 795 members (1 in 50), the Isle of Man 3,650 (a remarkable 1 in 8), Scotland 1,056 (1 in 1,522) and the five Welsh circuits 1,244 (1 in 435). As we have seen above, members were only part of the Methodist phenomenon. Wales was on the threshold of the expansion of the Welsh-language mission. The Isle of Man figures were to fall in the next few years, while the proportion of Methodists in the Channel Islands would increase. However, especially when compared with the local population numbers, Methodist membership shows the relative strength of these four different mission areas. Methodism had been much more successful in the islands.[38]

Language was an important reason for success or failure in these areas and Ireland. In Wales, Ireland and Scotland Wesley was against the use of the local language and as a result there was a relative failure, where otherwise the neglect by the Established Church might have rendered them ripe for success. In Wales and Ireland later attempts in the local languages after Wesley's death led to some progress, but the Methodist historian must always wonder what would have happened if an Ouseley and a Graham, a John Bryan or an Owen Davies had been let loose on the native speakers earlier. Admittedly men like Owen Davies were not fluent in Welsh and depended on locals like Richard Harrison and Edward Jones as the real experts in the language.[39] The exceptions to this before 1800 were in the islands. In the Isle of Man, despite Wesley's opposition to travelling preachers using the vernacular, the local preachers preached in Manx most of the time and were highly successful, not least in interpreting for their English colleagues. Wesley adopted a more enlightened attitude in the Channel Islands, the last of these four areas to be

---

[38] Census figures are taken from J. S. Watson, *The Reign of George III 1760-1815* (Oxford: Clarendon, 1960) 517. The first Channel Islands census was in 1821. The Isle of Man figures are taken from Frances Coakley's Manx Notebook on her website. Membership figures in the *Minutes* vol II.

[39] For Gideon Ouseley, Charles Graham and the Irish Mission see the next chapter.

opened, where he encouraged preaching in French as well as English, sending suitable preachers like Brackenbury and Adam Clarke who could preach in French. He received three native Channel Islanders into the itinerancy as the first of many, all preaching in their own language. The result in the Channel Islands as well as on the Isle of Man was the creation of a lively, stable and very successful native language Methodism, which was to bear fruit outside those areas as well.

Conference after Wesley tended to adopt a policy of benevolent neglect towards all these areas, at least after Coke's death. The result was a weakening, especially where Methodism had not already become strong. Only the islands were exceptions to this and even they received fewer resources and tended to have probationers appointed who would never return to the islands once they had left them.

CHAPTER 11

Ireland

'What is it but a secondary kingdom... a suburb of England, we are sunk in its shade;'
Sir Laurence Parsons in the Irish House of Commons in 1790.[1]

Introduction

This chapter deals with those preachers who came from Ireland and those who travelled to it. There were rather more Irish preachers than British preachers about whom we know little, because of the paucity of Irish records as a result of the great fire of 1922 in the Irish Public Record Office. Of the 210 preachers who are known to have travelled in Ireland in the period up to 1791, 106 were Irish-born and 104 born elsewhere, roughly equal numbers.[2] This hides the fact that those born elsewhere predominated in the early days of Irish Methodism (1747 to 1765), while after the mid 1780s those who travelled in Ireland were almost all Irish-born preachers.

Many English Methodists of Wesley's day and later thought of Wesley's diversion of resources to Ireland as a waste of time. Wesley, however, as with Scotland, disagreed strongly. An anonymous Methodist soldier deployed to Dublin in 1745 founded the first Methodist society there. This society invited the Moravians, and John Cennick, a former preacher for Wesley, went in 1746. Some were probably dissatisfied with him and invited Wesley. Certainly early in 1747 Thomas Williams, one of Wesley's preachers, arrived in Dublin and formed another society. He too invited Wesley.[3] Wesley described it as a 'Providential call' and stayed for a fortnight. Soon after Charles Wesley arrived and stayed from September 1747 to the following March when John himself returned. It was Charles, here as often elsewhere in the early days, who did the

---

[1] W. E. H. Lecky, *A History of Ireland in the Eighteenth Century* 3 vols (London: Longmans, 1892) 3: 7. Parsons was a Irish MP.

[2] Three other Irish-born preachers only served in Britain.

[3] Thomas Williams from Llanishen in Glamorgan had been one of Wesley's earliest preachers, but had been excluded in 1744. He was reinstated, but it is unclear as to when this happened. For more details on him see A. H. Williams in *WHS (I)* 2: pt 3 15-30. These Bulletins provide much information on individuals mentioned in this chapter. See also D. A. L. Cooney, 'The influence of the Army' in *WHS (I)* 7 (2001) 80-81.

real nurturing of the society, heartening it against the early persecution and opposition which its existence provoked. But after his second visit (August to October 1748) Charles never returned. By the 1750s John was going almost every other year in the spring and staying for up to four months at a time, returning for the British Conference. His ancestral family links to England's internal colony may have predisposed him to feel Ireland was important. The size of Ireland's population, three million in the early eighteenth century to England's five and a third million, made Ireland more important in the eighteenth century than it was to become in the early twentieth after famine and emigration. The fact that the majority of the population probably still spoke Gaelic was only a part of Ireland's opposition to 'Britishness' and a consequential danger to the authorities. Ireland was the most colonial part of the British Isles, being bled by a partly absentee Protestant ruling class. The army had its largest peacetime concentrations there. Roman Catholics, the majority of the population, were discriminated against and difficult to persuade to adopt Methodism. Yet despite all this, Ireland was to become much more of a success story for Methodism than the other large parts of the Celtic fringe, Scotland or Wales. When the numbers of Irish Methodists who emigrated and took their Methodism to the rest of the world are considered, the effect of Wesley's preachers in Ireland was much more than can be counted from modern Irish membership in the twenty-first century.[4]

Wesley's Policy in Ireland: John Smith

Wesley's work in Ireland has often been criticized. He depended too much on the army. This was partly because some soldiers were already Methodists before they came to Ireland, but he also made a point of preaching to them. Furthermore he needed their protection, several times receiving it. However, the army was unpopular. Wesley was closely linked to gentry of the Protestant Ascendancy such as Samuel Handy of the Midlands and the Gayers of Derriaghy, and he attacked the Catholics. Ward pointed out 'his habitual preaching in the courthouse must have had a chilling effect on the Roman Catholic population.'[5] He did not particularly encourage Irish speakers to

---

[4] Cooney, *Ireland* 26-45. This replaced all previous works on Irish Methodism and is basic reading behind this chapter. The Wesleys' mother's family, the Annesleys, had taken part in the New English settlement. The controversy over the possible paternal link with the Wesleys of Dangan is dealt with by Rack in *PWHS* 53 (2002) 117-19, who shows that whether or not there was an actual genealogical link, the Wesley brothers and their Irish 'cousins' thought there was in the mid eighteenth century. Pittock, *Inventing Britain* 45-6. For Irish Methodists overseas see N. W. Taggart, *The Irish in World Methodism 1760-1900* (London: Epworth, 1986).

[5] W. R. Ward, 'Was there a Methodist evangelistic strategy in the eighteenth century' in Tyacke, ed, *Long Reformation* 285-306. The Slackes of Annadale in Leitrim were another gentry family which was at some point Methodist.

preach in their native tongue, so someone like Thomas Walsh, the earliest and most important Irish speaking preacher of Wesley's day, spent most of his ministry in England, much in London. There are parallels here with other Celtic countries, as seen in the previous chapter. In Wales Wesley avoided Welsh speaking areas, leaving them to Howell Harris and the Calvinistic Methodists who had started first anyway. In Scotland, despite encouraging Duncan M'Allum and others to preach in Gaelic, there was very little real consistent effort in the Highlands. The instructive contrast is with the Channel Islands, where men who could speak French (Brackenbury and the Irishman Adam Clarke) were sent and supported through a period of persecution.

Wesley defended his mission to Ireland against those who said it was not worth the effort. The late Frank Baker's judgment was that it was worthwhile because 'the sturdy independence of the Irishman, his emotional fervour, his robust physique and dogged endurance, made him a tough prospect for the Methodist preacher, but a valiant champion once won over.'[6]

It was only after Wesley's death that the mission to Irish speakers was taken up by Thomas Coke and the Irish Conference, and men like Gideon Ouseley began their aggressive ministry. This last point was mirrored on a smaller scale in the Isle of Man where, despite a gigantic success, Wesley refused to allow the Bible to be translated into Manx.

One Irish individual mentioned in Chapter 5 was very significant, even though he was a travelling preacher for a relatively short time. John Smith was born in 1713 at the Clare in County Armagh, the third child in a large family, born near Tandaragee in Co. Armagh; his father was of Scots Presbyterian extraction, a farmer and linen handloom weaver. Smith was apprenticed at the age of eleven and at eighteen, having completed the apprenticeship, he joined the army, probably as many did to get away from his family. Having left the army, he wandered the country plying his trade. Still illiterate at 25 he married 'a managing woman' called Mary aged 22, and settled in neighbouring Newry on the edge of northern Ireland. He had become a Freemason and was known as being the foremost bruiser and cockfighter of Newry. Eventually Smith moved to Cootehill in the east of Co. Cavan with his family. He was converted at the age of 45 in early 1758 by Thomas Kead and became a class leader and then a preacher. By 1763 he was preaching out of his own neighbourhood in Co. Fermanagh and founded a society at Tonyloman.

He began to travel at the age of 53 in the summer of 1766, called out by Wesley to go to Fermanagh and Tyrone, and led a significant popular revival in the border regions of Ulster, both the Lough Erne rectangle and the Armagh triangle and much of the country in between. Smith converted at least fourteen of those who became Irish travelling preachers, including such leaders as John Bredin, Andrew Delap, Thomas Barber and James M'Donald. Out of the 106

---

[6] F. Baker, 'The Lay Pioneers of American Methodism' in A. Godbold, ed, *Forever Beginning 1766-1966* (Nashville: Abingdon, 1967) 172.

Irish born this is a high percentage in an astonishingly short period. He converted at least 500 and started 36 societies. He did not appear in the *Minutes* until 1767 when he went back to the Armagh circuit which included Newry. Even then his name was wrongly given as 'Jos'(sic) Smith. He began the Markethill society in 1767. In 1768 he preached at Charlemont and Magheralough forming more societies, but was given no station after 1771. Instead Wesley, who did not visit Ireland in 1772, had deliberately set him free from circuit responsibility that year so that he could act as a missionary. When Wesley censured him in a letter in June 1772 saying 'he should return to his business,' this was probably because Wesley had been misled by Thomas Wride who had a history of quarrels with his fellow itinerants and was likely to be unhappy about any preacher who had been stationed in his circuit. Possibly Smith was freed from circuit responsibilities as a result of what Wesley found out about him when he investigated Smith's behaviour properly. Smith had no station in the *Minutes*, but was anything but inactive for his last eighteen months. He met much persecution. In 1774 he was waylaid at Auchentain near Clogher by an opponent, a Mr Nixon, while he was travelling from Enniskillen to a Quarterly Meeting at Charlemont. He died in March 1774 at the age of 59 as a result of this beating, in the home of the local preacher Samuel Bates in Charlemont.[7] Methodism's strength in Ireland was the consequence of Smith's success in the north, particularly Fermanagh, Cavan, Monaghan, Tyrone and Armagh in the late 1760s and early 1770s.[8]

Origins of the Preachers

Importance of the Celtic Fringe

Of the 507 preachers whose country of birth is established, 109 (21.5%) came from Ireland. These figures should be compared with the membership figures nationwide in 1791. In that year 19.3 % of the total of Methodist members lived in Ireland, and so the percentage of preachers from there is slightly higher than we might expect, especially in view of the fact Wesley did not go until 1747. Wales in 1791 had only 0.7 % of the membership, Scotland rather more at 1.6%. All the Celtic countries provided more preachers than would have been expected from the membership numbers, Wales particularly so, though admittedly the numbers were still small.[9] Hempton has suggested that this

---

[7] Gallagher *JB* 20-2; C. H. Crookshank, *A Methodist Pioneer: The Life of J. Smith* (London: WCO, 1881); *PPIM* 9-11; *WJW* 22: 80 n81, 283 n31; *AM* 1782: 668-9; *WMM* 1836: 2; *DEB*; Crk 1: 161, 177-85, 188-95, 198-203, 210-3, 219, 2: 7, 12, 14, 20-2, 27-30, 35-41; *JWL* 5: 324-5; *JWJ(C)* 422n; Smyth. Bates, who was English-born, later became a travelling preacher.

[8] D. Hempton, *The Religion of the People: Methodism and Popular Religion* (London: Routledge, 1996) 39. For Smith see also Chapter 5 above.

[9] *Minutes* 1791: 243: answer to question 14. For numbers see note 2 above.

might be the result of the survival of 'folk revivalism' for longer in the Celtic periphery. This fits with Methodist success in rural North America and Cornwall, both also isolated from contemporary culture. He also points to the 'economic competition and cultural and religious conflict,' 'a way of affirming their Englishness without being (too) Anglican.' By this he meant that in those areas Protestant settlers wanted to show their distinctiveness from ordinary conforming Anglicans but were still opposed to Roman Catholicism. This might apply in the Irish context, though as we shall see many of the converts in these areas were of Scots Presbyterian ancestry and practice; but it is doubtful in Wales and nonexistent in Scotland. All preachers tended to travel in the areas from which they came.[10] However, the larger percentage from the Celtic fringe meant that a substantial proportion of preachers in England came from outside throughout Wesley's lifetime and for some time thereafter. This began early. James Massiot, a wealthy Huguenot from Cork 'had travelled some years in England,' preaching at Ryton near Newcastle in August 1755.[11] After Wesley's death few Irish preachers were transferred to the English work. The three exceptions to this rule were in 1794 and 1795, including Walter Griffith whose wife was ill. They came to England partly through Adam Clarke's influence, as did his close friend James M'Donald.[12] In Wesley's lifetime this practice had been common, as with William Myles.[13] At least twenty-five of these Irish-born preachers died in Britain which gives an idea of the high rate of traffic between the two countries among the preachers. Many others, such as Andrew Blair and John Bredin, returned to Ireland having spent time in Britain.[14]

Another reason for the high proportion of Wesley's preachers who came from the Celtic fringe was the relative poverty of those areas. Just as Dr Johnson suggested that the finest prospect seen by the Scot was the high road to London, so it might be said that the finest prospect seen by the Irish Methodist preacher was the boat to Chester or Bristol! The thirteen mentioned (in the previous paragraph and note 14) were very able, including six future Presidents of the Conference and three of the most important Methodist writers of the

---

[10] Hempton, *Culture* 18-20, 30.

[11] *WJW* 21: 158n; *JWL* 3: 141n. Massiot entered in 1751 and died in 1756.

[12] *WMM* 1827: 150-2. The name was usually spelt M'Donald in the eighteenth century, though his descendants all used Macdonald. Who made the decision that M'Donald should come to England? In Wesley's lifetime the decision was his. Presumably the British Conference decided, but who suggested it first? The third preacher was William West who in 1794 was 'brought out of Ireland at great expense' (*Pawson L* 2: 121-2). For more on Griffith see Chapter 14 below.

[13] *AM* 1797: 209-12, 261-5, 313-7. He asked to come to England.

[14] Others who died in Britain included James Byron, Lawrence Kane, Henry Moore, William Thompson, Adam Clarke, John Prickard, William Horner and Jonathan Hern. Convenient summaries of what is known about most of these can be found in *PPIM*.

period.[15] Wesley wanted his ablest preachers in key circuits. It was not surprising that many of these served in places like London in the latter years of Wesley's life. James M'Donald, himself Assistant Editor of the *Magazine* (to Benson), was the grandfather of the Macdonald sisters and so the ancestor of the authors Rudyard Kipling and Angela Thirkell and of the Prime Minister Stanley Baldwin.[16]

A further complication was that Wesley in his old age encouraged able young Irishmen, who were pointed out to him as possible itinerants, to come to England to improve their education and prepare themselves for the itinerancy. So Adam Clarke in 1782 was sent briefly to Kingswood, while James Byron in 1785 travelled with Wesley for almost a year before being sent to Norwich, and was then accepted as an English itinerant in 1786. Unlike Clarke, Byron is not known ever to have returned.

Counties of Origin of Preachers in Ireland

The numbers of preachers from many counties in Ireland are too small to be statistically significant. Few counties had many Protestants, from whom Methodists tended to draw. However, three of the most important were in the north where Hempton shows that Methodism became strongest from the 1760s onwards. Eleven preachers came from Tyrone, twelve from Fermanagh and seven from Armagh, all in the province of Ulster. Next were Limerick and Dublin with six, two towns where Methodism was strong, and Antrim with five. Though the origins of the majority of the Irish born preachers are not known, of those that are, a staggering 82% came from the province of Ulster.[17] When it is remembered that Ulster was the last province to be visited by Methodist preachers and that the Presbyterian north east was anything but fertile soil, this success is the more startling. Hempton has commented on the reasons behind the Lough Erne rectangle and the Armagh linen triangle. These were all places where most Protestants were Church of Ireland and Protestantism was relatively strong. Linen weaving was an important industry. I want to stress also the importance of an area closely linked to the Lough Erne rectangle but not identified or explained by Hempton, namely West Tyrone immediately east of Castlederg, stretching to Newtonstewart in the east, Drumquin to the south and the outskirts of Strabane to the north. It is a rough diamond shape with Donegal to the northwest and Fermanagh to the southwest (see Map 3). It was the basis of a circuit from 1779, called Lisleen after a small society south of Castlederg. Matthew Lanktree in the early nineteenth century

---

[15] The three were Myles, for whom see Chapter 1 above, Moore, Wesley's biographer, and Clarke, the greatest Methodist writer in the period after Wesley.

[16] Also of Frederic W. Macdonald, President of Conference. See F. W. Macdonald, *Letters of James Macdonald 1814-31* (London: Kelly, n.d. c. 1907-10).

[17] Appendix Table 12 and see map on page 41.

Ireland

Map 3: West Tyrone

reported it was called the 'college,' because it had been 'the great nursery for training itinerant preachers.' West Tyrone was where John Smith had some of his greatest successes. It is not clear why Methodism flourished there, and even less clear why so many preachers came from this relatively small part of Ireland in such a short period. It was close to the gentry family of the Boyles of Kirlish Lodge near Drumquin who supported Methodism, but there is no evidence that this was a reason until Alexander Boyle was converted in 1774. West Tyrone was significantly smaller than either the Fermanagh rectangle or the Armagh triangle, yet produced as many preachers as the former and more than the latter. It was dominated at least in the east and north by the Hamilton family, Earls of Abercorn, from their estate at Baronscourt, south of Ardstraw.[18]

West Tyrone

The eleven men from Tyrone all came from the west. Three were described as coming from 'near' Castlederg, one also being 'near Ardstraw' to the north east. Castlederg town itself was solidly hostile to Methodism until a slightly later stage. One preacher came from Lisleen, south of Castlederg close to Killen. Six were from the south east of Castlederg, stretching from Drumclamph east of Castlederg just south of the river Derg to Creevy, a few houses five miles away. Two of these six, the Brown brothers, had been born at Urney or Orney to the north near Clady, south west of Strabane, but when converted they lived with their widowed mother at Creevy, just south of Magheralough. The other came from Magheracolton, a little further to the east. Many were tenants of the Hamiltons, descended from Scots settlers brought in by the Hamiltons over a hundred years before.

The surname types are also interesting. In this area, half Protestant and half Catholic with a strong Scots settlement, of these West Tyrone eleven, seven had surnames of Scots origin (Stewart, Hamilton, Kerr...), while only two had Old Irish surnames (one being a former Catholic); one of those was mostly of Scots origin, Hugh Moore, whose ancestor had been a Volunteer defending Londonderry in the Protestant interest in 1689. Most of the others had surnames which could be either Scots or English. Admittedly, surnames only point to paternal origins, and intermarriage between both racial and religious groups was taking place. Identifying the surname type is an attempt to detect the community from which they came. Both Smith and Steele, two of the 'New English' names, could well be Scots.

Hempton pointed out that, as in England, Methodist societies often met in

---

[18] Hempton is dealing with the 'Lough Erne rectangle' and the 'Armagh triangle' rather than counties. It is not always clear what areas these cover. The circuits listed had many societies outside the rectangle and triangle and altered boundaries frequently. Counties, on the other hand, had permanent boundaries. See Hempton, *People* 35-48. The Lisleen circuit was renamed Newtownstewart in 1792.

villages outside towns and on the edge of parishes, where religious provision had been poor. This can often be observed about the siting of Methodist chapels today such as the one at Lisleen.[19] When the question of cohorts among these eleven is examined, all can be seen as late. There were three from cohort four but the vast majority entered in the 1780s and were cohort five. This was the period when West Tyrone had its Methodist success. Two of the eleven, Harper and Owens, became missionaries in the West Indies.

The preachers from West Tyrone included an unusual number of brothers, two Browns, two Smiths from Cavandarragh, two Stewarts from Drumclamph and two Kerrs.[20] The Browns and the Kerrs were two pairs of brothers who had entered by 1791. After Wesley's death James Stewart and James Smith joined their older brothers Matthew and Robert in the itinerancy, thus six of the eight having become preachers in Wesley's lifetime. They came from small hamlets in the area of Castlederg, places like Lisleen or Drumclamph rather than from Castlederg itself. This is reminiscent of Fermanagh, where Methodism was at first strong in the villages and countryside but was not well represented in the county town itself until later.

The Moore family of Drumclamph is particularly interesting. The survival of a nineteenth century family history by two successive Ebenezer Moores shows how Methodism began in Drumclamph. Mrs Moore, whose husband Charles was in the army, heard John Smith preach two counties away at Belturbet in Co Cavan in 1766. The Moores then moved to Drumclamph and were the first to welcome John Smith into the area and their home in 1769. Drumclamph was halfway between Londonderry and Fermanagh and a useful stopping point on the way.[21] By accepting the message Smith brought they provided the first converts and the meeting place for the society. They led a whole series of large family 'clans' to Methodism, not only the Moores and the family with which they were most closely intermarried, the Hunters, but also their neighbours the Stewarts, who married another daughter of the Moores, and the Caldwells who were relatively wealthy. This account gives a good picture of their family's spiritual life with its typical belief in signs and wonders, its self sufficiency, its business acumen in later setting up a shop in the growing Castlederg and its connections over a wide area, even with London. The travelling preacher whom the Moore family produced was Hugh Moore, a poet and musician who entered in 1777 and left in 1790 as a result of the hostility of Thomas Coke, at least according to his family. Lanktree described him twenty-one years later in 1811 in Drumclamph as 'a man of a fine countenance and heavenly conversation,

---

[19] Hempton, 'Methodism in Irish Society 1770-1830' *TRHS* (1985) 117-142 especially 124.

[20] Other Irish brothers were the two Saundersons from Co. Down, the two Price brothers from the shores of Lough Erne in Fermanagh and probably the two Magearys.

[21] A society had been formed by the very similar Gray family in Lislap, just south of Newtownstewart in 1766-7. Crk 1: 184-85.

once a travelling preacher.' He never married.[22]

The Army

At least six of the Irish-born preachers were in the army when they were converted. This was partly because Wesley and the Methodists frequently preached to them, partly because Methodism provided the sort of care that the itinerant soldiers needed. The soldier might be in Limerick this month, Galway next, and Dublin the month after. In each of these places he would be able to visit a Methodist society. He might well find the travelling preacher was the same man he knew in his previous station. Again and again the army was the reason for starting a society in a town. This was true of the Black Watch in Limerick in 1749 and Carrickfergus in 1752 and of the Royal Scots at Cashel in 1755. Sergeant Robinet of the Irish Dragoons was the instrument for the conversion of Gideon Ouseley.[23]

Huguenots and Palatines

Many Huguenot refugees from France had settled in Ireland after the 1680s, especially in the towns. Some of the first society to invite Cennick and then Wesley to Dublin were Huguenots by descent, notably William Lunell, a leading woollen merchant and banker, with whom both Wesleys stayed in Francis Street. He contributed £400 to the building of the first Methodist chapel in Dublin in Whitefriar Street. Another, Richard D'Olier, was Wesley's last host in Ireland. In Cork the wealthy Huguenot James Massiot has already been mentioned. There were many others scattered around Ireland, notably in the settlements at Portarlington and at Lisburn, who welcomed Methodism.[24]

The Palatines were German Protestants settled in Ireland on the Southwell estate in Co. Limerick after famines and persecution in what had become Catholic parts of Germany in the early eighteenth century. Good farmers and

---

[22] F. Baker, 'Hugh Moore and John Wesley: Some Unpublished Correspondence' *PWHS* 29 (1954) 112-16. Frank based this article on the MS account and notebook mostly by Ebenezer Moore in 1877 summarising the genealogy and giving an account of each family member, listing not only their dates of birth and death but also chronicling their spiritual state; these have been preserved in the WHS Library, Oxford ref B/MOO/MOO. These Moores are not known to be related to the much more famous preacher Henry Moore. The Hunters produced two prominent surgeons in early nineteenth century London, one of whom was buried at City Road next to Adam Clarke. Lanktree, *Narrative* 221. In the notebook it says of Hugh Moore 'A scandal about him here and Dr Coke who was his avowed enemy struck his name from the Minutes.' Hugh Moore played both flute and violin.

[23] Also Galway, Kilkenny, Nenagh, Cappoquin, and Thurles. Cooney, 'Army' in *WHS (I)* 7 (2001) 80-91.

[24] Cooney, 'The Huguenot Connection' in *WHS (I)* 7 (2001) 61-68.

strong Protestants, many adopted Methodism. Settlements of theirs in Ireland like Ballingarrane and Courtmatrix, both Co. Limerick, became strongly Methodist. As they flourished some families moved to other local estates like the Oliver estate in southern Limerick or to Adare, Pallaskenry and elsewhere. Some like Philip Embury later emigrated to America and were important in the setting up of Methodism there (see next chapter). They produced many local preachers like Philip Guier, who was admitted as a travelling preacher at the Irish Conference in 1752 but never travelled, but only a few itinerants like James Morris and possibly John Miller. Certainly Miller retained his strong German accent which sometimes made him difficult to understand. Still preserved at Ballingrane (the modern spelling) in the twenty-first century is a large cow's horn. It was probably a predecessor of this which was used to summon the whole community in Wesley's day when the travelling preacher arrived, so that he should not waste time before travelling on.[25]

Catholics in Ireland

Modern historians agree that in general Wesley had little success with the Catholic majority in Ireland.[26] So far as the preachers were concerned few came from Catholic backgrounds. Only six of the 109 Irish-born preachers were definitely brought up as Roman Catholic. However, there were at least fifteen others with surnames of Irish or Old English origin.[27] This means that their paternal ancestors arrived in Ireland pre-Reformation and that therefore some probably belonged to Catholic families. Of these fifteen several may well have been brought up Catholics. James M'Quigg was a fluent Erse speaker. Alexander Moore was encouraged by a zealous former Roman Catholic to attend Methodist preaching. Michael Murphy came from predominantly Catholic Gorey in Wexford and had a typical Catholic given name. On the other hand, Richard Dillon was an Anglican clergyman and presumably nurtured in the Church of Ireland, as Thomas Ryan, the landed attorney of Co

---

[25] The Palatinate, strongly Calvinist in the seventeenth century, had been inherited by a Catholic branch of the Wittelsbach family in the eighteenth. Most of the German settlers in Ireland came from there and had been much influenced by Pietism. Wesley already had links to the Germanic diaspora through the Moravians. Cooney (*Ireland* 125-26) thought Guier was allowed to stay in Ballingarrane all his life as a full time preacher. I think the fact that he stayed shows he never became a travelling preacher, though I agree he was accepted. There are many British examples of the same situation. The fact that Myles, who was a leader in Limerick Methodism where Guier had his business, called him a local preacher seems conclusive. Morris's chief claim to fame is that he converted Toplady. W. Crook, *Ireland and the Centenary of American Methodism* (London: Hamilton Adams, 1866) and *DOMBI* 265.

[26] Cooney, Rack, Kent and Hempton have all written to this effect.

[27] The surnames were Bourke, Darragh, Dillon, Dinnen, Jordan, Kane, Kead, M'Quigg, Mealy, Moore, Murphy, Rea, and Ryan. There were two Dillons and three Moores.

Armagh, probably was. John Dinnen was brought up a Presbyterian. Recently Cooney has used a similar analysis of the much larger number of members of the Methodist society in Dublin in 1788 to suggest that a sizeable proportion of them were likely to have been Catholic in background. Without necessarily accepting the derivation of all his surnames, his point holds; of the fifteen preachers with 'Catholic' surnames at least five and possibly more were originally Catholics. This would mean eleven of the 109 Irish born (10%). Some Catholics, having converted at this or later periods, emigrated to America or elsewhere to escape the persecution from former friends that they invariably suffered. Of the six definitely known, Owens and Coughlan became missionaries overseas; Bredin and Walsh spent long periods in England. Of the others with 'Catholic' surnames Bourke and Kane went to England. This supports Cooney's most recent suggestion that the relative success of Methodism among the Catholic population of Ireland has perhaps been underestimated.[28]

Entry, Education and Marriage

Wesley's Irish born preachers often entered young. The youngest was Andrew Coleman who entered at seventeen, and the oldest was John Smith from Cootehill at fifty-three. The average age was 25.7, younger than the average of 27 for all Wesley's preachers. This was because there were relatively few from Ireland in the early period. Furthermore, the Irish born preachers were clearly different when the cohorts are examined, unlike the overall situation. Few Irish preachers entered in the first few years and so I have put the first three cohorts together. Their average age of entry was 30.1. The cohort 4 average was 27.3, cohort 5's average 23.7. Thus in the early days it is clear that in Ireland at least, because there were few entries, Wesley would accept anyone, without regard to age. As the number of candidates grew, Wesley responded by becoming more selective and it was more difficult for older candidates to enter.

Wesley was careful to try and look after those who were younger, often to put them in their own circuit or with someone whom they knew. In 1787 William M'Cornock was allocated to his presumed relative William M'Cornock the older in the Castlebar circuit. John West, who also entered that year, was placed under the care of his possible relative William West in the Longford circuit. This last appointment was so successful that Wesley continued the pairing in the Londonderry circuit next year. Many on entry were promoted rapidly to Assistant. David Gordon, entering in 1786, found himself

---

[28] Cooney, 'Dublin Society'. He includes as 'old Irish' names like Dalton which are actually Old English but were Catholic. 'Relative' because the vast majority of the population remained Catholic. However, the point about religion still holds. Old English names in the list in note 21 above are Bourke, Dillon, and Jordan. For Ouseley's success in the early nineteenth century see Hempton, *People* 135.

the Assistant in 1787 in the key town of Cork, with the even more raw Andrew Jeffreys to help him who had only entered that year. George Henderson, who began 'On Trial' in 1787, was sent immediately to be the Assistant at Enniskillen, supported by the equally new Thomas Kerr. Next year John Stephenson in Killybegs and Matthew Stewart in his native Lisleen were both Assistants in their first year of travel, with two other 'On Trials' with them.

Wesley's preachers were trained in many different ways. For their use particularly Wesley established bookrooms in Cork and Dublin where preachers could read and continue to learn. The young Henry Moore described how in Cork in 1783 'in the book room, kept by that holy man Joseph Ward, I found what was indeed a treasure to me Mr Wesley's Works in 32 volumes. These I read, or rather devoured, one by one and chiefly on horseback; every sentence of them seemed life and spirit to my soul; and I am persuaded that this year's study was more to me than many years would be under the ablest masters...'[29]

Many English preachers who came to Ireland married Irish wives. This includes well known men like Thomas Rutherford, Samuel Bradburn, Richard Boardman, Joseph Cownley, and also John Cennick though by that time he was a Moravian not a Methodist. Such preachers often stayed longer in Ireland as a result. Similarly those Irish preachers who went to Britain often married British wives. Examples of well known Irish preachers who did this included William Thompson, Laurence Coughlan and William Myles. A rather less well known instance was William Horner from Strangford who married Miss George of Sevenoaks, a member of a family who entertained Wesley.[30] Hugh Saunderson, who is best known for being the reason why Wesley was arrested in Scotland, was later expelled and later still linked to Joanna Southcott. Before his expulsion he was married in 1775 to a Bristolian, Elizabeth Hayward. John Saunderson, who was possibly Hugh's brother, seems to have married in Scotland in 1796. Such preachers were likely to stay closer to the new wife's relations and not to return to Ireland.

Irish preachers who became missionaries often married in the countries where they went. Such were John Harper who married Henrietta Hawes in Antigua and Thomas Owens who married Henrietta Gibbon in St Kitts.[31]

---

[29] M. A. Smith (Mrs R.), *The Life of the Rev Henry Moore* (London: Simpkin and Marshall, 1844) 78-79. See also Chapter 4 above.

[30] *WMM* 1836: 1-16. John Pritchard married Hannah Day of East Brent in Somerset, possibly a relative of the travelling preacher Simon Day. There were also Walter Griffith's and Henry Moore's second wives.

[31] *IGI* for Hugh Saunderson's marriage. For Harper, Owens and other Irish missionaries see Chapter 13.

Development of Methodism

Women

As elsewhere, women played a major part. They were a majority of members in every society outside the army. In Dublin in 1788 they were 52% of the society. They often invited the preachers to the town or village, opened their homes, became class leaders, and were active correspondents of Wesley and others. Mrs Bennis of Limerick and Waterford wrote to preachers and to Wesley over a lengthy period. Wesley trusted her over a wide area of southern Ireland. On her judgement preachers moved or stayed. Mrs Dorothea Johnson of Lisburn nurtured Methodism in the north east. So did Anna Slacke of Annadale in the north west. Henrietta Gayer of Derriaghy entertained Wesley and nursed him when he seemed on the point of death. Alice Johnson invited the first Methodist preacher to Derryanvil. In many cases it was the wife or daughter who persuaded the husband or father to attend and become converted. The young Agnes Smyth persuaded her husband, Edward Smyth the Anglican clergyman, to join the Methodists. It was Mrs Moore who invited John Smith to Drumclamph, when her husband Charles Moore was more reluctant. There were even cases of women preaching, like Alice Cambridge, Margaret Davidson, and Anne Devlin who married a travelling preacher. Women read books and magazines, distributed tracts, founded and taught in Sunday schools. All Methodist societies began as cottage meetings, often led and always hosted by women. And for every named woman there were thousands of unsung heroines who faced mobs, fed and sheltered the itinerant preacher and were the mothers of the next generation of preachers.[32]

Circuits

In 1749 there was one circuit for all Ireland. In 1752 the first Irish Conference at Limerick reported six circuits, all in the south except for one called the 'North East.' This Conference accepted some of the first Irish preachers, John Fisher, Thomas Walsh and Thomas Kead. By 1765 there were eight circuits, with three in the north including Castlebar. In 1781 there were fourteen circuits of which all but five were in the north. Membership, mostly in the north, showed a giant upwards leap in the 1780s from 6,000 in 1783 to 14,000 in 1789. Even at this late stage Irish circuits were still large and difficult. Enniskillen, for example, had four preachers in 1771, which made it strong in Irish terms. They had an eight week circuit, so that in the ninth week each preacher was back at the point at which he had begun the cycle. In that period

---

[32] Hempton, *People* 179-188. R. Raughter, 'Women in the household of faith' in *WHS (I)* 7 (2001) 20-33. For the Dublin society see Cooney's analysis in *WHS (I)* 10 (2004-5) 58, who emphasizes also the importance of proximity. There were 23 Methodist households in the short stretch of Whitefriar Street.

he would have slept at fifty different places, as Crookshank put it 'some of them damp and others not very clean.' They generally preached 'two or three times a day and often their fare was potatoes and a little salt meat.'[33]

Alexander Moore was Matthew Lanktree's first Assistant when he entered in 1794 on the Cavan circuit. Moore received him 'with tender affection. After suitable advice and prayer, he presented me with a travelling plan and accompanied me part of the way to my preaching place. Before parting he took me by the hand and in the most solemn manner repeated the apostolic injunction to Timothy 2nd Epistle, iv 1, 2.' The plan of the itinerant's journeys was complex, but must be followed.[34]

The Irish Conference

From a relatively early stage Wesley encouraged the preachers in Ireland to meet in Conference. The first one was held at Limerick in 1752. Ten were present with Wesley, four of these preachers probably being Irish. The next Conference was in 1756 in Dublin. After that for a long time Wesley visited every other year and so Conference was usually in Dublin then. The procedure was otherwise similar to that in Britain. From 1782, however, Wesley delegated the presidency in the intervening years to Coke who developed a special relationship with the Irish preachers. Like Wesley Coke toured the country, though less extensively. 1782 was the first of the Annual Conferences, as well as the first not to be presided over by Wesley in Ireland. The next year Coke had the Irish *Minutes* printed separately for the first time, another stage in Conference's development. In Wesley's day the Irish Conference was always subject to the decisions of the British one, and each year from at least the 1760s several preachers would leave immediately after the Irish Conference to travel by ship to Britain to attend the Conference there. Irish stations were sometimes changed in Britain.[35]

General Assistants

From an early period Wesley appointed one of the Irish Assistants, usually the Dublin one, as the 'General Assistant for Ireland,' with a watching brief over

---

[33] Crk 2: 14. The circuit included, as well as Co. Fermanagh, most of Tyrone, Cavan and Leitrim and some of Donegal.

[34] Lanktree, *Narrative* 24. 2 Tim 4; 2 reads 'Preach the word; be instant in season, out of season; reprove, rebuke, exhort with all long-suffering and doctrine.' For the plan see the description of the Yarm circuit in Chapter 8.

[35] *HMGB* 4: 112. The four Irish were Thomas Walsh, James Morris, Thomas Kead and John Fisher, but Cooney says only the first two were Irish. However, Gallagher suggested Fisher and Kead were also of Irish origin. The British printing of the *Irish Minutes* always had minor differences, partly because of changes made in England, but also because the *Irish Minutes* had more details.

the whole country. This was similar to his practice in other areas such as America or Newcastle for the north of England. Over the years General Assistant was a key post only entrusted to particular individuals who were especially reliable. They might be English or Irish in origin; what mattered was that they must be trustworthy. At first Ireland was often treated as one circuit with local rounds within it. Though the Minutes of the Irish Conference of 1752 showed six circuits, the British Conference of 1753 listed one 'Ireland' circuit, to which twelve preachers were appointed. It was up to Mr Wesley and his General Assistant, that year Joseph Cownley, to decide who went where.[36] In July 1750 Wesley had left Michael Fenwick as General Superintendent, a title Wesley later used in America for Rankin and Asbury. It was actually enshrined in the *Minutes* in 1768 when the Assistants for Dublin (and Edinburgh for Scotland) were bidden to bring to Conference an exact account of all the Irish (or Scots) societies and their collections for the different Connexional Funds. Thomas Walsh early on, John Johnson in the early 1760s, Adam Clarke, Joseph Pilmore, William Thompson and Henry Moore all held this position. As such they received frequent letters from Wesley, often preserved, dealing with business relating to other circuits and preachers in Ireland. If one preacher died, resigned or was causing problems, it was through the Dublin Assistant that Wesley usually worked. In October 1782 he wrote to Thomas Rutherford, then at Dublin, about Boardman's death at Cork and the best way to solve the problem (Blair was sent from Dublin to take his place).[37] It should be noted that half of these names were Irish born preachers. However, none of them lasted in his job. In Ireland as in Britain Wesley found it difficult to persuade himself that he should delegate permanent responsibility to others. No satisfactory Methodist administration was set up in Ireland to take over on Wesley's death.

From 1782 Thomas Coke took some of the load from Wesley by presiding over the Irish Conference in the years when Wesley did not visit. He also did some preaching on tour in Ireland in those years, doing what Wesley would have done. However, his increasing interest in the West Indies and America meant that his time in Ireland was, like Wesley's own, relatively short. As we shall see, he continued to do this after Wesley's death, and it was valuable for Irish Methodism.

Balance of Irish or British-born Preachers

The first historian of Methodism in Ireland, William Smith, produced a useful table of British and Irish preachers. It started in 1765 with three Irish and eleven British in Ireland, and the Irish only overtook the British in 1777. There

---

[36] *Irish Minutes* 1867: 546.
[37] *Minutes* 1: 77-78; *JWL* 7: 144-45. Other General Assistants were Thomas Taylor, Mark Davis, James Rogers and Andrew Blair. Readers of Chapter 17 below might doubt Wesley's judgement over appointing Fenwick.

were in Ireland 15 Irish that year and 12 British preachers.[38] Originally all the preachers had been British. Wesley moved them around so much that as late as 1779 seven out of the thirteen Assistants, more than half, were still from Britain. Of the total number of preachers 12 out of 32 in Ireland (37.5%) were still British, with leading names like Bradburn, Rutherford, Boardman and the Hampsons among them. There were 28 Irishmen in the *Minutes* that year so that the Irish oversupply among the preachers had not yet started. In the 1790s the number of British-born preachers on the Irish stations was reduced to one in 1796 and none in 1800. The 1780s was the significant decade. The fifth cohort of Irish-born preachers was 56, over half of the total of 109. It was then that the growth in the number of Irish-born preachers enabled Wesley to reduce drastically those of British origin in Ireland, to use Irish preachers in relatively large numbers for missions abroad and to bring some over to Britain to help in leading the British Conference. This was also the moment when the number of preachers coming from the West Tyrone area rose. When the men from Fermanagh and the Armagh triangle are added we can see the importance of the change resulting from the success of John Smith and his successors in the Irish borderlands between north and south.

Thus in the 1780s Wesley brought a number of young Irish preachers to Britain. He sometimes promoted them to be Assistants over senior English preachers as with Lawrence Kane. In 1788 Kane, who had entered in 1783, was made Assistant in the Plymouth circuit over his seniors, the 28 year old Thomas Cooper who entered in 1781 and the 43 year old George Wadsworth who had entered in 1770.[39] While this also happened with some young British preachers, and some Irishmen like Henry Moore and Adam Clarke were clearly able, promoting Irishmen was not a popular policy. It may well have helped contribute to the backlash in the 1790s after Wesley's death, when relations between the two Conferences were strained, especially over money.

Wesley did use his Irish preachers in Ireland, as they composed the vast majority of the Irish Conference by the time of his death and served as General Assistant. An unusual man like John Smith was to have a major effect in the borderlands of the north. Though not prepared to do it for an Irish speaker as happened later, Wesley did experiment successfully with John Smith, setting him free from ordinary circuit work to be a missionary throughout Ireland with spectacular effect in the north.[40]

British preachers did not necessarily like going to Ireland, grumbling about the poverty, the weather and the bogs. Circuits were larger than in England, with fewer members and resources. Some said that their health had been ruined

---

[38] Smith, *Ireland* 164. Smith, born and brought up in England, converted in the Army in Ireland and then an Irish preacher, described the non-Irish as 'English.' I have used 'British' because Scots-born preachers like M'Nab and Dall both travelled in Ireland.

[39] Andrew Blair was another example of this and see Chapter 5 above.

[40] This paragraph acts as a counterpoise to Rack's view in *WHS (I)* 10 (2004-5) 12.

by their Irish travels. Nicholas Manners in his *Life*, printed in 1785, complained that 'the many black bogs send forth such quantities of corrupted particles into the air that it is unwholesome to some English constitutions.' It was not true, however, that 'from an early date it proved impossible to get English preachers to travel to Ireland,'[41] though Charles Wesley is an important example of a key preacher refusing to go to Ireland again at an early stage, and it could often be difficult for Wesley to get men to go there. It was thus the British preachers who refused to go in the 1790s, not the Irish who refused to receive them.[42]

Richard Bourke and Charles Graham

Richard Bourke was in some ways a typical Irish preacher in that nothing is known about his origins. With a name like his of Anglo-Norman origin he might well have been a Catholic originally. He was received 'On Trial' in 1765 but was given no station in the *Minutes* that year. His name is very common in Ireland especially in Connaught and Tipperary, and he may well have come from the Limerick society where in 1757 Thomas Olivers in writing to Mrs Bennis said 'Sister Bourk(e) can direct you.' This may have been Bourke's wife Lucia. He probably had financial problems before he entered, judging from the note in the 1766 *Minutes* 'RB remains On Trial till we know what his debts are.' In 1766 he was appointed to Athlone circuit, where he was the Assistant in his first year. John Wesley described him then in a letter to Charles as 'truly devoted.' Lucia Bourke probably appeared in the list of singers at Dublin in 1769. Their son entered Kingswood in November 1767 and was there at least until November 1770. Bourke therefore had entered the ministry married, probably older than the average. He was usually an Assistant, certainly over more experienced itinerants.[43] He had problems in supporting his wife in Irish circuits so John Wesley allotted an extra £5 to them in May 1770. Bourke was described as 'a great sufferer,' but no reason was given. Was it because of persecution, or because of the poverty he endured as a family man? Mrs Bennis got on well with him and successfully asked for him to stay a second year in 1769. Wesley moved him to England where there was more money for wives and families in 1771, and he died in Kent where Wesley preached his funeral sermon in 1778, praising him as 'a more unblameable character I have hardly known.' He possessed 'unwearied diligence and patience and his works do

---

[41] Ward, 'Evangelistic strategy?' 296. Manners, who was in Ireland 1759-60, is quoted in Bretherton, *Chester* 51. This also applied to Scotland and Wales.
[42] Crk 3: 76.
[43] Richard de Burgo was the medieval Anglo-Norman conqueror of Connaught. Bennis, *Correspondence* No 11; *JWL* 5: 53; *JWJC* 5: 221; *JWL* 5: 427; MS Kingswood Account Book 1767-70.

follow him.' His widow survived almost twenty years.[44]

John Smith's success in the northern borderlands was partly matched by Charles Graham's in Kerry, though this happened mostly after Wesley's death. But it was Coke and Wesley in 1789 who had selected him. Graham had been a wayward youth in Sligo, but was converted in 1770 aged 20. A local preacher in 1771, he was the leader in a local revival in Sligo around 1778. He began to preach in Erse under Coke's prompting in 1789 in his own circuit, and then went to Longford leaving his wife, two children and their farm to look after themselves. Graham was accepted at Conference in 1790 though married and forty because of the need for Irish preaching. John Wesley from England decided to send him as a missionary to the Catholic stronghold of Kerry where there was no society or congregation. He received 200 members in the year and more 'On Trial.' He became known as the 'Apostle of Kerry.' In 1791 he was in the neighbouring Limerick circuit, where he left 150 members in Mallow and 17 in Doneraile, both new societies.[45]

After Wesley

In many ways the development of Methodism in Ireland was that of the creation of a coalition, led by the preachers. There were women, Palatines, Huguenots, craftsmen and traders in the towns, as well as soldiers, a few gentry, many English immigrants and a large number of farmers and others from the Ulster border region from south Donegal and West Tyrone round to Co. Down. From 1791, though the number of members initially was still small, during the next 25 years the totals and their influence were to multiply thanks to the leadership of the preachers in control and particularly to the Irish Mission from 1799.

There were several developments in Methodism in Ireland after Wesley's death. The most immediate was the question of ordination, whether Methodists would have services in Church hours in competition with the Church, and if the preachers would administer Communion. In Britain this was decided in favour of separation and 'virtual ordination,' leading to the loss of influence of Church Methodists.[46] In Ireland at first it went the other way and the situation remained static for over two decades. Leadership came from Coke and Adam Averell, a gifted clergyman who gradually increased his commitment to Methodism to

---

[44] *JWL* 5: 189; Anon, *Wesleyan Takings* No 15; Bennis, *Correspondence* Letter 66; *WJW* 23: 75n. Payments to Lucia Bourke from the Preachers' Fund in the *Minutes*.

[45] W. G. Campbell, *The Apostle of Kerry* (Dublin: Moffat, 1868) 53, 73; *WJW* 23: 87n. Graham was probably the most successful missionary in Ireland.

[46] This is discussed elsewhere, notably below in Chapter 18. This section 'After Wesley' is largely dependent on Cooney, *Ireland* and articles in *WHS (I)*.

travel the country twice a year on preaching tours.[47]

The Irish Mission was the first new step. Wesley had not encouraged preaching in Gaelic, the language of the majority. It was not until after his death that Irish Methodists made a serious effort to reach the Catholic majority by preaching in Gaelic. In 1799, partly as a result of the 1798 rising and encouraged by Thomas Coke, they set aside three itinerants to preach in Gaelic throughout Ireland. It was a very similar time to the start of the Welsh mission in Britain in 1800. Both were due to Coke who encouraged and helped to select the preachers and made sure funds were available to each from the money he was raising. This was the beginning of the Irish mission of the 'black caps,' as they were called. Of the three men set aside two had entered in Wesley's day, James M'Quigg and Charles Graham.[48] The third, Gideon Ouseley, was to become the most famous both within and outside Ireland. They were successful in converting many Roman Catholics and also many Protestants. A noteworthy result was the rapid growth of Methodist members. From 16,227 members reported in 1799, membership grew to 26,700 in 1802. The increase occurred especially along the Ulster border in the districts of Enniskillen, Londonderry and Clones, and in odd southern circuits such as Wicklow and Limerick (including Kerry).[49] This continued, though at a much slower rate over the next twenty years, partly hampered by emigration which overtook growth after 1820. The Irish Mission did not create more influence for Methodism within Ireland. The period saw the rise of Irish nationalism and the invention of the 'boycott.' Those who deserted the Irish national cause, as Methodist converts were assumed to do by their former fellows, were singled out for especial hostility. The result was that most converts took the easy answer and emigrated to Britain, to America or elsewhere, rather than remain where they were known and persecuted. It was one of the reasons for the rapid growth of Methodism in the USA, to name but one of the places to which they went.[50] If there was an opportunity to convert the Irish Catholic majority, Wesley had missed it.

The period after Wesley's death also saw the unhappy division between the British and Irish Conferences. Coke thought he should preside, as he usually had in Wesley's absence. The Irish preachers, however, were as determined as

---

[47] D. A. L. Cooney, 'Bishop's Kin' in *Dublin Historical Record* 55 (2002) 21-42. Averell was also sent as an Irish representative to the British Conference from 1796, partly because of his status and partly because he could afford to travel.
[48] M'Quigg was an Irish speaker who edited the Bible in Gaelic. See Chapter 15 below.
[49] See Appendix One Table 13.
[50] The numbers are in the *Irish Minutes*. Suspicion must be attached to the 1802 figures because of the many circuits reporting in round numbers; 21 out of 37 reported a figure ending in zero. There is an account of the controversy as to the extent of the success of the mission in Cooney, *Ireland* 53-58. Cooney's criticism of Hempton's views here is supported by my work on USA obituaries of ministers who had come from the British Isles in the nineteenth century. The majority had been ministers or local preachers in Ireland rather than England.

the British that Coke should not assume Wesley's position. So, in 1791 when Coke arrived they told him he had no legal right to preside, since Wesley had made no such provision. Instead they elected John Crook, the only other leading member of the British Conference then in circuit in Ireland, as Chairman of the Committee of Preachers. It was a blow to Coke, though not one which led to hostility. In most years from then on if Coke was available he was sent by the British Conference to preside over the Irish Conference. This reconciliation with Coke was partly because he was prepared to travel around the Irish circuits gathering large numbers to hear him. No other British preacher of the period would do this.[51]

However, there was still a long term drift which led to divisions between the two Conferences. This was partly a result of the ending of young British preachers being sent to Ireland.[52] As the Irish Conference had become both independent and Irish-born, few British preachers were there apart from Coke who usually presided at Conference and one or two others often only visiting for the Conference. The only one who remained for most of the 1790s was John Crook, whom we met in the last chapter in the Isle of Man. Wesley had sent him to Ireland from 1781 to 1786 and again from 1788. He was familiar with Irish Methodism from his army days and Wesley made him his chief lieutenant in Ireland during the year (Wesley or Coke came for Conference). On Wesley's death he was Chairman of the Committee of Preachers there. Crook was Secretary of the Irish Conference in 1790 and 1792. In 1793, when Mather could not come to Ireland for Conference, Crook became president of the Irish Conference, perhaps the only minister on the Irish stations to hold this position until recently.[53] More important it was he who held the British and Irish Conferences together in the 1790s, an Englishman whom the Irish could trust. After John Crook's return to England in 1798 the division became more pronounced.[54] Coke himself tried to protect Irish interests, but had too little influence. He was widely suspected of having attempted to win himself too much power. Other preachers were suspicious of his 'rashness' as they called it. Modern historians may regret the blinkered defence of own immediate interests by both sides and lament the demise of Wesley who had spent British resources in many places where little immediate advantage had accrued. His successor, the British Conference, would not be so generous; admittedly it faced bigger

---

[51] Crk 3: 13-15, 49. Quoted by J. A. Vickers, 'Dr Thomas Coke and Irish Methodism' in *WHS (I)* 2 (1991) 2: 3.

[52] It was also because of the refusal of one British preacher, Joseph Sutcliffe, to follow the rules in Cork. He was quickly sent home.

[53] Cooney disputed this, but, unusually, his reasoning here is not clear (*Ireland* 128). Crook was English-born, stationed in Ireland at this point. It did not make him Irish.

[54] For Crook see Chapter 10 above.

problems.[55]

We have already seen the British Conference had 'forgotten' to send an Address to the Irish Conference in 1795. The financial question which arose was over the money which the British Conference used to pay to superannuated Irish ministers. In 1798 there was the rising of the United Irishmen against the British occupation. Mostly Catholic, there were some Presbyterians and Church of Ireland supporters involved, especially in the north. There were no Methodists. The British Conference, under the influence of the effect of the recent rebellion and very conscious that many Methodists had barely survived as a result, agreed in 1799 that the financial needs of the Irish Conference preachers should be paid before their own. However, a year later at the British Conference of 1800 Coke presented the Irish accounts, but found that the British preachers wanted more detail and refused to accept the Irish reasons for not printing the accounts, considering them insufficient.[56]

Next year the British Conference refused to pay and said that they would be unable to do so in future. The bills in question, amounting to £644 15s 42d, were returned unpaid. This was because the British Conference was itself in major debt of over £2000 despite much already having been contributed by the British ministers, the depression coinciding with a downturn of membership. The British had been generously supporting the new Irish Mission which they were later to take over and run completely. They had also cancelled the Irish debts to the Bookroom and encouraged them to set up their own Bookroom, giving them the right to publish and reprint any of the existing stock. Coke spent the next months travelling through Ireland and raising money to help set up the new Bookroom in Dublin, but the Irish still felt the blow. As their historian, William Smith, himself one of Wesley's preachers, said 'We were now orphans indeed!' Relations between the two Conferences, despite the special relationship over Missions, would never be so close again.[57]

A further source of friction was the appointment of the Legal Hundred in Britain. In Wesley's original choice there had been eleven preachers who were at that time stationed in Ireland. These included Irish and British born, just as there were some preachers then stationed in Britain and elsewhere who were of Irish origin. Ten preachers of the 1784 list had been born in Ireland. Over the years, as some died and others moved to Britain, this tended to reduce. By 1811 there were only two on the Irish stations. The Irish protested and as a result it

---

[55] For Coke, his chequered relations with other preachers and Ireland see Vickers, 'Coke' in *WHS (I)* and *Thomas Coke* 42-7, 73, 76, 112-3, 226-7, 242, 307-8, 344.

[56] MS letter at MARC from Coke on the 7th August 1800 to Thomas Barber at Longford re Irish claims on the Preachers' Fund.

[57] Smith, *Ireland* 174-178 and Crk 3: 173-4 dealt with this. Cooney does not mention it. A modern account is awaited from Robin Roddie who has prepared some materials on the question and to whom I am grateful for much information. Table 14 in Appendix One.

was agreed that in future there should be ten who were on the Irish stations.

Despite this friction, Irish Methodism prospered for the fifteen years from 1800. Numbers grew, the Irish missionaries continued to bring in new converts both Protestant and Catholic alike, and the British Conference supported schools in Ireland thanks largely to the leadership of Coke and Clarke. However, this broke down over the question of Communion and the relationship with the Church of Ireland. The agreement to remain as an adjunct to that church began to fracture in 1812 when a circular letter from the Belfast circuit pointed out that many Methodists were former Presbyterians and felt deprived of receiving Communion. Many Presbyterian and Church of Ireland churches refused Communion to Methodist members who petitioned for the administration of Communion by the preachers. This was put off but the issue did not go away. Next Coke, the possible reconciler who had maintained the Irish compromise, died on his way to India. Adam Averell, the Irish clergyman licensed as a deacon who was still touring the country preaching to Methodists, lacked the same standing most of all with the British Conference. He presided at the Irish Conference in 1814 and opposed the suggestion. The proposal was passed by a narrow majority of only ten. So the whole question of Communion was deferred for another year. Pamphlets were published by both sides which inflamed feeling. The next year the Irish born British president Walter Griffith was presiding.[58] The vote was against, but Conference asked Averell to provide Communion where there was a need. The Church of Ireland said that he as a deacon should not do this, and Averell who had celebrated it at (private) quarterly meetings therefore refused to do more. Eight Irish preachers, some of them in positions of leadership, under local pressure from lay leaders administered Communion during the year.[59]

In 1816 these eight were mildly disciplined and Conference this time decided in favour of administering Communion for eight of the circuits in the north. The opponents of this, the 'Church Methodists,' mostly leading laymen strong in Dublin and in the mid Ulster border region, met at Clones in October. They were supported by Averell but hardly any existing preachers, and so they chose for their first President Samuel Moorhead, who had left the itinerancy ten years earlier because of ill-health. Over the next two years they formed what were called the Primitive Wesleyans, getting the support of 8,000 members out of the 28,000 reported in 1816. Though the Wesleyans repaired most of their

---

[58] From 1815 to 2008 British Presidents presided at the Irish Conference.

[59] Averell had presided in Coke's absence because of illness in 1810 and so was asked again in 1814. The eight included Matthew Lanktree, Chairman of the Belfast District where the suggestion had originated and where the numbers of former Presbyterians were highest. Other senior preachers in the eight were Samuel Steele who entered in 1790, Thomas Kerr, entered in 1787, and William Hamilton, entered in 1788. Kerr and Hamilton were former Irish Missionaries, the latter being the preacher who had suggested the calling out of Ouseley as a Missionary in 1799.

losses over the next few years, the dispute clearly affected their purpose. Both sides had to concentrate on new buildings in place of people.[60]

Conclusion

An English Presbyterian doctor was visiting Co. Monaghan in 1810 and was impressed by how English his (Methodist apothecary) host and his guests sounded. At first he thought the guests were clergymen because one was asked to say grace. He discovered they were Methodist tradesmen in Clones, a place 'whose inhabitants if not rich in worldly wealth were rich in gospel grace for they were all righteous or Methodists which is the same thing.' 'The reason for this will be obvious upon reflection- a number of their preachers are Englishmen. Methodists hear more of their preachers than other sects- for not to mention Sunday, which is entirely spent in preaching and praying, they have sermons two or three times a week, and associate with them more in private.'[61] It is an interesting tribute for the body of Methodist preachers in Ireland from an unexpected angle. Monaghan and Clones were centres of the revival led by John Smith. The area was where he had been attacked, leading to his death. It is no accident that it became one of the strongest Methodist regions in the whole country or that this tribute should be set there.

---

[60] See D. A. L. Cooney, 'They met in Great George Street' *WHS (I)* 7 (2001) 34-48 for an in depth study of the original leaders of the Primitive Wesleyans. Of other Wesleyan preachers who joined them, Nehemiah Price had not been an itinerant since 1790, Joseph Armstrong had been a Supernumerary for 10 years, Lawrence Kane the same for a shorter time in England. Robert Smith, a Supernumerary since 1817, did not join them until 1820.

[61] R. P. Roddie, 'John Wesley's Legacy in Ireland' in *WHS (I)* 4 (1998) 1: 9-10.

CHAPTER 12

America to 1778

'It is now above a year since I left this city (Philadelphia): I set out with a consciousness of duty, and was determined to obey what to me was a call from above. I was totally unacquainted with the people, the road, and everything else, only I knew there a multitude of souls scattered through a vast extent of country... With this view I turned my face to the South and went further than a thousand miles through the provinces, visited most of the towns between Philadelphia and Savannah in Georgia, where I have preached the Gospel of Christ.'
Joseph Pilmore, June 1773, having completed his southern journey.

Introduction
Before the Preachers

The thirteen British colonies in North America in the early eighteenth century were divided from each other by geography and origin. It was difficult to travel from one colony to the next, since great estuaries divided them. No good bridges were built until later and these might easily be swept away. The land was heavily forested, so it was easy to be lost; Joseph Pilmore and Thomas Rankin, two early British itinerants there, emphasized in their Journals the number of trees. Pilmore on his journey almost drowned near the storm-ridden Carolina sands. Some colonies, like the former Dutch ones in the centre, were not even English by foundation. Many non-English groups, such as Germans, had moved particularly into the Middle Colonies. Religion was also one of the more important divisive factors. New England Puritans found little to approve in the Catholics of Maryland, the Quakers of Pennsylvania or the Anglicans of Virginia and Carolina. Their feelings were returned with interest. In each the Established Church lacked resources and resolute state backing from England, but defended what it had even more fiercely than in England. The most religious community was New England, but even here the strength of religion was weakening, partly because of Jonathan Edwards' insistence on new standards for admission to the church from 1750.[1] Throughout the colonies the lack of a local Bishop handicapped the Established Church, forcing Anglicans to go to England if they hoped to be ordained. The slave society in the South and Middle States encouraged a violent culture which brutalized black and

---
[1] For Edwards see Noll, *America's God* 45-50.

white alike, leaving Southern white males fixated on personal honour while their females were left to look after religion. In addition the colonies were part of a growing empire, belonging to what modern historians have described as 'a powerful fiscal-military state.' Since 1680 this had developed unusually large powers of money raising for the purpose of military expenditure. This led to increasing effort expended on colonial expansion from 1739 and more pressure on taxation in the colonies after 1760.[2]

The colonies were going through a period of great growth and consequential change. Many colonists in the 1770s had recently crossed the Atlantic. Those born there often moved westwards, and if not, then increasingly their children did. It was a mobile, rapidly expanding, prosperous society, another reason why the central government looked to augment its colonial revenues. The population was growing much faster than elsewhere in the British Empire. The 250,000 of 1700 had become 970,000 by 1750, and would be 5.3 million by 1800. Some of these colonists were Methodists already, moving from Ireland or Britain. The generation of soldiers in America, born a little before the American Revolution, was on average two to four inches taller than its British opponents. The most probable reason for this was the better nutrition in America. There were colonial elites, but they were more open to new ideas than their equivalents in England. Because they increasingly imported consumer goods from the mother country they were closely linked to ideas which were important there as well. Evangelical leaders in America criticized the wealthier colonists for this aping of London fashion. Traditional authority was more vulnerable in colonial society. America also remained different from Britain because of race. Black slaves and freedmen were economically and numerically important in the colonies. So, for different reasons, were the Native Americans, then referred to as Red Indians. As Wesley said in Georgia on his arrival there in 1735 'Beware America! Be not as England!'[3]

Why did not the Preachers come before 1769?

After all John Wesley had gone to Ireland in 1747 and Scotland in 1751. By 1760 the Connexion had been established nearly twenty years. Surely eighteenth century America was important enough to justify the sending of travelling preachers? The question on Sherlock Holmes' perceptive terms is why the dog did not bark. I want to suggest there were several reasons for this. Wesley's experience in Georgia in the 1730s had been deeply engrained in his

---

[2] R. Halpern and M. Daunton, eds, *Empire and Others: British Encounters with Indigenous Peoples 1600-1850* (London: UCL, 1999) 4.

[3] Andrews, *Methodists and America* 31-35; Winks, *Empire* Chapters 4 and 5; Noll, *Rise* 27-8, 41-3; *America's God* 106-7. The Wesley quotation is from R. P. Heitzenrater and P. S. Forsaith, *Wesley in America* (Dallas: Bridwell Library, 2003). The height statistics come from Heywood, *Childhood* 148.

conscious and sub-conscious memory. It had been a relative failure despite all his attempts to disguise it, and he would not venture down that route again until he was certain of success. Furthermore, there were other 'Methodist' preachers already there. From 1738 his friend George Whitefield preached regularly throughout the American colonies; indeed Whitefield's leaving for America had been the immediate reason for Wesley's first preaching in the open air. Whitefield had been most successful there working with the existing churches. Followers of Wesley in the colonies were logically encouraged to do the same. Finally, there was a lack of British Methodist resources. Numbers of preachers have been difficult to estimate, since the *Minutes* do not record everybody. However, it would seem that there were only about 108 travelling preachers in 1767 (104 according to the *Minutes* on the stations) for the 41 circuits that year. Wesley wanted three to each circuit, so resources were still scarce.[4] By 1769 the elderly Whitefield was not to continue his transatlantic ministry much longer. Sending preachers would not infringe his pastures. In addition, as America grew there was a need for both Wesley's preachers and Whitefield.[5]

The First Methodists in America

There were many factors which tended to the establishment of Wesley's Methodism in the thirteen British colonies in the eighteenth century.[6] Wesley's publications sold well even if his preachers had not yet arrived and the many problems of the colonial booksellers meant printed output in America was small. This was a gap the Methodist preachers could help to fill.[7] Individual Methodist migrants like the well known Philip Embury and Robert Strawbridge came from Ireland and elsewhere and began preaching. Others had come earlier but been less successful. The hostile Anglican Thomas Barton, who served in Pennsylvania from 1754, reported in 1763-4 that the 'Methodists and New Lights have roamed over the country leading captive silly women and drawing thousands to adopt their strange and novel doctrines.' Devereux Jarratt had come to England in 1762 for ordination and on his return to Bath parish south of Petersburg had begun his preaching on a large circuit in thirty counties in the tidewater area in Virginia and North Carolina. A man of high social status he had many failings and was difficult to work with, but he created a situation where Methodism was to reap the harvest. His support for the early Methodist preachers in America was vital for their success in the area. He was typical of some Anglican clergymen in America who looked favourably on Methodists, at

---

[4] For more details on this see Appendix Two.
[5] F. Baker, *From Wesley to Asbury: Studies in Early American Methodism* (Durham NC: Duke UP, 1976) 23-33.
[6] F. Baker, *Wesley to Asbury* Chapters 1 and 2.
[7] Rivers, *New Essays* 12.

least before 1784, and subscribed to many of the chapels they built.[8] The demobilized British soldier Captain Thomas Webb, who held the post of barrack-master at Albany in upstate New York, had been converted in 1765. He began to preach, helped the Methodists in New York to build their chapel in John Street and also formed a society in Philadelphia. He preached in at least four states, providing the valuable service of making the existing groups aware that they were not the only Methodists in America. Like other soldiers in other areas Webb proved to be a catalyst, coming back to Britain to carry the invitation which Wesley decided eventually to accept.[9]

In 1769 requests came again from several quarters to Wesley for preachers for America. As Baker pointed out, he responded over an extended period by dispatching matched pairs with one in charge, Pilmore and Boardman in 1769, Asbury and Wright in 1771, Rankin and Shadford in 1773, Dempster and Rodda in 1774. All these were volunteers from among the regularly stationed itinerants. There were also preachers arriving or already there, such as Embury who began preaching in 1768, Strawbridge who began earlier, Robert Williams, and later John King and Joseph Yearbury. Many American-born (with a few British-born like Glendenning) joined them from 1773, so that by the time the conflict began and most British-born preachers returned home there were sufficient American preachers to sustain the itinerancy during the war period. All the British-born preachers were mobile, some crossing the Atlantic without Wesley's blessing. This did not reduce their effectiveness or necessarily their acceptance. They were employed because of the need faced by the leaders, Pilmore and Boardman, and later Rankin and Asbury. In view of the requirements of the British Isles Wesley's generosity in this almost continuous sending of pairs of preachers should be praised. He was committed to the American mission; it was successful because of his steadfast commitment.[10]

Pilmore and Boardman

Joseph Pilmore to 1773

Pilmore[11] was important and successful, a little neglected by Methodist

---

[8] Andrews, *Methodists and America* has been most valuable for these chapters. For subscribers see Wakeley 94-97. The quotation is from Baker, *Wesley to Asbury* 24. For Jarratt see Jarratt, *Life* Foreword. For other soldiers see Hempton, *Empire* 20-21. Other sympathetic clergymen included Samuel Magaw.

[9] Bates, *Webb* 1-11. Webb married an American-born wife, so settled in America.

[10] Baker, *Wesley to Asbury*; Hempton, *Empire* 20; Andrews, *Methodists in America* 35-38. Wright went back to Britain in July 1774 see note 41 below. Each of the others sent have at least a paragraph in this chapter.

[11] There were many spellings of Pilmore. In the *Minutes* it was usually Pillmoor, sometimes Pilmoor, occasionally Pillsmore and once Pilsmore. However, in the baptismal register at Nunnington it was clearly Pilmore, and he signed himself the same

historians, in part because he later entered the Anglican ministry and also because he was not Asbury. Some have been led into false stories of his origin, even Baker who described him as never having been an Assistant though he had been one in Wales.[12] Boardman, aged thirty-one to Pilmore's twenty-six and travelled six years to Pilmore's four, was clearly more experienced. Wesley trusted Pilmore since he was made Assistant in 1770 over Boardman, though Wesley reverted to the latter in 1771 and 1772. The large distances of America meant each was practically independent of the other.

New light has been shed on Pilmore's origins thanks to recent research on a little known Quaker called Joseph Foord, later a maker of watercourses and an engineer in Yorkshire. Foord had an illegitimate son, born on the 31st October 1743 to his second cousin, the thirty year old Sarah Pilmore in the neighbouring village of Fadmoor, not 1739 as Pilmore in his old age told his vestryman Joseph Latimer, and historians have repeated ever since. This boy Joseph Pilmore, given his father's first name, was baptized at Nunnington eight miles south of Fadmoor in 1747 where Sarah was then living with her brother Francis. The father denied paternity but failed to convince either the York Consistory Court or the Quaker Meeting inquiry on the issue.[13] In 1754 Sarah married a yeoman of Fadmoor village, William Sleightholme. The eleven year old Joseph Pilmore was brought up by his stepfather whom he called 'father,' saying nothing about his early years, so that previous biographers accepted he was born in 1739. This is not true and he was therefore younger than he represented himself to be. Pilmore was a farm servant first at Muscoates near Nunnington, where he attended the week night meetings at Beadlam north of Nunnington led by Richard Conyers, the Evangelical vicar of Helmsley. This probably provided the connection with Wesley who certainly preached from Conyers' pulpit in 1764. Converted by Wesley around 1759 aged about 16,[14] Pilmore was sent to Kingswood to be educated as a preacher, where according to report he spent four years studying Latin, Greek, Hebrew and English Literature. Pilmore had travelled in Wales where he had been deputed by Wesley to deal with an angry class-leader in Pembroke.[15]

In 1768 Wesley received a letter from a British Methodist layman, Thomas

---

so I have settled for that.

[12] Telford described Pilmore as an Irishman! Baker, *Wesley to Asbury* 86.

[13] I. McLean, *Water from the Moors: The Life and Works of Joseph Foord* (Helmsley: North York Moors Parks Authority, 2005). McLean speculated about Foord's old age. He survived to a point when both his wife and family had predeceased him. Aged 72 in 1786 he declared his intention of going to the USA. Was it to see and be reconciled with the son whose paternity he had rejected so many years before, and who had in November 1785 been ordained priest there? It is an alluring thought, but unproven. See also J. H. Lenton, 'Joseph Pilmore's origins' *MH 44* (2006) 262-65.

[14] The parish registers of the whole area have been searched and only 1743 has provided a possibility. Ives, *DEB*. Sarah had a second son William Sleightholme in 1755.

[15] Pilmore, *South Wales* 69-72.

Taylor, in New York[16] about the needs of the small Methodist society there. Wesley appealed to Conference in 1768 and 1769. At the second Conference he appointed Pilmore to preach so he could listen to him. Pilmore passed the test and when Wesley called for volunteers for America there were two, Pilmore and Richard Boardman, and a collection of £70 to cover their passage and support the new society in acquiring a building.

Pilmore and Boardman arrived in 1769. During the voyage they built up a strong partnership which meant that Pilmore at least felt committed to support his fellow evangelist in whatever he was called to do. They found a society already established in Philadelphia, as well as the one in New York to which they were invited. They tended to concentrate on these societies in the cities, though both went out into the neighbouring area, and they preached at Trenton and Princeton and other points en route as they exchanged every four months. Pilmore's Journal shows him as far from Philadelphia as Matching, now Bethel Hill, more than twenty miles out, and preaching being established as far from New York as Rye, a similar distance north east of New York, close to Long Island Sound. The real criticism of the two preachers in New York is that they apparently made no effort to go up the Hudson, the most natural and strategic route inland.[17]

Pilmore established the Methodist deeds on which the original chapels in the two centres were held. He introduced Methodist innovations such as the Lovefeast and Watchnight services. Maser said he 'gave the Methodist people in America a sense of oneness with all Methodists everywhere.' He formed a number of societies, including two in Baltimore in his eleven day visit and a strong one at Norfolk, Virginia, and he carried Methodism into many areas which it had not previously penetrated. An exceptionally good preacher, his journey to the south laid the basis for the immediate expansion in the Chesapeake and Virginia, and eventual expansion into the Carolinas and beyond. The chief strengths of American Methodism were built on the foundations laid by Pilmore on this journey.[18]

Richard Boardman to 1773

Richard Boardman seems to have been baptized at Warrington Lancashire on the 19th February 1738, the son of John and Alice Boardman. Though he was presumably brought up as an Anglican, Warrington was a town where

---

[16] Not Thomas Taylor the itinerant. For the letter see Baker, *Wesley to Asbury* 73-83.

[17] F. E. Maser and H. T. Maag, eds, *The Journal of Joseph Pilmore Methodist Itinerant* (Philadelphia: Historical Society of Philadelphia Annual Conference, 1969).

[18] For Chesapeake Methodism see R. Richey, 'The Formation of American Methodism: The Chesapeake Refraction' in Hatch and Wigger, eds, *Shaping* 197-221. F. E. Maser, *The Dramatic Story of Early American Methodism* (New York: Abingdon, 1963) 46-47.

Timeline 3: Methodist Preachers in America

Year	Political Event	Methodist Event	Members	Circuits
1768		John Street Church New York		
1769		Pilmore and Boardman arrive		
1770	Boston Massacre	King in Maryland		
1771		Asbury and Wright arrive		
1772		Boardman to Boston, Pilmore to Virginia & Savannah		
1773	Tea Act, Boston Tea Party	Rankin and Shadford arrive. First Conference	1,160	6
1774	First Continental Congress	Dempster and Rodda arrive.		10
1775	Lexington (Apr) JW's 'Calm Address' (Sept)	Shadford's revival in Virginia	3,148	10
1776	American Declaration of Independence			
1777	Saratoga		6,968	15
1778		Rankin, Shadford and Rodda leave, Asbury hiding.		
1779		Fluvanna Conference	8,577	
1781	Yorktown		10,539	25
1783	Treaty of Versailles. Loyalists leave New York	Owings 1st preacher to cross Appalachians	13,740	39
1784		Coke & Asbury ordained. Christmas Conference. Methodist Episcopal Church		
1787	American Constitution agreed	Cokesbury College	25,342	63
1789	Washington President	Methodist Book Concern New York		
1792		1st Quadrennial General Conference, O'Kelly and Hammett schisms	65,980	136
1794		Camp meetings start. Bethel AME founded		
1796		Six Annual Conferences including Western		
1800		Whatcoat made Bishop		
1806		Death of Whatcoat		
1813				385
1816		Asbury's death, African Methodist Episcopal Church set up	214,000	

Nonconformity was relatively strong. In 1758 he was married in Liverpool and his child was baptized in Warrington a year later. By this time Boardman had become a shoemaker in Liverpool and had made the important decision to become a Methodist, being a select band member in Liverpool. However, nothing else is known about him before he began to travel in 1763.[19] After two years Wesley made him Assistant and kept him as this even though in 1768 he said Boardman had been unable to persuade the wealthy members at York to pay off the debt. Boardman suffered from periodic ill health probably caused by being out in all weathers. In September 1768, as Assistant in the Dales circuit, he was told by Wesley to supply Yarm. In January 1769 his wife and their new-born daughter both died and were buried at Barnard Castle. Since he was free from family ties he volunteered for America and was sent there as the senior preacher with Pilmore.[20]

In America Boardman went first to Philadelphia and then New York in 1769. He and Pilmore exchanged every four months on Boardman's insistence and against Pilmore's wishes. Boardman seems to have suffered poor health again. Baker felt he also still suffered from his double family loss in January 1769. He was found by Asbury to be 'weak in body' in 1771. One problem about Boardman is the lack of evidence, apart from a few of his letters. We have what others felt about him rather than his own thoughts. He was in the key position of Assistant for most of the time he was in America, but seems to have done little with it. In 1772 he went on a preaching tour to Boston, so was the first to introduce Methodism into New England, though the society he founded in Boston did not last because it was not given enough support.[21]

---

[19] For more details and why the older story about his birth in the North Riding is not correct see J. H. Lenton, 'More information on Richard Boardman' *MH* 44 (2006) 124-28. For sources see the next note. Warrington was then in Lancashire.

[20] Boardman left no journal, unlike Pilmore. Earlier accounts such as Lockwood had nothing before his entry to the itinerancy in 1763, except his birth said to be at Gillamoor very close to where Pilmore was born. There was no Boardman baptism there in the eighteenth century and a leading local historian refused to accept the story. Boardman's baptism, marriage and children's baptisms are in the *IGI*. He appeared in the 1759 list of Methodist members of society in Liverpool (Rose, 'South Lancashire'). For the rest see Myles; Crowther; No 50 in *Wesleyan Takings*; *JWL* 5: 85, 6: 107; *WJW* 22: 197 n36; *AM* 1783: 22, 472-3. Boardman, before he went to America, crossed the Derbyshire moors from the Leeds Conference on his way to Bristol and departure, stopping in the village of Monyash for the night and preaching to the small society on 1 Chronicles 9 verse 19. His recent loss of wife and child led him to take this text and preach about Jabez 'who was born with sorrow.' Mary Redfern was there converted, and ten years later called her only son Jabez Bunting. This story is in T. P. Bunting, *The Life of Jabez Bunting, D.D,* vol 1 (London: Longman, 1859) 8-9.

[21] *AM* 1795: 270-1; *Asbury Jol* 1: 8; seven copy letters of Boardman at Drew University.

The Departure of Boardman and Pilmore

Leaders of the New York society had complained to Wesley about both Pilmore and Boardman. This seems to be partly because of questions over the ownership of the chapel and also because they did not administer sufficient discipline in the societies. Asbury began in New York by purging a number of members who did not keep the rules of meeting and paying regularly.[22] Wesley's putting first Asbury and then Rankin in charge instead of Boardman and Pilmore was clearly a rebuke. Rankin's first Conference in 1773 omitted them both from the stations. This omission was an official rebuff coming as from Wesley himself, one which Boardman accepted but Pilmore did not. In the next six months both remained in America preaching and visiting friends. Only in December did Boardman decide to return to Britain. Pilmore, who really wanted to stay, decided he should go with him (he could not desert his friend) and so both took a boat home to face Wesley. Boardman was stationed by the next British Conference and continued until his death. Once back in England Boardman wrote from Warrington a letter to Philadelphia regretting his return. He died suddenly in 1782 in Ireland.[23]

Pilmore spent two years out of the itinerancy. In 1775 he was in York heading the procession at the funeral of Drummer Johnson, preaching the sermon.[24] In 1776 he was reconciled to Wesley by Fletcher and spent the next nine years in important circuits for Wesley such as Dublin, Norwich and York, usually as Assistant. Throughout this period Pilmore remained in touch with the Americans, particularly in Philadelphia. In 1785, peace in America having come and having obtained a letter of recommendation from Charles Wesley (not John!), he returned to America intending to remain this time. He was told that Asbury had instructed the (now independent) Methodists not to receive him. Pilmore therefore presented his letter to the newly ordained Bishop Seabury of the even newer Episcopal Church who received him well, ordaining him both deacon and priest. He then took up appointments in the Episcopal Church, first in Philadelphia and later in New York. He died in 1825.[25]

Some Problems for the Preachers

The chief problem for the first two preachers sent by Wesley was the lack of colleagues with the ability and determination to carry out what Wesley wanted

---

[22] See the extract from Wesley's letter to Pilmore in Chapter 4 above and F. Baker 'Early American Methodism: a Key Document' in *MH* 8 (1965) 12-13. For Boardman's later history see Lenton, 'Boardman.'

[23] Societies frequently complained and Wesley moved preachers anyway. *AM* 1783: 22, 472-3. Boardman's letter is at Drew 1646-5-6, dated the 19th March 1774.

[24] R. Burdekin, *Memoir of Robert Spence of York* (York: Burdekin, 1840) 35.

[25] MARC PLP Letters of the Wesley Family 2: 118-9 letter of Pilmore thanking Charles Wesley.

them to do, namely travel, visit, preach, gather together and care for the society. There were those whom Wesley had not sent who were acting as local preachers, often doing an excellent job but without the time to form and look after the societies. Philip Embury had founded the original society in New York, and in 1768 had built John Street church there, acting as preacher, treasurer, trustee and class leader as well as carpenter. However, he was also earning his own living and the burgeoning city was not his natural habitat. He preferred the small village community such as where he had lived in Ireland, so in 1770 he, his family and most of his Palatine friends moved upstate to Ashgrove where he farmed, developing a Methodist society there and being chosen as 'burgomeister,' that is leader of the settlement. It was a ready made opportunity for Boardman and Pilmore which they seem to have left for their successors to exploit. Embury carried out the first Methodist preaching mission in New Hampshire in 1772, but died suddenly at Ashgrove in 1773. Later still his community were to move across the border to Canada.[26]

The other Irish local preacher Robert Strawbridge, a dark-haired man who was an excellent singer, had settled at New Windsor near Sams Creek in Frederick County, Maryland. He began preaching services in his log house and then formed a society there. This society, meeting at his neighbour John England's house, was described by Asbury as the 'first in Maryland and America.' The date of his emigration and first preaching is not clear but certainly he had been preaching and building chapels in Maryland unknown to Wesley since at least 1766.[27] He welcomed Wesley's preachers but wanted to continue to give communion as he had done for some time. They told him to stop since it was opposed to Wesley's direct instructions. Strawbridge was shown on the stations several times. Eventually, as the supply of locally born American preachers increased, it was possible to enforce the rule even in 'his' area. In 1776 he moved to farm at Long Green Baltimore County, where he continued to serve as a local preacher and lay pastor until his death at the house of Joseph Wheeler near Baltimore in the summer of 1781. Strawbridge had been both an important reason for the growth of Methodism, particularly its strength in the Chesapeake area, and a stumbling block to the authority of the early preachers.[28]

---

[26] *WMM* 1827: 672, 717; Taggart, *Irish* 52-4; Baker, *Wesley to Asbury* 40-4; *Asbury Jol* 2: 60-1; P. J. O'Connor, *People Make Places: The Story of the Irish Palatines* (Coolamoran: Oireacht Na Mumhan Books, 1989) 72.

[27] Baker, *Wesley to Asbury* 31-40, 95-7; F. E. Maser, *Robert Strawbridge, First American Methodist Circuit Rider* (Rutland VT: Academy, 1983); Taggart, *Irish* 52-3; Barclay, *Methodism 1769-1849* 1: 17-23; Lednum 15-23; *PWHS* 13 (1922) 153-7, 39 (1973), 26; C. Yrigoyen and S. E. Warrick, eds, *Historical Dictionary of Methodism* (Lanham MD: Scarecrow, 1996); G. P. Baker, ed, *Those Incredible Methodists; A History of the Baltimore Conference of the United Methodist Church* (Baltimore: Baltimore Conference, 1972) 2-17.

[28] *DEB*; Lednum; *PWHS* 39 (1973) 26, G. P. Baker, *Incredible*.

Other preachers arrived in America who had not been sent by Wesley. Among the more important of these were Thomas Webb, Robert Williams and John King. Thomas Webb continued to preach as before around New York and Philadelphia, also playing a useful role in travelling back, appealing for more preachers and carrying correspondence from Europe. Without his personal appeals in Britain it is quite possible Wesley would not have felt the need to reinforce his preachers in America. It would be interesting to know Webb's view of the preachers Wesley sent. However, Webb also created a problem for the itinerants by wearing his redcoat to preach as a former officer. Methodists were in any case associated with the Loyalist cause in the popular mind. As opinion hardened and hostilities broke out, he could not remain and preach. The fact that he was a former British officer did not matter. So was Washington! But Webb's views were strongly Loyalist and he made them very clear. In the middle of the conflict he sent messages to the British commanders telling them when and where to attack. By staying until 1777 he made it more difficult for those who kept their opinions to themselves or their Journals.[29]

Williams and King were among the many young immigrants pouring into the colonies at this time. Robert Williams, probably of Welsh origin, had travelled three years not very satisfactorily for Wesley in Ireland. Wesley felt he had publicly opposed the Church, contrary to his instructions. Williams had no station in 1769 and decided to emigrate to America, a friend paying his passage. Wesley said he could preach in America if he did this under Boardman's direction. He arrived before Boardman but reported to the two official itinerants when they came. Pilmore thought Williams could preach suitably for rural areas not towns, but reckoned he was unable to carry out the pastoral work needed. Pilmore and Boardman had little option but to allow Williams to preach and he was sent to rural Maryland where Strawbridge was already prominent and he would be welcomed. Williams also worked around New York and in Baltimore and Virginia. He was very successful as a preacher, converting Jesse Lee in 1772, though less so as a pastor. Williams was important as the first publisher of Wesley's books in America and by 1775 he had been the catalyst for a large revival in Virginia which resulted in the creation of five new circuits. That year he married and located in Virginia, dying before the end of the year.[30]

---

[29] Bates, *Webb* 10-20.

[30] Williams was probably born in 1745, and so was 24 when he came to America. The fact that he appeared in Ireland on the stations under the guise of initials (see Chapter 15 below) indicates that Wesley had problems with him. For Williams see Lednum, 62-88, 100, 118-20, 134, 139-42, 151-3; *DEB*; F. Baker, *Wesley to Asbury* 44-9; *WJW* 22: 75 n43, 182 n78; Sprague, *Annals* 7: 11-13; *Asbury Jol* 1: 28, 46, 74, 85, 143, 160, 164; G. P. Baker, *Incredible* 17-19; Andrews, *Methodists and America* 40. 'Located' was the American term for leaving the itinerancy, settling in one place, usually marrying and becoming a local preacher.

John King was a local preacher from England who arrived in America in August 1770, appearing in the 1770 British *Minutes* as down for America. He was determined to preach whether licensed or not, earning from Wesley the description 'stubborn and headstrong,' a possible advantage in the pioneer situation of America, but one fraught with problems for the authority of those sent by Wesley to oversee his work. King was eventually licensed by Pilmore who found him both a 'particular trial' and an 'able minister,' sending him to Wilmington. By 1770 he was in Maryland and Baltimore, where he was the first Methodist to preach, and established Methodism there. In America he several times disappeared from the itinerancy, locating after his marriage to a Virginian in December 1775. He remained an active local preacher and frequently entertained Asbury, dying in the mid 1790s.[31] Webb, Williams and King, though not trusted particularly by Wesley or Pilmore, had been left virtually unsupervised by Boardman and Pilmore. Asbury and Rankin were more careful with them, but all three had a strong tendency towards independence and location.

A further problem facing the preachers was that of ill health. Nobody reading the journals of Asbury, Rankin and Pilmore can be anything but conscious of the way they fought against illness in order to preach. This was also true of Boardman and indeed most of the British preachers. Particularly in the southern and central colonies they were affected by what may have been malaria. Everywhere they faced the problems of frequent movement, insufficient or irregular meals and damp beds so their health suffered and many gave up under the pressure.[32]

Asbury, Rankin and Shadford

Francis Asbury to 1773

Francis Asbury was later to dominate American Methodism. The Methodist evidence tends to over-emphasize his importance and his judgements,

---

[31] For John King's origins see Chapter 3. See also G. P. Baker, *Incredible* 19-20; Lednum, 65-8, 141-4; F. Baker *Wesley to Asbury* 90-6; Barclay, *Methodism 1769-1849* 1: 33-4; W. G. Findlay and W. W. Holdsworth, *The History of the Wesleyan Methodist Missionary Society* 5 vols (London: Sharp, 1921) 1: 213-5; Moore, *Virginia* 51-6; E. Schell, 'Methodist Traveling Preachers in America 1773-99' in *MH* 38 (2000) 307-351; Maser, *Dramatic Story* 56-145; Sprague *Annals*; *Asbury Jol* 1: 29.

[32] *Asbury Jol* 1: 94-7 'a quartan ague,' 140 'Mr Rankin was sick,' Maser, *Dramatic Story* 111 'a stoppage and pain in my breast' (Pilmore). A further possible problem of stiff Methodist competition never materialised; in 1772 a party of Lady Huntingdon's preachers set out for America, declaring they would 'soon drive all the Methodist (Wesleyan) preachers from the continent of America.' In the event only two of the eight got there and those two suffered disasters. There was of course plenty of room in the colonies for different styles. Harding, *Countess's Connexion* quoting Rankin's Journal at MARC 2/91-2.

especially before the war. This book will attempt to put other views without minimizing his ultimate influence. The apparently unbaptized boy from the Black Country hamlet of Great Barr and the only surviving child of a religious mother, Asbury was probably apprenticed to the chape-filer John Griffin.[33] He was converted at sixteen, a local preacher at eighteen, and was acting as an itinerant in his own circuit before the age of twenty-one. The evidence shows that even then, right at the start of his travelling, he was concerned to spread the word by preaching to new areas, rather than just remaining in the traditional circuit round. In 1771 Asbury was sent by Wesley as junior to Boardman and Pilmore. In his *Journal* he immediately criticized them for remaining too much in the cities. His arrival resulted in Boardman and Pilmore making the journeys out to New England and the South in 1772 while Asbury and Wright remained behind. Asbury was unhappy with the way non-members were allowed into Methodist class and society meetings and also about some members not keeping the rules. In both New York and Philadelphia he purged many from the societies. In New York he brought financial stability to that society. However, his travels around the two cities differed little from those made by Pilmore, though he spent less time inside them. In October 1772 he received a letter from Wesley indicating that he was to be in charge as Assistant, a decision accepted by Boardman but resented by Pilmore. Asbury knew that his time would be limited as Wesley was intending to send Rankin out to take charge. In December he based himself further south in Baltimore, beginning to build it up as the great centre of early 'Chesapeake Methodism' it was to become. That month he held the first recorded Quarterly Conference, what in Britain was called the Quarterly Meeting, in Presbury's home nearby. Asbury used it to build up the fraternity of Methodism and the preachers and his authority as Assistant. Like Wesley he asked questions, but he did not always dictate the answers. Like the later Wesley he listened to what was said, in this case Strawbridge insisting on the administration of the sacrament, and 'connived' at Strawbridge's exemption from the rule. Asbury made extensive journeys in what had been Strawbridge's area, deepening the contact with young American preachers like Watters, Gatch and Owings, and establishing a lifelong alliance with Philip Otterbein, pastor in Baltimore and one of the founders of the German brethren in the colonies.[34]

---

[33] A chape-filer made fittings for scabbards, belt buckles, bucket handles etc. Baker, *Wesley to Asbury* 103-115; D. J. A. Hallam, *Eliza Asbury, her Cottage and her Son* (Studley: Brewin Books, 2003). The controversy over whether the apprenticeship was with Griffin or another friendly neighbour Thomas Foxall is in *MH* 42: (2005) 178-9.

[34] *Asbury's Jol*, published from 1788, is the main source. The MSS Journal was lost in a fire in 1836. The rules were about attendance, conduct, contributions and observance of the ordinances. He wanted seven preachers to 'spread seven or eight hundred miles and preach in as many places as we are able to attend' (entry for 22nd April 1772). page 41 and note 147 is the source for the financial improvement at New York. For Baltimore see pp 55-75 covering late November 1772 to early April 1773. See also Andrews

Thomas Rankin to the First American Conference

Thomas Rankin, born in 1738, was a Scot who had first come as a merchant's factor to Charleston in South Carolina in 1757. He had returned to his native Dunbar in June 1759 having gained knowledge of the colonies, though a different area from where he was to serve. He was an itinerant of considerable experience, having begun probably as early as November 1759 and having spent much time travelling with Wesley in 1770. Rankin was sent by Wesley in March 1773 to superintend the work in America, 'enough to overturn America' in Wesley's words. This was because Wesley was worried by the reports he received and wanted someone he could trust to enforce Methodist discipline on membership, class and band meetings, and mission outside the big cities.[35]

In June 1773 Rankin, George Shadford and Joseph Yearbury arrived. Within six weeks Rankin had summoned the first American Conference. This clearly stressed that British Methodist rules were to be followed, such as no administration of the sacraments, though Asbury's Journal shows that an exception was to be made for Strawbridge as long as he acted under the Assistant's direction. The first Assistant for Strawbridge's area was to be Asbury. The two pages of the first American Conference *Minutes* seem brief but were to the point. The preachers were in 'Connexion with the Reverend Mr John Wesley' and subject to his authority. The doctrine and discipline of the (British) Methodists applied to each one of them. They agreed on all the rules, such as non-members were not to be admitted to love-feasts or society meetings. Robert Williams, who had acted as printer, was to print no more without direct permission from Wesley. Rankin and Shadford were to take the traditional main stations of New York and Philadelphia and change in four months. Robert Williams and Richard Wright were sent south to Virginia. John King and the young American William Watters, the first native-born American to be accepted as an itinerant, were to take New Jersey (between the two original stations). Pilmore's foundation of societies was to be followed up properly since more itinerants were available. Asbury's Journal shows there were other complaints about Boardman and Pilmore expressed at the Conference though not in the *Minutes*. Apart from the 'living like gentlemen in the cities' there were accusations of money wasted, improper leaders appointed and many rules broken. If Rankin and Asbury could prevent it, this would not happen in future.[36]

Methodists and America 42-5. Since so much has been written on Asbury I am confining myself to a bare record of his part, except where new evidence has appeared, e.g. J. H. Lenton, 'William Orpe's letter of May 23, 1766 to Francis Asbury' in *MH* 44 (2005) 56-59. For the Quarterly Conference see Richey, *Conference in America* 22.

[35] *DEB, EMP* 5: 135-217.

[36] *Minutes MCA*. Rankin's MS Journal is at Garrett; I have used the copy made by Francis Tees held at Drew. *Asbury's Jol* 1: 85. The rule on admission was that if they came more than three times they must become members before they would be admitted

Meanwhile Baltimore, the new heartland in Maryland and originally Strawbridge's area which had recently been opened up by first Pilmore and then Asbury, was to be taken by four preachers, Asbury, Strawbridge, Yearbury and Abraham Whitworth, with Asbury in charge. Within six months Asbury had turned it into three circuits.

Rankin and George Shadford

George Shadford remains the one uncomplicated success of Wesley's preachers in America, a figure who has happily escaped controversy then and since. He was baptized on the 14th March 1738 at Scotter, not far from Epworth in the heart of strongly Methodist north Lincolnshire, the son of George Shadford and his wife Anne. His parents both attended the local parish church, his father kept a shop, and he had at least one brother and one sister. At the age of twenty Shadford joined the militia, and a year later he heard the Methodists preaching at Gainsborough. He was discharged and in 1762 converted. Shadford became a local preacher and then itinerant. He volunteered with others to go to America in 1772, having been preaching as an itinerant then for four years. Rankin deliberately chose him as someone he could trust to go with him to America. Shadford had spent his first year travelling with Rankin as his Assistant, so Rankin knew him well. John Wesley wrote to Shadford 'I let you loose, George, on the great continent of America. Publish your message in the open face of the sun and do all the good you can.' His American appointments included big cities like New York and rural areas such as Virginia. Wherever he went he attracted crowds, winning good opinions. His prayers were fervent and effective. In the Hanover and Brunswick circuits his success was so great that the rule against reappointment was ignored. In Virginia he arrived in May 1775 when there were 800 members. By May 1776 he reported 2,664. Though unwilling to take the Maryland oath, which required armed service against the King, Shadford retained his popularity even among strong Republicans. When later revivalist preachers appeared, their labours were always compared with his exploits in the Brunswick circuit. He set a standard few could match.[37]

Rankin in Charge 1773-1775

Rankin's Journal shows he looked upon his time in America 'as for a season.' Apart from anything else he had an arrangement in London with Mrs Bradshaw, whom he had originally met in 1770 and whom he married soon

---

again, since both were seen as useful for encouraging conversion.
[37] *EMP* 5: 184-6, 190-3, 202-8, 6: 137-81; *JWL* 6; 22-3; Lednum, 103-12. *Asbury Jol* 1: 219-20, 228; Moore, *Virginia* 56-7, 65-70. Shadford's former service in the militia made him declare 'I had sworn allegiance to the King twice and could not swear to renounce him for ever' G. P. Baker, *Incredible* 47.

after his eventual return.[38] Asbury as late as September 1773 similarly thought that he would return to Britain, writing to his parents that he hoped 'to be in England in less than two years,' having at the point of the letter writing done almost two years in the colonies.[39] Rankin was determined not only to administer Methodist discipline but also maintain its missionary profile. He spoke several times to John Brainerd, brother of the missionary to the Indians, and met with representatives of the Nanticoke tribe near Philadelphia. He commented favourably on the responsiveness of black slaves, freedmen, and their families to Methodism. He made contact with antislavery activists and lobbied members of the Continental Congress on the subject.

By the next American Conference *Minutes* in May 1774 at Philadelphia there were another 1000 members and a total of seventeen preachers. Of the ten Assistants five were American-born. There were ten circuits listed, but the key sentence in the *Minutes* was the last 'wherever Thomas Rankin spends his time, he is to be assisted.' This meant that Rankin, though down for the Philadelphia circuit with a three month exchange with Asbury as in the previous year, would actually travel where he thought fit, and so he was involved, for example, in the Virginia revival. Rankin also gave the American itinerants the same treatment received by British itinerants at the British Conference. Each received copies of the *Large* (disciplinary) *Minutes* of 1744 and the *Minutes* of the latest British Conference and formal certificates. This increased their feeling of fraternity, not least with their British brethren. Rankin had class papers printed on the British model with columns for name, state in life (married or single), state in grace ('s' for seeker, 'b' for born again), attendance and weekly contribution. The first known to survive is dated the 30th January 1775 in Maryland.[40]

At the same time the first moves were being made in preparation for the war which was to come. Rankin had arrived at the same time as news of the Tea Act which led to the Boston 'tea party' seven months later. The Continental Congress first met in September 1774, and the first skirmishes at Lexington and Concord were in March and April 1775.

Relations between Rankin and Asbury

Rankin, Asbury and Shadford were the chief British itinerants in America in this period with Rankin in charge. Rankin and Asbury had a relationship described by the editors of Asbury's Journal as 'strained compatibility.'[41]

---

[38] Rankin MSS Journal page 3 Sunday 13th January 1774. Rankin wrote up his Journal much later in Britain, while Pilmore's Journal seems almost contemporaneous, as was Asbury's, though there are marks of later editing.

[39] The letter is printed in *Asbury Jol* 3: 18. See also A. Godbold, 'Francis Asbury and his Difficulties with John Wesley and Thomas Rankin. *MH* 3 (1965) 3-19.

[40] *Minutes MCA*; Andrews, *Methodists and America* 46-7; G. P. Baker, *Incredible* 24.

[41] Wright and Yearbury returned to Britain at this point. Yearbury had been a local

Asbury's initial comment on Rankin is justly remembered 'He will not be admired as a preacher. But as a disciplinarian, he will fill his place.' For Asbury there were always others to do the preaching. Nobody else but Rankin and himself would be careful enough on the discipline. In December 1774 Rankin's Journal reported 'we talked over different matters regarding the work and removed some little and foolish misapprehensions which had taken place in his (Asbury's) mind.' Rankin had already set a pattern of making himself available to preside at Quarterly Meetings and setting up new circuits swiftly.

Though the pair had a whole continent in which to preach, they had different ideas. Asbury's Journal makes it clear the two men did not agree on stations. Asbury wanted to return to Baltimore and Rankin for the present was against it. However, Asbury, having written a letter to Wesley, showed it to Rankin as a sign of his loyalty to him and reported that 'Mr Rankin appeared to be very kind.'[42] Asbury also thought Rankin had spent too long in Philadelphia (ten months to February 1775). Whether he told Rankin this is not clear. Again it was ironic since Asbury had wanted to remain in Baltimore. At that point Asbury was seriously thinking perhaps he ought to go to Antigua, where there was a need for a preacher. It is also evident from Asbury's letters that he wrote a good deal to the American-born preachers and that Rankin had at times been suspicious of this, that Asbury might be 'stirring them up against those they must be in subjection to.'[43]

British Preachers and the War

James Dempster and Martin Rodda

In 1774 Wesley sent the final pair of British preachers to come to America in this period, James Dempster and Martin Rodda.[44] Like Rankin, these were

---

preacher before 1773 in Bradford on Avon, Wiltshire. Webb had persuaded him to go in April 1773 to America to become a travelling preacher. He took a supply of broadcloth with him which paid his return journey. F. Baker, *Wesley to Asbury* 61-2; Barclay, *America 1769-1849* 52-6; *EMP* 5: 185. Richard Wright, wrote Asbury, had been spoiled by gifts and lasted as a itinerant only for a similar period (*Asbury Jol* 1: 37).

[42] *Asbury Jol* 1: 80 3rd June 1770. Note also the beginning of the first sentence of the entry 'To my great comfort arrived Mr Rankin...' Rankin MSS Journal 19-20, Dec 5th 1774 and *Asbury Jol* 4th Dec 1: 140. Quarterly Meetings were held at Gunpowder Neck 1st, West Jersey 16th, Redley Creek in Newcastle Co 22nd and Trenton 29th August, and on Nov 1st William Duke was sent to form a new circuit on the other side of the Potomac. Rankin's Journal 15-6, 19.

[43] *Asbury Jol* 1: 149, 3: 20. The quotation is from a letter from Asbury to Edward Dromgoole, an Irish-born itinerant who had much success as a strong preacher, located, but whose collection of letters has survived.

[44] Asbury has a reference to three preachers arriving at this point. The third could be William Glendenning, but if so he had never been an itinerant in Britain and was therefore not an itinerant sent by Wesley like the others. Robert Lindsay is another

experienced itinerants, though perhaps not of Rankin's calibre. James Dempster was a thirty-four year old Scot, originally Presbyterian, who may have been educated at Edinburgh University and who had been travelling for ten years, mostly in Wales and Ireland, eight out of the ten as Assistant. He became ill, did not remain in the itinerancy and had left by May 1776 when he married. It would seem he wanted to settle in America, but did not want to remain neutral over the American cause. Instead by 1778 he had gone to Loyalist held New York, where he had previously served for a month, to help lead the Methodists there.[45]

Martin Rodda was a thirty-two year old Cornishman born in 1742, one of ten children of whom at least three became preachers. Martin was converted around 1756, began preaching by 1760 and was accepted by Wesley as an itinerant in 1763. He had had a dispute with a man in Pembroke and so he stopped itinerating and returned to Cornwall. In 1766 both he and his brother Richard began travelling by going to Wales. Like Boardman before him, he had married but lost his wife by death before he volunteered for America. He had been with Dempster in the previous year and it could be that Wesley chose him because of this, seeing the pair as compatible. A successful preacher in America, he helped to make the young Freeborn Garrettson an itinerant and should be credited with this. Garrettson was to be one of the most outstanding of the American-born itinerants, one of the very few who maintained a regular correspondence with Wesley.[46]

Unmarried Preachers

The preachers whom Wesley sent to America were without wives. Most were unmarried; some were widowed, though at least one (Rankin) had an understanding which blossomed into marriage on his return. This was because Wesley did not want to burden the nascent American societies with the cost of families and to make it easier for his preachers to go. There were several

---

possibility. He was an Irish-born preacher first stationed in 1774 in America. He returned to Europe in 1777 and then travelled on the Irish stations until 1788 when he was expelled (CJ). Like Glendenning there is no evidence he was an itinerant before he went to America. See *Asbury's Jol* 1: 135 24th October 1774. The Journal does have various other errors. For Lindsay see also Chapters 15 and 16 below.

[45] For Dempster's youth and education I am grateful to Margaret Batty (letter 14/6/1999). See also F. Baker, *Wesley to Asbury* 98-99; Wakeley 250-51; *JWJ(C)*; *MH* 38 (2000) 307-51; MS Letter from the preacher William Pitt to Bradburn 1770 in Queen's College Library, Melbourne, Australia; Sandford, *Missionaries* 30; Barclay, *Methodism 1769-1849* 1: 44. For more on New York in the war see Chapter 13 below.

[46] For Rodda's origins see Chapter 7 above. F. Baker, *Wesley to Asbury* 98-9; *EMP* 2: 295-323; *AM* 1784: 410-6; *WMM* 1827: 672-4; Pearce, *Wesleys in Cornwall* 7, 139; *JWJ(C)* 5: 427; R. D. Simpson, ed, *Life and Journals of... Freeborn Garrettson 1752-1827* (Madison NJ: Academy Books, 1984) 51.

results, the most significant being that this remained a sign of the difference between American and British Methodism into the early nineteenth century. In 1791 on Wesley's death the 200+ British travelling preachers had supported 100 wives, with at least 20 others married but unsupported because they had money of their own. On the other hand the American ministry under Asbury in the early 1800s was in Richey's words 'a band of single men'. This was no accident; it was the result of Wesley's original selection, backed up by the dominating authority and example of Francis Asbury himself. Those who married, as many did, usually had to locate. Few American preachers in this period had wives who were supported.

Another result was that the pool of those British preachers who could go to America was significantly smaller. Wesley was prepared to make exceptions to this rule as when he begged an obvious leader like the married Alexander Mather to go but without effect.[47] In addition, the preachers sent had experienced on average about five years of travelling in British circuits. The most important exception to this was the more senior Rankin.[48]

Methodist Success and the Revolution

It has also been argued that Methodist success helped to lead to the revolution against Great Britain, a consequence neither envisaged by Wesley nor advocated by him. Isaac[49] suggested that the previously loyal planters changed to a republican ideology because they felt threatened by the religious revivalists; these they saw as successfully creating a counter culture since the preachers questioned the morality of slavery. Slave-holding planters saw the republican doctrines of community giving new authority to their traditional structures. They became revolutionaries 'as a defensive response to the open rejection of deference that was increasingly manifested in the spread of

---

[47] Richey, *Conference in America* 57-8 also pointed out the social stigma of marrying an American itinerant.

[48] In 1774 there was even a suggestion that the (unmarried) Methodist clergyman John Fletcher should be sent out as Bishop for the colonies. Lord Dartmouth, the Evangelical politician who was Secretary for the Colonies, received a letter from Fletcher in which he thanked him for his 'gracious intentions.' Since Dartmouth filed it under 'patronage' it was clearly preferment. Forsaith suggests it should be linked to Rankin's slightly later letter to Dartmouth, referring to the proposal of an American Bishopric. Rankin wrote that the political strife would need to calm first. MS letter of Fletcher 19th September 1774 in the Papers of the Legge family at Staffordshire CRO D (W) 1778 V697 Box 2. Rankin's letter 29th December 1774 D (W) 1778/11/1041. I am grateful to Peter Forsaith for letting me read his unpublished paper 'Episcopacy, patronage and speculation: Fletcher of Madeley, North America and Lord Dartmouth's "gracious intentions."'

[49] R. Isaac, *The Transformation of Virginia 1740-1790* (Chapel Hill: Norton, 1982) 265. Isaac admitted, however, that his interpretation is speculative.

evangelicalism.' Certainly Methodism became very successful in Virginia, but there is no evidence that Virginians were more likely to become Patriots than the inhabitants of New England where Methodism had no hold yet. The 100 Virginian members gathered by Pilmore in 1773 had become 3,500 by 1778, over half the members in America. The general thesis, however, seems unlikely even if possible. The 3,500, though large in American Methodist terms, was still a very small proportion of the total population of the state and had no bearing on events in South Carolina and Georgia where Methodism at this point was still hardly noticeable. The opposite assertion by Clark that dissident Protestant denominations launched the revolution to defend themselves against the rising tide of Anglicanism can not be taken seriously so far as American Methodists were concerned. There was no rising tide from their point of view.[50]

The Coming of the War 1775-8

All Methodists were encouraged to attend the sacraments of the Church of England, which in the Middle Colonies had been easy since the Church was in the majority. However, even here problems arose with the coming of the War. Many clergy were Loyalist and therefore were prosecuted, forced out of their livings and went to New York or back to Britain. Among the Episcopalian clergy there were 63 Loyalists who left out of the total of 286.[51] Many of these Loyalists, like the British Methodist itinerants, were recent immigrants to the colonies, often sponsored by the Society for the Propagation of the Gospel. These tended to be the more loyal, the more likely to have been born in Britain and to have the most connections in British clerical circles.[52]

The Methodist and especially the British-born itinerants were also seen as Loyalists and many of them left for Britain, perhaps fifteen out of the total of fifty itinerants in 1777. Most of the British-born were pro-British, but followed

---

[50] J. C. D. Clark, *The Language of Liberty 1660- 1832 Political Discourse and Social Dynamics in the Anglo American World* (Cambridge: CUP, 1994). Methodism was growing rapidly and had no need to defend itself. Whether Anglicanism was growing faster than the population growth is not clear. Certainly many lay Methodists supported the revolution. American-born itinerants tended to keep resolutely neutral and suffered accordingly see below Chapter 13. 'Patriots' was the American term for what the British called rebels.

[51] Andrews, *Methodists and America* 62, correcting the earlier figures of 150 Loyalists and 123 Patriots. Other British-born itinerants who stayed active apart from Asbury were William Glendenning, John Littlejohn (located 1778), John Dickins, Edward Bailey who entered in 1777 and died in 1780, Robert Strawbridge (died 1781) and Edward Dromgoole (located 1778). See the lists in J. Lee, *Short History of the Methodists in the USA, beginning in 1766 and continued till 1809* (Baltimore: Magill, 1810) 319-24. Barclay listed four of Wesley's missionaries who lived and died on American soil despite the Revolution (*Methodism 1769-1849* 34n).

[52] G. M. Ditchfield, 'Ecclesiastical Policy under Lord North' in Walsh, *Church* 241.

the general no politics rule and kept their feelings to themselves. Their journals show little concern about what was happening on the political scene. By August 1775, however, Rankin had written a letter to Asbury suggesting that the British itinerants should leave. Asbury apparently replied that with a 3,000 membership increasing all the time it would be 'an eternal dishonour to the Methodists' if this happened, and shamed the others into staying. He was justified by the revivals of 1775-6 in Virginia and North Carolina which resulted in a large increase in Methodist membership. Asbury felt strongly, as he wrote to Shadford 'that as long as I could stay and preach without injuring my conscience, it appeared as my duty to abide with the flock.'[53]

However, Wesley, who had privately written to Lord Dartmouth in the Government that an 'oppressed people asked for nothing more than their legal rights,' changed his view and took a strong Tory line in his 'Calm Address to our American Colonies,' printed in September 1775. Martin Rodda came out openly as a pronounced Royalist, which made all the other preachers suspect also. In 1777 he circulated George III's proclamation, was arrested and brought before General Washington. Washington was reported to have asked him who he was. Rodda told him he was one of Mr Wesley's preachers. Washington replied 'Mr Wesley, I know; I respect Mr Wesley; but Mr Wesley, I presume, never sent you to America to interfere with political matters. Mr Wesley sent you to America to preach the Gospel to the people. Now go you and mind your own proper work: preach the Gospel and leave politics to me and my brethren.' On gaining his freedom Rodda left his circuit and sought refuge with the British fleet, then went to Philadelphia and returned to England in the spring of 1778.[54]

Rankin corresponded with Lord Dartmouth the Secretary for the Colonies, giving him the latest intelligence and suggesting concessions. Most Methodist preachers were pacifists and refused to serve and so many Methodists were imprisoned or persecuted. Thomas Webb was arrested in 1777 and held for a year at Bethlehem under parole. Eventually in August 1778 he was exchanged and in October 1778 the Webb family sailed for England.[55] Rankin had almost been arrested by the militia in August 1776 in Maryland. Many local societies were decimated by the hostilities.[56]

The Conference meeting of 1777 was well aware of the problems. It did not meet in a large town or city as all the previous ones had, but instead in a

---

[53] *Asbury Jol* 1: 161-3, 235, quotation dated 2 April 1777. Baker, *Wesley to Asbury* 98-9.
[54] The story of Washington and Rodda is in the *Wesley Banner* 1849: 17. Though it is late it is possible James Everett the editor could have heard the story from Rodda himself. It is quoted in Pearce, *Wesleys in Cornwall* 160n. See also for Rodda, Barclay, *Methodism 1769-1849* 1: 44; Lednum 150, 193-4; *PWHS* 33 (1961) 132: 39 (1973) 31-2; Andrews, *Methodists in America* 47-55.
[55] The American officer involved in the exchange, who had been released by the British, did not turn up. Eventually Washington ordered that his old comrade in arms be freed. Bates, *Webb* 19-22.
[56] Rankin's MS Journal 49.

preaching house at Deer Creek tucked away in the country in the Methodist Chesapeake heartland of Maryland. It reported almost 7,000 members and 36 preachers despite the conflict raging in the colonies. Neither Rankin nor Asbury appeared on the stations. Only Rodda, Shadford and John King of the preachers sent from Britain had their names printed, all as Assistants. There were fifteen circuits, though no preacher was listed for British-held New York. They all signed a covenant to remain loyal to their task as Methodist preachers and to choose a Committee of Assistants to carry out the role of the General Assistant and the 'old preachers who came from Britain.' This Committee included three young Americans and two Britons who had come to settle in America. The Conference was trying to remain loyal to its British Methodist roots and Wesley's preaching and practice, while adjusting to the anticipated loss of all the leaders whom Wesley had sent. In the event Asbury remained. Asbury reported the American itinerants' distress at the prospect of parting 'many wept as if they had lost their first born sons…thinking they should not see the faces of the English preachers any more.'[57]

The Methodist itinerants did not go easily. In January 1777, because of the danger, Asbury's Journal became more general, mentioning fewer places and names. In August Rodda was arrested, over two years after Lexington. In September Rankin and Rodda at last decided to leave. In March 1778 Asbury and Shadford met for the final time before Shadford and Spraggs went across the British lines to New York. The same month George Shadford finally and reluctantly joined Rankin and Rodda in leaving America.[58]

The Returned Preachers in Britain

It is interesting to follow the contrasting later histories of these three preachers. Martin Rodda who had been unhappy in America seems to have been dissatisfied with his reception in Britain when he returned. He desisted in 1781, for Wesley had not made him an Assistant as Rodda expected on his return.[59] George Shadford, however, had returned to the stations in England in June 1778. On the 17th December 1782 he was married in London (by Wesley himself) to someone whose name appears shortened as 'E Bai.' His wife must

---

[57] *Minutes MCA* 13-15; Baker, *Wesley to Asbury* 99-100. The Americans were Daniel Ruff, William Watters and Philip Gatch, the 2 Britons Edward Dromgoole and William Glendenning. *Asbury Jol* 1: 239; Richey, *Conference in America* 25-6.

[58] Andrews, *Methodists in America* 47-62; Baker, *Wesley to Asbury* 99; *Asbury Jol* 1: 188.

[59] Rodda's first job on leaving the itinerancy was a seller of 'spirituous liquors,' which supports Wesley's judgment. This information comes from Tom Albin's notes on Chubb Journal vol 2 at the New Room Bristol 23, for which I am grateful. Pawson thought Rodda had 'turned wicked' and should be forgotten. He apparently did not die until 1815. *Pawson L* 3: 27; Schell, 'Methodist Preachers,' which gives no source. See also Chapter 16 below.

have had means since she was never in the list of preachers' wives receiving money and his will left £100 to the Preachers' Fund, wealth he could never have had without her. He went as a Supernumerary in 1791 to Macclesfield but moved frequently after 1805, settling eventually in 1812 at Frome where he died in November 1816, leaving his widow to survive him. He was blind in his old age until he had a cataract operation.[60]

Thomas Rankin married soon after his return. His marriage meant he could not travel and he located in London, becoming one of Wesley's leading advisers and later publicly influencing him against Asbury. Wesley ordained him in February 1789 for the English work. Rankin's marriage weakened his position, however, as he was no longer travelling. He had only kept his position within the itinerancy on Wesley's special request. On his wife's death in 1796 he wrote he wanted no money. His fellow preachers in 1796 dropped him from the *Minutes* and gave him no obituary when he died in 1810.[61]

---

[60] *WJW* 23: 433; S. Tuck, *Wesleyan Methodism in Frome* (Frome: Tuck, 1814). Was it his wife's connections that made him move so much? The ministerial Waterhouse family, originally from New Mills, claim a descent from him, possess a book with his name in, and had a son christened 'Shadford' in the early 1850s (information from David Waterhouse 3/3/2007).

[61] At the Manchester Conference of 1787 Rankin publicly advised Wesley to recall Asbury from America (see Chapter 13 below under Harper). Asbury in 1816, close to his deathbed, said that Rankin had played the part of the early Christian leader Diotrephes influencing John Wesley against Asbury unjustly (*Asbury Jol* 3: 546-48). Diotrephes, according to 3 John v 10, was 'laying baseless and spiteful charges' against the writer. It should be recorded that the 'letter' which appears at *Asbury Jol* 1: 21-2 is the editors' mistaken reading of Carroll. Carroll meant Rankin had gone to Philadelphia in 1777 not that the letter was written then (H. K. Carroll, *Francis Asbury in the Making of American Methodism* (New York: Methodist Book Concern, 1923) 78). Asbury also accused Rankin of trying to sweep the American continent free of all the British preachers, telling them if they went home they would be ordained and could return after the war. In 1806 Asbury sent £95 to Rankin in settlement of the estate of Robert Williams, for whom they had been joint executors thirty years earlier. For more details on the controversy about Rankin's later ministerial status see Chapter 19 below. The Conference did not share Wesley's trust in Rankin.

Chapter 13

America from 1778

'I must ride or die.'
Francis Asbury

'When it was objected that we spoke for hire, it was answered, No – it was only a passing support.'
Asbury Jol New Jersey 22nd September 1783.

Asbury, the American Preachers and the War

Conferences without the British Preachers

1778 marked the worst point of the war for Methodism, with most of the English preachers gone and the forty-two-year-old Asbury in hiding. From then on the prospects for Methodism in America began to improve.

American Conferences continued to be held in 1778 and the following years but for some time the main Conference was held in the south in Virginia, usually without any British preacher because Asbury was in hiding in Delaware and unable to come south. The chief business was the question of the administration of the sacraments. Few clergy stayed in America. Though Devereux Jarratt who had remained did his best, he could not give Communion to all the Methodists in Virginia and Carolina, let alone baptize, marry and bury them as well. There was much pressure from the new converts of the revival for the preachers to do it themselves. The 1778 Conference at Leesburg and the 1779 Conference at Fluvanna, both in Virginia, had to face this problem. William Watters, the senior American preacher, presided at the first; Philip Gatch, another of the original five appointed, did so at the second. In 1778 there was a decrease of membership because of the war. Five circuits had to be discontinued in areas held by the British. However, new circuits were created in Virginia and Carolina. Watters was determined to 'stand in the gap,' to prevent a break with Wesley's rules which administering the sacrament would entail. Asbury had held his own Conference of mostly northern preachers earlier at his retreat, Judge White's, in Delaware. These sixteen preachers, including Watters, decided that Asbury should be General Assistant because he had been sent by Wesley and because of his seniority. The majority of the larger Fluvanna Conference, however, led by Gatch, agreed to administer the sacraments, a move opposed by Jarratt as well as a minority led by Watters and the northern preachers in touch with Asbury. While nineteenth century historians saw power flowing through Asbury and his northern conference, the Fluvanna Conference, apart from being both the legal Conference and the assembly of the larger number of preachers, has also now been seen by Richey as the fount of independent American Methodism. It 'lodged authority in conference, in a committee with apparent administrative and appointive powers elected by conference and in a presbytery also elected by conference.' He also emphasized that even at this stage the two wings had more in common keeping them together, though there might be different responses to the pressure since Asbury was not there in the south.[1]

Asbury and the War

Asbury was a deeply spiritual man whose Journal shows how often he needed to retire to the 'silent woods' for prayer and nourishment. He was able to survive from February 1778 by hiding from possible arrest and preaching relatively little. This was because influential Methodists in Delaware, particularly Judge Thomas White in Kent County, hid him and protected him. White, a Loyalist, was arrested and imprisoned for his pains. Asbury had to flee through a marsh to take refuge at Sudlersville, Maryland, until returning to White's house after his release. Asbury used his time for study and trying to keep in communication with Methodists throughout the colonies. He remained in White's house so long it was the only American place he ever called home. His Journal shows how he fretted at being unable to travel and preach. He was particularly low in September 1778 when he wrote in it 'My usefulness appeared to be cut off; I saw myself pent up in a corner; my body in a manner worn out; my English brethren gone, so that I had no-one to consult; and every surrounding object and circumstance wore a gloomy aspect.' Typically as a Methodist preacher he went on to hearten himself with a verse of Charles Wesley's he had often sung, ending

> For Thou, O Lord, art with me still;
> Thy friendly crook shall give me aid,
> And guide me through the dreadful shade.[2]

Asbury had written to Rankin in 1777 making it clear that 'the Americans

---

[1] Richey, *Conference in America* 26-8; 'Chesapeake' 202-3; Barclay, *Methodism 1769-1849* 58-65. Baker saw the unseen hand of Strawbridge behind the Fluvanna proposals which may well be correct. Andrews, *Methodists and America* 62-3.
[2] Andrews *Methodists and America* 59-61; *Asbury Jol* 1: 280 entry for the 15th September, and 441 for the 'silent woods.' 'Home' was mentioned 14 years later, September 15th 1792, when he felt ill and went 'home' to White's house *Asbury Jol* 1: 730. White also won over Richard Bassett of Dover, later Governor and Senator for Delaware (Lednum 272-6).

would become a free and independent nation, and that he was too much knit in affection to many of them to leave them.' This fell into the hands of American officers in early 1779 with the result that Asbury no longer had to hide. He also made contact with the Whig Governor of the state, Cesar Rodney, and became a Delaware citizen.

Asbury's mind had been supported at his lowest point in 1778 by the knowledge of several other factors. One was the continued success of Methodist preaching, especially in Virginia and North Carolina. Another was the continuing progress of the American-born itinerants. William Watters, Daniel Ruff and Freeborn Garrettson visited him and remained in close contact.[3] These preachers were joined by others. Twenty-eight new itinerants began to travel between 1777 and 1779 despite persecution. At least eight of the Maryland preachers were imprisoned and fined for not serving in the militia. After the Maryland Act of December 1777 was passed, demanding an oath of allegiance from all men and taxing those who did not comply at £100 a time, more were jailed and fined. Jesse Lee was drafted into the militia in North Carolina, having no choice about service as a wagon-driver until his release in 1780. Philip Gatch was tarred and feathered. Methodists were regarded as hostile to the Republic, correctly in view of Wesley's publication and the actions of Rodda, Rankin and Webb. The non-partisan stance of many others like Garrettson was seen as equally dangerous by most patriots.

Many influential Methodist laymen supported the Republic and influenced the Government to stop persecuting Methodists. Samuel Owings in Baltimore County, Maryland, was a colonel in the militia. Richard Dallam enlisted in the local Harford County Rifles. Jesse Hollingsworth of Baltimore organized supplies of food and arms to the patriots and was wounded in the process. Many other Methodists migrated westwards, looking for safety from war and persecution. It was remarkable that Methodism survived the war. This was the result of the work of British preachers before the war, especially Pilmore, Shadford, Williams, Rankin and Asbury. It was also thanks to the determination of Asbury in remaining in America and the loyalty he inspired. American itinerants and local preachers were loyal also to Wesley and to Methodism, despite the undoubted sufferings they endured.[4]

American and Methodist Success during the War

In 1780 Asbury was reconciled with the southern preachers and invited to ride

---

[3] The quotation is from Lednum 226. See also *Asbury Jol* 1: 299.
[4] Andrews, *Methodists and America* 39-40, 53-60, 64 emphasised the difficulties for the infant connexion, since the Methodists were deliberately calling on young able bodied Americans not to fight. It is interesting to compare Methodists with the other religious body linked to Loyalism, the Episcopalians. Noll showed (*America's God* 120-2) how much the latter suffered in the period 1770-1820, their period of 'suspended animation.'

through their circuits. He at once seized the opportunity and did just that, riding through much of North Carolina at the height of summer, though often unwell. The decision by these preachers confirmed the authority of Wesley and his deputy Asbury in America. Nevertheless, some southern preachers wanted more independence and power, and the problem of the sacraments remained. Jarratt was also reconciled to the preachers. The surrender of Cornwallis' British army at Yorktown in 1781 brought closer the prospect of an end to the war. In 1782 the continued growth of Methodism led to the setting up of two Conferences, one in the south and one in the north, both co-ordinated by Asbury. Asbury was aiming to strengthen his position by seeking the votes of the American preachers and trying to act according to their wishes. With peace imminent the country became quieter. The 1784 Conference reported nearly 15,000 members and 83 preachers, a better ratio than Britain. However, Asbury had many other problems. The Methodist connexion needed the same discipline that Rankin had provided before the war. New circuits had to be formed in the west and south. In the autumn of 1783 Richard Owings was the first preacher to cross the Appalachians, beginning a circuit there. By June 1784 Asbury had followed him over the Redstone Pass, but to man the new areas he needed many more preachers. Chapels had to be built and literature provided. Most of all he wanted his British leader to solve the problem of the sacraments before other churches seized the opportunity.[5]

Preachers in New York during the War

While the majority of the British preachers returned to Britain by mid 1778, the American-born preachers remained in most of the rebellious colonies (or newly independent States). However, there was a slightly different situation in New York. In the City and the surrounding islands a British army held the upper hand for most of the period until 1783. Daniel Ruff, the American-born preacher stationed there in 1776, left. Loyalist refugees from all over the other colonies flocked to New York to live. The Methodist preaching house on John Street remained open with a regular congregation, not shut or taken over as were most other religious buildings in the city. Indeed it was also used by the German Protestant Hessian troops for services in the evenings. Since the British preachers had gone home, the congregation turned to the Loyalist John Mann, trustee, class leader and local preacher since 1771, to maintain the worship. In 1778 he was joined by the Scot James Dempster and the American Loyalist Samuel Spraggs (who had entered as a travelling preacher in 1776), the latter fleeing from Frederick County where he was on circuit. They remained in New York in a kind of alternative circuit acting as the travelling preachers for the

---

[5] *Asbury Jol* 1: 345-462. Isaac Rollins, for example, was hostile.

remainder of the war period,[6] and Mann preached once a week in the chapel. A salary was paid to Spraggs from May 1778 to June 1783. New York was not cut off from its hinterland; the British and American authorities alike issued safe conduct for Whig and other women, men and even American officers to come into New York. Letters were frequent and American food and raw materials, much needed by the British Army, and British goods, ranging from china to tea and rum wanted by Americans, were bought and sold by both sides despite regulations against it. Many black slaves came into New York seeking freedom[7] and swelling the congregation at John Street.

Once peace was made Asbury lost no time in sending John Dickins, one of the better educated British-born preachers, to New York to care for the society. Asbury soon followed to stay for a week and preach, all before the British forces had evacuated New York. More than 30,000 Loyalists were shipped out on British ships, many to Nova Scotia. These included a large number of black Methodists, the local preacher John Mann and other Methodist lay leaders. Spraggs remained and became ordained as an Anglican. Dempster built a new life as a Presbyterian minister in Florida, New York State. Though some of these Loyalists in Nova Scotia moved on elsewhere, leading to the settling of Methodism in such diverse places as Sierra Leone and the Bahamas,[8] yet the settlement in the Maritime Provinces of Canada had a profound effect there in furthering the Methodist cause. The efforts of Spraggs, Dempster and Mann in maintaining and strengthening Methodism in New York during the war have rarely been acknowledged.

Coke, Asbury and the New British Preachers

Thomas Coke

The problem of the sacraments remained. Asbury had for some time been

---

[6] For Samuel Spragg or Spraggs see Andrews, *Methodists in America* 55, and Wakeley 253-66, 279-290, spelt 'Spragg' in the *Minutes* but 'Spraggs' in the old John Street accounts and elsewhere. Dempster had been at New York previously. See also *Asbury Jol* 1: 263, 440.

[7] J. L. Van Buskirk, *Generous Enemies: Patriots and Loyalists in Revolutionary New York* (Philadelphia: Pennsylvania UP, 2002) shows that the general 19th and 20th century idea that there was a strict separation was anything but true. Families divided by loyalties to the two sides communicated frequently, sending money and goods to each other. Parole meant captured British officers could return to New York to collect their belongings, just as a captured American officer from Maryland was allowed to go back to Maryland to get food supplies, and a leading American general (Charles Lee) could move relatively freely round New York. Whig was another term for Patriots.

[8] *Asbury Jol* 1: 440, 445-6. Some also returned, as did James Mann, John's brother, in 1791-2. For Nova Scotia see C. H. H. Scobie and J. W. Grant, eds, *The Contribution of Methodism to Atlantic Canada* (Montreal: McGill, 1992) 40. Robert Barry and Charles White were other Methodist leaders who went from New York to Nova Scotia.

appealing to Wesley to appoint him as General Assistant, which Wesley accepted in a letter of October 1783, and to solve the question of the sacraments. After much hesitation[9] Wesley in late 1784 ordained and sent his right hand man and fellow clergyman Thomas Coke. Coke was the archetypal itinerant like Whitefield, never really to settle on either side of the Atlantic and with two major spheres in Ireland and the West Indies to distract him from both Britain and the USA. Wesley also ordained and sent Richard Whatcoat and Thomas Vasey with Coke. Two other preachers ordained by Wesley for the West Indies, William Hammett and John Harper, ended up in the American ministry because of ill-health suffered on the mission field. Wesley made it clear that this was his final effort for America. There would be no more help from Britain.[10]

Wesley sent Coke to America ordained as a superintendent for the future American church, with orders to ordain Asbury to be co-superintendent with him and probably to set up an independent church. Asbury wanted to hold a Conference of all the preachers to ratify this. Coke, as had happened in England, wanted to do it alone. Asbury, the man in possession with the clear idea that in the new Republic the new church must be ratified by the votes of the preachers, got what he wanted, including those vital votes. Coke, however, first celebrated Communion. As an Anglican priest he had every right, but he allowed Whatcoat, ordained by Wesley in England, to celebrate with him. Similarly, Whatcoat also assisted Coke in baptizing at the first meeting of Coke and Asbury at Barratt's Chapel in Delaware before the Christmas Conference at Baltimore 1784.

Thomas Coke, the small and fiery Welshman from Brecon, was an apothecary's son who has had a chequered reputation attracting praise and blame over the years. Modern historians have given him more praise, which he particularly deserved for his work in America where he was 'determined not to stir a finger without his (Asbury's) consent.' Coke successfully adapted himself to a new continent, travelled vast distances in much worse conditions than he had ever seen before, allowed himself to play second fiddle to Asbury as he did to Wesley on the other side of the ocean, and helped to found one of the most successful churches of all time. Coke was given the right to have his name first on the letters from the two and when together he usually preached first. At the Christmas Conference it was Coke who presided but Asbury who emerged with the power. Coke sought in America to work with Asbury, accepting the journeys and preaching opportunities that Asbury thrust upon him. He did not start agitating against Asbury when Asbury refused to share the burden of stationing. A lesser man might well have complained about being cast only as

---

[9] Vickers, *Thomas Coke* 74-7 showed that Coke was aware in 1783 of the possibility that Wesley would send him to America. He did not sail until the 18th September 1784.

[10] For ordination see Chapter 18 below. For Coke see Vickers, *Thomas Coke*. Andrews, *Methodists in America* 66-8. Rankin argued against the ordinations but lost.

visiting evangelist. However, Coke without Asbury's knowledge did make overtures to the Episcopalians in April 1791 which were probably foolish. Asbury appreciated Coke's friendship and help, not least because Coke enabled him to keep in touch with his elderly parents and make sure he could get money to them for their needs.[11]

Christmas Conference 1784

Asbury did not accept at once what Coke said Wesley had planned, even with Wesley's letter. Instead he insisted that everything, from the setting up of a new church, through the liturgies Wesley had sent, to whether he and Coke should be the superintendents, should be accepted by the American Methodist preachers. With this in mind Garrettson was dispatched to summon as many preachers as possible while Coke went on a 900 mile tour of American Methodism. The Conference, which was held in Baltimore at Christmas in 1784 lasting two weeks, agreed to all the suggestions and acknowledged themselves in Wesley's lifetime as 'his sons in the Gospel.' However, the need for their agreement implied that they were with Asbury in declaring 'union but no subordination; connexion but no subjection.' It was appropriate for the new state that the new church set up to win it should also be independent of its former British master.[12]

One of the effects of the Christmas Conference and the setting up of the new church was the loss of some of Wesley's preachers to the Anglicans. John Coleman, Samuel Roe and Samuel Spraggs joined the Protestant Episcopal Church when that was created in 1785.[13] Pilmore returned to America the same year armed with a letter from Charles Wesley and was ordained in November 1785 in the Protestant Episcopal Church. Another result was the creation of Elders, later called Presiding Elders, to take control of groups of circuits. Twelve were appointed but each year thereafter the number grew. These included Whatcoat, Garrettson, Jesse Lee and James O'Kelly who kept the system growing; they were the local experts on whom Asbury depended. With them he devised the stations of the preachers before every Conference. At first the Elders also had the task of taking the sacraments to the people. Coke's other contribution was the use of liturgy by the new church. Wesley's Sunday Service, enthusiastically recommended by Coke, did get a place in America.

---

[11] Baker, *Wesley to Asbury* Chapter 9. Hallam, *Eliza Asbury* 58-81. For Coke's intentions before he went, see his striking letter to Wesley printed in Vickers, *Thomas Coke* 77-8. Coke's position between Asbury and the American Conference on the one hand and Wesley and the British Conference on the other was a difficult one. See, for example, his letter to Asbury of September 1791 printed *Asbury Jol* 3: 101-2.
[12] Heitzenrater 290-292.
[13] I am indebted to Ed Schell's card index of the early American preachers for the information on Roe and Coleman.

Though the book itself was dropped soon, the other services remained strongly alive, especially when incorporated into the Discipline of 1787.[14]

We should not overestimate the importance of 1784. The new church did not spring up ready made according to an imagined blueprint from Wesley. His various ideas were accepted in part only. The organization, discipline and liturgy of the church continued to develop over time, with experiments like the Baltimore Conference system and Asbury's Council appearing and departing. The number of Annual Conferences, nineteen in 1793, was reduced to seven in 1795. The powers of the Superintendents or Bishops changed. In 1792 the General Conference was set up though the first one lacked any *Minutes*. Only in 1796 did the General Conference legislate for specific boundaries for the Annual Conferences and in 1804 define the preachers as belonging to only one Conference. Methodism was developing to meet the society in which it was at work. 'Delegation,' creating a fairer system for the membership of the General Conference and strongly supported by Asbury, did not come until the legislation of the 1808 General Conference.[15]

Thomas Vasey

The other two British preachers whom Wesley sent in 1784, Vasey and Whatcoat, were both senior and experienced, much more so than any Wesley had sent earlier except for Rankin. Though Vasey was to return relatively speedily, Whatcoat remained and eventually was elected Bishop by the Americans themselves, a tribute to Wesley's choice. The lesser of these two was Thomas Vasey, a Durham man almost forty years old who had travelled for nine years though admittedly only twice as an Assistant. He was the orphan ward of a rich uncle who disinherited him when he became a Methodist. He appeared to have been an itinerant for a time in West Cornwall as early as 1773. The British *Minutes* said he began in 1775, but only his initials appeared for the first three years. Was this to protect him from his vengeful uncle?[16] After the Christmas Conference he served as an Elder in the American Church until 1787. He apparently married an American but was uneasy because of the new Republic. When a son was born, Vasey called him George, perhaps a

---

[14] For Presiding Elders see J. Kirby, *Episcopacy in American Methodism* (Nashville: Kingswood, 2000) 54-5.

[15] Richey, 'Chesapeake' 202. For the Baltimore Conference system, the Council and Conferences see Richey, *Conference in America* 37-9, 42-44, 44-54, 64-8.

[16] The *IGI* has Thomas Vasey baptized on the 25th August 1745 at St Helen's Auckland, son of Ralph Vasey (died 1746) and Mary Bouser. His older brother Richard Vasey (1741-92) of Hamsterley helped to bring him up. *City Road Magazine* 1871: 529-30; *WMM* 1827: 644-5. For the use of initials see Chapter 15 below. I am more doubtful than Wallington, who in *PWHS* 10 (1916) 156 made the suggestion of protection from the vengeful uncle, as to why Vasey appeared at first under his initials. Was he liable to quarrel as he was later so that Wesley had doubts about him?

provocation to Americans opposed to King George who had possibly overlooked the fact that Washington bore the same name. When his companion Whatcoat was not made a bishop in 1787, despite Wesley's expressed wishes, Vasey left the Methodists and accepted Episcopalian ordination by Bishop White of Philadelphia; he attacked Asbury as having cast off John Wesley's control.[17] Vasey's later history, though not always clear, shows he found it difficult to settle anywhere, and had an argumentative nature. He went back to Britain later in 1787 and was present at the 1788 British Conference. Wesley allowed him to accept an Anglican curacy but this was not satisfactory to him either. He returned to the British itinerancy at the 1789 Conference. By April 1790 he had gone back for a short visit to the USA, presumably with Wesley's consent since in the 1790 *Minutes* he was sent to Edinburgh.[18] He disagreed with the British Conference in 1794 (as he had with the American in 1787), taking the side of the Bristol trustees against Conference. In 1799 he spent some time arguing publicly in Conference about whether he or a colleague should be Superintendent at Bradford. He spent the period 1811 to 1826 as Reader at Wesley's Chapel in London and then retired to Leeds, dying there the same year.[19]

Richard Whatcoat

The better choice by Wesley was Richard Whatcoat, forty-eight years old in 1784, who had been travelling for fifteen years since 1769 and had been an Assistant every year since 1777 and three times even before that. He was ten or more years older than the next oldest among the British preachers sent. The most important reason for sending him in Wesley's mind must have been that he had known Asbury well when young, having been a local preacher nine years senior in Asbury's home circuit. Whatcoat lived close by in Wednesbury. Like Vasey he had lost his father early and like Boardman he had married but his wife died; in Whatcoat's case this was before he entered. A son seems to have been educated at Kingswood.[20]

---

[17] *WMM* 1827: 142; *DEB*; *Asbury Jol* 1: 472-74, 512, 520, 546-49. The 1882 picture of Asbury's ordination (Heitzenrater etc, *Wesley in America* 67) mistakenly shows Vasey as already ordained and in a white gown and stole not worn by Whatcoat or Coke.

[18] CJ; *WMM* 1827: 142; *JWL* 8: 212.

[19] Pawson thought poorly of Vasey, though this was usual for Pawson. *Pawson L* 2: 6; *PWHS* 22 (140) 126; Baker, *Wesley to Asbury* 103. Vasey's first (American) wife had died by 1798 which was perhaps the reason for at least one of his journeys across the Atlantic. He married Mary Wade at Aberford on the 30th December 1798 (*IGI*) and they had three children; all this is probably why he retired to Leeds. See also his MSS Letters 1792-1826 at MARC and the New Room; Atmore 536; *PWHS* 29 (1954) 178-81.

[20] Whatcoat was born on the 23rd February 1736, the son of Charles and Mary Whatcoat of Quinton, Glos, an early Methodist stronghold because of the sympathies of the clergyman Samuel Taylor whom the Wesley brothers visited regularly. Baker, *Wesley to*

Whatcoat served faithfully as a Presiding Elder on the American stations until he was eventually elected Bishop sixteen years later. In 1787 Wesley sent an instruction to the Americans to elect Whatcoat and Freeborn Garrettson as superintendents with the possible implication that Asbury could then go home. Asbury, sensitive to this and not wanting to go, put it all to the Conference as he had before. The American preachers were equally opposed to losing Asbury and also offended by Wesley's instruction to them to meet at another place and another time and elect Whatcoat. They also did not yet know Whatcoat well enough and refused to elect anybody, swayed by the senior American preacher and Presiding Elder James O'Kelly, who was opposing what he saw as all Wesley's anti-democratic schemes. Wesley complained that Asbury had not done enough to support Whatcoat. Asbury in fact had got Whatcoat to travel around as much as possible to be seen and heard throughout the whole church. Whatcoat in general supported Asbury and carried on with his preaching and administration. Holiness was his constant theme. When he lost his text in the middle of his sermon, he just took a new one! In 1800 the British Conference requested that Thomas Coke be allowed to concentrate on missions in the West Indies and Ireland. Asbury insisted on help for himself, and so in May 1800 Whatcoat was elected Bishop to assist Asbury. This was partly because Wesley had designated him earlier and partly because some thought Asbury wanted him, but mostly because Whatcoat had become universally loved for his simplicity. However, by then he was sixty-four and not well, unable to provide the kind of leadership the church needed.[21]

Whatcoat as Bishop frequently travelled with Asbury and often added a letter to the foot of what Asbury had already written. A preacher commented 'His dress was very plain, in Methodist minister style: the shad-belly coat and vest buttoned up snug to his neck.' By 1801 he was losing his sight. The revivalist Lorenzo Dow, to whom Asbury was often hostile, found real kindness from Bishop Whatcoat. In Whatcoat's sixty-sixth year he was still able to travel 3,077 miles. His health gradually became worse and from 1803 he suffered from the gravel. He died at the home of the former Governor Bassett in Dover, Delaware, on the 5th July 1806.[22]

Asbury 103-60, 191n wrongly said Whatcoat had travelled for 16 years. *Asbury Jol passim* especially 3: 346-7; Lednum, 404-6; *WJW* 23: 339 n30; Sandford, *Missionaries* 355-90; Charles Whatcoat, son of Richard, was in the *KS Reg* from 1774.

[21] Baker *Wesley to Asbury* 159 got Whatcoat's age wrong. Lednum 404-6, and the *IGI* show he was born in February 1736, so he was 64. *Asbury Jol* 3: 49; Wakeley; Sweet, *Methodists* 73-122; *JWL* 8: 73-4; Andrews, *Methodists and America* 197.

[22] Barclay, *Methodism 1769-1849* 130-1; Sprague *Annals* 7; 92-101; Sandford, *Missionaries* 355-90, Andrews, *Methodists and America* 209. Whatcoat's MSS Journal is at Garrett. There was an early biography by William Phoebus and a later one by Sidney Bradley.

Asbury, Coke and Wesley

Wesley had no choice over delegating power to Asbury. He was clearly in Wesley's image in both continual travel and organization. He was the only British preacher who remained through the Revolution and the only preacher who was identified with them enough for the newly independent Americans to accept. A sign of Wesley's trust in Asbury is that he put Asbury in the Legal Hundred at the first opportunity. With regard to Coke, Americans were always suspicious about where his loyalty actually lay. There were even derogatory remarks about King George to see if Coke would rise to them.

Rupp described Coke as 'a British loyalist, who was bound to be caught in the inevitable clash of loyalties (his part in the address offered to Washington was an embarrassment) whereas Asbury was completely identified with his American flock. (No English preacher could have referred to John Wesley as "Old Daddy").'[23] This is too simplistic. Asbury was loyal to his British roots in his correspondence with Wesley, trying to maintain Methodism as it should be. At the same time he had a clear idea of what the Americans in the aftermath of the Revolution would not accept. Wesley could not have such a vision. 'Old Daddy' was a way of making Wesley real to the American preachers who never knew him except as a faraway letter writer. Of course if Asbury had been in England he would not have used the expression. He was in a rapidly growing new country, very conscious of its own importance. He was seeking to naturalize Methodism in American culture and he succeeded. Pilmore is a good example of another English preacher who was equally attracted by America. Plenty of 'English' preachers in England wrote disrespectfully of Wesley behind his back in his lifetime to those whom they could trust like Pawson.

Once Wesley had decided to ordain Coke and the others and send them to America, and Asbury while accepting this had put it to a vote, Wesley had lost ultimate control. This remained with the American Conference. Wesley did not like that, even an ocean away. However, while rejecting Wesley's personal interference the Americans *chose* to remain loyal to his ideas and practice, the Methodist doctrines and the Methodist system. The first building at John Street was secured to 'those who preach no other doctrine than is contained in the said John Wesley's Notes upon the New Testament and his four volumes of sermons.' In 1784 at the Christmas Conference, where the new independent Methodist church was set up in America, the Book of Discipline adopted was in substance very close to the British *Large Minutes*. In 1808 the General Conference wrote in the restrictive rule that doctrine could not be altered. Even in free and republican America Wesley's ideas were to rule for ever![24]

---

[23] Baker, *Wesley to Asbury* 128-131. E. G. Rupp, *Religion in England 1688-1791* (Oxford: OUP, 1986) 434.

[24] R. J. Buchanan, 'The Development of "Doctrine and Discipline" in North American Methodism 1775-1808' in N. Semple, ed, *CMHS Papers 1997-8* (Toronto: n. p, 1999) 70-79.

Growth and Changes in American Methodism

Women

As elsewhere women played an important part in the growth of early Methodism in America. Women were a majority of the members of each society, often joining when young and single and with other female members of their family. It was women who hosted and cared for the early itinerants. Women's networks passed them on from homestead to homestead and town to town. In Philadelphia Mary Thorn, Mary Wilmer and Hannah Baker cared for the first preachers, Pilmore and Boardman. Both preachers wrote to them in gratitude long after they left America. Hannah Baker was still caring for itinerants as late as 1800. Priscilla Dorsey, wife of the ironmaster Caleb, was the first to invite preachers into her home at Belmont. Her daughters married into the Ridgeley family and ensured preachers were invited there as well. Strawbridge lived rent-free on Rebecca and Charles Ridgeley's Hampton estate. In 1775 Asbury had written in his Journal of his hostess Mrs Josias Dallam 'Sister Dallam has treated me with all the tenderness of a mother towards her son: and may He that will not forget a cup of water given in his name abundantly reward her!' Women persuaded their husbands to come and listen and, like Judge White, be converted as a result. A few are recorded as preaching. Many acted as class leaders, prayer leaders, gave large sums of money and created a network of friendly homes for the itinerants to rest in. When the preachers' houses were equipped, they gave, bought and loaned equipment. Their homes were places for the class and the society to meet. They welcomed the stranger and persuaded their husbands to treat the slaves better and give them their freedom. They brought up their children to expect special blessings from the visiting itinerant. Some married an itinerant, usually giving up everything in the process and often causing a rift with their own family like Catherine Livingstone.[25]

Black Methodists

It is estimated that one fifth of the over five million population in the USA in 1800 were of African descent, mostly in the south though in increasing numbers in the Middle Colonies, especially the cities. The slave system was harsh, but not as bad as in the West Indies. The main crop in the Chesapeake, tobacco, needed smaller groups of workers. Black and white workers worked alongside each other. The black slaves were more autonomous than those in the West Indies. It is significant that this was the area where Methodism did best in

---

[25] Richey, 'Chesapeake' 215-7; *Asbury Jol* 1: 150. For women preachers see C. A. Brekus, *Strangers and Pilgrims: Female Preaching in America 1740-1846* (Chapel Hill: North Carolina UP, 1998). For equipping the preachers' house in New York in 1770 see Wakeley 219-225; Andrews, *Methodists and America* 100-118.

America.[26] The 1780s was a period when antislavery legislation began in the separate colonies. It was supported by Methodists because their church had publicly espoused the elimination of slaveholding by its members at the 1780 Conference and in the first Discipline of 1785. One result was that many of the freed slaves especially in the Middle Atlantic States who were seeking for a church, found it in Methodism.

Recent research shows that Methodism in America as in Britain drew from all classes, particularly from lower social groups and all ethnic groups. German, Dutch, French and Swiss surnames appear frequently in the early society lists and church registers right from the start. In 1774 Rankin reported to Lord Dartmouth that 24% of all Methodist members in America were black. It is significant that Methodism persuaded more free blacks as a proportion of the membership to join than whites. When John Street church was built in New York in 1768 the list of donors included blacks. In 1782 William Black wrote in his journal about the 'wonderful work' among the poor negroes of Burchtown in Nova Scotia. In 1786 16.5 % of the female membership in New York City was black, which had risen to 23.5 % in 1791. In Baltimore City the percentage in 1800 was 34.8, over a third. This does not take into account the much larger number of black adherents (slaves, for example, were originally only adherents). This success was through the principled opposition to slavery of Wesley, the first leading religious figure to do this, followed strongly by the early British preachers in America. From their disembarkation they welcomed those who were black, opposed slavery, and encouraged Methodists who were slave-owners to manumit their slaves, as in the case of Richard Allen.[27] Coke particularly had been strong on this, where Asbury had been sometimes more cautious. From 1781 Asbury and other leading itinerants had sometimes taken the black preacher Harry Hosier with them on their journeys, especially to preach to black hearers but also as someone who was most acceptable to whites. This was a symbol that Methodism in America was against slavery and believed that the Spirit would work through Hosier as well as Asbury. Asbury's attitude to slavery was clear. He wrote in 1783 that on witnessing 'cruelty to a slave, I called for my horse, delivered my soul and departed.'[28]

Not all the British preachers always supported the black cause. Richard

---

[26] Noll, *Rise* 28-9; J. Walvin, *Black Ivory* (Oxford: Blackwells, 2001) 75-7.

[27] Betts, *Black* 16-17; Andrews, *Methodists and America* e.g. 46, 123-50, 280; Wakeley 69-72, 102-3. Rankin did not include slaves in membership figures. Even later, owners often prevented their slaves from being members.

[28] *Asbury Jol* 1: 403 onwards. Hosier's preaching career was some twenty-five years. Hosier acted as Asbury's servant and usually slept apart. Later Richard Allen refused an invitation on those terms. The quotation is from *Asbury Jol* 1: 442 where Asbury had gone to John Worthington's house in Maryland. Andrews, *Methodists in America* 139. It is important to realise that in Baker's words 'the modern edition of the Journal follows an expurgated text which sadly disguises his deep sympathy with the slaves.' Baker, *Wesley to Asbury* 121-2.

Whatcoat has often been seen as a saintly Bishop of the early American Church. Yet he may, as Presiding Elder 'Rev Mr W,' have opposed Richard Allen, the eventual founder of the African Methodist Episcopal (AME) Church. 'Degrading language' was used, presumably what the twenty-first century would describe as racist. Allen remained inside the Methodist Church despite this, because of his innate love for Methodism and of Freeborn Garrettson's concern for Allen echoing Asbury himself. Asbury remained concerned about Allen and the black population, even if he was not going to upset the white dominance of the Methodist Episcopal Church. In 1794 Freeborn Garrettson helped Allen found the new black AME church at Bethel within the ME Church, with Asbury preaching the first sermon.[29]

Admittedly the early antislavery rules made by Conference were modified, at least in the south. Lay slaveholders in Virginia made sure the regulations did not apply there as early as 1785. In 1804 the General Conference suspended the whole section on slavery south of Virginia in the *Discipline*. Nevertheless, the effect of slaveholding preachers like Garrettson and Gatch and of leading laymen emancipating their slaves in the Middle Atlantic states was impressive. Even in the Deep South Methodist preachers in the 1790s still bore their witness in favour of liberty. Methodists played a leading part in antislavery societies. Other Methodists left the south and settled in the free northwest of Ohio or Indiana, to get away from the hateful institution.[30]

Among the oppressed black people of America and in the West Indies Methodists had in a short period succeeded more than any other Christian group. Other churches had the evangelical experience of individual salvation. It was not just Methodism's denunciation of slavery and advocacy of freedom. It was also the Methodist 'sense of community, an extended family, an opportunity to meet neighbours, and a way of building an ethnic solidarity' that attracted them. To this social function was added 'an alternative value system in which African Americans could help each other sustain a dignified morality based on freedom of choice.' Further, the spiritual dimension allowed a 'particular commitment to the ecstatic rituals of conversion and baptism, and at least for some an eager aspiration for entire sanctification.' African Americans adopted Methodism because its emotionalism fitted their needs, for example in their use of spiritual songs. The heroes of the Old Testament became their friends. As they sang about Jericho or Samson, so they could imagine their own freedom. It was a Methodist church which Allen founded thanks to Asbury's

---

[29] Andrews, *Methodists in America* 144-8. John Wigger points out the reference may be to Willis. Allen had previously travelled with Whatcoat, when he found him 'a great strength in trouble and a father in Israel.' R. Allen, *The Life, Experience and Gospel Labours of the Right Reverend Richard Allen* (New York: Abingdon, 1960) 22.

[30] Andrews, *Methodists in America* 124-132, 225. Philip Gatch in old age is a good example of leaving the south. For use of the word 'liberty' see Wigger 'Fighting Bees' 213-4.

help that was 'the first social institution fully controlled by black men in America.' This would lead to the setting up of independent African Methodist churches in America and elsewhere.[31]

In both Britain and America Methodism did well in welcoming strangers, particularly important in America as a continent full of immigrants. Methodists were particularly successful on both sides of the Atlantic among the classes who were excluded from political and economic power: women, slaves, freedmen, miners. All these were groups seeking a separate identity and freedom. Methodism provided an important avenue and method of escape from their previous exclusion.

American Circuits

In Britain circuits consisting of as many as thirty or more societies were and still are the fundamental basis of Methodist organization. It is not an exaggeration to say that the modern Superintendent (the successor of Wesley's 'Assistant') is in the circuit the equivalent of the Bishop in his diocese. He or she has the power and the authority from Conference, though admittedly it is not always (or even usually) used. The pattern of the British circuit in the eighteenth century has already been explained above. The same system was the basis for the American organization. The preachers were to spend their time in travel round the small societies which met in people's houses in the evenings during the week. They preached outside whenever possible and stayed in ordinary Methodist homes, only returning to the circuit centre every third or fourth or even sixth weekend. By the early nineteenth century this was no longer the situation in America. It is important to chart the transition.

In 1782 there were twenty-six American circuits and of these only a couple, New Hope and Lancaster, were single-man stations. All the others had at least two preachers. Five circuits had three men and there were two with four. An interesting and probably typical circuit was Frederick, which had been formed from the north part of the Baltimore circuit in 1774. That year it had 175 members in sixteen preaching stations, seven to the west of the Potomac, nine to the east and two travelling preachers. Within the circuit there was a small society at Georgetown on the east bank of the Potomac in the south of the circuit, which had probably begun in 1773.[32]

---

[31] For the West Indies see Chapter 14. Hempton, *Empire* 24-25. The quotation is from E. Foner and O. Mahony, *America's Reconstruction: People and Politics after the Civil War* (New York: Harper, 1995) 92 quoted in Bayly, *Birth* 345. Walvin, *Black Ivory* chapter 12; Andrews, *Methodists and America* 153-4. See also W. Gravely, 'Many of the poor Affricans are obedient to the faith' in Hatch and Wigger, *Shaping* 175-195.

[32] See Chapter 8 above for the detailed explanation of what Wesley wanted a circuit to be. For the Frederick Circuit in 1773 see J. Donovan, ed, *Many Witnesses: A History of Dumbarton UMC 1772-1990* (Georgetown: Dumbarton UMC, 1998) 7-10.

By 1793 the position had changed a little nationally. There were then forty-six single-man stations, mostly in New England and in two other districts, Whatcoat's in the Chesapeake (Dover, Northampton, Dorchester, Kent) and McHemp's in Carolina (Bedford, Botetort, Green, Cowpattin). Ninety circuits, still the majority, had two preachers and six had three, while one had four and one five. By 1813 the number of single-man stations had grown to half the circuits in the connexion, 193; another 178 had two men. There were only eleven three-man circuits and three with four or five preachers, the cities of New York, Philadelphia and Baltimore. The New England Conference was two thirds single-man stations. New Conferences like Ohio and Tennessee were mostly the same. Virginia was half and half. Frederick Circuit had been divided in 1788 and again in 1794. In 1801 Georgetown, though still a small society according to William Watters, was separated off as a single-man station.[33]

Asbury opposed this change 'this growing evil of locality' as he described it in 1813.[34] But he was unable to stop it not just beginning but developing into a state where single-man stations had moved from being rare to becoming close to the norm. After his death the process continued unchecked and by 1840 it had become usual for single-man stations to dominate American Methodism. These single-man charges usually had only one church. The circuit rider had literally dismounted. By 1900 the idea of a circuit with many churches or societies as the responsibility of several ministers had been lost.

Why did this happen? Certainly it was because of demand. In America the pattern of one church one minister was most common in Congregational New England and this was where it was at first most common in Methodism. Circuits were still needed as a way to man the new frontier in the West where people were few and distances to ride long. The circuit system enabled Asbury to maintain the supply of the frontier circuit preachers because they only rode a one-man circuit, not the three-man circuit most common in Britain. Nathan Bangs was one of the leaders in the change, arguing it was needed so the preachers 'could discharge all their duties as pastors.' By 1840 all American circuits, even in the West, looked to grow and transform themselves into stations. There were many results of this, such as the reduction in the need for local preachers.[35]

Circuits in America were necessarily different from Britain, partly by their geographical size. One such difference in the early years was what Coke called 'the Preachers' mark, the split bush.' As he explained 'when a new Circuit is formed in these immense forests, the Preacher, whenever he comes in the first instance to a junction of several roads or paths, splits two or three of the bushes

---

[33] Donovan, *Witnesses*. The chance event that the national capital was founded on its doorstep accelerated these developments.
[34] *Asbury Jol* 3: 475 (Valedictory Address to McKendree).
[35] F. A. Norwood, *The Story of American Methodism* (Nashville: Abingdon, 1974) 131-2; Barclay, *Methodism 1769-1849* 2: 299-301.

that lie on the side of the right path, that the Preachers who follow him, may find out their way with ease.'[36]

Asbury's Later Years

Problems for Asbury and the Church: Hammett and Others

There were many problems for the expanding Methodist church in its first twenty or thirty years. One, which was directly related to British preachers, was that of division, because Asbury like Wesley himself had problems with delegation. Even leading preachers like Jesse Lee, James O'Kelly or Freeborn Garrettson might have to accept Asbury's stationing or leave. O'Kelly left in 1792 to set up the Republican Methodist Church.

A second split was led by William Hammett. He was an Irish itinerant who had become a successful missionary in the West Indies. In 1791 he became ill and Thomas Coke brought him to America to recover. He was put on the American stations but immediately assumed that he could demand any station he liked and receive it. He had built up a following in Charleston and wanted to remain as Assistant. When Asbury refused him this Hammett left, founding his own independent church and dividing the church in Charleston. His dispute with Asbury was both over the itinerant system and Asbury's centralized power. He claimed Asbury did not respect Wesley enough and that his own name had not been printed in the *Minutes*, and he wrote an attack on Coke in 1792. Hammett's new church was called the Primitive Methodist Church, the first breakaway Methodist church in America. He erected a new church building called Trinity in Charleston, South Carolina, and extended his work to several other places. He married a Miss Darrell in South Carolina in January 1794 and had a family. He even sent missionaries out, for example to the nearby Bahamas.[37] Hammett was popular at first and possibly may have made links with O'Kelly's more important division, but his church was declining by 1797. He bought slaves himself, settled on a plantation and became a 'man of the world.' He died in Charleston in 1803. Lorenzo Dow, the itinerant revivalist, later wrote that 'it appears' Hammett 'had died drunk.' Hammett's son Benjamin sued Dow for criminal libel. Dow was fined and sent to jail for a day but was pardoned by the son. All Hammett's churches returned to the Methodist Episcopal Church, though some followers went to the Bahamas.[38]

---

[36] Vickers, *Thomas Coke* 162-3.

[37] Baker, *Wesley to Asbury* 131-6. See Chapter 14 below for Hammett earlier. *DEB*; *MH* 10 (1971) 30-43; *PWHS* 8 (1912) 75-6, 9 (1914) 149, 28 (1952) 99-101; Schell, 'Preachers'.

[38] *AM* 1798: 501-2; *DEB*; *PWHS* 28 (1952) 99-101, 124; Taggart, *Irish* 11, 157-8; *Asbury Jol* 1: 667 n8, 674-5, 705-7, 738-9, 752, 766, 2: 42-4, 163, 423; *DOMBI*; Hammett's MS Journal, South Caroliniana Collection, University of South Carolina, Columbia SC.

Other difficulties included temporary declines in membership, frequent location by the preachers for marriage and a better material life, and also the kind of financial problems faced by the British Conference at a similar period. Already by 1790 the connexion owed the preachers over $1000; debts like these became larger over time.[39] As travel in the east became slightly easier, so Asbury and his itinerants headed west to the mountains and beyond where trails were still being made. In his journeys on horseback he would have a packhorse trained to follow carrying his baggage, much of it his correspondence as he oversaw the church from a continually moving base. Asbury himself found it difficult to ride because of his rheumatism and was using 'a little carriage' as early as 1798 and 'a very light stage wagon' from 1805.[40]

John Harper

John Harper like Hammett was an Irish missionary in the West Indies. In his case his wife of West Indian settler origin was ill and the reason why they had gone to the States, arriving in New England. She died there in May 1794 leaving three small children for the husband to support. Unlike Hammett Harper got on well with Asbury, helping him edit his *Journal* in 1798. It was he who told Asbury Rankin had made Wesley dissatisfied with Asbury and America. Harper was appointed to important circuits in the North and Middle Atlantic states before riding south with Asbury to Charleston in 1798. After the usual probationary period in America he was ordained as an Elder in 1796. The American Church had not accepted Harper's previous service either in Ireland or the West Indies, despite his closeness to Asbury. Even more strangely to modern eyes it did not recognize Wesley's ordination of Harper nine years earlier. (Even Asbury himself had not been ordained by Wesley!) In 1800 Harper suffered persecution because he had anti-slavery pamphlets from the north in his house. He located at Columbia in South Carolina in 1802-3 where he was an outstanding local preacher who helped to found the local church and the Mount Bethel Academy; he died in 1815. Like Hammett he had settled in the south and his family prospered, with his son becoming a Senator.[41]

---

[39] See above Chapter 9 for financial problems. Andrews, *Methodists and America* 213-6, Hempton, *Empire* 119-125.
[40] *Asbury Jol* 3: 170, 342. By 1801 he had sold it and was back on horseback (198).
[41] *MM* 1799: 262; *Minutes MCA* 1813; *Asbury Jol* 2: 159-60; Schell, 'Preachers'; J. A. Garraty and M. C. Carnes, eds, *American National Biography* 24 vols (New York: OUP, 1999 10: 130; copy of Ordination Certificate as Elder at Queen's College Melbourne says 5th August; email from Professor Heitzenrater 16/12/2003. The death date is from a newspaper cutting found by R. P. Stone of Wofford College SC.

Asbury's Last Years

Asbury scarcely changed his ideas and methods as he grew older. In 1796 the General Conference set up the system of six Annual Conferences including the Western, based among the new settlers entirely west of the Appalachians. There was the adoption of camp meetings firmly under the direction of the itinerants and the move towards one-man circuits and stations, but otherwise little change. Asbury continued to rise at dawn and frequently set off immediately, only to stop travelling at sunset. For the last seven years his health problems worsened and he had to preach resting against a table or stool because of the swelling in his legs. Even in his last two years, though weakened by pleurisy and crippled by rheumatism, he insisted on travelling as much as ever and on writing his Journal. John Wesley Bond, the preacher appointed to go with him as Joseph Bradford had gone with Wesley, carried him in his arms from the carriage into the church at Richmond, Virginia, to give his final sermon in early March 1816; he sat on a table to deliver his message. As an itinerant preacher he was determined both to journey and preach to the last. His preachers recognized the marks of the apostle. Asbury died at the house of George Arnold on the 21st March that year in Spotsylvania County, fifty miles north of Richmond, trying to get to the General Conference at Baltimore.[42]

Methodism's Success by 1816

Methodism continued to grow. Up to 1800 this had been particularly true of the Chesapeake region where it had become dominant, providing vital leadership for the rest of the connexion. After 1800 Chesapeake Methodists tended to move elsewhere, to Ohio, Kentucky and further west. By 1800 there were nationally 317 itinerant preachers and nearly 64,000 members. By 1810 it was 636 preachers and almost 175,000 members. By 1816 there were 214,000 members, more than 20,000 greater than British membership reported that year. As in Britain these numbers should be multiplied by at least four to reach the total number of hearers. Growth was particularly strong in the South and West where Methodism was already spreading beyond the Mississippi to Missouri and Arkansas. It did best in rural areas and by 1814 the movement which had begun unsuccessfully with the Wesleys in Georgia in the 1730s was coming full circle, opening a mission to the Wyandotte Indians in Ohio. By 1850 there were more Methodists in America than any other kind of Protestant. The rise in the proportion of Methodists in the population continued beyond 1850.[43]

---

[42] The last Journal entry was 7th December 1815, *Asbury Jol* 2: 797-807. He was then in South Carolina, over 400 miles south of Richmond. Baker, *Wesley to Asbury* 136-7.

[43] Richey, 'Chesapeake'; Hatch 'The Puzzle of American Methodism' in Hatch and Wigger, *Shaping* 27-8; *Minutes MCA*. Coke in his letter to Bishop White in 1791 multiplied by five and then added even more to allow for families. Andrews, *Methodists and America* 201, 225; Noll, *America's God* 168-9.

Why Did Methodism Have Such Great Success in America?

There were many reasons for Methodism's success. Hempton's emphasis on its symbiosis with society was certainly true. Methodism had an organization fitted for the rapidly expanding society of America. Hatch has argued it was exactly right for the new democratic Republic. The church possessed a system of primitive simplicity with 'accordion-like power of expansion into every corner of the country,' partly because Asbury espoused the practice of democratic votes, even if he actually remained in control. It was a system which was the same in every state. A Methodist from Delaware would feel at home if he moved to Ohio or later to Michigan or even California. It was the church for those excluded by the social elites of the new Republic, women, black people, settlers moving west and immigrants.[44] The organization cost little as the quotation at the beginning of the chapter hints; the itinerant only needed 'passing support' on his continual journeys in the new continent and could function almost anywhere. Asbury used the Methodist system to direct resources 'from centre to circumference' to supplement that passing support. He also insisted that the Presiding Elder must do on the small scale what he himself did on a larger scale, that is, visit, ride, preach and keep a check on what the other preachers were doing. Asbury pointed with some justice to this continual check at district level as the reason for Methodism's greater success in America compared with the more modest growth in Britain.[45]

Methodism had already honed its methods for moving into new and different societies; preaching inside and out, small groups meeting each week and the attention to personal salvation were some of these. New strategies were developed in America. The large Quarterly Meeting Conferences were lengthened to two days by the 1790s, becoming 'seasons of blessing;' thousands might attend to receive spiritual nourishment, thus differing from the more business-orientated British meetings. Later the open air camp meetings were encouraged with a very similar purpose, deliberately set to be overnight to increase the effect. They were organized by the preachers to be outdoor festivals and centres of pilgrimage, a way of bringing in those who came to mock. As the religious embodiment of community fairs they provided opportunities for many conversions and renewals of commitment.[46]

Methodism successfully adapted to the gigantic growth in the population (36% in the ten years from 1800 to 1810) which was much too fast for most denominations; it Americanized itself, adopting strategies like the single man station, copied probably from New England Puritanism. After 1770 many Americans migrated westwards altering society irrevocably, a process which

---

[44] Andrews, *Methodists and America* 221-239; Richey, 'Chesapeake' 218.
[45] *Asbury Jol* 3: 164 letter 1797 to Jesse Lee, 429 letter 1810 to Coke.
[46] Richey, 'Chesapeake' 208-210; Andrews, *Methodists and America* 226-9; Hempton, *Empire* 79-80.

assisted Methodism itself so attuned to the needs of a mobile society.[47] Richmond Nolley, a circuit rider on the Tombigbee Alabama circuit around 1812, was following fresh wagon tracks to the camp of a family just arrived in the area. 'What' said the father when he discovered Nolley's identity, 'have you found me already? Another Methodist preacher!' The man had left first Virginia and later Georgia, in the hope of breaking the church's hold on his wife and daughter and was dismayed to find the Methodist there 'before my wagon is unloaded.' Nolley offered him little comfort, telling him that not only were the Methodists everywhere in this world but that there would undoubtedly be Methodist preachers both in heaven and hell![48]

Undoubtedly the most important reason for Methodism's success was the preachers Wesley sent. They were already hardened itinerants, experienced in expansion on the margins of a growing society. Dempster and Rankin were Scots and Pilmore and Dempster had both recently served in Wales, while Dempster had travelled for almost six years in Ireland. Robert Williams, though not sent by Wesley, was a Welshman who had been on circuit in Ireland. Of those who arrived from 1784, both Hammett and Harper were Irishmen who had served with distinction in Ireland and in the West Indies, while Whatcoat had travelled in both Ireland and Wales. More than one third of the 'British' preachers in America actually came from Ireland. Thomas Coke himself, though not in America as much as the Americans would have wished, was a Welshman with intimate knowledge of Ireland and of other missionary areas as well. He became the Methodist missionary expert, unrivalled by any other Christian leader of his period. If Wesley was not to come in person, he sent his most important resource, his right hand man who could draw crowds almost as much as Wesley could himself. The Whitefield of his age, Coke spent three years in America over a twenty year period in nine different visits. Each of these contributed to the growth of Methodism in America.

By far and away the most significant of Wesley's preachers was Bishop Francis Asbury. In one letter to his parents he described himself as a country boy, not 'polite' enough for the cities. His concern for the rural areas was one of his strengths in America where the 'country' was always expanding. He was typical of the early Methodist itinerant who was usually originally from a rural area, even if he had moved to the town before conversion. Asbury, the ordinary preacher turned extraordinary itinerant with patience, determination and charm to win the inhabitants of a continent, found himself in the right place at the right time. He refused to desert his post during the Revolution though all the others might take what seemed wiser paths. His preachers served this Bishop without family or home and without special gown once he had heard Lee's acerbic comments, just as he served Wesley, because they knew that he had

---

[47] A. G. Schneider, *The Way of the Cross Leads Home: The Domestication of American Methodism* (Bloomington: Indiana UP, 1993) Chapter 3 Migration.

[48] I am indebted for this story to Wigger, 'Fighting Bees' 100.

faced all their difficulties. They felt that as Asbury's 'sons in the gospel' they should go where he sent them, however hard it might seem, because then 'all things would work together for good.' For Asbury it was indeed a choice between travelling or death.[49]

---

[49] Baker, *Wesley to Asbury* 143. The letter is printed *Asbury Jol* 3: 13-4. For the story of Lee and Asbury's robes see *Asbury Jol* 1: 481n. The quotations are from the reflections of the young itinerant James B. Finley when sent in the opposite direction from what he wanted. Schneider, *Domestication* 65.

CHAPTER 14

Missionaries

> 'And let our Bodies part
> To different Climes repair;
> Inseparably join'd in Heart
> The Friends of Jesus are.'[1]

Introduction

Walls has suggested the Protestant missionary ideal needed three factors to be consistently present: first a 'substantial corps of persons with the degree of commitment capable of sustaining such a life and with the intellectual equipment to further it. Second an organization that could mobilize and maintain such a force, and third sustained western access to specific locations with expectation of continued communication.' This chapter looks at the original corps of persons fulfilling that task in Methodism.[2]

There is some controversy about Methodist missionaries as to whether the term should include those who went as Methodist preachers to the thirteen colonies as described in the last two chapters. Birtwhistle had an interesting argument against describing as missionaries the preachers who went to 'their own kith and kin' in the thirteen colonies.[3] Mosley, in his database of British Methodist missionaries, does not include those who went only to the thirteen colonies. Perhaps part of the reason is that the official foundation of the Wesleyan Methodist Missionary Society was not till 1818. Nevertheless, nobody would doubt that those who went in the 1780s to the West Indies were missionaries, because of the large section of society which was not seen as 'Christian.' It could be argued that there were many in the other colonies who were equally 'heathen' in practice.

In my view those preachers who went to the thirteen colonies were very similar to those who were missionaries. Like them they had to be volunteers who went overseas. It is difficult to distinguish between Shadford going to the

---

[1] C. Wesley, *Hymns and Sacred Poems* 2: 317.
[2] A. F. Walls, 'Christian Missions and the Enlightenment' in D. Bebbington, ed, *Modern Christianity's Cultural Aspirations* (Sheffield: Academic Press, 2003).
[3] N. A. Birtwhistle, 'Methodist Missions' see the first subheading 'the First Half Century 1786-1838' in *HMGB* 3: 1-3.

colonies in the 1770s or Vasey going to the independent USA in 1784, neither of whom Mosley includes, and James Wray going to Nova Scotia in 1788, whom Birtwhistle and Mosley include. Moister in his *Heralds of Salvation* about missionaries included Shadford. Findlay and Holdsworth in their history of Wesleyan Missions had two chapters on American Methodist beginnings. Certainly Wesley and Coke treated the two groups in a similar way and there was movement between the independent USA and the fields where missionaries went. I shall make several comparisons between the two groups, but think they deserve separate chapters.[4] Their selection and training was similar. Some later transferred from one field to the other. All went to what were, at least at first, British colonies. In each case they had to cross the ocean knowing they might well not return. All were unmarried volunteers.[5] Few knew much about the country when they arrived.

Missionaries in my definition were those full-time preachers going abroad from the British Isles from 1786, including the five or six accepted into the British ministry by 1791, who were already local preachers overseas in the colonies. Most missionaries went out before Wesley's death in that year, but a few followed in the next twenty years, having already entered the itinerancy at home in Wesley's lifetime and volunteering later for missionary service. Two went to France, one to Gibraltar (all after 1791 though accepted as travelling preachers before), twelve to the British colonies in the maritime provinces of what eventually became Canada, and twenty-four, the largest number, to the British colonies in the West Indies. The total is thirty-seven because of Wray working in both the West Indies and Nova Scotia.

Beginning with his return from Georgia Wesley was for most of his life against his preachers going to be missionaries abroad. The well known quotation 'I look upon all the world as my parish' was said in the English context of parish clergy opposition to a stranger invading their prerogatives.[6] Methodism was not to be directly involved in 'overseas work' for thirty years. There were many reasons for this. Others such as Whitefield and the Moravians were attempting a world wide mission and were certainly successful at it. The insular Church of England of Wesley's day was not interested in mission overseas.[7] Wesley's own experiences in Georgia had been dispiriting and

---

[4] A. W. Mosley's database is at SOAS, London. W. Moister, *Heralds of Salvation, being Brief Memorial Sketches of Wesleyan Missionaries* (London: WCO, 1878) 36; Findlay and Holdsworth, *WMMS* vol 1. See below for details of the fields.

[5] Maser aptly wrote 'Wesley made a difference between preachers and missionaries. All preachers were expected to go where they were sent. Missionaries were challenged to volunteer for their fields of service' *Journal of Pilmore* 21.

[6] Admittedly Wesley specifically applied it to overseas as well and to Georgia where he had been 'for all the heathen (there) belong to the parish of Savannah or Frederica.' *WJW* 19: 67. The date in the journal was June 11th 1739, but it is not clear when the letter was sent or even to whom.

[7] 'Insular' is a description borrowed from John Walsh.

seemed unsuccessful. There was a shortage of preachers, so for him the needs were at home. However, gradually, his preachers became drawn into Ireland, Scotland, and eventually, in 1769, America.

The development of the British Empire, which historians are now seeing as radically changing in scope and character in the period 1760-1815, was a cause of the gradual expansion of where the itinerant Methodist preacher went. It was in this period that the 'Old British Empire,' relatively small and based on the Atlantic economy, was transformed. By 1815 it had become dominant over wide areas of both land and sea. Though it had lost the original heartland of the thirteen colonies, it was able to impose itself everywhere else its ships could sail, in the Mediterranean, across the Indian and Pacific Oceans, as well as inland in areas only reached easily by sea. Worldwide it was often British soldiers, or other government employed personnel sent by the imperial mother country, who formed the first Methodist groups and invited the first travelling preachers. As shipping developed so it became much easier to send and maintain missionaries anywhere in the transatlantic world of the late eighteenth century. As the British Empire developed, so did British Methodist missions.[8]

By the 1770s and 1780s the call to missionary work was becoming one which Wesley's preachers heard, even if Wesley resisted their offers; several volunteered to go abroad but none at first were accepted. Recorded offers rejected included ones from John Prickard and a Brettell brother for the West Indies in 1773, Prickard for Africa in 1777, Duncan M'Allum and another for Africa in 1778, Matthew Stewart (below) in 1785 and John de Queteville for Nova Scotia in 1791. There were others not recorded.[9] However, already at work in these areas were locals, some of whom later became travelling preachers. These included Nathaniel Gilbert and his brothers John and Francis in Antigua, the shipwright John Baxter, also in Antigua, and William Black and the Loyalist Mann brothers in Nova Scotia. Essentially the expansion was because of local action, what Rack described as 'accidents of individual enthusiasm.'[10]

Dr. Thomas Coke, the Anglican clergyman who joined Wesley in 1778, provided the spark to overcome Wesley's hesitation. Coke was an impulsive, enthusiastic and highly strung Welshman who could become irritable. Nevertheless, because of his enthusiasm, abilities and his prior ordination he was welcomed by Wesley and given a key post as his lieutenant, for example in Ireland (Chapter 11). He was 'mad about mission' and floated several schemes

---

[8] See for example Halpern, ed, *Empire and Others* 21-5, 43-45. Even in the former thirteen colonies the long arm of Britain's navy was still able to burn what would become the White House in the new nation's capital.

[9] There is a good summary of Wesley's complex motives and actions on this in Rack 471-88. See for the offers, Brettell and Prickard in *AM* 1789: 14-17; M'Allum etc in Tyerman 3: 272-3; Queteville in H. de Jersey, *Queteville* 66-7.

[10] Rack 476.

Timeline 4: Missionaries

Year	West Indies	British North America	Other Places
1760	N. Gilbert founded society in Antigua		
1766		Coughlan in Newfoundland	
1769		Pilmore and Boardman	
1773		Rankin 1st Conference	
1774	Death of N. Gilbert		
1775		Black family in Nova Scotia	
1778	J. Baxter shipwright in Antigua		Coke's Calabar scheme
1779	Death of F. Gilbert	William Black converted	
1781		W. Black first preached	
1783		Loyalists including blacks arrive	Coke 'Plan of Society Missions'
1784	Baxter ordained by Coke	Black present at Christmas Conference	Methodist Episcopal Church. Coke Bishop
1785		M'Coll in New Brunswick	
1786	Coke arrived Antigua, left 3 preachers	1st Conference	
1788	5 missionaries sent	J. Wray to Nova Scotia	
1789	3,433 members	William Black ordained	
1791			Death of Wesley. French mission
1792			Methodists in Sierra Leone
1796		Thoresby to Newfoundland	
1798			LPs to be considered
1800	11,120 members	Black to British Conference	
1804			M'Mullen died in Gibraltar after 6 weeks
1805	Death of Baxter		
1807			Society at Capetown
1811			G. Warren to Sierra Leone
1812	12 circuits	Black superannuated	
1814	17,000 members	1,570 members	Coke died going to Ceylon. 96 members Africa, 79 continental Europe
1818			WMMS founded

in Wesley's lifetime, as in April 1778 to set up a mission in Calabar in West Africa.[11] Even he, however, could not always persuade the eighty year old Wesley. In 1784 Wesley had deputed him to go to America and begin the Methodist Church there, ordaining him as Superintendent, a title later changed by the American Church to Bishop. In 1786 he was sent by Wesley to begin Methodist Missions in both the West Indies and British North America and became the Superintendent of missions in both places. In Europe when the 1789 French Revolution opened up a new avenue for missions closer to home, Coke seized on that as well. It could be argued that because of the shortage of resources Wesley had been right to delay and Coke was over ambitious. Certainly resources were thinly spread. The story of Wesley's preachers who were missionaries in this period was largely the story of Thomas Coke and his journeys, the men he took with him and left and the men he sent.[12]

Selection of Missionaries

Nowhere is there a list of selection criteria in the hand of Wesley or his coadjutor and successor Coke to suggest any differences between the qualities needed by preachers in Britain and those by preachers abroad. However, it is possible to deduce from the men they sent overseas the very similar but slightly different criteria they had in their minds. First, Wesley and Coke usually chose for missionaries those who did not have a wife, which was slightly different from the situation in Britain where married men were quite common under Wesley. This did not mean the men had not been previously married. In several cases widowers were sent whose wives had recently died. There were no exceptions to this rule for those who went from Britain and Ireland. Like those preachers who were sent to America they might marry abroad or on their return, but they were single when they were sent out. William Warrener, James Wray, Thomas Owens, Matthew Lumb and the others to the end of the century were all unmarried. Only local men like William Black and John and James Mann were exceptions to this rule, because they were accepted locally. A would-be missionary from Ireland who never went because he was married was Matthew Stewart, born near Castlederg in Western Tyrone, a wild youth who enlisted as a dragoon. Converted at Athlone as a result of attending Methodist meetings he had married by 1780. In 1785 he met John Wesley at Athlone, a meeting which led Wesley to have the army discharge him. Soon Stewart began to preach and offered to go abroad. John Wesley sent him a letter in November 1785 encouraging him to go to America with Coke in the summer of 1786, *if* he were a single man. The fact he was married clearly delayed his entry and meant

---

[11] The circular letter about this dated 15 April is in the Thomas Jackson Collection No 9 in the Methodist Missionary Society Collection at SOAS. See also Vickers, *Thomas Coke* 131-150. 'Mad about Mission' was the title of Cyril Davey's biography of Coke.
[12] Vickers, *Thomas Coke*.

when he did enter next year he had to stay in Ireland.[13]

Secondly, as with America, all who went, specifically volunteered for the field. According to Moister, Robert Gamble 'nobly offered himself as a Missionary' and William M'Cornock 'was led to offer himself as a Missionary for the West Indies,' both in 1788; in December they landed in Barbados and Dominica.[14] Coke spent much of his time and energy in Britain trying to encourage other preachers to volunteer for the mission field and not always succeeding. In 1788 he tried to persuade the twenty-five year old Joseph Sutcliffe in the St Ives circuit, then in his second year in the itinerancy, to go to Nova Scotia. Sutcliffe refused. John Braithwaite, an able young Cumbrian preacher stationed in London in 1793, wrote to his friend back in Cumbria 'Dr Coke has often endeavoured to press on me, (as he does with other young preachers) to go to America, the West Indies, or Sierra Leone in Africa.'[15]

Preachers who had volunteered to become missionaries, though their stations might appear on the *Minutes*, did not necessarily get there. Walter Griffith was an Irish preacher of ten years' experience whose wife was ill in 1794. The doctors recommended the West Indies for her health and so he came to the 1794 British Conference, was put down on the stations for St Kitts and was ordained by Coke in August. His wife became unable to travel and died early in 1795. He never went and remained in London for the rest of that year. Jonathan Crowther, an unmarried preacher also of some ten years' experience, had volunteered to go to the West Indies at the same Conference and was then ordained by Coke. Because of the controversy raging in Bristol over the question of the Conference's control of the chapels, he stayed there to support Henry Moore and found his future wife.[16]

Service on the British or Irish stations (or both) was also an important requirement for selection in this period, which meant preaching ability was also being assessed. Men who had no previous experience on the stations were soon to be sent quite early in the nineteenth century. Often missionaries among Wesley's preachers had considerable years of service behind them. John Stephenson and M'Cornock had done ten years first, William Warrener seven and Matthew Lumb five. Five years' experience was the average for those sent to the West Indies. Nobody went immediately, which had become the norm by the mid nineteenth century. Seniority was thus seen as useful while experience

---

[13] For Matthew Stewart see *WMM* 1827: 646, 1838: 237; *JWL* 7: 301; *Crk* 2: 48, 153-5.

[14] M'Cornock may have been married but his wife or widow is never mentioned, so if he had one she was dead before he went to the West Indies in 1788. For other West Tyrone Methodists see Chapter 11 above. Moister, *Heralds of Salvation* 1-14.

[15] Coke's 1788 letter to Joseph Sutcliffe, then in his second year of travel, suggested he should go to Nova Scotia, (Vickers, *Thomas Coke* 147-8). Vickers cited it as an example of Coke's care for the preachers. I would see it rather as an example of his attempting to use his persuasive powers, but not succeeding. Dickinson, *Braithwaite* 185.

[16] For Griffith see *WMM* 1825: 145-58. For Crowther see Tyerman BMM MAB B1245.

of preaching in the work at home was vital. So Hammett was described as 'a man of superior talents' and Werrill was noted for his hard work and 'loving deportment.' Fish, who had much experience, was described as 'a man of judgment and discrimination.' The same was true of those whom Wesley sent to the thirteen American colonies. Almost to a man they had had experience in the British Isles.[17]

As with preachers at home, age was not a factor; John Baxter was accepted despite the fact he was already forty. John Stephenson was sent when he was fifty-one. The average known age of those who went to the West Indies, the largest group, was in their mid thirties, slightly older than the average for acceptance among British travelling preachers of the period.[18] Language was not usually a criterion either, since missionaries were being sent at first to the West Indies or North America. When later in the 1790s Coke dispatched missionaries to France, Channel Islanders or those with French were selected.

The gradual dropping of the previous service criterion began at the end of the 1790s. In 1798 Coke used the *Minutes* of Conference to ask all District meetings to look for suitable local preachers in addition to travelling preachers. This is the first hint that those other than existing travelling preachers might be accepted. It did not have a major effect immediately. Missionaries were still usually experienced preachers for much of the first decade in the nineteenth century. When they ceased to be have previous service it often meant younger men were chosen. Admittedly later they became college-trained, so were a couple of years older, but the training rarely made up for the lack of home experience. It is interesting to wonder whether the experience of the early missionaries was perhaps part of the reason for their success in the early years. When younger missionaries went straight from college without training in home circuits this might well have led to more mistakes and perhaps a slowing down of Methodist expansion overseas after 1820.[19]

Throughout the period little explicit thought was given to the question of selection. Coke's letters, in general quite well preserved, act as a guide. There are more than sixty of his surviving from before Wesley's death; none deal with this issue. There are over fifty-three of Coke from 1791 to 1799, and so there are well over a hundred letters extant before a single one mentions the question of selection criteria thirteen years after missions began. Coke wrote to

---

[17] The apparent exception to the need for experience is John M'Vean sent to the West Indies in 1790. We know nothing of him before. He probably came from Ireland. He may well have been a full time missionary in Ireland for some time as others (whom we know almost as little about) were. P. Duncan, *A History of Wesleyan Missions to Jamaica* (London: Partridge and Oakey, 1849) 10, 24-5, 36.

[18] For age see above Chapter 5.

[19] Compare the request for volunteers for missionaries from 'preachers' (understand travelling) in 1797 to that of 1798 spelling out both 'local and travelling' in 1798, see *Minutes* (1812 ed) 380, 417.

Alexander Mather in October 1799 asking Mather to hear Christopher Harrison preach to see if he were suitable. At that point the standard of preaching was the important criterion. The letter shows what Coke expected of possible missionaries

> Very dear and respected friend
> I have desired Brother Harrison to preach tomorrow morning, if it meet with your approbation, before as many of the preachers as will be so kind to attend. I have in a great measure told him my mind in the subject. He ought not to go to the West Indies, unless he has abilities sufficient for the smaller Circuits of England...

Harrison was a pious young man who had volunteered as a missionary. He had already been assigned by the Conference to go to St Kitts. Coke was not happy about his lack of either previous service or abilities, said so, and did something about it. The result was that the preachers gathered together, agreed with Coke, overturned the appointment and Harrison left the ministry having never actually travelled. He was not an experienced itinerant; the other preachers did not think highly enough of his preaching and so he did not go. Coke's letters show that the selection of missionaries was not his main focus for the first fifteen years or so of Methodist missionary endeavour.[20] This example indicates that it was in late 1799 that the Conference was beginning to think of sending men who had no British or Irish experience since they considered Harrison. Coke was unhappy about it, partly because he was more expert on missions than the Conference which was advocating the change. In the next six years most men sent were experienced. Gradually by 1810 this had changed, partly because of the increasing number of appointments overseas to be filled and the shortage of existing itinerants who could be persuaded to go. After that point men going out had not done more than one year at home and many had done none. The only exception would be for an important post such as Chairman of the District, sometimes filled by a highly experienced minister.

It was as late as 1809 before Coke's letters revealed the full selection process for local preachers, that is those who had no experience of travelling at home at all. Coke that year wrote to the London Secretary of the Conference appointed Missions Committee

> Mr Bramwell very warmly recommends two single Local Preachers of this Society (it can hardly be called a Circuit) who are wanting to go to the West Indies. The Leaders, also, to whom I have spoken, give them an excellent character. Their names are Myles Dixon and George (or William) Poole. The Quarterly Meeting for Liverpool is over; But as Liverpool is in fact the Circuit,

---

[20] The best list of Coke's Letters is G. Lloyd, 'The Papers of Dr Thomas Coke: A Catalogue' *JRULMB* 76 No 2 Summer 1994. There are also substantial numbers of letters elsewhere, especially at SOAS. The letter quoted (PLP 28/10/6) was printed *WMM* 1850: 1168.

Prescot and St Helens being trifling or nothing, the Preachers are of the opinion, that by calling together all the official members of the 3 Chapels, they will to all intents and purposes be equivalent to a Quarterly Meeting. I have therefore given, or the Preachers have given notice accordingly; & on Thursday night they are to meet on the business. If they approve of the two young men Mr Bramwell will I think examine them on Friday. If they pass through these two stages with success, this will be all that I can do till I receive an answer from you. I therefore request that Mr Johnson favour me with a line by Friday evening's post, to inform me whether the Committee assent to my ordaining the two Brethren; if they meet with the approbation of the majority of the meeting of all the Official Members of the Liverpool Societies, & of those of the Preachers mentioned above.[21]

So by 1809 there were many stages in the selection process. Having established they were single and willing to go, then:
1) the local Superintendent, William Bramwell in the case here in Liverpool, must recommend them;
2) they must be approved by their local church, 'the Leaders' mentioned here;
3) their Quarterly Meeting must be prepared to recommend them;
4) their preaching must be heard by existing travelling preachers;
5) they must be examined as to doctrine not just by Coke himself but by two of his brethren, other travelling preachers.

Coke, having got the sanction of the Missionary Committee through its secretary Robert Johnson, would then ordain and send them.

Furthermore, the letter showed that Coke was prepared to ride roughshod over the official procedure if he thought well of the candidates and despite the fact that his knowledge of them was so slight that he was not sure of one of their names! Vickers admitted Coke's weakness in assessing the character of those who applied to go abroad.[22] In Coke's defence it should be said that his successors were not noticeably more successful over selection. It was not until 1817 that a questionnaire for candidates to fill in was introduced by the British Conference.[23] Unsurprisingly Coke's administration of missions in this period aroused opposition from many of his Methodist colleagues, not least the young and much more efficient Jabez Bunting! Coke's personal handling of all missionary affairs meant it was sometimes seen as a 'dictatorship.' Equally agreements with Coke might not be later honoured by Conference; for example,

---

[21] MARC PLP 28/17/3 Copy Letter of Coke to the Missionary Committee 3/10/1809. Original at SOAS, Home Committee Box I, read on microfiche, 1/1809 PLP (to Robert Johnson, Spitalfields London). Myles Dixon later went to Tortola and the Virgin Islands and died in 1857. The letter is typical of the general state of disorganization in which Coke lived over candidates, which was one of the reasons which annoyed the more organized members of the Committee, that he was not sure of one candidate's name. It was *George* Poole, who eventually went to St Vincent and died in 1847.
[22] Vickers, *Thomas Coke* especially 273-286.
[23] WMMS Committee Minutes January 1817 at SOAS.

missionaries did not necessarily 'offer for life' but Conference might later assume that. Hempton wrote of Coke's 'remarkable administrative incompetence' with regard to overseas missions.[24] Yet Coke was trying to run missions in several different areas including Ireland and Wales, while himself travelling the world. Communications in the age of sail were very uncertain, especially in winter in the northern hemisphere. The West Indies, then as now, suffered from hurricanes. Wesley had complained in the 1770s that his American preachers did not write to him enough. Coke lacked Wesley's charisma and perhaps received fewer letters because the missionaries had to travel much further and were subject to the vicissitudes of sea travel.

Training and Formation

Training was minimal, though most as we have seen were already travelling preachers in the British Isles. Many after 1784 seem to have been ordained to go abroad, unlike British preachers of the period.[25] There was little knowledge of or preparation for the field to which they were going. There were few books about the colonies available. They were encouraged to read what existed: the Moravian writings about the West Indies, the ever-popular *Life of Brainerd* by Jonathan Edwards,[26] or later the works of Coke himself about the West Indies. No specific list of books for missionary candidates to read was set by Conference until 1815. It was only in 1817 that the missionary secretaries were officially empowered by Conference to give reading and advice to missionaries before they set out. This is all a reminder that, though he tried to organize the training and formation of the missionaries, Coke was doing it by himself, without an office or a base, and travelling the Atlantic at the same time. System only came after his death, with Bunting in charge resident in London.[27]

Apart from encouraging preachers to volunteer, Coke often travelled out with them, using this as training. He wrote to and revisited them frequently. Training was similar to that for home preachers, limited if judged by modern standards and 'essentially on the job.' Local lay preachers were sometimes accepted, again usually unmarried. Local meetings which in America became Conferences were held frequently and preachers were often restationed every year. So in 1786 William Black, with Garrettson's encouragement, held in Halifax what he called his little Conference of the six preachers then in British America, the first of many. Vickers argued that Coke was very concerned about

---

[24] Hempton said he combined it with equally remarkable zeal. D. Hempton, *Methodism and Politics in British Society 1750-1850* (London: Hutchinson, 1986) 96.

[25] See for ordination and ordinary British preachers in this period Chapter 18 below.

[26] Published 1749, but very few Wesleyans made contact with Native Americans in this period.

[27] S. Potter, 'The Making of Missionaries in the Nineteenth Century' in M. Hill, ed, *A Sociological Yearbook of Religion* (London: SCM, 1975) 8: 112-114. *Minutes* 1817.

the missionaries' welfare, citing the fact that in winter he insisted they went by land to Falmouth and then by the Falmouth Packet rather than run the extra risk of sailing from London to Cornwall. It might cost £5 extra per missionary, but in Coke's eyes and those of the missionaries involved it was worth it. Sensibly he wanted to minimize for them the risks he himself had faced.

Why Were There so Many from Ireland?

Ten out of the thirty-seven missionaries were apparently from Ireland, more than one in four.[28] This is a higher proportion than the Irish preachers had in the total number of Wesley's preachers, roughly one in eight, and was the result of Coke's policy of approaching preachers in Ireland to go to the West Indies. Why did Coke do this? Possible reasons include that English preachers were better off and less likely to volunteer for the dangers of another country. Irishmen in general were more likely in the eighteenth century to emigrate than Englishmen. Among the 'British' preachers in America there was an even higher proportion of Irishmen, over one third of the total who had come from the British Isles. Coke, presiding over the Irish Conference every other year, was in a stronger position when asking for volunteers than in England, where senior preachers looked askance at his seeking influence and were suspicious of the Doctor's motives. Coke was also more independent of Wesley's influence when he was in Ireland. Wesley remained opposed to sending his best and most experienced men to the mission field. He might send Irishmen, young men, new or relatively new preachers possibly, but he remained reluctant despite Coke. Coke continued to be responsible for missions after Wesley's death. It was also the Methodist part-equivalent of the Church Missionary Society and London Missionary Society getting German or Dutch missionaries to fill the lack of British candidates in the 1790-1815 period. It was not as difficult for Coke to identify British Methodist candidates as it was for the CMS to find suitably educated Englishmen at a slightly later period, but he found it easier to use Irishmen.[29] One result was the large presence of Irishmen on the mission field, which was maintained for many years. In 1787, for example, there were eleven men stationed on the six circuits on the mission fields in Eastern British America and the British and Dutch West Indies. Of these, there was one American, Jessop, four who had been local preachers in the colonies before travelling full time, and six others. Of the six only two, Wray and Warrener,

---

[28] John Clarke, Daniel Graham, William Hammett, John Harper, James Lyons, William M'Cornock, Thomas Owens, John Stephenson and Thomas Werrill. John M'Vean was probably Irish.

[29] For Ireland see Cooney, *Ireland* and on Irish missionaries Taggart, *Irish*. See also Chapter 11 above. For the problems of the CMS and LMS see A. F. Walls, 'The missionary movement "a lay fiefdom"' in D. W. Lovegrove, ed, *The Rise of the Laity in the Evangelical Movement* (London: Routledge, 2002).

came from Britain. The other four, William Hammett, Thomas Owens, John M'Geary and John Clarke, all came from Ireland.

The West Indies

These islands had the largest number of Methodist missionaries in this period and comprised the most important field. Of the 802 preachers twenty-five were missionaries there including Thomas Coke, who admittedly spent most of his time elsewhere. In addition to Coke, Harper and Hammett spent time in America and Wray most of his time in Newfoundland. Of the twenty-four without Coke, at least ten were probably of Irish origin.[30]

The British colonies in the West Indies in the late eighteenth century were one of Great Britain's wealthiest resources. There were many mostly small islands, the centre of the valuable slave trade, producing large amounts of sugar and other crops for the British economy. Many fortunes, such as those of the Methodist Gilbert family and the economies of Methodist strongholds like Bristol and Liverpool, were based on them. The West Indian islands in the late eighteenth century had over 300,000 black inhabitants and almost a million by the time of emancipation, mostly a result of the importing of slaves from Africa. Blacks outnumbered whites by seven to one in most islands. Slaves suffered more in the West Indies than in America. The gang system and the conditions of work were worse than the task system more common in the Chesapeake area in America. In the early eighteenth century the failure of the slaves to maintain their numbers by breeding was a sign of the poor conditions they endured. Planters were in general reluctant to see their slaves converted and baptized, partly because the idea of slaves not working on Sunday was not wanted by the owners. There had been some successful attempts at preaching to the slaves, for example by the Moravians who arrived in 1732 in the Danish island of St Thomas and spread a little, reaching the largest British island of Jamaica in 1754. A group of black Baptists arrived there in 1784 and also spread.[31]

The story of early Methodism in the West Indies is well known. The key was Antigua in the Leeward Islands where a 37 year old planter called Nathaniel Gilbert III, went to England in 1757, met Wesley and became a

---

[30] The 25 were John Baxter, William Brazier, John Clarke, Coke, Thomas Dobson, William C. Fish, Francis Gilbert, Robert Gamble, Daniel Graham, William Hammett, Joseph Harper, John Lynn, James Lyons, Matthew Lumb, William M'Cornock, John M'Vean, William Meredith, Thomas Owens, Benjamin Pearce, James Richardson, George Skerritt, John Stephenson, William Warrener, Thomas Werrill, and James Wray. For brief obits of fourteen of these, see Moister, *Heralds of Salvation*. Brazier and Skerritt were like Baxter employed locally, in St Kitts in their case, before becoming missionaries (Vickers, ed, *Journals of Coke* 109).

[31] Walvin, *Black Ivory*.

Methodist. His brother Francis became a preacher in England for a time. Nathaniel, who had two of his slaves baptized by Wesley in Wandsworth in 1758, went back to Antigua in 1759 and founded a society with regular preaching. The protection he gave through his social position (he was the Speaker of Antigua from 1763 to 1769) enabled the societies in the island to grow. Though he died in 1774, the society remained in existence without any itinerant preachers, thanks partly to members of his family, notably Francis who died in 1779 and Francis' widow Ann who died in 1816.[32] The black and mulatto class leaders Sophia Campbell and Mary Alley played an important part in keeping the society together. Modern historians reckon they must have preached both in this period and later. They are symbolic of the hundreds, if not thousands, of women and men who lived locally who did far more than the traditional heroes, Gilbert, Baxter or Coke, to ensure the long-term success of Methodism in the Caribbean. These 'intermediaries,' as described by modern historians, played a vital part in fitting Methodism to the local culture.[33]

The Gilbert family influence was widespread. Nathaniel's second wife was a Lynch, and the Lynches became prominent Methodists in Antigua. Nathaniel's nephew Melville Horne, curate to John Fletcher, was another Methodist itinerant preacher and later the first Anglican missionary in West Africa. Nathaniel's sister Grace married Captain Thomas Webb who played such a vital part in America. A niece Alice Bannister married Nicholas Mosley Cheek, like Horne a Methodist itinerant turned Anglican clergyman. Another nephew, John Gilbert, was a local preacher in Antigua until his death in 1833. His marriage to the educated mulatto Alice Hart in 1798 was a symbol of the importance of Methodism in the growing and influential mulatto community. The activist Methodist societies gave the mulattoes something to do, using their talents as class leaders, stewards and preachers. By providing cheap bibles and teaching them to read, it gave them a passport to education and encouraged thoughts of equality.[34]

In 1778 the local preacher John Baxter came as a naval shipwright to the dockyard at English Harbour in Antigua. There he made contact with the society and encouraged them. By the early 1780s he was a fulltime preacher, though not yet recognized. He went to America and was ordained by Coke and Asbury after the Christmas Conference of 1784. Baxter returned to Antigua fully authorized to preach and deliver sacraments. The famous meeting two

---

[32] FB Origins is updated by R. Glen, 'A Tangled Web: the Gilberts of Cornwall and the Gilberts of Antigua' in *PWHS* 53 (2001-2), 216-227. Ann Gilbert (nee Walsh) remained in Antigua to 1791 as steward, class leader and local preacher. See also D. U. Farquhar, *Missions and Society in the Leeward Islands 1810-1859* (Boston: Mount Prospect Press, 1999) Chapter 1.

[33] P. D. Morgan, 'Encounters between British and indigenous peoples c1500-c1800' in Halpern, ed, *Empire and others* 53.

[34] FB Origins; Farquhar, *Leeward Islands* 9; Glen, 'Tangled Web'.

years later on Christmas Day 1786, when Thomas Coke and three missionaries going to Nova Scotia were blown off course and came ashore to be greeted by Baxter and the societies, was therefore not surprising, at least for Coke who must have expected to meet Baxter once he realized where he was. Coke recognized the West Indies' need and left three of his four missionaries there. From then on Methodism spread across the British West Indies, going also to Dutch colonies like St Eustatius. Only whites, free blacks and mulattoes were members at first, but the growth among slaves was also startling. By 1820 the West Indies district reported 20,000 slave members, five and a half thousand free blacks and coloureds, and almost 900 white members. As in Britain, most who attended were not members. Methodism had played a major part in the Christianizing of the black population of the West Indies before their eventual emancipation in 1834. Baxter did not die until 1805. Ordained as an Elder by the American Conference, his long term service provided important continuity, not only over the period before Coke's arrival but also into the nineteenth century and when other missionaries fell victim to local diseases.[35]

In 1800 Coke claimed 'between fifty and sixty thousand under instruction, of all of whom we are in hopes that we shall be able in time through the Grace of God to give a good account. And the Lord has been pleased to raise up about 50 Preachers among the Negroes.'[36] Walvin described the influence of Christianity in the British West Indies between 1783 and 1838 as 'seismic.' Because so many slaves had become Christians, it was difficult for the planters to argue in Britain against the abolition of slavery. Methodism's success in the West Indies led to the strong opinion of British Methodists that freedom for black slaves there must be right. The part played by Methodists in the abolition of slavery despite the rule of 'no politics' is indubitable. Methodists gave money, signed petitions and voted. When Wilberforce was liable to lose his seat in 1807, every Methodist travelling preacher in Yorkshire was told to call for prayer (and votes) in his congregations.[37]

Missionary Life in the West Indies

In the West Indies in St Vincent Matthew Lumb reported 'I generally preach

---

[35] *AM* 1788: 382, 1791: 444, 501, 1797: 81-2; *MM* 1803: 505, 1806: 142-3, 426, 1807: 92-3; D. S. Ching, *For Ever Beginning: Two Hundred Years of Methodism in the Western Area* (Kingston: Methodist Church (Jamaica), 1960) 16; Sandford, *Missionaries* 318; *DOMBI*; Tyerman BMM B1237 at MARC; Atmore 531; Myles.

[36] Anonymous in *MM* January 1800, but almost certainly Coke see *HMGB* 3: 10.

[37] Walvin, *Black Ivory* 168. For Wilberforce see Lyth 207-8, quoting a circular 'widely distributed in the Yorkshire circuits,' 20 October 1806, signed by 13 leading Wesleyans, urging support for Wilberforce. A second circular was issued a few days before the poll in May 1807 by the York ministers (Joseph Taylor, Joseph Drake and Daniel Isaac) 'earnestly pressing the necessity of exertion and soliciting subscriptions;' both references I owe to Ted Royle.

twelve and some times fourteen times in the week; besides riding and talking much with the poor Negroes...I often walk four or five miles, and leave my horse standing in the stable, and I find it does me good.' Lumb was the tough Yorkshireman who had survived the Dales and Scotland and would not be defeated by the climate. In 1793 a group of planters in St Vincent passed an Act which forbade preaching to both slaves and free blacks. Lumb continued to preach and was promptly jailed. His friends supplied him with food; he continued to preach through the bars. Coke's influence in London secured the annulment of the Act and Lumb was released, but his health had suffered and he was forced home.[38]

Archibald Murdock was born near Forkill Co. Armagh in Ireland in 1767. Converted early he began to preach and started as an itinerant at Ballyshannon in 1790. He volunteered to be a missionary and was appointed to Africa in 1796 but did not go. He was then sent to the West Indies in 1798, aged thirty-one where he did six years.[39] This is a letter to Coke in April 1804 from Tortola

> Rev and dear Sir,
> I inclose you the Accounts of our receipts and expenditure, in Johannes, dollars and parts of dollars, as the exchange here varies. The number in Society is as follows Blacks and Coloured 2070, Whites 38. About 440 of these attend the Sacrament of the Lord, and 345 meet in Band as well in Class. Mr Thompson arrived here on the 28th of January, and shortly after, I was seized with a fever, which confined me four weeks. The Physician who attended me gave me up as past recovery: But it pleased God to spare me a little longer.
> March 15, Mr Thompson was seized with a fever, having taken cold at the Courthouse, He still lingers under it, but I hope there is no danger of his life. These things, the want of a good opportunity, and Mr Brownell's requesting me to delay going to St Kitt's, have kept me here yet: But I hope to go very shortly. May our gracious Lord pour out abundantly, his blessing upon you, and your labours, and upon the Conference!
> Your humble and affectionate servant in the Gospel, A. Murdock[40]

This letter illustrates many of the problems of missionary life in the West Indies. Finance came first in the letter. It was always a major concern and a complex one, because of the different currencies which were legal tender. As a result sometimes missionaries got into debt. Numbers were also important and

---

[38] *AM* 1791 612. Findlay and Holdsworth, *WMMS* 2; 55-6. For Matthew Lumb earlier see Chapters 8 and 10 above. On his return he speedily married Ann Wilson, a Scot whom he had presumably met before going to the West Indies. Pawson's view in 1797 was that Lumb was receiving too much money from Methodism in his illnesses (*Pawson L* 2; 127). For Lumb's later history see Chapter 18 below.
[39] *WMM* 1849: 95; *Crk* 3: 71, 76, 107, 115, 5: 38, 198, 6: 86; *PPIM*; Smith, *Ireland* 241.
[40] *MM* 1804: 523-4. In 1803 Murdock had been appointed the Superintendent in St Kitts but had not yet moved from Tortola. John Brownell was still in St Kitts. Thomas Isham and Edward Thompson the other ministers had been ill.

the ratio reported here of whites to blacks was typical. Health was a recurring problem and could not be counted on. It was difficult to keep to the Methodist timetable. It was advantageous when missionaries could visit each other frequently. Tortola was a Methodist stronghold, where travel in the circuit was often by boat to similar islands belonging to the British Virgin Islands.

Little more is known about Murdock. He returned later that year because he was ill, but was able to resume his ministry in Ireland until 1839 when he superannuated to Longford at the age of seventy-two, moving eventually to Dungannon where he died aged 81 in 1851. He had married someone much younger than himself some time after his return and his widow, Mary Murdock, died a year later at Dungannon.[41]

The Maritimes

In what became known as British North America or later Canada possibly eleven of the missionaries, two of Irish origin, served in Newfoundland, Nova Scotia and Prince Edward Island, later known as the Maritime Provinces. Of these eleven two, M'Geary and Wray, (in the United States and West Indies respectively) had already appeared elsewhere.[42]

William Black

In contrast to the West Indies, in the provinces of British North America in this period most preachers were home grown. There were many who came from the USA, whether as Loyalist refugees like the Mann brothers or sent by the American Conference like William Jessop, Daniel Fidler or Joseph Cromwell. However, the most important was the Yorkshire born William Black, a Methodist who had come to Nova Scotia with his family at the age of fourteen in 1775. In the spring of 1779 he was converted in Halifax and began to preach in 1781, marking the beginning of his (self determined) itinerancy. One of the most important decisions to be made by Black and the other leaders of the infant church in Nova Scotia and the other Maritime territories was where to go for help. Was it to Britain or the USA or both? With Wesley's blessing and Coke's direction it was at first more to their continental neighbours in the new

---

[41] *WMM* 1849: 95, 1088, 1852: 605.

[42] William Black, Henry Brians, Lawrence Coughlan, John Hoskins, William Jessop, John M'Geary, James and John Mann, William Thoresby, Thomas Whitehead, James Wray. Of these Black and the two Manns were locals. Coughlan was sent out by the SPG after being ordained. He had been a Methodist travelling preacher and often in Newfoundland he behaved like one. Hoskins was a local preacher, who behaved in some ways like an itinerant. There were three others of Wesley's preachers who had entered the itinerancy before 1791 but served later as missionaries in other places. They were M'Mullen of Irish origin in Gibraltar and Mahy and de Queteville in France. For the two last see Chapter 10 above.

United States. Black visited the States several times, notably for the Christmas Conference of 1784 asking for preachers for Nova Scotia and he was given two. In the first flush of enthusiasm at the creation of the new church in America in 1784, under the spur of their new Bishop Coke, missionaries were designated not only for Nova Scotia but also for the West Indies. Those for the West Indies never got there. Black returned in 1789 to Philadelphia where he was ordained Elder/Bishop by Coke.[43] Several American preachers came to the Maritimes including Freeborn Garrettson. Most, like Garrettson, regarded the United States as their country and went back soon. There were also some from Britain like James Wray.

Eventually in 1800 Black made the journey to Britain, attended Conference there and returned with more missionaries to be succeeded by others. British missionaries found it much more difficult to go back to their home country. Black was the father of Methodism in the Maritime Provinces of Canada, his constant concern being to get other preachers to help. Because Black lacked the power that Coke had in the West Indies in stationing, missionaries there helped to choose whether or not they would move and so tended to stay in the same place. Black himself set the example by staying near Halifax and Duncan M'Coll stayed at St Stephen, while the Mann brothers remained at the places they had originally settled in Nova Scotia. Black, who married twice and had a number of children, superannuated in 1812 and died of cholera in 1834.[44]

The reasons for his decision to turn to Britain rather than the US were many. Black himself was a Yorkshire Methodist and many of the new settlers had come from the mother country bringing their Methodism with them. They naturally looked back to the old country and expected it to help. Those who had come from New England and the other more southern colonies were Loyalists like the Manns. Though they retained many contacts yet their ethos was one of loyalty to the British crown and connection, and they preferred British Methodism to the independent Methodism of the United States. Preachers who came from the US were much more easily able to go home than those from Britain and they did. Only Cromwell and Fidler stayed for any length of time. Cromwell eventually became ill and went back. Fidler, though he built up a very close relationship with Black, eventually did the same. America was warmer, less inhospitable, and their home. They were loyal to the Republic and, at times of tension between the two countries, were suspect in the Maritimes

---

[43] Jeremiah Lambert died first, Samuel Rudder never appears to have got there, see Vickers, ed, *Journals of Coke* 43-4, 163.

[44] http://www.mun.ca/rels/meth/texts/origins.html (accessed 4/2/2003) for H. Rollmann, *Origins of Methodism in Newfoundland*; Scobie & Grant, eds, *Atlantic Canada*; E. A. Betts, *Bishop Black and his Preachers* (Sackville NB: Tribune Press, 1976); G. A. Rawlyk, *The Canada Fire: Radical Evangelization in British North America 1775-1812* (Montreal: McGill, 1994) 21-45. St Stephen was the only strong Methodist area in New Brunswick.

which were too close to Maine for comfort. Finally, Asbury was all too conscious of the needs of his expanding country. As the population swelled and moved west, so he wanted his preachers back to follow the settlers.

Coke never visited the Maritimes. He sent a number of preachers but many of the early ones were diverted, often by him to the West Indies and elsewhere. He wrote regularly to William Black, James and John Mann and others there. Though Coke had theoretical authority in the area, since he never came his actual power was limited.

William Thoresby

One British preacher who went for two years to Newfoundland was William Thoresby. Another Yorkshireman, one of several brothers who became itinerant preachers, he began preaching in 1784 in the Oldham area and went out to travel in his own circuit in 1785. In 1795 Coke asked him to consider being a missionary. At the 1796 London Conference he was asked if he had any objections to going to Newfoundland. He agreed apparently to do a two year term and sailed on the 30th August from Poole in Dorset. It was a stormy voyage and on September the 18th he remembered the verse printed at the start of this chapter, which he had sung at Conference. He wrote 'My mind in contemplation returned to England and visited my friends in their assembling together...although we are absent in body, we are present in spirit.' On October the 7th he and his companion George Smith landed at Conception Bay. He found much to do. Measles was hitting some of the isolated communities and there was much demand for burials and baptisms. In January 1797 he wrote about a journey from Carbonear to Port de Grave

> We had to go ten miles in an open boat, old and leaky, the wind blew strong and intensely cold; however we got safe to Port de Grave the same day; glory be to God. I have preached four sermons here and not in vain; some are convinced of the evil of sin, others are blest with a feeling sense of God's love. I met the society and joined some new members; the people are very loving and kind. Jan 11th. I went in a skiff half a league to Bareneed and stayed one night, after preaching in a house full of hearers; they all appear at present to be determined for the kingdom of God, and in the morning I preached to them, and after preaching buried a child; and set off in a boat two thirds of a league to Cupids, and walked two miles to Brigus. I preached to a tolerable congregation and the night following likewise; and on Saturday evening I met the society, gave them tickets and joined some members and backsliders...

He was the Superintendent of the station and hardworking, 'A Preacher of attractive talents' according to Findlay and Holdsworth. He found the climate difficult, wearing at one point two pairs of gloves, two pairs of stockings and a pair of buskins (boots) on his legs, yet 'it was with difficulty I escaped being bit by the frost' while preaching in the church. He suffered much from the local lice and gave a blow by blow description of how he took his clothes off and embarked on regular battles with the insects, picking off and crushing them one by one. He returned in 1798 losing his box of possessions on the sea journey. He married Mary Bickford of Ashburton on the 20th August 1798. Seriously ill in June 1806 he superannuated to Ashburton that year and died on the 26th August aged 46, leaving two young daughters and his widow.[45]

Life as a missionary in this period was very uncertain. In the West Indies they were subject to storms and hurricanes, in Nova Scotia to cold and equally fierce storms. Travel between the islands was not easy. In his journeys Coke recounts all sorts of problems ranging from shipwreck, via being captured by a privateer, to his dinghy almost sinking. Persecution was always likely. Lumb was put in jail in St Vincent for preaching without a licence. Methodists were whipped in St Eustatius for worshipping together.[46]

Marriage and Family

Some missionaries married local wives and costs then escalated. In the West Indies John Harper married Henrietta Hawes in 1789. There was a shortage of white women there as in other colonies. A black or mulatto wife would create problems within West Indian society. Benjamin Pearce married in Barbados, also in 1789.[47] Thomas Owens married the relatively wealthy Henrietta Gibbon in St Kitts in 1791.[48] Otherwise of these early preachers they were local and married already (Baxter, Black, etc) or they only married on or after their return to Great Britain. The exception was the later missionary John Stephenson who went out with his wife and family in 1798, more typical of the nineteenth century situation where single men chosen as missionaries were expected to get married before they went.[49] Lumb married in 1793, apparently on his return,

---

[45] W. Thoresby, *A Narrative of God's Love to William Thoresby* (Redruth: Bennett, 1801); *MM* 1807: 420; G. Lloyd, ed, *The Papers of Joseph Benson* (Manchester: MARC, 1991) PLP 7/10/7 17; Findlay & Holdsworth, *WMMS* 1: 270-1; Anon, *Ashburton Methodist Church: A Brief History* (Ashburton: Ashburton Methodist Church, 1994); *IGI*.

[46] Licences could only be granted to those with twelve months' local residence, as Coke said, a measure designed to prevent the itinerant Methodists preaching. The capture by a French privateer was 1804/5.

[47] St Michael, Barbados 9th July 1789 (*IGI*). Melville Horne argued for marriage with indigenous women in Africa, but this had little contemporary support (M. Horne, *Letters on Missions: Addressed to the Protestant Ministers of the British Churches* (Bristol: Bulgin and Rosser, 1794) 50, 65-7, 72). I owe this reference to Suzanne Schwarz.

[48] Anon, *Wesleyan Takings* No. 170.

[49] The classic nineteenth century story was of Thomas Adams, sent to Tonga in 1842, being told he must find a wife to take with him in eight weeks. He found Maria French of Taunton. Their granddaughter proclaimed the hasty marriage an unqualified success. G. E. Harrison, *Methodist Good Companions* (London: Epworth, 1935) 88-104.

and Warrener married in 1800, three years after he came back. Similarly in the Maritimes Thoresby married when he came back to Britain. The importance of the part played by these missionary wives, even though they were few at first, cannot be overstated. Much work is now being done on what they did. Their influence on the local environment in terms of dress, food, education, nursing, child rearing and general cleanliness was for the next missionary period.[50]

Death, Leaving or Return

Nine of the missionaries died on station or travelling to it, a much higher percentage than among those itinerant preachers who stayed at home. The most famous and the oldest was Thomas Coke, dying in his cabin in the Indian Ocean in 1814 on his way with the first Methodist missionaries to Ceylon. The rest died equally suddenly but relatively young, usually of tropical diseases against which they had no defence. This was especially true of the West Indies. Daniel Graham having 'preached some years in Ireland,' volunteered for missionary work and 'crossed the ocean to carry the gospel to the negroes in the West Indies.' He first went to Jamaica and arrived in Barbados in the early months of 1793. He died in August 1793 of yellow fever aged 33.[51] The Yorkshireman Robert Gamble, having served three years in Britain, offered himself as a missionary to the West Indies in 1788, going there with Matthew Lumb and Coke in October. He landed first at Barbados and then went to St Vincent in December where he was left by his fellow Yorkshireman Lumb. In February 1791 he was seized at St Vincent by a 'putrid fever,' probably typhus. He was ill for sixteen days and died.[52] William M'Cornock, sent to Dominica in 1788, died in 1789 within six months of his arrival. Thomas Werrill or Worrell, sent to Barbados in 1790, died of fever in 1791. John M'Vean seems to have died in 1797. Benjamin Pearce, who started in Barbados in 1788 and had a family by 1793, died in Grenada in 1795. In Gibraltar James M'Mullen arrived with his wife in September 1804 to face an outbreak of yellow fever. By the end of October both were dead and their infant daughter an orphan. At least five and probably six of these early deaths on the field were of Irishmen, emphasizing the sacrifice made by Irish Methodism for missions. The high mortality shows the impressive self sacrifice of the men who continued to volunteer and later of the women who went with them.[53]

Similarly ill health forced many to leave either the ministry or the colony.

---

[50] Bayly, *Birth* 334-5.
[51] The quotations are from *PPIM* 26-7. See also T. Coke, *An Account of the Rise and Present State of the Methodist Missions* (London: WCO, 1804) 59, and Moister, *Heralds of Salvation* 8-9.
[52] Atmore; *PWHS* 33 (1962) 120; Baker, *Wesley and Church* 317 citing licence in MARC; Moister, *Heralds of Salvation* 3-4.
[53] Moister, *Heralds of Salvation* 1, 4, 9, 20; Findlay and Holdsworth, *WMMS* 2: 66-7.

The Irishmen Harper and Hammett went to the United States because of their ill-health, where they joined the American Methodist Episcopal church and in each case later left the ministry. George Skerritt and William Brazier, both local candidates entering in 1789, were forced to leave the ministry because of ill health after two years. The Irishman John Clarke, who had suffered so much on the journey out that Coke reported his hair falling off, was sent to St Vincent in January 1787, but left the itinerancy in 1790. In 1799 there was a *Minute* which codified what was already happening, saying that preachers in the West Indies who were ill could go to Bermuda or the Continent of America to recuperate, if a physician recommended it.[54]

Thought of return to the British Isles was at first and before 1791 non existent. In the 1790s a few missionaries like Thoresby had agreed the length of time they would spend on the station. In the 1800 Conference there was an attempt to prevent this by saying all preachers must agree to go out for ten years. This was wildly over optimistic. Many preachers never made two. The rule had to be modified and in 1802 became six years.[55] Some were able to return home eventually, though illness usually caused this. Lumb, imprisoned in St Vincent in 1792, had to leave it in 1793. William Warrener, having served eleven years, came back to Great Britain in 1797. John Stephenson came back in 1802. Lumb and Stephenson had both suffered from the hostility of the planters and had spent time in prison. William Fish, a missionary by 1792, returned to Britain in 1805 having done thirteen years, mostly in Jamaica. Richard Patterson was in the *Minutes* as a missionary in 1791 and returned safely to Britain. Having come home their treatment tended to be poor, Scotland or rural circuits in Cornwall or Cumbria being common stations.[56]

Short periods of service abroad, therefore, were a characteristic of these early missionaries. In the West Indies only the locally recruited John Baxter served for what would be described as a long term in the twentieth century from 1784 to 1805, and he returned to Britain for 1800 to 1801, being stationed at Newbury for the year. In the Maritimes there were several locally recruited preachers who managed long stretches in a more favourable environment, but nobody from Britain. In the West Indies twelve years (Thomas Owens) or thirteen (William Fish) were long terms. More usual were the three years of Robert Gamble or the two of James Lyons. The two men who went on to America had both served the West Indies relatively well first, Hammett five years and Harper seven.

---

[54] For Clarke's hair see Vickers, *Journals of Coke* 73 'Brother Clarke's hair falls off wonderfully.' *Minutes* 2: (1799) 14.

[55] *Minutes* 2: 58, 139.

[56] P. Howard's paper on 'returned empties' at the MMS History Conference of 2005.

Finance, Organization and Thomas Coke

Finance was not easy. Apparently Coke raised the sum of £1,167 in 1787. This was a good ratio for the eleven missionaries on station that year, but the number of missionaries rose sharply. By 1791 there were twenty-four but the money did not rise in proportion. Coke and Wesley seem to have assumed that they or later the home church and its missionary organization would find the cost of outfit and travel to the mission field, but that the missionary would be largely supported by the locals once he got there, as in the thirteen colonies earlier. Since the British Connexion remained in charge and most Methodists in the West Indies were black and poor, this was never the case. Certainly in Nova Scotia and many islands in the West Indies, being supported by the societies was not practicable for much of the time. Similarly, there were places as in Newfoundland where most fishermen did not over-winter, and some other islands where money was never enough. In Newfoundland, for example, missionaries were forced to supplement their meagre stipend by taking pupils and teaching, or by doing other secular work.[57] This prevented consistent itinerant work. Local money raising was always poor. Buildings were erected with heavy debts which were not paid off. Missionaries overdrew on their accounts and spent too much money on buildings. In the West Indies the largely poor black societies found it difficult to support the missionary, let alone build the churches he was asking for. Coke did raise money for the cause, but the published figures show that this was only £620 in the year 1792/3, a sum which had to face not only current expenditure of £2,788 but also long standing overspending and debt.[58] It was a sum which had to be spread over an ever larger number of circuits. This was partly because of lack of publicity or what later periods described as missionary education. The *Arminian*, later *Methodist, Magazine* which in the nineteenth century seemed to be full of missionary reports had very few in the 1780s and 1790s. There were printed accounts of Coke's Journals but these referred to America more than the West Indies. Only from 1800 do we find regular printing of missionaries' letters to Coke, and even these tended to be relatively short extracts not the whole letter and were often at first several years out of date, so the readers would not learn the current situation and needs. In contrast the *Evangelical Magazine* founded in 1793 from the first had many missionary reports.[59]

For most of the period under review Thomas Coke *was* the only missionary

---

[57] Vickers, *Thomas Coke* 134-9 and 266 n2; N. W. Taggart, 'Missionary Finance and Administration under Coke 1784-1813' *WHS (I)* 12 (2006-7), 44-54; N. Semple, *The Lord's Dominion: The History of Canadian Methodism* (Montreal: McGill, 1996) 29, 35-7.

[58] Coke said the West Indies alone cost £1,200 per annum in 1794 (Vickers, *Thomas Coke* 261).

[59] A. Porter, *Religion versus Empire? British Protestant Missionaries and Overseas Expansion 1700-1914* (Manchester: Manchester UP, 2002) 48.

organization. Just as John Wesley was the fulcrum of everything in Methodism while he lived, so Thomas Coke was for Methodism overseas, whether it was the USA, the West Indies, France or British North America. Coke was the prime mover and organizer but he did not and could not solve the problem of control, which was only met when the Wesleyan Mission House was set up at the end of the decade in which he died.[60] It was highly appropriate that as the one who travelled so much by ship he should die on board, going on the greatest adventure of all to the east. However, like Wesley it was obvious he too needed help. A Committee for the Management of the Mission Affairs was set up by Conference in 1790. As well as Coke it included Alexander Mather, Thomas Rankin, Henry Moore, Adam Clarke, John Baxter, William Warrener and Matthew Lumb. Of these the last three were existing missionaries in the West Indies. Rankin had been the Superintendent in the United States and Clarke had been a missionary in the Channel Islands. Only Mather, Wesley's senior adviser, and the young Irishman Moore had no relevant experience. Or perhaps Wesley thought of Ireland as a mission field? But when and where would the committee meet? It seems unlikely that it could ever be got together and we hear no more of it.[61]

After Wesley's death Conference in 1792 set up another committee to 'examine accounts, letters and missionary candidates.' This was to assist Coke and act for him when he was overseas. It included the president of Conference and eight British travelling preachers, but was not recorded in the *Minutes*. It was not until 1804 that an effective committee of 'Finance and Advice' was formed, consisting of all the preachers stationed in the London circuits under Coke's own presidency. Coke wrote to this Committee in the letter quoted above, and much of their correspondence remains showing that unlike previous attempts they actually had influence. Like many committees they were cautious. Coke came into conflict with them over several issues, not least their 'frugal spirit.' He had been frequently to the West Indies and understood the problems. The Committee was composed of senior preachers whose most distant station had been Ireland fifteen years earlier.[62] Coke seems to have remained in real control until his death. When he died in 1814 Conference appointed two of the London preachers to act as Secretaries to run the nascent organization, the usual principle of two needed to do one great man's work, leading to the eventual establishment of the Wesleyan Mission House Secretariat.[63]

The preachers in the West Indies at first met Coke in Conference whenever he visited them. In 1794 a note appeared in the *Minutes* 'There is to be no

---

[60] Porter, *Religion* 37.
[61] *Minutes* 1: 240 (1790).
[62] 'Frugal spirit' is Coke's phrase. Lloyd in *JRULMB 76 No 2 Summer 1994* 254 ref 28/12/23.
[63] Peirce, *Polity of the Methodists* 722; *Minutes* 2: 240 (1804).

general conference in the West Indies the ensuing year: 1 Because the expense will be enormous on account of the war. 2ndly, Because of the great dangers from the French Privateers who infect those seas. 3rdly, because the removals of preachers in the West Indies are very few.' After 1806 such meetings became called District meetings or Synods on the model of what happened at home, with Chairmen appointed by London and a Secretary elected locally.[64]

Coke has had a bad press over mission as over America and elsewhere. Piggin described him as 'an unrealistic optimist' for writing to his companion Thomas Squance about their journey to Ceylon that they 'might expect fine weather all the way.' He also suggested that Coke prevented the development of an efficient organization like the CMS or the LMS, and that he was incapable of delegating responsibility.[65] Porter went further describing Methodist missions as 'a fragile one-man band, a construction constantly at risk from Coke's impulsiveness, his chaotic personal control, swelling debts, and a complete lack of any financial or administrative system.'[66] Coke at least knew the foreign field. The Missionary secretariat under Bunting which succeeded him lacked overseas experience and were rarely able to understand the difficulties of missionaries. They were no better at delegation either. Coke's enthusiasm meant over a hundred missionaries went out and were supported on the field. The growth of the number of members overseas by the time of his death from the nil of 1786 to the 18,747 reported in 1814 testifies to the immense importance of his inspiration. His contribution was not ended by his death. Robert Newton, the greatest missionary advocate of the next period, was inspired by his mentor Coke.[67]

Conclusion

Missionaries abroad, under Wesley or Coke, were treated very similarly to travelling preachers at home. Like them they received little training, apart from the regular epistle from their leader to which they were expected to reply even more regularly. Like those in the British Isles they might be moved at any time from circuit to circuit, from area to area such as between islands in the West Indies, or from home to abroad and back again. The chief criteria for selection were their abilities to preach and travel. The early Methodist missionaries hailed from many diverse backgrounds. They were of different ages. Their common pattern was to be single and volunteers, eager to spread the message and build up groups who were often already in place, from Antigua to the Cumberland Valley in Nova Scotia. We know little about these men, partly

---

[64] *Minutes* 1: 289.
[65] S. Piggin, *Making Evangelical Missionaries 1789-1858* (Abingdon: Sutton Courtenay Press, 1984) 68.
[66] Porter *Religion* 32.
[67] *Minutes* (1814) 32. For Coke's influence on Newton see Birtwhistle in *HMGB* 3: 27.

because the bureaucracy which would give information about them had yet to begin. There may well be more material to find. But we shall never be able to answer most of the questions we would like to ask. As at home, local workers were also very important. Again we know little about them unless like Baxter they joined the itinerancy. The black and the women leaders among them are especially under-recorded. Women, even more than in Britain, were important in the early colonial churches. As in America, the part played by Wesley's preachers in Christianizing the black population of the West Indian islands was to be highly significant for the future. Equally important was the foundation of Methodism in Canada.

It is questionable whether in this period the romantic view of the missionary being inseparable from his brother at home, as given in the hymn at the beginning of the chapter, was true. The ideas certainly provided spiritual and mental support as shown by the experience of Thoresby on his way to Newfoundland. But, though selection and training might be similar in being very little, there was only minimal information coming back to the preacher at home from the one overseas. There was very little understanding of the problems faced by the missionary. If the missionary did return he was treated worse than his brother who had remained in Britain all the time. The pattern of lack of understanding and interest had been set by Wesley himself and despite all Coke's efforts was not significantly altered until the setting up of the official Wesleyan Methodist Missionary Society in 1818.

CHAPTER 15

Why Did Men Leave?

'You say some of my friends say I am too severe upon some who travelled with me. I should be sorry if this charge was true... Mr Fugill... when at home for years, yea for many years he was quite happy (felt right with God), yet he was a well known drunkard, a thief, a swearer, if not an adulterer to the last, and yet his words on his deathbed were "I walk and talk with God" and the cats (did) eat his face when he was dead... But I am quite of your mind, that we can only be justified in exposing persons who are dead in order to warn others.' Pawson's letter to Atmore 1st February 1802, after the publication of Atmore's *Methodist Memorial* in which many of Pawson's views on his former fellow itinerants could be found.[1]

Introduction

Leaving the itinerancy was something which Wesley (and the Conferences which followed him) did not want publicized. Dying in the work, that is in harness as an active itinerant, would be celebrated in many different ways.[2] Leaving, whether because of ill health, marriage, personal reasons or more critically doctrine or unsuitability, let alone expulsion, was different, not to be made much of, and often preachers literally 'disappeared' from the *Minutes*, usually never to return. Even an examination of the Conference Journal may reveal nothing, least of all the reason which might emerge in someone's reminiscences fifty years later.[3] One of the ways in which Wesley tried to disguise the problems he was having with some of his preachers was to print their initials rather than their names in the *Minutes* of Conference. They and he knew who they were and where they were supposed to be. Others who read the *Minutes* might guess but did not know, so if these preachers did not arrive or left during the year the whole problem was less public. Some of Wesley's

---

[1] *Pawson L* 3: 57-8. More than two paragraphs of other examples given by Pawson have been omitted from this quotation. William Fugill entered in 1748, was stationed with Pawson in the Haworth circuit in 1763, where he 'shook the foundations of the circuit' and was expelled at the following Conference. Wesley allowed him to return in 1767, but sent him to the Manchester circuit where Pawson was his Assistant. Again he was excluded. Pawson therefore had suffered from him more than most.
[2] See Chapter 20 below.
[3] See my *DOMBI* article on 'Ministry, Men who Left.'

preachers spent much of their time on the stations half-hidden behind these initials. Michael Fenwick, who entered as early as 1749, was usually not on the stations for the whole of his career. The only time his name was there in full was when after forty years he was sent in 1789 to the new mission station of Bideford. In the 1770s his initials usually appeared, as he journeyed from Hull in 1772 to Kent in 1778. Charles Wesley had several times got rid of him in the 1750s only for John to allow him back.[4]

Pawson, as in the quotation at the start of the chapter, has sometimes been accused of painting his colleagues too blackly. In this case he and Atmore (unlike Wesley or Conference) were printing details about men who had died, with the motive of warning others. Cases like Fugill's, though often notorious at least within a particular area, were not the majority of those who left the itinerancy at any period. Pawson had a genuine concern about the behaviour of the itinerants. His letters again and again show he feared a lowering of standards and pleaded for better behaviour from and stern discipline for those preachers who fell below the levels expected. If sometimes he over-egged the description, such as his phrase 'and the cats eat his face,' the Biblical reference was to dogs rather than cats in the story of Jezebel in 2 Kings 9 vv 30-37, yet he tried to keep to facts.

Reasons for Leaving

149 preachers left but no cause was given and there is no basis for conjecture. For the other 278 known to have left, often several reasons were given and it is an interesting judgement as to which was most important. For example, John Bennet left in 1752. He accused John Wesley of 'acting like a Pope.' He suspected Wesley of trying to have the house at Bolton made over to him and he was accused by other Methodists of differing over doctrine. Valentine, his biographer, suggested many causes (such as preaching with Whitefield and Dissenting ministers and Bennet's suspicion of preachers loyal to Wesley). Surely the key was the jealousy between Bennet and Wesley over Grace Bennet, formerly Murray, in what can be described, in summarizing the type of reason, as a very 'personal' one.[5] The most common factors which led to preachers leaving are important and revealing (Appendix One Table 15).

---

[4] There was an important article on this use of initials by A. Wallington, 'The Initialled Preachers in the Early *Minutes* and in Hall's *Circuits*' *PWHS* 10 (1916) 154-7. Other examples were Thomas Vasey, above Chapter 13, Thomas Wride and Isaac Waldron. For more on Fenwick see below Chapter 17; *CWJ* 2; 90-1; *AM* 1780: 495; *PWHS* 2 (1900) 65, 10 (1916) 155-6; his MS letters in MARC and the Manchester A/C Book.
[5] For Bennett see Valentine, *Bennet*.

Marriage

Marriage was cited 73 times as the reason for leaving, covering more than the decision to marry, settle down and travel no longer, though this happened most often. (Many married and remained itinerants, as in Chapter 6 above.) William Dufton was one who married and then left. He began to travel in 1773, and when Assistant in Grimsby circuit in 1784-5 he encouraged the young Alexander Kilham when he entered in 1784 after helping Brackenbury in the Channel Islands. Dufton was described as 'a wise father' and someone who 'assisted greatly in my studies.' In 1791 he married and left next year, probably because of the marriage. He had done almost twenty years.[6] A slightly different example was Francis Walker. Entering in 1744 from Tewkesbury, he left to marry and settle down in his native Gloucestershire as a farmer and local preacher after or perhaps in 1753. Despite this he still came out and travelled sometimes. In 1755 he was listed as a 'chief Local Preacher.' John Jones' notes on Conference showed him as present at the 1758 Conference and appointed Assistant in Wales. In March 1762 Walker travelled with John Wesley from Hereford to Church Stretton, and according to Curnock went to Ireland with Wesley in April. He was present at the Bristol Conference close to his home in August 1771, where he signed the letter from the itinerant preachers. In the early days preachers moved easily from local to itinerant, despite being married and settled.[7]

On occasion leaving was as a result of offending against the rules on marriage such as not getting the permission of his colleagues or of the lady's parents. Joseph Fenton was a local preacher from Pudsey near Bradford, a young man of great ministerial promise, who was sent to Hull to 'fill up a chasm in the itinerancy,' probably in 1771. However, he married suddenly and without consulting his brother itinerants. He was forced to leave and next Conference returned to Pudsey, continuing as a local preacher.[8]

Jonathan Edmondson's case shows the importance of following the marriage regulations in Wesley's day. Entering in 1786 he moved circuit each year as was usual, in 1789 being stationed at York. On the 6th August 1789 just after Conference he married Mary Gunniss of Spilsby from his 1787 circuit, at Otley, near his home in Keighley. He was still on trial aged twenty-two and had not asked permission. For these offences, and since there was no

---

[6] The quotations are from Francis Truscott when he entered the ministry in the Pembroke circuit in 1787. *WMM* 1850: 5; Myles; *JWL* 6: 351, 8: 75; *WJW* 8: 337; R. Treffry, ed, *Select Remains of the Rev. Francis Truscott* (Helston: Roberts, 1833); J. Blackwell, *Life of the Rev. Alexander Kilham* (London: Groombridge, 1838) 72-3, 83. Wesley was unhappy with Dufton's unpopularity in Pembroke.

[7] Atmore said the city of Gloucester was where he settled and died. *WJW* 20: 80n, 21: 353 n71; *JWJ(C)* 4: 492, 5: 427.

[8] For Fenton see Stamp, *Methodism in Bradford* 64. Robert Lindsay did not get his wife's parents' permission, as described in Chapter 6 above.

accommodation in York for her, Wesley suspended him until the next Conference (1790). Wesley did not deal with it all himself as he usually had done previously. He was giving Conference the final decision. So Edmondson and his wife went home from York where he had been sent, back to Keighley. Next year before the 1790 Conference a daughter was born, but the mother died as a result of the child's birth. Conference listened to Edmondson's plight, had pity and continued him on trial, sending him to nearby Bradford where he could visit his daughter regularly. Next year (1791) he was received into Full Connexion a year late, and thirty years later he was elected president of the Conference. However, he had lost almost a whole year, and it was probably only his wife's premature death that saved him from expulsion since she would no longer require support. This would appear to indicate Conference's firmness in contrast with Wesley's lenience, and illustrates the transition of power away from Wesley at the end of his life beginning before his death.[9]

The rule 'a preacher who marries while on trial, is thereby set aside' (*Large Minutes* 1770) was therefore enforced only much of the time, not the strict rule it was after Wesley's death and well on into the twentieth century. In at least one case it was said that the man had entered in order to find himself a wealthy wife. This was Peter Dean who in his first year found the widow of a Captain Bishom in Norfolk and married her. He then left the itinerancy and Atmore told how Dean later died feeling he was cursed because of his previous offence.[10]

Marriage was often an important factor in leaving, but perhaps slightly more important early on at the time of the first cohort. Many married men had entered and then found it impossible to continue. There was no suggestion then of a marriage allowance and those who did marry could expect nothing for their wives.

Unsuitable

The next most common reason for leaving (69 men) was 'unsuitability.' This usually meant lacking what Wesley called 'gifts and graces' for the work. It might cover 'a weakly constitution' which was the reason given by Atmore for Wesley's former coachman Edward Slater who left in 1776 after six years.[11] It also included 'an incorrigible coxcomb,' Wesley's description of John Heslup who gave up in 1768 after seven years,[12] and a 'trifler,' the Irish preacher

---

[9] *Pawson L* 1: 83; *JWL* 8: 279; Tyerman BMM. For the whole question of Wesley's lenience see below Chapter 17.

[10] Atmore 56-58. He confessed that 'in commencing an Itinerant Preacher' he had no other motive 'than to obtain a rich wife! And he added "The Lord has given me my desire, and His curse with it- and now I am ruined for ever!"'

[11] Atmore. See 'John Wesley's 1770 Will' in *PWHS* 54 (2003) 35.

[12] *JWL* 5: 70-4, 92, 107-8.

William Brandon who ceased to travel in 1790 after a single year.[13] An 'unsuitable' person was someone incapable of doing the difficult job properly, like the English preacher Robert Blake, who gave up in 1784 after six years having left his appointment in Athlone in Ireland three times without the Assistant's permission. Marriage could well have played a part in this judging from James Creighton's account of him in London later in 1784 'R(obert) Blake is here still; I don't (know) rightly what scheme he is upon: some say he is going to join the Quakers or Indepe(ndents). He has married an ungodly woman.' Interestingly Seymour printed a letter from the Countess of Huntingdon to Blake dated the 13th July 1784. From Berkhamsted he had applied to be one of her preachers. She refused. 'I am exceeding cautious about who I receive out of other connexions... I must request that your parting with Mr Wesley be exactly proper.' It clearly had not been and he was unsuitable for the Countess as well.[14]

The local preacher James Ridley from Manchester was sent out to travel in Scotland in 1788. When the Manchester folk heard, they sent after him because they knew he was a bankrupt. The Scots sent him away at once. Similarly the otherwise unknown T. Alsop prompted John Wesley to write to Charles in April 1748 'T. Alsop is not equal to Reading.'[15] John Abraham was an Anglican clergyman in northern Ireland who became a keen Methodist in 1776 as a result of Edward Smyth. Wesley invited him to London because he wanted him to administer communion there. He came in 1778, but there were problems. John Wesley considered Abraham was not adapted to the itinerancy. Charles Wesley, who might be supposed to be in favour of him, wrote in 1783 that he 'was quite unmanageable.' John Wesley eventually declared Abraham 'totally unqualified for a public preacher,' partly because he would not take advice from others. He went back to Ireland, later returning to London, but was declared to be insane.[16]

---

[13] The quotation about Brandon 'trifling' is from CJ. Little else is known about him, except his year was in the Belfast circuit.

[14] *EMP* 4: 262; Seymour 2: 476; *JWL* 7: 156-7, 165, 167, 249. The MS Letter Book of James Creighton consists of copies of letters sent by the Irish clergyman James Creighton (1739-1813) in London to his sister in Ireland, and is at the World Methodist Museum, Lake Junaluska NC. It has been little used, partly because of its size.

[15] For Ridley see *Pawson L* 1: 76; Bendall, *Yours Affectionately* 82. For Alsop see *WJW* 26: 310. The letter continued 'nor can John Jones ride long journeys.' The context led Baker to describe Alsop as 'apparently a preacher who is not otherwise known.' Rogal described him as 'Thomas Alsop' which is probable but lacks any evidence. SJR vol 1.

[16] *JWL* 6: 218, 177; J. B. Leslie, *Clergy and Parishes of the Diocese of Derry* (Enniskillen: Ritchie, 1937) 291; MS letters of JW to Alexander Knox 20/5/1776, 20/12/1778, 25/1, 4/6, 31/7/all 1779, 7/2/1784 (copies at WHS Library).

'Personal'

This category came next highest with 68 men. Many of Wesley's hearers only heard the part of his message which they wanted, that about their need for personal salvation. Notions of sacrifice and belonging to an often hostile Church they never really accepted and this often became a stumbling-block later. The Scots itinerant Alexander M'Nab, partly because of his Presbyterian upbringing, did not like Wesley intruding Edward Smyth into what M'Nab saw as 'his' pulpit at Bath in 1779. M'Nab had entered at the age of twenty-one in 1766 and so by 1780 was an experienced married itinerant who had been the 'Superintendent' or 'General Assistant' for Scotland when stationed in Edinburgh in 1776. Wesley had described him as one of his best preachers. When M'Nab, as Assistant in Bristol, objected to Smyth being allowed to preach on Sunday evenings at a Methodist chapel within his circuit, Wesley took strong action. Usually this affair has been described from Wesley's point of view. It is interesting to read M'Nab's

> I strenuously remonstrated against to Mr Wesley and firmly withstood Mr Smyth; and threatened, that if he would not desist from the Claim he had extorted from Mr Wesley, I would complain to my Brethren the Preachers, whom I considered as being all concerned in the Cause. This opened a Field for a paper-war between Mr Smyth, and me. Mr Wesley supported Mr Smyth, and for that Reason many Letters passed between him and me also. And my Fellow-labourers[17] joined with me in Two Letters to him complaining of Mr Smyth's extorted Permission. After Six or Seven Weeks Mr Wesley, Mr C Wesley, Dr Coke, and Mr Bradford came down Post-haste from London to Bath. Without speaking a Word to us the Preachers, Mr Wesley that Evening in the Society, utterly condemned us; and justified Mr Smyth. The next morning he called us all together and in the presence of my friends excluded me from the Connection, and would not allow me to speak one Word in my own Defence.

Wesley's account centred on M'Nab's refusal to obey him 'Whoever, therefore, violates the conditions, particularly that of being directed by me in the work, does ipso facto disjoin himself from me. This Brother M'Nab has done.' M'Nab was forced to leave. He certainly saw it as personal.[18]

---

[17] The other preachers in the Bristol circuit that year were John Valton and John Bristol. John Bristol certainly supported M'Nab, because he left also, 'turning Calvinist' and apparently becoming a Calvinist pastor in Sheffield by 1782. Valton may have been more equivocal. According to Valton's account there were 'heavy trials' for him because of 'a dispute between the superintendent (M'Nab) and the clergyman Mr Wesley had stationed at the new chapel in Bath.'(*EMP* 6: 98). He does not say what he did or said, but he remained an itinerant, the more use to Wesley since it was his second year in the circuit, while M'Nab had been in Scotland until the previous August.

[18] For the rest of M'Nab's story see Chapter 17. Sources for this are *EMP* 6; 98; *AM* 1784: 389, 1789: 629; *MM* 1808: 491; *JWL* 5: 155, 219, 346, 6: 268, 355, 375; Atmore; *Pawson L* 1: 20n, 2: 136; *PWHS* 7 (1910) 132-5. The quotation is from the MS M'Nab

Very often personal hostility to Wesley, as for John Bennet mentioned earlier, might be the most significant of the reasons for leaving. Michael Moorhouse, who apparently entered in 1773, was in Newcastle in 1777 where his wife died in childbirth. Moorhouse later blamed neglect by the Assistant, John Crook, for this. Next year in Melton Mowbray Moorhouse was pulled down by a mob, imprisoned and pressed for the army. He did not actually leave until 1786 when he circulated anonymous letters and later pamphlets which accused Wesley of favouritism. 'Some preachers' wives dine on Potatoes and buttermilk, some preachers could use umbrellas.' Moorhouse claimed fourteen years' service and to have been turned out without a hearing. He attacked the Deed of Declaration from which he had been left out.[19] It is not surprising that he departed after all that.

It could be 'personal' problems with the other itinerants which caused some to give up their calling, as with the 'stubborn' John King who did not get on with the others in America. Often we do not know the real reasons which may be merely hinted at. Martin Rodda, whose details are above, was a good example. He left the itinerancy the first time after a quarrel with a man in Pembroke and then returned to it. We might think nothing of this first occasion but after coming back from America he was upset when Wesley did not make him an Assistant and left in 1781. This appears therefore as 'personal' in the list. He became a liquor seller according to the layman Chubb and 'wicked' according to Pawson. The historian's suspicious mind wonders whether he was too fond of liquor. What was the real reason? Was he touchy? Did he feel upset by his experience of war, armed conflict and 'preaching politics' in America? Was he ill, suffering from what in the twenty-first century might be called 'American War Syndrome?'[20]

Expelled

Both John and Charles Wesley were prepared to expel preachers if they would not depart quietly when asked. Some were publicly forced out as a lesson to all, even if they would go quietly. The total of 49 expelled in relation to the total number of those who left is not large, and this was because Wesley and Conference after him much preferred it if men left without arguing and no publicity was aroused. Most who left in the classic phrase 'disappeared' with no trace occurring in the published *Minutes*. After 1784 there should have been

---

letter to Christopher Hopper February 2nd 1780 MARC PLP 72.34.2.

[19] The 14 years service is possible since he remained 'on trial' in 1773. *JWL* 6: 375, a letter to Thomas Taylor who had written to Wesley 'being very uneasy on account of the expulsion.' Clearly Taylor, a senior itinerant, sympathized with Moorhouse and felt there was some force in his criticism. *Pawson L* 1: 85; *AM* 1810: 167; Tyerman 3: 468; *JWL* 7: 335, 8: 144; *PWHS* 26 (1948), 126-7; Blackwell, *Kilham* 29-30.

[20] For John King and Martin Rodda see Chapter 12 above.

a mention in the Conference Journal, but even this did not always occur and the historian has to scour all the stations to see if in fact the minister still appeared there or not.[21]

Often no reason was given officially; sixteen of those expelled, however, were so treated because of unsuitability, eight for drunkenness and thirteen for immorality. James Wheatley, the famous example for immorality, had been accepted as a travelling preacher at least by 1744, possibly earlier. In 1751, after much investigation by both the Wesley brothers, they expelled him for 'horrid practices' with seven women in the Bradford on Avon area. James Thom, who probably entered in 1782, had a difficult marriage. He disappeared several times from the stations between 1792 and 1803, probably because of this, and again in 1809, committing bigamy in Ireland in 1812.[22] There was also David Barrowclough, who got his maid with child in 1803 while his wife was pregnant. In America Joseph Cromwell was admitted by Asbury in 1778. Asbury admired him immensely saying that 'the power of God attended him in every place,' yet in 1797 he was expelled for 'immoral conduct.' In 1802 Asbury recorded Cromwell's death from alcoholism.[23] Barnabas Thomas, a Cornish preacher, was another notorious drunkard, though he may have left rather than being expelled. Probably born in 1734 he entered in 1764 and married a 'pious peaceable woman of considerable property in Scotland' who never received allowances. By 1782 Pawson described him as 'not very acceptable to the people' (of York) saying his preaching was 'exceeding dry,' while in 1785 John Wesley said he could not preach at 5 am or keep a circuit. In 1786-8 Thomas failed to keep lists of members in his circuit. He superannuated in 1788, eventually to Leeds, where Atmore said he became a recluse and died of a violent fever in 1793 while Conference was sitting. Pawson suggested it was a result of his alcoholism, saying he was delirious.[24]

Alcoholism did not always lead to expulsion. Billy Brammah was rebuked by Wesley for his fondness for spirits, and especially for trying to use spirits to cure his 'dropsy.' Despite all this, though Wesley only once allowed him to be an Assistant and never repeated the experiment, he did not expel him.

---

[21] *Hill's Arrangement* appeared from 1819 every five years or so, see K. B. Garlick in *PWHS* 40 (1975) 2-5. Indexes of ministers' names only appeared in the *Annual Minutes* from 1823. They do not appear in the more generally used *Collected Minutes*.

[22] E. J. Bellamy, *James Wheatley and Norwich Methodism in the 1750s* (Peterborough: WMHS, 1994) 26-29; G. Lloyd, ed, *Catalogue of the Adam Clarke Papers* (Manchester: MARC, 1991) 12 quoting MAM PLP 25/3/12. Interestingly Mrs Thom was still supported by the Connexion in 1801 and 1802 though her husband did not appear anywhere on the stations in those years.

[23] Barclay, *Methodism 1769-1849* 2: 35.

[24] Atmore; *EMP* 4: 49-50; *PWHS* 31 (1957) 10-15, 37 1970) 166; *Pawson L* 1: 44, 3: 57, 141-2; *JWL* 5; 178,7; 262, 266; *Bedford St Paul's Circuit Class Book 1781-1806* (Bedford: Bedfordshire CRO, 1977); *JWJ(C)* 5: 427.

Brammah, who entered in 1762, was still an itinerant when he died in 1780.[25]

Accusations against the itinerants were not always correct. James M'Quigg, the author of the Bible in Erse, was expelled for immorality by the Irish Conference in 1815, following an accusation from a woman. It was only after his death that he was discovered to be innocent. Malicious prosecutions for scandal were often because of opposition to Methodism; just as in an earlier period such prosecutions against clergymen were often made by Dissenters.[26]

Henry Taylor provides the best example of how the process of dealing with charges worked in the period immediately after Wesley. Taylor's case was one mixed up with the controversies within Methodism. He died in 1798 after a very chequered career which can be followed partly through Pawson's eyes. Taylor had been a Methodist local preacher in Rossendale when very young. After some 'foolish behaviour' around 1776, according to another Lancastrian Bardsley, he joined the Independents becoming Minister to their Holcome Lane chapel in Bacup. Next Taylor was minister for the Particular Baptists who built him chapels at Rawtenstall and then Crawshawbooth (around 1779). His church failed and so he moved to Chester, followed by Cannon Street, Birmingham 'for some years' until 1788. That year Taylor rejoined Methodism, this time as a travelling preacher despite the fact that he was married with a large family already. 'Never had we received so large a family as his into the Connexion.'[27] 'At his own desire he was sent to Scotland at great expense,' yet became 'weary of Scotland in one year...' In June 1797 when Taylor had been Superintendent of the Sheffield circuit for two years, and in view of the fact that charges seemed to be likely to be brought, Pawson as an old friend of his family sent him a letter summing all this up prior to Conference. Taylor thought the letter very severe. He had been sympathetic to Kilham, had thought of leaving Methodism and went so far as to join the Methodist New Connexion at their meeting at Ebenezer, held during the Leeds Conference when he sent in his resignation. Mary Barritt persuaded him to withdraw it. When he returned, Taylor declared 'It is one thing to read men's (sc Kilham's) writings, and another to see them act.' The charges against him had been brought by a 'Mrs S.' to whom he had already sent money, the action of a guilty man. Kilham thought he had been spared by the 1797 Conference so that Taylor would desert Kilham. Kilham was also aware of Taylor's conduct to other women such as one in Sheffield. Taylor received money from Conference, after which new

---

[25] For Brammah see D. A. L. Cooney, 'Irish Methodists and the Demon Drink' in *WHS (I)* 2: 4 (1992) 33. The rebukes, all in the 1770s, are in *JWL* 5: 347, 6: 17-18.

[26] Spaeth, *Church in Danger* 128.

[27] All the quotations are from *Pawson L* unless otherwise stated. Atmore; *Pawson L* 1: 144, 163, 2: 62, 122; M. Taft, *Memoirs of Mrs Mary Taft, formerly Miss Barritt, Written by Herself* (London: the author, 1827) 2: 14; J. Hargreaves, *Life of the Rev John Hirst* (Rochdale: Littlewood, 1816) 134-145; G. Lloyd, ed, *Personal Papers of Samuel Bardsley* (Manchester: MARC, 2001) 1: 14.

charges were brought against him to the District meeting in the autumn of 1797 where he was accused of immorality in an earlier circuit (North Shields, Newcastle circuit). He was therefore suspended by his District meeting until the 1798 Conference. Taylor returned to his original home in the Blackburn circuit where 'Mr T's affairs coming to light proved a curse to many.' He moved to Liverpool and decided to get out of the country altogether and start again as a teacher in a school in West Indies. He died at sea on his way to the West Indies, probably before the next Conference. There was no obituary and so he was treated as having resigned. Had he lived he would have been expelled.[28]

Many were excluded because they did not keep to Wesley's regulations. His preachers were laymen and must not ape the clergy and think they could administer communion or baptize. In the 1760s several tried to get ordained by the Greek Orthodox Bishop Erasmus without Wesley's permission. When Wesley found out about it they were forced out, for as he wrote to Joseph Thompson in 1772 'Whoever among us undertakes to baptize a child is ipso facto excluded from our Connexion.' Similarly in 1783 he wrote to Benson 'I do not, and never did consent that any of our preachers should baptize as long as we profess ourselves to be members of the Church of England.'[29]

Health

Continual travel, ill-treatment, preaching outside in all weathers, little food and damp beds were all recipes for ill-health. 54 men gave up as a result. Itinerants suffered from aching limbs and bruised heads because of their repeated travel and the persecution they often received. The poor food led to intestinal diseases and to emaciation. Damp beds, often the only ones that could be found, led to the major killer consumption or tuberculosis. Psychologically preachers were liable to depression as a persecuted minority. They suffered from nervous disorders and hysterical fits. Nosebleeds, bleeding lungs and ulcerated wounds were all reported, as were 'Closed throats, cankers and ulcers.'[30]

Pain was the great leveller. Everybody suffered from pain to a greater or lesser extent, whatever might be the efforts of their medical attendants. A leading itinerant like Asbury might write in 1772 to complain that 'I find a degree of effeminacy sticking to me, but abhor it from my very heart.' Still

---

[28] Atmore; *WMM* 1845: 433-40; *Pawson L* 1: 144, 163, 2: 62, 122, 128; J. Entwisle, *Memoir of Joseph Entwisle* (Bristol: Lomas, 1848) 157; Taft, *Memoirs* 1: 58, 2: 14; Letters, G. Lloyd, ed, *Catalogue of the Early Preachers Collection* (Manchester, MARC, 1995) DDPr 2/32; J. Grundell & R. Hall, eds, *The Life of Mr Alexander Kilham* (Nottingham: Sutton, 1799) 189-92. For the MNC and Kilham see Chapter 16.

[29] For Erasmus see *PWHS* 38 (1971-72) 83-102; Burdon, *Authority and Order* 52-56; *JWL* 5: 330, 7: 179. For baptism see Holland, *Baptism* 108, which shows by 1785 such otherwise loyal preachers like Atmore and Thomas Taylor were baptizing regularly.

[30] For ill-health as a cause of death rather than leaving see Chapter 20 below.

twenty-five years later he could write he was 'subject to the greatest effeminacy by my gloomy and nervous affections.' The evidence seems to be that continual pain was the enemy which threatened, as he saw it, to emasculate and weaken him and make him unable to do his job properly. Similarly, John Valton wrote about being 'sorely depressed with various dejections and temptations.'[31]

There were at least nine examples of those who abandoned the itinerancy because of mental problems. Enthusiastic religious preachers of any period were often described as mad because they were so at variance with their society. Some actually became mad. William Freemantle and Peter Price, who thought they were called to preach to the American Indians in the early 1760s, were forced out of the itinerancy because of 'losing their reason' in 1766. The two suicides which took place (below, Chapter 20) were described as deranged. The American preacher who was very successful in Britain in the next period, Lorenzo Dow, was not nicknamed 'Crazy Dow' without reason.[32]

Doctrine

In comparison with all these other reasons for leaving, doctrinal differences involving only forty-two men were relatively low. Doctrine was only an important reason for the first two cohorts, twenty-three men among the first cohort, representing almost a fifth of those where reasons were given, and eight men, one tenth, in the second. After that the number of those leaving because of doctrinal differences was very small. What kept cropping up among these early preachers, at least for twenty-one of the men who left over doctrine, were Antinomianism, 'Calvinism' and opposition to the Wesleyan doctrine of perfection. The first of these might well be described as moral rather than doctrinal in any case. Again these were only prominent early on among the first cohort with fifteen cases, over half of the twenty-three who left over doctrine. Often it was partly because of their 'Calvinist' upbringing, as with Bennet or John M'Gowan, and so they became Dissenting ministers of Calvinistic churches.[33]

One example involving 'doctrine' was Thomas Newall who began to travel in 1761 when he went to the Whitehaven circuit. Having travelled in Ireland and at one point acted as Assistant in London, Newall vanished from the stations in 1775, but in April 1776 he had reappeared at Epworth. According to a lady in the Isle of Wight, when he was in the Wiltshire South circuit in 1776-7, he 'neither preaches truth nor experience, and avoids the name of Jesus.'

---

[31] *Asbury Jol* 1: 44-5, 2: 326; *EMP* 6: 65. The psychological origins of this were examined by Juster, *Doomsayers* 104-133. For drugs used to ease death see Chapter 20.

[32] For Price and Freemantle see *Pawson L* 3: 143-4. For the transatlantic Methodist evangelist Dow see *DEB* where he is described as 'a gaunt, unkempt and effeminate figure,' 'guided by inner lights, visions and voices.'

[33] See below for John M'Gowan.

Dyson, who reported this last fact, thought Newall had left very soon afterwards. In fact he remained on the stations until 1780 and was preaching as a local preacher as late as 1786.[34]

Persecution

Most travelling preachers in Wesley's day suffered persecution at one time or other, even if conditions improved in most places as the century went on, and most did not let it daunt them or prevent them from travelling while they were physically capable. New places, such as the Channel Islands in the 1780s, usually resulted in mistreatment for whichever preachers were the pioneers, though those who followed might do better. Persecution usually took the form of stone and dirt throwing, often acts of charivari and some times ill treatment such as led to the demise of John Smith in Ireland in 1774. Death was an unusual result, but being forced to give up the itinerancy was more common. Certainly the eighteenth century was a rough period and in an age without a police force riots were a frequent happening. Anti-Methodist riots were usual, and the treatment received from the mob was no different from that of other unpopular religious groups, such as Catholics in the London Gordon Riots of 1780 or the anti-Dissenter riots of 1791 which drove Priestley out of Birmingham. The early Methodist William Seward was killed at Hay-on-Wye in 1740.[35] Later preachers like Thomas Beard in Newcastle and John Smith and John M'Burney in Ireland all died as a result of mistreatment by mobs. Others were more fortunate and survived, though often forced to retire. Methodist houses were pillaged or pulled down. Methodist supporters were maltreated and wounded. At Cardiff firecrackers aimed at the Methodists burned several women badly.[36]

Impressment

As in America, another form of persecution which caused men to leave was the press gang. This had been almost used against Howell Harris himself as early as 1739, when he confided to his diary that 'if I had staid (sic) in Cardiff, I should be pressed next morning, that some were actually in the house where I

---

[34] It was rare for Newall to be Assistant in his nineteen years travelling, a substantial period. *JWL* 4: 164-5, 169-70, 241-2, 6: 212; *MM* 1816: 7; Dyson (1865) 89-90; *Crk* 2: 13; Manchester Circuit Account Book; Bennis, *Correspondence* letter 22; MS letter of Eliza Cooke to Adam Clarke 1786 at Bridwell Library, SMU.

[35] For riots see the first serious analysis in G. Rudé, *The Crowd in History 1730-1848* (Etobicoke: John Wiley, 1964) and Porter, *English Society* 100-04. For Seward see G. Lloyd, ed, *The Letters of William Seward 1703-40* (Manchester: MARC, 2004).

[36] For more details of such persecution see D. D. Wilson, *Many Waters Cannot Quench* (London: Epworth, 1969). Beard's death may have been because of impressment (next).

was for that purpose'. In the following years it was used several times against lay exhorters of the Calvinistic Methodists in Wales. So Roger Williams was pressed in 1744 and wrote to Harris about his experience as a soldier at Gloucester. The fear of the press gang had a real effect on several preachers and altered where they went.[37]

John Nelson was the standard example of the use of the press gang against a leader among Wesley's preachers. His wife had already lost a child because of the ill-treatment of the local mob. Nelson was told that several local clergymen and innkeepers had agreed he should be pressed. On the 4th May 1744 he was arrested, having preached at Adwalton close to Bradford, and pressed, being held in Bradford's dungeon under the butcher's shop in Ivegate. Taken to York and on to Durham in the army he refused to use weapons, reproved the swearing around him and preached to his fellow soldiers and others in and outside the towns to which he was taken. Thanks to Lady Huntingdon and a substitute being found for him by Shent, Nelson was released after almost three months on the 28th July. 1744 was a crisis for military manpower as the Government, threatened by a Jacobite invasion, needed to impress men quickly; it was therefore a bad year for Methodist preachers.[38]

Thomas Beard, who seems to have entered the itinerancy in 1743, was pressed in York in 1744 and held for some time with Nelson. Though eventually released, he seems to have died in Newcastle possibly as a result of his treatment in the army. Charles Wesley wrote a lengthy poem in his honour which is one of the major sources for him.[39] John Downes was also arrested and pressed for a soldier in Lincolnshire in April 1744 and held until June that year.[40] The other important preacher impressed was Thomas Maxfield. He was Wesley's 'first Son in the Gospel,' as significant in the south as John Nelson was in the north and so as critical a target for the enemies of Methodism as Nelson. Maxfield was pressed into the army in 1745 and apparently released by 1746 when he was present at Conference.[41]

Three later preachers suffered from impressment. William Thompson, the Irish born preacher, had hardly entered the itinerancy when in December 1756 he was pressed for the army near Whitby. It is not clear when Thompson, who was only 23, was released, but he was certainly back preaching in Ireland by the summer of 1757 when he was received on trial as a preacher. William

---

[37] Tudur, *Harris* 142-4.
[38] *EMP* 1: 90-139 is the classic account of Nelson in the army.
[39] There is little contemporary evidence for Beard. Myles and Atmore blamed the mobs, Tyerman the army. *WJW* 9: 438-9, 20: 32 n63; *Pawson L* 3: 52 correcting the date in Atmore; *PWHS* 31 (1931) 171; Myles; Tyerman 2: 126; Tyerman, *Whitefield* 2: 105-6; Tyerman BMM; Jackson, *Charles Wesley* 1: 386-7; Benson, *Apology* 161.
[40] For Downes see Chapter 4 above and *WJW* 20: 25, 28-9; Jackson, *Charles Wesley* 1: 385.
[41] For Maxfield see Chapter 2 above. Pearce, *Wesleys in Cornwall* 85-7; Tyerman 1: 454.

Hitchens, an experienced preacher who entered in 1745, was arrested in January 1757 at Bradford Wiltshire. He was imprisoned on the bridge there but freed by the impressment commissioners in February.[42] Also in 1756 Peter Jaco, the pilchard fisherman from Penzance who had entered in 1753, was impressed in his native Cornwall 'at Grampound I was pressed for a soldier; kept under a strong guard for several days, without meat or drink, but what I was obliged to procure at a large expense.' He was soon released by the local commissioners.[43]

Impressment had been used in 1743-6 and again in 1756-7, often near the coast where the country seemed to be most in danger and manpower was shortest. Each point was a time in the British wars with France when there was particular danger, such as the Jacobite Rebellion of 1745-6 and the outbreak of the Seven Years' War in 1756 when Britain was isolated and in danger. The Act used (18 Geo II c.10) was one which encouraged the pressing of vagabonds and migrants. Travelling preachers with no clear means of support might well come into this category. It was an excuse for clergymen and innkeepers who saw their means of existence threatened to remove their chief opponents. It is notable that the Wesleys travelled about these same areas without any successful threat being made. Both appeared to have more visible means of support and often local gentry friendships and influence. With the exception of Cornwall and Wiltshire, all the impressments took place in the North, mostly in Yorkshire. As Yorkshire was the major centre of Methodism by the second half of the 1740s, this is understandable. The press gang was also used against Methodist preachers who were not part of the Wesleyan connexion; Harding cites two instances in the south where the Countess's Connexion was stronger than Wesley's, again usually close to the coast.[44]

Trade or Business

Early Methodist preachers found it very difficult to make ends meet and if married with a family it might well be impossible. Even after allowances were brought in for wives and then children it was still difficult, as these were not always paid or paid in full. Such early leaders as Bennet, Nelson, Hopper and Jacob Rowell all found themselves earning money in different ways to eke out their allowances. There was always the danger that this could take over so that it became more time consuming than their work as an itinerant. In 1768 Wesley

---

[42] For Thompson see Atmore and *PWHS* 2 (1900) 215-6, 6 (1908) 4-8, 7 (1910) 70. For Hitchens see *WJW* 9: 465-6, 21: 86-8; *PWHS* 6 (1908) 115.

[43] *EMP* 1: 264.

[44] The Act of 1745 gave bounties to parishes per man impressed. The example of Michael Moorhouse being pressed, above, was also in time of war, that of American Independence. At Gwennap in Cornwall the press gang, when asked, refused to press Wesley, Shepherd and others *WJW* 20: 74-5. Harding, *Countess's Connexion* 892.

brought to Conference the question 'Should Itinerant Preachers follow trades?' The reply was 'We advise our brethren who have been concerned herein to give up all and attend to the one business' (of being an itinerant). Two years later in London, presumably since the 'advice' had not been taken to heart, the question came forward again, and this time the judgment was expressed with more firmness

> It is agreed by all the brethren now met in Conference, this 9th day of August 1770, that no Preacher who will not relinquish his trade of buying and selling, of making and vending pills, drops, balsams or medicines of any kind, shall be considered as a Travelling Preacher any longer; and it shall be demanded of all those Preachers who have traded in cloth, hardware, pills drops, balsams or medicines of any kind at the next Conference, whether they have entirely left it off or not.
> But observe, we do not object to a Preacher's having a share in a ship.[45]

Twenty-four itinerants were forced out, many as a result of this regulation in the late 1760s and early 1770s. Most were traders with medicines and are dealt with in the next chapter. Some were trading with cloth, such as Joseph Yearbury who took cloth from his native Wiltshire with him to America in case he failed as a travelling preacher. Others traded with hardware, probably from Birmingham or the Black Country, another major Methodist centre.[46]

The lack of restriction on shares in ships is interesting. Preachers lived in towns and cities which were major seaports, notably London, Bristol, Liverpool, Whitehaven and Dublin. Others knew the ports of the east coast, like Lynn, Hull, Whitby, Hartlepool or Newcastle, or those of the south, like Portsmouth, Plymouth or St Ives. Some of their society members owned shares in ships, often relatively small proportions such as a sixteenth. It was inevitable that the wealthier preachers might also own such shares. Because this did not involve their time, Wesley was prepared to allow it.

Other Reasons

Among the other possible categories of reasons for leaving were the thirty men who were opposed to the itinerancy, one of the leading marks of the Methodist preacher. One revealing example of Wesley's attitude to leavers over this issue was John Ellis, who entered in 1762 and was about to stop travelling because of the hardships involved when he died in the summer of 1772. Wesley's reaction was to write 'I was not sorry at John Ellis's Death when I heard he had decided to travel no more.'[47] Ten men wanted more money, while seven needed to look after other members of the family (usually aged parents). The final group of six

---

[45] *Minutes* 1: 90.
[46] For Yearbury see Chapter 12 above.
[47] *PWHS* 29 (1954) 150.

were those not put by Wesley in the Legal Hundred in 1784. It is worth noting the very low numbers in this last category. Successive historians have emphasized the crisis of 1784, partly because of the importance of those involved and partly because we know more about that period than earlier ones. But in numerical terms the offence Wesley gave to the total preacher body by this act was not significant, certainly not when compared to other reasons suggested for preachers leaving.[48]

Class

Chart 4 in Chapter 3 analyzed by class those who left and those who died in the work. The numbers in each group were small. Classes A and B were more likely to leave than die in the work. This was because, since they were gentry or belonged to the professions, it was easier for them to find another means of supporting themselves. Groups C, E and F were all more likely to die in the work than leave. It was particularly true of group E, the 'manufacturers.' The link between Methodism and the new industrial society of the late eighteenth century is again emphasized.[49]

It is instructive to realize that belonging to a lower class than the Wesleys was not a factor in why men left, or at least not apparently. Historians since Marx have tended to see class warfare at the heart of most problems. Yet no preachers left because of the aristocratic or class nature of Wesley's control. Wesley was a member of a relatively well connected, well-educated clerical family. The preachers, who came mostly from ordinary backgrounds, did not resent his authority but accepted it as natural because of the society they lived in. Stirrings can be seen later after the French Revolution, especially in Kilham's writings, but in Wesley's lifetime class was not a problem. Wesley's opposition to democracy was well known but was not an issue. Partly this was because, though he claimed to be against 'democracy,' a term which then meant rule by the mob such as in the Gordon Riots, in fact he was working with the spirit of the age in terms of the Enlightenment in so many ways. Lay trustees and stewards were given major responsibilities just as his lay preachers were given complete charge of large circuits as his 'Assistants.' Wesley asked laymen and laywomen to take on tasks previously reserved for the clergy. He gave a voice in class and band meetings to the poorest members of society. He lived an abstemious life that was a public rebuke to the conspicuous expenditure of the aristocracy.[50]

---

[48] The six were Atlay, the two Hampsons, William Eels, Pilmore and William Moore. Historians who have emphasized 1784 included Hampson, Tyerman, and Simon.

[49] For explanation of the groups see Chapter 3 above.

[50] Noll, *Rise* 225. Cf. Hempton, *People* 77-90; Rack 360-380; Walsh, *Church* 16-17. Rack is particularly useful here.

Areas and Leaving

Some areas in England produced preachers who were more likely to leave (Appendix One Table 16). Others produced fewer who left, the north midlands being the area with the lowest proportion of leavers at 28%. Very similar was Yorkshire at 29%. Next came Lancashire and the north at 32%. In other words, those who came from England north of a line from Wrexham to the Wash averaged fewer than a third leaving. In contrast was the south of England and especially the south east, the area which tended not to produce Methodist preachers. Preachers coming from London and East Anglia averaged 58.3% leaving, the southwest 49%, the south 47% and the midlands 44%. The midlands had the whole range from industrial counties like Staffordshire and Warwickshire, producing men who tended to stay (eight out of ten did), to the more southerly Gloucestershire where out of fourteen entrants nine left. Areas which produced more Methodist preachers were likely to produce preachers who lasted and died in the work. Areas producing few preachers found that even those they did produce had a tendency not to stay the course. Perhaps the hardships of travelling and the temptations of settling down were too much, so they left knowing there were more opportunities for other employment. Certainly the results are skewed slightly because where the origins are not known at all, the preachers were most likely to leave; but this is since less is known about those who left.

The only sizable Methodist county which did not fit this theory was Cornwall, which produced the high number of 38 entrants; but of these 21, substantially over 50%, left. Is this linked to the fact already discussed that Cornishmen tended to enter early on in the first three cohorts and not at later periods? So, just as a lower percentage of Cornishmen entered after 1770 than had previously, more of those who had already entered from Cornwall left the itinerancy. Or was it simply that because Cornishmen entered early, most left because they were *early* entrants who were more likely to leave?[51]

As already seen for preachers from the Celtic fringe, one of the results of this was that preachers who came from the periphery tended to be sucked towards the centre. Just as many Irishmen (and the few Welsh and Scots) found themselves in England, so in England it was northerners who tended to preach across the south, partly because fewer southerners became preachers in relation to membership, and also because those southerners who did start lacked the "stickability" needed for the Methodist itinerant's life. As with the Irish it may well be that there were fewer alternative opportunities in the north for bright young men than in London in particular and the south in general. This is similar to the findings on class, in that the lower social groups with fewer alternatives were more likely to stay as preachers until they died.

In London, the largest and most important circuit in 1788, there were nine

---

[51] See Chapter 3 for discussion of areas of origin.

preachers listed after John Wesley. The only southerners were Joseph Bradford and Peard Dickinson, originally from Somerset and Dorset in the south west peninsula. There were two Irishmen Henry Moore and James Creighton, a Welshman Thomas Coke, two Scots Thomas Rankin and Alexander Suter, and two from the north John Atlay and Samuel Bradburn. None were from London, the south-east or even the midlands. Only Atlay and (probably) Rankin left the itinerancy. London could often be different from the rest but the shortage of southerners was one factor present throughout the connexion in Wesley's lifetime and afterwards.

Conclusion

Some men were undoubtedly eccentrics whom Wesley might have excluded for their behaviour, but did not. George Sykes (1761-1826) is said to have once slid down the pulpit stair-rail to illustrate how easy it was for a Christian to backslide and how difficult to return. On another occasion when his hearers refused to listen to him, he turned his back on them.[52] William Ashman wore a red night cap in the pulpit, goodness knows why![53] Thomas Wride, however, must be the prize eccentric among the preachers. Wesley said his language was too bad for the fishwives of Billingsgate. Wesley wrote to him 'You bite like a bulldog. When you seize you never let go.' In 1775 while supposed to be riding with Wesley to guide him around the circuit, he 'loitered behind' so that Wesley failed to find the place where he was supposed to preach and went on to the next appointment. Wride found it very difficult to get on with his fellow preachers. In Norwich he had problems with the singers as well as his younger colleagues, and was locked out in the street.[54] Wesley had to move him from the circuit. Yet Wesley had faith in him and his preaching when few others had. In 1790 he wrote to him 'I hope you have NOW got quit of your queer, arch expressions in preaching, and that you speak as plain and dull as the rest of us.'[55] There was another side to his character, for Wride was a mechanical genius in regulating clocks and watches. He used his ingenuity for 'suspending fire-irons to make them fall off at any given hour.'

Wesley himself had a sense of fun which he shared with at least some of his preachers. In August 1775 he wrote the brief letter (this is all there was) to the young preacher Samuel Bradburn, suffering in the very poor Brecon circuit and down to his last shilling

---

[52] J. T. Slugg, *Woodhouse Grove School Memorials and Reminiscences* (London: Woolmer, 1885) 312-3; Mary Taft MSS in JRULM 104.4.14-15.
[53] *JWL* 8: 104.
[54] *JWL* 7: 304-5. Byron was from Northern Ireland. For Wride see also Chapter 17 below.
[55] *JWL* 6: 353; Wride's MSS letters, poems, prescriptions, will, etc at MARC.

Dear Sammy
Trust in the Lord and do good; so shalt thou dwell in the land, and verily thou shalt be fed.
Yours affectionately
J.Wesley

With this letter Wesley sent some banknotes. Bradburn replied in similar vein

> I have often been struck by the beauty of the passage of scripture quoted in your letter, but I must say I never saw such *useful explanatory notes* upon it before.[56]

Preachers left the itinerancy in general because they found it too hard. They needed great reserves of physical energy and stamina which relatively few could maintain over a twenty year period and more. The continual travel in all weathers, the lack of money, proper food and shelter, the difficulty of supporting wife and children, and, most important, poor health largely caused by all these factors were the overwhelming reasons why men left. Personal quarrels played a part but not a large one. Doctrine after the early years was rarely a factor. Temptations such as alcohol, money or women did not bulk as large as contemporary rumours, spread partly by opponents, tried to show. Those who came from wealthier areas were less able to face the strain of itinerant travel, or more likely wanted to leave and settle down in one place, knowing they could more easily find alternative employment. As the next chapter shows, when conditions for the itinerant improved over time, the proportions of those leaving became smaller. The chapter after that will focus on John and Charles Wesley's own part in the disciplinary and leaving process. Were they a major factor in driving men out, or was John in particular too lenient in allowing men to remain or to return when they should have been barred for ever?

---

[56] *JWL* 6: 177. The biblical quotation is from Psalm 37: 3. Bradburn was 25 and in his third circuit.

CHAPTER 16

Numbers and Destinations of Leavers

> 'Rarely two in one year out of the whole number of persons (preachers) have either separated themselves or been rejected by us.'
> John Wesley letter to Rev Samuel Walker 3rd Sept 1756.

Numbers of Leavers over Time

Wesley's defence of his preachers in 1756 as printed above was not true, either for itinerants during the decade up to 1756, or for itinerants in the future. He continued in the same vein to Walker 'A great majority have all along behaved themselves as becometh the gospel of Christ, and I am clearly persuaded still desire nothing than to spend and be spent for their brethren.'[1] Most of the travelling preachers at any one time remained within the itinerancy, but over the period of Wesley's lifetime and the next thirty years 427 (53%,) so just over half, of the 802 Wesley's preachers left the itinerancy. This was a loss which in the nineteenth century would have been seen as a disaster.[2]

Chart 10 below, based on Table 17 in Appendix One on the numbers of

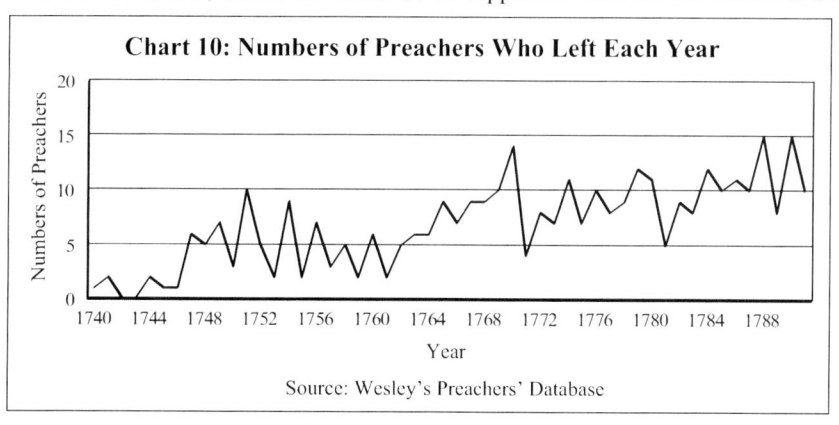

Chart 10: Numbers of Preachers Who Left Each Year

Source: Wesley's Preachers' Database

---

[1] *JWL* 3: 193.

[2] It could be argued this was because so many doubtfuls have been included in the list. In other words these may well not have entered at all, which applied to half itinerants like Shent as well as to Anglican clergyman friends of Wesley who dropped out in the 1750s. If the doubtfuls are not included, even so the total is almost fifty percent.

leavers each year, shows that until 1746 Wesley's estimate that only one or two preachers left in a year was accurate. In 1747 six men left and from then on the average number of those leaving over a ten year period never dropped below four. Admittedly the raw number of leavers in a single year could be as low as two as it was in 1755, the year before the quotation. The *numbers* that left each

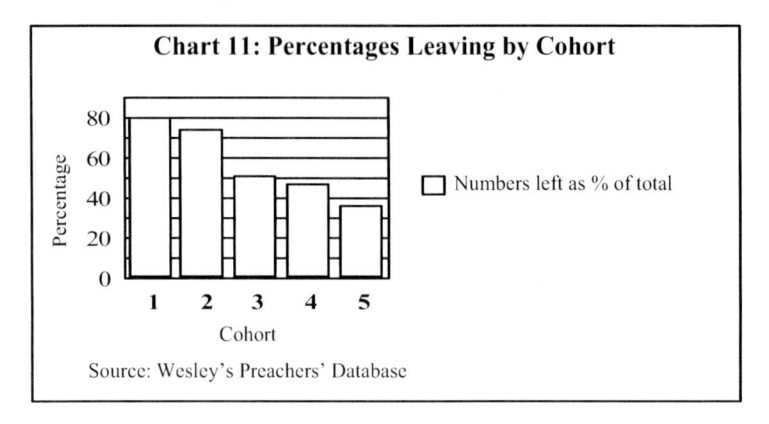

Chart 11: Percentages Leaving by Cohort

Source: Wesley's Preachers' Database

year show a gradual increase over time. Total numbers of those who left declined from the first cohort to the second (Table 1 in Appendix One), but then remained relatively stable. This was because the *proportion* leaving decreased significantly over time as the cohorts succeeded each other (see Chart 11 above). In the first cohort the percentage of those who left was 80. In each succeeding cohort it declined, reaching a low of 36% in the final cohort during Wesley's lifetime, less than half the original figure. It is worth noting that this decline in the percentage of those leaving continued through the nineteenth century and into the twentieth. In the eighteenth century it was a large and very significant decrease. The large majority of the first cohort having left, only 20% succeeded in remaining and 'dying in the work.' Yet the last and largest cohort, the men who had entered in the 1780s, would mostly remain and die in the work. Only a minority of those entrants would leave because the life of a travelling preacher had become easier as circuits became smaller, men were allowed to stay longer, and provision improved in terms of better accommodation, more regular stipend and allowances for wives and children. The territory covered by these itinerants had expanded to much of the world, where conditions were often worse. If preachers who served elsewhere, in Scotland, Ireland, America or the colonies were removed, then an even higher proportion died in the work. The Wesleyan itinerant body, so fluid and with most preachers likely to leave in the 1740s, had settled down by 1791.

The Leaving Process

Wesley, followed later by Conference, tried to keep quiet the process of preachers leaving. Usually, as we have seen in the previous chapter, there was no blame involved. The man was ill or aged, or was about to marry a wife and settle down and would remain as a local preacher wherever he lived. In any case a public spectacle was never made of it. Wesley described leaving as some 'separating themselves' and some being 'rejected by us.' The latter were those referred to as expelled in the Conference Journal, usually a rare occurrence. Most preachers themselves chose to leave against Wesley's wishes, but even when a weak preacher was encouraged to leave or the man was expelled, Wesley wanted as little publicity as possible. Robert Lindsay was expelled in 1784 according to the (private) Journal, but no reason for this was given in it. In the public printed *Minutes* Lindsay was, among others, described as 'desisted from travelling.'[3] Reasons for the preacher leaving tended to be omitted in the *Minutes* also, even though most were sound. Sometimes the man concerned published pamphlets justifying himself, as did Michael Moorhouse and John Helton.[4] Wesley rarely deigned to reply to these, though his successors were less able to carry out this policy. The basic principle to say as little as possible about why it happened, the process of leaving and what the man did afterwards was usually successfully maintained, with little evidence left for the modern historian. The total numbers of leavers each year appears at the end of the book in Table 17 in Appendix One. They show that when Wesley began to print the names of those who 'desisted' in the *Minutes*, there were always more who left than those listed, usually in fact double the number to which Wesley was prepared to admit. When Conference took over the decision concerning what should appear in the *Minutes* there was even less openness, since they admitted to fewer than half of those preachers who actually left. Often the individual just 'disappeared.'[5]

The process of leaving might take some time. Thomas Halliday was a preacher who suffered from alcoholism which eventually led to his expulsion. He was an Englishman who entered in 1766, being first stationed in the Dales

---

[3] CJ; *Minutes* 1: 166.

[4] J. Helton, *Reasons for Quitting the Methodist Society, Being a Defence of Barclay's Apology* (London: Fry, 1778); M. Moorhouse, *The Defence of Mr Michael Moorhouse: Written by Himself* (Leicester: Ireland, 1789).

[5] 'Disappeared' as a term for ministers first appeared in modern works on the ministry such as KBG. It reflects exactly what happened so far as the *Minutes* are concerned. Sometimes reasons for the leaving would appear in CJ but not in the printed *Minutes*. Sometimes no reasons appeared anywhere. Sometimes nobody was listed as desisting even in the MS Journal, though preachers had left. Often the *Minutes*, printed later, had more men listed as desisting than CJ, even though that was the legal document. This was because later editors knew of other men who had desisted and put them in, so presuming to 'correct' the acts of the Conference! There were many reasons for this. Partly the compilers of CJ and *Minutes* could and did make mistakes. Sometimes the information was lacking. The references could be to Irish ministers or men on the missions, so perhaps the information came late. But rarely did they catch up the following year.

circuit for half a year. He was then sent to Ireland where he remained, apart from spending May and June 1767 in the Manchester circuit, probably in place of Paul Greenwood. Halliday was successful in his visit to Fermanagh in 1768. He did not appear in the *Minutes* of 1770 or 1771. In most of his circuits in Ireland in the 1770s he was only shown by initials. This indicated he already had problems in Wesley's view, though he may still have been travelling throughout. Halliday's drink problem was probably the reason why he never permanently returned to Britain, unlike most British preachers who went to Ireland. In 1780 he suffered severely from persecution at Clara near Cavan in the north of Ireland, where he was beaten, stripped and nearly drowned.[6] As a result he was not in the *Minutes* in 1781 and 1782, presumably recovering from his ill-treatment. He was the second travelling preacher who went to Drumclamph in west Tyrone. There Halliday said he had been travelling a long time[7] and that the Moore family who were giving him hospitality were the first large 'unitedly' Methodist family he had seen. The Preachers' Fund gave him £12 in 1782 and again in 1784 and 1785. For most of that period he was a supernumerary[8] either in Athlone or Castlebar, two large circuits in the west of Ireland. According to the later Irish Methodist historian Crookshank 'His complaint (alcoholism) was brought on by fatigue, exposure and abuse which drove him to stimulants for relief and he became a slave to the intoxicating cup.' Halliday was finally expelled at the 1786 Conference for 'scandalous and open crimes,' according to a letter from the twenty year old Dublin Methodist James Freeman to his sister Charity. The manuscript Conference Journal that year said the expulsion was for 'habitual drunkenness.' The *Minutes* simply said 'desisted' and gave no reason. He died repentant.[9] The process had therefore taken well over ten years from the first appearance of the problem in the 1770s, via the use of initials, periods of complete absence from the *Minutes* and some part-time ministry as a Supernumerary, to complete expulsion in 1786. The repeated warnings, suspensions and (probably) letters he must have received have left little or no trace.

---

[6] *Crk* 1: 198, 2: 29, 55, 77, 91; Steele, *Barnard Castle* 82; MS Manchester Circuit Account Book; *WJW* 22: 277n.

[7] The first preacher at Drumclamph was John Smith who also suffered much ill-treatment. MS notes of Moore family of Drumclamph at WHS Library B/Moor/Moo 15 and see Chapter 11 above. It is difficult to date the Drumclamph story, but it appears to be 1769-70, so Halliday had only travelled three or four years then. It seemed a long time to him and he had certainly travelled a long way!

[8] For the Methodist term 'supernumerary' in the eighteenth century see Chapter 19 below.

[9] *Crk* 2: 160-1; *PWHS* 10 (1916) 157; *AM* 1783: 48; Myles; *ICA* 19th December 1941. The 'scandalous and open crimes' may refer more to the man expelled with him, George Dice, who was expelled for adultery (CJ). For a more detailed account of Halliday's repentance and deathbed see *PWMM* 1828: 158-9.

Destinations of Leavers

What happened to those preachers who left? Very often it is sheer chance as to whether they turn up elsewhere in the historical record. If they remained as Methodists, and especially as Methodist local preachers, there may well be some record, but even then it did not always happen. Of the 426 preachers who left, 254 have no identifiable destination. The remainder of this chapter is devoted to an examination of known destinations and the common and diverse patterns they present.

Local Preachers

180 men are known to have had jobs after they left, see Table 18 in Appendix One.[10] There is evidence that at least 87 men remained as local preachers, so still active in Methodism. A good example was James Jones from the heart of the Black Country who had probably become a preacher as early as 1743. From 1749 to 1758 he was apparently stationed as Assistant for the Staffordshire circuit, as Baker put it 'in an unique position as half-itinerant.' He was a wealthy man with property who built the first Methodist chapel in Staffordshire at Tipton Green in 1750. After he married and left the itinerancy in 1758 he settled near Birmingham and died in 1783.[11] Many maintained good relations with Wesley, who sometimes stayed with them. The claim was made by the descendants of William Orpe, who left in 1777 to get married and look after his father's farm, that Wesley visited him at his farm at Prestwood near Ashbourne more than once and preached to around 80 people.[12] Similarly Wesley stayed with John Undrell or Underhill, who had left also in 1777 to become a local preacher in Birmingham.[13] There was no clear date for when many preachers left, for such preachers were often in a state of having been half itinerant for some time, Joseph Jones, Francis Walker and William Shent all being in this

---

[10] Some men returned after they left and 8 who had jobs remained. See also Chapter 17.

[11] Jones lived for a time at Handsworth (MS letter to Charles Wesley 24/12/59 MARC DDCW 6/31) and built 64 High Street West Bromwich later the Elms, (H. H. Prince, *Romance of Early Methodism in and around West Bromwich and Wednesbury* (West Bromwich: the author, 1925) 63-4), where he kept a carriage and servants. He intrigued against the Assistant Mather c1760-1 (*EMP* 2: 180). He had at least one son Masfen who was educated at Kingswood in 1770 (Kingswood MS Account Book 1766-70 at Kingswood School). *WJW* 20: 10-2, 21: 92, 242, 26: 286, 485; *PWHS* 4 (1907) 116-7, 14 (1922) 27-8, 42 (1979) 25; J. L. Waddy, *'The Bitter Sacred Cup': The Wednesbury Riots 1743-4* (London: WMHS, 1970) 10, 37-8; Valentine, *Bennet* 193.

[12] For Orpe see J. H. Lenton, 'William Orpe's letter of May 23rd 1766 to Francis Asbury' *MH* 44 (2005) 1: 56-9; Myles; MS Letters of Mrs Ida Johnson (descendant of Orpe) 12 March and 3rd April 1997.

[13] He was the 'John Andr' in Wesley's diary wrongly identified by W. R. Ward. Later he went bankrupt. Myles; *WJW* 23: 443, 481; *PWHS* 39 (1973) 145.

position.[14] A number of others are described below.

Dissenting Ministers

Fifty-seven became Dissenting ministers, a slightly larger proportion than those who were Anglican clergymen afterwards.[15] These tended to have Dissenting origins, or have been from lower social groups such as carpenters or shoemakers. Some were both craftsmen and Dissenters. John M'Gowan (1726-1780), an example of this, was the son of an Edinburgh baker, brought up as a Presbyterian. At nineteen he joined the Jacobites, fighting for Charles Edward Stuart at Culloden. Escaping the massacre after the battle, like many others he headed south, reaching first Durham and then Stockton. There he was converted by John Unthank, a farmer and local preacher, and became a local preacher himself, helping Unthank to introduce Methodism at nearby Darlington. It is not clear when he began to travel but there was one payment made to him as an itinerant on the Cheshire or Manchester Round in March 1755.[16] Soon afterwards, 'embracing the Calvinistic system,' M'Gowan left Methodism and became first an Independent minister and then a Particular Baptist minister at Hill Cliff Church near Warrington. In 1758 he moved to Bridgnorth in Shropshire. He was discouraged by relative failure in Bridgnorth, though he stayed there eight years. In 1766 he became minister of the Devonshire Square Church in London, a larger and more fashionable church than any of his preceding appointments. There he wrote several works, such as 'the Shaver' (about the expulsion of young Methodists from St Edmund Hall in 1768). Like many other London Dissenters he was buried at Bunhill Fields;[17] he had returned to his Dissenting roots like John Bennet and others.

Another man who became a Dissenting minister was John Whitford. He was a Cornishman like many of Wesleys earliest preachers, probably an exhorter heard by Wesley in July 1747 and described as 'much blessed in the work.' He had entered by 1748 when he was accepted as an Assistant. Wesley heard him preach at Bristol in March 1750 at 5-00 am and, as a result of hearing him, wrote dryly that he 'no longer wondered at the deadness of his hearers.' It is

---

[14] For Jones see Chapter 8, for Walker see Chapter 15, for Shent see Chapter 3 above.

[15] 32%, slightly above the 26% of the Anglican clergy, though some of those were already clergy before becoming preachers. It is much more difficult to determine whether some of the Dissenters had preached before to Dissenting congregations, though certainly some had.

[16] R. Trotter, *The Centenary of Bondgate Chapel...Darlington* (Darlington: Dresser, 1913) 6-7; *PWHS* 2 (1900) 65 quoting Manchester Circuit Account Book, 3. His first Dissenting pastorate was geographically at the centre of his former circuit. Briggs in *DEB* thought he had settled in Warrington earlier as a weaver in which case he was returning to a place he knew before. As a Dissenter he tended to be known as Magowan.

[17] Myles 123; *DEB*; *DNB*; J. Ivimey, *History of the English Baptists* 4 vols 4: 318 (London: the author, 1811-30), from whom the quotation comes.

interesting that Wesley still needed him and he was not dropped by Wesley on account of this lack of fire.[18] He did not leave until he chose to along with others in 1754, a departure probably made official at the 1755 Conference.[19] Whitford, as a Dissenting minister, served the Independent Church at Bolton from 1756 until 1758 or 1759, though already pronouncing himself 'sick of the congregation' there as early as 1756! He appeared as a minister in York in the early 1760s and then minister at Cleckheaton from around 1762 or 1763 until 1766. In 1762 he married Hannah Brooke at Birstall and went on to have at least two children who were baptised at his next church at Thornton near Bradford. There he also kept a school, but problems occurred over property and, according to Peel, 'he did not meet the expectation of the people and soon after removed.' He was the Minister of the Olney Independent Meeting in Bedfordshire from 1775 onwards, so serving at least five different churches in his career as Dissenting minister.[20] With both these preachers there is a pattern of unsettled ministry, ended in M'Gowan's case after he reached London, but apparently not in Whitford's.

Clergymen

Seventeen of those who left were already clergymen of the Church of England or occasionally Ireland, such as Henry Piers or John Abraham.[21] It is not surprising that when these decided to cease helping Wesley as his preachers, they went back to their original profession, which in reality they had never left. The 1740s, and to a lesser extent the 1750s, was a period of more mobility in and out of Methodism when boundaries were still unclear. Of the twenty-four who had not been clergymen, but who succeeded in becoming ordained, ten (the largest group) were from the first cohort. Many of them had been to university or had relatively wealthy backgrounds. John Jones, Charles Graves and Thomas Williams had all been to university.[22] Because of this it was easier for them to be ordained since they could prove sufficient education. Few if any of these gained promotion within the Church. Most found their Methodist background meant Bishops and others were suspicious of them and so they found it difficult to obtain livings. Frequently they only gained poorly paid

---

[18] *WJW* 20: 182, 249 n70, 323.

[19] *WJW* 486 n69, 21: 8; Myles 77, 449; Tyerman 2: 57, 187; Rack.

[20] The marriage and the baptisms are in the *IGI*. Baker, *Grimshaw* 250; *CWJ* 2: 116; Lloyd, *Labourer's Hire* 20; Peel, *Spen Valley* 106-7; J. G. Miall, *Congregationalism in Yorkshire* (London: Snow, 1868) 243, 249. The chapel at Thornton was at Kipping. I owe the last reference to Colin Dews.

[21] For Piers, who was Vicar of Bexley and supported Methodism throughout the 1740s, see Chapter 2. For Abraham see Chapter 15. He left twice, the second time in 1783. See *JWL* 6: 218, 7: 177.

[22] Jones was a medical graduate, Graves a friend of Charles Wesley while at Magdalen College, Oxford, Williams also at Jesus College, Oxford at the same period, see *A.O.*

posts, such as chaplaincies to workhouses or hospitals, or went to Ireland or the colonies where others did not want to go. Those who held livings had often become Methodists later and then found no further promotion.[23]

John Haughton (? 1720-1781) from the first cohort was a preacher who became a clergyman in Ireland.[24] He first appeared as a Methodist weaver of Chinley End, Derbyshire, very close to John Bennet whom he must have known well. He began as a preacher in 1741 or 1742 and so was one of the first lay preachers, certainly in his area. He encountered persecution in the Staffordshire riots in 1743 and 1744 and again in Cork in 1749 and 1750. He travelled widely, preaching in London, Bristol, Lancashire and Ireland as well as his native Cheshire. In 1752 in Bristol the steward, who had exacting standards on preaching, was impressed by him, reporting 'a pretty sermon enough and tolerably connected.'[25] He had gone first to Ireland as one of the pioneers with Charles Wesley in 1747 and Ireland was where he spent most time, being Assistant in Dublin in 1756. Having served almost twenty years as an itinerant, and after preaching very successfully in Ireland in 1760, he was led to resign and receive Episcopal ordination. It was easier for Methodists to be ordained in Ireland where there were fewer candidates with suitable qualifications; Bishops, such as the Bishop of Londonderry who was prevailed upon slightly later to ordain Maxfield, might look rather more favourably upon Methodists.[26] Who ordained Haughton is unknown, but there is a pointer in the fact that his two preferments in the Church of Ireland were both in the Londonderry diocese, so it was probably the same Bishop. Haughton was first Curate of Dunboe from 1766 to 1776, and was then promoted to being Rector of Kilrea from 1776 to 1781 where he was also a Justice of the Peace. Haughton welcomed Methodist preachers to Kilrea and Wesley himself stayed with him. He died early in 1781.[27]

---

[23] Bateman and Piers are examples of the end to promotion.

[24] His name also appears in a number of similar forms, notably 'Houghton' (in Atmore for example) and 'Acton.' He is said to have had a brother Nicholas at Stockport (A. Strachan, *Recollections of the Life and Times of the Rev George Lowe* (London: Mason, 1848) 29-30). The only Nicholas Haughton born at this period in the *IGI* was baptized at Gee Cross Independent chapel Hyde, the son of Nicholas and Phebe Haughton whose older son John was born 29th April and baptised 9th May 1720 at the same place. John Haughton was a common name, so it is probable, not proven.

[25] Bennet also had a high opinion of Haughton (Valentine, *Mirror of the Soul* 81-4, 152-9). *WJW* 20: 338 n92; *PWHS* 36 (1968) 179; Smith *Meth* 1: 195; Myles; Manchester MS Circuit Account Book; MS Bristol Stewards Journal 30.

[26] *WHS (LC)* 10: (1969) 177-9; *WJW* 20: 338 n92, 26: 402; Myles. The Bishop of Londonderry was William Barnard, died 1768.

[27] *WJW* 23: 90 n48; Leslie, *Clergy of Derry* 213, 234. John Haughton had a son of the same name born in 1774, educated at Trinity College Dublin and Cambridge, who in the nineteenth century was Vicar of Middleton, not far from where his father had been brought up, *AC*.

The preachers who entered later and who subsequently became clergymen were also better educated and connected, though much fewer in number. There was James Rouquet (1730-1776), a preacher of Huguenot descent among the second cohort. He had been educated at Merchant Taylors' School in London (where he was converted under George Whitefield) and St John's College, Oxford. He had been appointed by Wesley in 1751 or 1752 to reopen Kingswood. While there he was expected to preach to the local Methodist societies. When Rouquet left for a curacy at Sandhurst, Gloucestershire, he was ordained deacon by the Bishop of Gloucester in September 1754 but did not stay there long. At the 1755 Conference in Bristol he was listed as a semi-itinerant. As a clergyman Rouquet was involved in benevolent work such as prison and hospital visiting, and he married the wealthy Miss Sarah Fenwick in September 1756 in London with Wesley as a witness. He remained friendly with Wesley, helping him at Bristol in March 1772 and introducing Captain Thomas Webb to Methodism. He was in return relied upon by Wesley, who left him all his potentially valuable manuscripts in his 1768 will and made him a trustee in the 1770 will.[28]

Nicholas Mosley Cheek (1745-1805) from the third cohort of preachers possessed a second name belonging to a leading Manchester family which owned clerical livings. His mother, Elizabeth Mosley, was the sister of Sir John Parker Mosley 1st Baronet who was Lord of the Manor of Manchester. Cheek was a Methodist member and local preacher in Manchester in the early 1760s, who began to travel as an itinerant in 1764 or 1765. After preaching in circuits from Yorkshire to South Wales he had left by early 1769 when he had become a student at Trevecca seeking ordination. He next appeared at Warsop in Nottinghamshire and was later rector of Rolleston in Derbyshire, both livings owned by the family.[29] Later still Melville Horne from the fifth cohort, like Cheek connected to the Methodist Gilbert family, was first an itinerant preacher and then a curate at Madeley as well as being a preacher; he left Methodism after Wesley's death to become the first missionary in West Africa.[30]

Forty-seven, over a quarter of those leavers who had known destinations, either returned to their previous clerical occupations or became clergymen. More than half thus became clergy or ministers. It can be argued that this

---

[28] A. B. Sackett, *James Rouquet and His Part in Early Methodism* (Chester: WHS, 1972); *PWHS* 9 (1914) 11-4, 123-5, 12 (1920) 32-3, 19 (1934) 88-9, 39 (1973) 48, 45 (1985) 72-3, 54 (2003) 33; *AO*; MS Diary of a Bristol Steward 1752-4 passim; *WJW* 20: 472, 21: 129n, 22: 359n.

[29] I am most grateful to Henry Rack for sending me a summary of Cheek's career which elucidates many of the problems surrounding information on Cheek and the Mosley family. Myles and Crowther said he entered the ministry in 1764, while Ward said 1765. *WJW* 21: 427 n46, 22: 103n, 158, 200 n60; *PWHS* 18 (1932) 132.

[30] *WJW* 24: 12 n60; MSS letters at Cheshunt College in Countess of Huntingdon's Archives 19/1/69; J. Macdonald, *Memoirs of the Rev Joseph Benson* (London: Blanshard, 1822) 83-4. For the Gilbert connections see Chapter 14 above.

demonstrates the high standards of the Methodist preachers in that so many of those who left Methodism, even though some at least had left because they were seen as unsatisfactory by the Methodists, were able to find acceptance elsewhere. It also shows that Methodists thought of themselves as part of the Church of England, since it was so common for clergy to become Methodist preachers as well and for former Methodist preachers to be ordained within the Church.[31]

Founding Breakaway Methodist Groups

In Wesley's lifetime relatively few tried to found other *Methodist* groups, a tribute to his charisma. Though a number set up or joined Independent churches, taking with them some of their Methodist hearers, they usually did not adopt the Methodist 'brand.' John Bennet on leaving took with him several societies though most of these failed. He was reduced to being only the pastor of the meeting house at Warburton in Cheshire by the time he died.[32] When John Edwards left in 1754 taking many of his Methodist congregation in Leeds with him, he became minister of a pre-existing Independent chapel and did not seem to have tried to persuade other Methodist societies in the circuit to join him.[33]

On the 1st April 1769 the Cornish-born preacher James Brownfield (1744-1803) had married in Whitby a rich wife who was older than he was. The *Congregational Church History* said his wife was the daughter of William Skinner, after whom Skinner Street in Whitby was named since Skinner was the developer of the area, and that Brownfield began his pastorate of the Church in May 1770. As with Edwards, Brownfield took some Methodist members from Whitby with him when he left the circuit in April 1770, but he did not target other societies in the circuit. He became the minister of the Silver Street Chapel which he built in the middle of Skinner's new development on the fashionable West Cliff, remaining there for many years until his death.[34]

---

[31] 180 preachers who left have known destinations so the percentage was 53.3 who became ministers or clergy. Admittedly ordination did not necessarily lead to preferment.

[32] Valentine, *Bennet* 278.

[33] For Edwards see above Chapter 3 and Bennet MSS; Atmore; Baker, *Grimshaw*. 242, 250; Myles. Edwards had three children by 1752. There were also hints of personal problems with the leading Leeds Methodist Shent, see *JWL* 3: 185 and Bennet MSS.

[34] For Brownfield see *PWHS* 21 (1938) 170; *WMM* 1907: 456; *WJW* 22: 234 n91; Myles; S. Foot, ed, *Methodist Celebration: A Cornish Contribution* (Redruth: Dyllansow Truran, 1988) 23; St Mary's Whitby MS Parish Register at the Library of the Whitby Literary and Philosophical Society; *Whitby West Cliff Congregational Church Year Book 1894-5*. The Parish Register described him as a tailor (1772-3), perhaps his job before he was an itinerant, and schoolmaster (1776-9). His wife was Rebecca

In 1784 there was an attempt by John Atlay and William Eells, who had been excluded from the Legal Hundred by the Deed of Declaration, to set up independent Methodist societies with the Methodist 'brand.' In Yorkshire the Dewsbury Trustees, who had not settled their chapel on Wesley's Deed, much to his annoyance, provided them with one base. William Eells' native northeast provided them with another at North Shields and from 1788 to the early 1790s they struggled to create their own breakaway denomination. They were not successful.[35]

After Wesley's death there were rather more attempted schisms. The radical itinerant Alexander Kilham (1762-1798) with William Thom and others, who had pushed hard for reform after Wesley's death to break immediately with the Church and give laymen more power, formed the Methodist New Connexion in 1797. The New Connexion had solid support in the new towns in the north and the north midlands such as Sheffield and Manchester. Its strength lay among its prosperous laymen such as John Ridgway of Hanley, with much support also among local preachers and Sunday school teachers. Its weakness was the lack of ministerial leadership. Too few existing Methodist itinerant preachers joined it. Kilham himself worked too hard trying to serve all the causes that he had founded and as a result suffered an untimely death in February 1798. The later breakaway movement in Ireland known as the Primitive Wesleyans, though proportionately stronger, had a similar weakness.[36]

There were other less significant schisms which involved Wesley's preachers after his death. John Boyle, the preacher brought up in the Isle of Man detailed in Chapter 10, married a Cornish wife and eventually left to settle with his Cornish relations, keeping a school near Truro. He was to set up a number of societies around him, which became known as 'Boylites.' These were later taken over by the emerging Bible Christian denomination, another Methodist offshoot.[37] With all these defections within Methodism the immediate cause was almost always organization not doctrine.

Schoolmasters

At least thirteen preachers were known to have become schoolmasters, mostly from later cohorts, though the small numbers preclude drawing too many

---

Skinner. Another and less successful attempt was by John Blades who set up the Millenarian Bladites in 1779, but failed, going to America (Tyerman 3: 536-7).

[35] For Atlay see Tyerman 3: 552-8; *PWHS* 5 (1906) 241, 18 (1932) 131; and Chapter 6 above. For Eells see *WMM* 1845: 15; Tyerman 3: 558; *Pawson L* 1: 71-5, 99, 102-3, 118; *WJW* 22: 47 n23, 396n. Atlay seems to have given up by 1791; Eells was buried at Dewsbury in 1792.

[36] For Kilham see Chapter 6 above and Blackwell, *Kilham*. For Ireland see Chapter 11. For the MNC see Ward, *England 1790-1850* 37-9, 85-91, 170-174. Other MNC towns were Halifax, Dudley, Hanley, Newcastle-on-Tyne and Ashton-under-Lyne.

[37] See above Chapter 10.

conclusions from this. Some had taught before entering and were simply returning to their old jobs. Some were either clergymen or Dissenting ministers and were combining it with that profession in order to support themselves. This was true of John Boyle (above) and John Hampson senior and Mark Davis (below). Most were seeking alternative employment, and the learning they had acquired as a result of Wesley's training often meant they were sufficiently skilled to act as a schoolmaster.

John Catermole, a preacher possibly from Norfolk, began to travel between 1756 (when Myles said he entered) and 1762 when he appeared as travelling in nearby Lincolnshire. The author of several useful tracts he was sent to Cornwall but got no further than Kingswood. Some thought him melancholy and Atmore described him as 'a trial to himself' and not acceptable to the people. Catermole was not on the stations between 1768 and 1770, but reappeared as Assistant over Francis Asbury in 1770 in the large Wiltshire South circuit. He withdrew early that year, leaving Asbury with many problems. He had opened a school on Portsmouth Common within the circuit that year, though it is quite possible it was already open or at least that he already had pupils. He continued as a local preacher as long as he was able, appearing in 1784 in Story's notebook of members in the Salisbury circuit as a schoolmaster living in Cross Street in Portsmouth along with his wife Mary, eventually dying in 1799.[38]

John Hampson senior (1730-1795) left the itinerancy twice, the second time being in 1785 when he had been omitted from the Deed of Declaration the previous year. He moved to Southborough in Kent as the Minister of a Dissenting meeting; this did not provide sufficient income and so Wesley obtained for him a post in a Methodist founded Charity School nearby. Not only Wesley but also his brother preachers were concerned for him and he received £12 p.a. from the Preachers' Fund from 1792 onwards until his death. Hampson preached occasionally in Methodist chapels and was described by Pawson ambiguously, and probably deliberately, as 'as much a Methodist as he had ever been.'[39]

Mark Davis was a well educated Irishman from a respectable Dublin family who became an itinerant in 1756. Charles Wesley treated him as a confidant, writing to him about problems with his brother John over separation from the Church. Davis left in 1769, partly because he wearied of travelling on horseback and partly because he disagreed with many of the preachers. By 1772 he had been ordained, was curate at Coychurch near Bridgend in Glamorgan and then, marrying a second time, settled in Leyton near London

---

[38] Two John Catermoles were baptized in Norfolk in the 1740s (*IGI*). Atmore; *JWL* 4: 275-8, 315, 6: 13; Myles; MS Story Notebook 6, Baker Collection, Duke 78; Lyth 304; *Pawson L* 3: 140 n1 quoting Stamp's MSS History of Methodism in Hampshire.

[39] Atmore; *JWL* 4: 132; *Pawson L* 3: 52; *PWHS* 10 (1916) 199.

where he made his living as a schoolmaster until his death.[40]

Physicians

Many of Wesley's preachers travelling on their circuits were practised in caring for the physical as well as the spiritual problems of Methodist members and hearers. They were behaving like the eighteenth century clergy, who were often the sole educated source of remedies in rural areas and felt bound to care for their parishioners. Some branched out for themselves in a large way; Matthew Lowes sold his eponymous 'Lowes' Balsam' in his circuits in the north. Such examples were common because Wesley himself gave this kind of advice. Wesley's letters were full of it. His *Primitive Physick* was one of the most popular publications of the day. Every preacher was expected to familiarize himself with its contents and carry a copy. In 1764 the Moravian pastor at Haverfordwest described 'one of Mr Wesley's journeymen preachers, who carries about an electrifying machine and acts the doctor...' This was probably Thomas Taylor.[41]

In 1768, and even more strongly in 1770, all trading by preachers was prohibited (see Chapter 15). As a result Matthew Lowes, who had sold his balsam for some time while travelling, was forced out. He was born at Whitfield in Northumberland in 1721, became an itinerant in 1751 and in 1756 married Isabella Perkyns from Middleton-in-Teesdale, their growing family eventually extending to eleven children. Between 1758 and 1771 he travelled in the three northern circuits of Yorkshire, Newcastle, and the Dales, though in fact he spent much of all this period in Whitehaven. The new regulation hastened a retirement brought on by his asthma. He went to live in Newcastle where he continued to support himself by making and selling balsam, doing a tour as local preacher that meant two or three sermons each day.[42]

Many preachers who remained itinerants prescribed for different friends. Francis Asbury did so for his host Henry Fry in 1804, while Robert Costerdine carried out an operation to remove a cyst on Robert Derry's head in 1770. If they left, these were skills they might well use. In America William Phoebus,

---

[40] Myles; Crowther; *JWL* 5: 29, 329, 6: 29, 67; *JWJ(C)* 4; 158n, 8: 36, 121; *MM (I)* 1804: 516-20; *Crk* 1: 105; *PWHS* 23 (1941) 7-14. Davis is another example of a leader of a religious society, in his case in Dublin, being persuaded to join the Methodists with his society. John Wesley would have welcomed him back a second time in 1773, but Mather and Olivers objected; see Lloyd, *Early Preachers* DDPr 1/41-8.

[41] D. Madden, 'Experience and the Common Interest of Mankind: The Enlightened Empiricism of John Wesley's Primitive Physick' in *British Journal for 18th Century Studies* 26 (2003), 41. *PWHS* 15 (1926) 63; *EMP* 5: 22; A. W. Hill, *John Wesley among the Physicians* (London: Epworth, 1958). For Taylor in Pembrokeshire see above Chapter 10. Wesley was a great encourager of electrification.

[42] *AM* 1795: 462, 525-9, 577-81; *EMP* 5: 160; Atmore; Tyerman 3: 71-2; *JWL* 4: 56, 163-5, 170, 180, 320, 5: 64, 184, 205, 288-9.

who was born in 1754 in Maryland and entered the itinerancy in 1783, located in 1792 to take up the practice of medicine.[43]

At least twelve preachers became physicians, surgeons, doctors, druggists or 'quacks' of some kind. They included James Kershaw as Doctor or 'quack,' and Dr. John Whitehead who attended Wesley and had a substantial practice in London. Whitehead was even being asked to preach to Conference.[44] George Hudson, who was born at Keighley in 1738, was living at Tong near Bradford in the late 1750s. He began to travel in 1760, but in 1780 Bradburn said 'after many years... he fell into sin, disgraced himself, and was expelled.., confessed, found peace... preaching as ...local preacher in the Otley Circuit' where he died before 1818. His gravestone there described him as 'George Hudson of Middleton, (Ilkley parish) gentleman... eminent... successful... in surgical operations... preaching the gospel in connection with the Wesleyans for half a century...'[45]

It was a period when interest in medicine was growing. Recent research shows medicine was attracting more participants; because society was becoming more prosperous, there was an expanding demand for their services and the consequent rewards increased.[46] It was even possible to combine these professions or jobs. William Tunney was first found in the Derby circuit, probably as a local preacher, before the 9th October 1773. By 1774 he had entered the itinerancy and then travelled until 1781 when he left, parting on good terms with Wesley who wrote to him affectionately. He settled in Nottingham as teacher, doctor and local preacher, carrying out baptisms there from 1787 to 1791, an interesting example of a local preacher acting against Wesley's wishes on the question of baptism during Wesley's lifetime. 'Dr' Tunney was described in 1789 as 'well, keeps a school in Nottingham and does

---

[43] *Asbury Jol* 2: 431. For Costerdine see B. J. Biggs, *Ellen Gretton and her Circle* (Gainsborough: Lincolnshire Methodist Historical Society, 1999) 17, for Phoebus see Barclay, *Methodism 1769-1849* 2: 12-13.

[44] For Kershaw see Atmore. For Whitehead, who became a schoolmaster, then gained an M.D. at Leyden under Dr Barclay, see *WJW* 23: 340 n80. The thirteen only included one from the last cohort.

[45] Others apart from those named here include John Floyd, Thomas Dancer, John Ingham, John Trembath, John Hosmer, Richard Elliott and John Tregortha. For Hudson see *MM* 1818: 51; *PWHS* 22 (1940), 117-8; *Crk* 1: 140-2; *JWJ(C)* 5: 427; Blanshard, *Bradburn* 82; MS Life of Pawson 20a. Hudson was in Ireland in 1760 where he made Margaret Davidson a member. At the 1771 Conference it may well be his signature (no 51) on the preachers' letter. Pawson in Bristol 1772 said 'we found (him) to be a mere trifler.' In Keighley in 1779/80 Bradburn described him as one who 'by his misconduct brought great reproach upon his brethren.'

[46] R. and D. Porter, *Patients' Progress: Doctors and Doctoring in 18th Century England* (Oxford: Polity Press, 1989) 18-22, 126.

pretty well, preaches sometimes, &, and is friendly as usual.'[47]

Farmers

Agriculture was the major industry of the day in which most people worked, even if they worked elsewhere as well. Eleven preachers who had been farmers eventually returned to it. Six of the eleven belonged to the first cohort, like Jonathan Brown referred to in Chapter 6. From the fourth cohort came John Whitley mentioned in Chapter 5. Both had been farmers before they entered and returned to the family farm which other members of the family had been running in their absence. John Trembath combined farming with being a doctor, which was a more profitable way of making a living.[48]

Jonathan Maskew, born at Otley in the West Riding of Yorkshire, had probably by 1744 become William Grimshaw's handyman, living with him at Sowdens in Haworth, acting as a farmer in looking after the glebe, dressing Grimshaw, travelling with him and preaching. He preached widely throughout the north and was then called into the itinerancy by John Wesley. Maskew travelled for ten years and left in 1759 when he married Mrs Margaret Clegg of Dainhead near Rochdale, settling down again as a farmer. He continued to preach over the whole area from Halifax to Rochdale where he was well known. For a time he became the minister of a Calvinistic society in the area, but eventually he renewed his old doctrines and ceased to serve the Calvinists. He died aged 81 in 1793.[49] There were many different kinds of farmers, varying from small holders like William Darney and hill farmers like Maskew and Brown, via tenants like Whitley or yeomen like William Allwood, to relatively well-off men like Orpe.

Shopkeepers

There were many businessmen described specifically as shopkeepers amongst the preachers. The town of Redruth provided an interesting example in Francis Woolf. Born in 1740 he had become a wigmaker, married and had four or five children of whom two were alive when he went out to preach in 1768. In 1782 Woolf was in poor health and retired from the itinerant ministry to Redruth,

---

[47] Myles; Nottingham Methodist Baptismal Register in Nottingham County Record Office; *JWL* 6: 342, 378, 7: 42, 69; Lloyd, *Papers of Bardsley* BRD1/26; London Stewards Book 1760s-1804, Hanby letter MARC PLP 48.55.11 both at MARC.

[48] Others not mentioned in this section were Joseph Jones, and John Hall, both from the first cohort and the Irishman George Henderson of the fifth cohort. For Trembath see *WJW* 20: 96 n68, 188 n8, 205, 358, 23: 250 n58, 26: 589-91.

[49] *AM* 1780; 317; *MM* 1798: 473-8, 510-4, 567-71, 603-7, 1802: 320; *EMP* 1: 244, 4: 198-227; Atmore; Baker, *Grimshaw* 98-9, 148-50, 170, 248-53; *GHR* 71-4, 83-5; Valentine, *Bennet* 189 n53; Valentine, *Mirror of the Soul* 167, 183-4; Manchester Circuit Account Book.

having lost two wives in four years, though a four year old daughter survived. Wigs were out of fashion so he joined his brother-in-law's drapery business in Fore Street and married again. Richard Andrew, another Methodist, had married Woolf's sister Jane in 1760; no children had survived so Woolf and his family represented a future for the business. By 1791 Francis Woolf was one of the leading inhabitants of the town and his brother-in-law had retired. He was a local preacher and had been Society Steward, class leader and trustee for the flourishing Methodist society at different times. He had five more children and by his death in 1805 had made enough money to leave the four children who survived him two houses or business premises each, in addition to bequests of money. Right to the end of his life he continued to visit as class leader, calling on a dying Methodist just before his own death.[50]

There was a range of different kinds of shopkeepers among those preachers who left, including at least two grocers, Thomas Colbeck and James Oddie. Colbeck had inherited his shop in Low Street in Keighley. It remained there in the care of others when he went off preaching, and by the early 1750s he had settled down as Circuit Steward, not preaching outside the large Haworth circuit. He was Grimshaw's close associate and executor. He married the 'like-minded' Mrs Sarah Sharp of nearby Otley in 1765. When he died in 1779 his wife inherited the shop and after five years married another retired preacher, James Oddie. When the marriage did not work she returned to Otley, leaving Oddie still running the shop.[51] Michael Fenwick and William Shent were barbers, Shent with a Leeds shop on Briggate. Other shopkeepers included James Wild, with a shop in Sheffield, Peter Mill, the hatter and hosier in Hull,[52] Daniel Bumstead, the wine merchant of Bishopsgate Street in London, and Martin Rodda, the liquor seller in Manchester. Richard Burdsall was to be a successful hardware merchant in York.[53] As several had run shops before they became preachers it was easy for them to resume their previous occupation. This was the case with William Roberts who settled as a bookseller in Tiverton, and Jasper Winscom, the successful Winchester ironmonger and haberdasher.[54]

---

[50] Woolf, *'dear Franky'*.

[51] The marriages are in the *IGI*. Baker, *Grimshaw* 253, 260; *MM* 1801: 432; *WJW* 20: 241 n31, 459; Lyth 304; Copy of Philip Hardcastle MSS in Baker Collection, Duke; *DOMBI*; MSS Laycock's Notebook in Keighley Library 137; Valentine, *Mirror of the Soul* 158; Atmore; *GHR* 360-9; *Pawson L* 1: 73-5.

[52] For Fenwick see the 1760 part letter to CW MARC EMV 143 and see *DOMBI* for Shent. For Wild's shop see *AM* 1780: 335-6. Mill retired for health reasons in 1795 and went to Hull (*MM* 1807: 337-44).

[53] For Bumstead see Atmore, for Rodda see Chapter 12, for Burdsall's shop built into the York city wall opposite Bootham Bar see H. Lee, *Ploughshare of Prayer: A Memoir of the Lyth Family of York in the Nineteenth Century* (Leeds: WHS Yorks, 1987) 2-6.

[54] For Roberts (1728-1797) see Atmore; Hayman 18-21; for Winscom see Chapter 17.

Other Businesses

At least ten men went out to set up their own business. There is little information about what the concern was, because usually the *Minutes* say only 'entered into business.' Some were shopkeepers like Jonathan Hern who, after spending twenty-two years as an itinerant, set himself up in Barnard Castle when he was expelled. Sometimes the business failed. This happened to William Underhill in Birmingham, later employed by his fellow Methodist Julius Hardy as a traveller for his button making enterprise. It was presumably also the case with Peter Dean, whose concern in London was unsuccessful. The Irish preacher James Wilson left in 1787, 'entered into business' and then emigrated to America after this failed.[55] William Hitchens or Kitchings was a hatter in Bristol. Thomas Rankin, Wesley's Superintendent in America, had been a Supernumerary in London for some time, supported partly by his wife. When he left in 1796 he 'entered into a small business of a commercial nature.' At least two, John Oliver and James Oddie, had shares in ships before they left which might well have provided income when they left.[56]

John Tregortha was a Cornishman who travelled from 1786 to 1790. When he left he set up as a bookseller and druggist in Burslem in the Potteries, which had been his second circuit. In 1796 he began printing as well, for Sunday Schools, Wesleyan Methodists and later even the Primitive Methodists. He was a local preacher and also Treasurer of the Wesleyan Methodist Sunday School in Burslem. He died in 1821, leaving behind him a tradition in Burslem that nothing was as 'old as Tregortha.'[57]

Many returned to the enterprise in which they had worked before they entered, or, as with many of the shopkeepers, maintained the shops thanks to their wives and other members of the family; sometimes they were half itinerants, travelling for several months and then returning. James Thwayte was a jeweller and silver-smith in London who began to preach in 1758. He travelled with Wesley frequently and also by himself, preaching and meeting the societies. His 'Labours were crowned with considerable success,' but Wesley never gave him a circuit. In 1764 he was one of those preachers who were ordained by Erasmus and began to administer communion. As a result he was expelled on the 7th February 1765. He remained settled with his establishment in London but also became an Independent minister. Later the

---

[55] For Dean, Underhill and Hern see Chapter 15 above for why they left. For Wilson see *Asbury Jol* 1: 766 n77.

[56] For Rankin see Chapters 12 and 19. For Hitchens see Atmore and *JWL* 5: 178. John Oliver (entered 1759, left 1784) needs to be distinguished from the better known hymn writer Thomas Olivers. The information on shares in ships come from Tyerman 3: 71.

[57] Myles; R. Simms, ed, *Bibliotheca Staffordienses* (Lichfield: Lomax, 1894); *PWHS* 5 (1906) 190-2, 22 (1939) 15-20; Foot, *Celebration* 23. I owe the Simms reference to John Anderson. James Lawton also became a printer.

business failed.[58] Two others had concerns in London. Samuel Tooth was a builder, timber merchant and undertaker, and William Holland ran a painting business in Basinghall Street.[59] Thomas Broadbent was a corn merchant in King's Lynn and Richard Henderson kept a lunatic asylum at Bristol, according to Atmore 'based on the principle of love.' William Jenkins, who had originally trained as an architect, went back to that profession.[60]

Others – the Wide Variety

Preachers had come from all levels of society and from many different types of jobs. This was mirrored in the similar variety to which they went when they left. Some had offices, sometimes within Wesley's movement; Matthew Errington worked for nearly forty years as the Book Steward at the Orphan House at Newcastle. Robert Bell went back to his former occupation as an Excise Officer.[61] William Briggs was an officer of the Custom House in London. The Irish preacher John Murray became the steward for a lady's estate in Ireland. John Gibbs became Master of the Workhouse at Warminster.[62] However, there was also clearly a tendency to move into the professions; Arthur Kershaw became a journalist. Others who had been craftsmen moved into trade or business; the former carpenter Samuel Tooth became a builder and timber merchant. Richard Williams became a mine captain in Cornwall.[63] But there were still some who belonged to the lower strata of society, like the smallholder and the hedger already mentioned. There were craftsmen, the carpenter Philip Embury or the skinner William Linnell.[64] John Haime became a button-mould maker. Thomas Hardwick went back to being a stone-cutter, as did Francis Scott to being a joiner.[65] Nebuchadnezzar Lee enlisted in the army.

---

[58] The quotation is from an anonymous document, possibly by Myles, in *PWHS* 22 (1940) 140-3. For Thwayte see also *PWHS* 38: (1971) 85, 22: (1940) 140-43; *JWL* 4: 287, 290-1; Myles; W. Wilson, *History and Antiquities of Dissenting Churches and Meeting Houses in London* 4 vols (London: Edwards, 1808-14) 4: 319.

[59] For Holland see Chapter 2, for Tooth, who travelled less than one year but built City Road, and whose oldest daughter was the executrix of Charles Wesley's daughter Sally see *WJW* 23: 191n and Stevenson's *City Road*.

[60] For Broadbent see *WMM* 1845: 711; *Cirplan* 12: 4 Issue 92 Lent 2001 100-1; Will in Norfolk CRO. For Henderson, who left in 1771, see Atmore; *WJW* 23: 224 n33, and for Jenkins see Chapter 10.

[61] For Errington see *WJW* 26: 86, 480, and for Bell *WMM* 1826: 96/7; *JWL* 5: 70, 163.

[62] For Briggs see Stevenson, *City Road* 30, 38, for Murray see *Pawson L* 3: 22, for Gibbs see *City Road Magazine* 1876: 298.

[63] For Kershaw see *JWL* 6: 51, 71; *DNB*. For Williams see *JWL* 7: 201-2, 257.

[64] For Embury see Chapter 12, for Linnell see *WHS Cul* 40 (1997) 15-17.

[65] For Haime see B. J. Biggs, *The Wesleys and the Early Dorset Methodists* (Gillingham: Woodsorrel, 1987); for Hardwick see G. Lloyd, *Methodist Biographical Index* (Manchester: MARC, 2004) 1: 168, for Scott see *WJW* 20: 102 n87.

Samuel Rogers and Victory Purdy both returned to being the Kingswood colliers they had been before.[66] John Wilkinson resumed his shoemaking. Benjamin Beanland was typical of these at the bottom of the social pyramid, being described as very poor for many years and spending some time in prison for debt. He died very suddenly in great obscurity.[67]

Common Patterns

Most of those leaving who are known remained Methodists, as can be seen from the number who continued to act as local preachers and leaders. Even if they went elsewhere they usually maintained good relations, as Pilmore did in America. The famous names like Bennet and Kilham left with great publicity, but most left without public knowledge. Even Robert Lindsay from Ireland, who had served as an itinerant in two continents for thirteen years, was reported after he left to have settled in the East Indies where he led a class.[68] Returning to their previous jobs was a strong tendency, true not only for those who were clergymen, but for farmers, teachers, craftsmen, shopkeepers, and many others. Out of the 81 whose jobs are known both before and after being itinerant, over half 45 (56%) took up the same occupation afterwards though this was not always possible. Francis Woolf found it necessary to take a similar job because his original one had changed with the pressures of fashion.

The society in which they lived was one of many people doing several jobs at once or doing seasonal jobs. It is not surprising therefore that when they ceased to be itinerant preachers they went back to combining several different jobs and/or changed jobs frequently, sometimes with the seasons. David Trathen had lost his farming job and was on the streets hedging and ditching when he turned to selling medicines. For most, such detail of information is simply not available, but he was probably one of many in a mobile society going to whatever occupation would bring in a little money.[69]

---

[66] For Lee see *PWHS* 9 (1914) 166-7; for Rogers see Myles 38; for Purdy see J. B. Edwards, *Victory Purdy 'the Kingswood Collier'* (Bristol: New Room, 1984).

[67] For Wilkinson see Laycock's Notebook BK 15/1/3/18c; for Beanland see *Pawson L* 3: 24 and Atmore.

[68] Irish *Minutes* 1867 and see note 3 above.

[69] *WJW* 23: 250 n58. For the society see Chapter 3 above.

CHAPTER 17

Preachers Returning to the Itinerancy

'Charles Wesley was of a very suspicious temper... John Wesley had far more charity in judging of persons in general (except the rich and the great) than his brother had.'
Pawson.[1]

Introduction

Of the 802 preachers who entered in Wesley's lifetime 426 left (53%), as shown in the previous two chapters. Of these leavers seventy preachers returned, at over 16% a relatively high percentage of those who left. One reason for these figures, particularly in the early days, was the lack of differentiation between travelling and local preachers and the relative ease of moving 'out' or 'in.' As time went on this differentiation became clearer and changes happened less as a proportion of the total number of preachers. A factor working in the opposite direction was that from 1765 Conference *Minutes* were printed each year so becoming easier to show that the individual preacher left or remained.

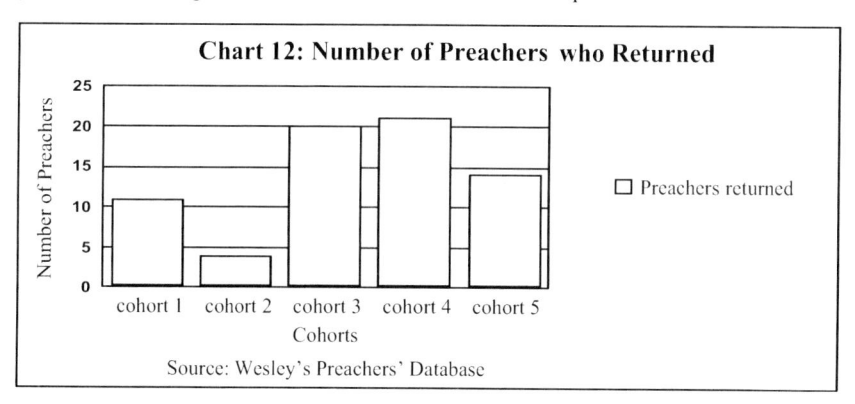

Chart 12: Number of Preachers who Returned

Source: Wesley's Preachers' Database

---

[1] Pawson MS Memoir of Whitehead quoted Tyerman 3: 297. Earlier versions of parts of this chapter have appeared as J. H. Lenton, 'John Wesley and the travelling preachers' JRULMB 85: 2 and 3 (2005) 99-110 and 'Charles Wesley and the preachers' in K. G. Newport and T. A. Campbell, eds, *Charles Wesley: Life, Literature and Legacy* (Peterborough: Epworth, 2007) 88-108.

Chart 12 on the previous page shows the numbers of those returned, arranged by their cohort of entry. It is based on Table 19 in Appendix One. Table 20 there also shows very few returning before 1765, and the lack of printed *Minutes* before then was probably the major reason.

Why did preachers return as such a high proportion of those who left? One important reason was the personality of John Wesley and it is fair to say that the large number of those who came back must show his tolerance in their being allowed to return. Almost two thirds of those who returned (43) left again. The fact that so many departed after being allowed to return shows John was probably too lenient. There were even a select few who re-entered a second time. Some, like Michael Fenwick whose life is detailed below, may have left three times or even more.

Not everyone agreed with John's policy of allowing men to return easily. In particular Charles Wesley, his younger brother and co-leader at least for the first twenty years, felt that John's standards were too low and many should not have been allowed to travel in the first place. Charles was often the main reason men left, just as John was the reason they were allowed back. Charles was not alone in his views for many later critics, both inside and outside the connexion and historians to the present, have felt the same about too many preachers being allowed to stay or return. Pawson, who had much personal experience of John Wesley allowing men to remain who should have been thrust out much earlier, expressed his views in the quotation above.[2] Charles was perhaps more hard-headed here than John and, despite being seen as the more emotional of the two brothers, was in this instance at least the more practical. This chapter will focus on these men who left and returned, their relationships with the two brothers and John Wesley's leniency. How far was Charles a major factor in driving men out? Was John in fact too relaxed in allowing men to remain or to return when they should have been barred for ever?

Charles and John

The Importance of Charles

Charles has typically been seen as the inspired hymn writer and little more. Modern historians have been pointing to his other skills, not least his preaching and leadership of the movement in the early years.[3] On the 15th March 1760 the itinerant preacher Francis Gilbert wrote to Charles Wesley about his fellow travelling preachers, describing them as those 'who are in Connection with your Brother & You.' For Gilbert, as for most Methodists of the period,

---

[2] This was in a private document after Wesley's death. Pawson's views on John Wesley were complex and can be read in Tyerman and in an important article by Rack 'Wesley Observed' *PWHS* 49 (1993) 11-17.

[3] G. Lloyd, *Charles Wesley and the Struggle for Methodist Identity* (Oxford: OUP, 2007).

preachers and ordinary members alike, the two brothers were of equal importance and the preachers were best defined as being in connexion with *both* of them. Later, certainly from the nineteenth century perspective, Charles may have been seen as less important than his elder brother, but not in 1760.[4]

John Wesley later declared he had invited the preachers to be his 'sons in the Gospel.'[5] However, the first reference to 'sons' in John's published *Journal* shows it was his brother Charles who was acting the more important fatherly role. On March 8th 1741 John wrote to the preacher John Cennick 'You came to Kingswood upon my brother's sending for you. You served under *him* as a son.' It had been Charles who had begun the whole process of encouraging lay itinerant preachers, or at least that is the implication of this early example. This was probably slightly earlier than the story about Maxfield dated by Baker as January or March 1741.[6] In the previous year Charles had taken Maxfield on a preaching tour with him, so helping to train one of the most important lay preachers *before* John's recognition of Maxfield as a preacher. It was Charles who was the pioneer in Cornwall and the first to preach outside in Dublin.[7] During the 1740s he travelled shoulder to shoulder with the itinerants, suffering persecution with them as least as much as John did. Charles was the better preacher, the more fiery evangelist, the one who stayed on to face persecution at Wednesbury or Cork where John was usually even then sticking to what already seemed his predetermined timetable. But it is certain it was John as organizer who decided the stations of the preachers, moved them, and invited them to Conference. In time it became clear that John was the more important. For fifty years John travelled throughout the Connexion, carrying on a correspondence with individuals in every circuit, checking up on the preachers. John was very much the leader of Methodism and this is shown not least by his work with the preachers. Charles's place in the movement may have been second to that of John in the later years, but not necessarily always at the beginning. When the preachers wrote to Charles, they usually ended the letter by describing themselves as 'your affectionate son in the Gospel,' exactly the same as in their correspondence with John.

---

[4] MS letter of Francis Gilbert at Bristol to CW MARC PLP MAM 2/54. Francis Gilbert (1725-79) was the younger brother of Nathaniel Gilbert, planter of Antigua. He fled to England where he became a Methodist and began to travel as a preacher in 1758. He had money and probably acted as a local preacher after 1764 when he was living first in Kendal and later in Chester.
[5] Lenton, *My Sons* 3.
[6] The story is examined in detail in Chapter 2. *WJW* 19: 186. The emphasis is mine.
[7] July 15th 1743 in Cornwall to John's August 29th. Pearce, *Wesleys in Cornwall* 28, 69. In Ireland John went first on the 9th August 1747, but only for a fortnight and preached inside. Charles was first to preach on Oxmantown Green and stayed from September 9th to March 20th. He was also first to travel and preach inland in Ireland and was the real founder of Wesleyan Methodism in Norwich in 1754 (Bellamy, *Wheatley* 172-8).

Was John Wesley Too Lenient?

There has been a controversy in Methodist historiography from the eighteenth century about Wesley's lenience towards the preachers. Charles Wesley particularly, but also Methodist preachers such as Pawson, regarded John's standards for the laymen he accepted as full time itinerant 'Sons in the Gospel' as too low. John Wesley was prepared to forgive and allow those who left to return to the itinerancy, without demanding any more of them. On the other hand, many preachers who left and also some outside the movement regarded him as often too much of a dictator, 'Pope John' consulting only his particular friends and even them insufficiently. Wesley certainly had an iron will.[8] As Vivian Green neatly put it, he was 'granite in aspic.'[9] He had a strong conviction of being always in the right, rarely admitting mistakes even if he had changed his mind. Historians from the contemporary John Hampson onwards have complained about his refusing to alter his opinions. Hampson, who with his father resented Wesley's treatment, said when individuals opposed Wesley 'He treated them as the mariners treated Jonah, he threw them overboard or.... to borrow his phraseology he "commended them to God."'[10] Pawson said the same 'He had some very great weaknesses. His natural temper was extremely warm and he had not always power over it, but on many occasions broke out sometimes to the grief of those who loved him. In the government of the preachers... he was extremely fond of power... He would never suffer it to be called into question, much less would he share it.'[11]

After Wesley's death Pawson pointed out his vulnerability to those who flattered him 'Some who knew him well thought he loved it. His ear was certainly too attentive to hear his own praise. Many there were who took advantage of this great weakness... deceived and misled him and greatly injured others...' Joseph Benson, as a young tutor at Kingswood in 1769, had a similar view of Wesley

> But so it is, and so it has ever been: you have had the misfortune to mistake your friends and enemies. Whoever has made a point (in order to gain your favour) to contradict you in nothing, but professed implicitly to follow your direction and abide by your decision, especially if they added thereto the warmest expressions of regard for you and told you a tale of their being saved from sin and perfected in love, they never failed to gain your favour in an high degree... On the other hand, whoever... could not in conscience acquiesce in your bare ipse dixit but have

---

[8] J. D. Walsh, *John Wesley, 1703-1791: a Bicentennial Tribute* (London: Dr Williams' Trust, 1995) 8.
[9] V. H. H. Green, *John Wesley* (London: Nelson, 1964) 127.
[10] J. Hampson (junior), *Memoirs of the late Rev. John Wesley, A.M.* (Sunderland: Graham, 1791) 107-200. This is increasingly seen as a relatively fair and unbiased contemporary account by a former preacher.
[11] *PWHS* 49 (1993) 17.

believed it their duty to call in question some things you have advanced, ... have in general stood low in your esteem.[12]

Benson had been educated for the Anglican ministry. He had standing outside the connexion and had been appointed to Trevecca by Lady Huntingdon so he was able to see more deeply than the majority of the preachers. He had clearly criticized Wesley to his face and was paying the penalty.

Early 1750s

Charles Purging the Preachers

During the 1740s the order of Methodist itinerants was gradually being established. Men came and went, usually without any record. The whole principle of paid, full-time itinerancy was still to be established. They preached, or did not, without necessary recognition either by the Wesleys or by Conference which itself was still to be properly agreed. In general though Charles doubtless had strong views on the suitability of the preachers, he felt that these were shared by his brother whose travels he also shared.

Early in the 1750s this began to change. Conference became held regularly and the preachers expected to attend it. John Wesley embarked on ever widening tours which meant he saw any one society or preacher (and Charles) less frequently. When Charles Wesley married in 1749 and settled in Bristol later that year, his relationship with the preachers and John started to change. This was inevitable as Charles' domestic situation had an effect on his travels and therefore on his previously close engagement with the preachers in the work of the Revival. The early period of Charles' ministry and his relationship with the preachers and his brother had come to a close. From 1751 onwards Charles took it on himself, with John's sometimes reluctant agreement, to purge the preachers, examining most and turning quite a few out of the itinerancy. Charles' predilection for the Church of England meant that this was the main focus of his concern in relation to the preachers for much of the next forty years.[13]

This first happened at a Conference Charles Wesley held at Leeds in September 1751. Assembled with him and two other clergymen (Grimshaw and Milner) were eleven preachers, including Nelson, Shent and Bennet, so most of the leading preachers in the north. According to Charles' account the meeting began with a hymn

---

[12] *PWHS* 49 (1993) 17; *JWL* 5: 157-59, 164-65, Benson to Wesley late November 1769. The reply by Wesley on December 3rd is also important for how Wesley saw himself.

[13] There is more detail on this in Lenton, 'Charles Wesley and the Preachers'. See also Charles' MS Preachers (1751) at MARC. Maldwyn Edwards suggested in *Family Circle* (London: Epworth, 1946) 110-111 that Charles was influenced by his oldest brother Samuel who died in 1739.

Arise thou Jealous GOD arise
  Thy sifting power exert,
Look through us with thy flaming eyes
  And search out every heart.

Our inmost souls thy Spirit knows,
  And let him now display
Whom thou hast for thy glory chose
  And purge the rest away

Charles then continued

> After prayer I began, without design, to speak of the qualifications, work and trials of a preacher; and what I thought requisite in men who act in concert. As to preliminaries and principles we all agreed... At Three we met again. But first I talked to Mortimer, whom I admitted; and to William Darney, whom I rejected.[14]

Darney was to be the first of many preachers who were suspended by Charles from the itinerancy. He soon returned, though his career was to be chequered and he probably eventually left the itinerancy but not Methodism in 1768. Charles said that at the same time Webb and Trathen 'came afterwards but were not admitted.' Thomas Webb, who had preached alongside Charles Wesley in Wednesbury and elsewhere in 1744, was permanently excluded, apparently for preaching Calvinism. David Trathen, a Cornishman accused of preaching predestinarianism, was also forced to leave at this time by John Wesley, but for his actions rather than his beliefs; at least according to Bennet's account.[15]

Seven others were similarly purged then, in addition to Webb, Trathen and Darney.[16] How well did Charles know the details of the lives, beliefs and conduct of those whom he was removing? Charles named one preacher as 'James' Watson, though the only Watson was a Matthew Watson. He was a local preacher in Leeds scarcely known to Charles, which is perhaps why he had difficulty in even getting his name correct. Ten preachers were purged by Charles in 1751, which out of the sixty-nine or so available to the brothers was a high proportion. No wonder John let at least five, possibly six, back. Charles'

---

[14] *CWJ* 1: 584-5. For Darney see *WJW* 20: 171 n12, 26: 537. See the more detailed account of the purging in 1751-2 by Heitzenrater in Newport and Campbell, *Charles Wesley* 486-514.

[15] For Webb (who sometimes appears as John Webb) see *AM* 1779: 315; *WJW* 20; 111 n15, 26: 487 n15; *CWJ* 2: 345, 348-9; Valentine, *Mirror of the Soul* 215. For Trathen see *CWJ* 1: 583, Valentine, *Bennet* 147n, 174-5, 259, 265; Valentine, *Mirror of the Soul* 154, 159, 188-94, 215.

[16] The seven were Thomas Westell, James Wheatley, Eleazer Webster, Robert Gillespie, 'James Watson,' Michael Fenwick and John Maddern.

argument was that 'the tinner, barber, thatcher, forgot himself with his business and immediately set up for a gentleman,' and therefore needed to be purged. He was not always right.[17]

An example of one preacher who was allowed back within a year was Robert Gillespie who had been an itinerant since 1748. He had been expelled by Charles in 1751 but was allowed to return, presumably by John, in 1752. Little is known about him apart from the letter Charles wrote to Bennet

> Your last helped on the work of God for which he has sent me into his vineyard at this time: and it supplied me with more abundant proof of R.G.'s utter unworthiness to preach the Gospel. I have accordingly stopped him, and shall tomorrow send him back to his proper business. A friend of ours (without God's counsel) made a preacher of a tailor. I with God's help shall make a tailor of him again.
> You will not (I am persuaded) rejoice in evil, but in evil prevented and good secured by this thing. And pray earnestly for me, that the Lord may guide and direct me in my most important concern - to purge the Church, beginning with the labourers.
> For this end, I say again in God's name, come and help me. On [the] 6th of September I trust to see Leeds: on Wednesday, September 11th to meet in conference as many of the preachers as can be got together. Bring all you can; and give notice everywhere I have silenced another scandalous preacher, and sent a third back to his trade.

It is clear Gillespie did not stay purged for he is found preaching in the Isle of Wight in the Wiltshire circuit in 1753.[18] Though Charles removed some of the preachers, it would appear that John allowed many of those spurned by Charles to return, so Charles' effect on preacher numbers was more limited than he would have wished and the high rate of preachers returning was part of the complex relationship of the two Methodist leaders at this point.

Purging the preachers should, of course, be seen as part of Charles' high view of their calling. This is supported in this last letter by his clear belief that

---

[17] For Fenwick see below. Matthew Watson was assisting in one place in the 1747 and 1751 *Minutes*, listed after Shent and before Appleyard, so local to Leeds. He was invited by Charles to the September Conference at Leeds with a note. He was still preaching in the area in 1753, 1756, and 1758/9. Nelson said he was buried on the 10th November 1763 having preached 17 years (*GHR* 80, 256). Charles' notebook (mostly 1751) DDCW 8/5 in *CWP* II 87-8 shows ten excluded. The five definitely allowed back were Michael Fenwick, Robert Gillespie (details below), William Darney, Thomas Westell and John Maddern. The doubtful one was Eleazer Webster, listed as a 'chief Local Preacher' in the Haworth circuit in the 1755 *Minutes*. Trathen, Wheatley and Webb did not return. Watson was not a travelling preacher.

[18] F. Baker, *Charles Wesley as Revealed by his Letters* (London: Epworth, 1948) 86. See also Heitzenrater 185, which makes it clear 'RG' was Robert Gillespie. *WJW* 26: 530 n15 provides the Isle of Wight reference.

the recipient Bennet, a lay preacher himself, would only want to help Charles. Relationships between the brothers at this point were uneasy. On the one hand John wanted Charles to travel more; on the other Charles, when he did travel, was using his power to purge below-standard preachers whom John later allowed to return. No wonder each regarded the other with some concern.

Preachers Administering Communion

John Wesley found a main cause of controversy with his preachers was over Methodism's relationship with the Church of England and whether the preachers should administer Communion. Charles Wesley cared even more than his brother about this and felt John forgave men too easily on the issue. John Wesley's compromise, to remain inside the Church and encourage his followers to attend her sacraments while breaking her rules on lay preaching and preaching in other parishes, brought conflict in every generation. Each cohort of preachers included some who could not follow Wesley's logic and felt that they should be able to administer Communion as much as any erring local cleric. They were trusted by Wesley to preach the gospel and to look after the pastoral needs of the societies. Why could he not trust them with this as well? Their congregations often wanted it. Certainly, as Charles Wesley said, the more ambitious of the preachers aspired to it.

In October 1754 Charles Perronet administered Communion in London while Thomas Walsh did the same in Reading. Both were strong favourites of John, who without Charles' pressure on him would have agreed that they should do this. Though Perronet was forced to leave, Walsh remained a travelling preacher until his death in 1759. Even Charles Perronet was allowed by John Wesley to return in 1755 before being forced out on the same issue in 1756. Again in 1760 three preachers administered Communion in Norwich. Again Charles pressed John to expel them. It was only after Grimshaw insisted also that John eventually acted at Conference and the preachers concerned agreed not to do it any more.[19]

There was then a pause on this for over twenty years. John Wesley eventually gave way over ordaining preachers, first for America (1784) and then the West Indies and Scotland.[20] America and the West Indies did not immediately affect Methodist practice in England because few preachers returned from there in Wesley's lifetime; but several had returned from Scotland to England within a couple of years and more followed. Preachers like Pawson and Hanby, who had been ordained for Scotland, came back to England and found they were refused permission to administer Communion, as asked by local Methodist society members. They were annoyed. Thomas Hanby was in open revolt, prepared to be 'martyred' for his beliefs, secure in

---

[19] Baker, *Charles Wesley* 92, 102-03; Lenton in *JRULMB* 85 (2003) 101-2.
[20] For much more detail on ordination see Chapter 18.

the knowledge that Wesley could not survive indefinitely and his removal would secure general administration by the preachers. Hanby, despite directly opposing Wesley's wishes, survived to become one of the presidents after Wesley's death. Had it been twenty or thirty years earlier Charles Wesley would probably have seen to it that John expelled him.

Examples of Leniency

Leniency over Time

For John Wesley there were far more examples of leniency than harshness when dealing with his ordinary preachers as opposed to his possible rivals like Bennet.[21] An early incident is contained in the *Minutes* of the first Irish Conference in 1752. 'Is there any objection to the behaviour of Thomas Kead? A. He hath been charged with idleness and lightness; but we are convinced both those charges are false.' It is not clear whether Wesley's judgement on Kead was sound. On the one hand Kead was later responsible for the important conversion of John Smith and the formation of a society in 1758 in Cootehill, Co. Cavan. On the other, when Kead was in Dublin in July 1760 filling in for Peter Jaco, the leading Irish layman William Lunell thought he was responsible for the congregation being 'thinner than ever.'[22]

The suggestion of John's leniency, according to John Kent, was particularly true of the 1760s when 'Charles Wesley constantly complained to his brother about what he held to be the low quality of the majority of itinerants. He accused John of preferring 'grace' (which in this case meant the ability to obtain conversions) to 'gifts', by which Charles meant administrative and intellectual qualities, combined with strength of character.'[23] It was also true of the 1750s. I suspect that Charles was more interested in educational attainment and potential rather than the administrative and evangelical qualities more appreciated by John. 'Grace' for John also included the determination to innovate and persevere despite the hostility which greeted them in so many places, a determination found in some of John's favourites such as Mather or Adam Clarke.

It is difficult to discover differences in standards between the decades. The low figure in Table 19 in Appendix One of those who returned from cohort 2 does not mean necessarily that Wesley was being less lenient with them. Certainly it was the smallest cohort in the first place and therefore would be expected to produce the fewest number anyway. It could simply mean fewest preachers left and that might mean higher standards. The higher numbers in the 1760s were partly because of the growing body of itinerants, but also was the result of the printing of annual *Minutes* from 1765 which provide far more

---

[21] For Bennet see Valentine, *Mirror of the Soul*.
[22] *Crk* 1: 120-3; *PWHS* 16 (1928) 17; *PPIM* 1, 3; Rowell's notes in *Minutes* 1: 716.
[23] Kent, *Wesley and the Wesleyans* 65.

details of both leavers and those re-entering. To the end of his life John Wesley was lenient with his preachers about returning to the itinerancy, and indeed may even have become more lenient as time went on. Certainly the figures in Table 19 seem to indicate this. Of this total of seventy who returned, forty-four (63%) were married, This was in line with what might be expected in view of the lack of evidence for many of those who left, whether or not they returned.[24] At least twenty-eight (40%) were known to be local preachers while they were not travelling. In fact the real number and percentage was probably much higher, as for leavers where over half of those known were local preachers.[25]

Most preachers (thirty-eight or 54%) were out of the itinerancy for two years or less. These had frequently experienced a health problem which cleared up with rest. Others who were punished for breaking the marriage regulations or for other reasons were often allowed back soon, another example of Wesley's habitual leniency on this subject. Thomas Cooper, who entered the itinerancy in 1781 though still On Trial, became engaged in 1785 to a local girl, Ann Pawninton of Mistley in his Colchester circuit; he asked Wesley to let him stay a third year, rather than go the three hundred miles to Cornwall where he was being sent. When Wesley refused, Cooper left, married Ann and preached in a chapel built for him at Manningtree. However, seventeen months later by January 1787 he was helping the local Assistant Joseph Algar and had been reconciled to Wesley. Cooper then took his wife in February to the Birmingham circuit, where he was re-stationed in August. In 1788 she died leaving a young child. Cooper remarried locally and travelled for another thirty years.[26]

Of the preachers who returned, the majority, forty-three (or 61%) left the itinerancy again, while twenty-five (36%) died in the work. There were two for whom it is unclear whether they left or not, and these will be considered in the next chapter on retirement and superannuation, because it is not certain whether they superannuated or left. The logic of this high percentage of leavers a second time is that Wesley was too lenient and should not have readmitted them to the itinerancy, since the problems Wesley had already identified had not changed. David Evans and Thomas Wride were both preachers whom Wesley expelled or forced to leave but allowed back within one or two years. In each case this caused problems for their fellow-itinerants. Evans had to be expelled again. Wride appears to have remained despite the continuing problems, but his colleagues must have wished he had not been allowed back. Hugh Saunderson

---

[24] Similar to the 65% in Table 10 for the preachers overall and the 81% reported above in Chapter 6 for those who died in the work. Fifteen of the preachers who returned were of Irish origin (21%), four from Scotland (6%) and two Americans (3%) which again compares well with Chapter 3 above.

[25] Chapter 16 above.

[26] For twenty (29%) the gap was only one year; for another eighteen (26%) the gap was between one and two years. For Cooper see *WMM* 1835: 1-14, 81-92; *JWL* 7: 136, 363, 8: 87; Tyerman BMM.

and Jasper Winscom were also shown leniency by Wesley. In Winscom's case after Wesley's death Conference got rid of him by asking him to go to a circuit in faraway Norfolk, so leading to his resignation.[27]

Wesley became more lenient over time, as Table 19 which deals with those preachers who returned shows. From 1765 to 1790, Wesley's last Conference, the numbers of those returning grew steadily. In Wesley's later years there are other examples of increasing leniency. Thomas Hanby at the 1775 Conference was an experienced preacher with over twenty years travel, known for speaking his mind such as later when he refused to obey Wesley in using his ordination in Scotland for administering communion in England. He commented that year 'we have had a very loving and agreeable Conference and I think Mr. W(esley) is not near so overbearing as he was.'[28]

John Fenwick

There are two other interesting examples, the two Fenwicks, John and Michael, who both left and returned, in Michael's case several times.[29] They may have been related, but none of the sources say or suggest this. John Fenwick was a man of property from Newcastle who entered about 1750 and left soon after 1758. In eight years he had travelled in Ireland (twice), Cornwall, Bristol, East Anglia and Yorkshire, as well as his native Newcastle, journeys quite typical for the early Methodist itinerant. His letter from Bristol in late 1758 to John Wesley has survived in which he reported to John about the situation at Bristol, especially on how Mrs Molly Wesley, John's wife, had seized some of Wesley's letters. It shows Wesley was trusting John Fenwick with his most private business.

Having left the itinerancy and settled back in Newcastle Fenwick acted in general as a good Methodist, for example as a man of wealth helping poorer Methodists. But in 1775 the preacher there, Benson, wrote to Wesley explaining how Fenwick had tried to make Wesley think Benson and others had opposed the woman preacher, Elizabeth Hurrell.[30] Despite this Wesley allowed Fenwick to return as an Assistant for the new Whitehaven circuit in 1777. For the next few years he travelled in northern circuits often acting as the Assistant, in other words trusted by Wesley. Certainly he was 'dealing plainly' with

---

[27] For these four preachers see Lenton in *JRULMB*. 85 (2003) 104-7.
[28] *WJW* 22: 460n.
[29] There were actually three Fenwicks, John and Michael, dealt with here, and William Fenwick of Hainton near Epworth, who entered in 1747, but probably only 'preached in one place' and left relatively soon afterwards. For William see *WJW* 20: 60 n48, 159; *EMP* 1: 71; *Minutes* for 1747 and 1758.
[30] Turner *HBA*; *AM* 1780: 511, 1781: 479; *EMP* 2: 135; *WJW* 22: 333 n70; *JWL* 3: 74, 4: 320, 5: 31, 51, 6: 138, 184-6; Lloyd, *Early Preachers* DDPr 2/16; Manchester Circuit Account Book; Todmorden Account Book 3; Valentine, *Mirror of the Soul* 226. The letter from Fenwick is at MARC Box letters to JW 2/43 Fenwick November 1758 to JW.

Wesley. According to his letter to Benson in November 1769 that meant telling Wesley the unflattering truth and being trusted and appreciated for this. So in 1783, though the *Minutes* said he was at Burslem in the Potteries, John Fenwick was actually in London in September correcting the press for Wesley. The 1785 Conference Journal recorded him as expelled for drunkenness. Despite this the *Minutes* that year had him down for London as a Supernumerary, so had Wesley reprieved him again after Conference? In 1786 Wesley sent him as Assistant to Epworth, where there were quarrels between the preachers, partly because, according to Wesley, Fenwick 'did the right thing in the wrong manner.' He died at the end of the Methodist year, being buried at St Andrews, Epworth on the 24th June 1787. John Fenwick's somewhat chequered history showed Wesley being lenient with him on several different occasions, clearly because Wesley thought he could be useful.[31]

Michael Fenwick, the Eternal Repentant Preacher

The story of John Fenwick becomes that of an average preacher when compared to that of Michael Fenwick. Michael was the one of Wesley's preachers who was again and again forced to leave and then accepted back, an extreme example of the process not only because it happened so often, but also because Charles was much involved in the process. It is difficult to be sure how many times it happened. It is even uncertain whether at the end Fenwick had left or died in the work. Michael Fenwick seems to have come, like John Fenwick, from the northeast. In 1749 Michael was accepted as a travelling preacher for the first time. In his first three years he was found in Ireland, London, Leeds and Newcastle. John Wesley described him as 'an excellent groom, valet de chambre, nurse and upon occasion a tolerable preacher.' This explains the relationship with John who was again prepared to put up with the less good side of Fenwick because of his other worthy qualities.[32] Charles felt Fenwick's preaching was far too bad for him to be allowed to continue and in 1751 wrote in Leeds about him

> I went to the room that I might hear with my own ears one of whom many strange things had been told me. But such a preacher have I never heard, and hope I never shall again. It was beyond description. I cannot say he preached false doctrine or true, or any doctrine at all, but pure unmixed nonsense. Not one sentence did he utter that could do the least good to any one soul. Now and then a text of Scripture, or a verse quotation was dragged in by the head or shoulders. I could

---

[31] *WMM* 1823: 351, 1850: 5-6; CJ; *JWL* 5: 165, 7: 189, 279, 349; National Burial Index.
[32] *Minutes* 1: 710; *AM* 1780: 494; Manchester A/C Book; *Crk* 1: 75-6, 85; Tyerman 2: 219.

scarce refrain from stopping him. He set my blood a galloping and threw me into such a sweat that I expected the fever to follow.[33]

Charles Wesley wanted to set Fenwick up in business again to work with his hands and according to a later letter to Charles he did just that, 'instantly taking him off his fine horse and fixing him in a public barbershop there.'[34] Fenwick recorded that he went to London as a barber and then to Glasgow where 'I remained for near eight weeks labouring with my own hands and teaching the people to sing our hymns, until... having full liberty I was called to visit both high and low, teaching and exhorting from house to house.' It was a good example of the usefulness of the half-itinerant preacher to the Connexion. John Wesley met Fenwick, allowed him to return and by 1754 he was back as a travelling preacher in the Manchester Round.[35] In 1755 and again in 1757 he accompanied John Wesley on much of his tour in both England and Ireland.[36] In November 1756 Fenwick's delay in bringing money from the north to London annoyed John Wesley. While travelling south with Wesley next year Fenwick fell asleep under John Wesley's preaching at Clayworth, near Retford, according to *Wesley's Journal*. Having travelled a long way with Wesley, Fenwick became irked by the lack of other references to himself in Wesley's published *Journals*. He then caused trouble for the Irish preacher Thomas Walsh by spreading rumours about a possible marriage for Walsh to a widow. As a result of all this John Wesley decided, as recorded in the 1758 *Minutes*, that Fenwick must return again to his business and cease to itinerate.[37]

Next year Fenwick had abandoned his trade to itinerate again, so presumably John had been lenient with him once more. In December 1765 Wesley would only allow him to stay in Newcastle if he obeyed the Assistant Christopher Hopper in everything. In 1767 Fenwick was to go to Ireland from Newcastle.[38] He appeared on the stations having definitely returned to the itinerancy from 1771 to 1779, but only under his initials, a sign of the worry he was causing John Wesley.[39] Fenwick was not stationed anywhere for the next few years after that. Atmore described him in this period as 'always attending the place of Conference but not permitted to be actually present at Conference after 1784.'[40] We depend for our information about him on the stray references which are

---

[33] *CWJ* 2: 77-8; cf. Baker, *Charles Wesley* 85. The letter has not survived.

[34] The letter apparently by Fenwick, though also catalogued as by Thomas Ellis to Charles is MARC EMV 143. Fenwick's account was supported by Charles in *CWJ* 2; 90-1.

[35] MARC EMV 143, Manchester A/C Bk.

[36] Tyerman 2: 219, 277-8.

[37] *EMP* 3: 280; *WJW* 21: 117 n57; *JWL* 3: 180, 211; *PWHS* 5 (1906) 185; *Minutes* 1: 712.

[38] *JWL* 4: 319, 5: 25, 31, 51.

[39] Crowther; *PWHS* 10 (1916) 154-6.

[40] Tyerman 2: 219, 277-8, 3: 351, 522; Atmore.

available. In 1785, for example, Fenwick was preaching in Bedale in the Yorkshire Dales. In January 1788 he was allowed to go from Bolton to help Robert Dall in Dumfries.[41] In 1789 Fenwick was sent from Hexham to Bideford (he was not listed in the stations in the *Minutes* but added by Coke in the Conference Journal for that year) to help Bardsley mission the new area. Though Fenwick had been travelling for forty years he was still prepared to encourage Bardsley when he wavered, and go himself to brave the local Whig peer Lord Fortescue in his stately home to demand protection from the mob.[42]

He continued in this way for the rest of his life. In 1790 he was acting as an itinerant in the Dales circuit, from where he was supposed to have sent a letter to King George III. Over the next few years he was found preaching in such diverse places as Potto in the North Riding, Wantage in Berkshire, Bedford and York.[43] According to Atmore he was not 'acknowledged as a (travelling) preacher for several years before his death... but his preaching occasionally was connived at, and a small pittance of £12 was allowed him annually by the Conference to preserve him from want and distress.' Most of this he is supposed to have given away. He died as he had lived in an unusual fashion, being struck by lightning in a mill where he had retreated for shelter in a storm on the Wolds near Bridlington.[44]

Michael Fenwick is an excellent example of how lenient Wesley was. It becomes impossible to describe how often he was forced to leave and then allowed back by Wesley. He was unusual in his eccentricities, his mimicking of Wesley even down to his writing, his longevity and that we know so much about him, including at least five of his letters. His career shows how easy it was for Wesley to take the simple way out by letting the errant preacher back, even if towards the end of his life Fenwick was confined to pioneer work and occasional appearances. It is not surprising that nineteenth century Methodist historians were confused as to whether he died in the work or not.[45]

Wesley's Leniency

Whitehead summed up the common view in his lifetime of Wesley's leniency

> No man was ever more free from jealousy or suspicion than Mr. Wesley, or laid himself more open to the impositions of others. Though his confidence was often abused, and circumstances often took place which would have made almost any

---

[41] *WMM* 1830: 781; Tyerman 3: 522; *JWL* 8: 34.
[42] Fenwick's letter to Bardsley about his visit to Fortescue is in the Baker Collection, Duke, dated from Marcham near Barnstaple 25th December 1789. CJ; *JWL* 8: 186-7.
[43] Strachan, *Rev George Lowe* 116-27; *AM* 1795: 391; *WMM* 1839: 586.
[44] Atmore; *Minutes passim*.
[45] For example Myles said he died in the work, Atmore that he left. The letters are those listed in notes 34 and 42 above, two quoted in Tyerman 3: 591-2, (one now at Duke) and a copy of one written just before Fenwick's death in June 1796, now at Drew.

other man suspect every body around him, yet he suspected no one: nor was it easy to convince him that anyone had intentionally deceived him... And when facts had demonstrated that this was actually the case, he would allow no more than that it was so in that single instance. And if the person acknowledged his fault, he believed him sincere and would trust him again.[46]

There were many preachers who benefited from his tolerance. Wesley had to judge his preachers by what they said to him, what they did, and by what others, often too kind and generous, said of them. James Deaves, the former Irish preacher, put it well in 1772 when he wrote of Wesley

I hold him to be no judge at all of the bulk of them (the preachers), for he never heard them, and what he hears of them, is this the channel of some very good hearts, but weak heads. Had he the gift of discerning spirits, he might know a good man but that may not make a good preacher.[47]

Wesley himself admitted his own tendency to leniency. Writing about his choice of men for the Legal Hundred in 1784 he said 'I am not infallible. I might mistake and think better of some than they deserved. However I did my best and if I did wrong it was not the error of my own will but of my judgment.'[48]

Lenience over Marriage

One example of this increasing leniency is the question of his preachers' marriage; Wesley was lenient towards some of his itinerant preachers over marriage, perhaps (especially in his old age) recognizing his own failings in this respect. His encouragement of Bradburn, where 'he bullied the girl's reluctant guardian into consenting and then married the couple on the spot in the family drawing-room' is well known.[49] An interesting and previously unknown example is George Gibbon (1744-1816), an itinerant originally from County Durham who as a forty year old was stationed in Sheffield in 1784 where he met the twenty year old Rebecca Trickett. In 1785 Gibbon was stationed in Liverpool. Presumably, when he told Wesley about his wish to marry her, he not only got Wesley's agreement to the marriage but was in 1786 sent back to live in Sheffield for their first year of marriage.[50] Once his leading preachers had married Wesley often allowed them to remain close to where their wives' family or business interests were. So William Thompson remained in Scotland

---

[46] Whitehead, *Wesley* 2: 470.

[47] James Deaves' copy letter 31st January 1772 Craigavon Museum, Northern Ireland.

[48] *WJW* 13: 249.

[49] Rack, 'Betsy'. Her stepfather was a wealthy Dublin jeweller, Mr Karr.

[50] The Gibbon-Trickett marriage is based on the *IGI* entry at St Peter's Sheffield for 7th June 1786.

after his marriage in Edinburgh in 1769 until his wife's mother died in 1782, and Thomas Rankin was allowed to locate in London after 1783.[51] The Irishman Adam Clarke in 1786 fell in love with Mary Cooke, the twenty-seven year old daughter of a wealthy Trowbridge widow. In 1787 he proposed to Mary and was accepted. However, Mary's mother was much less accommodating and banned Clarke and all other Methodists (except Wesley himself, who was at first against the marriage) from the Cooke house in Trowbridge. Wesley had made it a rule that no preacher could marry against their fiancée's parent's wishes. After a lengthy winter (1787-88) of clandestine and at one point intercepted correspondence between Trowbridge and the Channel Islands (where Clarke was stationed) the couple were married, Wesley having changed his mind and written in their favour to Mrs Cooke. Next year (1789) they were sent to nearby Bristol, with Adam (who had entered in 1782) made Assistant over senior preachers like Wadsworth (entered 1770) and Hodgson (entered 1779). The mother remained unreconciled as late as 1794.[52]

Did It Matter?

Did his leniency matter? John Wesley has had a bad press on this, from Charles Wesley to Roy Hattersley. Recently Hempton has suggested that he was too lenient with the enthusiast George Bell in 1762. His 'tactic was to wait and see the results of Bell's ministry, which in this case produced greater damage than would have been the case if he had acted promptly.' Hempton blamed Wesley's caution on his 'predilection for religious enthusiasm.' With his own preachers Wesley was certainly lenient. Men who left were allowed back, when the fact of their leaving again afterwards shows they should not have been. Some who left, like the older Hampson, were looked after in their old age, when Wesley could have washed his hands of them and pleaded shortage of means. He was lenient also over their education, not insisting sufficiently that they learn and read. Thomas Hanson's neglect of his Latin and Greek when he became an itinerant[53] is by no means untypical. Wesley's generous behaviour to Joseph Algar who opposed him to his face in the 1784 Conference was again typical of Wesley. Algar, who had only travelled two years, spoke in the debate on the Deed of Declaration and complained. Fletcher fell on his knees before Algar

---

[51] Atmore.
[52] The main source for this is the MSS Mary Cooke Correspondence held by Bridwell Library, SMU, Dallas. The clandestine correspondence of Adam and Mary in 1787-8 was carried out through the assistance of Miss Peacock of Bath. Copy letters in the Peacock Letterbook show that she acted as the post box. Other main sources are Smith, *Mrs Clarke* and Clarke, *Life*. For Mrs Cooke's continued hostility see Pawson's letter to Eliza Cooke, the second sister, printed in *Pawson L* 2: 6-8. See also W. Jones, *Memoirs of Adam Clarke* (London: MacGowan, 1838) 173-4. Page Thomas pointed me to the letterbook.
[53] Hempton, *Empire* 39-40; Kent, *Wesley and the Wesleyans* 91.

and begged him not to divide the societies. The fact that Wesley did not hold all this against the twenty-four-year-old Algar and from 1785 made him Assistant for the next three years shows how far in his old age Wesley was prepared to allow his preachers license to do (almost) what they pleased.[54] His lenience was a factor in building up the self-importance of the Wesleyan itinerancy, something which was to be carried too far in the 1830s and 1840s.

After Wesley

So far as cohorts are concerned, Table 19 shows cohorts 3 and 4 had the largest numbers of those who returned, twenty and twenty-one; but cohort 5, which had by far the largest number of entrants, had only fourteen leaving a second time. Table 20 in Appendix One shows a drastic reduction in the number of preachers who returned after 1791. This was because John Wesley was no longer in charge. The Conference of travelling preachers which succeeded him had a very different policy and was much stricter, as above with Winscom. After Wesley's death fewer left but it was much harder to return. One who did so was Richard Elliott, Arkwright's former coachman, who travelled from 1790 to 1803. He left to become a druggist in Huddersfield in that year, remaining a local preacher. 'Weary of this way of life' in 1811 Elliott returned to the itinerancy, a rare example of such return by that date.[55] The other major area where Conference remained as lenient as Wesley had been was over health or care for the family. Joseph Cross had left for health reasons in 1790. In 1791 Conference allowed him back.[56] Philip Hardcastle had been allowed by Wesley to leave in 1786 to take care of his aged parents at Bluecoat Farm, Lund House Green, Pannal near Harrogate. In 1796 he was permitted to re-enter.[57] The others who came back were allowed to return by the Irish Conference (2) or in America (2) or the colonies (1),[58] all of which were much shorter of manpower than the British Conference at home. Wesley's preachers had no mind to be as

---

[54] The story of Algar and Fletcher is found in Tyerman BMM 1 MAB B1234. Algar's age depends on those given below his portraits in the *Arminian Magazine* (*AM* May 1786, August 1798), which may well be two years out. He had not been included in the Legal Hundred, but he had far less cause to complain than seniors like the older John Hampson or Joseph Pilmore.

[55] For Winscom see n 26 above. For Elliott see *MM* 1813: 708, 1814: 881-7; *Pawson L* 3: 101-9. It should be noted there were others who returned like Richard Watson who had entered after Wesley's death. Total numbers of returners in the nineteenth century were still much lower than in Wesley's lifetime.

[56] K. B. Garlick MS notebook at WHS Library, Oxford Brookes.

[57] R. Corbridge, *Heritage. The Story of the Methodists of Pannal* (Harrogate: Pannal Methodist Church, 1984).

[58] The two who returned in Ireland were Thomas Davis in 1798 and James Jordan in 1792; the two in America were Robert M'Kay or McCoy and Thomas Whitehead, the missionary being Thomas Dobson, who returned in 1799.

lenient as John had been. They agreed with Pawson that Wesley had been too lenient. Nobody left a second time because so very few had been allowed to return under Wesley's successors.

Conclusion

Wesley followed his own 'Rules for an Assistant' as given first in the Conference *Minutes* of 1744 '4. Believe evil of no one. If you see it done, well. Else, take heed how you credit it. Put the best construction on every thing. You know the judge is always supposed to be on the prisoner's side.' He was therefore reluctant to judge his 'Sons in the Gospel' too hastily. His leniency should be seen as Wesley's carrying out in his own life the Christian witness to 'Judge not and you will not be judged,' unlike the more practical or clear-sighted of those who surrounded him, such as Pawson or Charles Wesley.[59]

---

[59] *JB's Minutes* 15; *St Matthew's Gospel* 7: 1.

Chapter 18

Ordination

'Ordination is separation.'
Lord Mansfield.

Introduction

Three groups of Wesley's preachers were ordained. The first were those already ordained in the Church of England or Ireland, like the Wesleys themselves. There were many of these, especially in the first cohort. The famous ones were well known men like Fletcher of Madeley or Grimshaw of Haworth. Fletcher was so gifted as to be designated by Wesley as his successor; less well known were Wesley's attempts to draw him into the Methodist circuit system, by making him the Assistant of the local Methodist circuit.[1] There were also other clergymen, some of whom flitted in and out briefly, especially but not only in the early years. The most important were those who lived in London and acted as 'Communion providers' in Wesley's later years for his congregations at the Foundery, West Street and City Road, preaching there and in the country as well. John Richardson (1733-92), who came to London in 1762 and died there thirty years later, James Creighton in London from 1783 to his death in 1819, and Peard Dickinson (1758-1802) were the most notable and long lasting of these.[2]

The second group, of whom there were many, was those who left the itinerancy and then became ordained in the Church of England.[3] Thirdly there were the men ordained by Wesley or others during his lifetime or afterwards who remained within the Methodist Connexion,[4] including such a well known preacher as Coke.[5] Many were the chief leaders of Methodism in the period that

---

[1] For many early preachers who were clergymen see Wood, *Brothers in Arms*; A. B. Sackett, *John Jones - First After the Wesleys* (Chester: WHS, 1972) and *James Rouquet*.
[2] For Richardson see *PWHS* 15 (1926) 3-4, 172, 21 (1937-8) 97-101 and Stevenson, *City Road* 375-6. For Creighton see Chapter 15 above and for Dickinson see *MM* 1802: 483-4, 492, 527 and Stevenson, *City Road* 396-8.
[3] See Chapter 16.
[4] Townsend, Workman, and Eayrs, *New History* 1: 372 suggested twenty-seven of these were by Wesley himself, an excellent estimate; 100 years later I can only add two more.
[5] Coke falls into two of the three groups, being already a clergyman and then ordained

followed Wesley. Ordination was also given to many Methodist missionaries of the period from 1784 into the early nineteenth century, such as William Warrener.[6] It is important to discover why Wesley decided to ordain them when he had resisted similar pressures for most of his life, and it is interesting to see what the preachers thought about it. There is also value in examining what Wesley's immediate successors believed about ordination, their practice being slightly different from either Wesley's or the high nineteenth century Wesleyan practice which was the eventual solution to the question. This whole issue of ordination is still a living one today as modern British Methodism discusses bishops, ordination and the doctrine of the historic episcopate and 'succession.' For this chapter I am investigating the ordinations of the third group and in the period after Wesley.[7]

Wesley's Change of Mind

Pressure for Ordination

From the early days preachers were admitted to the status of travelling preacher in a solemn service. Joseph Cownley in 1747 had the New Testament put in his hands with the words 'take thou authority to preach the Gospel.'[8] Preachers were given pastoral authority over the societies and often hoped for ordination in the Church of England, which would make them more like the Wesleys and the Wesleys' original friends. In 1760 Nicholas Gilbert, a Cornishman who had been travelling as an itinerant for ten years, wrote from his circuit in Cornwall to Charles Wesley in Bath. Most of the letter was, as Charles succinctly described it, 'N. Gilbert's diffidence' about himself. At one point the diffident Gilbert brought up the latest rumour about ordination and his hopes for himself. 'It runs in my Head, that your Brother & you intend to apply to Mr. (John) Gambold[9] (who I apprehend is a Bishop) for the ordination of some of the Preachers. This is purely conjecture. Is there any reason for this Conjecture? If it is so, I hope I may be a Candidate.' This kind of hope was rarely put on paper to the Wesleys, but was common among their preachers and to be ordained and settle down in the Church was why many left. John Haughton and Joseph Pilmore were merely two of the many disappointed itinerants who left with this purpose in the fifty years up to Wesley's death.[10]

---

by Wesley as Superintendent for the American church, see below.
[6] See for all these Chapters 12-14 above.
[7] Most of these were listed in *PWHS* by the Rev Eddie Lacy 33 (1962) 118-21.
[8] *EMP* 2: 7. See Chapter 4 above for more detailed discussion.
[9] This letter is in the MARC, Nicholas Gilbert, Redruth, MS letter to Charles Wesley 24th September 1760 DDPr 1/33. John Gambold (1711-71) was linked to the Holy Club in the early 1730s, an Anglican priest, and from 1754 Moravian Bishop.
[10] For Pilmore see Chapter 12 and for Haughton Chapter 16 above.

Timeline 5: Ordinations

Year	Events England	Elsewhere
1783	Lady Huntingdon preachers ordained	
1784	Coke, Whatcoat, Vasey ordained	Coke ordained Asbury, Baxter, Black
1785	Death of Fletcher. Preachers ordained for Scotland	Coke ordained Johnson in Scotland
1786	Atmore and others ordained for Scotland, Warrener and Hammett for overseas	
1788	March: Death of Charles Wesley. August: Mather ordained for England	
1789	Rankin and Moore ordained. Korah Sermon	
1791	March: Death of John Wesley. August: Hopper ordained by Hanby etc	Sept: Coke ordained 2 preachers for France
1792	Early: Bradburn and others ordained at District meetings. Conference: Virtual ordination agreed	
1793	Coke publicly ordained 2 preachers	
1797	Barritt and Townsend ordained for Scotland at Conference by Coke	
1798		Braithwaite ordained in Scotland
1808	Ogylvie ordained by Coke	
1816		Primitive Wesleyans separate in Ireland
1820	Bunting proposed laying on of hands	
1836	Conference ordained by laying on of hands	
1839	Moore helped to ordain missionaries	
1844	Death of Moore	

Events in 1784

For over forty years the Wesley brothers refused to even consider requests for ordination. Again and again the Conference *Minutes* return to the subject of relations with the Church. The Wesleys' reply was consistent: they must not separate from the Church. However, eventually in 1784 John changed his views.[11] As a result some travelling preachers towards the end of Wesley's life were ordained as *Methodist* preachers by Wesley or his associates and by the laying on of hands. Later his successors eventually agreed how ordinations for nineteenth century Methodist ministers should be carried out.

Many of these early ordinations took place secretly in someone's room rather than publicly, partly because Wesley was concerned about possible hostility from both his brother Charles and other Church Methodists. Many, both inside and outside Methodism, saw such acts as in direct opposition to the Church of England, as Charles forcefully pointed out at the time. His poetic comments on the ordination of Coke as 'Superintendent' for the new American Church gave a flavour of his opposition to what John Wesley was doing

> So easily are Bishops made
> By man's or woman's whim
> Wesley on Coke has laid his hands
> But who laid hands on him?

'Ordination is separation' was the legal opinion of Lord Mansfield, Lord Chief Justice of the King's Bench, given to his old school-friend Charles Wesley. John Wesley himself refused to accept this view and remained convinced to his death that he, his preachers, and the members of the Methodist societies were still within the Church. That he was still welcomed into Anglican pulpits and to Anglican communions after 1784 shows that it was not an unreasonable belief. Gregory has argued that ordination was not in fact separation 'the case for John Wesley as "Church of England man" rests then on his own statements, and the fact that he did not actually join another church. He saw himself as a member of the church even if others did not.' John Wesley viewed the Church according to the twentieth article of the Church of England as 'that body of faithful people in England among whom the pure word of God is preached,' so doctrine and behaviour were more important than institution and organization. Since he believed the doctrine and behaved according to what he saw as the rules, he remained an Anglican.[12]

---

[11] For a recent examination of Wesley's views and how they developed see Burdon, *Authority* Chapters 4-5.

[12] Baker, *Wesley and the Church* 273. See also Gregory's perceptive analysis of the discussion on this: '"In the Church I will live and die:" John Wesley, the Church.. and Methodism' in W. Gibson and R. C. Ingram, ed, *Religious Identities in Britain 1660-*

On the other hand, to Charles and many Church Methodists ordination was a step too far and some left the Methodist Society as a direct result. Three American preachers abandoned Methodism and joined the Episcopalians.[13] There were only three British preachers who did the same, one being Joseph Pilmore who went to America to do it. So far as the other two were concerned, John Hampson junior and Edward Smyth, it seems to have been other factors which were more important than Wesley's ordinations, though these may well have played a part. Edward Smyth was already an Irish clergyman who separated himself from Wesley in 1784 and took many Methodists in Dublin with him to the new Chapel, Bethesda, which his brother had built. As we have seen over M'Nab and Bath, it took very little to provoke controversy where Smyth was concerned. The other preacher, John Hampson junior, was more concerned about being left out of the Legal Hundred in the Deed of Declaration. In each case Wesley's ordinations may have played a part, but we have no evidence to support the speculation.[14]

All these questions are of interest to many in the twenty-first century looking at modern ways of bringing Wesley's successors and other Christian churches together. In the twentieth century the ordinations led to controversy at the time of the Conversations with the Church of England in the late 1950s and 1960s. One book, for example, written at that time by Edgar Thompson, concentrated on Wesley's ordination of Coke to superintend the new church in America.[15]

Wesley's Reasons for Changing His Mind

The chief reason for Wesley changing his mind over ordaining some preachers was the need in North America, where 15,000 Methodist members looked to the Methodist preachers, none of whom were ordained, and where there were few Anglican clergymen and even fewer who were not hostile to Methodists. The American societies were in danger of schism on the issue of whether or not the preachers should give them the sacrament, with Asbury finding it increasingly difficult to hold the American born preachers back. Reg Ward pointed out that the real problem was the separation of America from Britain. The American Episcopalians had exactly the same problem and far less freedom of action. The expedients they were driven to were almost as radical as Wesley's, with one leader, White, suggesting a scheme similar to Wesley's

---

1832 (Aldershot: Ashgate, 2005) 147-178, the quotations being from 155 and 166. For references to Wesley's preaching in churches see for example *WJW* 8: 181 (Whitby) and 194 (Diss).

[13] For the three, Coleman, Roe and Spraggs, see Chapter 13 above.

[14] For Smyth and Hampson see *DEB*.

[15] E. W. Thompson, *Wesley: Apostolic Man* (London: Epworth, 1957); cf. A. R. George in *HMGB* 2: 143-160 which has a good though now dated reading list.

solution in 1782;[16] another, Seabury, received his ordination as a Bishop from Scottish non-jurors in Aberdeen, something on which some modern Anglicans might well still frown today. Seabury had arrived in England from America seeking ordination in 1783 and only received it in November 1784, when he finally despaired of more orthodox means. In other words, he was seeking and not gaining ordination for a whole year during which time Wesley decided to ordain Coke and the others and send them to America. Thus he stole a march on the Episcopalians which they might well feel was the result of the Church of England's intransigence. In March 1783 the Countess of Huntingdon had had ordained six students from her Trevecca College (by two Anglican clergy supporters).[17] These other ordinations at the same period in a similar way for comparable situations provide a useful backcloth for Wesley's actions which have usually been studied in isolation. Lady Huntingdon, for example, had been considering the merits of ordination since as early as 1774. When looked at in this context Wesley's actions seem sensible and, once he had decided to ordain, speedy. As George said, the ordinations in Methodism by Wesley and others were the consequence of steps taken over forty years earlier in the decision to create an order of lay preachers. They marked the culmination of a process which had been developing over a long period. Wesley did this despite the fact that all his advisers opposed except Coke,[18] just as most of Lady Huntingdon's friends were against what she had done. Harding pointed out that the persecution suffered by the Countess's Connexion was neither worse nor better than it was before the ordinations, and the same was true about Wesleyan Methodism.[19] The suggestion that Wesley was an old man overborne by Coke has been dealt with thoroughly and ruled out by Vickers. Wesley's explanation in his letter 'to the American brethren' was cogent and well argued. He was following in the steps of Lady Huntingdon, partly because of the hostility of the English bishops to ordaining for America. Their refusal was because of perceived legal problems, and so strong that it was impossible for Seabury to overcome it directly, despite his being seen as a loyal member of the Church of England, unlike Wesley. It was not hasty or ill-thought out. It was Wesley reacting like others in similar positions to the new political entity which had been created on the other side of the Atlantic.[20]

---

[16] Thompson, *Wesley* 63; Ward, *Faith and Faction* 231. White's scheme is explained in Vickers, *Thomas Coke* 181-2. See also Chapter 13 above.

[17] Schlenther, *Countess* 154; Harding, *Countess's Connexion* 310. This was for Britain rather than America, so not as close a parallel as the American Episcopalians. Some American bishops were ordained later than Seabury with the consent of Parliament, see Noll, *America's God* 120.

[18] Thompson, *Wesley* 12; Heitzenrater 287.

[19] Harding, *Countess's Connexion* 321.

[20] On this 'grand diversion' see C. N. R. Wallwork, 'Three Bridges to Melchizedek' in J. Strawson, ed, *Church and Theology* (Buxton: Church in the Market Place, 2004) 118-9; Vickers, *Thomas Coke passim*. Burdon, *Authority* 57-8 pointed out the legal problems.

Ordinations under Wesley

Total Numbers

Once John Wesley had ordained for America it was likely he would go on to ordain elsewhere. Charles predicted this in a letter to John of 1785 'When once you began ordaining in America, I knew, and you know, that your preachers here would never rest till you ordained them.'[21] The first of Wesley's ordinations was in 1784, that 'turning point' year of the Deed of Declaration and Coke's first journey to America. Wesley used the term 'ordain' in his Diary. However, the actual certificate(s) said 'set apart,' which shows that he retained some doubts about the advisability of what he was doing. Coke was 'ordained' or 'set apart' in Dr. Castleman's house in Bristol on the 2nd September 1784. Coke was to have the same status as Wesley in America, that is be able to ordain like Wesley himself.[22] The result was that thirty-five British travelling preachers were ordained by the laying on of hands before Wesley's death in 1791, mostly (29) by Wesley himself, the remainder by the coadjutor he had appointed, Thomas Coke. Where Coke ordained it was either in America, the West Indies or Scotland, in other words where Wesley was not going to be present. The number of ordinations was significant, averaging five or six a year, about 18% of the total received on trial by the British Conference each year.[23] The countries they were ordained for were also significant. The proportions in relation to the total number of British Methodist preachers were low. Since there were over 300 preachers at the time in the British Conference this was only one in eight of the total number who had been ordained by Wesley's death. Wesley in England asked other Anglican presbyters such as Coke and James Creighton to assist in the ordinations. Coke overseas usually could not find such help but included other Methodists who had been ordained such as Asbury, Whatcoat and Vasey.[24]

The comparison should first be made with the practice in the new American Methodist Church, which provided Wesley's official reason for the original ordinations. Of the 811 American preachers before 1799 studied by Schell,[25] only 127 were ordained, about one in six. Relatively few American preachers were ordained at first. It was only by about 1790 that higher proportions began to be ordained in the USA. Compared to British Methodism, however, this was still a large number and a significantly higher percentage.

---

[21] Letter 14/8/1785 quoted J. R. Tyson, ed, *Charles Wesley: A Reader* (Oxford: OUP, 1989) 434.

[22] The full text is in Thompson, *Wesley* 10 replacing earlier incorrect printed versions.

[23] The average received on trial each year in this period was thirty.

[24] The best evidence is supplied in the ordination certificates, listed elsewhere in this chapter, or in *PWHS* 33 (1962) 118-21. These are minimum numbers, since more may have been ordained, but the evidence has not survived.

[25] *MH* 38 (2000) 307, 351.

Scotland

On this side of the Atlantic the largest number ordained, fifteen, was for Scotland, a much higher proportion of the Methodist preachers who served there than in any other group or country in the British Isles. Wesley had long resisted the argument put to him that Scots Methodists expected preachers there to be ordained and to administer Communion. In 1785 he gave in (Pawson said too late).[26] Wesley published a defence of his ordinations for Scotland 'The Scotch ministers had refused to admit Methodists to Holy Communion or to baptize their children unless they ceased to be Methodists.' Swift showed that the evidence of Wesley's own preachers was that these ministers were of the Presbyterian establishment.[27] The Church of Scotland being Presbyterian, Wesley had no scruples about setting up in opposition to it. It was not, he said, separation from the church, for the Methodists were never linked to the Church of Scotland, and the Church of England had no concern with Scotland since they were not the established church there. He ignored completely the Episcopalian Church in communion with the Church of England, which admittedly was absent from most areas of Scotland in Wesley's day, with less than 1% of the total population and was bitterly divided anyway.[28]

The process of ordination came in two stages, to the offices of deacon and presbyter or elder usually on two successive days. Almost all were by Wesley with others assisting. However, there were instances of Coke performing the ordination. Robert Johnson, for example, was ordained by Coke in Scotland as a deacon in 1785. He was not ordained as a priest until 1786 when Wesley performed the ceremony.[29]

Wesley remained opposed to those ordained for Scotland performing ministerial functions in England when they returned there, as Thomas Hanby did. He ordered them to put away their gowns and not to give communion. When Hanby refused, a major dispute developed where Hanby was saved by Wesley's age, his colleagues covering for him and Wesley's eventual death. It seems that only some of the Methodist preachers in Scotland were ordained, four out of the ten stationed there in 1785, seven out of the fourteen on station

---

[26] Rack 230.
[27] Swift, *Scotland* 55 n2; G. W. Anderson, 'Wesley's ordinations for Scotland' and W. Jamieson, 'A New Departure 1st August 1785' *WHS Scotland* 16 (October 1985) 3-8.
[28] K. Robbins, 'Religion and Community in Scotland and Wales' 366 in Gilley and Shiels, ed, *Religion*.
[29] Robert Johnson, who appeared on the stations first in 1783, was received into Full Connexion and sent to Scotland as Assistant in Inverness in 1784, but not ordained then. Ordained deacon by Coke on the 24th October 1785, he was at 5 am on the 27th May 1786 ordained presbyter by Wesley at Edinburgh for Scotland. *PWHS* 36 (1967) 36; Baker, *Wesley and the Church* 395. George in *HMGB* 2: 152 described the use of presbyter in place of elder as 'isolated,' though there may well have been other certificates of the period with similar wording which have not survived.

in 1786 and so on.[30] Usually but not always it was the Assistants in the five large circuits of Edinburgh, Aberdeen, Dundee, Inverness and Glasgow who were ordained, the last only being an independent circuit from 1788. Glasgow, as a large town, usually had an ordained preacher there even before it was a circuit. Wesley did not feel it necessary to have all the preachers in Scotland ordained. He did want one preacher in each large circuit to be able to dispense the sacrament. As with modern British Methodism he allowed 'dispensation to administer communion' on the basis of deprivation, though these modern terms were not being used. He did not ordain for Ireland or Wales, where the Anglican Church remained the official Church and there were many clergy to dispense the sacraments.

The West Indies

The second largest number of preachers known to be ordained (fourteen) was those who served the chief Methodist foreign mission area of this period, the West Indies. Again Wesley defended what he did on the grounds of need and distance from the few Anglican clergy in the islands, so again the purpose was to provide communion. Each island was relatively separate and sometimes difficult of access. John Baxter, possibly William Brazier (both local residents) and Thomas Werrill were ordained by Coke. The majority, however, were all ordained by Wesley in Britain before they crossed the ocean. Wesley's general practice, therefore, was to ordain most missionaries himself before sending them out. Until Wesley's death Coke only ordained those who lived in the West Indies and could not be ordained by Wesley.[31]

England

In 1786 Wesley was urged to ordain for 'a desolate place in Yorkshire.' (It would be fascinating to know who urged him and where the place was!) After a debate at Conference he refused.[32] Pressure from the preachers was increasing,

---

[30] Six out of the sixteen in circuit in 1787, five out of thirteen in 1788, six out of eighteen in 1789 and 1790. (Numbers include the Berwick circuit 1785-7; this circuit did not exist after 1787 for some time). Each year many, but not all of the preachers ordained the previous year, stayed on in Scotland, making the numbers correct so far as we know. It could also be that certificates, our chief source for these ordinations, have simply not survived for many preachers in Scotland.

[31] Those ordained by Wesley were Robert Gamble, Joseph Harper, Matthew Lumb, William M'Cornock, Thomas Owens, Benjamin Pearce, and William Warrener. For more details on these and others in the West Indies see Chapter 14.

[32] In addition to the numbers given here of the travelling preachers ordained, Wesley ordained a local preacher called Woodhouse of Owston in the Epworth Circuit, and appointed him to administer the sacrament in Church hours. Smith, *Meth* 2: 11. It is not clear when this was, or what was Smith's source, but the implication is it was late in

especially from those who like Pawson and Hanby had been ordained in Scotland but had since been stationed back in England. Similarly there was increasing unrest among the Methodist people, at least according to interested parties like Pawson and Hanby. The ordinary society member, they said, wanted to receive communion from their own preachers. Most importantly in March 1788 the chief opponent of ordination, Charles Wesley, died.[33] So, in August that year, John Wesley broke his own rule by ordaining Alexander Mather for England. Significantly, Mather, like Coke and unlike those ordained for Scotland, was ordained as Superintendent; in other words in Wesley's mind, with his brother dead, he was hoping Mather would succeed to Wesley's own position among English Methodists. Next year Wesley ordained two more preachers in England, Thomas Rankin and Henry Moore. All three ordinations were significant; Mather (age 55, travelled 31 years) and Rankin (age 51, travelled 28 years) were both senior preachers and advisers, members of his inner Cabinet and Scotsmen to whom Wesley had given much responsibility over the years.[34] Moore was a much younger Irish preacher (age 37, travelled 11 years) whom Wesley had favoured, bringing him to England and giving him key jobs. All three were able leaders based usually in London near Wesley. Fletcher had died in 1785, John Wesley's brother Charles in 1788. John knew that the idea he had clung to for so long that he would be succeeded by an Anglican clergyman like himself was not going to be possible. There was still Thomas Coke but Wesley recognized the unpopularity of the Doctor among the preachers, his major responsibilities across the world, relative inexperience and fallibility, and was therefore giving others like Mather as Superintendent an importance in the inevitable struggle for the succession. Wesley's actions here did not bear fruit, except as we shall see below through the survival of Moore. Wesley was not wanting those he ordained to administer the sacraments in competition with the Church of England. They were to act as 'prophets' or Methodist preachers, not 'priests' or Anglican clergy. It would also give them status among their brethren.[35]

British North America

For British North America there were eight ordained of whom William Black,

---

Wesley's life. The late appearance of the story is not a reason to doubt it. The fact of a local preacher being ordained simply emphasises the fact that to Wesley there was no difference between him and the travelling preachers since both were lay.

[33] Burdon, *Authority* 66-70 has a very useful section on this, on which this paragraph is largely based.

[34] For Rankin see chapters 12 above and 19 below. For Moore see later in this chapter. *HMGB* 2: 152.

[35] The reference is to Wesley's sermon 57 first preached in March 1789, later called the Korah Sermon, which Outler relabelled 'Prophets and Priests.' *AM* 1790: 230-5, 286-90; *WJW* 4: 72-82; Burdon, *Authority* 70-6.

brought up in Nova Scotia, and the brothers John and James Mann, natives of the American continent, were ordained by Coke because they never came to England. Wesley ordained John Clarke, William Hammett and James Wray, who were sent out from Britain. Asbury ordained the American William Jessop.

After Wesley

After Wesley's death early in 1791 the position in British Methodism changed at once. In the uncertainty the only sure point was that many of the leaders of Wesley's preachers sought ordination if they had not already received it. Therefore more preachers were ordained by others among the leading group, at least eighteen altogether. George called those who carried out the ordinations at District meetings 'separatists.'[36] Yet eventually these became the majority.

In 1792 the Conference agreed that ordination should not happen without its authorization on pain of exclusion for any ordaining or being ordained.[37] They agreed that reception into Full Connexion (without the laying on of hands) by the Conference should be understood as the equivalent of ordination or 'virtual ordination.' George denied that this was so and suggested that Conference was saying simply ordination was not needed for administration of communion. He suggested that the virtual ordination idea was a later one of Atmore's which then became generally accepted. Whichever view is correct, what happened was that in addition to the reception into Full Connexion ordinations of preachers by laying on of hands continued with the consent of Conference, usually between Conferences for those who could not attend, both for missionaries (mostly by Coke) and (at a reduced level) for Scotland. The main area for which the missionaries were ordained was still the West Indies, though there were a couple for Canada and two, Mahy and de Queteville, for France. At least two of those ordained for the West Indies never went, Jonathan Crowther in 1794 and John Burdsall sometime after 1796. Neither these two, nor John Townsend ordained at Leeds in 1797, have appeared in lists previously published.[38] Whereas with Wesley it seems likely that most certificates survived and few more are to be discovered, after Wesley the reverse is true. Probably more were ordained, especially for overseas, whom we are unlikely to learn about because the certificates, not having Wesley's famous name on them, have been lost.

---

[36] A. R. George in *LHQR* 1951: 164; cf. F. Baker in *PWHS* 24 (1944) 102.

[37] There were three reasons for this position see Walsh in *HMGB* 1: 281.

[38] The lists are in an article by J. C. Bowmer in *PWHS* 36 (1967-8) 36-40, 111-4. For Burdsall see Lyth 173-4 for the story of how Burdsall's father, the renowned local preacher Richard Burdsall, wrote to Coke and begged successfully that he be released from his engagement. Crowther's account of his ordination and subsequent failure to go overseas is in his MS Autobiography at Duke and Tyerman BMM MAB B1245. For Townsend see note 41 below.

Scotland

Scotland remained a problem. Apparently in 1793 the Conference decided not to ordain for Scotland any more and to forbid the wearing of gowns and bands there as elsewhere. Conference was to find it difficult to maintain this line and clearly did the opposite by allowing or even performing actual ordinations on at least four occasions. Almost certainly there must have been others not recorded.[39] In 1797 both John Barritt and John Townsend were ordained for Scotland by Coke and others at Conference. For John Barritt we only have his letter of that year 'Several preachers this year were ordained and I was one, for Scotland; as the Scotch clergy refuse to give us the Lord's Supper or baptize our children.'[40] Townsend's ordination for Scotland was significant because in his case the certificate survived. He had been received into Full Connexion at Wesley's last Conference in 1790; in 1797 he was being sent to Glasgow in Scotland and was therefore ordained by the Conference. The certificate stated that he was 'authorized by the Conference to administer the Sacraments of Baptism and the Lord's Supper.' Townsend understood it as ordination since he endorsed it as that. It was signed by Coke and Bradburn as president and secretary, so it was the officers of the Conference acting as such who ordained Townsend.[41]

In March 1798 John Braithwaite was ordained at Edinburgh for Scotland as a result of the decision at the previous Conference. He was the second minister in the Edinburgh circuit. We know about this from his biography which stated 'The certificate is in front of me' and reproduced it, but the original has not survived. He was ordained by Duncan M'Allum, the senior of the Scottish ministers and Chairman of the District, Thomas Warwick, his friend and Superintendent of the Edinburgh circuit that year (for whom Braithwaite had recently performed his second marriage), and Dr. Thomas Olivers Warwick, son of the latter and an old boy of Kingswood and a local layman and doctor.[42] Presumably Conference had authorized the ordination to be held in Scotland. The presence among the ordaining party of a layman is even more interesting. It is the only example of a layman's name being on an ordination certificate. The Conference had therefore altered its mind, at least by 1797 if not earlier, under pressure from Scotland.

Finally there is the strange case of the Scots-born John Ogylvie (1763-1839), ordained by Coke and others in August after the Conference of 1808, a year when Ogylvie was appointed for Chester. Had it been during Conference we might presume that Ogylvie was going north to Scotland. It cannot have been a change on the stations since it was immediately after Conference. So were other ministers like Ogylvie ordained for England as well, as Vickers has suggested?

---

[39] *HMGB* 3: 270-1.
[40] Thompson, *Barritts of Foulridge* 5.
[41] Townsend's certificate was held by John Simon c 1910. *PWHS* 7 (1910) 165-6.
[42] Dickinson, *Braithwaite* 309-11.

Certainly it is possible. With only one example it is difficult to know whether this was perhaps a case of Coke doing an occasional favour for a friend, one opposed to Conference policy, but he knew he was strong enough to avoid any retribution.[43]

The Mission Field

Coke and others after his death continued to ordain for the mission field;[44] he ordained Myles Dixon, George Poole and John Charrington for the West Indies in 1809. William Jewett and Thomas Dobson were ordained by him in 1810. He ordained his seven companions for India in December 1813 before he left on his final voyage there. Two missionaries were ordained by Atmore and others (as an ex-president?) in November 1819.[45] Some missionary ordination certificates have survived, probably partly because the ordinand became famous as a pioneer. Those ordaining these future missionaries included one or two Missionary Secretaries, like Thomas Coke, Robert Alder, Jabez Bunting or Elijah Hoole, an ex-president or other leading minister and occasionally a foreign visitor. Henry Blaine Foster in 1835, about to go to the Caribbean, had the American Wilbur Fisk among the group ordaining him.[46] These ordination certificates were perhaps as important for the missionaries as first membership tickets became for lay Methodists and were preserved with similar care. Almost certainly many others ordained for the mission field did not have their certificates survive.

Ordination by Conference 1836

Several questions have been raised about those of Wesley's preachers who survived to 1836. For a long period in the early nineteenth century the Wesleyan Conference had followed the practice of virtual ordination by reception into Full Connexion and refused to ordain new ministers by laying on of hands, with the exception of some missionaries proceeding overseas considered in the last paragraph. Methodist theologians when defending their practice said that reception into Full Connexion by the Conference was the equivalent of ordination. This seems to have been because after Wesley the

---

[43] *PWHS* 26 (1947) 30-1; Vickers, *Thomas Coke* 202.
[44] Coke's letters are listed and described in *JRULMB* 76: 2; 285-6 PLP 28/17/12-15. These 1809 ordinations are not listed in *PWHS* 36 (1967) 36-40. Known ordinations by him were listed by Vickers, *Thomas Coke* Appendix C.
[45] John Shaw was ordained then. *PWHS* 36 (1967) 36-40.
[46] Most certificates are at the School of Oriental and African Studies where the Methodist Missionary Society Archives are held, including Joshua Marsden ordained in 1802 for Nova Scotia, Samuel Young for South Africa in 1823, Thomas Jones for the West Indies in 1824, William Wood in 1828, Henry Wilkinson for the Gambia and Henry Foster for the West Indies in 1835.

preachers were concerned that no hierarchy should develop among themselves. They feared fresh ordinations would upset the existing settlement. Few wanted ordination on those terms.[47]

It was Jabez Bunting from the chair in Conference in 1820 who first proposed that the young preachers should be received by the imposition of hands. It was too early.[48] His time had not yet come on this point and there was uproar. In 1822 there was another debate in Conference reported in Entwistle's memoirs. 'On one point all agreed; that the old method of admitting into full connexion had all the essentials of Scripture ordination, and that its validity was not to be questioned. But some contended for the imposition of hands as a circumstance sanctioned by Scriptural ordination and usage of the ancient church, and which would add much to the solemnity and impressiveness of the ordinance.' After discussion, no vote was taken. The question was raised again in Conference in 1824 and 1828, each time without result, but the mere fact of its being considered shows that a strong group was pressing for action on the question.[49]

Eventually in 1836 the Wesleyan Conference decided to reverse the practice they had followed since the 1790s and physically ordain the probationers by the laying on of hands. The proposal that year was carried with only two dissenting votes showing the complete change from the previous view. The ordinations were to be carried out as a high point in the Conference proceedings, and separate ordination services did not develop until later. Conference did not call for those preachers who had survived since they had been ordained by Wesley to be associated with this new departure. Why was this? Probably they did not think of the question of 'apostolic succession,' regarded as so important later. The survivors were all superannuated and in most cases infirm. It has also been suggested that the only survivor was the eighty-four year old Henry Moore, who had ironically been specifically ordained for England by Wesley nearly forty years before. Moore had certainly quarrelled with his brethren over a number of issues and no longer came to Conference. On the other hand, he was still well enough and would have come had he been invited.

In fact there were four others still alive among the preachers belonging to the Conference that year who had been ordained, to say nothing of those in America who had been ordained by Coke or Asbury, in addition to Henry Moore.

James Bogie, who was to die in April 1837, was aged seventy-nine. He had been ordained by Wesley for Scotland and later acquired a Scots wife. In 1836 he was living at Low Hill, Liverpool. His obituary reported that for his last two

---

[47] J. D. Walsh in *HMGB* 1: 281, but see note 53 below for it being suggested by 1815.

[48] Another example of the situation after Wesley of the president being still unable to carry business and an important one in view of who was president that year (see Chapter 9 above). Smith, *Meth* 3: 35.

[49] *PWHS* 16 (1935) 148-53; George, *LHQR* 1951: 164.

years, 1835-7, he was in declining health and so he was probably too infirm. Matthew Lumb had been ordained by Wesley in 1788; a returned missionary from the West Indies, he was the last of these five to die, in 1847. In 1836 he was living at Otley with his daughter, though he died at Harrogate. His obituary also reported that his mental 'faculties had been maimed for several years' before his death.[50]

John Ogylvie, ordained by Thomas Coke for Scotland as late as 1808, was in his early seventies in 1836. He died in 1839 at Dulow in Cornwall when his obituary reported that he had 'lived retired among his children' and had 'little intercourse with his brethren' (the other ministers). Since one son was an Anglican clergyman in Cornwall, all this may explain why no Methodist thought of asking him to share in the ordination of preachers. The final preacher was John de Queteville, the Channel Islander ordained by Coke to go to France in 1792. He did not die till 1843. He was living in his home on the island and still acting as editor of '*Le Magasin Methodiste,*' the Magazine of the French Methodist church. He could well have been asked, but perhaps in the islands he was cut off from the main stream of British Methodism.[51] In addition, these last two were ordained by Coke, not Wesley. Certainly Henry Moore thought that important and it is likely that others agreed with him.

Why Not Use Henry Moore in 1836?

This brings us back to Henry Moore. Living in London at the heart of Methodism, the preacher ordained by Wesley with this very purpose in mind, Moore was still active and did not die until 1844. He was very concerned about the question and certainly thought he should have been asked.[52] Jonathan Crowther twenty years before had hinted at how the process might work.[53] Despite his ripe years, why was he not asked? The doctrine of ministerial ordination, as formulated by Alfred Barrett and accepted by Conference at this time, was that the ordaining body was the Conference represented by the president and ex presidents. Moore was, of course, an ex-president and so should and would have been asked to preside or at least assist in modern circumstances, but he was at odds with his brethren. He had managed to antagonize them over several different issues. Because he was the sole survivor of the three executors of Wesley's will, Wesley's manuscripts were still in his possession. He claimed the right to control the preaching at City Road and to

---

[50] Bogie's wife came from Dumfries. *WMM* 1837: 878, 1847: 411, 922. Yet the eleven years before his death is perhaps too long for the 'several' mentioned.
[51] *WMM* 1839: 764; de Jersey, *de Queteville*.
[52] Smith, *Moore* 123.
[53] J. Crowther, *The Life of Thomas Coke* (London: Edwards, 1815) 44, 55: 'he ought to consecrate some bishops and then he, and they, ought to ordain the preachers in general.'

have free housing on the premises. Conference was insistent on its right to control who was appointed as the Superintendent who would occupy the prestigious Wesley's House. It did not want it monopolized by Moore. There were also other causes of friction between Moore and the other preachers. It is true that modern ideas of 'succession' were not present at the time. Nobody thought it important!

In August 1837 Moore wrote to the then president of Conference (Edmund Grindrod 1837-8) on the whole question as follows

> The Scriptural way of ordination by imposition of hands was allowed by the Apostles, and since their time has been allowed by the Church in every age. Mr Wesley allowed this and ordained-first for America-secondly for Scotland -and thirdly for England 'when the time should come'... I am the only person now alive that Mr Wesley committed that power to, and I know that he committed it for the purpose that it should become a common thing, whenever it should be judged by the Conference best to adopt it.[54]

Moore was not entirely accurate here. Lumb was still alive though Bogie had died since the Conference of 1836. Admittedly Lumb had been ordained for the West Indies. Moore was the only survivor of the three preachers Wesley had ordained for England.

Perhaps as a result of the views expressed in this letter Moore *was* included in the ordination of four missionaries in 1839 on the 14th April, though he had not been involved in 1836.[55] These four were George Pope for Canada, John Garrett, Edward Squarebridge and William Arthur for India. Since Arthur went on to become President of Conference in 1866 Wesleyan ministers since 1866 (and Methodists from 1932) can claim to be in an 'apostolic succession' from Wesley himself via Henry Moore. Another similar succession line was pointed out by George. Atmore, ordained by Wesley for Scotland in 1786, ordained William Shaw for South Africa in 1819. In 1865 Shaw was President and ordaining the ordinands that year, one year earlier than 1866. Not all 'Wesley's Preachers' in the twenty-first century are concerned about this![56]

Conclusion

Ordination was what many itinerants wanted. Most of the Methodist people outside England and Ireland before the end of the eighteenth century wanted it for their preachers. In America it became possible after 1784 and by 1800 it was a normal stage in the itinerant's career after his time on probation. In Britain before 1786 ordination was impossible because of Wesley's opposition. Gradually over the next fifteen years it became usual for missionaries and for

---

[54] *PWHS* 9 (1914) 153-4 quoting Smith *Meth.*
[55] N. W. Taggart, *William Arthur* (Peterborough: MPH, 1993) 5; *PWHS* 24 (1919) 103.
[56] A. R. George in *HMGB* 2: 154.

many preachers going to Scotland. In England the practice was much more random. Though Wesley had ordained at least three men for England before his death, the way in which his preachers behaved after his death, in rejecting ordination by imposition of hands while carrying out many 'personal' ordinations and administering the sacraments wherever the people asked for them to deflect the popular demand, meant that no solid agreement on the validity and principles of ordination was reached. When eventually Wesleyan Methodism decided to ordain all its new preachers in full connexion by the imposition of hands, this was done without reference to or using those whom Wesley or Coke had ordained. 'Succession' from Wesley was seen as less important than the power of Conference and the equal rights of each minister. Yet by the late 1860s an 'apostolic succession' from Wesley had developed for British Methodist ministers.

Chapter 19

Retirement

'Q. What are the rules relating to the Preachers' Fund?
A. As to the subsistence of those who are so entirely worn out, that they cannot preach at all;
1. Let every Travelling Preacher contribute half-a-guinea yearly, at the Conference…'
Minutes of the 1765 Conference.

The Problem

When the Wesleys began to use itinerant lay preachers there was no provision for those who became old. The original preachers were mostly young and able to look after themselves, such as many of their Anglican clergy friends. Sometimes there were neither wives nor families to support. They had not then spent long travelling. When they wanted to marry many chose to separate themselves from Wesley and deliberately joined other groups who might support them and their families even in old age such as the Moravians, the friends of George Whitefield or the Dissenters. Others, like William Shent or John Nelson, were only partly itinerant and maintained a shop or trade with which they supported themselves and their families, something on which they could fall back if they became less active preachers. Nor was retirement an idea which appealed to John Wesley himself or was common in the eighteenth century. Wesley's oft-repeated ideal was that 'he would cease at once to work and live.'[1] Since he had no intention of ever retiring himself he saw no need for his preachers to do so either, let alone organize provision for them. Equally, the eighteenth century had no retirement system. Nobody expected to retire at sixty-five or seventy. If they got to such age, which was unusual, they struggled

---

[1] Charles Wesley's hymn ran 'O, that without a lingering groan, I may the welcome word receive; my body with my charge lay down, and cease at once to work and live!' John Wesley quoted it frequently during prayers at his house at City Road in his last year and usually used it as the last hymn in services he took on his final tour in 1790. J. Telford, *Life of Wesley* (London: Wesleyan Bookroom, 1902) 345-6. The hymn was omitted from modern British Methodist hymnbooks, presumably because modern Methodists expect a protracted period between work and death!

on. This was as true of politicians, financiers, monarchs, bishops and clergy as it was of coalminers, carpenters and tinkers. Few could afford retirement. If they stopped working they often regretted it. Widows of preachers were especially vulnerable as immediately homeless and without support.

In the eighteenth century most people were conscious of the ubiquity and inevitability of death. Each year at the beginning of Conference the Methodist preachers sang Charles Wesley's question with a feeling of surprise 'And are we yet alive, and see each other's face?'[2] However, as time went on there were many preachers who had served for twenty years or more, some with wives and families to support. Few had financial resources they could call upon for help in prolonged illness or old age. The itinerant system was particularly difficult for the elderly because of its constant unremitting travel and effort in preaching and visiting. Even the aged John Wesley retreated to his chaise. Some of his itinerants wanted to devise a system of financial support for his 'worn out' preachers. Christopher Hopper, who had entered in 1749, expressed the question forcibly in a letter to Charles Wesley in 1759 after ten years service

> If a Methodist preacher live till he be weak and worn out with travelling, I apprehend he must either be ordained or turn Dissenting teacher, or sit down by his own fire (if he has one) or be cast out and rejected like an old superannuated Hottentot left in his hut to die in mercy in his old age. Now Sir, if matters should come to this conclusion, I'll ask you in the fear of God, which of these would you have an poor worn out brother to choose? All this and more has been answered with one word: 'You want faith,' 'You've lost your zeal.' This may be soon said but still I'm to believe that true faith, though above, never contradicts sound reason. However, be as it will, I'm a Methodist yet, & if my brethren will do me justice, I think they never saw anything in my whole deportment very bad, but there were some born to find fault, & those are the unhappy men. I've preached since I was married, as I did before, but those men say, He is silent; I've kept my Circuit constantly, which is I suppose some three hundred miles in a month, as before[3]

Hopper's complaints bore fruit in four years time when Conference set up the Preachers' Fund to deal with the problem.

Preachers' Fund

Pawson later reported that at the 1763 Conference 'it was said that several of the Preachers… asked what they should do for support if they should live to be

---

[2] J. McManners, *Death and the Enlightenment* (Oxford: OUP, 1981) 439. Number 707 in *Hymns and Psalms*, it was and is traditionally sung at the beginning of the British Conference. It was first published in 1749 in *Hymns and Sacred Poems*. For its use in America see Richey, *Conference in America* 128-9.

[3] MS letter at Emory University, printed *HMGB* 4: 141-2. It was to the more sympathetic Charles that Hopper wrote, not to his more inflexible brother.

Chart 13: Preachers' Fund

Year	Annual Income for the Fund				
	Annual Subscription	Entry Fee	From Preachers	Other income	Total
1763	£0.10.0				
1765	£0.10.6	1g*			
1771	**	**			£63.8.5
1780					£87.
1790					£695.8.7
1794			£380.7.0	£795.4.2	£1,175.11.2
1796	1g	2g			£1,249.17.3
1798				Merciful Fund	
1813	£1.11.6	10g		£3,378	

Year	Main Change	Annual Expenditure		
		Preachers	Widows	Total
1763	Fund set up			
1765	First printed Minutes	£10***	£40 total***	
1771	First payment noted	5g	5g	£36.5.0
1780	First support for Preachers' wives	£16	£7	£120.5.0
1790	Wesley's last Conference	£17.11.4	£14.3.1	£583.11.0
1794	First time lay donations noted separately	£17.12.8	£14.10.9	£718.0.0
1796	Major increase	£21.5.1	£16.10.6	£922.6.0
1798	New Annuitant Society	All payments in these 2 columns are average per person from 1790 onwards		
1813	Auxiliary Fund			£2,374.2.0

Key
*   guinea.
**   1765 level probably maintained until 1796.
***   fixed at that level, but no actual payments known.

Source: *Minutes*

past their labour.' The result was the setting up of the Preachers' Fund for 'old or worn out preachers,' though John Wesley himself 'did not approve as he always thought it worldly.'[4] Each travelling preacher was to contribute ten shillings a year. No rules survive for how much support would be provided or criteria as to who exactly would receive help or when they would receive it; something was to be paid to the 'old or sickly' preachers and to the widows and children of those preachers who had died. A new group of 'supernumerary' preachers was established to help in those circuits where there was most need; they would receive payment from those circuits.[5] With the first regular printing of the *Minutes* in 1765 a more complex system appeared in the rules for the Preachers' Fund (see Chart 13). A reason for this printing may well have been to make it clear who should be supported by the new Fund and how it would be financed. Very few preachers could not preach at all and qualified at that time for help from the Fund.

Each active travelling preacher was to contribute half a guinea at each Conference to this Fund, which was slightly more than had been previously agreed. New entrants to the scheme had to pay one guinea at their entry. Superannuated preachers, that is those who were allowed to retire because they could not preach at all, were to receive £10 p.a. and their widows a final payment of £40. Nobody was entitled to anything unless they had paid at least two guineas and so three years service was a minimum for qualification. Equally, if they retired without the agreement of Wesley and the Conference they would receive nothing. The generosity over back payments was shown in the rule that any preacher who 'neglects paying his subscription for four years' was excluded.[6] The following year those who did not bring or send their subscription to the Conference were fined half a crown, a sure sign that many had not contributed.[7] Contributions to the Preachers' Fund were also solicited from those who were not preachers, in other words from wealthy laymen. There is no evidence as to how much this provided until 1794 when lay contributions were significantly almost twice as much as the total contributions by preachers.[8] In addition, there were provisions for the widows and children of

---

[4] Quotations from Pawson in *EMP* 4: 27. Since there were no ordinary *Minutes* surviving for 1763 this is the only source apart from the new edition of the *Large Minutes* cited in note 6 below. For the significance of Wesley's opposition see p 411 below. The *Minutes* have been the main source for everything in this Chapter about the Preachers' Fund.

[5] Tyerman 2: 478-79. For a definition of supernumerary see page 372 below.

[6] *Minutes* 1: 49-50. It was also stated that the fund must never be reduced below £100, which would certainly limit payments at first. Further definition of superannuating and how it differed from being a supernumerary is explained in more detail below. See also Chart 13.

[7] *Minutes* 1: 58. Half a crown was two shillings and sixpence since there were four crowns to the pound.

[8] Lloyd, *The Labourer's Hire* 28-38 is the best summary for this Fund providing the best

'worn-out' preachers; they were expected to support themselves as far as possible.

The success of the whole system depended on the amounts subscribed being sufficient and the numbers of those who received money being limited. While the total of active preachers grew each year and those preachers allowed to retire were few, it had a chance. This situation was true for most of the next twenty years. However, Wesley was never clear about where the help would come from for the travelling preachers, let alone the 'worn-out' ones; he was always acting hand to mouth, seeking support from wherever money was available and raiding this fund and other sources so that the London Stewards were often called upon for help simply because they had the greatest resources.[9]

Levels of Support

The level of support provided by this fund to 'worn-out preachers' was low. The first we know about how much was paid was in 1771, when the fund was already eight years old and £36 and five shillings was distributed to a total of six annuitants, four of them widows and two former preachers. Five of them received five guineas each, which seems to have been the standard payment then. Of these Mary Penington (1726-1802) had been born the well-connected Mary Teare of Athlone, her brother being Rector there. She was converted by Wesley in her twenties and brought her parents into the society. She married the preacher William Penington[10] in 1765. They had a daughter, another Mary, in 1766, and the new mother became a long-term beneficiary of the Preachers' Fund after her husband's early death in 1767. Mary Penington lived with her mother and daughter in Athlone until at least 1785. Wesley frequently stayed there on his Irish visits and suggested in 1771 to the Methodist Limerick shopkeeper Thomas Mason that Mason should marry Mary, but nothing seems

---

commentary on the *Minutes*. He said 1763 was relatively early as few then had service of over fifteen years and other financial provisions for them were still sketchy. However, his discussion on page 31 does not seem to realise the importance of lay contributions to the Fund, presumably because they were not listed until 1794 and not regularly then. *Minutes* 1: 73. In 1767 a rule was made that the Fund must never be allowed to fall below £500, which implies that well wishers' subscriptions must have been at least half the total by that period, if it was to pay anything that year.

[9] FB Polity 253. MS London Stewards Accounts at MARC show Cornelius Bastable received small payments in 1766 and 1768 though not appearing in the *Minutes* and in 1766 being apparently in poor health at Bristol (MS letter Fl/T 1.3/5 at MARC).

[10] *Minutes* 1: 100. The two former preachers were Samuel Levick and Richard Lucas. The widows who received the standard amount were Elizabeth Oldham, Elizabeth Dillon and Mary Penington. It is not clear why Elizabeth Standring received £10. Only about Mary Penington is much known, thanks to Crk (1882) 5-19; cf. *WJW* 20: 270 n63. For William Penington see page 148 above. 'Penington' is the most common spelling for him, 'Pennington' more common for her, but I have omitted her 'n' for consistency.

to have come of it.[11] After her mother's death, and her daughter's marriage in 1785 to the soldier and future itinerant Joseph Burgess, Mary Penington travelled with them until she died on the 9th June 1802. The last payment she received from the Preachers' Fund was £15 in 1801.[12]

Heitzenrater calculated that an income of £30 per annum was the level below which poverty appeared in the eighteenth century, so that most labourers, small craftsmen and manual workers were poor.[13] Those who were superannuated or their widows were well below that level. Levels of payment did rise as Chart 13 shows. Presumably there could be some help from local societies in addition, since the *Large Minutes* said that widows and children were to receive £10 per annum. The money given from the Fund to the preachers and their widows could be varied at Wesley's discretion each year on the basis of what he saw as their need. Sometimes mistakes meant that payment did not happen, leading to double amounts the next year, but these did not provide luxury![14]

Being a Supernumerary

The term 'Supernumerary' means literally being over the numbers needed on the circuit. 'Superannuated' derives from being 'over the years,' so having completed the total of years expected for a preacher. In the 1770 edition of the *Large Minutes* Wesley defined a Supernumerary preacher as one 'who can preach four or five times a week.' Baker[15] explained the term Supernumerary

> From 1767 several names appear, followed by the term 'supernumerary.' This seems to imply that they were extra preachers for the circuit in which they were stationed, carrying only a small load of responsibility and paid by the circuit. This was usually done after a severe illness, as in the case of Christopher Hopper, whose name is the first thus to appear and who returned to the full work in the following year.

From 1765 and into the nineteenth century a Supernumerary was distinguished from a 'superannuated' preacher: the former was still subject to stationing and

---

[11] *PWHS* 32 (1959) 63; *Crk* 1: 208; *WJW* 22: 190; *JWL* 5: 254. Telford's note in the last said the Molly Penington referred to was the daughter, but since she was only four years old in May 1771 and Wesley referred to her as being 'of middle age, well tried, of good sense and of deep experience' it must be the widow in her forties not the daughter.

[12] *WJW* 24: 137; *Crk* (1882); *Minutes* 2: 106. Earlier there were more widows than preachers receiving money, but by 1796 there were 27 preachers and only 19 widows.

[13] Heitzenrater, *The Poor* 18.

[14] Lloyd, *The Labourer's Hire* 31. For a failure to pay which was made up the following year, see for example *Minutes* 1: 358 where Parson Greenwood received £64, half of which should have been paid the year before.

[15] *HMGB* 1: 250-1; cf. Heitzenrater 234.

supported by 'normal' circuit or connexional funds; the latter was regarded as being 'worn out' and received a pension from the Preachers' Fund. The first was expected to preach in his circuit frequently, though he was no longer able to preach twice a day. Nothing was expected from the second, who might or might not be able to preach. Being a Supernumerary was essentially a temporary status. The Supernumerary still appeared on the stations. If he died in the 1780s he received an obituary unlike those who had superannuated.

In 1767 the first Supernumeraries were listed in the *Minutes*: John Johnson and Christopher Hopper, who had written the 1759 letter to Charles. Hopper was a Supernumerary only for a year, but John Johnson superannuated the following year and 'dropped' to being only a local preacher in 1770.[16] Another example was Robert Empringham, who was born in Lincolnshire and entered the itinerancy in 1771. In 1778, having travelled the Methodist world, he was back in his native Grimsby circuit suffering from ill health. At the 1779 Conference he disappeared from the stations and retired in the Grimsby circuit. By March 1780 he had recovered enough for Wesley to suggest he should go to Whitby to help 'as they need a Supernumerary preacher.'[17] In 1782 he was able to resume a full ministry. Though it was possible that being a Supernumerary was the first step to becoming completely retired as with John Johnson, many men like Empringham and Hopper were able to resume the complete itinerant ministry after a year or so as a Supernumerary.[18] In 1783 George Snowden (who had entered in 1769) and in 1787 John Shaw (who entered in 1763) both spent a year as a Supernumerary, in each case resuming the full ministry the following year.

Supernumeraries could be very active, using their energy in different ways since they were not travelling as much as an ordinary itinerant. Thus John Atlay, the Book Steward, appeared as a Supernumerary preacher in London from 1784 to 1788 because he was concentrating on Wesley's publishing business, by then an important revenue stream for Methodism. He continued to preach but not as much as the other preachers in the circuit.

A further instance of the way this Supernumerary stage could be a transitional one was Robert Carr Brackenbury.[19] Brackenbury was sui generis a Cambridge-educated wealthy landowner who had become a Methodist preacher to whom Wesley could appeal when he wanted a one-man mission in an area;

---

[16] Heitzenrater 234, 278.

[17] *Minutes*; *JWL* 7: 8-9.

[18] Empringham received no money from the Preachers' Fund in 1781 or 1782. However, in 1781 John Furz, also listed as a Supernumerary that year but a much more senior preacher, received £12 from the Fund; of the other Supernumeraries Richard Seed, Joseph Bradford, and William Boothby also received nothing from the Fund like Empringham. Wesley was already allowing money to be paid from the Fund to a special case like Furz.

[19] Perhaps the best relatively modern account of Brackenbury remains L. F. Church, *More About The Early Methodist People* (London: Epworth, 1949) 117-125.

he 'travelled irregularly for forty years' as Eayrs put it.[20] As a French speaker Wesley had persuaded him to lead the mission in the Channel Islands in 1783. In 1790 Brackenbury returned, the mission having been established and he became a Supernumerary preacher within his own circuit (that year Gainsborough). After Wesley's death he retained the relationship with Conference, many of whose members had benefited by staying in his house and reading his books. In 1791 Brackenbury emerged to go to Portland in Dorset to start a mission. Though his time there was shorter, yet again he preached, founded societies and built chapels, providing a base for other preachers.[21] He finished as a Supernumerary in the Spilsby circuit, but was always one who might go and preach at the other end of the country at a moment's notice.

Superannuation

A preacher who had superannuated had reached a permanent condition and would not return, drawing money from the Preachers' Fund and being listed each year in its accounts. He would not, in the 1770s or for some time after, receive an obituary in the *Minutes*. The first obituary for a preacher in this position was Robert Swindells in 1783. He had ceased to appear on the stations and had superannuated ten years before. He was an exception.[22] After Wesley's death Conference drew another line in this minefield. In 1793 it ruled that 'every Preacher shall be considered as a Supernumerary for four years after he has desisted from travelling, and shall afterwards be deemed to have superannuated' (quoted Baker as above). As late as 1808 this distinction had not been abandoned and all superannuated preachers did not appear in the stations. Wesley's preachers mostly did not superannuate, but died in the active work. The modern situation of the British Methodist minister retiring when he or she reaches a certain age and drawing superannuation payments for the remainder of his or her life was definitely not open to Wesley's preachers.

In 1803 the first list of all superannuated preachers was printed, listed by circuit. Thirty names were given for England and five for Ireland, but of these only five appeared on the English (and four on the Irish) stations as Supernumeraries who retained their ministerial status in the *Minutes*. They were listed there according to wherever they resided.[23] In other words most of the retired preachers were still not called Supernumeraries. There was a long period going on well into the nineteenth century when this status was not yet

---

[20] Workman, Eayrs and Townsend, *New History* 1: 317.
[21] Brackenbury tried to make it impossible for anyone to write his biography. Sources include Smith *Raithby*; *PWHS* 13 (1922) 68, 20 (1936) 169, 28 (1952) 170-4, 33 (1961) 12, 5l; Moore *CI* 18-59; Biggs, *Early Dorset* 27-33; *Wesley Banner* 1851 110, 267; DEB.
[22] *Minutes* 1: 159. For more on obituaries see the next chapter.
[23] *Minutes* 2: 179.

clear. Most men retired and were left out of the *Minutes*. If they died they did not receive an obituary. It therefore becomes difficult to determine whether or not they left. If there were payments from the Preachers' Fund until their death I have assumed they died in the work. An obituary also showed they died in the work but, as we have seen, obituaries did not necessarily appear until into the nineteenth century for those who had retired. There is usually no consensus in the evidence for these problems. The next section deals with some examples to illustrate this.

Individual Preachers in Retirement

Joseph Jerome

Joseph Jerome entered in 1783 probably from the wider Nottingham area, and he travelled until 1792 when he disappeared from the *Minutes*.[24] He returned to the stations in 1794 at Leicester as a Supernumerary and so presumably had been ill. In 1795 he was at Derby, still as a Supernumerary. In 1796 there was no record again so probably he was too ill to act as a Supernumerary and had left, though in 1799 he received three pounds from the connexion as 'an act of mercy.'[25] It is an interesting example of how the system of support for sick preachers was in the process of change after Wesley's death, and how, as we have seen in Chapter 15, prolonged sickness meant leaving the itinerancy. There was no obituary for Jerome and his date of death is unknown.[26]

Joseph Sanderson

Joseph Sanderson, a Yorkshireman from Birstall, entered in 1775 and was put in the original Legal Hundred by the Deed of Declaration early in 1784. Later that year he left the itinerancy and so was removed from the Legal Hundred after only five months. He was, according to his own account, 'burried (sic) alive in one town' in Dundee for 1784-5.[27] He had set up as a merchant there but returned to the full work in 1786, serving for two years in Newcastle and Aberdeen.[28] In 1788 Sanderson appeared as a Supernumerary going to Dundee

---

[24] He always appears as 'Jerom' in the *Minutes* but Jerome appears elsewhere and is the modern version. Another version was 'Jer(r)am.'

[25] This is all based on the *Minutes* though Myles said he left in 1798. *MM* 1804: 100; Myles; National Burial Index (version one), J. Everett, *Adam Clarke Portrayed* (London: Hamilton Adams, 1843) 1: 154-5.

[26] He could be the early nineteenth century local preacher Jerram in Nottingham.

[27] A. J. Hayes, *Edinburgh Methodism 1761-1975 The Mother Churches* (Edinburgh: the author, 1976) 51-6; *PWHS* 1 (1898) 38, 10 (1916) 88, 94-7, 11 (1911) 7-12. He always spelt his name Sanderson but in the *Minutes* it always appeared as Saunderson.

[28] Described as a merchant of Dundee in the Feu Charter of Arbroath Methodist church 1784 see G. W. Davis, *Arbroath Methodism: the Story of Wesley's 'Totum Kirkie'*

once more, after which he was not in the *Minutes* for three years so had probably left, though Wesley stayed with him at Dundee on the 18th May 1790.[29] He returned to the full work for the second time in 1792, became Chairman of the Aberdeen District in 1793, and was suggested by Pawson to Atmore for ordination in 1794. He became a Supernumerary again in Edinburgh in 1796 and then moved around in and close to Scotland until 1806, when he finally disappeared from the *Minutes*.[30] He was described by his descendant, the historian John Smith Simon, as 'a half-itinerant' in business who possessed means, and so was able to send the future itinerant David M'Nicoll to college. There was no obituary, which raises the question as to whether he left or died in the work. His family's tradition was that he was ordained by Wesley and did die in the work. The first is unlikely in view of Pawson's suggestion since Pawson should have known about an earlier ordination; the second is likely but cannot be proved. Sanderson was someone who did not remain a full itinerant because of his business. The help that he could still give to the connexion in Scotland, where there were greater distances and a shortage of itinerants, was very useful. His preaching was later described as distinguished which may well have encouraged other preachers to try to retain him. As late as 1806, however, his name was removed from the *Minutes* without an obituary, though he may have died that year. Presumably his brethren felt he had not been doing enough and so was not worthy.[31]

Thomas Rankin

We have already met in Chapter 12 Thomas Rankin as Wesley's Superintendent in America until the Revolution. He returned from America in late 1778 and early the following year married Mrs Bradshaw, a wealthy widow, whose business kept him in London. As a result from 1783 to 1796 his name appeared as a Supernumerary in London by special request (at least at first) of John Wesley. During this time he remained active, preaching and leading classes, so that in February 1789, when Wesley wanted to ordain someone for England for after his own death the best person he could think of, in addition to the young Henry Moore and the senior adviser Alexander Mather, was Rankin.[32]

However, Rankin's brethren among the preachers had a different view. Myles and Crowther, both fellow preachers present at Conference, described

---

(Arbroath: the author, 1996) 5.
[29] *WJW* 24: 317n.
[30] Listed as Aberdeen 1798, Alnwick 1801, Dundee 1802 and Glasgow 1805 (*Minutes*).
[31] *PWHS* 10 (1916) 88, 94-7. Myles said he left in 1800 which was too early. Harrison, *Companions* 45-52.
[32] *Pawson L* 1: 17, 94-9, 129, 144; *PWHS* 9 (1914) 152-4, 13 (1922) 16, 24 (1944) 79-80, 33 (1962) 119-21; Baker, *Wesley and the Church* 281; Stevenson, *City Road* 400-2.

him as having left in 1787. Duncan, the later historian of the Annuitant Society, described him as 'not a Supernumerary in the ordinary acceptance of the term.'[33] In 1796 his name was removed from the *Minutes* though he remained the active preacher he had been, continuing to preach at least once a week and lead a class until his death in 1810. His wife had died in April 1798 and on her death he wrote that he wanted no money.[34] When he died he did not receive an obituary in the *Minutes*, a striking omission for one who had once been so prominent and so close to Wesley; there was an obituary in the *Magazine* that year which said he 'had been a preacher in the Connexion of the late John Wesley about fifty years,' implying he had been until his death.[35] Some modern historians agree, but contemporary opinion was more often that he had left.[36]

The last years of Thomas Rankin, therefore, show that even famous men who were counted as preachers might not receive any listing in the *Minutes* or an obituary there, even if they were still active as Rankin was as late as 1810. It was only towards the end of the next decade that obituaries for those who had retired became standard.

John Watson Junior (1749-1837)

John Watson junior was the son of the Irish itinerant of the same name. He began to travel in 1771 and officially entered at the 1772 Irish Conference. By at least 1778, like so many other Irish itinerants, he was travelling in Britain. In 1785 he lost his voice recovering from a violent fever and became unable to preach in large chapels. As a result he appeared on the stations as a Supernumerary, first at Bedford and then Leicester, Aberdeen, Penzance, St Austell and Pembroke, giving what help he could. He received money from the Preachers' Fund from at least 1786 to 1796 and then again from 1798. He died aged 88 on the 2nd April 1837 at Bath where he had been for twenty-one years at the home of his niece. He was not able to do a full itinerant's job from 1785, but could help actively in a number of different circuits for probably twenty years at least. It is not clear at what point he was no longer able to help. Watson had survived long enough to have a continued listing on the stations, so

---

[33] *PWHS* 2 (1900) 219, 22 (1940) 119-20, 38 (1971) 30-1; P. Duncan, *Wesleyan Ministers' Annuitant Society: A Critical Examination* (London: Mason, 1858).

[34] *Pawson L* 1: 17, 94-9, 129, 144; *PWHS* 9 (1914) 92-3; *EMP* 5: 135-217; *AM* 1779: 182-98; *MM* 1799: 71-6, 1811: 561-895.

[35] *MM* 1810: 281. The full obituary in *MM* 1811 described him as 'Minister of the Gospel.'

[36] W. R. Ward thought he died in the work in *WJW* 22; 19 n82. Hills only restored him to the list of those who died in the work in 1936, 126 years after his death! Of contemporary writers only Atmore agreed, having Thomas Rankin in his list of preachers 'now labouring' in 1801. Myles, Crowther and even Jesse Lee in America, all followed the *Minutes* and said he left.

receiving an obituary in the *Minutes*.[37] He is an example of what became the regular system in the nineteenth century under which 'worn-out' preachers would be supported by the Connexion without question, so long as they had sufficient service behind them.

Wesley and the Preachers' Fund

Other Connexional Funds were set up in the 1760s such as the General Fund, established 1761. Wesley regarded all these as subject to him, on which he could draw if he needed money for some other part of Methodism. He did this with the Preachers' Fund and the receipts from the Bookroom. By the early 1780s the Preachers' Fund was paying out each year to retired preachers significantly less than the income received. As a result, when faced with major financial problems in the 1780s as the number of married preachers rose and proved too great a burden for the circuits, Wesley raided this retirement fund for payments to wives saying 'What can I do? Must the work stand still? The men and their families cannot starve. I have no money. Here it is; we must use it. It is for the Lord's work.'

Many of his preachers objected and in 1784 the practice was stopped when the fund ran too low. However, as it picked up in the later 1780s he milked it again. In 1791 one of the first acts of the newly independent Conference was to forbid such use of the Preachers' Fund.[38] As a result of his raids the fund found itself in difficulty in the later 1790s as the number of annuitants swelled when more of Wesley's preachers retired.

Reasons for and against Retirement

Not Wanting to Retire

Admittedly many of the preachers did not want to retire and were determined to remain itinerant as long as they could. Wesley himself set the example of not retiring but paradoxically tended to insist that if his preachers could not do the whole work of a preacher they must retire. In America there were leaders like Asbury and Whatcoat who died while still travelling as Bishops. After Wesley's death this tendency increased, at least among those who were leaders in the Connexion. This was partly because Conference did not want to insist on retirement in cases where the individual had contributed so much to Methodism. Coke was the pattern for all missionaries, dying at the age of sixty-six in his cabin on the long voyage to India in 1814. Pawson, despite a distressing and crippling illness, died in harness in the Wakefield circuit at the

---

[37] *WMM* 1837: 397, 709, 1840; 959; Myles.
[38] *Minutes* 1: 334, 338, 367. The Wesley quotation comes from the letter the Stewards of the Fund wrote to the Methodist people in 1795. Lloyd, *Labourer's Hire* 31-2.

age of sixty-eight in March 1806.[39] The prime example was Samuel Bardsley, the oldest preacher in the connexion at time of his death at Delph on his way from Conference to his new circuit at Manchester in 1818 at the age of eighty-two. Some junior preachers had agreed to ensure he would never need to superannuate, by supporting him in whichever circuit he was. Bardsley had travelled fifty years.[40] Thomas Taylor, pioneer in Pembrokeshire and elsewhere, was eventually forced to retire in 1816, at the age of seventy-eight. Until then he had maintained his preaching and travelling around the circuit. Three months later he died having travelled fifty-five years. Dying in the pulpit like Downes in 1753 was regarded as ideal yet rarely achieved.[41]

Reasons for Retirement

Usually the reason for retirement was ill health, often caused by the stresses of the itinerancy, such as accidents while travelling. Thomas Longley, who was born in 1743 and entered the itinerancy in 1780, was involved in a coach accident in 1806. He was concussed and fractured his shoulder blade. His journal ended and he became a Supernumerary that year, dying three years later.[42] John Allen, who came from Chapel-en-le-Frith in the Peak District, entered in 1765 at the age of twenty-six, superannuated because of asthma and arthritic illness in 1799 and died in 1810.[43]

There were preachers addicted to smoking like Thomas Kelk (1768-1836) of whom Everett said he 'could master anything but his pipe, by which he was always mastered, to the prejudice of his health and the frequent annoyance of those who truly loved him.' Kelk had to superannuate at the age of sixty in 1828.[44] There were a few preachers who had some money like Rankin, often from a wealthy wife but sometimes with a business or property as in her case; they wanted to retire partially in order to concern themselves with the business while retaining as far as possible the preacher's status and privileges. Rankin was allowed to remain in the *Minutes* for some time, but not indefinitely. A similar case was that of William Blagborne, whose marriage to a wealthy wife enabled him to decline his stipend in 1793.[45] Born in 1754 he entered in 1785 and in the 1790s travelled in key circuits. In 1799 Blagborne was chosen with two others to act as 'Accountant' to manage the Bookroom accounts, which shows how much he was trusted by the other preachers.[46] In 1802 he

---

[39] Pawson's realistic description of his last illness is in *Pawson L* 3: 127-136, 149.
[40] Jackson, *Recollections* 167-71.
[41] For Taylor see *MM* 1816: 945-7. For Downes see Chapter 20.
[42] Appleby, *Longley* 4.
[43] *MM* 1810: 356-7, 1812: 1-10, 81-90; *DEB*; Tyerman BMM 1.
[44] Shaw, *Camelford* 19.
[45] MS London Stewards' Account Book. See also Lenton, *My Sons* 33 for the wife.
[46] *Minutes* 2: 24: Robert Lomas was the Bookroom Steward, John Leppington and

superannuated, living first in Bath and then in York since his wife's income presumably allowed him to retire early, there being no suggestions of health problems. His continued prosperity is shown by his gift of £100 to the new chapel at Fulford on the outskirts of York in 1805.[47] In 1806 Blagborne's wife died suddenly leaving him with four young children, but his financial prosperity remained since he was able to give £25 to Wilberforce's election campaign next year. In 1808 he returned to the active work serving at Stroud.[48]

Where Retired Preachers Lived

Preachers often went to live with one or more of their surviving children. This was particularly applicable when they became widowers (and was even more true for preachers' widows) though it meant much geographical mobility, especially for those who lived with ministerial children. This care for parents in the extended family was common in the society in which they lived. William Thompson was the Irish-born first president after Wesley's death. His wife died during 1797-8. In April 1799 he was forced to retire from the itinerancy and was given the large sum of £31 10s to furnish a house close to his daughter's home in Birmingham. Alexander Suter, having retired in 1812, settled with his wife at their son's in Halifax in 1814 and died there. His Cornish-born widow Mary survived until she died thirty-four years later in Halifax. John Townsend died suddenly aged fifty-six in 1818 at Manchester where he had been a supernumerary from 1817. His widow died in December 1836 at Northampton aged seventy-seven, having lived from 1819 with one or other of her sons-in-law Peter and John M'Owan.[49] Alexander Mather was Superintendent of the London circuit in 1800.

> In the spring of that year he was completely laid aside; and from that time, until death brought a welcome release, he was an almost constant sufferer. At

---

Blagborne the Accountants appointed to keep a check.

[47] Lyth 289.

[48] MS letter 1806 at Bridwell Library, SMU of James Wood BPF 1/34-5; Lyth 208; *Minutes* 3: 11. His later history was unusual. He left in 1809 according to Myles, disappearing from the *Minutes* and emigrating with his family to New York, where he was received by Asbury as a Methodist preacher. Later he returned to England and was eventually buried as one of Wesley's preachers at Wesley's Chapel at City Road. Such transatlantic journeys make health problems even more unlikely.

[49] See Chapter 6 'Children as insurance' in MacFarlane, *Marriage*. For Thompson see Atmore; *Minutes* 2: 4; *Pawson L* 2: 148-51. Pawson typically thought it was too much money. For the Suters see *MM* 1817: 639, 708; *WMM* 1846: 200, 1848: 922. For the Townsends see *MM* 1818: 70; *WMM* 1837: 79.

midsummer he came to reside with his son, Dr Mather, then an eminent medical practitioner in York.[50]

An interesting example of how a preacher who had a little money might retire is Christopher Hopper, one of the early preachers whose complaint in 1759 on behalf of his older and possibly poorer brethren had led to the setting up of the Fund in 1763. The description came from his friend George Escricke, being written after Hopper's death in 1801

> About sixteen years ago, Mr Hopper having built a house adjoining the chapel at Bolton-le-Moors, from that time his wife and family resided there; while he continued his itinerant labours in the neighbouring circuits till the Conference of 1790; when, finding the infirmities of old age increasing, and being no longer capable of doing the work of an evangelist, he desisted, and from that period his labours were principally confined to Bolton; though he generally paid an annual visit to his friends in Yorkshire and the adjacent Circuits.

Hopper, born in December 1722 and still in his thirties in 1759, was therefore in his sixties when he built the house and sixty-seven when he superannuated, having travelled forty-one years. He did not die until 1802 when he was seventy-nine. His activities as listed by Escricke during these twelve years were typical of most retired preachers who wanted to be 'active supernumeraries.'[51]

After Wesley

In 1796 there were new levels of support laid down and the contributions of the preachers increased.[52] In 1795 Conference agreed to settle the fund on a legal basis which would take advantage of the Act of Parliament protecting Friendly Societies. However, they did not carry out this resolution. Another criticism was that widows who remarried were still to be paid by the fund. This caused a number of the younger preachers led by Adam Clarke and Henry Moore to take matters into their own hands. In 1798 and 1799 they took steps to set up their own Annuitant Society protected by the Act.[53]

There were no fewer than twenty-seven rules for the new Society. Only

---

[50] Lyth 189. The manse, Wesley's House, would be needed in August.

[51] *EMP* 1: 225-6. Hopper was by some distance the member of the first cohort who travelled longest. He probably travelled furthest as well, having served in Wales, Scotland, Ireland as well as England by the 1760s.

[52] Contributions were raised to one guinea each year and two guineas entry fee. The standard benefit for a superannuated preacher or widow was fixed at twelve pounds a year, but increased by one pound a year for each year served beyond twelve. In practice these levels of payment were not always met because so little money remained of what had been raised. In any case even twelve pounds a year remained extreme poverty. Lloyd, *Labourer's Hire* 32.

[53] Lloyd, *Labourer's Hire* 32-35.

preachers under forty-five could join, though until 1799 those up to fifty were also to be allowed in. Entry subscription was one guinea for those under thirty, rising to five guineas for those between forty-five and fifty. The annual subscription was also fixed at one guinea. Benefits were restricted to those declared supernumerary or superannuated by Conference, thereby putting the two groups together. Seventy-three of the preachers enrolled immediately with Thomas Roberts as Treasurer and both Clarke and Moore on the Committee. Treasurers of the Funds were usually preachers who were wealthier than the rest.[54] Next year Conference took steps to adopt the scheme. All preachers were to be allowed in, on payment by the Conference to the new Fund of £6,000, being regarded as the profits of the Bookroom which had been given by Wesley to the preachers.[55] In 1813, as a result of Clarke's detailed explanation of the whole plan in the *Magazine* a large increase took place in the donations from the Methodist people. At the same time the subscription to the Preachers' Fund was increased to ten guineas for admission and one and a half guineas for the annual subscription.[56]

The two categories of Supernumeraries and those who had superannuated had therefore been united. Those whom the Conference allowed to superannuate, officially those who had done forty years travel but in practice often a shorter period, received an allowance until their death. Their widows if they survived also received an allowance. By 1817 there were forty-eight such preachers receiving allowances, double the number of twenty years earlier. In the next twelve years the number doubled again and the burden on the funds without the donations of the people would have been unsustainable.[57] There was never in this period a satisfactory solution to this problem.

For most of Wesley's preachers who survived beyond 1815 the process was simple. Having done their forty years or so they became relatively active Supernumeraries, often for long periods. The final one to die John Hickling, billed as the 'Last of Mr Wesley's Preachers' because he was the last of those who had been accepted by Wesley, was a good example of this. He had entered in 1790 and in 1838 retired having served for forty-eight years. He settled in

---

[54] For the wealth of Roberts see Chapter 6 above. For Clarke's wealth see M. Edwards *Adam Clarke* (London: Epworth, 1942) 13. Appointing the wealthy as Treasurers has been the almost invariable Methodist practice at least until the late twentieth century.

[55] Lloyd, *Labourer's Hire* 35-6. Conference also separated the subscriptions of the preachers from the donations of the people, one fund to be called the Preachers' Fund, the other (eventually) the Merciful Fund, a title changed to Auxiliary Fund in 1813. 73 preachers represented only a fifth of the total number of British active preachers in 1799 (333), but many of these were over fifty or not at Conference.

[56] Lloyd *Labourer's Hire* 36; Brown, *Nonconformist Ministry* 194; Peirce, *Polity of the Methodists* 492. In 1813 the Auxiliary Fund subscriptions amounted to £2,635, compared to the previous year's £1,922. The Auxiliary Fund used the donations to it to supplement the Annuitant Society's payments to the superannuated preachers.

[57] Peirce, *Polity of the Methodists* 309.

Audley, Staffordshire, taking 150 services a year, and died twenty years later in November 1858, lecturing until a fortnight before his death.[58]

Between 1763, when the Preachers' Fund was set up, and 1859 when John Hickling the last Supernumerary among Wesley's preachers died, great changes had taken place. The numbers of those retired and dependent on the funds had increased beyond recognition. The receipts for the fund came more from the laity than from the preachers themselves, the rules had changed out of recognition and the payments made to the dependants were regular and strictly regulated. If supernumeraries and their widows were still poor, this was because the standards expected by contemporary society had also changed. Mid-Victorian relative prosperity had replaced the penury of society before the Industrial Revolution.

---

[58] See Chapter 1 above, *WMM* 1858: 114, 1859: 837; *PWHS* 26 (1947) 15-6, 27 (1949) 4. Hickling would certainly have received his expenses for his travels. He would probably also have received a fee.

CHAPTER 20

Death

'His days of pain & grief are o'er:
Rejoice for him who weeps no more'
Charles Wesley excerpt from 'on the death of W. Hitchin October 29th 1773.'

Introduction

Death was very important to the early Methodists. They hoped to be examples of the maxim 'Our people die well' and most did. This 'ritual of happy dying' or 'Evangelical Endings,' as it has been variously described, was one in which the sufferer 'said he was happy, felt the Love of God in his heart, that he was going to heaven and was not afraid to die.' Welcoming death was a tradition going back to the Puritans and beyond. John Wesley declared in his classic account that it was also the result of conversion.[1] Death mattered; early nineteenth century obituaries contained long descriptions of the death compared with the rest of the life. No twenty-first century biographer would dream of doing the same. The *Arminian Magazine* had far more space devoted to deathbed scenes than the Calvinist *Gospel Magazine*. Wesley saw the potential for popular appeal of such vivid accounts long before his competitors.[2] This was partly because of the assumption that death was in God's hand, rather than the doctor's.

However, during the eighteenth century doctors grew in confidence in their ability to remove pain and make death a more peaceful 'falling asleep.' One of the reasons for this was the increasing and widespread use of opium in copious quantities. It was prescribed in large amounts by physicians such as Erasmus Darwin in Shrewsbury and was also available in nostrums such as Dover's Powders or Godfrey's Cordial. The public process of dying was therefore to some extent orchestrated by doctor, family and friend as well as the preacher himself. As the physician Benjamin Rush put it 'Opium has a wonderful effect

---

[1] *WJW* 9: 158; W. A. Chambers, 'John Wesley and Death' in J. Stacey, ed, *John Wesley: Contemporary Perspectives* (London: Epworth, 1988) 150-161; Hempton, *Empire* 67; H. D. Rack 'Evangelical Endings: Death-beds in Evangelical Biography' *JRULMB* 74 (1992) 39-56.

[2] J. A. Newton, *Susanna Wesley and the Puritan Tradition in Methodism* (London: Epworth, 1968) Chapter Eight 'Holy Dying' 201-207.

in lessening the fear of death. I have seen patients cheerful in their last moments, from the operation of this medicine upon the body and mind.'[3] Spiritual strength was certainly there for the Methodist preacher on his deathbed, though the doctor might often help to remove the pain associated with death. However, sometimes it went wrong; the early Irish preacher Thomas Walsh, on his deathbed in Dublin in 1759, was given too strong a dose of laudanum leading to what has been described as his 'tortured state of mind.'[4]

Death while on Circuit

The early preacher John Downes experienced the most impressive death in the active work, dropping down dead in the pulpit at West Street, London, on the 4th November 1774, having just finished his sermon.[5] John Oldham, who died in 1762, underwent a more usual death, as described by his wife to Wesley

> Every round my husband took lately, being doubtful when he took horse whether he should drop by the way, he carried a paper in his pocket, telling who he was and whither he was going. This day five weeks, being exceeding weak, he feared he should not be able to preach. But I said: 'My dear, go into the pulpit and the Lord will strengthen thee.' Neither did he speak in vain: many were comforted; several justified. One of these said, 'He is going to rest soon, and I shall go with him.' He died in triumph the next Lord's Day.[6]

Andrews, in her recent work on the American Methodists, used Jesse Lee's lists of preachers to discover the numbers who died in the active work in America. She claimed 79 % of Lee's first generation of preachers died while on circuit; also that 63.1% of the American preachers whose age was known and who died in the field were under forty. The first figure depends on excluding those who left who were in a majority. Lee himself wrote in 1810 that, of the 125 American preachers in his first generation (up to 1785), ten were alive and twenty-five had died in the work. When his figures are updated from Ed Schell's list and the database, they come to twenty-eight dying in the work, only 21%, a very different figure.[7]

---

[3] A. G. Schneider, 'The Ritual of Happy Dying among Early American Methodists' *Church History* (1987), 348-63; Porter, *Patient's Progress* 144-52.
[4] O'Glaisne, 'Walsh' 7.
[5] Downes, having married the wealthy heiress Dorothy Furley 10 years earlier, had settled in London, so though he appeared in Myles, Garlick and Hill's as a preacher who died in the work, he was no longer active in the *Minutes*. Baker described him in this period as only a local preacher. He had certainly been a travelling preacher earlier. *AM* 1787: 105-6; MM 1813: 217-22; *WJW* 22: 435-36, 26: 476-81.
[6] *WJW* 22: 174-5.
[7] Andrews, *Methodists and America* 216-9; Lee, *Methodists in USA* 320-324.

In Britain the case was different.[8] Some of those who died while on circuit were elderly like Sammy Bardsley whom the junior preachers had resolved to support in the field so he would not have to retire.[9] It would seem that conditions were a little easier in Britain than in America by the end of the century. Out of the 802 British preachers 144 died while travelling on circuit (18%), only slightly different from the States. The comparison of the different cohorts shows that death on circuit was least likely in the early days when most left and fewer than 15% are known to have died while on circuit. Both the third and fourth cohorts, those who entered after 1760, show a high percentage of those who died while on circuit, at between 40 and 45%. After 1780 the final cohort found it more possible to retire, since Wesley died in 1791 and the Conference which succeeded him was more lenient about the criteria and improved financial provisions came in (Chapter 19 above). Again, of the 144 who died while on circuit, five were or had travelled in America and another nine were or had been missionaries. Each figure is higher than the percentage of the total that had travelled in America or as missionaries because conditions abroad were harsher than in Britain. The average age of death for those who died in circuit was just over 53, not particularly young. Admittedly there were a number of men whose ages were not given but who were described as young, usually in their first five years of travelling. It tended to be the more elderly whose age was exactly recorded.[10]

Age at Death

The oldest of the preachers who died in circuit were usually those, like Benson, who were well known and so much appreciated by their fellow-preachers that none wanted to see them retire; they were allowed to remain when others would have already superannuated. Admittedly Benson was Editor in London rather than an ordinary circuit preacher. Where ages are known the most senior was the Irish-speaking Methodist missionary Charles Graham, who collapsed on his horse's back after the Irish Conference in 1823 going to his next appointment. He died at Athlone after a long and painful illness aged seventy-four in April 1824 and was buried at Abbey Street, Dublin.[11]

The claim that the preachers died young[12] is not borne out by the overall figures either (Chart 14 below based on Table 21 in Appendix One). Andrew

---

[8] See Table 21 in Appendix One.
[9] For more examples of this see Chapter 19.
[10] Andrews, *Methodists and America* 217; Lee, *Methodists in USA* 316-39.
[11] For Benson see *DOMBI*. For Graham see *WMM* 1824: 499; F. J. Cole, *The Cavalry Preachers* (Belfast: WHS (I), 1945) 11, 13.
[12] For example R. Watson, *The Life of John Wesley* (London: Mason, 1845) 216 'Under the severity of labour... many a fine constitution was broken, and premature death was often induced.'

Chart 14: Wesley's Preachers: Number of Deaths at Any Age

Source: Wesley's Preachers' Database

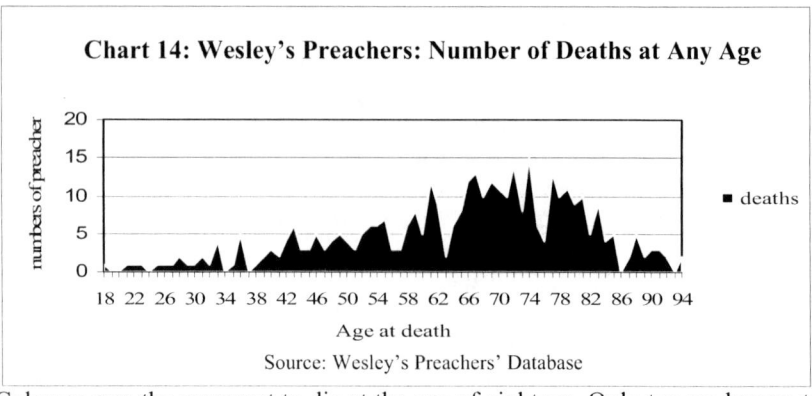

Coleman was the youngest to die at the age of eighteen. Only ten are known to have died under thirty and the average age of death recorded is almost sixty-five. There were ten who made ninety years old or more; Joseph Sutcliffe and Thomas Ridgeway were the joint oldest dying at ninety-four. Most of these entered after 1779. Of the ten ninety year olds, seven entered in the 1780s and two in the 1770s. 14% of the American preachers were known to have reached ninety or more. At a time when expectation of life at birth was around thirty-six, this average of sixty-five represents a considerable improvement for those who became travelling preachers in Britain.[13] Certainly the 802 Wesley's preachers had by definition at entry already passed the period of infancy when highest mortality took place, but the average British male aged twenty was probably dead by forty-five like his American cousin.[14]

These figures compare well with the recent study by Schell of the American travelling preachers who entered between 1773 and 1799. His total of 819 preachers studied is similar in size to my 802 (28 appear in both lists). They belonged to a slightly later generation than the British preachers, including some of my last two cohorts. Of these American preachers the dates of both birth and death (and hence age) are known for 263 of them. Schell pointed out that the average lifespan for the preacher was sixty-five, in an age where the average American male aged twenty would probably be dead by forty-five.[15] This was very similar to their British brethren, so both British and American preachers outlived the norm for their societies by a long way.

Reasons for Death

The reasons given for death in the second half of the eighteenth century often differed from how early twenty-first century medicine would explain them and

---

[13] Rule, *Vital Century* 9. The age at death is known for 368 of the British preachers.
[14] I am indebted to Bill Graham for this point. In France in the same period a twenty year old could expect to live to 51. McManners, *Death* 100.
[15] *MH* 38 (2000) 307.

may be unhelpful. In his discussion of the causes of death in 1750 Thomas Short included 'teething' for children, 'headach' and 'megrim' for adults. He cited being 'aged' as the reason for as many as two in fourteen of all adult deaths.[16] 'Paralysis,' common in the contemporary accounts of final illnesses, often meant stroke and may or may not have led to death. Cause of death was not important to the writer of a preacher's obituary, the historian's main source, and was often not mentioned except incidentally even in the lengthiest of accounts.

Richard Watson suggested that the lifestyle of Wesley's preachers tended towards an early death. Continual travel in all weathers leading to frequent accidents, lack of regular meals, sleeping in strange 'damp' beds or no bed at all, encountering mobs throwing stones or worse, persecution and imprisonment are all well known and documented.

On the other hand, Schell's American study suggested many reasons for preachers' later deaths, their 'hard, active, alcohol-free lifestyles, loving support from spouses and families, and a vibrant religious faith.' Examining how far this applied in Britain is interesting. The 'hard, active lifestyle' remained true for British preachers into the nineteenth century, though already by 1800 many English circuits had become easier, with regular country walks and a return to the preacher's home each night. On the other hand, 'damp beds' continued to be blamed for many deaths and more withdrawals from the work.

'Alcohol-free life styles' was not true of eighteenth century or early nineteenth century Britain and I would question how far it was true in America before 1800. Wesley drank alcohol, if abstemiously, and so did his preachers, for there was little else to drink. Certainly 'spirituous liquors' were forbidden (see the *Large Minutes* 1780) as were drams (1765). But beer was often regarded as a temperance drink in contrast to distilled spirits. Good Methodists like Hugh Bell of Halifax Nova Scotia brewed beer.[17] Tea was still difficult to get in many parts of the British Isles, and water everywhere was disease ridden. It was only after Chadwick's development of safe state-provided water in the towns of the next century that temperance came to mean not drinking alcohol. At least eight preachers left because they became drunk. Often preachers stayed at inns. Not all were like the Christopher Inn at Bath where the Methodist owner, who entertained Wesley among others, shut it on Sundays.[18] Some preachers were even landlords, such as Benjamin Pearce who kept the Cross

---

[16] T. Short, *New Observations, Natural, Moral, Civil, Political and Medical on City Town and Country Bills of Mortality* (London: Longman and Millar, 1750) 199-201.

[17] M. I. Campbell, *No Other Foundation: The History of Brunswick St United Church with its Methodist Inheritance* (Hantsport NS: Lancelot, 1984) 92-4. See also G. T. Brake, *Drink: The Ups and Downs of Methodism's Attitude to Temperance* (London: Oliphants, 1974).

[18] For the leavers because of drink see Chapter 15 above. Church, *More About* 10. The eight preachers represent only 3% of those for whom a reason is known.

Keys in Bradford-on-Avon where class meetings were held in the little whitewashed room behind the bar.[19] Most preachers were abstemious and doubtless their health benefited from this, but their lives were certainly not 'alcohol-free.' 'Loving support from spouses and families' would be even more true in Britain where a higher proportion of preachers was married than in America. Married preachers found that their wives often encouraged their husbands to eat while they themselves went hungry in order to eke out the preacher's allowance so that it lasted until the payment at the next Quarter Day.[20]

The 'vibrant religious faith' was likely to have been a reason for longevity. The itinerants were determined to preach despite weakness and illness, regular ascetic fasting and an attitude which said that 'pain is more salutary than pleasure.' A letter to Mary Fletcher suggested that the 'suffering in the scarlet fever ... would draw the patient closer to God.' However, John Fletcher is said to have hastened his death not just by fasting, but also by denying himself sleep.[21]

Other important factors tending towards a longer life included the help preachers received from local Methodists who gave them their own food when they were hungry. Most preachers before Wesley's death were still looked after by different individuals for most of the time as they travelled their rounds.[22] So in 1788, right at the end of Wesley's life, the *Minutes of Conference* read 'many of our preachers have been obliged to go from the house of one friend to another for all their meals.'[23] Significantly they worked hard to make what they had last longer.

However, perhaps most important was the fact that the preachers were not liable to accidents in mine or factory, nor so much out of doors in all weathers as the agricultural labourer, and were able to avoid living in the worst sources of infection. Thus Wesley's preachers tended to survive longer than the average for the period.

Suicide and Mental Instability

Suicide was thought of in the eighteenth century as 'the English disease.'[24] Certainly in London the suicide rate increased dramatically in the first half of

---

[19] Church, *More About* 10.

[20] Schell's argument about support from spouses is less likely to be important in America in the eighteenth century when relatively few Methodist preachers married before location. Many married when they retired.

[21] I owe these references to Phyllis Mack's keynote lecture to the 2003 Wesley Conference in Manchester, published in *JRULMB* 85 (2005) 157-176.

[22] Chapters 6 to 8 above.

[23] *Minutes* 1: 214.

[24] McManners, *Death* 428. See for further discussion G. R. Taylor, *The Angel Makers* (London: Heinemann, 1958) Chapter 6.

the century. Two of Wesley's preachers were known to have committed suicide. One was William Collins who hanged himself in 1797. He had entered perhaps from Limerick and probably in 1776 when he was placed on trial in Ireland, since Wesley described him as 'a prophet in his own country' leading a revival there in 1771. Under Wesley Collins was almost always an Assistant after his first year of travel. He was transferred to English circuits because he 'had too much self esteem' and 'his wife was too expensive for Irish Circuits.'(!) His fellow preachers found him difficult to work with since he did indeed think too highly of himself. His Assistant John Pawson even described him as 'wicked' and brought a complaint against him to the 1789 Conference;[25] Collins was interviewed for ninety minutes by Wesley, Pawson and John Peacock for disparaging the latter pair, Collins' fellow Leeds' preachers. As a result Collins did not go to his next circuit (Colne) until December, causing yet more trouble for the Assistant there, Charles Atmore.[26] Collins told the eighteen year old Mary Barritt in 1791 that she would be expelled if she did not stop exhorting and praying in meetings, but Conference ordered him from the Colne circuit for 'immorality.'[27] Collins' troubles became even worse. Atmore said he preached 'nonsense' at Worcester in 1794. The 1796 Conference convinced him that he was 'sunk in the estimation of Conference and people.' Collins became deranged, was again ordered from his circuit and at that point hanged himself. In an age when the King of Great Britain could be manhandled and imprisoned by his doctors, it might be seen as strange that Collins was still being allowed his freedom for so long.[28]

The other suicide was Joseph Bradford, formerly Wesley's travelling companion and favourite. Like Collins, but with much more reason having supported the aged and failing Wesley for some time, he was left money in Wesley's will. After Wesley's death Bradford became president and was then given the prestigious and much sought after post of Governor of Kingswood School. He too became gradually 'deranged,' which may in his case have meant Alzheimer's disease, and he committed suicide in 1808.[29]

Certainly these two suicides were connected with mental instability. Care of such cases was then in its infancy. The continual stress of the itinerant's life was such that mental problems almost certainly were more common among Wesley's preachers than has been realized. Some others among those who left, about whom we know little and certainly not the cause of death, may have had

---

[25] Haire, *Wesley's Visits* 114; *WJW* 22: 365n, 24: 288-9d; *Pawson L* 1: 71, 90-1, 2: 111-3.

[26] *WJW* 24: 288-9d; Lloyd, *Personal Papers* 1: 72.

[27] Wesley, forgiving as ever, left Collins money in his will. *JWJ(C)* 8: 342; Taft, *Memoirs* 1: 11-21.

[28] Taft, *Memoirs*; *Pawson L* 2: 111-3, 3: 43; *PWHS* 32 (1959) 74.

[29] No 54 in *Wesleyan Takings*; Ives 108; C. A. Bradford, *The Life of the Rev Joseph Bradford* (London: R. F. Hunger, n.d. c 1931); MS Crowther's Memoirs 62 (at Duke).

similar problems. We know about Collins and Bradford because they died in the work.

Tuberculosis

Tuberculosis, or consumption as it was called at the time, was a major killer of most of the population, holding the kind of place held by cancer or heart disease today. Many preachers in the age groups up to sixty died of it, just as happened in the rest of the population. When Wesley wrote his own epitaph at the age of fifty, it was because he thought he was dying of consumption.[30] The preachers who succumbed were usually young, and had often travelled very little. A high proportion of them were Irish, because living conditions were worse in Ireland. Among the last three cohorts, so from 1760 on, they were often able to superannuate before they died because tuberculosis was a gradual wasting disease of which we have several harrowing descriptions.[31] At least seventeen died from it and, of the nine where we know the age of death, the youngest was Andrew Coleman at eighteen and the oldest was Duncan Wright at fifty-five. The disease was usually blamed on 'damp beds and long rides.' The damp beds were often the best the travelling preacher could find, even when Methodists were taking him in. The long rides were the result of large circuits and travelling in all weathers. Joshua Marsden in the Cumberland circuit in Nova Scotia in the winter of 1800 wrote that sleeping in damp beds brought on a cold which laid him up for eight weeks. 'Friends watched my bed with affectionate attentions and marked every step of my disorder with peculiar anxiety; prayer was made for my recovery in every part of the settlement; and the minds of the people were remarkably affected, for they deemed my affliction a judgment upon them.' They were quite right. It was![32]

Accidents

A relatively high number died as a result of accidents, usually associated with the travel necessary for the itinerant. Some got lost like Joseph Algar in the Isle of Wight in 1795 who fell into some water and was in danger of being drowned while crossing Parkhurst Forest. He was fortunate to escape.[33] Others fared less

---

[30] R. P. Heitzenrater, *Faithful unto Death; the Last Years and Legacy of John Wesley* (Dallas: Bridwell Library, 1991) vii, 15. Wesley lived nearly 40 years more, dying of 'a small cold.' For ill health causing men to leave the itinerancy rather than killing them see Chapter 15 above.

[31] For example William Minethorpe's death described in *MM* 1808: 401-2.

[32] E.g. *Minutes* 1803: 168 where 'they laid the foundations of a consumption of which he died' for the young William Jackson. J. Marsden, *Narrative of a Mission to Nova Scotia...* (London: Kershaw, 1827) 33.

[33] Dyson (1865) 185.

well. Several fell off their horses. They were not usually as heavy as the corpulent John Shaw who fell off his horse in 1793 in the Pocklington circuit and bruised his hand. In Shaw's case mortification (gangrene) set in and spread to his elbow, eventually killing him. A similar account is given of the death of John Livermore after a fall from his horse in 1783 at Charlemont in Ireland. Little is known of him except he was 'considerably advanced in years' when he entered the Irish itinerancy in 1778.[34]

Roads were not good despite the development of turnpikes in the eighteenth century. Some preachers died as a result of coach accidents early in the next century. On the 26th July 1823 George Sargent died two days after the coach overturned in which he and eight other preachers were travelling on their way to the Sheffield Conference; another preacher was killed and six others suffered various injuries in the same accident.[35] The Irishman John Darragh, Chairman of the Clones District, died in 1806 after a fall from a gig when travelling from Clones to Limerick. He dislocated his arm and mortification set in.[36]

Other Cases of Gangrene

Surgery in the eighteenth century was primitive with no pain killers apart from alcohol and laudanum and no antiseptics. The repeated use of surgical instruments without any cleansing led to sepsis, gangrene and death. A typical early example was Thomas Beard, pressed into the army for preaching in 1743. In 1744 he became 'sunk under (his) burden ... fever increasing, (he was) bled, his arm festered, mortified and was cut off....two or three days later' he died at Newcastle.[37] In 1765 Alexander Coates, who was also stationed at Newcastle, received a major blow or contusion to his leg leading to mortification of the limb. As a result he died at the Orphan House, Newcastle on Tyne, being then the oldest preacher in the connexion.[38]

Diabetes and 'Dropsy'

Thomas Bartholomew was reported as dying in February 1819 having been ill with diabetes for several years. He had apparently remained in the active work despite his illness and was able to study the Polyglot Bible towards the end of 1818.[39]

Dropsy was what the eighteenth century called oedema, the chief symptom

---

[34] *Pawson L* 1: 138-9. Atmore said the fall was little thought of at first.
[35] *WMM* 1823: 633, 1824: 73-8.
[36] *Crk* 4: 10, 24; M. Lanktree, *The Biographical Narrative of Matthew Lanktree* (Belfast: Wilson, 1836) 180-2.
[37] Benson, *Apology* 16.
[38] *WMM* 1844: 3-4; Atmore; *WJW* 22: 23 n96; Lloyd *Biographical Index*.
[39] *MM* 1820: 564-5, 695-96. Diabetes is not mentioned in the official obituary.

being the accumulation of watery fluids in the lower parts of the body especially the ankles and the abdomen. It was associated with heart problems. At least six preachers seem to have died of it. William Brammah was suffering from it in the 1770s. Wesley in 1773 suggested a sensible regimen

> I am concerned on account of poor William Brammah. He cannot, he will not take advice. Spirituous liquors in all dropsically disorders are deadly poison. Indeed they give a little present ease, but they lay the foundations for ten thousand more pain than that which they remove. I say once more (1) let him wholly abstain from these; (2) let him never scream or preach too long; (3) let him eat early and light suppers; (4) let him never sit up till ten; and then he will be as well able to preach in the morning as I am.

Brammah did not die until June 1780, so perhaps he listened to Wesley. His obituary described him as having had much weakness and pain.[40] Another preacher who died as a result of dropsy was the Irishman Andrew Blair, who had taken the waters at Bath for the illness in 1792.[41]

Deathbeds

McManners suggested that death became more of a private concern for the family than a community event in the eighteenth century.[42] This was certainly not true for Methodism where preparation for death was a concern for the whole Methodist community who were likely to visit the afflicted. The deathbed was seen as a chance for all, including those not yet converted, to come and learn and see the importance of dying well. Those dying grasped the opportunity to testify to their faith and demonstrate their certainty for the life to come. Often family and friends would gather to sing hymns around the bedside.

It has been suggested that the local society had been able, at least at first in early Methodism, to share in the sacrament of Holy Communion with the dying member. Bowmer stated

> In the early days of Methodism, before the Lord's Supper was... administered in the preaching houses and when at the same time the Methodists were refused it at the parish churches, they would have been denied this ordinance had they not taken advantage of the opportunities of Communion with the sick. The permission which Canon law gave to ...communicate with the sick accounts for the large

---

[40] The quotation comes from a letter to Ann Bolton in the Oxfordshire Circuit, *JWL* 6: 17-18. For Brammah see *PWHS* 36 (1968) 169-177.
[41] For Blair's death see *WJW* 23: 348. Others who died of oedema included Robert Smith senior, John Cricket, Joseph Thompson and James Wood.
[42] McManners, *Death* 234.

numbers of communicants which John Wesley, in his diary records for these sick-room celebrations.[43]

The actual references for this cited by Bowmer are not satisfactory at least where administration by John Wesley is concerned. The picture Bowmer gave is in my view overstated and, so far as large numbers for sick-room celebrations is concerned, incorrect; in most places Methodists were not refused Communion. There are no references to large groups communicating with the sick, but there were many occasions where large groups received Communion from the Wesleys at Methodist homes or in preaching-houses. Further, and most important, there were no references to Communion in the accounts of preachers dying.[44]

To die well was what Hindmarsh described as the final part of the whole process of conversion and the Christian life. When Thomas Taylor died suddenly in 1816, the editor of the *Magazine*, his old friend Benson, lamented that his 'death was so sudden that he experienced little or nothing of the *formality* of dying.'[45] This whole process can be illustrated by the death of Jane Allen in 1779 as recounted by her preacher husband John.

> On the 30th June last she was seized by the epidemic distemper. At first we were not apprehensive it was the fever; though she herself judged it was, and believed it

---

[43] J. C. Bowmer, *The Sacrament of the Lord's Supper in Early Methodism* (London: A. & C. Black, 1951) Chapter 10. Compare for Anglican practice Jacob, *Clerical Profession* 186, 211.

[44] Bowmer gave five references for John Wesley giving Communion to the sick or dying; two of these are not there in the new edition of Wesley's diaries. Of the three remaining only one showed another person present at the bedside. Bowmer also had rather more examples from Charles, four of Communion for dying persons (two with others definitely present), five for the sick (again two with others present). None of the sick or dying were known preachers. Several were Anglican clergy or their wives. Much greater numbers were present at ordinary Communions, for example 22nd July 1739 where 25 were mentioned at John's Communion at Mrs Williams', but there is nothing to show she was unwell. The evidence for Charles related to 1738-1750. John's references were from 1763 to 1782, despite a much longer published *Journal*. See also *HMGB* 1: 269; *WJW* 9: 531n1, Chambers, 'Wesley and Death' 160-61. For Wesley's death see R. P. Heitzenrater, *The Elusive Mr Wesley* (Nashville: Abingdon, 1984) 2: 143-158, where again there is no reference to Communion. In John's *Journal* the only other reference for Communion is that in 1751 in Ireland to a local Methodist, Rose Longworth, with no others except her husband known to be present, probably given by a friendly local clergyman (*WJW* 20: 436-7). I am grateful to Bill Gibson, Henry Rack, John Walsh and Martin Wellings for their views on this question.

[45] The death of Taylor is in *MM* 1816: 947. The italics were Benson's own emphasis. See also Hindmarsh, *Conversion Narrative* 255-259, citing Robert Roberts' death in 1799 as an instance of someone too ill to testify to his faith on his deathbed (*MM* 1800: 392), this being the chief reason for his friends' regret.

was the messenger of death. As her fever increased, and her end drew nearer, she was happier and happier. She said very little to me about dying, because she was sensible it would give me more affliction than I should be well able to bear. But to others she spoke freely concerning it; and with the greatest composure she said 'I shall soon be

> 'Far from a world of grief and sin,
> With God eternally shut in.'

The Tuesday before her death she seemed to be quite transported with joy. When I went up stairs, I found her with heaven in her look, repeating the following lines:

> 'The world recedes; it disappears!
> Heaven opens on my eyes! My ears
>   With sounds seraphic ring!
> Lord lend your wings! I mount! I fly!
> O grave, where is thy victory?
>   And where, O death, thy sting?'

On Friday she seemed like one from above. There was in her such a spirit of love and gratitude as I never saw before in any creature. She thanked and blessed everyone that did the least thing for her. She often prayed that God would reward me for all my kindness to her; and broke out, 'My Lord! My God! My Father! My Husband! My Friend! I long to see thee!' When she could speak no longer, I desired her if her soul was happy, to lift up her hand. This she immediately did; and soon after fell asleep.[46]

Despite his concern for the use of deathbeds for spiritual purposes, John Wesley found it difficult to sympathize with his preachers when their children or wives died, unlike his more feeling brother Charles. Where Charles would write long sympathetic letters, John would pen a less sympathetic short one, as for example to Bradburn on his loss of his wife in 1784. 'He that made the heart can heal the heart.' But he spoilt this with a decidedly unsympathetic letter to Charles saying that 'the loss of his (Samuel Bradburn's) wife will be one of the greatest blessings which he has ever met with.'[47] An interesting observer of all this was the Irish Methodist clergyman James Creighton, resident in London in the 1780s

> PS the wives of two preachers died lately at Bristol, one of them an old woman... The other Mrs B-n, her Husband is in grief unspeakable... Deaths... As to Mr W(esley) he has no feelings about these things. He wishes to get as much work

---

[46] *EMP* 6: 245-6. Jane Allen was probably the daughter of a preacher (Westell) as well as the wife of one.
[47] *JWL* 8: 315, 323. Letter to Samuel Bradburn in February 1786 after the death of his first wife.

out of his preachers and when they are gone there is no more about them, only he enquires how they died.'[48]

Wills

Many preachers left wills, the majority leaving most of their possessions to their families. The other beneficiaries often mentioned were the 'family' the preachers had in the itinerancy. Rankin left a number of items to his surviving friends among the travelling preachers; William Jenkins received his 'boots with standing up tops,' while Robert Johnson those with turned down tops, Mr (Richard) Rodda the 'best wig,' and Walter Griffith his 'Coat and blue Cloak.' To Benson Rankin bequeathed the more valuable 'manuscripts of American journal' (now in the USA) 'and short account of my life with my Gold Studs set with a lock of Mr Wesley's hair.'[49] Asbury, who had no family remaining after his mother's death in 1802, had little money until 1813 when Methodists in Maryland left him $2,000. His will, made during that year, left all his effects to the American Book Concern, the chief support of the travelling preachers there. Their poverty and that of their widows and children had long been the chief object of whatever money he had available.[50]

Burials and Ceremonies Following Death

Before the late eighteenth century Europeans accepted death as a constant companion. During this period society began what has been described as an attempt 'to separate the living from the dead,' at least in the towns. The use of coffins and the process of embalming increased. Burials began to be prohibited in churches, often for medical reasons. Parishioners were no longer always buried even in the graveyard outside their church, but instead cemeteries were moved to the outskirts of towns, separated from the parish churches to which they had belonged. These new cemeteries helped to destroy the cultural dominance and self-reliance of the parish, as had the Methodist preacher himself.[51]

Increasing ceremonial surrounding death was generally adopted and Wesley's followers reflected this practice. Funeral monuments became more elaborate and classical in design. For example, Wesley's body was first buried in 1791 in three separate caskets, the inner one of lead with a Latin inscription

---

[48] MS Creighton Letterbook at Junaluska 23-4 March 30th 1786.
[49] MS will of Rankin at Drew University NJ.
[50] *Asbury Jol* 2: 732-3, 3: 472-3.
[51] A. Rusnock, *Vital Accounts: Quantifying Health and Population in 18th Century England and France* (Cambridge: CUP, 2002) 137; J. McManners, *Death* 303-311; T. W. Laqueur, 'Cemeteries, Religion and the Culture of Capitalism' in J. Garnett and C. Matthew, eds, *Revival and Religion since 1700* (London: Hambledon, 1993) 187.

and the outer made of oak. In 1828 the outer one was replaced with one in Portland stone. The coffin was placed in a vault in the ground *behind* Wesley's Chapel in City Road, London. The vault, which had been prepared at his instructions, was large enough to contain more coffins and others were added later, including those of some of his preachers. Over it was placed a substantial stone monument. The important points were that it was not in officially Anglican consecrated ground, it was a large and significant structure and it was not just outside but behind the chapel he had built. In addition, the monument was elaborated over time. Pilgrims to the tomb then and today must pass through the church building. Worshippers in the church did not need even to think about the grave.[52]

None of these points was necessarily true for his preachers. As usual we do not know what happened to most of them. However, for over half (67) of those we do know (128) the bodies were buried in the ordinary local parish churchyard and not Methodist ground. Almost everybody looked to the parish church for the rites of passage. For baptism, marriage and burial most Methodists went to their local parish church in the eighteenth century and in many cases long into the nineteenth century. Often Methodism did not own much land, certainly none to use for burials.

Where Did Burials Take Place?

Grimshaw, Fletcher and Charles Wesley were all buried in their parish graveyards because they were clergy of the Church of England. John Milner, as the long time vicar of rural and remote Chipping in Lancashire, was interred in the chancel within his own parish church in 1777. Since the leaders of Methodism were being buried in the traditional places, other preachers followed their example.[53] Some former preachers were even buried inside, such as Thomas M'Geary in 1797 in the parish church at Keynsham where he had been the parish schoolmaster.[54] As Lloyd and Gregory have shown, until 1791 most Methodists thought of themselves as good members of the Church of England anyway. This changed in the following thirty years in Britain and (somewhat later) in Ireland. For most of the 1790s in Britain the question of separation from the Church was anything but decided. In Ireland this decision was not taken until 1816/7, when a new generation of Methodists had grown up. Even in England many Methodist congregations still attended their parish church in the morning in the 1820s, as they had done under Wesley. Of course they expected to be buried in Anglican churchyards and often they were. The last of Wesley's preachers to be thus buried was the respected ex-president of Conference, Jonathan Edmondson, as late as 1842. By that time few of those

---

[52] Heitzenrater, *Faithful unto Death* 24; *JWL* 8: 114.
[53] *WHS N. Lancs* 22: 7-9.
[54] Ives 104-5, 107-8.

who had entered in Wesley's lifetime were left.[55]

Most of the other half of Wesley's preachers (about 40%) were buried on Methodist premises, sometimes actually within the church building, where the burial place is known. John Wesley had an ambivalent attitude to burial in consecrated ground and he himself had been opposed to the consecration of ground for burial since at least 1764. So in the letter quoted above, in which he said to Benson that no preacher could baptize, he went on 'Much more may be said for (lay preachers) burying the dead.'[56] After Wesley's burial many of his preachers or their families chose to be buried at the unconsecrated City Road, London, and the coffins were usually added to Wesley's vault behind the chapel there. Other Methodist premises were also utilized. Jonathan Coussins' body, for example, was buried in a casket in the chapel at Diss.[57]

Methodist burial grounds seem to have existed from at least 1778, when burials are recorded at Greetland and South Parade Chapel, Halifax. Halifax was a large growing parish with many contiguous settlements; the Anglican provision was inadequate to meet the demand for burial ground. Others were set up at both Mount Zion at Bradshaw near Halifax in Yorkshire (January 1779) and at the newly constructed City Road Chapel, London, where the chapel had been opened at the end of November and the first burials were recorded as December 1779.[58]

The twelve known remaining Wesley's preachers were buried in other graveyards, usually Nonconformist. This was mostly because they had become Dissenting ministers like John Bennet, and so were buried in what was seen as Dissenting ground, often that belonging to the congregation they had served. Bennet's body was buried at Chinley, outside the Independent chapel there, later to be joined by that of his widow Grace, (formerly betrothed to Wesley and who had returned to Methodism after her husband's death).[59]

Liturgy and Funeral Orations

Services for the burial of the dead had been carried out by Wesley's preachers

---

[55] *PWHS* 19 (1935) 179; *HMGB* 2: 140.

[56] *WJW* 9: 531-3 n1; *HMGB* 1: 269; *JWL* 7: 179.

[57] *PWHS* 34 (1963) 58-60 which explained that the body was reinterred elsewhere in the 1960s and Chapter 2 above.

[58] Yorkshire FHS, 'Monumental Inscriptions of the Mount Zion Graveyard' http://mountzionhalifax.free.fr/FullSeach.php (accessed 2/3/2007). The first Methodist buried there was Susanna Child of Ovenden aged 28, who died on the 7th January 1779. Stevenson, *City Road* 309. The Countess of Huntingdon's Connexion first recorded burials one year earlier at Clerkenwell in 1778. W. Leary, *My Ancestors were Methodists* (London: Society of Genealogists, 1993) 35 and 46 for Greetland and South Parade.

[59] Valentine, *Bennet* 230. The tomb and chapel still stand, though now dwarfed by the nineteenth century railway viaducts.

long before Wesley's death in 1791, apparently with his consent.[60] The service for the communion of the sick was retained by Wesley from the Book of Common Prayer for his American Sunday Service of 1784, which was reprinted in Britain in 1786. In that book the order for the burial of the dead had had excised from it both the committal and the prayer of thanksgiving which followed in the original. However, British Methodists normally used the Book of Common Prayer for funeral services, as for example for Thomas Coke's in the Indian Ocean in 1814.[61]

Funeral sermons were common in the eighteenth and nineteenth centuries. These could celebrate the deceased and were often printed. To the twentieth century sociologist a funeral was 'a social rite par excellence. Its ostensible object is the dead person but it benefits not the dead but the living.'[62] Methodist preachers sought to improve the opportunity by preaching to the mourners on both the challenge of death and the good life of the departed. When John Nelson died in Leeds his body was carried in procession to his native Birstall for burial. As they walked the numbers swelled and William Shent gave out appropriate hymns to be sung. Afterwards he preached a funeral sermon at the door of the cottage where Nelson had lived. The singing of hymns was a deliberate innovation introduced by Wesley to create a positive mood.[63]

The literary success in the eighteenth century of books like Young's *Night Thoughts* was followed by a whole genre of sombre meditations and poetry. Young was much read by Methodists.[64] What was important was that the funeral should not be showy or expensive. Wesley himself was determined that for him there should be no hearse or carriage.[65]

Obituaries

The first obituaries of preachers did not appear in the *Minutes* until 1777. 'John Slocomb, at Clones; an old labourer, worn out in the service. John Harrison, near Lisburn: a promising youth, serious, modest and much devoted to God' were the first, with two others that year. For some time obituaries were always equally short. Many preachers who died in the work might receive no recognition, not just those who had left or, as discussed in the previous chapter, had retired. Gradually the reading of obituaries became a recognized part of Conference and their printing a part of the *Minutes*, something in which the

---

[60] *Minutes* 1: 314.
[61] Baker, *Wesley and the Church* 234-255; C. N. R. Wallwork, 'Wesley's Legacy in Worship' in Stacey, *Wesley* 84-6; Vickers, *Thomas Coke* 366.
[62] McManners, *Death* 291-2.
[63] Church, *More About* 252; D. M. Chapman, *Born in Song: Methodist Worship in Britain* (Warrington: Church in the Market Place, 2006) 221-2.
[64] Church, *More About* 104.
[65] *JWL* 7: 171-2.

achievements of the past generation could be celebrated and the early deaths of the young lamented, like Harrison. It was part of the fraternal ritual of Conference. The single sentence describing the dead man's character became longer. By the early nineteenth century three or more sentences were expected and eventually a whole paragraph. What was included also became stereotyped. Not everything Wesley included in the 1777 obituaries remained. It did not matter where the preacher died, so it was usually omitted. How he died was sometimes included. The length of the obituary tended to vary with the preacher's importance to and length of time in the connexion. So in 1801 Alexander Mather who had travelled for forty-two years, received thirty-two lines, John Poole who had travelled thirty years, had fourteen, while John Furness who had only done six years, was accorded a mere five lines. By 1806 the obituary was slightly more standardized, with nobody receiving fewer than eight lines and useful details of service to the connexion highlighted. Thus Jonathan Coussins, whom we met in Chapter 2, was described as

> A man of very mild temper, clear in Christian experience and in the doctrines of the Gospel. He was an acceptable and useful Preacher, and gained the love and esteem of the people wherever he went. He commenced a travelling preacher in the 23rd year of his age and finished his course in the 49th, on the 31st October 1805. He bore the affliction, (the palsy) which caused his death, with invincible patience and calm resignation to the will of God. He died at Diss near Norwich, where he first began his itinerant labours. He is now happily delivered from a world of trouble pain and death. He rests in paradise; he is at present with his Lord; and all tears are for ever wiped away from his eyes.

Even so the previous year Joseph Algar had been dismissed with the single rather grudging sentence 'After travelling many years, we trust he died in the Lord.'[66]

Conclusion

Death was seen as the final proof and element of conversion. Hindmarsh makes the excellent point that the later editors of the *Lives of the Early Methodist Preachers* felt the need to add on a deathbed account to their memoirs when they were republished later. Many preachers had worked in occupations like mining, which made them very aware of the close presence of death.[67] Joy, as in Charles Wesley's verse at the beginning of this chapter, was usually present. John Cricket typified the Methodist view of death as a homecoming, in his final illness refusing medical help. 'It is of no use' he said, 'I tell you I am going home' and with that, he died.[68]

---

[66] *Minutes* 2: 323-6, 271.
[67] Hindmarsh, *Conversion Narrative* 255-9.
[68] Dyson (1865) 184-5.

CHAPTER 21

Conclusion

'My heart is as a fount of love to the cause of God, to the preachers and missionaries. I esteem them the most valuable body of men the world has in it.'
Dying words of the preacher William Saunderson in Brechin, Scotland, 1810.

Introduction

William Saunderson (1748-1810) was biased. Brought up as a Dissenter in Birstall, he and his wife had only joined Methodism after the death of their infant daughter in 1772. His older brother Joseph had become an itinerant in 1775 and, belatedly, William followed him in 1788. After almost forty years doing his utmost for Methodism he felt that the combined efforts of the preachers had ensured their success. Each preacher might himself be frail, fallible and liable to break down and leave, yet the ability of the Methodist system to find a ready replacement for him meant that together they were a significant force.[1] When Brownfield, one of the three preachers on the Yarm circuit, left the itinerancy in 1769, then the worst that could happen was that there would be a gap of a month instead of a fortnight before the coming of the travelling preacher to a village. At best Wesley would send another preacher immediately and there would be no gap at all, or the Assistant would get a local preacher to become full time for a period. This was how the young Samuel Bradburn had started. 'Mr John Oliver... sent me sometimes through the circuit in his place.'[2] The itinerant system was therefore flexible enough to deal with such emergencies easily, so that many locals would not notice the difference. This chapter will assess the preachers' collective importance, the reasons for it and also the reliability of what some historians, especially recent ones, have said about them.

---

[1] Harrison, *Companions* 47-53, with the quotation at 53; *AM* 1810: 202-3, 1812: 321-7; *PWHS* 10 (1916) 88, 94-7. Jacob, *Clerical Profession* 304-6 argues that the Anglican clergy of the period were also a homogeneous group, a unifying force focussed on London.

[2] See Chapter 8 above for the Yarm circuit. Blanshard, *Bradburn* 35 for Bradburn. Oliver was his Assistant. For the continuation of Bradburn's story see Chapter 5 above.

Jesuits?

Niall Ferguson recently suggested the use of counter-factual arguments in history, the 'what if' questions which some historians despise, but most consider at some point.[3] Macaulay did this, being the first to compare Wesley favourably to Ignatius Loyola and his itinerants to the Jesuits. In a brilliant passage in his Essay on Ranke's *History of the Popes* he suggested 'Place Loyola at Oxford. He is certain to become the head of a formidable secession. Place Wesley at Rome. He is certain to be the first general of a new Society devoted to the interests and honour of the Church.' As Walsh aptly stated 'Wesley formed what was in part a new preaching order like that of the friars and in part a lay devotional fraternity'...embracing 'that principle of mobility' which was so important for Methodism.[4] Wesley's preachers were indeed an itinerant order, trying to serve Jesus, devoted to poverty and obedience if not chastity (though the American preachers came close here in their early days), as they followed the hoof marks of the founder whom they revered. Whether Loyola was like Wesley I doubt, but the preachers who claimed to be Wesley's 'Sons in the Gospel' might have had a similar role to the Jesuits if there had been an Anglican Pope far-sighted enough to become Wesley's patron. Certainly Wesley wanted to remain in the Church of England, and if the Archbishop of Canterbury had possessed more power and used it to promote and guide him, then his preachers could have become a pioneering order within the Church. During Wesley's lifetime the Conferences of his preachers passed resolution after resolution that they wished to remain within the Anglican Church.

The travelling preachers of John Wesley should be seen as part of this recurring pattern of Christian rebirth and mission over the centuries, a model which was imitated also by both Anglicans and Dissenters. Wesley's 'sons' were a Protestant religious order drawn together by common experiences and loyalties, meeting regularly each year in Conference and obeying the letters and commands of a leader every bit as much as the followers of Loyola did. To those who say that many of Wesley's men 'left' unlike members of religious orders, it should be pointed out that many Jesuits and others abandoned their vows during the Catholic Reformation. Luther left his Augustinian monastery, and later the general of the Catholic Reformation Capuchin order, Ochino, fled to Geneva in 1542. Like the Counter-Reformation orders Wesley's preachers were mobile in an age which had become more so than previously. This was especially important on the frontiers of society, as in America for Catholics in

---

[3] N. Ferguson, ed, *Virtual History: Alternatives and Counterfactuals* (London: Macmillan, 1998) Chapter 1 Introduction: Virtual History: Towards a Chaotic History of the Past.

[4] T. B. Macaulay, *Essays Critical and Miscellaneous* (London: Phillips, 1856); Walsh, *Church*.

Mission Preaching and Methods

Itinerancy

Neither Loyola's Jesuits nor Wesley's preachers were by any means the first to adopt a strategy of mission preaching, let alone preaching in the open air. Christianity's apostolic age had both methods as standard and the Didache gives a good picture of the succeeding period in Syria where it was equally important.[6] This model continued, especially in missionary situations and was true of most of Europe during the Middle Ages. Recent late Medieval and Early Modern scholarship has shown that such patterns still existed in many places. The Friars from Francis and Dominic onwards provided hugely popular evangelists throughout medieval Europe. It has been suggested, however, that these tended to be hit and run missions, something not unknown in Methodism. John Wycliffe's Lollards fulfilled a similar function, though one more opposed by the authorities in late fourteenth century England and later. Duffy argued that the Catholic Reformation had a much more successful and permanent mission in 'the revivalist cycle of the parish mission.' This included 'sermons preached at dawn,' 'catechizing of children in the afternoons.... and the great catechism ...of all the parish in the evening.' He suggested that 'the most effective and characteristic Counter Reformation machinery for renewal was the itinerant preaching of revival by specialized bands of religious.' Duffy argued that similar attempts in Protestant England in the period 1560-1700 were a failure, though they did also occur. In the 1570s Bishop Barnes of Durham drew up 'circuits' (sic!) for his licensee preachers, though few except the well known Bernard Gilpin actually ventured along them. Because there were too few parish clergy, itinerating preachers were a feature of English Protestant life at least up to 1662. Even after the Restoration this same pattern can be seen both among those ministers ejected as Nonconformists and their successors on the one hand, and in the growth of religious societies inside the Church of England on the other. If Duffy's point is correct, the spiritual hunger partly unmet by the Church of England was a reason for the success of Wesley's preachers after 1740.[7]

---

[5] R. P. Hsia, *The World of Catholic Renewal 1540-1770* (Cambridge: CUP, 1998) 29; Hempton, *Empire* 15.

[6] The Didache was printed in M. Staniforth tr, *Early Christian Writings* (London: Penguin, 1968) 225-237.

[7] E. Duffy, 'The Long Reformation: Catholicism, Protestantism and the Multitude' 34-39, 47-64 in N. Tyacke, ed, *England's Long Reformation 1500-1800* (London: UCL, 1998).

Mission Methods

Itinerant preachers usually worked with and alongside the local regular clergy. Just as the Orders of the Catholic Reformation worked with the diocesan bishop and his parish priests, so Wesley's preachers attempted to work through the parish ministries of Grimshaw of Haworth, Sellon of Breedon, Fletcher of Madeley, and later John Crosse of Bradford, David Simpson of Macclesfield and John Eyton of Wellington. As Gregory has shown, the Methodist itinerants were essentially working, at least for Wesley's lifetime, within the Church of England's existing boundaries.[8] Methods used were also similar. Like the Counter Reformation orders, Wesley's itinerants used ritual and drama. In watch-night services, lovefeasts, the comfort and conversion of condemned criminals[9] and outdoor meetings they 'laboured for the Lord.' They held cottage prayer meetings, later Sunday Schools, processions and camp meetings. If the regular confessional was the 'decisive weapon of the Counter Reformation,' so the class meeting, with its elements of confession and fellowship, was the eighteenth century Methodist equivalent of a decisive weapon, as in the story of Jonathan Coussins.[10] Even Catholic pilgrimage and the search for relics were replicated by the Methodists and others who made pilgrimages to Madeley, Bristol, Epworth, Gwennap, City Road and elsewhere, to see or hear the Wesleys or the Fletchers; or they later wrote to Mary Tooth asking for a memento of Mrs. Fletcher, or placed a piece of Wesleyana on the mantelpiece. Unlike the Catholic revivalists the Methodist preachers used music as an important part of their ritual and Charles Wesley's hymns and the tunes to which they were set became key reasons for the success of the revival. Indeed the attitude of devoted Methodists towards their hymns has usefully been compared to that of the Catholic faithful towards relics of the saints. Each was sacred, holy, to be prized and meditated upon as part of the personal discipline of the believer. As Watson has said, they not only contained 'the fundamental truths and tenets of Methodist doctrine,' but 'did so in a way which made them memorable to successive generations.'[11]

Many of these methods were first adopted by an itinerant and then encouraged and accepted by the Wesleys, or later in America by Asbury. They were most effective. In America, for example, one in eight Americans attended

---

[8] J. Gregory, '"In the Church I will live and die": John Wesley, the Church of England, and Methodism' in W. Gibson and R. Ingram, *Religious Identities in Britain 1660-1832* (Aldershot: Ashgate, 2005).

[9] P. Lake and M. C. Questier, 'Prisons, priest and people' in Tyacke, *Long Reformation*. 195-233.

[10] Duffy, 'Long Reformation' 64-5. Chapter 2 for Coussins. Eighteenth century Methodists refused to accept the parallel, see D. Butler, *Methodists and Papists: John Wesley and the Catholic Church in the 18th Century* (London: DLT, 1995) 190-1.

[11] C. N. R. Wallwork, 'Wesley's Legacy in Worship' in J. Stacey, ed, *Wesley* 94-97; J. R Watson, ed, *Companion to Hymns and Psalms* (Peterborough: MPH, 1988) 22.

at least one Methodist camp meeting in the year 1813.[12] But whatever the methods used, the preachers were itinerant travellers who were replacing the local religious associations of each parish by a religion of the heart, united by a national conference to which they could all go, a group characterized by openness and exchange, not location.

A Mission Strategy?

Ward looked at the question of whether the Methodists had an evangelistic strategy in the eighteenth century. He suggested that the Methodist group, which included Whitefield, Harris and the Countess of Huntingdon as well as the Wesleys, was until Frederick Prince of Wales' death in 1751 thinking in terms of a political revolution which would include religious reform, giving them at least some control of patronage. Ward also poured scorn on the idea that 'these clergymen had no plan at all... only went hither and thither wherever they had a prospect of saving souls from death.' He suggested this idea of a providential call was being taken by historians to mean that Methodism had no real strategy and resulted 'from a fit of absence of mind.'[13]

Ward argued that on the macro level Wesley, the great survivor, had an overall plan of going to the poor, to those who needed him most. Though this happened in the early years in Cornwall or Newcastle Rodell has shown that in the Bedford and Northampton area he rarely stayed with the poor in the period 1750-90. Usually Wesley stayed with wealthy sympathizers, clergy like Berridge of Everton in that area, Milner of Chipping or Grimshaw of Haworth elsewhere. Frequently these do not appear on the list of members of the Methodist societies. Sympathetic they may have been but they were neither poor nor strictly speaking Methodists.[14] On the micro level he and his preachers went where there was hospitality. After the early years Wesley himself never tried new places. His preachers did, but even they for the most part kept to established parts. A new preacher like Miles Martindale might try the Wirral as a mission area, but in general by the 1780s preachers kept to where the previous year's preachers had been.[15] There were new invitations from keen and key lay people, like the Palatines in Ireland, but from an early stage a tendency existed in British Methodism, against which Wesley tried to fight, to stick to the known paths and, as Ward pointed out, to recruit more and more from the children of members. This was less true of American Methodism under Asbury and his

---

[12] Noll, *America's God* 248.

[13] W. R. Ward, 'Was there a Methodist Evangelistic Strategy in the eighteenth century?' in Tyacke, *Long Reformation.* 285-305.

[14] Rodell, 'The best house by far.' In the area he surveyed, Wesley stayed most (40 nights) with William Cole, the High Sheriff of Bedfordshire, not a member.

[15] *AM* 1797: 3-9, 53-60. In Ireland Charles Graham was similarly sent to Kerry see Campbell, *Apostle of Kerry* and Chapter 11 above.

successors, with its camp-meetings aimed at all-comers, partly because of the more mobile society on the other side of the Atlantic. Trying fresh places was a regular strategy in the early days and as late as 1763 John Manners was intending to try new places in the York circuit. The strategy became more difficult to put into practice as Methodism expanded and untouched areas became fewer, but in 1780 Zachariah Yewdall was preaching where Methodists had not preached before, in Pembrokeshire at Selvidge and again at Wick in Glamorgan in 1781.[16] The most common strategy adopted by Wesley and his preachers was to go where there was a clear opening or an invitation. The increase in the number of preachers available to Wesley in the 1780s enabled him to push ahead in Britain, in Ireland and overseas. The question of numbers (see Appendix Two) decided what Methodism's strategy was and whether he could accept the openings available.

The Preachers and Wesley

Circuits Founded by Preachers

Historians have tended to concentrate on Wesley and forget the contributions of other Methodists, especially of laywomen and laymen. Many of Wesley's preachers were not at all dependent on Wesley, though attracted by him. Recent research has shown that there were several of importance who, like William Darney or John Bennet, had founded their own circuits and societies and were to merge them later into the larger whole. Darney's Round is well known from Laycock's classic account.[17] Valentine's important book gives a valuable picture of Bennet's Round in the 1740s in Cheshire, Lancashire and North Derbyshire; but there were several others.[18] Nelson had been creating a round of societies near Birstall after his conversion and before Wesley accepted him as a preacher in 1742. The Society at St Ives, which drew Wesley to Cornwall in 1743, was absorbed into Methodism and became the foundation of the powerhouse that was West Cornish Methodism. Wesley said of them, not quite relishing their independence 'They took me into their fellowship, and not I them.'[19] Other similar preachers included Thomas Lee with his group of societies in Nidderdale in 1748, Thomas Mitchell, and in Ireland the society led by Mark Davis in Dublin. In Norwich James Wheatley handed over the society he had created at the Tabernacle to Wesley in 1758, though admittedly Wheatley's motives were rather different and Wesley was never going to take Wheatley back! Anglican clergy did this as well. Grimshaw's round based at Haworth, but including much of West Yorkshire and some of Lancashire, is

---

[16] Chapter 8 above; Eastwood, 'Yewdalls' Chapter 3.
[17] *GHR.*
[18] Valentine, *Bennet.*
[19] For St Ives and Cornwall see Shaw, *Cornish Methodism* 14-15.

well documented.[20] Less known are the societies in South Wales founded by Philip Thomas, who was curate of Gelligaer near Merthyr Tydvil in 1744 and later curate to John Hodges of Wenvoe and friendly with the Wesleys. By 1746 he had his 'own' society near Neath and formed other Methodist societies in Glamorgan in this period. In 1753 he was presented to the livings of Michaelston and Sully by Mrs Jones of Fonmon. It seems his societies were taken over by the Wesleys who could provide continuity.[21] Similarly, in East Cornwall and West Devon the clergyman George Thomson, who had a little circuit between Port Isaac and Bideford, came to work closely with the Methodists. All these show Wesley as the supreme organizer of other people's societies, both those of clergy and those formed by laymen. It also demonstrates how Methodism was very happy to work within the Church of England and was at first seen by clergymen to be doing this.[22]

Historians in the past have viewed the preachers as dependent on Wesley. The Methodist legend was focussed too much on its (undoubted) heroes. Knox, in his criticism of Wesley, said he was not a great organizer because he was unable to delegate.[23] Though Wesley did have difficulties in working with equals, yet someone whose successful lieutenants included John Nelson, Christopher Hopper, Thomas Taylor and Francis Asbury was certainly able to delegate, though Wesley did not always appreciate the results of their work. One of the purposes of this book has been to rescue the whole body of preachers, not simply the more famous leaders, from the obscurity of much of earlier Methodist history writing and give them the rightful place they deserve. The cadre which these itinerants formed was not only to provide the men and methods for advancing through much of the British Isles, but also to spread to America and to other areas where Britons settled or had influence. Methodist preachers on horseback were known, attractive figures and their success in England and elsewhere was a result. Historical writing has also focussed on 1738 and the conversion of the Wesley brothers, often to the exclusion of later periods. The events of the next fifty years, and especially the rise of that cadre of preachers, a group we can now date to the 1740s for its size, rules, regular conferences, circuits and societies, were of more long term importance. The modern President who sits in Wesley's chair is, as such, still a figure-head, while the real power in modern British Methodism resides elsewhere, in the Connexional Team, with the Chairs of Districts and Superintendents of circuits

---

[20] For Lee see *AM* 1780: 25-32, 140-5, 1787: 70-1. For Mitchell who had several preaching places round Guiseley see *AM* 1780: 313-25. For Davis see *Crk* 1: 102-5. See also Chapter 2 above. For Wheatley see Bellamy, *Wheatley* 181-9.

[21] For Glamorgan see Williams, *Wesley in Wales* 21 n1, 25.

[22] Shaw, *Cornish Methodism*. Fletcher's societies in east Shropshire provide another example.

[23] R. Knox, *Enthusiasm: a Chapter in the History of Religion* (Oxford: Clarendon Press, 1954) 428-430.

and in the Circuit Meetings, with the successors of those ordinary preachers.

Organization

Hempton has recently cast doubt on Wesley's genius for organization, describing what Wesley did as a 'ragbag of pragmatic innovations borrowed from Moravians and Quakers, or suggested to him by other free lance itinerant evangelists, most of whom he later fought with.' This is a reference to men like Whitefield, Bennet and David Taylor, each of whom suggested innovations to him. Thus Bennet was responsible for the introduction of the Quarterly Meeting. Certainly in later years Wesley may have wished to give the impression of a fully formed plan for evangelism which he had implemented. There was no plan. Movement forward to new areas depended on being invited, or on individual preachers' initiatives rather than Wesley's direction. His organization, however, depended on those who carried out the ideas and it was their determination, persistence and commitment that mattered, not where the original idea had come from. Once there was an invitation (as with America in 1769) Wesley and his lieutenants would use the existing organization to seize the opportunity, and Wesley continued to give regular support to the new areas which he expected to expand and produce new preachers in their turn. His real greatness lay in his ability to borrow the new ideas and implement them, while transforming them to suit the situation in which he found himself across a far broader constituency and with much more success than anybody else. His wide pastoral effectiveness over an area beyond the British Isles is testimony to the success of his organization. It did not matter that it was assembled in a haphazard fashion over more than twenty years. What was important to him, to Methodism then and to his heirs today looking back, was that it worked. That was always the test for Methodists. The methods may have been a ragbag, but they were pragmatic, and they were a success.[24]

Hempton went on to explain that what gave Methodism its preponderance was 'energy, mobility, perseverance and will.' He was referring to Wesley himself, but these qualities were also present in his preachers. Nelson and Hopper of the first cohort, Lee, Hunter and Rowell of the second, Benson, Pawson, Mather and Thomas Taylor of the third did thirty or more years' service. Their energy, mobility, perseverance and will equalled Wesley's own. His preachers showed the same qualities, vitally important in maintaining the morale and ethos of the organization that was being built. These itinerants also were capable of thinking and acting for themselves. This was particularly true in America with Asbury or Freeborn Garrettson, but it was also applicable to preachers like Hopper, Nelson, Bennet, Thomas Taylor, or Walsh and John Smith in Ireland or John Crook in the Isle of Man. Methodism was undoubtedly

---

[24] Hempton, *Empire* 16.

an active agent in the transformation and transference of religious culture.[25]

Hempton emphasizes the importance of the mobile laity in the spread of Methodism. He is correct, but this does not minimize the importance of Wesley's preachers who, in the view of most people of the period including usually themselves, were lay in any case. They were needed to exploit the openings created by the mobile lay part-timers. Pilmore and Asbury were in the end more important than Captain Webb and Philip Embury.[26]

Preachers Controlling Wesley

In an important insight Kent described Wesley as 'caught up in a religious movement that he could not control as he wanted.' 'Once he had accepted his leading role in what became a Wesleyan subculture, his reactions to the unexpected religious experiences he encountered then hardened into a confident system.' It was indeed his travelling preachers, the order that he had created, who came to control him, immersing him in a religious subculture which carried him along increasingly towards separation, ordination and the setting up of the Legal Hundred.[27] This was certainly the view of Charles Wesley and it should not be dismissed, as some previous historians have done, just because it came from him. As early as 1763 the Preachers' Fund was established against John Wesley's wishes for the benefit of the preachers.[28] By the 1780s his British and Irish preachers were able to exert considerable control over John Wesley on most issues, and what he did in Britain and Ireland was in general what they wanted. Similarly in America only Asbury, not Wesley nor even Coke, was able to control the new American Church, and Asbury only succeeded by transferring vital decisions to the preachers such as the election of a Bishop, not to Wesley's nomination. The story told by Smith of Wesley and Henry Moore, with Wesley giving way to Moore over whom to admit to communion, is a good example of the way his preachers had taken a controlling position.[29]

However, on one important issue, remaining within the Church, John Wesley continued to withstand the strong swell of preacher opinion until his death. To judge from the correspondence of Pawson, Hanby and other leading preachers in the 1780s there was strengthening antipathy among them to the

---

[25] Hempton, *Empire*. For support for my view that Hempton is wrong here see, for example, A. R. George, 'John Wesley: the Organizer' in Stacey, ed, *Wesley* 108-114. 'Transference' refers to the spread to other areas.
[26] Hempton, *Empire* 30.
[27] Kent, *Wesley and the Wesleyans* 191.
[28] Chapter 19.
[29] Smith *Meth* 1: 649-50. Moore had taken his class-ticket away from a wealthy member who attended the theatre. Wesley, who was about to admit him to communion, gave way to Moore's protest.

Methodists remaining within the Church.[30] Yet it is clear that Wesley led the majority of Methodists to feel they were still within the Church right up to his death in 1791, despite giving way partially on the question of ordination. The fact that the Database shows so many Methodist preachers continued to attend the Church of England for the rites of baptism, marriage and funerals long after 1791 shows the strength of the desire to remain within the Church, if only in a residuary form for these rites of passage. Even after Wesley's death separation was not inevitable, if the leadership of the Anglican Church had been at all interested in retaining Methodism.

Methodism after Wesley
Mission beyond the British Isles

Methodist growth overseas was a natural result of growth at home. This book has sought to show that the original growth in centres with maritime connections, Bristol, London and Cornwall, led easily to Methodism moving first to the rest of the British Isles and then to other parts of the transatlantic community. Methodism was always strong at the margins, whether in Cornwall or the Isle of Man or the American frontier. The thirteen American colonies took their natural place after Ireland and before the West Indies and Canada. The numbers and strength of the mission work, first in the American colonies and then elsewhere especially in the Caribbean, was important because of the effect on those countries. There were also even wider repercussions. Not only did this lead to Methodist missions to India and Ceylon (1813), to Africa (1811), in the South Seas (1815) and even in China (1851), but there was an effect back in Britain. Missionaries returned. Mass produced engravings and word pictures used in missionary education helped to create the globalized world in which we live today. The old assertions found it more difficult to survive in a world of cultural diversity. The men whom Wesley sent to America usually returned to Britain. Though mostly conservative in their outlook they all had had the ideas of a new world impressed upon them, ideas which were to become more pressing in the age of the French Revolution.[31] And there were important effects overseas as well. Methodism, successful in America among the colonists, was even more successful among the black population there. By 1813, of the 210,000 plus members in the USA, a fifth were black, a larger proportion than blacks were in the total population.[32] Methodist ideas of

---

[30] *Pawson L* 1: 35-125.

[31] The Methodist Missionary Society Collection of pictures at the School of Oriental and African Studies in London has over the last few years become one of the main sources of pictures for the modern media of the non-European world in the nineteenth century. Pilmore is an example of a Methodist preacher who, though he had returned from America, was unable to get the idea of America out of his mind and went back.

[32] Noll, *America's God* 168.

liberation and strength through unity became important among indigenous peoples from Native Americans via Tonga and Fiji and China to Sri Lanka and Ghana. The equality of all peoples before God was a powerful idea which encouraged the rise of local Christian sects. National leaders, from the Ojibways in nineteenth century Canada to Nelson Mandela, were Methodist trained and often preachers themselves. Methodists set up their printing presses wherever they went. One of the first tasks of the missionary was to write down the local languages, translate the Bible and the hymns into them and then print these. The explosion of print in the developing world was not only because of Methodism, but Methodists played an important part in that process. It is also worth pointing out that the missionary was a pioneer of scientific collection and categorization, and played an important part from the late eighteenth century for at least 200 years. Methodists like Soothill in China and Edwin Smith and Parrinder in Africa have their own place in the world academic pantheon. 'Globalization' was both a help to and a result of the spread of Methodism.[33]

Unity and Strength

Wesley's preachers remained together after his death, despite many predictions to the contrary. Part of their strength was that unity, forged as we have seen in their meeting each year in Conference. Part was also the system of itinerancy which, by transferring preachers each year from Ireland to Cornwall or Scotland or East Anglia and the like, ironed out differences and brought circuits more closely together. Methodists were united in their loyalty to Wesley, the man who faithfully travelled the three kingdoms and preached to all. By his last years this had become a royal progress which no good Methodist dare miss, in case it was Wesley's last. But they were also loyal to the preachers who like Wesley, travelled the three kingdoms, at least in his lifetime. They were the men he had appointed, who travelled less distance but more miles locally, visited each home and society class, administered the same discipline and preached the same doctrine whether in Ireland or Accrington. If a preacher died on circuit someone would be sent to take his place, while the local preachers filled in meanwhile. Interregnums, which caused problems for other churches, were always much shorter or non-existent.

The result of all this was the strong professional feeling of unity expressed in the hymn at the opening of Conference. Wherever they were, in whatever continent they were sent to serve, however difficult the situation was, they were

---

[33] E.g. Bayly, *Birth* 347-351, 357-63. For Methodism and print see the Proceedings of the 2006 MMS History Conference on disk. William Soothill became Professor of Chinese at Oxford, Geoffrey Parrinder Professor of the Comparative Study of Religions at King's College, London. Both were Methodist missionaries and remained ministers in academic life. For Smith see W. J. Young, *The Quiet Wise Spirit* (Peterborough: Epworth, 2002).

'Mr Wesley's preachers' and they knew that they were serving God's kingdom and that His purposes would triumph. They could go to America, as William Blagborne did in 1810, and be recognized there as having the status of a Methodist travelling preacher.[34]

Wesley's Preachers after 1791

Despite this basic unity, Wesley's death in 1791 led to some divisions among Wesley's preachers. Where previously these had been masked by their common loyalty to Wesley, or at least by his consistent will, his removal led to problems which at times were to cripple his heirs seriously. As Pawson, writing to Asbury in 1803, said about British Methodism 'we have not had since the death of Wesley any proper government. We are a very large body without a head.'[35]

A dispute over the right to control Wesley's papers and books led to an immediate breach among his executors, between the former preacher Dr Whitehead on the one hand and the preachers Thomas Coke and Henry Moore on the other, resulting in a flurry of publications. A second and more serious division was the result of the large number of Methodists who wanted complete independence from the Church of England, and so ordination for all the preachers and the right for the Methodist members to receive the sacrament of Holy Communion from them. These were opposed by many who were called Church Methodists, especially in such places as London and Bristol but also Dublin and elsewhere. Some left the Society in the 1790s in order to remain within the Church. In Ireland the division was delayed for twenty years but was more serious in terms of losses when it came.

The next schism was over the question of the authority of the preachers. Many wanted to share it with the lay members. Those radical Methodists, of whom Kilham was the fervent proponent, clashed with the more conservative majority. Kilham was forced out, and those who sympathized with him had to decide whether to remain or follow him into the New Connexion. There were also divisions between Wesley's preachers in Ireland and those in Britain.[36] British Methodists should regret the decision no longer to station British preachers in Ireland, and similarly to station fewer and mostly younger preachers in Scotland and the Isle of Man.[37] This was partly because of the demands of the mission field to which Bunting and his contemporaries turned the energies of the British Methodist Church. Youthful enthusiasts, many of high calibre, were sent to Africa and India often to die there, but not as had

---

[34] For similar international specialisms developing into different professions but feeling the same problems and needs see Bayly, *Birth* 21. For Blagborne see *Asbury Jol* 3: 428.

[35] *HMGB* 4: 304 quoting MS letter at Garrett. Pawson also said the preachers refused to have discipline applied to them and that they were increasingly conforming to fashion.

[36] Chapter 11.

[37] Chapter 12.

happened under Wesley to Ireland.

The final important division came after 1820 when the younger preachers led by Bunting criticized and sidelined the surviving remaining leaders of Wesley's own preachers. Adam Clarke was attacked for 'the irregularity of his mode of establishing schools in Ireland' and, more seriously, for his views on the Eternal Sonship. He was not elected president for the fourth time and was forced to become a Supernumerary in 1831 against his own wishes. Henry Moore was sidelined in London.[38] Younger men who spoke out against Bunting, like James Everett or Samuel Dunn, were excluded from power and the 'better' stations. They felt discriminated against. George Whitfield, a trusted friend of Wesley who had drafted him in to run the vital Bookroom after Atlay's desertion, was granted only 'derisory obituaries (which) show he suffered the common fate of many of Wesley's inner circle who survived into the age of Bunting, of being forgotten.'[39] It was a process already in motion in 1810 when Rankin was denied an obituary. All this could be seen as personal and trivial, but it led to the partial disruption of 1835 and the loss of loyalty from much of the local preacher body symbolized by the creation of a separate Local Preachers' Mutual Aid. Most significantly it produced the 1849 Disruption when 100,000 members were lost, many never either to return to Wesleyan Methodism or join another Methodist body. It could be argued that British Wesleyan Methodism never recovered from the anti-Bunting feuding of the period 1830-50.[40]

Yet despite these divisions, each time they occurred most Methodist preachers were moderates seeking unity rather than division. Wesley had appealed to them to treat each other equally and to stay together. This made a great impression. In 1797 few preachers followed Kilham, though many had corresponded favourably with him beforehand. William Bramwell, the leader of the revivalists in the generation following Wesley, resigned at Conference in 1803. But he was persuaded to return, much to the disgust of Sigston and other lay leaders who wanted an itinerant preacher figurehead.[41] This pattern of ministerial solidarity was repeated later again and again. Few ministers followed the 'three expelled' in 1849. The preachers' desire for unity, their corporate loyalty to the 'Living Wesley' of Conference when their 'Father' was no longer with them, overcame the strains and stresses of internal divisions. In Ireland the division leading to the Primitive Wesleyans was very similar, with few existing preachers among those who separated.[42] A generation after 1849

---

[38] Edwards, *Clarke* 22-4, 33-4. Bunting was the author of the quotation from the motion. Bunting and his friends were suspicious of all the surviving preachers who had been personally associated to Wesley. For Moore see Chapter 18 above.
[39] Ward's shrewd words in *WJW* 23: 219 n4.
[40] Ward, *England 1790-1850* is the best modern account of these divisions.
[41] *Pawson L* 3: 92, 98, 100, 118, 120; Ward, ed, *Early Correspondence* 11.
[42] Chapter 11.

laymen were to be admitted to become members of the Wesleyan Conference.

Another important effect of these divisions was the political stance of the Connexion. Under Wesley Methodism had been non-political, but holding also something of a traditional country party attitude. In the turmoil of the revolutionary 1790s and in the early nineteenth century Wesleyanism became more 'Tory' and solidly conservative, losing reformers and radicals first to the New Connexion, later the Primitive Methodists, followed by the Wesleyan Methodist Association and the Wesleyan Reformers.[43]

The Semmel Thesis

In 1973 Semmel produced a book which challenged other historians on Methodism, arguing that potentially damaging revivalism was channelled into foreign missions after Wesley. While under Wesley the British Isles always had clear priority, later first Coke and then Bunting, supported by and often driven on by the other preachers, turned the efforts of Wesleyan Methodism into the organization of overseas missions and away from home missions.[44] Piggin's important rebuttal in 1980 argued, among other points, that Semmel was only looking at the surface, and that Coke and Bunting did not oppose revival. Certainly Bunting and the other Wesleyan leaders wanted controlled revival, run by themselves as the ministers of the Wesleyan Church.[45] But it is also true that the machine that became the Wesleyan Methodist Missionary Society (WMMS) raised money, educated the Methodist people and sent outside the country some of the best young men produced within Methodism for the next 140 years, a change from what had happened under Wesley. Chapters 12-14 above have shown that this was beginning under Wesley. £50 for America in 1769 represented a relatively large proportion of Methodism's money in that year and was a much smaller proportion of the total than the £124,000 spent by WMMS in 1849.[46] Bunting felt strongly that improving money raising for

---

[43] Bayly, *Birth* 102 aptly described this Wesleyan stance as 'a form of Conservative Enlightenment,' improving society by the application of rational benevolence to the problems of poverty, while standing against social revolution or the expropriation of property.

[44] See Chapter 14 above. B. Semmel, *The Methodist Revolution* (London: Heinemann, 1973).

[45] S. Piggin, 'Halévy Revisited: The Origins of the Wesleyan Methodist Missionary Society: An Examination of Semmel's Thesis,' *JICH* (October, 1980) 9.1, 17-37 and 'A Marxist Looks at Methodism: A critique of E. P. Thompson's assessment of the role of Methodism in an age of Revolution,' in J. S. Udy and E. G. Clancy, eds, *Dig or Die*, (Sydney: WMHS, 1981) 290-305. The idea has not been much discussed by later historians except Piggin, though Macquiban suggested the move to OM as a reason for the decline after 1840 of giving to the Strangers' Friend Society. I am indebted to Stuart Piggin, who also provided references and summarized his views on the whole question.

[46] See Chapter 12 for the £50 given to Pilmore and Boardman. They did take other

Overseas Missions (OM) would improve all money-raising within the church. The modern historian looking at this may feel that, though he could well have been right, yet there must have been a ceiling of money which could have been raised and the more of this that went to OM, the lower the proportion that would be left for work at home. In this sense at least foreign missionary work must have been conducted at the expense of home missions.[47] George Morley admitted in 1813 that it would 'diminish the Number of Preachers at home ... that we might maintain a greater number of Missionaries.'[48] As Piggin pointed out this was also true of other churches who equally put more money and personnel into overseas work, but the change was more noticeable in Wesleyanism since it had for its first eighty years so much emphasized mission within Britain itself. We have already noted the little mention of overseas mission in Methodist literature such as the *Magazine* before 1810. By 1850 the flagship *Wesleyan Methodist Magazine* had a seventh of its mammoth 1,333 pages devoted to Missionary Notices alone. As Piggin suggested, this change for Methodism was more a mark of its triumphalism than of pressure from outside.[49] It was not for its participants a conscious change, but there were effects. This change in ethos should be seen as a natural stage in the development of Methodism. While it was a young movement it concentrated on its mission within the country, as did Primitive Methodism from 1810 to around 1880. In maturity it naturally turned its eyes to the wider world, partly because mission at home was becoming more difficult. The wider ramifications and the details of this major change have yet to be properly assessed.[50]

Secularization

Many historians have seen the progress of secularization in Europe as the most important development since the Reformation. Methodism grew in opposition

---

things of value, not least themselves, two trained and experienced itinerants. For the 1849 figures see WMMS *RJ* 157.

[47] This is the fifth and last of the questions Piggin posed in 'Halevy Revisited' 19. Piggin pointed out on page 31 that the Methodist leaders who opposed the change swiftly joined the missionary bandwagon, once Home Missionary giving via the Contingent Fund increased.

[48] J. Nichols, *A Report of the Principal Speeches Delivered at the Formation of the Methodist Missionary Society... Leeds* (Leeds: Nichols, 1813) 19.

[49] The 1850 *WMM* had 193 pages for missionary notices with other articles such as three on 'Incidental results of Christian Missions in South Africa' outside that number. Cf. Piggin, 'Halevy Revisited' 28-9; *HMGB* 2: 120.

[50] I am not suggesting that Home Missions ceased, simply that less of the connexion's effort was directed that way and more went to Overseas Missions. I am indebted to a number of friends for their comments on this topic, especially John Walsh who drew my attention to Piggin's opposition to Semmel's thesis. British Methodist finance in this period and its sources is a subject to which I hope to return.

to the major secular trend in the world in which it began.[51] Methodists and Evangelicals in general saw themselves as the opponents of latitudinarianism and the Enlightenment.[52] The title of Rack's biography of Wesley 'Reasonable Enthusiast' encapsulates the paradoxical nature of the man and the movement. If Wesley was more reasonable than many of his supporters or preachers, yet the whole movement by weakening the Established Churches and increasing religious pluralism helped the trend in Western Europe and America to move to first toleration and then the encouragement of alternative beliefs. The plausibility of religion suffered and this led to no belief at all. As Berger suggested, Methodism by being an agent of pluralism ultimately helped to bring about its own decline.[53] The real strength of secularization at different times has come under increasing question, some historians suggesting it was a later phenomenon than previously thought.[54] Nevertheless the itinerancy, more than any of the other institutions of Methodism, stood against the manners and mores of secular society. Methodist preachers did not receive the college training expected by the polite society of clergymen and occupants of pulpits. Instead the itinerant gave up everything that was materially important in order to concentrate on spiritual matters and the preaching of the Gospel. What made it worth the material sacrifice to the Methodist preacher was the knowledge that he was owned by God, by the people of God, and by his brothers in the itinerancy.

Connexionalism and the Pastoral Task

One of the legacies of Wesley's preachers was the idea of connexionalism, partly resurrected by Beck in the last years of the twentieth century. This was about interdependence, through spiritual fellowship, consultation (those letters!), government by lay conferring (Conference, Quarterly Meetings and later Synods), and oversight by Wesley and others acting as his eyes. Because Wesley's preachers were and remained basically united and a brotherhood sharing the same spiritual father, the limited organization was a seamless robe which, despite the failings of individual preachers, was always being repaired. No preacher was the same, but all sang Charles Wesley's verses from the same hymn book to the same tunes, followed the same discipline, went back to meet each other at the same Conference and travelled the circuits even in the worst

---

[51] See for instance Hempton, *Empire* 189-201.

[52] The point is made for America by Noll in *America's God* 13-14 and at length later.

[53] P. Berger, *The Sacred Canopy: Elements of a Sociological Theory of Religion* (New York: Anchor, 1969). J. Gregory, 'Charles Wesley and the 18th century' in Newport and Campbell, *Charles Wesley* 26-8 argues Methodism reflected as well as opposed the Enlightenment.

[54] C. G. Brown, *The Death of Christian Britain: Understanding Secularisation, 1800-2000* (London: Routledge, 2001) argued it was not until the 1960s.

weather. If the preacher left, some one else would fill his boots. The idea of 'connexion,' of support from different societies for other societies in the circuit, other circuits for each circuit, the 'Connexional Funds' such as the Preachers' Fund to which every circuit contributed and on which each could call if in need, was one which was there from the earliest times. By 1791 this practice of connexionalism was well established and in the nineteenth century it was to be much further developed.[55]

The 'Pastoral Authority' of the preachers, the importance of their pastoral work and the authority this gave them over the laity, was a subject specifically developed by Barrett and others in the nineteenth century. It was sometimes a cause of division, when it was seen as unreasonable and undemocratic, but it had good effects as well. Carter has reminded us that the Wesleys were concerned that there should be a 'ministry that trained souls in holiness and watched over them in love.' Wesley's preachers knew well that this was their chief task after preaching. Any one might be able to preach and convert, to act the evangelist like Whitefield. But could those souls be gathered in and trained in the Christian religion? By staying in a different home with a new family each night on his circuit the preacher watched over the spiritual development of many households and individuals. Overnight hospitality was to decline in the nineteenth century, with the reduction in need because of the smaller circuits. Yet Methodism continued to believe in growth in the Christian life, and turned its energies to this increasingly after 1800, not least worldwide. Schools, colleges, hospitals and the different outworkings of the late nineteenth century Central Missions were important ways of building up the Christian body.[56]

Standards

The chapters on leaving and why preachers left might lead to the assumption that, because of the high number of cases of problem preachers at any period, general standards of preaching and pastoral care must have suffered. This was not the case. Reasons for leaving were not usually connected with standards, but health and family life. The existence of some who left was itself a mark of the high standards that the Wesley brothers, and the Conference after them, maintained. A large number of diaries, journals, letters and other private documents which have survived from this period illustrate this. The spiritual powerhouse which comprised Wesley's preachers had their greatest effect on the lives of thousands across eighteenth century Britain and her dependent territories.[57]

---

[55] B. E. Beck, 'Some reflections on Connexionalism' in *Epworth Review* 18: 2 (1991) 48-59, 3: 43-50; *DOMBI*. For the Preachers' Fund see Chapter 19.
[56] D. Carter, *Love Bade Me Welcome* (Peterborough: MPH, 2002) 131.
[57] See for example the work of Tom Albin, beginning with T. R. Albin, *Full Salvation: the Spirituality of Anna Reynalds of Truro 1775-1840* (Redruth: CMHA, 1981).

Rewriting Methodist History

Methodist history was written by those who won, by John not Charles, by the preachers who stayed not those who left, by Coke and Moore not the Church Methodists, by male not women preachers. Too much of early British Methodist history has been seen through the prism of John Wesley's extensive writings. This book has tried to give a voice to those who left like Bennet or Pilmore,[58] and to those who remained but were written out such as Mary Taft or George Whitfield. The ordinary itinerant who stayed or left has had his daily life portrayed, often by his own words. The book has used their correspondence both to the Wesley brothers and others, rather than the Wesleys' letters to them. Similarly in America Methodism has been seen as largely the creation of Asbury. Chapters 12 and 13 in this book have shown the importance of the parts played by those other British preachers whom Wesley sent, as well as Asbury. The large number of Methodist itinerants represented in this book has enabled a wide cross section of Methodist society in the period 1740-1820 to be celebrated and a mine of information displayed, in aspects of their lives usually hidden in the past. Hopefully this has meant successfully rewriting some of the previously accepted assumptions about the preachers. Many returned to the local preacher status from which they had come and a substantial number of these returned again to the itinerancy. Their essential 'layness' assisted the movement in spreading faster and surviving even in places of great difficulty, where expensive clergy would never have remained. The promotion by Wesley of younger preachers to be his Assistants in the circuits was another factor which aided growth, particularly in the 1780s and 1790s. The fact of extra, previously 'hidden' preachers available to Wesley and his successors shines a different light on their effectiveness.

History of Methodism and the Preachers

This book has tried to fill the gap in Methodist historiography about the preachers, rather than be another history of the rise of Methodism, but inevitably it casts much light on early Methodism generally. It has proved impossible not to deal with this because it was intertwined so much with their lives. Most of the 802 preachers who entered before the death of Wesley have been mentioned in the book, some with considerable detail.[59] The new sources available to the genealogist and historian via the internet have enabled new facts such as the 'wealthy wives' to emerge, which allow the modern historian

---

[58] Other good though less well known examples have been Alexander M'Nab in Chapter 15 and Michael Fenwick in Chapter 17.

[59] The total number of preachers is that arrived at a particular point in time and including 'probables.' Two years before publication it was 799. In another 5 years it could be 805. The exact numbers do not matter, because the proportions arrived at as a result will vary little.

to observe more rounded characters, with parents, wives, families and friends to act as counterpoint to the picture of the itinerant preacher always riding round or changing his circuit. The sometimes dry statistics from the database have often provided new insights on the rise of Methodism, such as Wesley's use of younger preachers, and are always capable of being lit up by stories about the individuals, whose 'labours for the Lord' inspired others, not least their successors.

Wesley's preachers were an order created by the Wesleys as part of the Methodist movement they founded. They were essentially part of the society from which they came. Their origins were typical of that mobile society, especially from the areas in the north and north Midlands where Methodism became strongest. They married and had children, they travelled in circuit, attended Conference, they were ill, they retired and died in patterns which fitted the Methodism they helped to create and the society in which they were at work. The step of creating lay itinerant preachers at the beginning of the 1740s in England led on to the other changes seen above, from the creation of vital parts of the organization such as the society, the circuit and the Conference, to later developments like Kingswood School, the Preachers' Fund and ordination. The separate church had eventually been created *because* of the new order of preachers.[60]

Wesley's Preachers: Wesley's Memorial

Howard described the itinerancy as Wesley's true memorial. It would be equally apt to say that the itinerants themselves were his true memorial. By 1791 both John and Charles Wesley and many of the original itinerant preachers had died. But a large number, larger than previously realized, remained of the experienced travelling preachers to mould the increasing numbers entering upon the itinerancy.[61] The 'bright succession' of these preachers carried forward the movement to the next generation. They presented the message to future Methodists as well as to the world. As the key people who sparked the rising Evangelical revolution of their day, these 'joiners' in eighteenth century Methodism were able, by the example of their lives and the power of their preaching, to persuade others to join their Methodism.[62] Their success can be seen in the continuance of Wesley's Methodism compared with those other early Methodists, Whitefield or the Countess of Huntingdon, or

---

[60] *HMGB* 2: 159-60.

[61] P. Howard, 'Developments in the Itinerancy 1780-90' in WHS/WMHS Conference Report (WHS, 1983); Appendix Two below.

[62] See Fr Kay, 'Childhood Personality and Conversion' 217 in L. Francis and Y. Katz, eds, *Joining and Leaving Religion: Research Perspectives* (Leominster: Gracewing, 2000). The term 'bright succession' comes from Doddridge's ordination hymn, verse 4, no. 211 in the current *Hymns and Psalms*, 'So shall the bright succession run...'

with the Moravians. Saunderson said on his deathbed in the quotation at the start of this chapter that the Methodist preachers and missionaries were the most valuable body of men the world possessed. Though an itinerant himself, his insight remains important for the wider view. The efforts of the many itinerants bound together in a common purpose had more effect than the sum of the individual's achievements. The world since Saunderson's day has been a different and a better place as a result. Smith, in his massive history of Methodism, stated 'the institution of lay preaching …lay at the foundation of Methodism. Without it the Connexion could not have come into existence.'[63] The actual personnel of the lay preachers, the itinerant ministry, were even more important in maintaining and ensuring that Methodism flourished and its influence increased.

---

[63] Smith *Meth* 1: 305.

Appendix One: Tables

Table 1: Wesley's Preachers by Cohort

Cohort number	Entry dates of cohort	Preachers Total no. No.	Preachers Total no. % of total preachers	Left No.	Left As a % of cohort	Died in the work No.	Died in the work As a % of cohort
1	1740 to 1750	144	18%	115	80%	29	20%
2	1751 to 1760	84	11%	59	70%	25	30%
3	1761 to 1770	135	17%	69	51%	66	49%
4	1771 to 1780	149	19%	68	46%	81	54%
5	1781 to 1790	273	35%	99	36%	174	64%
N/A	Not assigned to a cohort	17	100%	17	100%	-	-
Total		802		427		375	

Source: Wesley's Preachers' Database

Table 2: Wesley's Preachers by Countries of Birth

Country	Number of preachers
England	349
Ireland	109
Scotland	18
Wales	18
Other	13
Total	**507**

NB: countries of birth not known for 295 preachers
Source: Wesley's Preachers' Database

Table 3: Wesley's Preachers by English Counties of Birth

County	Total No.	1	2	3	4	5	None	Died	Left
BDF	1	-	1	-	-	-	-	-	1
BKM	2	-	1	-	1	-	-	1	1
BRK	2	1	-	-	1	-	-	1	1
CHS	14	2	4	2	2	4	-	8	6
CON	37	14	3	10	3	6	1	16	21
CUL	5	-	1	-	2	2	-	4	1
DBY	9	1	-	1	1	6	-	8	1
DEV	9	-	1	1	2	5	-	7	2
DOR	3	1	-	-	2	-	-	1	2
DUR	9	2	-	2	5	-	-	7	2
ESS	1	-	-	1	-	-	-	-	1
GLS	14	6	-	2	4	1	1	5	9
HAM	1	-	1	-	-	-	-	1	-
HEF	1	1	-	-	-	-	-	1	-
KEN	4	2	-	1	-	1	-	1	3
LAN	30	2	3	8	5	12	-	19	11
LEI	7	2	-	2	1	2	-	2	5
LIN	19	2	2	6	-	9	-	14	5
LND	6	1	1	1	1	2	-	3	3
MDX	2	-	-	-	2	-	-	1	1
NBL	15	3	1	2	4	5	-	9	6
NFK	8	3	-	-	-	4	1	4	4
NTH	2	-	-	1	1	-	-	1	1
NTT	1	-	-	-	1	-	-	-	1
OXF	1	1	-	-	-	-	-	-	1
SAL	3	2	-	-	-	1	-	1	2
SFK	2	-	-	1	-	1	-	-	2
SOM	4	1	1	1	1	-	-	3	1
SSX	2	1	-	-	-	1	-	1	1
STS	7	1	-	2	2	2	-	5	2
WAR	3	-	-	-	-	3	-	3	-
WIL	5	-	2	1	1	1	-	4	1
WOR	4	1	-	-	2	1	-	2	2
YKS*	3	-	3	-	-	-	-	-	3
ERY*	3	-	2	1	-	-	-	2	1
NRY*	22	-	-	9	5	8	-	18	4
WRY*	78	12	10	14	11	31	-	55	23
Totals	339	62	37	69	60	108	3	208	131

NB: counties of birth not known for 10 English-born preachers
County abbreviations are Chapman county codes.
* The list is ordered alphabetically but the Yorkshire Ridings have been placed together with Yorkshire.
YKS = Those from Yorkshire but no Riding known.
Source: Wesley's Preachers' Database

Table 4: Wesley's Preachers by Region of Origin

English born only

Area	Number of preachers born	Percent
Yorkshire	106	31%
North and Lancs (inc. Lancs, Cumbria, N'land, Durham)	59	17%
North Midlands (i.e. Lincs, Notts, Derbys, Cheshire)	43	13%
Midlands (i.e. Warks, Worcs, Staffs, Salop, Herefordshire, Leics, Glos)	39	12%
South West (i.e. Cornwall, Devon, Somerset, Dorset)	53	16%
South (i.e. Oxon, Wilts, Berks, Kent, Sussex, Hants)	15	4%
London and East Anglia (i.e. London, Bucks, Beds, Herts, Essex, Middlesex, Northants, Norfolk, Suffolk)	24	7%
Total	**339**	

NB: region of origin not known for 10 English-born preachers
Source: Wesley's Preachers' Database

Table 5: Wesley's Preachers by Religious Upbringing

Category	Number	Percent
Church of England or Ireland	65	40%
Methodist	40	25%
Dissenter	37	23%
Roman Catholic	9	6%
'Religious'	10	6%
Total known	**161**	

NB: religious upbringing not known for 641 preachers
Source: Wesley's Preachers' Database

Table 6: Wesley's Preachers by Class

Class	Left	Died
A	5	1
B	36	26
C	7	11
D	23	20
E	8	17
F	25	32
Totals	104	107

NB: class not known for 591 preachers. See for definitions Pages 46-48.
Source: Wesley's Preachers' Database

Table 7: Standard of Education of Wesley's Preachers

Cohort	Level 1 No.	Level 1 %	Level 2 No.	Level 2 %	Level 3 No.	Level 3 %	Total No.
1	16	72%	5	23%	1	5%	22
2	6	38%	2	12%	8	50%	16
3	6	29%	6	29%	9	42%	21
4	8	40%	6	30%	6	30%	20
5	13	41%	8	25%	11	34%	32
N/A	-		1	100%	-		1
Totals	49	44%	28	25%	35	31%	112

NB: standard of education not known for 690 preachers
Source: Wesley's Preachers' Database

Table 8: Wesley's Preachers' Age at Leaving School

Cohort	11	12	13	14	15	16	17	18	19	20	21	Total known
1	-	-	-	-	1	2	5	7	-	-	-	15
2	2	-	2	2	1	-	2	2	-	-	-	11
3	-	-	1	4	1	1	-	2	1	-	-	10
4	-	1	2	1	3	2	2	-	-	-	-	11
5	1	1	2	4	-	4	2	1	-	-	1	16
Total known	3	2	7	11	6	9	11	12	1	-	1	63

NB: age at leaving school not known for 739 preachers
Source: Wesley's Preachers' Database

Appendix One: Tables

Table 9: Age of Wesley's Preachers on Entry

Age	Number of preachers known	Age	Number of preachers known
16	1	39	3
17	3	40	5
18	3	41	2
19	19	42	1
20	15	43	-
21	27	44	2
22	38	45	1
23	29	46	2
24	26	47	-
25	24	48	-
26	18	49	-
27	27	50	-
28	22	51	-
29	15	52	1
30	12	53	1
31	15	54	2
32	18	55	1
33	7	56	1
34	6	Total (aged 16-56)	369
35	7		
36	5		
37	6		
38	4		

Mode = 22
Mean = 27
Median = 25

NB: age on entry not known for 433 preachers
Source: Wesley's Preachers' Database

Table 10: Marriage Totals by Cohort

Cohort	Already married at entry No.	Already married at entry As a % of cohort	Married No.	Married As a % of cohort	Not known to have married No.	Not known to have married As a % of cohort	Total
1	17	12%	82	57%	62	43%	144
2	10	12%	52	62%	32	38%	84
3	24	18%	95	70%	40	30%	135
4	19	13%	99	66%	50	34%	149
5	22	8%	186	68%	87	32%	273
N/A	1	6%	4	24%	13	76%	17
Total	93	12%	518	65%	284	35%	802

Source: Wesley's Preachers' Database

Table 11: Age at Marriage of Preachers and Their Wives

Age	Before entry	During travel	After leaving	Total	No. of wives marrying at given age	Age	Before entry	During travel	After leaving	Total	No. of wives marrying at given age
15	-	-	-	-	1	50	-	-	-	-	-
16	-	-	-	-	-	51	-	-	-	-	-
17	-	-	-	-	1	52	-	1	-	1	1
18	1	-	-	1	4	53	-	1	-	1	-
19	-	-	-	-	1	54	-	-	-	-	-
20	6	1	-	7	3	55	-	1	-	1	-
21	5	-	-	5	5	56	-	1	-	1	-
22	5	1	-	6	6	57	-	1	-	1	-
23	-	2	-	2	7	58	-	-	-	-	-
24	4	9	1	14	6	59	-	-	-	-	-
25	5	8	2	15	6	60	-	1	-	1	-
26	-	10	2	12	9	61	-	-	-	-	-
27	1	10	2	13	4	62	-	-	-	-	-
28	2	9	2	13	10	63	-	-	-	-	-
29	-	17	2	19	2	64	-	-	-	-	1
30	-	14	1	15	7	**Total (15-64)**	**32**	**174**	**20**	**226**	**112**
31	-	11	2	13	6						
32	-	10	-	10	3						
33	-	11	-	11	5						
34	-	5	1	6	4						
35	2	9	-	11	1						
36	1	10	1	12	4						
37	-	3	-	3	1						
38	-	3	-	3	1						
39	-	3	-	3	4						
40	-	4	-	4	1						
41	-	3	1	4	1						
42	-	3	2	5	1						
43	-	3	-	3	-						
44	-	2	-	2	1						
45	-	2	-	2	3						
46	-	1	1	2	1						
47	-	3	-	3	1						
48	-	1	-	1	-						
49	-	-	-	-	-						

Mean marrying age of preachers: 31.3

Mean marrying age of wives: 29.2

NB: age at marriage not known for 294 preachers (excluding those not known to have married)

Source: Wesley's Preachers' Database

Appendix One: Tables

Table 12: County of Birth of Wesley's Preachers: British Isles outside England

Wales	
County	Number of preachers
Brecon	3
Pembroke	3
Monmouth	2
Glamorgan	2
Cardigan	2
Denbigh	1
Montgomery	1
Total known	14

Scotland	
County	Number of preachers
Angus	3
Midlothian	2
Perth	2
Aberdeen	2
Argyll	1
East Lothian	1
Fife	1
Total known	12

Channel Islands	
Island	Number of preachers
Jersey	2
Guernsey	1
Total known	3

Ireland			
County	Number of preachers	County	Number of preachers
Fermanagh	12	Down	2
Tyrone	12	Leitrim	2
Armagh	7	Sligo	2
Dublin	6	Tipperary	2
Limerick	6	Cavan	1
Antrim	5	Offaly	1
Donegal	4	Roscommon	1
Londonderry	4	Waterford	1
Cork	3	Wexford	1
	(continued right...)	Total known	72

Source: Wesley's Preachers' Database

Table 13: Irish Membership Growth by Circuit 1799-1802

District	Circuit	1799	1802	Change
Dublin	Dublin	1,020	1,112	92
	Wicklow	200	406	206
	Carlow	310	462	152
	Longford	540	468	498
	Drogheda (1802)		570	
Cork	Cork	379	420	41
	Bandon	270	410	-6
	Youghal (1799)	146		
	Skibbereen	160	250	90
Limerick	Limerick	291	560	269
	Birr	400	250	67
	Roscrea (1802)		217	
	Waterford	260	277	17
	Mountrath	400	420	20
Athlone	Athlone (1799) / Tullamore (1802)	545	600	55
	Castlebar	240	240	-
	Sligo	580	900	320
	Boyle	400	536	136
Clones	Clones	700	1,209	509
	Ballyconnell	520	1,600	1,080
	Cavan	450	860	410
	Monaghan (1802) *		800	800
Enniskillen	Enniskillen	600	1,660	1,060
	Ballinamallard	690	1,540	850
	Brookborough	620	1,160	540
Londonderry	Londonderry	314	473	384
	Rathmelton (1802)		225	
	Newtownstewart	560	1,344	784
	Ballyshannon	370	1,050	680
Belfast	Belfast	482	558	76
	Coleraine	471	651	180
	Lisburn	620	620	-
	Downpatrick	442	620	178
Newry	Newry	420	491	71
	Dungannon	587	749	162
	Charlemont	760	1,028	268
	Tanderagee	1,300	1,460	160
Totals		**16,047**	**26,196**	**10,149**

Where circuit names only existed in either 1799 or 1802 this is indicated and the change in membership is shown corrected to match the geographical area.
* Monaghan was partly created from circuits in the Newry and Dublin districts as well as the Clones district.
Sources: British *Minutes* for 1799, Irish *Minutes* for 1802.

Table 14: Irish Preachers' Fund Payments Recorded in the British *Minutes*

Year	To nearest £	
	Income	Expenditure
1794*	136	116
1795		112
1796	178	71
1799		119
1800		76
1801	124	58
1802	121	64
1804	128	33
1805	171	37
1806	177	215

Gaps are where no income figures are known.

* It is known that in 1794 £87 came from the preachers and £49 from the people.

Table 15: Reasons Why Wesley's Preachers Left (by Cohort)

	Reasons for leaving (more than one reason applies to some preachers)	Cohort 1	2	3	4	5	N/A	Total	Rank *
A	Opposed Church of England/Ireland	7	1	0	2	0	1	11	16
B	Business	12	1	4	3	4	0	24	10
C	Not in Legal Hundred	0	2	1	3	0	0	6	20
D	Doctrine	23	8	4	5	2	0	42	7
E	To be clergyman	14	6	3	4	1	0	28	9
E*	Already clergyman returned	7	2	1	2	2	0	14	13
F	To be Dissenting minister	13	8	6	9	8	0	44	6
H	Health	8	4	12	9	13	0	46	5
H (M)	Mental health	1	2	3	0	2	1	9	18
I	Itinerancy problems	12	2	4	3	9	0	30	8
M	Marriage	26	9	12	12	14	0	73	1
N	Antinomianism, Calvinism, or opposed perfection	15	2	1	2	1	0	21	11
O	Aged parents, other family needs	1	1	3	1	1	0	7	19
P	Personal difficulties JW/preachers	24	7	11	13	12	1	68	3
Q	To become a Quaker	0	0	1	1	0	0	2	22/23
R	Too old	0	0	0	1	1	0	2	22/23
T	Alcoholism/Drunkenness	4	1	3	3	1	0	12	15
U	Unsuitable	15	7	20	13	12	2	69	2
W	Sexual immorality	3	1	3	3	6	0	16	12
X	Expelled	10	5	7	10	14	3	49	4
Y	Opposed Methodist polity	1	2	2	2	5	1	13	14
Z	Supported the Church	0	0	0	0	4	0	4	21
£	Money eg bankruptcy, embezzled	2	2	1	3	2	0	10	17
	Total leaving	115	59	69	68	99	17	427	

* Rank: 1 is the most common reason for leaving and 23 is the least.
Source: Wesley's Preachers' Database

Table 16: English Preachers Leaving by Area

Area	Total number born in area	Those who left No.	%
Yorks	106	31	29%
North and Lancs (inc. Lancs, Cumbria, N'land, Durham)	59	19	32%
North Midlands (i.e. Lincs, Notts, Derbys, Cheshire)	43	12	28%
Midlands (i.e. Warks, Worcs, Staffs, Salop, Herefordshire, Leics, Glos)	39	17	44%
South West (i.e. Cornwall, Devon, Somerset, Dorset)	53	26	49%
South (i.e. Oxon, Wilts, Berks, Kent, Sussex, Hants)	15	7	47%
London and East Anglia (i.e. London, Bucks, Beds, Herts, Essex, Middlesex, Northants, Norfolk, Suffolk)	24	14	58%
Total	339	126	

Source: Wesley's Preachers' Database

Table 17: Wesley's Preachers: Numbers Left

Year	Wesley's Preachers' Database	Minutes	Journal	Year	Wesley's Preachers' Database	Minutes	Journal
1740	1			1766	7	2	
1741	2			1767	9	5	
1742	0			1768	9	2	
1743	0			1769	10	6	
1744	2			1770	14	5	
1745	1			1771	4	0	
1746	1			1772	8	2	
1747	6			1773	7	4	
1748	5			1774	11	4	
1749	7			1775	7	2	
1750	3			1776	10	5	
1751	10			1777	8	4	
1752	5			1778	9	7	
1753	2			1779	12	4	
1754	9			1780	11	5	
1755	2			1781	5	2	
1756	7			1782	9	6	
1757	3			1783	8	3	
1758	5			1784	12	5	4
1759	2			1785	10	8	3
1760	6			1786	11	7	7
1761	2			1787	10	0	0
1762	5			1788	15	5	5
1763	6			1789	8	4	8
1764	6			1790	15	2	0
1765	9	0		1791	10	5	5

NB: year of leaving only known for 356 who left (427 left in total).
Sources: Wesley's Preachers' Database, *Minutes* (information available from 1765) and Conference Journal (information available from 1784).

Appendix One: Tables

Table 18: Destination of Leavers among Wesley's Preachers

Job	Number
Dissenting minister	57
Clergyman	47
Other business	21
Teacher	13
Physician, surgeon etc	12
Farmer	11
Craftsman	7
Shopkeeper	7
Labourer, etc	6
Office-holder	5
Other	3

NB: 180 known. Total is more because some had several known occupations.
Source: Wesley's Preachers' Database

Table 19: Wesley's Preachers: Returners by Cohort

Cohort	Returned Number	As a % of total returned
1	11	16%
2	4	6%
3	20	28%
4	21	30%
5	14	20%
Total	70	100%

Source: Wesley's Preachers' Database

Table 20: Dates of Return of Wesley's Preachers

Year	Preachers returned
1746	T Williams
1747	
1748	
1749	
1750	
1751	
1752	J Maddern
1753	
1754	M Fenwick *
1755	W Darney, C Perronet
1756	
1757	
1758	
1759	M Fenwick *
1760	J Kershaw (1760 or earlier)
1761	
1762	
1763	
1764	
1765	M Fenwick *, J Oliver
1766	J Deaves
1767	W Fugill
1768	M Rodda, W Whitwell
1769	J Stephens
1770	J Crowle, J Peacock
1771	W Baynes, M Fenwick *
1772	J Barry
1773	W Minethorpe, B Thomas
1774	N Manners, R Hayward, J Watson senior
1775	T Ryan
1776	J Hampson senior, J Fothergill, R Davis, J Pilmore, J Robinson
1777	J Fenwick
1778	J Bristol, Jos Jones

Year	Preachers returned
1779	G Wadsworth, R Swan, D Evans, S Day
1780	A M'Nab, G Gibbon
1781	J Beanland, J Abraham
1782	J Christie, T Wride
1783	
1784	
1785	R Condy, R Lindsay
1786	J Howe, T Cooper, H Robins
1787	J Roberts
1788	W Church, J Wiltshaw, W Wilson
1789	T Vasey, J Ramshaw, J King (US), M Fenwick *
1790	W Franklin, C Bond, R Phillips
1791	J Cross
1792	J Jordan, R M'Kay (US), J Sanderson
1793	J Lyons junior
1794	J Jerom
1795	
1796	P Hardcastle
1797	
1798	T Davis
1799	T Dobson
1800	
1801	
1802	
1803	
1804	T Whitehead (US)
1805	
1806	
1807	
1808	
1809	R Elliott

NB: Many dates are not known.
* M Fenwick returned several times.
US = United States.
Source: Wesley's Preachers' Database

Table 21: Wesley's Preachers: Number of Deaths at Any Age

Age	Number of deaths	Age	Number of deaths
18	1	58	6
19	-	59	8
20	-	60	5
21	1	61	12
22	1	62	9
23	1	63	2
24	-	64	6
25	1	65	8
26	1	66	12
27	1	67	13
28	2	68	10
29	1	69	12
30	1	70	11
31	2	71	10
32	1	72	14
33	4	73	8
34	-	74	15
35	1	75	6
36	5	76	4
37	-	77	13
38	1	78	10
39	2	79	11
40	3	80	9
41	2	81	10
42	4	82	5
43	6	83	9
44	3	84	4
45	3	85	5
46	5	86	-
47	3	87	2
48	4	88	5
49	5	89	2
50	4	90	3
51	3	91	3
52	5	92	2
53	6	93	-
54	6	94	2
55	7	Total (where age is known)	368
56	3		
57	3		

Mean age of death for all known = 64.9. For those who died in the work the age of death is usually known; for those who left it is usually not known.
Source: Wesley's Preachers' Database

Table 22: Wesley's Preachers: Numbers Received On Trial and Total Number of Preachers

Year	Received On Trial - In Ireland (per Database)	Received On Trial - Total (per Database inc. Ireland)	Received On Trial - Total (per *Minutes* inc. Ireland)	Travelling preachers - Definite	Travelling preachers - Possible	Supernumeraries
1740				4	6	
1741				5	9	
1742				17	24	
1743				25	31	
1744				32	39	
1745				33	40	
1746				34	43	
1747				36	77	
1748				46	63	
1749				56	68	
1750		6		57	66	
1751		9		61	69	
1752		4		60	67	
1753		10		71	78	
1754		4		64	74	
1755		4		66	77	
1756		8		73	79	
1757		6		69	76	
1758		9		71	84	
1759		9		69	76	
1760		8		70	78	
1761		12		79	85	
1762		16		88	95	
1763		9		88	92	
1764		13		94	101	
1765	4	12	12	102	108	
1766	3	15	6	103	107	
1767	2	13	9	108	113	1
1768	2	19	12	99	109	1
1769	3	14	12	116	125	1
1770	4	13	18	120	128	4
1771	3	13	8	128	131	1
1772	4	15	11	136	140	1
1773	2	13	12	142	149	2
1774	3	16	15	148	156	0
1775	3	13	9	153	157	2
1776	6	19	13	165	168	1
1777	3	13	10	167	171	0
1778	4	15	12	169	172	1
1779	7	15	11	167	169	0
1780	7	18	11	172	177	2
1781	1	9	9	177	182	3
1782	3	15	15	188	192	2
1783	8	23	11	188	195	5
1784	5	15	8	195	203	7
1785	3	27	20	213	221	7
1786	10	41	39	240	249	8
1787	13	33	32	258	269	11
1788	14	32	30	271	285	14
1789	11	27	25	287	298	11
1790	12	38	23	304	319	14

Sources: *Minutes* and Wesley's Preachers' Database
See text in Appendix Two for explanation.

Table 23: Wesley's Preachers: Length of Service / Number of Years Travelled on Circuit

Number of Years	Number of Preachers	Number of Years	Number of Preachers
<1	19	30	13
1	51	31	10
2	24	32	9
3	32	33	16
4	19	34	5
5	26	35	13
6	27	36	12
7	34	37	6
8	19	38	9
9	18	39	12
10	10	40	12
11	20	41	3
12	21	42	5
13	18	43	5
14	17	44	5
15	14	45	6
16	12	46	-
17	9	47	4
18	9	48	2
19	16	49	4
20	11	50	6
21	10	51	4
22	12	52	-
23	8	53	1 (J Wood)
24	8	54	-
25	8	55	1 (T Taylor)
26	8	56	-
27	4	57	-
28	12	58	-
29	11	59	1 (R Reece)

802 preachers, 131 no record shown.
Mean length of service = 17.4 years.
Source: Wesley's Preachers' Database

Appendix Two: Total Numbers

'And some there be, that have no memorial.'
Ecclesiasticus 44: 9.

Early Preachers and Differences between the Cohorts
Existing Estimates

John Wesley liked counting! It was partly a question of control; others have pointed out how difficult it was for him to work with equals. One result of his need to be in charge was his habit of checking numbers, for example, by getting someone to list members for him. Methodists have liked counting ever since. Richard Whatcoat noted every meal in his Journal. Peter Cartwright in America reckoned that he had preached a total of 14,600 sermons.[1]

The question of the total number of Wesley's preachers in the eighteenth century is an important one and has been referred to frequently in this book. In this Appendix the questions and discussion are brought together. Those who do not find this question of interest should stick to the book proper. Those like me who find the details of individual preachers of interest will read on. From a relatively early period Methodists and non Methodists alike have assumed that the totals given on the stations in the *Minutes* were correct, and that those who appeared there represented the maximum extent of the men available to Wesley for stationing. Wiser historians have qualified this by saying 'the number that appears in the *Minutes*.' It is my contention that we cannot rely on the *Minutes*, certainly for the period before the 1765 *Minutes* were printed, and to a lesser extent afterwards even into the early nineteenth century. A distinguished historian such as Heitzenrater, writing relatively recently about the 1745 Conference, said 'three clergymen and six lay preachers (out of twelve) attended.' Rupert Davies writing in 1989 suggested as many as fifty for 1745, a very different estimate.[2] I would argue that among the lay preachers at least twenty-nine 'could' have attended that year rather than either twelve or fifty. Baker, though less recent, said there were 39 circuits in 1758 'served by 25

---

[1] Andrews, *Methodists and America* 260-1.
[2] Heitzenrater 152; *WJW* 9: 16.

Assistants and 49 other travelling preachers,' a total therefore of 74 preachers. My figures would be 83 preachers that year, a slightly higher total which includes both a clergyman like Grimshaw and twelve doubtfuls, because a much closer estimate is available than for the earlier period.[3] Older totals are equally disparate. Tyerman, for example, suggested there had been thirty-nine preachers by 1744. He was not including clergymen.[4]

Travelling Preachers Not Listed in the Minutes

There was a steady number of preachers who at any one time were not listed in the printed *Minutes* after 1765, forming a substantial total when looked at over the whole period. It is not necessary to rehearse the arguments and individuals already cited above (Chapter 2). Other examples of preachers not listed in the *Minutes* include Henry Boyd, who wrote a friendly letter from Banff to Robert Dall in 1789, which included

> I love all who love you in Ayr – give my love to them all. I do not know where I may be stationed next year. I have little choice, except I do not want a walking Circuit.
> (A Secret) I have some thoughts on intimating a desire of marriage to Mr Wesley by way of letter from a proposal of my friend, viz. as she has proposed to keep herself free from Conference or Circuit charge for a time. But I am afraid. Fear not say you.[5]

Clearly from his language Boyd was a travelling preacher on circuit, describing to a former colleague his hopes and fears at Conference time. Dall, in his unpublished 'Reminiscences,' said that Boyd had 'Travelled for some time.'[6] Boyd's name never appeared in the *Minutes*, so but for this letter and those reminiscences nothing would have been known about him.

A similar example was that of John Francis. He appeared in Myles and Crowther as entering in 1774 and leaving in 1776. There was, however, no mention of either event in the *Minutes*. Again it would be tempting to say that Myles and Crowther, who usually based everything on the printed *Minutes*, made a mistake with his name, except that there was a signature (of a preacher) in the general letter written at the Conference of 1771 which cannot be fitted with any known preacher. The signature is not clear and was interpreted (for example by Rogal) as Fisher. Yet 'Francis' is much closer to the signature as it appears than Fisher especially as John Fisher, the only travelling preacher of

---

[3] FB Polity 232.
[4] Tyerman 1: 450 named them. His numbers could fit with Davies's estimate but not Heitzenrater's.
[5] *PWHS* 26 (1947) 22-25 quoting Dall Reminiscences MA 3181.
[6] MS associated with Robert Dall at MARC MA 3181/13. Copy of Dall Reminiscences in hand of great-grand-daughter.

that surname, disappeared after 1760.[7] The likelihood therefore is that Francis *was* a preacher travelling, recognized, but not on the stations for at least five years in the 1770s.

Another query involves John Hampson senior, who had married and apparently settled down in Cheshire in 1765. Yet in December 1768 in his *Journal* Pilmore stated in faraway Pembrokeshire 'I arrived in Haverford-West and was happy to find Mr Hampson had been with them and preached in my absence.'[8] The Chester circuit in which Hampson was a *local* preacher was large and did extend into North Wales, but not to the southern end of Wales and Pembroke. On this evidence Hampson therefore was travelling again in 1768, if only briefly, yet there was nothing about him in the *Minutes* either that year or in 1769.

There were many who appeared at one moment but were itinerating rather longer, an example of this being Thomas Hoskins. The *Minutes* showed him as entering in 1776, but not being appointed to the stations that year. The next year he was on the stations, and in 1778 his death was recorded with a note that he was in his second year of travel. The logical conclusion if he was in his second year was that he had been travelling in 1776 and should be counted for that year, even though no station existed for him.[9] Similarly, though with more concrete proof, the Hayfield-born (Derbyshire) preacher John Barber was actually available to Wesley for stationing from early 1782, though not on the stations in the *Minutes* until 1783 at Northampton. He was shown in the *Minutes* in 1782 as On Trial, but not on the stations. Barber himself said he had been interviewed and sent by Wesley to Birmingham in March 1782, 'remained' there, and was eventually in 1783 'sent back' to Northampton, so he must have been there also at some point in the intervening period.[10]

Another group concerned those who were not listed in the *Minutes*, usually for one year only, but were still in fact travelling on the stations. They were shown as on the stations the following year but with no hint of having left or come back. Thus in 1781 Thomas Mitchell did not appear on the stations and was not mentioned in the *Minutes*. He was travelling the next year and was then stationed in Bradford next door to his home circuit of Keighley. His autobiography shows he was in the London circuit in 1781.[11] The London Stewards' book confirms this. He received quarterly payments like all the other

---

[7] There is a facsimile printed of the letter and signatures in *JWJ(C)* 5: 427. John Francis' name appears before John Goodwin near the bottom of the left hand column.

[8] Pilmore, *South Wales* 83.

[9] Also known as 'Hosking.' *Minutes*.

[10] Tyerman BMM MAB B1236, *Minutes*. *Hill's* actually had him as entering in 1781, presumably at Conference, but I can find no contemporary evidence for this, and assume it is a later reading back from Tyerman's MSS.

[11] *EMP* 1: 257. Mitchell was born at Bingley in the West Riding. In 1781 he had travelled for over thirty years, having entered in 1748. He was to superannuate in 1784 and die in 1785.

travelling preachers that year, which proves he was still travelling and therefore available to Wesley for stationing.[12] I have not included in my estimates all who miss a year like this, only those who do not have a 'Desisted' in the first year or a 'Returned On Trial' in the year they came back, since these had clearly left. Thomas Gill entered in 1786 and was on the stations that year. Next year in 1787 he was not on the stations or mentioned in the *Minutes*, but in 1788 he was there again and in 1790 was received into Full Connexion having done his four years' probation. I would argue that he was actually available to Wesley in 1787, the year he did not appear. To show the likelihood of this it is interesting to note that in May 1788, hence three quarters of the way through the Methodist year of 1787-8, he was married at Otley to Elizabeth Ritchie's cousin, allowed to marry while still on trial. Now why would Wesley show such favour to a preacher who had left? Gill must have been still travelling that year. It is, as elsewhere, a case of a mistake being made in the *Minutes*. They were full of them.[13]

It is also worth pointing out that this discussion so far has been all about the period from 1765 to 1791 and all the examples quoted come from that time. There was also the earlier period up to 1765 where, because we have no regular printed *Minutes*, it has been much more difficult to assess. It is clear that from the 1740s to 1765 there could yet be many more travelling preachers to discover. The 1754 preaching plans for London, in Wesley's handwriting, show at least two preachers for whom there has been no other evidence that they preached for Wesley. Supposing other circuit plans were available for other circuits or even for London itself during these twenty plus years up to 1765, how many other occasional preachers who were full time for a short period would be revealed?[14]

An important element in the uncertainty for before 1765 was the so-called half-itinerants, already referred to in Chapter 2 above. They were men listed as such in those *MS Minutes* which have survived. Some had been itinerant or were to be. All had some sort of job or trade which would support them for some of the time. They were a halfway house between the local preacher, with whom this book is not concerned except when he was someone who had been or was to be a travelling preacher, and a travelling preacher who was by definition full time and supported by the local Methodist people. Such half-itinerants were by definition less costly to support than full itinerants. They might use their other job to support a wife, children or other dependants as well as themselves. From the early 1740s to 1765 William Shent was a barber with his shop under a barber's pole in Briggate, Leeds. The town was flourishing

---

[12] MS London Stewards Book at MARC.

[13] *WMM* 1838: 314; *WJW* 24: 82 n, 244d. Elizabeth Ritchie of Otley was a well known correspondent of Wesley.

[14] Heitzenrater 190 see Chapter 9 above note 16. The two were Robert Haigh and Joseph Swain.

and Shent thought he could support himself at his shop any time he wanted. He could (and did) go off for several months. In 1751 he was first preaching in Newcastle and later in Musselburgh in Scotland.[15] In April 1754 he preached twelve times over two weeks in London. In November 1759 he was in Scotland again preaching at Dunbar. None of these places were anywhere near Leeds. However, his business suffered, which was probably why he curtailed his tours and became a local preacher again. Shent was listed as a half-itinerant at Conference 1755 (with eleven others!).[16] There were a number described at different points as preaching in one place. But if some of their preaching is tracked, they were certainly not preaching in one place only. There was, for example, a list of thirty-eight who assist 'only at one place' in the *Minutes* of the 1747 Conference. Not all were known apart from this list, and it is rarely clear where that 'one place' might be. Most, however, were known to have preached in places at least fifty miles apart. John Appleton, the Shrewsbury currier, preached in Manchester and Stockport in 1748 and 1749 as well as his native Shrewsbury.[17] Henry Lloyd appeared in many parts of Wales. The same 1747 *Minutes*, which described John Maddern as preaching 'in one place,' dispatched him to London for the next quarter and then his native Cornwall for the one after. Since in the previous January he had appeared preaching at Woodley in John Bennet's Round on the way to Nelson at Birstall, the description of their preaching as being 'in one place' is frankly not true. It is impossible to separate such men from the itinerant preachers that year described as 'Assistants.'[18]

Some historians have not counted these half-itinerants as travelling preachers. Admittedly there is often more doubt about them, especially those for whom there is no other evidence. But in this period, when evidence is scarce and preachers could preach and travel for years without leaving any trace in the records, I have included them on the grounds that they mostly did travel. Even for those for whom there is no other evidence, the balance of probability is that they did travel if only for a short period. This, therefore, increases the total number beyond some older estimates.

Some of Wesley's preachers, in the words of Ecclesiasticus placed at the head of this Appendix 'have no memorial.' Despite that, they played an important part in the development of Methodism. New estimates for the total numbers of Wesley's preachers are therefore needed.

---

[15] Tyerman 2: 118; *DOMBI*; *WJW* 20: 160n57.
[16] *MM* 1811: 647; *PWHS* 25 (1945) 35; *EMP* 5: 159; Tyerman 2: 118 and Colman 20 at MARC.
[17] *AM* 1779: 418 and Valentine, *Mirror of the Soul* 192.
[18] *JB's Minutes* 49. For Lloyd see Chapter 10 above.

Anglican Clergy

One of the possible reasons for higher numbers in the database than previous estimates is that more Anglican clergymen have been included. If they accepted Wesley's authority at some time, appeared on the printed stations or preached regularly to Methodist societies within the connexion, they have been claimed for the database. Melville Horne or William Ley were definitely preachers since they travelled first and became clergy later. Similarly William Grimshaw and Thomas Coke were obvious Methodist leaders who cannot be excluded from the list of 'John Wesley's Preachers' simply because they were clergy first and Methodist preachers later. More controversial could be the inclusion of clergy like Henry Piers or Richard Thomas Bateman. They are in the database because in the 1740s it is more difficult to distinguish between the three different categories given above. Bateman and Piers certainly preached to Methodist societies. They never appeared on those stations which were printed, but undoubted Methodist (lay) preachers were not there either. Later clergymen who were sympathetic such as Cornelius Bayley (1751-1812) or B. B. Collins (1754-1807) have not been included in the database. In Bayley's case the *Dictionary of National Biography* described him as a Methodist preacher. There is no *Methodist* evidence that he went to preach to them despite his partiality, but he could have done. Methodists frequently went to St James' in Manchester to hear him and receive the Sacrament. The estimates therefore do not include Anglicans such as Bayley or Collins.[19]

New Estimates

The estimates of numbers that appear in this book are therefore just that. Admittedly I am giving figures including doubtfuls, such as some only mentioned as half itinerants, as well as minimum numbers. But the existence of Boyd, Holdsworth and Martin who never appeared in the Minutes, or Barry who 'desisted' in the Minutes without ever appearing before on the stations, shows that these new 'maximum' estimates are more likely to be an underestimate than an overestimate. These estimates include the doubtfuls among the preachers available for stationing to Wesley or the Conferences that succeeded him.

It is possible, therefore, to arrive at new approximations for the numbers of travelling preachers who were available for stationing at any one time in the eighteenth century. It should be emphasized that these encompass all preachers, those stationed in Ireland, later the British preachers stationed in America, and missionaries stationed in the West Indies; Supernumeraries and those in jobs such as Book Steward or 'travelling with Mr Wesley' are similarly included. Table 22 in Appendix One shows that the numbers moved rapidly and

---

[19] I would argue the *DNB* is notoriously poor on Methodism and does not constitute evidence which should be accepted. In retrospect I regret not including Collins.

substantially upwards in regard to the period up to 1747 for doubtfuls or 1749 for those who were definite. The reason for the high figure for doubtfuls in 1747 was because that year the *Minutes* listed those who preached in one place, with thirty names given. Such a list was rare. Most of these thirty names never appeared elsewhere and must remain dubious, but for Christopher Hopper it marked the start of a major career as an itinerant preacher. Hopper was chosen to preside by his fellow-preachers when Wesley was ill at Conference in 1780. In addition, it should be said that the average circuit in 1747 was large, so the 'one place' often covered a wide area.[20]

There was then a plateau in numbers for the whole of the 1750s until 1760. From 1761 to 1765 the figures moved upwards again steadily, and from then were relatively close to the figures taken from the *Minutes*. However, the new estimates remain higher than figures based only on the *Minutes* and except in the 1750s the number of Methodist preachers available to Wesley at any one time increased. The reasons for the plateau in the 1750s were important. It was a period when the original group of Anglican clergy and others who had joined the Wesley brothers in the hot dawn of the Evangelical revival were growing older and colder. Meriton, Bateman and others were no longer supportive. John's brother Charles married, settled down and hardly travelled north except occasionally to Conference. John Bennet, that important preacher who had brought many societies to the Connexion, left and set up on his own. Several other leading preachers like John Edwards, Samuel Larwood and Charles Skelton married and left the connexion, sometimes taking significant groups with them. Wesley's main expansionist effort in this decade was spent in Scotland. He lacked the help of his brother in this venture, which he had had in the late 1740s in Ireland, and he enjoyed less success. In Yorkshire there was competition from other groups like the Moravians and the more widely spread Inghamites. In Cornwall far fewer came forward to help there in comparison to the 1740s. The economic situation may well have played a part in the dramatic rise in the number of preachers in the 1740s and the plateau which followed. Trinder and others pointed to the economic distress of the early nineteenth century which tended to coincide with revival.[21] More men offered for or were persuaded into the itinerancy in bad years when they found it more difficult to make a living by other means. The war period of the 1740s had brought real economic hardship but the late 1740s and the 1750s showed some improvement. The result for Wesley was that there were fewer new preachers available to him. It was only in the early 1760s as more new preachers became available that he could resume the outwards expansion which led to the missioning of other areas in England, Northern Ireland, America and elsewhere

---

[20] *Minutes*. William Martin entered in 1772 according to Atmore, dying in his third year. He is not in the *Minutes* at all. For Holdsworth see above Chapter 1 and for Barry Chapter 7.

[21] Trinder, *Industrial Revolution* 185.

overseas. There were later smaller plateaux in the supply of preachers, from 1765 to 1769 and from 1775 to 1780. The second of these was during the depression which coincided with the first years of the American War of Independence. This, if the logic of the argument above is followed, should have led to more preachers rather than fewer. Certainly these two later and smaller plateaux are less easy to explain.

Some estimates have tried to omit preachers in America, Ireland and on the mission field from the figures. This obviously leads to different numbers being cited. I would contend that in Wesley's lifetime at least the British itinerants formed one unit, deployed by one man. From 1784 the transatlantic unity was broken by the creation of the independent church in America under Asbury. After 1791 the independence of the Irish Conference took more preachers away. The British Conference in the early nineteenth century should be easy to count. Yet still in the twenty-first century inaccurate estimates are being made for the numbers in the British ministry. Kent, for example, wrote of no more than about 200 preachers even at the end of the eighteenth century. When the stations for 1800 are carefully examined, I cannot count fewer than 242, over 20% higher than Kent's estimate. This is after deducting all Supernumeraries, those preachers in Wales, Scotland, Ireland and Foreign Missions, those who supported themselves like George Smith in the Hull circuit, and those who 'could not conveniently travel' that year like William Heath.[22] And then we must remember there were those like Holdsworth or Boyd who did not appear on the stations. Even these numbers as given can only be approximate. This is particularly true for the period before 1765 when my totals should be regarded more as 'guesstimates.' However, the figures throughout indicate the minimum number of preachers, which may well have been a little higher at all periods. These totals are consistently above most earlier estimates. It is this final point which is important. There were more of Wesley's preachers active at any one time throughout the eighteenth century than historians have thought. Their impact was therefore greater and more widely spread and felt.

Numbers who Entered Each Year

As argued above in Chapter 5, preachers did not just enter at Conference as has often been assumed. Historians have thought that by looking at the totals that were received 'on trial' each year they could see how many were entering, and therefore spot changes and growth. The process was more complex than this; for instance there were many who had already entered in terms of serving on the stations for some time, often even for several years before their names appeared in the *Minutes*.

Where there were *Minutes* before 1765 and numbers of those on probation given, these were usually some way below those actually beginning to travel

---

[22] Kent, *Wesley and the Wesleyans* 91. The stations were printed in *Minutes* 2: 44-50.

that year and often bear little relationship. The figures given were of preachers who probably had begun their itinerancy since the previous Conference. The most interesting and substantial growth in numbers only came in 1761 after which most years had twelve or more new preachers. Previously, between 1750 and 1760, the number of new preachers each year was only ten or fewer, with as little as four in each of 1754 and 1755, not enough to make up for losses. Further, there were frequently mistakes in the *Minutes*, usually but not always omissions and these were not just occasional individuals but statistically significant amounts. For example, historians have looked at the raw numbers received on trial in 1785 (sixteen) and 1786 (thirty-nine) and noted the large rise in the second of these years. This was the more evident since eighteen new entrants on trial had been reached as early as 1775 so there appeared to be a plateau of probationer numbers over those ten years. 1786 marked a new move forward. However, when the stations are examined for 1785 no fewer than eight new preachers can be actually found on the stations, none of whom was formally received on trial that year, so that the number of new itinerants available to Wesley then was in reality twenty-four not sixteen. In turn the number of new itinerants actually available to Wesley in 1786 was not the thirty-nine preachers who appeared On Trial in the *Minutes* but in fact forty-two.[23] The real contrast should be with the thirteen or fifteen new itinerants each year in the 1760s and 1770s, an earlier plateau which had been stable for almost twenty years. The rise in 1786 enabled Wesley to create new circuits, expand existing ones, mission new areas like north Devon[24] and still have preachers to send abroad to the West Indies and elsewhere. The rapid expansion of Methodism in the 1790s was because of this sudden surge of increased manpower of preachers from 1786 who by the next decade were the leaders of the expansion into new areas.

Wesley's Empirical World View

This more precise quantification of his preachers would have appealed to Wesley. It has been pointed out that Wesley through his writings (especially that ego-document we know as his own lengthy *Journal*) built up a world view in which empirical reality of places and times and people were of primary importance. It would rebut critics who asked if his preaching had any effect and was one major reason why he wanted all his preachers to keep journals and write him letters about their experience. Many did, though only some were published. In this way Wesley could measure and even 'prove' his preachers'

---

[23] Some may question why the new estimates occasionally show more received in the Minutes than are in my new estimates. This is because men showed as admitted on trial that year had actually been available at least one year earlier and are therefore shown there. This applies for example to years like 1770.

[24] See the story of Michael Fenwick in Chapter 17 above for north Devon.

effectiveness and utility. His Methodist people were to put usefulness first, and if they were useful then they must be both doing what God wanted and improving themselves and the nation. It is from these personal journals and diaries, written by his preachers, that much of the information about them has been derived. The journals helped them to build up their own self-understanding, reinforced by the collective unity of the preachers in Conference described above.[25]

Length of Service

Chart 15: Number of Years Travelled on Circuit

Source: Wesley's Preachers' Database

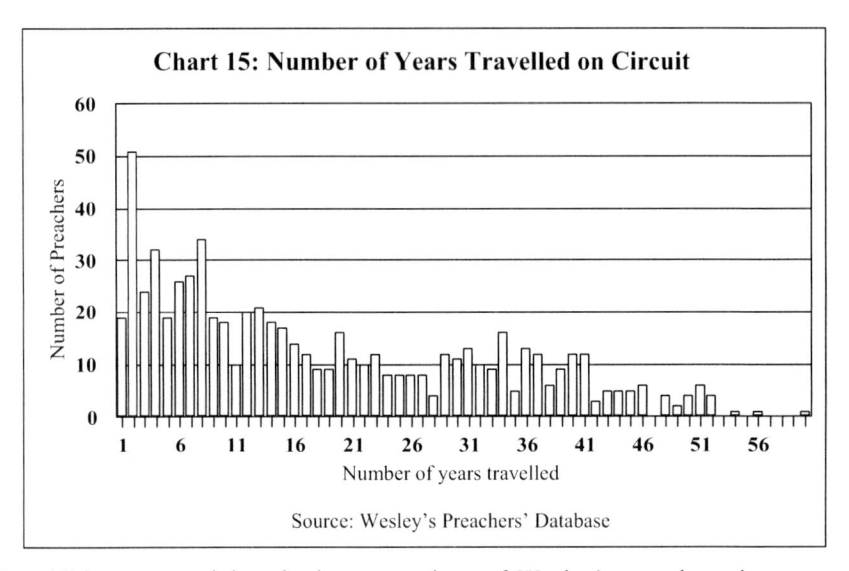

In addition to examining the larger numbers of Wesley's preachers than was previously thought, it is valuable to look at their length of service, as shown in Table 23 in Appendix One and Chart 15 above. Table 23 also names those preachers of John Wesley who travelled longest.

Chart 15 shows that while the largest numbers were those who did only a handful of years, yet there were sizable numbers doing over twenty years. The longest number of years travelled was 59, achieved by the nineteenth century president Richard Reece. Immediately behind him came the veteran who has often appeared in this book in other guises, Thomas Taylor who did 55, and another president James Wood who did 53. Six preachers reached fifty years. Admittedly one is tempted to question the amount of effort these men were able

---

[25] For a discussion of ego-documents such as journals see Dekker, ed, *Egodocuments*. For Wesley's use of the *Journal* to build the world view of the Methodist people see in Dekker's book Mascuch, 'John Wesley Superstar.' For the preachers in Conference see Chapter 13 above.

Appendix Two: Total Numbers 451

to put in during their later years. However, the historian needs to recognize the continuity which such preachers were able to provide for the Wesleyan Connexion, both under Wesley and after his death. 164 preachers did thirty years or more, fifty-nine of them forty years or over. Together they were able to use their experience to change the world in which they lived.[26]

---

[26] Wesley's Preachers' Database. Reece (1765-1850) was born in Cheshire and well connected.

Appendix Three: List of Preachers in the Database

Abraham, John
Acutt, John
Adams, Thomas
Adamson, William
Ainsworth, John
Algar, Joseph
Allen, John
Allen, Thomas
Allwood, William
Alsop, T
Anderson,
Anderson, James
Ansel, Thomas
Appleton, John
Appleyard, Samuel
Armstrong, Francis
Armstrong, Gustavus
Armstrong, Joseph
Armstrong, Robert
Asbury, Francis
Ashman, William
Atkins, John
Atkinson, William
Atlay, John
Atmore, Charles
Aver, William
Bailey, Edward
Baldwin, George
Barber, John
Barber, Thomas
Bardsley, Samuel
Barker, William
Barnes, Thomas

Barritt, John
Barrowclough, David
Barry, James
Bartholomew, Thomas
Bastable, Cornelius
Bateman, Richard Thomas
Bates, Samuel
Baxter, John
Baynes, William
Beanland, Benjamin
Beanland, John
Beard, Thomas
Beaumont, John
Bell, James
Bell, Robert
Bennet, John
Bennets, John
Benson, Joseph
Biggs, Benjamin
Biggs, William
Black, John
Black, Thomas
Black, William
Blackwell, Richard
Blades, John
Blagborne, William
Blair, Andrew
Blake, Robert
Bland, Charles
Blow, Robert
Blundell,
Boardman, Richard
Bogie, James

Bond, Charles
Boone, Charles
Booth, John
Boothby, William
Botts, Samuel
Bourke, Richard
Boyd, Henry
Boyle, John
Brackenbury, Robert Carr
Bradburn, Samuel
Bradford, Joseph
Braithwaite, John
Brammah, William
Bramwell, William
Brandon, John
Brandon, William
Brazier, William
Bredin, John
Brettel, Jeremiah
Brettel, John
Brians, Henry
Bridge, Robert
Briggs, William
Brisco, Thomas
Bristol, John
Broadbent, John
Broadbent, Thomas
Brocklehurst, William
Brook, Thomas
Brown, George
Brown, Hugh
Brown, Isaac
Brown, John

Brown, Jonathan
Brown, Thomas
Brownfield, James
Bryant, Thomas
Buckingham, William
Bumstead, Daniel Wallett
Bumsted, Daniel
Burbeck, Edward
Burdsall, Richard
Burgess, Joseph
Burnet, John
Burt, James
Butterfield, William
Button, George
Byron, James M'Kee
Carlill, Thomas
Carthy, Clayton
Catermole, John
Catlow, Jonathan
Cennick, John
Cheek, Nicholas Mosley
Cherry, Thomas
Christian, John
Christie, James
Church, William
Clarke, Adam
Clarke, John
Clough, James
Coates, Alexander
Coates, Richard
Cocker, Jeremiah
Cockson, John
Coke, Thomas
Colbeck, Thomas
Cole, Joseph
Coleman, Andrew
Colley, Benjamin
Collins, William
Collins, William jr
Condy, Richard
Cooper, Thomas
Corbett, Thomas
Cornish, Richard
Costerdine, Robert
Cotty, James
Coughlan, Lawrence
Coussins, Jonathan
Cowen, William
Cowmeadow, John
Cownley, Joseph
Cox, William
Crabb, William
Craddock, Richard
Crane, William
Cricket, John
Creighton, James
Crook, John
Crosby, John
Cross, John
Cross, Joseph
Crossley, Thomas
Crouch, Thomas
Crouch, William
Crowle, Jonathan
Crowther, Jonathan
Crowther, Robert
Crowther, Timothy
Dall, Robert
Dancer, Thomas
Darney, William
Darragh, John
Davies, Owen
Davis, John
Davis, Mark
Davis, Robert
Davis, Thomas
Day, Simon
Dean, John
Dean, Peter
Deaves, James
Delap, Andrew
Dempster, James
Denton, John
Denton, William
Dice, George
Dickinson, Peard
Dieuaide, William
Dillon, John
Dillon, Richard
Dinnen, John
Dixon, Thomas
Dobson, Thomas
Doncaster, John
Donovan, George
Dowling, Blakely
Downes, John
Drake, Robert
Drew, Richard
Dufton, William
Duncan, John
Dunn, Thomas
Dunstan, Edward
Easton, John
Eastwood, James
Eden, Thomas
Edmondson, Jonathan
Edwards, John
Edwards, Samuel
Eells, William
Elliott, Richard
Elliott, Thomas
Ellis, John
Ellis, Thomas
Ellis, William
Embury, Philip
Empringham, Robert
Entwisle, Joseph
Errington, Matthew
Evans, David
Evans, Edward
Evans, James
Felton, William
Fenton, Joseph
Fenwick, John
Fenwick, Michael
Fenwick, William
Ferguson, Peter
Ferguson, William
Fish, William C
Fisher, John
Fletcher, John William
Floyd, John
Foster, Henry
Fothergill, Joseph
Francis, John

Appendix Three: List of Preachers in the Database   455

Franklin, William
Frazier, Francis
Freemantle, William
Fugill, William
Furness, John
Furz, John
Gaffney, James
Gamble, Robert
Garnett, Joseph
Gates, Samuel
Gaulter, John
Gibbon, George
Gibbons, Edward
Gibbs, John
Gibbs, Phil(l)ip
Gilbert, Francis
Gilbert, John
Gilbert, Nicholas
Gill, John
Gill, Thomas
Gill, William
Gillis, John
G----h,
Gillespie, Robert
Glasbrook, James
Glascot, John
Godwin, John (?)
Goodwin, John
Gordon, David
Gore, James
Gouldston, John
Grace, John
Graham, Charles
Graham, Daniel
Graham, John
Graham, William
Grandage, William
Grant, John
Graves, Charles C
Greaves, Thomas
Greaves, Thomas
Green, John
Green, William
Greenwood, John
Greenwood, Parson

Greenwood, Paul
Griffiths, John
Griffiths, Michael
Griffith, Walter
Grimshaw, William
Guier, Philip
Guilford, Joseph
Guthrie, George
Hacking, John
Haigh, Robert
Haime, John
Hainsworth, William
Hall, James
Hall, John
Halliday, Thomas
Hamilton, Andrew
Hamilton, Andrew jr
Hamilton, Frederick
Hamilton, William
Hammett, William
Hampson, John sr
Hampson, John jr
Hanby, Thomas
Hanson, Thomas
Hardcastle, Philip
Hardwick, Thomas
Harmer, John
Harper, John
Harper, Joseph
Harris, Howell
Harris, William
Harrison, John
Harrison, Lancelot
Harrison, Robert
Harrison, Thomas
Harwood, William
Hathway, John
Haughton, John
Hayter, George
Hayward, Robert
Healey, John
Heath, William
Helton, John
Henderson, George
Henderson, Richard

Hern, Jonathan
Heslup, John
Hetherington, Thomas
Hewett, Thomas
Hickling, John
Highfield, George
Higley, R
Hindmarsh, James
Hindmarsh, William
Hitchens, Samuel
Hitchens, Thomas
Hitchens, William
Hobart, Samuel
Hodgson, Samuel
Hodges, John
Holder, George
Holdsworth, John
Holland, William
Holmes, John
Holmes, William
Hopkins, Robert
Hopper, Christopher
Horne, Melville
Horner, William
Hosking, Thomas
Hoskins, John
Hoskins, William
Hosmer, John
Houghton, Richard
Howe, John
Hudson, George
Hudson, James
Humphreys, Joseph
Hunt, Richard
Hunter, William sr
Hunter, William jr
Hunter, William (III)
Hurley, James
Hurley, John
Hutton, Thomas
Ingham, John
Inglis, Andrew
Irwin, James
Isherwood, Francis
Jackson, Daniel

Jackson, Edward
Jaco, Peter
Jane, John
Janes, Thomas
Jefferys, Andrew
Jenkins, Herbert
Jenkins, John
Jenkins, William
Jerom, Joseph
Jessop, William
Johnson, John
Johnson, Robert
Johnson, Thomas
Johnson, William
Jones, James
Jones, John
Jones, Joseph
Jones, Thomas
Jordan, James
Joughin, William
Joyce, Matthias
Kane, Lawrence sr
Kay, Duncan
Kead, Thomas
Keighley, Joshua
Kelk, Thomas
Kelshall, Stephen
Kerr, John
Kerr, Thomas
Kershaw, Arthur
Kershaw, James
Kershaw, John
Kilham, Alexander
Kessel, Andrew
King, John
King, John
Knight, Titus
Kyte, Charles
Langston, John
Larwood, Samuel
Lawton, James
Lee, Joseph
Lee, Nebuchadnezzar
Lee, Thomas
Leech, John

Leggatt, Benjamin
Leicester, William
Lessey, Theophilus sr
Levick, George
Levick, Samuel
Ley, William
Liddicot, Antony
Light, Benjamin
Lilly, Isaac
Lindsay, Robert
Linnell, William
Livermore, John
Lloyd, Henry
Lomas, Robert
Longbottom, James
Longley, Thomas
Lovebond, J
Lowe, George
Lowes, Matthew
Lucas, Richard
Lumb, Matthew
Lumley, William
Lynn, John
Lyons, James sr
Lyons, James jr
M'Allum, Duncan
M'Burney, John
M'Cadden, James
M'Cornock, William sr
M'Cornock, William jr
M'Donald, James
M'Donald, Michael
M'Evoy, John
M'Geary, John
M'Geary, Thomas
M'Gowan, John
M'Kay, Robert
M'Kersey, John
M'Mullen, James
M'Nab, Alexander
M'Neese, John
M'Quigg, James
M'Vean, John
Maddern, John
Magor, John

Mahy, William
Malcomson, John
Mann, James
Mann, John
Manners, John
Manners, Nicholas
Manning, Charles
Marshall, Michael
Martin, William
Martindale, Miles
Maskew, Jonathan
Mason, John
Massiot, James
Mather, Alexander
Mather, Ralph
Maxfield, Thomas
May, Edward
Mayer, Thomas
Mealy, John
Meggott, Samuel
Meredith, William
Meriton, John
Meyrick, Thomas
Mill, Peter
Millard, Henry
Miller, James
Miller, John
Miller, Robert
Miller, Robert
Milner, John
Minethorp, William
Mitchell, Samuel
Mitchell, Thomas
Moon, John
Moore, Alexander
Moore, Henry
Moore, Hugh
Moore, Joseph
Moore, William
Moorhead, Samuel
Moorhouse, Michael
Morgan, James
Morgan, John
Morley, John
Morris, James

Appendix Three: List of Preachers in the Database 457

Morris, John
Mortimer, Samuel?
Moseley, Abraham
Moss, Richard
Mott, Thomas
Moulson, John
Mowat, George
Murdock, Archibald
Murlin, John
Murphy, Michael
Murray, John
Myles, William
Naylor, Robert
Nelson, John
Nelson, John jr
Newall, Thomas
Newton, Booth
Nicholls, Stephen
Norman, William
Norris, John
Oddie, James
Ogylvie, John
Okeley, Francis
Oldham, John
Oliver, John
Olivers, Thomas
Orpe, William
Osborn, John
Owens, Thomas
Palmer, William
Parkin, Jonathan
Patten, Archibald
Patterson, Thomas
Pawson, John
Payne, Thomas
Peacock, Christopher
Peacock, John
Pearce, Benjamin
Pearce, John
Penington, William
Percival, William
Perfect, James
Perronet, Charles
Perronet, Edward
Perronet, Vincent

Perry, Richard
Pescod, Joseph
Phillips, George
Phillips, John
Phillips, Richard
Pickford, Robert
Piers, Henry
Pilmore, Joseph
Pipe, John Sanders
Pitt, William
Poole, John
Price, John
Price, Nehemiah
Price, Peter
Prickard, John
Prior, William
Pritchard, John
Pritchard, Jonathan
Proctor, Stephen
Prosser, Thomas
Pue, Hugh
Purdy, Victory
Queteville, John de
Ramshaw, John
Randal, Samuel
Rankin, Thomas
Rawlins, Thomas
Rea, James
Readshaw, Thomas
Reddall, John
Reece, Richard
Reeves, Jonathan
Rennick, James
Reynolds, John
Rhodes, Benjamin
Richards, Thomas
Richardson, James
Richardson, John
Ridall, James
Ridgeway, Thomas
Ridley, James
Riles, John
Rippon, Edward
Roberts, John
Roberts, Robert

Roberts, Thomas
Roberts, William
Robertshaw, Jeremiah
Robins, Henry
Robinson, Jasper
Robinson, Thomas
Robotham, John
Rodd, William
Rodda, Martin
Rodda, Richard
Rodda, Thomas
Roe, George
Rogers, James
Rogers, Samuel
Rogerson, Thomas
Roorke, Thomas
Roots, William
Rouquet, James
Rowell, Jacob
Rowell, Matthew
Rushton, George
Russen, Benjamin
Rutherford, Thomas
Ryan, Thomas
Sandoe, John
Sargent, George
Satles, James
Saunders, Henry
Saunders, John
Saunders, William
Saunderson, Hugh
Saunderson, John
Saunderson, Joseph
Saunderson, William
Savage, George
Scholfield, James
Scott, Francis
Scott, Robert
Seccomb, Thomas
Seed, Richard
Sellor, Vince
Sellon, Walter
Severn, William
Seward, Thomas
Shadford, George

Shaw, John
Shaw, Thomas
Shearing, Isaac
Shelmerdine, William
Shent, William
Shepherd, William
Shorter, George
Simmonite, Thomas
Simpson, John
Simpson, John
Simpson, Thomas
Simpson, William
Skelton, Charles
Skelton, James
Skerritt, George
Skinner, James
Slater, Edward
Slocomb, John
Smith, Francis
Smith, John
Smith, John Sugden
Smith, Robert sr
Smith, Robert
Smith, Samuel
Smith, Thomas
Smith, William
Smyth, Edward
Snowden, George
Spargo, John
Stamp, John
Standring, John
Steel, Richard
Steele, Samuel
Stephens, James
Stephens, John
Stephenson, John
Stephenson, William
Stevens, William
Stewart, Matthew
Steward, Thomas
Story, George
Story, Nicholas
Strawbridge, Robert
Sutcliffe, Joseph
Suter, Alexander

Sutty, Robert
Swain, Joseph
Swan, Robert
Sweeny, Edward
Swindells, Robert
Sykes, George sr
Tattershall, Thomas
Tatton, Thomas
Taylor, David
Taylor, Henry
Taylor, Joseph
Taylor, Robert
Taylor, Samuel
Taylor, Samuel
Taylor, Thomas
Tennant, Thomas
Thom, James
Thom, William
Thomas, Barnabas
Thomas, Philip
Thomas, Roger
Thomas, William
Thompson, Jonathan
Thompson, Joseph
Thompson, Thomas
Thompson, William
Thoresby, Richard
Thoresby, William
Thorpe, John
Thwayte, James
Tizard, George
Tobias, Thomas
Tooth, Samuel
Townsend, John
Trathen, David
Tregortha, John
Trembath, John
Trethewey, Thomas
Truscott, Francis
Tucker, Joseph
Tucker, William
Tunney, William
Tunnycliffe, Charles
Turnough, John
Undrell, John

Valton, John Francis
Vasey, Thomas sr
Verner, Thomas
Wadsworth, George
Waldron, Isaac
Walker, Francis
Walker, James
Walker, John
Walker, Peter
Walker, Thomas
Walker, William
Walsh, Richard
Walsh, Thomas
Ward, Nathanael
Warrener, William
Warwick, Thomas
Wasley, John
Watkins, Christopher
Watkinson, Richard
Watson, James
Watson, John sr
Watson, John jr
Watson, Matthew
Watts, Richard
Wawne, George
Webb, Thomas
Webster, Eleazer
Wells, Samuel
Werrill, Thomas
West, John
West, William
Westell, Thomas
Whatcoat, Richard
Wheatley, James
Wheeler, John
Whitaker, William
Whitehead, John
Whitehead, Thomas
Whitfield, George
Whitford, John
Whitley, John
Whitley, John
Whitwell, William
Wild, James
Wilkinson, John

Appendix Three: List of Preachers in the Database

Wilkinson, Robert	Wiltshaw, John	Wray, James
Williams, Enoch	Winbey, William	Wride, Thomas
Williams, James	Winscom, Jasper	Wright, Duncan
Williams, Richard	Wittam, John	Wright, Richard
Williams, Robert	Wood, James	Wrigley, Francis
Williams, Thomas	Wood, Samuel	Wyment, Thomas
Willis, Mark	Wood, Thomas	Yearbury, Joseph
Willis, Thomas	Woodcock, Samuel	Yewdall, Zachariah
Wilson, James	Woodrow, John	
Wilson, William	Woolf, Francis	

Bibliography

Primary Sources

Manuscripts

Bartholomew, Thomas MS Notebooks at Keighley Library.

Bastable, Cornelius MSS Letters of in MARC, JRULM Fletcher/Tooth Collection Fl/T 1/35.

Bennet, John MSS at MARC BNNJ Colman box.

Black, William MSS Letters at United Methodist Archives, Drew University, Madison, NJ (Drew) 1646.

Blair, Mrs Andrew MSS Diary extracts from in Biog Cuttings Files at WHS Library Oxford Brookes University B/Blair/Mrs.

Boardman, Richard MSS copy Letters of at Drew 1646.5.

Bradford, Joseph MS Letter of in Baker Collection Perkins Library, Duke, NC (Duke) Box 14 presidential book.

Bradford, Joseph MSS Letters of at Drew 1647-3-1, 56.

Broadbent, Thomas MS Will of in Norfolk County Record Office, Norwich.

Butts, Thomas MSS Diary in Baker Collection, Duke.

Chubb, James MSS Journals of at New Room Bristol.

Clarke, Adam MSS Letters of at Bridwell Library, SMU, Dallas.

Clarke, Adam MSS Letters, Sermons etc at MARC.

Coke, Thomas MSS Letters of at MARC PLP 28/.

Coke, Thomas MSS Letters of in Thomas Jackson Collection, and Home Committee Box I, MMS Collection, School of Oriental and African Studies, London.

Conference Journal, MS at MARC.

Cooke, Mary, Eliza, etc MSS Letters of at Bridwell Library, SMU, Dallas.

Cownley, Joseph MSS Letters of at MARC DDPr1/104.

Creighton, James MS Letterbook of at the World Methodist Museum, Lake Junaluska NC.

Crook, John MS Letter of at MARC DDPr 2/17.

Crook, John MS Letter of at New Room, Bristol.

Crowther, Jonathan MS Volume 'Life and Travels of a Methodist preacher...Jonathan Crowther written by himself' in Duke Box 4.

Dall, Robert MSS Papers of in MARC MA 3181.

Deaves, James copy Letter of at Craigavon Museum, Northern Ireland.

Deed of Declaration 1784 MS at MARC.

Everett, James MS Scrapbook f 420 at MARC.

Fenwick, Michael MSS Letters of, EMV 143, Box Letters to JW 2/43 at MARC.

Fletcher, John MS Letter of at Staffordshire Record Office, Stafford D (W) 1778 V697 Box 2.

Fletcher, Mary MSS Letters in Fletcher/Tooth papers at MARC MAM Fl/T.

Gilbert, Francis MSS Letters of in MARC DDPr 1/32 2-3 and PLP MAM 2/54.

Gilbert, Nicholas MS Letter of in MARC DDPr 1/33.

Hanby, Thomas MSS Letters of at MARC PLP 48.55.11.
Hardcastle, Philip copy of MSS in Baker Collection, Duke.
Harper, John Ordination Certificate of at Queen's College, Melbourne, Australia.
Holland, William MS Letter of in National Library of Wales, Aberystwyth.
Hughes, John MS Journal of at National Library of Wales, Aberystwyth.
Jackson, Thomas MSS Collection in the Methodist Missionary Society Collection, SOAS, London.
Jenkins, William MSS Papers of at MARC.
Jones, James MS Letter of at MARC DDCW 6/31.
Keighley Methodism MS Notebook, (Laycock's) in Keighley Public Library BK 15/1/3/18c.
Kingswood MS Account Book 1766-70 at the Wesley Centre Kingswood School, Bath
Leeds, MS History of Methodism in at Leeds City Library.
London Stewards' Book 1760s-1804 MS at MARC.
M'Nab, Alexander MSS Letters of at MARC PLP 72.34.
Manchester Circuit Account Book in Manchester Central Library and (as copied by M. Riggall) 2 vols in possession of Rev H. D. Rack, Manchester.
Mather, Alexander MS Letter of at Museum of World Methodism, Lake Junaluska, British Presidential file.
Mather, Alexander MS Letter of in BPF 1/10-12 Leete Collection, Bridwell Library, SMU, Dallas.
Mather, Alexander MSS Letters of at MARC DDPr 1/41-8.
Mercer, John MS Letter of at MARC PLP 17.1.
Moore family of Drumclamph MSS Notebooks of at WHS Library B/Moo/Moo.
Moore, Henry MSS Letters of at MARC Folio Letters of the Methodist Preachers vol 5.
Nelson, John, MSS Letters of at MARC PLP 78.53.
Nottingham Methodist Baptismal Register in Nottingham County Record Office.
Olivers, Thomas MSS Letters of at MARC DDPr 1/41-8.
Orp, William, MS Letter of at the United Methodist Archives, Drew.
Pawson, John MS Life of in MARC.
Peacock, John MSS Letters of at MARC.
Percival, William MSS Letters 1778-99 in MARC.
Perfect, James MS Letter 1779 in MARC.
Pescod, Joseph MSS Letters, Sermons, Notes, in MARC PLP 83.32.
Pilmore, Joseph MSS Letters of at MARC in Letters of the Wesley Family vol II.
Pitt, William MS Letter of preacher at Queen's College, Melbourne, Australia.
Preachers, MS List of those On Trial 1803-31 at MARC.
Rankin, Thomas MSS Journal and Will of, copies at Drew.
Rankin, Thomas MS Letter of 29 Dec 1774 D (W) 1778/11/1041 at Staffs RO, Stafford.
Rouquet, James MS Letter of at MARC.
Rowell, Jacob MSS Notebooks of in Durham County Record Office M/BC 83-85.
Simpson, Thomas, MS Letter of to Benson at Duke.
Smyth, David MS 'Short Account of the Life of the Late John Smyth Methodist Preacher' in MARC (C 319 Diaries box S TS).
Staffordshire Circuit Stewards Account Book 1768-93 MB/1/1 at Birmingham City Library.
Stamp, John S. 'The History of Methodism in Hampshire', 2 vols c. 1827 MSS in MARC.

Story, George MSS Notebooks etc in Baker Collection at Duke.
Sutcliffe, Joseph MS History of Methodism at MARC.
Taft, Mary MS Diary in Birmingham University Library (copy at MARC).
Taft, Mary MSS Letters of at MARC PLP 104/4.
Taylor, Thomas MS Letter of in Loose Presidential volume, Baker Collection, Duke.
Taylor, Thomas MS Letter of at Bridwell Library, SMU BPF1/23-4.
Thom, Mrs Mary MS Letter of in MARC PLP 106-2-54.
Todmorden MS Account Book 1748-1793 at Keighley Public Library. BK15/1/1/3a.
Tyerman, L. MSS Biographies of Methodist Ministers A-D in 15 Vols in MARC (MAB B 1234 onwards).
Tyerman, L. MS Biography of Jonathan Crowther at Duke.
Tyerman, L. MS Biography of Dr John Whitehead in 3 folios at MARC.
Vasey, Thomas, MSS Letters at MARC.
Vasey, Thomas MSS Letters at the New Room.
Wesley, Charles MSS Letters at MARC W4/46.
Wesley, John, MSS Letters of (unpublished) at Bridwell Library, SMU.
Wesley, John MSS and copy Letters in WHS Library.
Wesley, John MSS Notebooks at MARC in Colman Collection.
Wesleyan Methodist Missionary Society Committee Minutes at SOAS.
Whitby, St Mary's MS Parish Register at the Library of the Whitby Literary and Philosophical Society, Whitby.
Wolverhampton, MS Baptismal Register of the Noah's Ark Chapel 1793-1825 Wolverhampton City Archives (under Darlington Street).
Wood, James MS Letter of at Bridwell Library, SMU BPF1/34-5.
Wride, Thomas MSS Letters, Poems, Prescriptions, Will, etc at MARC.
Wright, Duncan MSS Letters of at MARC PLP 115.823.
Yewdall, Zachariah MS Diary of in MARC Diaries Box vol 1.
Yorkshire FHS 'Monumental Inscriptions of the Mount Zion Graveyard' http://mountzionhalifax.free.fr/FullSeach.php (accessed 2/3/2007).

Books

Allen, R. *The Life, Experience and Gospel Labours of the Right Reverend Richard Allen* (New York: Abingdon, 1960).
Anon *Wesleyan Takings* 2 vols (London: Hamilton Adams, 1845 and 1851).
Asbury, F. *Journals and Letters,* E. T. Clark, J. M. Payton and J. S. Potts, eds, 3 vols (London: Epworth, 1958).
Asbury, F. and T. Coke, eds, *Doctrine and Discipline* (Philadelphia: Tuckniss, 1798).
Atmore, C. *The Methodist Memorial* (London: Hamilton Adams, rev. ed. 1871).
Baker, F, ed, *The Works of John Wesley* (Oxford and Nashville: OUP and Abingdon, Bicentennial Edition 1965).
Bedford St Paul's Circuit Class Book 1781-1806 (Bedford: Bedfordshire CRO, 1977).
Bendall, M, ed, *Yours Affectionately John Wesley The Rev. John Wesley and his Correspondents A Catalogue of Letters at Wesley's Chapel, London* (London: Wesley's Chapel, 2003).
Bennet, John's Copy of the Minutes of the Conferences of 1744, 1745, 1746, 1747 and 1748; with Wesley's copy of those for 1746 (London: WHS, 1896) WHS Occasional Publication No. 1.

Bennis, T. *The Christian Correspondence of Mrs Elizabeth Bennis* (Philadelphia: Graves, 1807).
Benson, J. *An Apology for the Methodists* (London: Story, 1801).
Blackwell, J. *Life of the Rev. Alexander Kilham* (London: Groombridge, 1838).
Bowmer, J. and J. A. Vickers, eds, *The Letters of John Pawson,* 3 vols (Peterborough: WMHS, 1996).
Bulmer, A. *Memoirs of Mrs Elizabeth Mortimer (Miss Ritchie)* (London: Mason, 1859).
Bunting, T. P. *The Life of Jabez Bunting, D.D,* vol. 1 (London: Longmans, 1859).
Burdekin, R. *Memoir of Robert Spence of York* (York: Burdekin, 1840).
Carvosso, W. *The Efficacy of Faith in the Atonement of Christ, Exemplified in a Memoir of William Carvosso. Written by Himself* (London: Mason, 1847).
Chilcote, P. W. *Her Own Story: Autobiographical Portraits of Early Methodist Women* (Nashville: Kingswood, 2001).
Chubb, J. *The Bristol Journal of James Chubb* (Bristol: New Room Booklets No. 8, 1988).
Clarke, A. *Memorials of the Wesley Family* (London: J. & T. Clarke, 1823).
— *The Miscellaneous Works of,* J. Everett, ed, (London: Tegg, 1836-7).
Clarke, J. B. B. ed, *Account of the Life of Adam Clarke, Partly Written by Himself* 3 vols (London: T. S. Clarke, 1833).
Coke, T. *An Account of the Rise and Present State of the Methodist Missions* (London: WCO, 1804).
Coke, T. and H. Moore *Life of the Rev. John Wesley* (London: Paramore, 1792).
Crook, W. *Ireland and the Centenary of American Methodism* (London: Hamilton Adams, 1866).
Crookshank, C. H. *Days of Revival: History of Methodism in Ireland* (Clonmel: Tentmaker Press, 1994).
— *Memorable Women of Irish Methodism* (London: WM Bookroom, 1882).
Crowther, J. *The Methodist Manual* (Halifax: Walker, 1810).
— *A True and Complete Portraiture of Methodism* (London: Edwards, 2nd ed. 1815).
— *The Life of Thomas Coke* (London: Edwards, 1815).
Curnock, N. ed, *John Wesley's Journal,* 8 vols (London: Epworth, 1938).
Dickinson, R. *The Life of the Rev. John Braithwaite* (London: Broadbent, 1825).
Dyson, J. B. *Methodism in the Isle of Wight* (Ventnor: Burt, 1865).
Early Methodist Preachers, T. Jackson, ed, 6 vols (London: WM Bookroom 1865).
Edwards, J. C. 'Memoir of John Blewett of Truro' in *Bible Christian Magazine* 1844: 227-36, 251-7, 274-80.
Entwisle, J. *Memoir of Joseph Entwisle* (Bristol: Lomas, 1848).
Everett, J. *Adam Clarke Portrayed* (London: Hamilton Adams, 1843).
Foster, J. *Alumni Oxonienses: The Members of the University of Oxford 1715-1886,* 4 vols (Oxford: Parker, 1888).
Greenwood, W. *Memoir of the Life, Ministry and Correspondence of the Late Rev George Sykes of Rillington* (Malton: G. Barnby, 1827).
Gregory, B. *Sidelights on the Conflicts in Wesleyan Methodism* (London: Cassell, 1898).
Grundell, J. and R. Hall, eds, *The Life of Mr Alexander Kilham* (Nottingham: Sutton, 1799).
Hampson, J. (junior) *Memoirs of the late Rev. John Wesley, A.M.* (Sunderland: Graham, 1791).
Hargreaves, J. *Life of the Rev John Hirst* (Rochdale: Littlewood, 1816).

Hastling, A. H. L. and W. P. Workman, eds, *The Register of Kingswood School 1748-1910* (London: KOGU, 1910).
Heberden, W. *Observations on the Increase and Decrease of Different Diseases and the Plague* (London: Payne, 1801).
Helton, J. *Reasons for Quitting the Methodist Society, Being a Defence of Barclay's Apology* (London: Fry, 1778).
Hill's Arrangements (London: WCO, 1819-1968).
Holder, G. *A Short Account of the Life of Mrs Mary Holder* (Whitby: Horne, 1836).
Horne, M. *Letters on Missions: Addressed to the Protestant Ministers of the British Churches* (Bristol: Bulgin and Rosser, 1794).
Ivimey, J. *A History of the English Baptists* 4 vols (London: the author, 1811-30).
Jackson, T. *Life of Charles Wesley* (London: Mason, 1841).
— ed, *Charles Wesley's Journal*, 2 vols (repr. Kansas City: Beacon Hill Press, 1980).
— ed, *EMP* (London: WCO, 1865-8).
— *Recollections of My Own Life and Times* (London: WCO, 1873).
Jarratt, D. *The Life of Devereux Jarratt: An Autobiography* (Cleveland: Pilgrim Press, 1995).
Jersey, H. de, *Vie Du Rev. Jean De Queteville* (London: Mason, 1847).
Jessop, W. *Account of Methodism in Rossendale and Neighbourhood.* (London: WCO, 1880).
Jones, W. *Memoirs of Adam Clarke* (London: MacGowan, 1838).
Kimbrough, S. T. and O. A. Beckerlegge, eds, *The Unpublished Poetry of Charles Wesley* 3 vols (Nashville: Abingdon, 1992).
Kingswood Register (Frome: KOGU, 1910).
Lanktree, M. *The Biographical Narrative of Matthew Lanktree* (Belfast: Wilson, 1836).
Laycock, J. W. *Methodist Heroes of the Great Haworth Round 1734-1784* (Keighley: Rydal Press, 1909).
Lednum, J. *A History of the Rise of Methodism in America* (Philadelphia: the author, 1859).
Lee, J. *Short History of the Methodists in the USA, beginning in 1766 and continued till 1809* (Baltimore: Magill, 1810).
Lelievre, M. *Histoire du Methodisme dans les Isles de la Manche 1784-1884* (London: WCO, 1885).
Lloyd, G. ed, *Catalogue of the Adam Clarke Papers* (Manchester: MARC, 1991).
— ed, *The Papers of Joseph Benson* (Manchester: MARC, 1991).
— ed, *Catalogue of Wesley Family Papers* (Manchester: MARC, 1992).
— ed, *Catalogue of the Papers of Charles Wesley,* 2 vols (Manchester: MARC 1994).
— 'The Papers of Dr Thomas Coke: a Catalogue.' *JRULMB* 76: 2 (Summer, 1994).
— ed, *Catalogue of the Early Preachers Collection* (Manchester: MARC, 1995).
— ed, *Catalogue of the Fletcher Tooth Papers* (Manchester: MARC, 1997-).
— ed, *Catalogue of Early Methodist Personal Papers* (Manchester: MARC, 2000).
— ed, *Personal Papers of Samuel Bardsley* (Manchester: MARC, 2001).
— ed, *The Letters of William Seward 1703-40* (Manchester: MARC, 2004).
Lyth, J. *Glimpses of Early Methodism in York* (York: Sessions, 1885).
Macdonald, F. W. *Letters of James Macdonald 1814-31* (London: Kelly, n.d. c. 1907-10).
Macdonald, J. *Memoirs of the Rev Joseph Benson* (London: Blanshard, 1822).
Manners, N. *Some Part of Life and Experience of... Nicholas Manners* (York: 1785).

Marsden, J. (Anon) *The Conference or Sketches of Methodism* (London: Blanshard, 1816).
— *Narrative of a Mission to Nova Scotia...* (London: Kershaw, 1827).
Maser, F. E. and H. T. Maag, eds, *The Journal of Joseph Pilmore Methodist Itinerant* (Philadelphia: Historical Society of Philadelphia Annual Conference, 1969).
McGregor, J. J. *Memoir of Mrs Alice Cambridge* (Dublin: 1832).
Minutes of the Methodist Conferences Annually held in America 1773 to 1813 Inclusive (New York: Hitt and Ward, 1813).
Minutes of the Methodist Conferences from the First Held in London..., vols I-V (London: 1812-24 and 1862).
Moister, W. *Heralds of Salvation. being Brief Memorial Sketches of Wesleyan Missionaries* (London: WCO, 1878).
Moorhouse, M. *The Defence of Mr Michael Moorhouse: Written by Himself* (Leicester: Ireland, 1789).
Morgan, J. *The Life and Death of Mr Thomas Walsh* (London: Cock, 1762).
MS Minutes of Conference (London: Occasional Publication of the WHS no. 1, 1896).
Myles, W. *A Chronological History of the People called Methodists,* (London: Cordeux, 4th ed. 1813).
Nichols, J. *A Report of the Principal Speeches Delivered at the Formation of the Methodist Missionary Society... Leeds* (Leeds: Nichols, 1813).
Osborn, G. *Outlines of Wesleyan Bibliography* (London: WCO, 1869).
Pawson, J. *A Chronological List of all the Travelling Preachers now in the Methodist Connexion* (Liverpool: J. M'Creery, 1795).
Phoebus, W. *Memoirs of the Rev. Richard Whatcoat* (New York: Allen, 1828).
Pilmore, J. *Narrative of Labours in South Wales in the Years 1767 and 8* (Philadelphia: Staveley, 1825).
Place, F. *Illustrations of the Principles and Proofs of Population.* (London: Allen and Unwin, 1930).
Rhodes, E. *Memoir of Mrs Elizabeth Rhodes, Widow* (London: Mason, 1829).
Sandford, P. P. *Memoirs of Mr Wesley's Missionaries to America* (New York: Lane, 1843).
Seymour, A. C. H. *The Life and Times of Selina, Countess of Huntingdon,* 2 vols (London: Painter, 1839-40).
Short, T. *New Observations, Natural, Moral, Civil, Political and Medical on City Town and Country Bills of Mortality* (London: Longman and Millar, 1750).
Sigston, J. *A Memoir of the Life and Ministry of Mr William Bramwell,* (London: Nichols, 2nd ed. 1820).
Slugg, J. T. *Woodhouse Grove School Memorials and Reminiscences* (London: Woolmer, 1885).
Smith, G. *History of Wesleyan Methodism,* 3 vols (London: Longmans, 1857-61).
Smith, M. A. (Mrs R.) *The Life and Correspondence of Mrs Adam Clarke* (London: Partridge and Oakey, 1851).
— *The Life of the Rev. Henry Moore* (London: Simpkin and Marshall 1844).
— *Raithby Hall* (London: Wertheim, 1859).
Smith, W. *History of Wesleyan Methodism in Ireland* (Dublin: Doolittle, 1830).
Sprague, W. B. *Annals of the American Pulpit,* vol VII (Methodist) (New York: Carter, 1970).
Stamp, W. W. *Wesleyan Methodism in Bradford* (London: Mason, 1841).

Steele, A. *History of Methodism in Barnard Castle and the Principal Places in the Dales Circuit* (London: Vickers, 1857).
Stevenson, G. J. *History of City Road Chapel* (London: Stevenson, 1872).
Strachan, A. *Recollections of the Life and Times of the Rev George Lowe* (London: Mason, 1848).
Taft, M. *Memoirs of Mrs Mary Taft, formerly Miss Barritt, Written by Herself* (London: the author, 1827).
Telford, J. ed, *John Wesley's Letters* (London: Epworth, 1931).
Thomas, P. ed, *'I Am Your Affectionate Brother J Wesley'* (Dallas: Bridwell Library, 1994).
Thoresby, W. *A Narrative of God's Love Towards William Thoresby* (Redruth: Bennett, 1801).
Townsend, W. J. *Alexander Kilham the First Methodist Reformer* (London: MNC Bookroom, 1889).
Treffry, R. ed, *Select Remains of the Rev. Francis Truscott* (Helston: Roberts, 1833).
— *Memoirs of the Life of the Rev. Joseph Benson* (London: Mason, 1840).
Tuck, S. *Wesleyan Methodism in Frome* (Frome: Tuck, 1814).
Valentine, S. R. ed, *Mirror of the Soul: The Diary of an Early Methodist Preacher John Bennet 1714-54* (Peterborough: MPH, 2002).
Venn, J and J. A. *Alumni Cantabrigienses A Biographical List of all Students at.. Cambridge... to 1900* (Cambridge: 1924-54).
Wakeley, J. B. *Lost Chapters Recovered From The Early History Of American Methodism* (New York: Carlton, 1858).
Ward, J. *Historical Sketches of the Rise and Progress of Methodism in Bingley* (Bingley: Harrison, 1863).
— *Methodism in the Thirsk Circuit* (Thirsk: Peat, 1860).
Ward, W. R. ed, *The Early Correspondence of Jabez Bunting* (London: Royal Historical Society, 1972).
Watson, R. *The Life of John Wesley* (London: Mason, 1845).
Wesley, C. *Hymns and Sacred Poems* (Bristol: Farley, 1749).
Wesley, J. *The Christian Library* 50 vols (Bristol: Farley, 1749-55).
Wesleyan Methodist Missionary Society *The Report of the Jubilee Fund of the Wesleyan Missionary Society 1863-68* (London: WMMS, 1869).
West, R. A. *Sketches of Ministerial Character* (London: Simpkin and Marshall, 1849).
Whitehead, J. *The Life of the Rev. John Wesley, M.A, Sometime Fellow of Lincoln College, Oxford*, 2 vols (London: Couchman, 1793-6).
Whittemore, T. ed, *The Life of John Murray: Preacher of Universal Salvation* (Boston: Trumpet, 1833).
Wilson, D. *Methodism in Scotland: a brief sketch* (London: Ogylvie, Brown & Co, 1850).
Wilson, W. *History and Antiquities of Dissenting Churches and Meeting Houses in London* 4 vols (London: Edwards, 1808-14).
Young, D. *Origins and History of Methodism in Wales* (London: Kelly, 1893).

Secondary Sources

Albin, T. R. *Full Salvation: the Spirituality of Anna Reynalds of Truro 1775-1840* (Redruth: CMHA, 1981).
Anderson, G. W. 'Wesley's ordinations for Scotland' *WHS Scotland* 16 (October, 1985) 3-6.
Andrews, D. *The Methodists and Revolutionary America 1760-1800: The Shaping of an Evangelical Culture* (Princeton: Princeton UP, 2000).
Anon, *Ashburton Methodist Church: A Brief History* (Ashburton: Ashburton Methodist Church, 1994).
Anon. *Methodist Chapels in Kirklees* (Huddersfield: Kirklees, 2000).
Appleby, C. *Thomas Longley in Cornwall 1798-1801* (Redruth: CMHA, 1983).
Baker, F. *Charles Wesley as Revealed by his Letters* (London: Epworth, 1948).
— 'Thomas Maxfield's first sermon' *PWHS* 27 (1949-50) 7-15.
— 'Hugh Moore and John Wesley: Some Unpublished Correspondence' in *PWHS* 29 (1954) 112-6.
— 'The Origins of Methodism in the West Indies: the Story of the Gilbert Family' *LQ & HR* (1960) 9-17.
— *William Grimshaw 1708-53* (London: Epworth, 1963).
— 'Early American Methodism: a Key Document' in *MH* 8 (1965) 12-13.
— 'The Lay Pioneers of American Methodism' in A. Godbold, ed, *Forever Beginning 1766-1966* (Nashville: Abingdon, 1967) 169-77.
— 'Polity' in *HMGB* 1: 211-256.
— *John Wesley and the Church of England* (Nashville: Abingdon, 1970).
— *From Wesley to Asbury: Studies in Early American Methodism* (Durham NC: Duke UP, 1976).
— *John Wesley, London Publisher 1733-91* (London: Wesley's Chapel, 1984).
— *A Union Catalogue of the Publications of John and Charles Wesley* (Stone Mountain GA: Zimmermann, 2nd ed. 1991).
Baker, G. P. ed, *Those Incredible Methodists; A History of the Baltimore Conference of the United Methodist Church* (Baltimore: Baltimore Conference, 1972).
Barclay, W. C. *Early American Methodism 1769-1849*, 2 vols (New York: Board of Missions, 1949-50).
Barry, J. and C. Brooks, eds, *The Middling Sort of People: Culture Society and Politics in England 1550-1800* (London: Macmillan, 1994).
Bates, E. R. *Captain Thomas Webb* (London: WMHS, 1975).
— 'The Wives of Wesley's Preachers' *WHS Br* 15 (1975) 1-3.
Batty, M. *Bygone Reeth... History of Methodism in Reeth.* (Reeth: Reeth Methodist Church, 1985).
— *Stages in the Development and Control of Wesleyan Lay Leadership 1791-1878* (Peterborough: WMHS, 1988).
— *Vincent Perronet 1693-1785 The Archbishop of the Methodists* (Emsworth: WMHS, 2002).
Bayly, C. A. *The Birth of the Modern World 1780-1914* (Oxford: Blackwell, 2004).
Bebbington, D. *Evangelicalism in Modern Britain: A History from the 1730s to the 1980s* (London: Unwin, 1989).
— ed, *Modern Christianity's Cultural Aspirations* (Sheffield: Sheffield Academic Press, 2003).

Beck, B. E. 'Some reflections on Connexionalism' *Epworth Review* 18: 2 (1991) 48-59, 3: 43-50.
Bellamy, E. J. *James Wheatley and Norwich Methodism in the 1750s* (Peterborough: WMHS 1994).
Berger, P. *The Sacred Canopy: Elements of a Sociological Theory of Religion* (New York: Anchor, 1969).
Best, G. M. *Continuity and Change: A History of Kingswood School 1748-1998* (Bath: Kingswood School, 1998).
Bett, H. *Early Methodist Preachers* (London: WHS Lecture no. 10, Epworth, 1944).
Betts, E. A. *Bishop Black and his Preachers* (Sackville NB: Tribune Press, 1976).
Biggs, B. J. *The Wesleys and the Early Dorset Methodists* (Gillingham: Woodsorrel, 1987).
— *Ellen Gretton and her Circle* (Gainsborough: Lincolnshire Methodist Historical Society, 1999).
Birtwhistle, N. A. 'Methodist Missions' in *HMGB* 3: 1-116.
Bishop, M. 'Wesley and his Schools at Kingswood' in Lenton, *Vital Piety* 16-24.
Blanshard, T. *The Life of Samuel Bradburn, the Methodist Demosthenes* (London: Elliott Stock, 1870).
— *Methodism in the Shotley Bridge Circuit* (Consett: Jackson, 1872)
Bowmer, J. C. *Pastor and People: A Study of Church and People in Wesleyan Methodism 1791-1858* (London: Epworth, 1975).
— *The Sacrament of the Lords Supper in Early Methodism* (London: A. & C.Black, 1951).
Bradford, C. A. *The Life of the Rev Joseph Bradford* (London: R. F. Hunger, n.d. c.1931).
Brake, G. T. *Drink: The Ups and Downs of Methodism's Attitude to Temperance* (London: Oliphants, 1974).
Brekus, C. A. *Strangers and Pilgrims: Female Preaching in America 1740-1846* (Chapel Hill: North Carolina UP, 1998).
Bretherton, F. F. *Early Methodism in and around Chester* (Chester: Phillipson, 1903).
Brooks, C. 'Apprenticeship, Social Mobility and the Middling Sort.' in Barry and Brooks *Middling Sort* 52-83.
Brown, C. G. *Religion and Society in Scotland since 1707* (Edinburgh: Edinburgh UP, 1997).
— *The Death of Christian Britain; Understanding Secularisation, 1800-2000* (London: Routledge; 2001).
Brown, K. D. *A Social History of the Nonconformist Ministry in England and Wales 1800-1930* (Oxford: Clarendon Press, 1998).
Buchanan, R. J. 'The Development of "Doctrine and Discipline" in North American Methodism 1773-1808' in N. Semple, ed, *CMHS Papers* 1997-8, (Toronto: n.p, 1999) 70-79.
Burdon, A. *Authority and Order: John Wesley and his Preachers* (Aldershot: Ashgate, 2005).
Butler, D. *Methodists and Papists: John Wesley and the Catholic Church in the 18th Century* (London: DLT, 1995).
Campbell, M. I. *No Other Foundation: The History of Brunswick St United Church with its Methodist Inheritance* (Hantsport, NS: Lancelot, 1984).
Campbell, W. G. *The Apostle of Kerry* (Dublin: Moffat, 1868).

Carroll, H. K. *Francis Asbury in the Making of American Methodism* (New York: Methodist Book Concern, 1923)
Carter, D. *Love Bade Me Welcome* (Peterborough: MPH, 2002).
Chamberlain, J. S. '"A regular and well affected diocese" Chichester in the eighteenth century' in Gregory and Chamberlain, eds, *National Church*
Chambers, W. A. 'John Wesley and Death' in Stacey ed, *Wesley* 150-161.
Chapman, D. M. *Born in Song: Methodist Worship in Britain* (Warrington: Church in the Market Place, 2006).
Chick, E. *Methodism in Exeter* (Exeter: Drayton, 1907).
Chilcote, P. W. *John Wesley and the Women Preachers of Early Methodism* (Metuchen: Scarecrow, 1991).
Ching, D. S. *For Ever Beginning: Two Hundred Years of Methodism in the Western Area* (Kingston: Methodist Church (Jamaica), 1960).
Church, L. F. *Early Methodist People* (London: Epworth, 1948).
— *More About The Early Methodist People* (London: Epworth, 1949).
Clark, J. C. D. *The Language of Liberty 1660-1832 Political Discourse and Social Dynamics in the Anglo American World* (Cambridge: CUP, 1994).
Clarke, J. N. and M. S. Anderson, *Methodism in the Countryside; Horncastle Circuit 1786-1986* (Horncastle: Cupit, 1986).
Coad, J. G. *The Royal Dockyards 1690-1850* (Aldershot: Scolar Press, 1989).
Coakley, F. 'The Rise of Manx Methodism' (accessed 5/3/2006) http://www.isle-of-man.com/manxnotebook/methdism/rise/rise/htm.
Cole, F. J. *The Cavalry Preachers* (Belfast: WHS (I), 1945).
Colley, L. *Britons: Forging the Nation 1707-1837* (New Haven: Yale UP, 1992).
Collins, V. T. '"Walking in Light, Walking in Darkness:' The Story of Women's Changing Rhetorical Space in Early Methodism' in *Rhetoric Review* (1996) 336-54.
Cooney, D. A. L. 'Irish Methodists and the Demon Drink' *WHS (I)* 2: 4 (1992) 33.
— 'The Bennis Family of Limerick, Huguenots, Methodists, Friends' MS in WHS Library, Oxford Brookes.
— 'A Wedding in St Bride's' *Dublin Historical Record* 48 (1995) 19-39.
— '20 Reduced Widows' *Dublin Historical Record* 50 (1997) 44-54.
— *The Methodists in Ireland: a Short History* (Dublin: Columba, 2001).
— 'They met in Great George Street' *WHS (I)* 7 (2001) 34-48.
— 'The Huguenot Connection' in *WHS (I)* 7 (2001) 61-68.
— 'The influence of the Army' in *WHS (I)* 7 (2001) 80-91.
— 'Bishop's Kin' in *Dublin Historical Record* 55; (2002) 21-42.
— 'Dublin Methodist Society Membership 1788' *WHS (I)* 10 (2004-2005) 44-62.
Corbridge, R. *Heritage: The Story of the Methodists of Pannal* (Harrogate: Pannal Methodist Church, 1984).
Crookshank, C. H. *Memorable Women of Irish Methodism* (London: W. M. Bookroom, 1882).
— *A Methodist Pioneer: The Life of J. Smith* (London: WCO, 1881).
Cumbers, F. *The Bookroom* (London: Epworth, 1956).
Cunliffe, N. *The Beckoning of the West: A Lancashire Odyssey* (Blackpool: N. Lancs Methodist History Group, 1992).
Currie, R. 'A Micro-Theory of Methodist Growth' *PWHS* 36 (1967-8) 65-73.
— A. Gilbert, and L. Horsley *Churches and Churchgoers: Patterns of Church Growth in the British Isles since 1700* (Oxford: Clarendon, 1977).

Dallimore, A. A. *George Whitefield: the Life and Times of the Great Evangelist of the 18th Century Revival* 2 vols (Edinburgh: Banner of Truth, 1970).
Davidoff, L. and C. Hall *Family Fortunes: Men and Women of the English Middle Class 1780-1850* (London: Routledge, 2002).
Davies, R. E, A. R. George and A. G. Rupp, eds, *History of Methodism in Great Britain* (London: Epworth, 1965-88).
Davis, G. W. *Arbroath Methodism: The Story of Wesley's 'Totum Kirkie'* (Arbroath: the author, 1996).
— *The Robert Dall Story 1745-1828* (Arbroath: the author, 1995).
D'Cruze, S. 'The Middling Sort in 18th Century Colchester: Independence, Social Relations and the Community Broker' in J. Barry and C. Brooks, eds, *The Middling Sort of People: Culture Society and Politics in England 1550-1800* (London: Macmillan, 1994) 189.
Davison, J. *Chronicles of Lealholm and Glaisdale* (n. pl: Duck, n. d, c. 1991).
Dekker, R. ed, *Egodocuments and History* (Rotterdam: Verloren, 2002).
Dictionary of Evangelical Biography 1730-1860, D. Lewis ed, (Oxford: Blackwell, 1995).
Dictionary of National Biography (Oxford: OUP, 1886).
Dictionary of Methodism in Britain and Ireland, J. A. Vickers ed, (Peterborough: MPH, 2000).
Dictionary of Welsh Biography (London: Honourable Society of Cymmrodorion, 1959).
Ditchfield, G. M. 'Ecclesiastical Policy under Lord North' in Walsh, *Church* 228-46.
Dobree, B. ed, *The Letters of Philip Stanhope, Lord Chesterfield* (London: Eyre and Spottiswoode, 1932).
Donovan, J. ed, *Many Witnesses: A History of Dumbarton UMC 1772-1990* (Georgetown: Dumbarton UMC, 1998).
Doughty, W. L. *John Wesley: His Conferences and His Preachers* (London: WHS Lecture no 10, Epworth, 1944).
Dreyer, F. *The Genesis of Methodism* (London: AUP, 1999).
Duffy, E. 'The Long Reformation...' in N. Tyacke *England's Long Reformation 1500-1800* (London: UCL,1998).
Duncan, P. *A History of Wesleyan Missions to Jamaica* (London: Partridge and Oakey, 1849).
— *Wesleyan Ministers' Annuitant Society: A Critical Examination* (London: Mason, 1858).
Earle, P. 'The Middling Sort in London' in Barry and Brooks, eds, *Middling Sort* 141-58
East, D. *My Dear Sally: The Life of Sarah Mallet, One of John Wesley's Preachers* (Emsworth: WMHS, 2003).
Eastwood, D. 'The Yewdalls of Eccleshill and Calverley' (Timperley 1997) (copy in MARC).
Edwards, J. B. *Victory Purdy 'the Kingswood Collier'* (Bristol: New Room, 1984).
Edwards, M. *Adam Clarke* (London: Epworth, 1942).
— *After Wesley* (London: Epworth, 1935).
— *Family Circle* (London: Epworth 1946).
Ehrman, E. *Dressed Neat and Plain: The Clothing of John Wesley and his Teaching on Dress* (London: Wesley's Chapel, 2003).
Elliott-Binns, L. E. *The Early Evangelicals: A Religious and Social Study* (London: Lutterworth, 1953).

Farquhar, D. U. *Missions and Society in the Leeward Islands 1810-1859* (Boston: Mount Prospect Press, 1999).

Feather, J. *The Provincial Book Trade in Eighteenth Century England* (Cambridge: CUP, 1985).

Federation of Family History Societies, National Burial Index, Burials 1538-1825 (CD-RomDisc 1 2001).

Ferguson, N, ed, *Virtual History: Alternatives and Counterfactuals* (London: Macmillan, 1998).

Field, C. D. 'Adam and Eve: Gender in the English Free Church Constituency' *JEH* 44 (1993) 63-79.

— 'The Social Structure of English Methodism 18th -20th Centuries' *British Journal of Sociology* 28 (1977) 2: 199-225.

Findlay, W. G. and W. W. Holdsworth *The History of the Wesleyan Methodist Missionary Society* 5 vols (London: Sharp, 1921).

Foner, E. and O. Mahony *America's Reconstruction: People and Politics after the Civil War* (New York: Harper, 1995).

Foot, S. ed, *Methodist Celebration: A Cornish Contribution* (Redruth: Dyllansow Truran, 1988)

Forsaith, P. S. '"A dearer country" the Frenchness of the Rev Jean de la Flechere of Madeley: A Methodist Church of England Vicar' in R. Vigne and C. Littleton, eds, *From Strangers to Citizens: The Integration of Immigrant Communities in Britain, Ireland and Colonial America 1550-1750* (Brighton: Sussex Academic Press, 2001) 519-26.

— 'The Correspondence of the Rev John W. Fletcher; Letters to the Rev Charles Wesley considered in the context of the Evangelical Revival', D Phil thesis at Oxford Brookes 2003.

— http:// www.methodist.org.uk (Heritage) (accessed 12/12/2008).

Gallagher, R. H. *John Bredin: Roman Catholic Schoolmaster and Methodist Preacher* (Belfast: WHS (I) 1960).

— *Pioneer Preachers of Irish Methodism* (Belfast: WHS (I) 1965).

Garlick, K. B. *Wesley's Chapel: An Illustrated History* (London: Wesley's Chapel, n. d. c. 1978).

— *Mr Wesley's Preachers* (London: Pinhorns, 1977).

— MS Notebook of at WHS Library.

Garraty, J. A. and M. C. Carnes, eds, *American National Biography*, 24 vols (New York: OUP, 1999).

Gay, J. D. *The Geography of Religion in England* (London: Duckworth, 1971).

George, A. R. 'John Wesley: the Organizer' in Stacey, ed, *Wesley*.

Gibson, W. *The Church of England 1688-1832* (London: Routledge, 2001).

Gilley, S. and W. J. Shiels, eds, *A History of Religion in Britain: Practice and Belief from Pre-Roman Times to the Present* (Oxford: Blackwell, 1994).

Glen, R. 'A Tangled Web: The Gilberts of Cornwall and the Gilberts of Antigua' *PWHS* 53 (2001-2002) 216-227.

Godbold, A. 'Francis Asbury and his Difficulties with John Wesley and Thomas Rankin' *MH* 3 (1965) 3-19.

Graham, W. T. 'Pupils in the Gospel' in P. Taylor ed, *Wesley Papers* (Lutterworth: Wesley Fellowship, 2002).

Gravely, W. 'Many of the poor Affricans are obedient to the faith' in Hatch and Wigger,

Shaping 175-195.
Green, R. *The Works of John and Charles Wesley: A Bibliography* (London: Kelly, 1896).
Green, V. H. H. *John Wesley* (London: Nelson, 1964).
Gregory, B. *Autobiographical Recollections* (London: Hodder, 1903).
Gregory, J. *Restoration, Reformation and Reform 1660-1828* (Oxford: Clarendon, 2000).
Gregory, J. and J. S. Chamberlain, eds, *The National Church in Local Perspective: The Church of England and the Regions 1660-1800* (Woodbridge: Boydell, 2003).
— ed, *John Wesley Tercentenary Essays JRULMB* 85: 2 and 3 (Summer and Autumn 2003) 1-431.
— '"In the Church I will live and die": John Wesley, the Church of England, and Methodism' in W. Gibson and R. Ingram, eds, *Religious Identities in Britain 1660-1832* (Aldershot: Ashgate, 2005) 147-78.
— 'Charles Wesley and the 18th century' in Newport and Campbell, *Charles Wesley* 18-39.
Hallam, D. J. A. *Eliza Asbury, her Cottage and her Son* (Studley: Brewin Books, 2003).
Halpern, R. and M. Daunton, eds, *Empire and Others: British Encounters with Indigenous Peoples 1600-1850* (London: UCL, 1999).
Harding, A. *The Countess of Huntingdon's Connexion* (Oxford: OUP, 2003).
Harrison, G. E. *Methodist Good Companions* (London: Epworth, 1935).
Hastings, J. J. *Misterton Methodism Past and Present* (Gainsborough: Newbold and Humphries, 1928).
Hatch, N. O. and J. Wigger, eds, *Methodism and the Shaping of American Culture* (Nashville: Kingswood, 2001).
— 'The Puzzle of American Methodism' in Hatch and Wigger, *Shaping* 23-40.
Hayes, A. J. *Edinburgh Methodism 1761-1975 The Mother Churches* (Edinburgh: the author, 1976).
Hayman, J. G. *The ..Methodist Revival... in North Devon* (London: WCO, 1881).
Heitzenrater, R. P. *The Elusive Mr Wesley* (Nashville: Abingdon, 1984).
— 'A Critical Analysis of the Ministry: Studies since 1948' in E. D. Dunlap, ed, *Perspectives on American Methodism.*
— *Faithful unto Death: the Last Years and Legacy of John Wesley* (Dallas: Bridwell Library, 1991).
— *Wesley and the People Called Methodists* (Nashville: Abingdon, 1995).
— 'John Wesley's principles and practice in preaching' in Sykes, ed, *Beyond the Boundaries* 12-40.
— ed, *The Poor and the People Called Methodists* (Nashville: Abingdon, 2002).
Heitzenrater, R. P. and P. S. Forsaith, *Wesley in America* (Dallas: Bridwell Library, 2003).
Hempton, D. 'Methodism in Irish Society 1770-1830' *TRHS* 1985 117-142.
— *Methodism and Politics in British Society 1750-1850* (London: Hutchinson, 1986).
— *The Religion of the People: Methodism and Popular Religion* (London: Routledge, 1996).
— *Religion and Political Culture in Britain and Ireland* (Cambridge: CUP, 1996).
— *Methodism: Empire of the Spirit* (New Haven: Yale UP, 2005).
Heywood, C. A. *A History of Childhood: Children and Childhood in the West from Medieval to Modern Times* (Oxford: Polity Press, 2001).

Hill, A. W. *John Wesley among the Physicians* (London: Epworth, 1958).
Hill, B. *Women, Work, and Sexual Politics in Eighteenth Century England* (Oxford: Blackwell, 1989).
Hindmarsh, D. B. *The Evangelical Conversion Narrative* (Oxford: OUP 2005).
Hitchcock, T. *English Sexualities 1700-1800* (London: Macmillan, 1997).
Holland, B. G. *Baptism in Early Methodism* (London: Epworth, 1970).
Holmes, J. *Religious Revivals in Britain and Ireland 1859-1905* (Dublin: Irish Academic Press, 2000).
Howard, P. 'Developments in the Itinerancy 1780-90' in WHS/WMHS Conference Report (WHS, 1983).
— 'Returned Empties' unpublished paper at the MMS History Conference, 2005.
Hsia, R. P. *The World of Catholic Renewal 1540-1770* (Cambridge: CUP, 1998).
Hughes, G. T. 'Welsh-speaking Methodism' in Madden, *Methodism in Wales* 23-38
Hymns and Psalms (London: MPH, 1983).
International Genealogical Index http://www.familysearch.org/Eng/Search/ (accessed 4/5/1996).
Isaac, R. *The Transformation of Virginia 1740-1790* (Chapel Hill: Norton, 1982).
Ives, A. G. *Kingswood School in Wesley's Day and Since* (London: Epworth, 1969).
Jacob, W. M. 'John Wesley and the Church of England 1736-40' in *JRULMB* 85 (2003) 57-71.
— *The Clerical Profession in the Long Eighteenth Century 1680-1840* (Oxford: OUP, 2007).
Jago, J. *Visitation Studies in the Diocese of York* (London: Chapman, 1999).
Jamieson, W. 'A New Departure 1st August 1785' *WHS Scotland* 16 (October 1985) 7-8.
Jemison, M. M, ed, *A Methodist Courtship: Love Letters of Joseph Benson & Sarah Thompson* (Atlanta: Emory, 1945).
Jenkins, G. H. *The Foundations of Modern Wales 1642-1780* (Oxford: OUP, 1993).
Jenkins, P. 'Church, Nation and Language: The Welsh Church 1660-1800' in Gregory and Chamberlain, eds, *National Church* 265-284.
Johnson, I. MS Letters of Mrs 12 March and 3rd April 1997.
Jones, D. C. '*A Glorious Work in the World:' Welsh Methodism and the International Evangelical Revival 1735-50* (Cardiff: Wales UP, 2004).
Jones, M. P. '"Her Claim to Public Notice:" The Historiography of Women in British Methodism' in R. Sykes, ed, *God's Own Story* (Oxford: Applied Theology Press, 2003) 273-86.
Juster, S. *Doomsayers: Anglo-American Prophecy in an Age of Revolution* (Philadelphia: Pennsylvania UP, 2003).
Kay, Fr 'Childhood Personality and Conversion' 217 in L. Francis and Y. Katz, eds, *Joining and Leaving Religion: Research Perspectives* (Leominster: Gracewing, 2000).
Kent, J. H. S. *Wesley and the Wesleyans* (Cambridge: CUP, 2002).
Kirby, J. *Episcopacy in American Methodism* (Nashville: Kingswood, 2000).
Knighton, D. G. 'English-Speaking Methodism' in Madden, ed, *Methodism in Wales* 1-22.
Knox, R. *Enthusiasm: a Chapter in the History of Religion* (Oxford: Clarendon Press, 1954).
Lake, P and M. C. Questier 'Prisons, priest and people' in Tyacke, ed, *Long*

Reformation.
Lambert, F. *Inventing the 'Great Awakening'* (Princeton: Princeton UP, 1999).
Laqueur, T. W 'Cemeteries, Religion and the Culture of Capitalism' in J. Garnett and C. Matthew, eds, *Revival and Religion since 1700* (London: Hambledon, 1993) 183-200.
Lawrence, A. 'The Question of Celibacy' in *JRULMB* 85 (2003) 177-193.
Leary, W. *My Ancestors were Methodists* (London: Society of Genealogists, 1993).
Lecky, W. E. H. *A History of Ireland in the Eighteenth Century* 3 vols (London: Longmans, 1892)
Lee, H. *Ploughshare of Prayer; A Memoir of the Lyth Family of York in the Nineteenth Century* (Leeds: WHS Yorks, 1987).
Lenton, J. H. 'James Glazebrook: a Protégé of Fletcher and his Double' *WHS Shropshire* NS 4 (1998) 4-5.
— *My Sons in the Gospel: An Analysis of Wesley's Itinerant Preachers* (Wolverhampton: WHS lecture, 2000).
— 'John Wesley's Itinerant Preachers' *Cirplan* 12: 4 (2001) 94-97.
— 'John Wesley and the travelling preachers' *JRULMB* 85 (2003) 99-110.
— '"Labouring for the Lord" Women Preachers in the 19th century' in Sykes, *Beyond the Boundaries* 58-86.
— 'The Education of John Wesley's Preachers in J. H. Lenton ed, *Vital Piety and Learning* (Oxford: Applied Theology Press, 2005) 25-37.
— 'Who were John Wesley's Own Preachers' *MH* 43 (2005) 227-38.
— 'William Orpe's Letter of May 23, 1766 to Francis Asbury' *MH:* 44 (2005) 56-59.
— 'Joseph Pilmore's Origins' *MH* 44 (2006) 262-65.
— 'More information on Richard Boardman' *MH* 44 (2006) 124-28.
— 'Charles Wesley and the preachers' in Newport and Campbell, eds, *Charles Wesley* 88-108.
— 'Wesley's Preachers 1740-1791, compiled and edited by' (accessed 2/8/2008) http://www.gcah.org/site/c.ghKJI0PHIoE/b.3945307/.
Leslie, J. B. *Clergy and Parishes of the Diocese of Derry* (Enniskillen: Ritchie, 1937).
Lloyd, A. K. *The Labourers Hire: The Payment and Deployment of the Early Methodist Preachers 1744-1813* (Cheshire: WHS Lecture, 1968).
Lloyd, G. 'Croakers and busybodies: The extent and influence of Church Methodism in the late 18th and early 19th Centuries' *MH* 42 (2003) 20-32.
— 'Sarah Perrin (1721-87): Early Methodist Exhorter' *MH* 41 (2003) 79-88.
— *Methodist Biographical Index* (Manchester: MARC, 2004).
— *Charles Wesley and the Struggle for Methodist Identity* (Oxford: OUP, 2007).
Lunn, H. (Sir) *Chapters From My Life* (London: Cassell, 1918).
Lysons, K. *A Little Primitive* (Buxton: Church in the Market Place, 2001).
Macaulay, T. B. *Essays Critical and Miscellaneous* (London: Phillips 1856).
MacFarlane, A. *Marriage and Love in England 1300-1840* (Oxford: Blackwell, 1986).
MacInnes, J. *The Evangelical Movement in the Highlands of Scotland 1698-1800* (Aberdeen: Aberdeen UP, 1951).
Mack, P. 'Religious Dissenters in Enlightenment England' *History Workshop Journal* 49 (2000) 1-24.
— 'Does gender matter? Suffering and salvation in eighteenth-century Methodism' *JRULMB* 85 (2003) 157-76.
McEllhenney, J. G. 'Itinerancy Is Dead But It Can Live Again' in *Quarterly Review* 23

(2003) 59-70.

McLean, I. *Water from the Moors: The Life and Works of Joseph Foord* (Pickering: North York Moors Authority, 2005).

McManners, J. *Death and the Enlightenment* (Oxford: OUP, 1981).

Madden, D. 'Experience and the Common Interest of Mankind: The Enlightened Empiricism of John Wesley's Primitive Physick' *British Journal for 18th Century Studies* 26 (2003) 41.

Madden, L. ed, *Methodism in Wales: A Short History of the Wesley Tradition* (Llandudno: Methodist Conference, 2003).

Maddox, R. L. three articles on John Wesley's surviving books *MH* 41 (2002-3) 1: 342-370, 2: 49-67, 3: 118-133.

Mascuch, M. 'John Wesley Superstar' in R. Dekker ed, *Egodocuments and History* (Rotterdam: Verloren, 2002) 137-148.

Maser, F. E. *Robert Strawbridge, First American Methodist Circuit Rider* (Rutland VT: Academy, 1983).

— *The Dramatic Story of Early American Methodism* (New York: Abingdon, 1963).

Mathias, P. 'The Social Structure in the 18th Century: A Calculation by Joseph Massie' *Economic History Review* 2nd series 10 (1957-8) 30-45.

Miall, J. G. *Congregationalism in Yorkshire* (London: Snow, 1868).

Milburn, G. E. and M. Batty, eds, *Workaday Preachers* (Peterborough: Epworth, 1995).

Mills, Joan '"What are our thoughts on Women preachers?" The Women Itinerant Preachers of the Bible Christian Church', Bristol MA thesis, n.d. c. 1992.

Moore, R. D. *Methodism in the Channel Isles* (London: Epworth, 1952).

Moore, M. H. *Sketches of the Pioneers of Methodism in North Carolina and Virginia* (Greenwood, SC: Attic, 1977).

Morgan, P. D. 'Encounters between British and indigenous peoples c1500-c1800' in Halpern, ed, *Empire and Others:* 42-78.

Nayler, J. *Charles Delamotte John Wesley's Companion* (Wesley Bicentenary Manuals no. 10, London: Epworth, 1938).

Newport, K. G. and T. A. Campbell, eds, *Charles Wesley: Life, Literature and Legacy* (Peterborough: Epworth 2007).

Newton, J. A. *Susanna Wesley and the Puritan Tradition in Methodism* (London: Epworth, 1968).

Nicolle, E. T. *The Town of St Helier* (Jersey: Bigwood, 1931).

Noll, M. A. *America's God* (Oxford: OUP, 2002).

— and G. A. Rawlyk, eds, *Amazing Grace: Evangelicalism in Australia, Britain, Canada and the United States* Oxford, OUP, 1994).

— *The Rise of Evangelicalism* (Manchester: IVP, 2004).

Norwood, F. A. *The Story of American Methodism* (Nashville: Abingdon, 1974).

O'Connor, P. J. *People Make Places: The Story of the Irish Palatines* (Coolamoran: Oireacht Na Mumhan Books, 1989).

O'Glaisne, R. 'Our Blessed Thomas Walsh' *WHS (I)* 2: 7 (1994) 5-7.

Olleson, P. *Samuel Wesley: The Man and his Music* (Woodbridge: Boydell and Brewer, 2003).

Osborn, M. F. 'Some Notes on Early Methodism in Rochester' *WHS (Lond)* 21 (1980) 4-8.

Pearce, J. *The Wesleys in Cornwall* (Truro: Bradford Barton, 1964).

Peel, F. *Nonconformity in the Spen Valley* (London: Senior, 1891).

Peirce, W. *The Ecclesiastical Principles and Polity of the Wesleyan Methodists* (London: WCO, 1873).

Pickles, H. M. *Benjamin Ingham, Preacher among the Dales, Forests and Hills* (Skipton: Pickles, 1995).

Piggin, S. 'A Marxist Looks at Methodism: A Critique of E. P. Thompson's Assessment of the Role of Methodism in an Age of Revolution' in J. S. Udy and E. G. Clancy, eds, *Dig or Die*, (Sydney: WMHS, 1981) 290-305.

— 'Halévy Revisited: The Origins of the Wesleyan Methodist Missionary Society: An Examination of Semmel's Thesis,' *JICH* 9.1 (October, 1980), 17-37.

— *Making Evangelical Missionaries 1789-1858* (Abingdon: Sutton Courtenay Press, 1984).

Pike, G. H. *Wesley and his Preachers: Their Conquest of Britain* (London: Fisher Unwin, 1903).

Pittock, M. G. H. *Inventing and Resisting Britain: Cultural Identities in Britain and Ireland 1685-1789* (Basingstoke: Macmillan, 1997).

Pocock, W. W. *History of Wesleyan Methodism in Some of the Southern Counties of England* (London: WCO 1885).

Podmore, C. J. *History of the Moravian Church in England 1728-60* (Oxford: Clarendon, 1998).

Porter, A. *Religion versus Empire? British Protestant Missionaries and Overseas Expansion 1700-1914* (Manchester: Manchester UP, 2002).

Porter, R. *English Society in the 18th Century* (London: Penguin, 1982).

Porter, R. and D. *Patients' Progress: Doctors and Doctoring in 18th Century England* (Oxford: Polity Press, 1989).

Potter, S. 'The Making of Missionaries in the Nineteenth Century' in M. Hill, ed, *A Sociological Yearbook of Religion* (London: SCM, 1975) 8: 103-124.

Prince, H. H. *Romance of Early Methodism in and around West Bromwich and Wednesbury* (West Bromwich: the author, 1925).

Pritchard, F. C. *The Story of Woodhouse Grove School* (Bradford: Woodhouse Grove, 1978).

Rack, H. D. 'Evangelical Endings: Death-beds in Evangelical Biography' *JRULMB* 74 (1992) 39-56.

— 'Wesley Observed.' *PWHS* 49 (1993) 11-17.

— '"But Lord, let it be Betsy" Love and Marriage in Early Methodism' *PWHS* 53 (2001) 1-13.

— 'Wesley Portrayed: Character and Criticism in Some Early Biographies' *MH* 43 (2002) 90-114.

— *Reasonable Enthusiast* (Peterborough: Epworth, 2nd ed. 2003).

— 'John Wesley and Ireland' *WHS (I)* 10 (2004-5) 3-13.

Raughter, R. 'Women in the household of faith' in *WHS (I)* 7: 20-33.

Raven, J. 'The Book Trades' in I. Rivers ed, *Books and Their Readers in 18th Century England: New Essays* (London: Leicester UP, 2001) 1-34.

Rawlyk, G. A. ed, *Aspects of the Canadian Evangelical Experience* (Kingston: McGill, 1997).

— *The Canada Fire: Radical Evangelization in British North America 1775-1812* (Montreal: McGill, 1994).

Remond, R. *Religion and Society in Modern Europe* (Oxford: Blackwell, 1999).

Richey, R. 'The Formation of American Methodism: The Chesapeake Refraction' in

Hatch and Wigger, *Shaping* 197-221.
— *The Methodist Conference in America: A History* (Nashville: Kingswood, 1995).
Rivers, I. ed, *Books and their Readers in Eighteenth Century England* (Leicester: St Martins, 1982).
— ed, *Books and Their Readers in 18th Century England: New Essays* (London: Leicester UP, 2001).
— 'Dissenting and Methodist Books of Practical Divinity' in Rivers, ed, *Books: New Essays* 128-64.
Robbins, K. 'Religion and Community in Scotland and Wales' 363-80 in Gilley and Shiels, ed, *Religion*.
Rodell, J. '"The best house by far in the town": John Wesley's personal circuit' *JRULMB* 85 (2003) 111-122.
Roddie, R. P. 'John Wesley's Legacy in Ireland' in *WHS (I)* 4 (1998) 1: 3-21
Rogal, S. J. *A Biographical Dictionary of 18th Century Methodism* 8 vols (Metuchen: Scarecrow, 1997-99).
Rollmann, H. 'The Origins of Methodism in Newfoundland' (accessed 4/2/2003) http://www.mun.ca/rels/meth/texts/origins.html.
— 'Laurence Coughlan and the Origins of Methodism in Newfoundland' in C. H. H. Scobie and J. W. Grant, eds, *The Contribution of Methodism to Atlantic Canada*, (Montreal: McGill, 1992) 53-76.
Rose, E. A. 'Methodism in South Lancashire to 1800' *Transactions of the Lancashire and Cheshire Antiquarian Society* 81 (1982) 67-91.
Rosman, D. *The Evolution of the English Churches 1500-2000* (Cambridge: CUP, 2002).
Rosser, J. *Wesleyan Methodism in the Isle of Man* (Douglas: Quiggin, 1849).
Roux, T. *Le Methodisme en France* (Paris: Librairie Protestante, 1940).
Royle, E. 'Methodism and Education' in Lenton, ed, *Vital Piety* (Oxford: Applied Theology Press, 2005).
— *Queen Street Chapel and Mission, Huddersfield* (Huddersfield: Huddersfield Local History Society, 1994).
Rudé, G. *The Crowd in History 1730- 1848* (Etobicoke: John Wiley, 1964).
Rupp, E. G. *Religion in England 1688-1791* (Oxford: OUP, 1986).
Rule, J. *Albion's People* (London: Longmans, 1992).
— *Vital Century: England's Developing Economy 1714-1815* (London: Longmans, 1992).
Rusnock, A. *Vital Accounts: Quantifying Health and Population in 18th Century England and France* (Cambridge: CUP, 2002).
Sackett, A. B. *John Jones - First After The Wesleys?* (Chester: WHS, 1972).
— *James Rouquet and his Part in Early Methodism* (Chester: WHS, 1972).
Schell, E. 'Methodist Traveling Preachers in America 1773-99' *MH* 38 (2000) 307-(351).
Schlenther, B. S. *Queen of the Methodists; The Countess of Huntingdon and the 18th Century Crisis of Faith and Society* (Bishop Auckland: Durham Academic Press, 1997).
Schneider, A. G. 'The Ritual of Happy Dying among Early American Methodists' *Church History* (1987) 348-63.
— *The Way of the Cross Leads Home: The Domestication of American Methodism* (Bloomington: Indiana UP, 1993).

Semmel, B. *The Methodist Revolution* (London: Heinemann, 1973).
Semple, N. ed, *Canadian Methodist Historical Society Papers* 1997-8 (Toronto: CMHS, 1999).
— *The Lord's Dominion: The History of Canadian Methodism* (Montreal: McGill, 1996).
Shaw, T. *A History of Cornish Methodism* (Truro: Bradford Barton, 1967).
— *Methodism in the Camelford and Wadebridge Circuit 1743-1963* (Camelford: The Author, 1963).
— *A Methodist Guide to Cornwall* (Peterborough: MPH, 2005).
Shipley, D. C. 'The Ministry in Methodism in the 18th Century' in G. O. McCulloh, ed, *The Ministry in the Methodist Heritage* (Nashville: Abingdon, 1960) 11-31.
Schlenther, B. S. *Queen of the Methodists; The Countess of Huntingdon and the 18th Century Crisis of Faith and Society* (Bishop Auckland: Durham Academic Press, 1997).
Schneider, A. G. *The Way of the Cross Leads Home: The Domestication of American Methodism* (Bloomington: Indiana UP, 1993).
Scobie, C. H. H. and J. W. Grant, eds, *The Contribution of Methodism to Atlantic Canada* (Montreal: McGill, 1992).
Simon, J. S. *John Wesley*, 5 vols (London: Epworth, 1921-28).
— 'Elections to the Legal Hundred' in *PWHS* 13 (1922) 14-21.
Simms, R, ed, *Bibliotheca Staffordienses* (Lichfield: Lomax, 1894).
Simpson, M. ed, *The Cyclopedia of Methodism* (Philadelphia: Everts, 1887).
Simpson, R. D. ed, *Life and Journals of ... Freeborn Garrettson 1752-1827* (Madison NJ: Academy Books, 1984).
Slugg, J. T. *Woodhouse Grove School Memorials and Reminiscences* (London: Woolmer, 1885).
Snape, M. F. *The Redcoat and Religion* (Abingdon: Routledge, 2005).
— 'The Church in a Lancashire Parish: Whalley 1689-1800' in Gregory and Chamberlain, eds, *National Church* 243-63.
Spaeth, D. A. *The Church in an Age of Danger* (Cambridge: CUP, 2000).
Stacey, J. ed, *John Wesley: Contemporary Perspectives* (London, Epworth, 1988).
Staniforth, M. tr, *Early Christian Writings* (London: Penguin, 1968).
Stone, L. *The Family, Sex and Marriage in England 1500-1800* (London: Penguin, 1979).
Stout, H. *The Divine Dramatist: George Whitefield and the Rise of Modern Evangelicalism* (Grand Rapids: Eerdmans, 1991).
Sweet, W. W. *Religion on the American Frontier vol 4: The Methodists* (Chicago: University of Chicago Press, 1946).
Swanson, R. N. ed, *Gender and Christian Religion: Studies in Church History no 34* (Woodbridge: Boydell, 1998).
Swift, W. F. *Methodism in Scotland: The First Hundred Years* (London: WHS lecture no. 13, Epworth, 1947).
— *The Romance of Banffshire Methodism* (Banff: Banffshire Journal, 1927).
Sykes, R. ed, *Beyond the Boundaries* (Oxford: Applied Theology Press, 1998).
— ed, *Gods Own Story: Some Trends in Methodist Historiography* (Oxford: Applied Theology Press, 1993).
Taggart, N. W. *The Irish in World Methodism 1760-1900* (London: Epworth, 1986).
— 'Missionary Finance and Administration under Coke 1784-1813' *WHS (I)* 12 (2006-

07) 44-53.

— *William Arthur* (Peterborough: MPH, 1993).

Taylor, G. R. *The Angel Makers* (London: Heinemann, 1958).

Taylor, I. *The Macdonald Sisters* (London: Weidenfeld, 1987).

Taylor, Roger 'Wesley's Preachers: An Analytical Study in Legible Longhand' in WHS Library Oxford Brookes, Biographical Cuttings files (B/WES/TAY).

Telford, J. *Life of Wesley* (London: Wesleyan Bookroom, 1902).

Thackray, J. and W. J. Dutton MS Notes on William Allwood in Biographical Cuttings files, WHS Library.

Thomas, P, J. H. Lenton and H. D. Rack, 'John Wesley's 1770 Will' *PWHS* 54 (2003) 29-38.

Thompson, E. W. *Wesley: Apostolic Man* (London: Epworth, 1957).

Thompson, E. *'This Remarkable Family:' The Barritts of Foulridge 1750-1850* (Barnoldswick: the author, 1981).

Thompson, W. H. *Early Chapters in Hull Methodism 1746-1800* (London: Kelly, 1895).

Thomson, D. P. *Lady Glenorchy and her Churches-The Story of 200 Years* (Perth: Munro, 1967).

Townsend, W. J. *Alexander Kilham the First Methodist Reformer* (London: J. C. Watts, 1889).

Townsend, W. J, H. B. Workman and G. Eayrs, *A New History of Methodism* 2 vols (London: Hodder, 1909).

Trinder, B. S. *The Industrial Revolution in Shropshire* (Chichester: Phillimore, 2000).

Trotter, R. *The Centenary of Bondgate Chapel...Darlington* (Darlington: Dresser, 1913).

Tudur, G. *Howell Harris 1735-50 From Conversion To Separation* (Cardiff: Wales UP, 2000).

Turberfield, A. *John Scott Lidgett: Archbishop of British Methodism?* (London: Epworth, 2003).

Turner, J. H. *Halifax Books and Authors* (Brighouse: Brighouse News, 1906).

Turner, J. M. *John Wesley* (Peterborough: Epworth, 2003).

Tyacke, N. ed, *England's Long Reformation 1500-1800* (London: UCL, 1998).

Tyerman, L. *Life of John Wesley,* 3 vols (London: Hodder & Stoughton, 1870-71)

— *Wesley's Designated Successor* (London: Hodder, 1882).

Tyson, J. R. ed, *Charles Wesley: A Reader* (Oxford: OUP, 1989).

Valentine, S. R. *John Bennet and the Origins of Methodism and the Evangelical Revival in England* (London: Scarecrow Press, 1997).

Van Buskirk, J. L. *Generous Enemies: Patriots and Loyalists in Revolutionary New York* (Philadelphia: Pennsylvania UP, 2002).

Vickers, J. A. *Thomas Coke Apostle of Methodism* (London: Epworth, 1969).

— 'Dr Thomas Coke and Irish Methodism' in *WHS (I)* 2 (1991) 2: 3.

— *A Short Guide to the Memorials at Wesley's Chapel* (London: Wesley's Chapel, n.d. 1995).

— ed, *Dictionary of Methodism in Britain and Ireland* (Peterborough: Epworth, 2000).

— ed, *The Journals of Thomas Coke* (Nashville: Kingswood, 2005).

Vickery, A. *The Gentleman's Daughter: Women's Lives in Georgian England* (London: Yale UP, 1998).

Virgin, P. *The Church in an Age of Negligence. Ecclesiastical Structure and Problems of Church Reform 1700-1840* (Cambridge: Clark, 1989).

Waddy, J. L. *'The Bitter Sacred Cup': The Wednesbury Riots 1743-4* (London: WMHS,

1970).

Wakefield, G. S. ed, *A Dictionary of Christian Spirituality* (London: SCM, 1983).

Wallace, C. 'Eating and Drinking with John Wesley' *JRULMB* 85 (2003) 137-155.

Wallington, A. 'The Initialled Preachers in the Early *Minutes* and in Hall's *Circuits*' *PWHS* 10 (1916) 154-7.

Walls, A. F. 'The missionary movement "a lay fiefdom"' in D. W. Lovegrove, ed, *The Rise of the Laity in the Evangelical Movement* (London: Routledge, 2002).

— 'Christian Missions and the Enlightenment' in D. Bebbington, ed, *Modern Christianity's Cultural Aspirations* (Sheffield: Academic Press, 2003).

Wallwork, C. N. R. 'Three Bridges to Melchizedek' in J. Strawson, ed, *Church and Theology* (Buxton: Church in the Market Place, 2004) 118-124.

— 'Wesley's Legacy in Worship' in Stacey, ed, *Wesley* 83-98.

Walsh, J. D. 'Origins of the Evangelical Revival' in G. V. Bennett and J. D. Walsh, eds, *Essays in Modern Church History* (London: Black, 1966) 132-162.

— 'The Church and "Anglicanism" in the Long Eighteenth Century' in Walsh, *Church* 1-64.

— *John Wesley, 1703-1791: A Bicentennial Tribute* (London: Dr Williams' Trust, 1995).

— 'Methodism and the Origins of English Speaking Evangelicalism' in Noll et al, eds, *Evangelicalism* 19-37.

Walsh, J. D, C. Haydon and S. Taylor, eds, *The Church of England c 1689-1833* (Cambridge: CUP, 1993).

Walvin, J. *Black Ivory* (Oxford: Blackwell, 2001).

Ward, W. R. *Religion and Society in England 1790-1850* (London: Batsford, 1972).

— *The Protestant Evangelical Awakening* (Cambridge: CUP, 1992).

— *Faith and Faction* (London: Epworth, 1993).

— 'The Evangelical Revival in Eighteenth Century Britain' in Gilley and Sheils ed. *Religion* 252-72.

— 'Was there a Methodist Evangelistic Strategy in the eighteenth century' in Tyacke, ed, *Long Reformation* 285-306.

Warne, A. *Church and Society in Eighteenth Century Devon* (Newton Abbot: David and Charles, 1969)

Watkins, O. S. *Soldiers and Preachers Too* (London: WCO, 1906).

Watson, J. R. *Companion to Hymns and Psalms* (Peterborough: MPH, 1988).

— *The English Hymn: A Critical and Historical Study* (Oxford: Clarendon, 1997).

Watson, J. S. *The Reign of George III 1760-1815* (Oxford: Clarendon, 1960).

Watts, M. *The Dissenters,* vol 2 (Oxford: Clarendon, 1995).

Wedley, J. F. *History of Methodism in the Stourport Circuit from AD 1781 to AD 1899* (Stourport: Stourport Printing Co, 1899).

Whaling, F. 'The Development of Methodism in Scotland Part 1 to 1791' *WHS Cul* 45 (2000) 2-20.

White, E. M. 'Women in the Early Methodist Societies in Wales' *Journal of Welsh Religious History* 7 (1999) 95-108.

Whitby West Cliff Congregational Church Year Book 1894-5.

WHS Conference 1983 Report (typescript in WHS library).

Wickes, M. J. L. *The 1851 Census in Devon* (Devon: Wickes, 1990).

Wigger, J. 'Fighting Bees: Methodist Itinerants and the Dynamics of Methodist Growth 1770-1820' in Hatch and Wigger, *Shaping* 87-133.

Wilder, J. S. 'The Early Methodist Preachers and their contribution to the 18th century Revival in England' New College, Edinburgh University. Dissertation 1948.
Williams, A. H. ed, *John Wesley in Wales 1739-90* (Cardiff: University of Wales Press, 1971).
— *Welsh Wesleyan Methodism 1800-58* (Bangor: Methodist Press, 1935).
Williams, A. R. *Legends of the Severn Valley* (London: Folk Press, 1925).
Williams, C. *The Methodist Contribution to Education in the Bahamas* (Gloucester: Sutton, 1982).
Wilson, D. D. *Many Waters Cannot Quench* (London: Epworth, 1969).
Wilson, K. *The Island Race* (London: Routledge, 2003).
Winks, R. B. ed, *The Oxford History of the British Empire. vol 4: Historiography* (Oxford: OUP, 1999).
Wood, A. S. *Brothers in Arms: John Wesley's Early Clerical Associates* (Nantwich: WHS, 1992).
— *Thomas Haweis 1734-1820* (London: SPCK, 1957).
Woolf, T. and G. *'dear Franky:' The Life and Times of Francis Woolf 1740-1807* (Southampton: n. p. 1995).
Wright, J. *Early Methodism in Yarm* (Billingham: Billingham Press, 1950).
Wrigley, E. A. and R. S. Schofield *The Population History of England 1541-1871* (Cambridge: CUP, 1989).
Young, W. J. *The Quiet Wise Spirit* (Peterborough: Epworth, 2002).
Yrigoyen, C. and S. E. Warrick, eds, *Historical Dictionary of Methodism* (Lanham MD: Scarecrow, 1996).

Journals

Arminian Magazine.
Bathafarn.
Bible Christian Magazine.
British Journal for 18th Century Studies.
Cirplan.
City Road Magazine.
Cornish Methodist Historical Association Journal (1960-).
Evangelical Magazine.
History.
Irish Christian Advocate (1883-1971).
John Rylands University Library of Manchester Bulletin.
Journal of Ecclesiastical History.
Journal of Imperial and Commonwealth History.
London Quarterly and Holborn Review.
Magazin Methodiste des Iles de la Manche.
Methodist History.
Methodist Magazine (Irish edition) (1804-22).
Methodist New Connexion Magazine.
Methodist Recorder Winter Number.
Primitive Methodist Magazine.
Primitive Wesleyan Methodist Magazine.

Proceedings of the Wesley Historical Society.
Quarterly Review (USA).
Wesley Banner.
WHS Bulletin of the Bristol Branch.
WHS Cumbria Journal.
WHS (I) Bulletin of the Irish Branch of the WHS.
WHS Journal of the Lancashire and Cheshire Branch.
WHS Bulletin of the London and Home Counties Branch.
WHS North East Branch Bulletin.
WHS North Lancashire Branch Bulletin.
WHS Scotland Journal.
Wesleyan Methodist Magazine.

General Index

Additional information found in a footnote is identified by the addition of 'n' to a page number. Footnoted sources are not indexed.

Abbott, Benjamin, 49
Aberdeen, 183, 184
　circuit, 182
Abney House seminary, 63
Abraham, John, 295, 317
Adams, Mrs Maria (née French), 283n
Adams, Thomas, 32, 283n
Adams, William, 14
Addingham, Yorkshire, 42
Adwalton, Bradford, 303
Alder, Robert, 361
Alderney, 191, 192
Algar, Mrs Elizabeth (née Emblem), 93
Algar, Joseph, 82, 93, 340, 346-47, 392, 401
Allen, Jane (Mrs Butterfield), 80
Allen, Mrs Jane (née Westell), 102, 104n, 395-96
Allen, John, 49, 101-102, 124, 379
Allen, Richard, 255, 256
Alley, Mary of Antigua, 277
Allwood, Mrs Mary (formerly Mrs. Davison), 93
Allwood, William, 93, 98, 325
Alpraham, Cheshire, 134
Alsop, T, 295
America
　AME church, 256
　Black Methodists, 254-57, 412
　Christmas Conference, 248, 249-50, 253
　Conference, 18, 159-60, 162, 171, 232, 239-40, 243-44, 250, 261
　General Conference, 166, 250
　Methodism in, 12, 407-408
　'Quarterly Conference', 231, 262
　Revolutionary War, 237-40
　sacraments in, 238, 243, 247-48
　other refs: 2, 69, 89, 92, 172, 199, 214, 219-41, 347, 353-5, 387, 388, 389, 390n, 406-7, 410, 411, 412-13, 420, 448
Anderson, James, 124
Andrew, Richard, 326
Andrews, Dee 386
Anglican clergy, 86
Annadale, Co. Leitrim, 208
Annuitant Society, 381-82
Antigua, 276-77
Antrim county, 200
Appleton, John, 51n, 445
Armagh, 211
　county, 200
Arminian Magazine, 23, 29, 66, 67n, 149, 151n, 155, 286, 385
Armstrong, Joseph, 218n
Arrivé, Pierre, 190
Arthur, William, 364
Asbury, Francis
　and American Methodism, 18, 69, 89, 108, 159, 162, 227, 230-35, 240, 247-64, 282, 298, 378, 406, 407-8, 411, 420
　and blacks, 255-7
　and Coke, 248-50, 253
　and the Conference, 159-60, 162, 232, 243-44, 248-50, 253, 261
　and discipline, 227, 231-2, 235, 298
　health, 230, 246, 260-1, 300-301
　and marriage, 89, 92, 119, 237, 260
　ordinations, 355, 359
　and Rankin, 234-35, 241, 260
　and the Revolutionary War, 243-47

and the sacrament, 247-8, 353
and Wesley, 36, 222, 231, 241, 246-9, 251-3, 409
will, 397
other refs: 7, 84, 132, 322, 323, 397, 410
Ashman, William, 308
'Assistant', 11, 35, 81-83, 140
Atherton, William, sons of, 117n
Athlone, 295, 371
circuit, 212, 314
Atlay, Mrs Jane (née Spencer), 93
Atlay, John, 93, 308, 321, 373
Atmore, Charles, 84n, 122, 162, 184, 298, 300n, 322, 344, 359, 361, 364, 391, 393n
Methodist Memorial, 13
daughter, 119
sons, 117n
Auchentain, Co. Tyrone, 198
Auxiliary Fund, 382n
Aver, William, son of, 114
Averell, Adam, 213-14, 217

Bacup, Lancashire, 147
Bahamas, 247, 259
Bailey, Edward, 238n
Baker, Frank, 7, 11, 128, 152, 197, 222, 223, 372, 386n, 441
Baker, Hannah, 254
Ballacharry, Isle of Man, 188
Ballaclague, Isle of Man, 188
Ballingarrane (Ballingrane), 205
Baltimore, 224, 230, 231, 233, 235, 255, 258
Bangs, Nathan, 258
Bannister, Alice (Mrs Cheek), 277
baptism, 119-20, 248, 300, 324
Barbados, 284
Barber, John, 443
Barber, Thomas, 197
Bardsley, Samuel, 51, 71, 122, 124, 184, 299, 344, 379, 387
Barnard, William, Bishop of Londonderry, 318n
Barnard Castle, Co. Durham, 226
Barnes, Richard, Bishop of Durham, 405

Barrett, Alfred, 363, 419
Barritt, John, 69, 360
Barritt, Mary, (Mrs. Taft), 35, 104, 152n, 156, 299, 391, 420
Barrowclough, David, 93, 298
Barrowclough, Mrs Mary, (née Hirst), 93
Barrule, Isle of Man, 188
Barry, James and Isaac, 116
Barry, Robert, 247n
Bartholomew, Thomas, 50, 94, 112, 393
daughter, 119
sons, 114
Barton, Thomas, 221
Bastable, Cornelius, 371n
sons, 114
Bateman, Richard Thomas, 31, 60, 318n, 446, 447
Bates, E. Ralph, 91
Bates, Samuel of Charlemont, 198
Bath, 377
Christopher Inn, 389
Baxter, John, 43n, 90, 103, 267, 271, 276n, 277-78, 285, 287, 357
Bayley, Cornelius, 63, 86, 446
Baynes, William, 63
Beanland, Benjamin, 329
Beard, Thomas, 302, 303, 393
Beaumont, John, 49, 55, 80
sons, 113
Bedale, Yorkshire, 344
Bedford, 407
circuit, 178
Bell, George, 346
Bell, Hugh, of Halifax NS, 389
Bell, Jane (Mrs M'Kersey), 88
Bell, Robert, 328
Bellafeason, Isle of Man, 188
Belturbet, Co. Cavan, 203
Bennet, Mrs Grace (formerly Murray, née Norman), 94, 106, 292, 399
Bennet, John,
his circuit, 129, 136, 408, 447
Dissenting background, 23, 45, 118, 301, 399
marriage, 94, 106, 292
secession, 320, 329, 420, 447

General Index 487

and Wesley, 155, 292, 297
  other refs: 22, 40, 86, 304, 318,
    335, 338, 410
Bennis, Mrs Elizabeth, 97, 208, 212
Benson, Joseph, 58-59, 63, 66, 67, 68,
    94, 157, 167n, 170, 184, 334-5,
    341, 387, 395, 397, 410
  sons, 114, 117
Benson, Mrs Sarah (née Thompson),
    94
Berger, Peter, 418
Berkshire, 43
Berridge, John, 407
Berrisford, Mrs Elizabeth (Mrs
    Murlin), 100n, 161n
Bible Christians, 187, 321
Bickford, Mary (Mrs Thoresby), 283
Bideford, Devon, 344
Biggs, Benjamin, 47
Bingley, Yorkshire, 42
Birmingham, 43, 186, 305, 380, 443
Birstall, 40, 42, 135, 143, 317, 408
Birtwhistle, N. Allen, 265, 266
Black, William, 63, 70-71, 100, 255,
    267, 269, 274, 280-82, 358-59
Black Country, 305
Blackwell, Ebenezer, 65
Blades, John, 321n
Blagborne, William, 379-80, 414
Blair, Andrew, 83, 199, 210n, 394
Blake, Nanny, of Wadebridge, 144
Blake, Robert, 295
Bland, Charles, 50
Boardman, Richard, 7, 80, 207, 210,
    211, 222, 223, 224-27, 229, 230,
    231, 232, 254
Bogie, James, 90, 362-63, 364
Bolton, Lancashire, 317
  chapel at, 381
Bond, John Wesley, 261
Book Room, 148, 167-8, 379, 382, 415
  trustees, 167-68
Booth, John, 81n
Boothby, William, 373n
Bosanquet, Mary, *see* Fletcher, Mrs.
    Mary
Boston, Mass, 226
Botternell, Cornwall, 144

Boulton, Matthew, 101
Bourke, Mrs Lucia, 92n, 212
Bourke, Richard, 68, 92, 206, 212-13
Bourne, Hugh, 59
Bowen family of Llwyn-gair, 175
Bowmer, John, 394-95, 395n
Boyd, Henry, 442, 446, 448
Boyle, Mrs Elizabeth (née Magor), 187
Boyle, John, 52n, 187, 321, 322
Boyle family of Kirlish, 202
Brackenbury, Robert Carr, 7, 66, 121,
    190, 194, 197, 373-74
Bradburn, Mrs Elizabeth ('Betsy'), 69,
    95, 101, 207, 345, 396
Bradburn, Samuel,
  debts, 66
  family, 118, 118-19
  president, 167n, 360
  publications, 67
  trade, 48
  Wesley and, 36, 69, 308-9, 403
  wife, 69, 95, 101, 207, 345, 396
  other refs: 40, 73-74, 77, 102, 211,
    308, 324
Bradford, Joseph, 94, 103, 167n, 308,
    373n, 391
Bradford, Joseph jr, 116
Bradford (Yorkshire), 37, 42, 303
Bradford-on-Avon (Wiltshire), 304,
    389-90
Bradshaw, Mrs (Mrs Rankin), 88, 376
Bradshaw, Yorks, 399
Brainerd, John, 234
Braithwaite, John, 142, 187, 270, 360
Brammah, Mrs Mary, 161
Brammah, William, 137, 298-99, 394
Bramwell, Mrs Ellen (née Byrom), 47,
    81
Bramwell, William, 46-47, 80-81, 97,
    272-3, 273, 415
  son, 114
Brandon, William, 295
Brazier, William, 276n, 285, 357
Brecon, 176, 177
  circuit, 175
Bredin, John, 61n, 66, 197, 199, 206
Brettell, Jeremiah, 63, 83n, 123n, 267
Brettell, John, 91n, 123n

Bridgerule, Devon, 37
Bridgnorth, Shropshire, 316
Briggs, Mrs Elizabeth (née Perronet), 53
Briggs, William, 53, 328
Brisco, Thomas, 81
Bristol, 43, 51, 276, 318, 412, 414
    circuit, 168
    New Room, 159
Bristol, John, 296n
British North America, 247, 266, 280-83, 285, 286, 358-9, 413
Broadbent, John, 59
Broadbent, Thomas, 328
Broad Marston, Worcestershire, 18
Brooke, Hannah of Birstall, 317
Brown, Callum, 184
Brown, George, 106, 203
Brown, Hugh, 203
Brown, John, 98, 124
Brown, Jonathan, 124, 325
Brown, Kenneth, 116-17
Brownell, John, 279n
Brownfield, James, 137, 151, 320, 403
Brownfield, Mrs Rebecca (née Skinner), 151, 320-1n
Bumstead, Daniel, 326
    niece, 124
Bunting, Jabez, 8n, 10, 96, 110, 165, 168, 226n, 273, 274, 288, 361-2, 414-5, 416-7
Burdon, Adrian, 15-16, 352n, 354n, 358n
Burdsall, John, 359
Burdsall, Richard, 124, 326
Burgess, Joseph, 52, 118n, 372
    daughter, 118
Burslem, Staffordshire, 327
Butterfield, Mrs Jane, 80
Butterfield, William, 80
Button, George
    daughter, 120
Butts, Thomas, of Bristol, 57-58
Byrom, Ellen (Mrs Bramwell), 47
Byron, James M, 69, 116, 199n, 200

Calabar, West Africa, 269
Caldwell family, 203

Calvinism, 301
Calvinistic Methodism, 176, 303
Cambridge, Alice, 208
camp meetings, 262, 407, 408
Campbell, Sophia of Antigua, 277
Canada, *see* British North America
Cardiff, 174, 302
Cardigan, 176
Carlill, Thomas, 108, 150, 176
Carmarthen, 175
Carrickfergus, 204
Carter, David, 419
Cartwright, Peter, 441
Cashel, 204
Castlebar, 208
    circuit, 136, 314
Castlederg, West Tyrone, 202, 203
Castletown, Isle of Man, 185, 187, 188
Catermole, John, 63, 322
Catlow, Jonathan, 77-78, 80, 124
Catlow, Sarah (Mrs Edmondson), 78
Cennick, John, 8, 32, 33n, 36, 195, 204, 207, 333
Chafer, Mrs Elizabeth (Mrs Sargent), 96
Channel Islands, 39, 190-94, 302, 374
Charlemont, Co. Armagh, 198
Charleston, SC, 259
Charrington, John, 361
Cheek, Nicholas Mosley, 59, 277, 319
Chepstow, 175
Chester circuit, 176, 443
Chesterfield, Earl of, 58
Children's Fund, 110
Chipping, Lancashire, 398, 407
Christian Library, 65-66, 133, 146
Chubb, James, 69, 123, 156, 166
Church, William, 81n
Church Methodists, 37, 318, 398, 414
Church of England, 3-6, 23-24, 45, 266
    in America, 49, 238
    clergy, 4, 221-2, 316n, 317-20, 446, 447;
    see also ordination
    Methodist relations with, 157, 158, 160, 338, 404, 409, 411-12, 414
circuit quarterly meeting, 129
circuits, 127-52

General Index 489

in America, 257-59
Irish, 208-9
Clara, Co. Cavan, 314
Clark, Helen (Mrs Thomas), 91
Clarke, Dr Adam
   and the Annuitant Society, 381-82
   in the Channel Islands, 7, 191, 194, 197
   family, 116, 117, 124
   in Ireland, 210, 211, 217, 415
   marriage, 346
   and missions, 287
   portrait, 149
   presidency, 167, 171n, 415
   probation, 63, 76, 153, 200
   scholarship, 59, 67, 200n
   and Wesley, 339, 346
   other refs: 7, 102, 104, 132, 144, 162, 199, 199n
Clarke, John, 275n, 276, 276n, 285, 359
Clarke, Mrs Mary, 104, 105
class meeting, 406
Cleckheaton, Yorkshire, 317
Clegg, Mrs Margaret (Mrs Maskew), 325
Clones, 214, 217, 218, 400
Coates, Alexander, 183, 393
'cohorts' of preachers, 31-2, 203
Coke, Dr Thomas
   and American Methodism, 89,159, 166, 248-49, 253, 255, 263
   and Ireland, 10, 197, 209, 210, 216, 217;
   Irish mission, 197, 213-14
   and missions, 176, 180, 183, 190-1, 192, 197, 217, 252, 263, 266, 267-9, 270, 271-9, 280-2, 283,284, 286-88, 378, 416
   ordination of, 349, 352
   ordinations by, 355, 356, 359, 360, 360-61
   and the preachers, 81, 102, 167, 203, 214-15
   other refs: 58, 101n, 149, 164, 168n, 169, 170, 191, 192, 308, 344, 354, 358, 414, 446
Colbeck, Mrs Sarah (née Fletcher), 108
Colbeck, Thomas, 50, 108, 326
   son, 114
Colby, Isle of Man, 188
Cole, Joseph, 150
Coleman, Andrew, 61n, 79, 206, 387-88, 392
Coleman, John, 249
Colley, Mrs Anne (née la Croissette), 53
Colley, Benjamin, 53
Collins, Brian Bury, 124, 446
Collins, William, jr, 117
Collins, William, sr, 117, 391
Colne, Lancs, 37
   circuit, 122, 136, 142
Columbia, SC, 260
Communion, sacrament of, 232, 338-39
   in America, 238, 243, 247-48
   of the sick and dying, 394, 400
   see also sacraments
Condy, Richard, 43n
Conference, 9, 62, 72, 131, 153-72, 305, 413, 448
   annual address, 166
   committees, 165
   Journal, 161, 169, 298
   laymen, 416
   presidency, 169-71, 409-10
   printed Minutes, 163-64
   See also under America; Ireland; Isle of Man
   connexionalism, 418-19
Conyers, Richard of Helmsley, 223
Cooke, Mary (Mrs Clarke), 104, 105, 346
Cooke, Sarah (Mrs Bradburn), 101
Cooney, Dudley, 57, 206
Cooper, Thomas, 63, 91, 211, 340
   children, 120
Cootehill, Co. Monaghan, 339
Cork, 185, 204, 207, 318, 333
   book room, 207
   circuit, 139
Cornwall, 2, 4, 40, 43, 175, 199, 307, 333, 408, 409, 412, 447
   Benson in, 170

Boylites in, 187
Costerdine, Robert, 83n, 89, 130, 323
Coughlan, Lawrence, 190, 206, 207
Countess of Huntingdon's Connexion, 43, 85-86, 304
Courtmatrix, Co. Limerick, 205
Coussins, Jonathan, 27-29, 106, 399, 401, 406
Coussins, Mrs Penelope (née Newman), 27-8, 106
Cowmeadow, John, 82
Cownley, Joseph, 51, 53, 65, 71, 75, 88, 104, 115n, 118n, 164, 168, 207, 210, 350
Coychurch, Glamorgan, 322
Crane, William, 68
Creevy, West Tyrone, 202
Creighton, James, 90, 285, 308, 349, 396-97
Cricket, John, 19, 83, 99n, 394n, 401
Croissette, Elizabeth la (Mrs Colley), 53
Cromwell, Joseph, 132-33, 280, 281, 298
Crook, John, 7, 52, 80n, 82, 106n, 185-87, 215, 297, 410
Crookshank, Charles, 55
Crosby, John, 50, 100
Crosby, Sarah, 17, 34, 35, 98
Cross, John, of Bradford, 406
Cross, Joseph, 347
Crouch, Thomas, 31
Crowther, Jonathan, 12, 110, 123-4, 152, 270, 359, 363, 376, 442
  family, 121, 123-24
Crowther, Robert, 106n, 123-4
Crowther, Timothy, 80, 123-4
Crumlin, Alexander, 109
Cumbria, 4
Currie, Robert, 43
Cutler, Ann, 35

Dales circuit, 142, 168
Dalkeith, Midlothian, 136
Dall, Mrs Margaret (formerly Stevenson), 125
Dall, Robert, 48, 109, 181, 183, 344, 442
  family, 125
Dallam, Mrs Josias, 254
Dallam, Richard, 245
Dancer, Thomas, 51, 324n
Darlington, 316
Darney, William, 22, 40, 67, 115n, 129, 150, 182, 325, 336, 337n, 408
Darragh, John, 393
Dartmouth, Earl of, 237n, 239
Davidson, Margaret, 208, 324n
Davie, Mary (Mrs Richards), 94, 106
Davies, Mrs (formerly Mrs Hemmings) of Ealing, 178
Davies, Owen, of Llanrhaiadr-ym-Mochnant, 176, 177-80, 193
Davies, Rupert, 441
Davis, Mark, 210n, 322-23, 408
Davis, Thomas, 347n
Day, Hannah (Mrs Pritchard), 207n
Day, Mrs. Grace, 98
Day, Simon, 51n, 98
Dean, John, 106n
Dean, Peter, 294, 327
Deaves, James, 345
Deed of Declaration, 169, 171n, 297, 321-22
Delamotte, Charles, 33n
Delamotte, Elizabeth (Mrs Holland), 31, 53
Delap, Andrew, 197
Dempster, James, 183, 222, 235-36, 246-7, 263
  sons, 117n
Denbigh, 176
Denbigh, Mary, of Keighley, 50
Derbyshire circuit, 17
Derriaghy, Co Antrim, 208
Derry, Robert, 323
Derryanvil, Co. Meath, 208
Devlin, Anne, (Mrs George Brown) 208
Devonshire circuit, 137-38
Dewsbury, Yorkshire, 321
Dice, George, 314n
Dickins, John, 238n, 247
Dickinson, Mrs Elizabeth ('Betsy', née Briggs), 53
Dickinson, Peard, 51n, 53, 118n, 168n,

General Index 491

308, 349
Didache, 405
Dieuaide, William, 39n, 192
Dillon, Mrs Elizabeth (Mrs John), 371n
Dillon, John, 52
Dillon, Richard, 205
Dinnen, John, 206
Diss, Norfolk, 399
Dissent, 2-3, 5, 45, 316-17, 367, 399
Dixon, Myles, 272, 273n, 361
Dobinson, Mrs, 17
Dobson, Thomas, 276n, 347n, 361
D'Olier, Richard, 204
Dominica, 284
Doneraile, Co. Cork, 213
Dorsey, Priscilla, 254
Doughty, W. Lamplough, 15
Douglas, Isle of Man, 185, 187, 188
Dow, Lorenzo, 252, 259, 301
Downes, Mrs Dorothy (née Furly), 386n
Downes, John, 15, 58, 91n, 303, 379, 386
Drew, Richard, 82
Dromgoole, Edward, 235n, 238n, 240n
Drumclamph, West Tyrone, 202, 203, 314
Dublin, 51, 195, 200, 204, 206, 208, 209, 318, 333, 408, 414
  book room, 207
  Whitefriar Street chapel, 204
Duffy, Eamon, 405
Dufton, William, 293
Duke, William, 235n
Dumfries, 125, 344
Dunbar, 182
Dunboe, Co. Derry, 318
Duncan, Peter, 377
Dundee circuit, 182
Dungannon, Co. Tyrone, 186
Dunn, Samuel, 415
Dupuy, Anne (Mrs Thomas Taylor), 53

East Anglia, 307
East Midlands, 43
Eayrs, George, 374

Eden, Thomas of Broad Marston, 18
Eden, Thomas, itinerant, 18, 80n
Edinburgh, 150, 182
Edmondson, Jonathan, 50, 78, 124, 293-94, 398
Edmondson, Mrs Mary (née Gunniss), 293-94
Edmondson, Mrs Sarah (née Catlow), 78
Edwards, John, 49-50, 51, 320, 447
Edwards, Jonathan, 22, 25, 219, 274
Edwards, Maldwyn, 43
Eells, William, 83, 321
Elliott, Richard, 47, 324n, 347
Ellis, John, 52n, 305
Ellis, Mary (Mrs Olivers), 100
Ellis, William, 86
Emblem, Elizabeth (Mrs Algar), 93
Embury, Philip, 52-3, 205, 221, 222, 228, 328, 411
Empringham, Robert, 82, 373
Enniskillen, 207, 214
  circuit, 208-209
Entwisle, Joseph, 6, 362
Epworth, Lincolnshire, 140, 342
Erasmus, Bishop, 157, 300, 327
Errington, Matthew, 328
Erskine, John, 181
Escricke, George, 381
Evangelical Magazine, 286
Evangelical Revival, 21-26
Evans, David, 83, 340
Everett, James, 415
Everton, Bedfordshire, 407
Eyton, John, 406

Fadmoor, Yorkshire, 223
Faragher, Robert, 189
fasting, 123
Fenton, Joseph, 293
Fenwick, John, 141, 341-42
Fenwick, Michael, 83, 210, 292, 326, 332, 336n, 337n, 342-44, 420n
Fenwick, Sarah (Mrs Rouquet), 319
Fenwick, William, 341n
Ferguson, Niall, 404
Fermanagh, Co., 200, 203, 211, 314
Fidler, Daniel, 280, 281

Field, Clive, 15, 33-34, 46, 47, 48
field-preaching, 9, 146-7, 152
finance,
    circuit 95-6, 109-10, 122, 125, 148-9, 155, 165, 372-3
    connexional 95-6, 110, 114, 148, 155, 163, 165, 180, 215-6, 299-300, 305, 367-8, 370-8, 379-80, 381-3, 416-7
    missions at home 180
    overseas missions 224, 269, 279, 283, 286-8, 416-7
    personal 96-8, 101-3, 106, 107-8, 121-2, 124, 125, 155, 212, 304-5, 375-7, 381, 397, 414-5, 368
    other refs 156, 175, 180, 204, 214, 232, 236-7, 262,
Findlay and Holdsworth, *History of WMMS*, 266
Fish, William C, 102, 108, 271, 276n, 285
Fisher, John, 208, 209n, 442-43
    wife, 96
Fishguard, Pembrokeshire, 175
Fisk, Wilbur, 361
Fletcher, John, 51, 52-53, 53, 86, 92, 101, 103, 106, 164, 227, 237n, 346-47, 358, 390, 398, 406
Fletcher, Mrs Mary, née Bosanquet, 35, 53, 66, 103, 107, 406
Flint, 176
Floyd, John, 63, 324n
Fluvanna Conference, 243
Foord, Joseph, 223
foreign missions, 165, 265-89, 357, 359, 361, 412, 414, 416-7
Forsaith, Peter, 53
Forward Movement, 168n
Foster, Henry Blaine, 361
France, 191, 192, 266, 269, 271, 359
    French language, 190-93, 194
    war with, 304
Francis, John, 442-43
Francis, Molly (Mrs Maddern), 94n
Frederick circuit, 257-58
Freeman, James of Dublin, 314
Freemantle, William, 43n, 301
French, Maria (Mrs Adams), 283n

Friars, 405
Fry, Henry, 323
Fugill, William, 291
Fulford, Yorkshire, 380
Full Connexion, 153, 359n, 361-2
Furly, Dorothy (Mrs Downes), 386n
Furness, John, 51, 401
Furz, John, 98, 373n

Gallatin, Colonel, 182
Gamble, Robert, 270, 276n, 284, 285, 357n
Gambold, John, 350
Garlick, Kenneth, 15
Garrettson, Freeborn, 7, 236, 245, 249, 256, 259, 281, 410
Garrett, John, 364
Gatch, Philip, 231, 240n, 243, 245, 256
Gaulter, John, 146
Gay, John, 43
Gayer, Henrietta, of Derriaghy, 208
    family of, 196
George, Raymond, 354, 359
George, Miss, (Mrs Horner), 207
Georgetown, 257, 258
G—h, itinerant, 17
Gibbon, Dorothy (Mrs Wright), 100
Gibbon, George, 345
Gibbon, Henrietta (Mrs Owens), 207, 283
Gibbs, John, 328
Gibraltar, 266, 284
Gilbert, Mrs Ann (née Walsh), 277
Gilbert, Francis, 51, 106, 267, 276n, 277, 332-33
Gilbert, Grace (Mrs Webb), 277
Gilbert, John, 118, 267
Gilbert, Nathaniel, 267, 276-77
Gilbert, Nicholas, 40, 350
Gill, Thomas, 444
Gillespie, Robert, 336n, 337, 337n
Gillies, Dr John, 182
Gilpin, Bernard, 405
Glamorgan, 176-77, 409
    circuit, 175
Glasgow, 182, 185, 357
Glassbrook, James, 79
Glendenning, William, 222, 235n,

General Index 493

238n, 240n
Glenorchy, Lady, 182
Gloucestershire, 307
Goldhawk, Norman, 26
Gordon, David, 206-207
Gore, James, 76, 151
Gospel Magazine, 385
Gower, the 175
Graham, Charles, 213, 214, 387
Graham, Daniel, 275n, 276n, 284
Grampound, Cornwall, 304
Grant, James, 59
Graves, Charles, 317
Gray family of Lislap, 203n
Greaves, Thomas, 79
Green, Miss (Mrs Olivers), 102
Green, William, 83
Greenwood, Parson, 372n
Greenwood, Paul, 25-26, 78, 314
Greetland, Yorkshire, 399
Gregory, Benjamin, 121
Gregory, Jeremy, 398, 406
Grenada, 284
Gresford, Denbigh, 176
Grey, Sarah (Mrs Kilham), 88
Griffith, Walter, 199, 217, 270, 397
Grills, Hannah (Mrs Suter), 91
Grimsby circuit, 373
Grimshaw, William, 40, 63, 92, 101, 114, 121, 129, 325, 335, 338, 349, 398, 406, 407, 442, 446
Grindrod, Edmund, 364
Guernsey, 185, 190
Guier, Philip, 39n, 61n, 205
Guilford, Mrs, 161
Gunnis, Mary (Mrs Edmondson), 293
Gwennap Pit, 134
Gwynne, Marmaduke, 174-75
   family, 93

Haddock, Ann (Mrs Holmes), 106
Haigh, Robert, 444n
Haime, John, 52, 71, 89, 328
Hainsworth, William, 80, 107n
'half-itinerant', 35, 315, 343, 376, 444-45
Halifax, 2, 42, 380, 399
Hall, James, 84, 85

Hall, John, of Bristol, 8, 325n
Hall, Martha, née Wesley, 111
Halliday, Thomas, 68-69, 313-14
Hamilton, Dr James, 150
Hamilton family of Baronscourt, 202
Hammett, William, 217n, 248, 259, 263, 271, 275n, 276, 276n, 285, 359
Hampson, John, jr, 114, 117, 211, 334, 353
Hampson, John, sr, 17, 68, 81, 83, 89, 117, 211, 322, 346, 443
   sons, 114
Hanby, Thomas, 19, 167, 338-39, 341, 356, 358, 411
Handy, Samuel, 196
   conversion, 25
Hanson, Thomas, 346
Hardcastle, Philip, 347
Harding, Alan, 85-6
Hardwick, Thomas, 328
Hardwicke's Marriage Act, 87, 94
Hardy, Julius, 327
Harper, John, 203, 207, 248, 260, 263, 275n, 276, 276n, 283, 285, 357n
Harris, Howell, 8n, 32, 156, 176, 197, 302
Harrison, Christopher, 272
Harrison, John, 400-401
Harrison, Lancelot and Thomas, 117
Harrison, Richard, 193
Harrison, Robert, 118n
Hart, Alice (Mrs Gilbert), 277
Hartlepool, Co Durham, 137, 305
Haskins, Mrs Elizabeth, née Richards, 103
Haskins, Mrs Martha, née Potts, 103
Haskins, Thomas, 103
Hastings, Lady Margaret, 100
Hatch, Nathan, 262
Haughton, John, jr, 318n
Haughton, John, sr, 318, 350
Haverfordwest, 175, 323
Hawes, Henrietta (Mrs Harper), 207, 283
Haworth Round (circuit), 40, 78, 150, 408, 408-9
Hay-on-Wye, Brecon, 175
Hayward, Elizabeth (Mrs Saunderson),

207
Hayward, Robert, 83
Heath, William, 448
Heitzenrater, Richard, 70, 90, 157, 158n, 372, 441
Helmsley, Yorkshire, 223
'helpers', 35
Helton, John, 68, 313
Hemmings, Thomas, 178
Hempton, David, 30, 133, 198-9, 202-3, 262, 274, 346, 410-11
Henderson, George, 207, 325n
Henderson, John, 113, 114, 115
Henderson, Richard, 114, 328
Heptonstall, Yorkshire, 42
Hern, Jonathan, 97, 109n, 199n, 327
Heslup, John, 294
Hey, William, of Leeds, 42
Heywood, Lancs, 147
Hickling, John, 10, 382-83
Higginson, Agnes (Mrs Smyth), 99
Highfield, George, 52n
Hill Cliff, Warrington, 316
Hill's Arrangement, 15, 297-8
Hindmarsh, D. Bruce, 15, 29, 395, 401
Hirst, Mary (Mrs Barrowclough), 93
Hitchens, William, 123n, 303-304, 327
Hoadly, Benjamin, Bishop of Bangor, 174
Hodges, John, of Wenvoe, 409
Hodgson, Samuel, 346
Hogg, Alexander, *New Spiritual Magazine*, 149
Holder, George, 106, 107
Holder, Mrs Mary ('Polly') née Woodhouse, 107, 187-88
Holdsworth, John, 19, 446, 448
Holland, Elizabeth (Mrs Delamotte), 31
Holland, William, 31-32, 53, 176, 328
Hollingsworth, Jesse, 245
Holmes, Mrs Ann (née Haddock), 106n
Holmes, Janice, 48, 49
Holmes, John, 106n
Holmes, William, 144
Holywell, Flint, 176
home missions, 417

Hoole, Elijah, 361
Hopper, Christopher
 illness and age, 368, 372, 373, 381
 marriage, 89, 94-95, 98
 portrait, 149
 president, 166, 447
 in Scotland, 7n, 182, 184
 trade, 304
 Wesley and, 71, 409
 other refs: 61n, 180, 343, 410, 447
Hopper, Mrs Jane (née Richardson), 88, 94-95, 98
Horbury, Yorkshire, 42
Horncastle, Lincolnshire, 140
Horne, Melville, 132, 277, 283n, 319, 446
Horner, William, 141n, 199n, 207
Hosier, Harry, 255
Hoskins, John, 61n
Hoskins, Thomas, 443
Hosmer, John, 324n
Houghton, Pembrokeshire, 175
Howard, Peter, 128n, 129n, 137n, 140n, 421
Howe, John, 151
Huddersfield, 42, 347
Hudson, George, 324
Hughes, Hugh Price, 168
Huguenots, 2, 52-53, 204, 319
Hull circuit, 141
Humphreys, Joseph, 8
Hunter, William, jr, 117
Hunter, William, sr, 117, 410
Hunter family of West Tyrone, 203
Huntingdon, Countess of, 295, 303, 354, 421
Hurrell, Elizabeth ('Betsy'), 35, 341
Hutton, Thomas, 81n
Hutton Rudby, Yorks, 137
hymn-singing, 24, 72, 133, 134, 156, 244, 256, 282, 335-6, 368, 400, 418,

infant mortality rates, 112-13
Ingham, Benjamin, 29, 100
Ingham, John, 324n
Inghamites, 447
Inglis, Andrew, 183n

General Index 495

Inverness, 183
  circuit, 183-84
Ireland, 3, 10-11, 39, 54, 58, 61, 92, 96, 141, 195-218, 284, 307, 333n, 357, 392, 398, 414
  annual address to, 166
  book room, 216
  Communion, 217
  Conference, 159, 171, 208, 209, 214-17, 347, 448
  Gaelic, 214
  General Assistant, 209-10
  Irish Mission, 213, 214, 216
  missionaries from, 275-76
  see also Primitive Wesleyans
Isbell, Digory, of Trewint, 144-45
Isham, Thomas, 279n
Isherwood, Francis, 124
Isle of Man, 4, 185-89, 197, 412, 414
  Conference, 186, 188-89
  Manx language, 186-7
itinerancy, 7-19, 22-6, 35-6, 46-9, 67-70, 127-31, 136-48, 151, 404-405, 413, 418
itinerants, *see* preachers

Jackson, John, RA, 151
Jackson, Thomas, 66
  Early Methodist Preachers, 13-14
  sons, 117n
Jaco, Peter, 149, 304
Jamaica, 284
Janes, Thomas, 43n
Jarratt, Devereux, 101, 221, 243, 246
Jeffreys, Andrew, 207
Jenkins, William, 82n, 176, 178, 328, 397
  sons, 113
Jerome, Joseph, 375
Jersey, 190
Jessop, William, 280, 359
Jesuit Order, 404
Jewett, William, 361
Johnson, Alice, 208
Johnson, Mrs Dorothea (Mrs King), 106, 208
Johnson, John, 80n, 105, 106n, 210, 373

Johnson, Robert, 95, 273, 356, 397
Johnson, Dr Samuel, 115
Johnson, Thomas, 49, 149, 161
Jones, Edward, 193
Jones, Griffith, 22
Jones, James, 139n, 315
Jones, John, 63, 101n, 106, 161, 317
Jones, Joseph, 51n, 135, 315, 325n
Jones, Mrs of Fonmon, 409
Jones, Robert, of Fonmon Castle, 174
Jones, Thomas, 361n
Jordan, James, 347n
Joyce, Mathias, 89

Kane, Lawrence, 54, 89, 199n, 206, 211, 218n
Kay, Duncan, 183n
Kead, Thomas, 197, 208, 209n, 339
  wife, 96
Keighley, Yorkshire, 42, 50, 293-94
Keighley, Joshua, 140
Kelk, Thomas, 379
Kent, John, 42, 58, 166, 339, 411, 448
Kerr, John, 203
Kerr, Thomas, 203, 207, 217n
Kerry, 213
Kershaw, Arthur, 328
Kershaw, James, 67, 117, 324
Kershaw, John, 15n, 29, 117n
Keynsham nr Bristol, 398
Kilham, Alexander, 88, 102, 293, 299, 306, 321, 329, 414, 415
Kilham, Mrs Hannah (née Spurr), 106
Kilham, Mrs Sarah (née Grey), 88
Killybegs, Co. Donegal, 207
Kilrea, Co. Derry, 318
King, Mrs Dorothea, 106
King, John, 12, 54, 99, 103, 222, 229, 230, 232, 240, 297
King's Lynn circuit, 168, 178
Kingswood School, 59, 62-63, 110, 113, 114-15, 116, 157, 223, 319, 391
Kingswood Fund, 163
Kirlish, West Tyrone, 202
Kitchings, William, *see* Hitchens
Knight, Titus, 61n
Knowlden, Martha (Mrs Rogers), 105
Knox, Ronald, 409

Kyte, Charles, 49

laity, 306, 408, 411
Lambert, Jeremiah, 281n
Lancashire, 5, 307
Lange, Johann, 128n
Lanktree, Matthew, 200, 203, 209, 217n
Larwood, Samuel, 447
Lawder, Jane (Mrs Lindsay), 95
Lawton, James, 327n
Lee, Jane (Mrs Roberts), 103
Lee, Jesse, 229, 245, 249, 259
Lee, Nebuchadnezzar, 328
Lee, Thomas, 22, 86, 89, 153-55, 408, 410
Leeds, 42, 50, 107, 159, 186, 320, 335
 circuit, 168
Leesburg Conference, 243
Legal Hundred, 95n, 159, 167, 216-17, 253, 306, 321, 345, 353, 375, 411
Leggett, Benjamin, 49
Leppington, John, 379n
Lessey, Theophilus, 51n, 113
Levick, Samuel, 371n
Ley, William, 68, 446
Leyton, nr London, 322-23
Lilly, Isaac, 12, 104n
Limerick, 185, 200, 204, 209, 371
 circuit, 213, 214
 Conference of 1752, 77
Lincolnshire, 42
Lindsay, Mrs Jane (née Lawder), 95
Lindsay, Robert, 95, 235-6n, 313, 329
Linnell, William, 328
Lisburn, 204
Lislap, West Tyrone 203
Lisleen, West Tyrone 202, 203
 circuit, 200
Littlejohn, John, 238n
Livermore, John, 393
Liverpool, 51, 159n, 180, 185, 186, 276, 305
Livingstone, Catherine, (Mrs Garrettson), 254
Llanlleonfel, nr Garth, Brecon, 174
Llanrhaidr-ym-Mochnant, Montgomery. 176.

Llanusk, Gwent, 177.
Llanwynno, Glam, 177.
Lloyd, Kingsley, 97, 110
Lloyd, Gareth, 398
Lloyd, Henry or Harry, of Rhydri, 177, 445
local preachers, 18-19, 271, 293, 315-16, 340, 357-8n
 Manx, 186
 in Scotland, 184
 Local Preachers' Mutual Aid Association, 415
Lollards, 405
Lomas, Robert, 124, 379n
London, 44, 51, 54, 305, 412, 414
 circuit, 171, 307-8, 443, 444
 City Road Chapel, 107, 349, 398, 399
 Devonshire Square Church, 316
 Foundery, 107, 159, 349
 Hinde Street chapel, 178
 infant mortality rates, 112
 St Luke's, Old Street, 107
 Stewards' Book, 16-17, 371, 443
 West Street chapel, 349
Londonderry, 214
 circuit, 206
Longley, Mrs Martha, 112
Longley, Thomas, 80n, 112, 379
Lord's Supper, *see* Communion
Lowes, Mrs Isabella (née Perkyns), 323
Lowes, Matthew, 323
Loyola, Ignatius, 404
Lucas, Richard, 68, 371n
Lumb, Mrs Ann (née Wilson), 279n
Lumb, Matthew, 49, 142, 183, 189, 269, 270, 276n, 278-79, 283, 285, 287, 357n, 363, 364
Lunell, William, 204, 339
Lunn, Henry, 168n
Luxulyan, Cornwall, 134
Lynch family of Antigua, 277
Lynn, John, 276n
Lyons, James, jr, 117
Lyons, James sr, 80, 117, 275n, 276n, 285

General Index 497

Macaulay, Zachary, 132
Macclesfield, 241
  circuit, 139
Macdonald family, *see* M'Donald
Mackrill, Agnes (Mrs Yewdall) 100n
Macquiban, Timothy, 416n
Maddern, Mrs Francis, 94n
Maddern, John, 94n, 115n, 336n, 337n, 445
Madeley, Shropshire, 37, 319
Magheracolton, West Tyrone, 202
Magheralough, West Tyrone,198
Magor, Elizabeth (Mrs Boyle), 187
Mahy, William, 39n, 90, 280n, 359
  family, 192
Mallow, Co. Cork, 213
M'Allum, Duncan, 58, 183, 197, 267, 360
Manchester, 37, 42, 44, 51, 159, 178, 319, 321
  circuit, 16, 139, 150
Mann, James, 247n, 267, 269, 280, 281, 359
Mann, John, 90, 246-47, 267, 269, 280, 281, 359
Manners, John, 123, 128, 408
Manners, Nicholas, 15n,123, 212
Mansfield, Earl of, 349, 352
Marsden, Joshua, 61-62, 361n, 392
Martin, William, 446, 447n
Martindale, Miles, 49, 52n, 59, 89, 407
Maryland, 230, 245
Maser, Frederick, 224
Maskew, Jonathan, 54-55, 84n, 325
Mason, John, 59, 83, 149, 150
Mason, Thomas, of Limerick, 371
Massie, Joseph, 46
Massiot, James, 52, 199, 204
Massiot, Martha (Mrs Cownley), 88
Mather, Alexander,
  marriage, 89, 96, 97-98
  on missionary committee, 287
  obituary, 401
  ordination, 358, 376
  son, 120, 381
  Wesley and, 71, 182, 237, 339
  other refs: 48, 51, 73, 111, 146, 167, 168n, 170, 181, 272, 380-81,

410
Maxfield, Thomas, 8, 32-33, 51n, 101n, 303, 318, 333
Maxwell, Lady Darcy, 182
M'Burney, John, 302
McManners, John, 394
M'Coll, Duncan, 281
M'Cornock, William, jr, 117, 206
M'Cornock, William, sr, 117, 206, 270, 275n, 276n, 284, 357n
M'Coy, Robert, 347n
M'Donald, James, 197, 199
  family, 117, 200n
Melton Mowbray, Leicestershire, 297
Mercer, John, 188-89
Meredith, William, 276n
Meriton, John, 12, 31, 447
Merryweather, George, of Yarm, 137
Metcalfe, Henry, 49
Methodism
  membership, 6
  rural, 44
  spirituality, 26-30
'Methodist', 29-30
Methodist New Connexion, 299, 321, 414, 416
Meyrick, John, 129
M'Geary, John, 95, 203n, 276, 280
M'Geary, Thomas, 63, 203n, 398
M'Gowan, John, 58, 301, 316, 317
Michaelston, Pembrokeshire, 409
Midgley, Mary, of Sheffield, 1
Mill, Peter, 84-85, 181, 183n, 326
Mill Row, Lancashire, 147
Miller, James, 18n, 39n
Miller, John, 55, 205
Miller, Robert, 118, 147
Milner, John, 335, 398, 407
Minethorpe, William, 99
Minutes of Conference, 11, 17-19, 441, 448-49
  Irish, 209
  Large Minutes, 157
  obituaries, *see under* preachers
  printed, 163-4
  stations, 18-19
Mitchell, Thomas, 52n, 75, 83, 168, 408, 443

M'Kay (or M'Coy), Robert, 347n
M'Kersey, Mrs Jane, (née Bell), 88
M'Kersey, John, 88
M'Mullen, James, 280, 284
M'Nab, Alexander, 132, 183, 296, 420n
M'Nicoll, David, 376
Moister, William, 266
Mold, Flint, 176
Monaghan, 79n, 218
Monmouth, 176
Moore, Alexander, 205, 209
Moore, Mrs Anne (née Young), 93, 104, 112
Moore, Charles, of Drumclamph, 203, 208
Moore, Henry,
   and Annuitant Society, 381-2
   in Ireland, 210, 211
   marriage, 93, 104
   on missionary committee, 287
   ordination, 358, 362, 363-64, 376
   presidency, 167n
   Wesley and, 207, 411, 414
   other refs: 178, 199n, 200n, 308, 415
Moore, Hugh, 120-21, 202, 203
Moore family of Drumclamph, 202, 203, 208
Moorhead, Samuel, 217
Moorhouse, Henry, 49
Moorhouse, Michael, 67, 297, 313
Moravians, 53, 128, 266, 276, 367, 422, 447
Morgan, James, 81
Morgan, John, 74
Morlais, Pembrokeshire, 175
Morley, George, 417
   daughter, 118
Morris, James, 57, 205, 209n
Mort, James, 145
Mosley, Albert, 265, 266
Moss, Richard, 68, 92, 98-99
Mowat, George, 117, 140, 183n
Mowat, James, 117
Mowat, William, 117
M'Quigg, James, 59, 205, 214, 299
mulattoes, 277

Murdock, Archibald, 279-80
Murdock, Mrs Mary, 280
Murlin, Mrs Elizabeth (formerly Mrs Berrisford), 100n, 161
Murlin, John, 83, 84n, 100n, 106n, 150
Murphy, Michael, 205
Murray, Mrs Grace *see* Mrs Bennet)
Murray, John, 328
Musselburgh, East Lothian, 182
M'Vean, John, 271n, 275n, 276n, 284
Myles, William, 11-12, 79, 199, 207, 376, 380n, 442

Naylor, Robert, 13
Nelson, John,
   conversion, 51
   death, 400
   impressment, 52n, 303
   marriage. 89, 98, 135
   as preacher, 48, 134, 135, 408
   trade, 304, 367
   and Charles Wesley, 36, 135, 335
   and John Wesley/Conference, 40, 155, 156
   other refs: 7, 49n, 144, 409, 410
Nelson, John (grandson), 106n, 124
New England, 258
New York, 246-47, 222, 224, 226, 227, 231, 233, 236, 246-47, 255, 258
   John Street church, 246, 253, 255
Newall, Thomas, 301-302
Newcastle, 42, 297, 305, 323
Newcastle, Duke of, 5
Newman, Penelope (Mrs Coussins), 27-8
Newton, Robert, 288
Nile, Molly, of Botternell, 144
'no politics' rule, 278
Noll, Mark, 26
Nolley, Richmond, 263
Norfolk, VA, 224
North Midlands, 307
North Shields, 321
'North Wales' circuit, 175
Northallerton, 137
Northampton, 407, 443
   circuit, 143
Norwich, 308, 338, 408

Nottingham, 324
Nova Scotia, 247, 255, 392

Oddie, James, 100, 108, 326, 327
Oddie, Mrs Sarah (née Thompson), 100
Ogden, Halifax, Mount Zion chapel, 145
Ogylvie, John, 360, 363
   son, 114
Ohio, 258
O'Kelly, James, 249, 252, 259
Oldham, Mrs Elizabeth, 371
Oldham, John, 386
Oliver, Mrs Elizabeth, 161
Oliver, John, 327, 403
Oliver estate, Co. Limerick, 205
Olivers, Mrs Mary (née Green), 100, 102
Olivers, Thomas, 48, 51-2n, 75, 100, 102, 143, 150, 176, 178, 212, 327n
Olleson, Philip, 111
Olney, Buckinghamshire, 317
ordination, 183, 192, 213, 338, 349-65
   for America, 248, 353-5
   'virtual ordination', 359, 361
Orney (Urney), West Tyrone, 202
Orpe, William, 91, 315, 325
Osborn, George, 168n
Osmotherley, Yorkshire, 137
Otley circuit, 324
Otterbein, Philip, 231
Ouseley, Gideon, 197, 204, 214
Owen, Miss, schoolmistress, 114
Owens, Thomas, 203, 206, 207, 269, 275n, 276, 276n, 283, 285, 357n
Owings, Samuel, 231, 245, 246
Oxford, St Edmund Hall, 316

Paisley, 185
Palatines, 53, 204-205, 228, 407
Palmer, William, 43n
Parkin, Jonathan, 50-51, 54
Parrinder, Geoffrey, 413
Patterson, Richard, 285
Pawninton, Ann (Mrs Cooper), 340
Pawson, Mrs Frances (formerly Mrs Wren), 106, 140, 145, 167n

Pawson, John,
   Atmore and, 13n, 139n, 162, 291, 292
   baptizing, 120
   and Conference, 158, 161-2, 298
   correspondence, 13n, 253, 298, 299, 411-12, 414
   fasting, 123
   health, 378-79
   marriages 92, 101, 106, 107, 122
   and Methodism after Wesley, 414
   and other preachers, 13n, 101, 105, 116, 136, 148, 158, 253, 291-92, 298, 299, 322, 334, 348, 376, 391
   portrait, 149, 150
   in Scotland, 136, 184; ordination for, 19, 338, 358
   Wesley and, 15, 71, 83, 120, 140, 161, 332, 334
   other refs: 84n, 100, 143, 150, 163, 410
Payne, Thomas
   Mary (daughter), 116
Peacock, John, 49, 84, 391
Pearce, Benjamin, 276n, 283, 284, 357n, 389-90
Peel, Isle of Man, 185, 187
Pembroke, 176, 223
   circuit, 175
Penington, Mrs Mary, 371-72
Penington, William, 61n, 148, 371
Pentre Llifior, Montgomery, 176
Penzance, revival, 187
Percival, William, wife of, 120
perfection, 301
Perkyns, Isabella (Mrs Lowes), 323
Perrin, Sarah, 34
Perronet, Charles, 338
Perronet, Elizabeth (Mrs Briggs), 53
Perronet, Vincent, 52-53, 60
Pescod, Joseph, 100, 104
Pescod, Mrs Sarah, 104
Peterhead, Aberdeenshire, 182
Philadelphia, 222, 224, 226, 227, 231, 235, 239, 258
Philipstown, 143
Phoebus, William, 323-24
Piers, Henry, 31, 60, 317, 318n, 446

Piggin, Stuart, 288, 416, 417
Pike, G. Holden, 14
Pilmore, Joseph
   in America, 7, 219, 222, 222-24, 229-32, 233, 238, 245, 249, 253, 254, 263, 329, 411, 412n
   Anglican orders, 50, 227, 249, 350, 353
   illegitimacy, 50, 55, 223
   in Ireland, 210 , 227
   at Kingswood, 63, 223
   in Wales, 223, 263, 443
   other refs: 254, 329, 420
Pipe, John S, 98, 132
Placey, Northumberland, 44
Plymouth, 43, 305
   circuit, 211
politics, 416
Polperro, Cornwall, 134
Ponsanooth, Cornwall, 134
Poole, George, 272, 273n, 361
Poole, John, 82, 401
Pope, George, 363
Portarlington, Co. Laois, 204
Porter, Andrew, 288
Porter, Roy, 127, 185
Portsmouth, 43, 305, 322
Portsea, Hampshire, 37
Potto, Yorkshire, 344
Potts, Martha (Mrs Haskins), 103
preachers
   from the Army, 51-52, 195, 196, 204, 328-9
   clothing, 150
   'cohorts', 31-2, 89-93, 301, 307, 339-40, 441
   conversion, 27-29, 50-52
   database, 9, 31
   daughters, 110, 114, 118-19
   death, 284, 368, 385-401
   diet, 122-23
   'disappeared', 313n
   doctrine, 157, 160, 171-2, 301-2
   drink, 69, 298, 389-90
   education., 57-62
   expulsion, 69, 291, 297-300, 335-8, 340, 342
   family, 109-25
   first, 8n, 32-33
   ill-health 131, 226, 284-5, 300-01, 347, 373, 375, 377, 379, 392-4
   horses, 142-4
   impressment, 302-4, 393
   marriage, 80-81, 87-108, 161, 163, 207, 269-70, 283-84, 293-94, 345-46
   obituaries, 13, 18, 19, 374-75, 400, 400-401, 415
   persecution, 198, 206, 214, 245, 279, 302, 314, 318
   portraits, 149-51
   probation, 73-86, 153
   reading, 64-7
   retirement and superannuation, 367-81
   returning to itinerancy, 227, 331-48
   social class, 46-9, 55, 306
   spiritual growth 26-9, 61-2, 64-70, 73-5, 86, 132-5,
   stationing, 139-42, 162, 163-4, 281-2, 333
   suicide, 390-91
   'superannuation', 372-75, 382
   'supernumerary', 370, 372-74, 374, 382
   titles, 35-36
   trade, 304-305, 323-4, 325-9
   use of initials, 229n, 250, 291-2, 314, 332n, 343
   widows, 105-6, 368, 370, 371, 372, 381
   wigs, 150
   wills, 397
   withdrawal, 151, 291-329, 331, 339-341, 342, 347, 419
   wives of, *see* marriage *above*
   see also finance, ordination
Preachers' Fund, 110, 157, 163, 178, 314, 322, 367, 368-72, 378, 382, 383, 411
'Presiding Elders', 249
Prestwood, nr Uttoxeter, 315
Price, John, 203n
Price, Nehemiah, 203n, 218n
Price, Peter, 43n, 301
Prickard, John, 95, 199n, 267

General Index 501

Priestley, Joseph, 302
Primitive Methodism, 44n, 416, 417
  in Isle of Man, 189
Primitive Wesleyans, 217-18, 321,
  414, 415
Princeton, NJ, 224
Pritchard, Mrs Hannah (née Day),
  207n
Pritchard, John, 63, 143, 162, 207n
Probus, Cornwall, 134
'prophet's chamber', 144-45
Publow, nr Bath, school at, 114, 116
Purdy, Victory, 51n, 329

Queteville, Henry de, wife of, 191
Queteville, John/Jean de, 39-40n, 59,
  190-91, 267, 280n, 359, 363

Rack, Henry, 43, 47, 53, 107-8, 267,
  418
Ramsey, Isle of Man, 185
Randolph, Mary (Mrs Roberts), 102
Rankin, Mrs (Mrs Bradshaw), 88
Rankin, Thomas
  in America, 182-83, 219, 222, 227,
    230, 232-35, 237, 239, 240, 241,
    245, 248n, 255, 263
  marriage, 88, 106n, 327, 376, 379
  ordination, 358
  retirement, 346, 376-77
  Wesley and, 68
  other refs: 143, 287, 308, 397, 415
Rawlins, Philip, 80
Redruth, Cornwall, 325-26
Reece, Richard, 168, 450
Reeves, Jonathan, 52n
Religious Census, 1851, 3
religious societies, 22, 405
Reynolds, John, 59, 82-83
Rhodes, Benjamin, 59n, 97
  daughter, 118
  'Itinerants' Anthem', 127, 142n
Rhydri, Glamorgan, 177
Richards, Elizabeth (Mrs Haskins),
  103
Richards, Mrs Mary (née Davie), 94,
  106
Richards, Thomas, 33, 63, 94, 106

Richardson, James, 276n
Richardson, Jane (Mrs Hopper), 94
Richardson, John, 349
Richey, Russell, 89, 153, 244
Richmond, VA, 261
Ridall, James, 107n
Ridgeley, Rebecca and Charles, 254
Ridgeway, Thomas, 388
Ridgway, John, of Hanley, 321
Ridley, James, 295
Ridley, William, 151
Ritchie, Elizabeth, 94
Roberts, Mrs Jane (née Lee), 103
Roberts, Mrs Mary (née Randolph),
  102
Roberts, Robert, 84, 155
Roberts, Thomas, 92, 102-103, 382
  family, 119
Roberts, Mrs Thomas (née Wogan),
  102
Roberts, William, 326
Robin Hood's Bay, Yorkshire, 107
Roch, Pembrokeshire, 175
Rochdale, Lancashire, 146
Rochester, Kent, 145, 186
Rodda, Martin, 123, 222, 235-36, 239,
  240, 245, 297, 326
Rodda, Richard, 89, 106, 123, 397
  family, 121, 145
Rodell, Jonathan, 407
Roe, Hester Ann, (Mrs Rogers), 105,
  112
Roe, Samuel, 249
Rogers, James, 92, 105-6, 168, 210n
  daughter, 118
  marriages, 105-106
  sons, 120
Rogers, Samuel, 329
Rolleston, Derbyshire, 319
Roman Catholics, 2-3, 45
  in Ireland, 3, 196, 199, 202, 205-
    206, 212-3, 214, 217
Rouquet, James, 52, 53, 63, 319
Rouquet, Mrs Sarah (née Fenwick),
  319
Rourke, Mrs, 161
Rowell, Jacob, 84n, 123n, 137, 161,
  304, 410

Rowell, Mrs Jane, 97
Rowland, Daniel, 22
Royle, Edward, 42, 137n, 278n
Rudder, Samuel, 281n
Ruff, Daniel, 240n, 245, 246
Rule, John, 44
Rutherford, Mrs Isabella (née Young), 112, 119, 120-1, 207
Rutherford, Thomas, 84, 85, 93, 112-13, 120, 132, 210, 211
Ruthin, Denbigh, 180
Ryan, Sarah, 34, 99
Ryan, Thomas, 205-206

sacraments, *see* baptism; Communion
St Austell, Cornwall, 134
St Eustatius, 278, 283
St Isaac, Cornwall, 134
St Ives, Cornwall, 134, 305, 408
St Just, Cornwall, 134
St Vincent, 278-79, 284, 285
Salisbury circuit, 136
Sampford Peverell, Devon, 6
Sandhurst, Gloucestershire, 319
Sandoe, William, 82
Sargent, Mrs Elizabeth (formerly Chafer), 96
Sargent, George, 96, 118, 393
Sargent, John, 118
Sa(u)nderson, Hugh, 123n, 203n, 207, 340-41
Sa(u)nderson, John, 123n, 203n, 207
Sa(u)nderson, Joseph, 375-76, 403
Sa(u)nderson, William, 403, 422
Scarborough, Yorks, 186
Schell, Ed, 355, 386, 388, 389, 390n
Schwarz, Suzanne, 16
Scotland, 3, 7n, 39, 52n, 58, 107, 142, 180-85, 198, 360-61, 414, 447
 Cambuslang revival, 22
 ordination, 356-57
 Scots language, 180
Scott, Francis, 48, 328
Seabury, Bishop Samuel, 227, 354
Seccomb, Thomas, 54
secularization, 417-18
Seed, Richard, 90n, 373n
Sellon, Walter, 12, 52, 63, 86, 406

Sellon, Walter jnr, 114
Selvidge, Pembrokeshire, 408
Semmel, Bernard, 416
Sevenoaks, Kent, 207
Seward, William, 302
Shadford, George, 52, 222, 232, 233, 240, 245, 265-66, 266
 wife of, 240-41
Shaford, Lancashire, 147
Sharp, Mrs Sarah (Mrs Colbeck, née Fletcher), 108, 326
Shaw, John, 361n, 373, 393
Shaw, William, 364
Sheffield, 1, 40, 50-51, 159n, 321, 345
 Carver Street chapel, 178
 circuit, 299
Shent, William, 16, 19, 40, 42, 89, 303, 315, 320n, 326, 335, 367, 400, 444-45
Shipley, David, 15
Short, Mally, of Stratton, 144
Short, Thomas, 389
Sierra Leone, 247
Sigston, James, 415
Simon, John Smith, 376
Simpson, David, 406
Simpson, John, 31
 family, 117
Simpson, Thomas, 115, 140, 183n
Simpson, William, 118
Skelton, Charles, 49, 447
Skerritt, George, 276n, 285
Skinner, Rebecca (Mrs Brownfield), 151, 320-1n
Skirrow, John, 79
Slacke, Anna of Annadale, 208
Slater, Edward, 140, 294
slavery, 219, 247, 254-57, 256, 276, 278
Sligo, 213
Slocomb, John, 400
Smith, Edwin, 413
Smith, George, 282, 411, 422, 448
Smith, James, 203
Smith, John, 49, 57, 197-8, 202, 203, 206, 208, 211, 218, 302, 314n, 339, 410
Smith, John Sugden, 50

General Index   503

Smith, Mrs Mary, 197
Smith, Robert, 203, 218n, 394n
Smith, Samuel, 79
Smith, Sydney, 46
Smith, William, 52, 89, 210, 216
Smyth, Mrs Agnes, née Higginson, 99, 208
Smyth, Edward, 55, 59, 90, 99, 208, 295, 296, 353
Snowden, George, 82, 373
Soothill, William E, 413
Southborough, Kent, 322
Southcott, Joanna, 207
southern England, 42
Spencer, Jane (Mrs Atlay), 93
Spensley, Hannah (Mrs Thom), 91
Spittal, Pembrokeshire, 175
Spraggs, Samuel, 246-47, 249
Squarebridge, Edward, 364
Staffordshire, 307
   circuit, 16, 136
   riots in, 318
Stamp, John, 106n
Standring, Mrs Mary, 371n
Staniforth, Sampson, 14, 52n
Steel, Richard, 90
Steele, Samuel, 217n
Stephens, John, 168
Stephenson, John, 207, 270, 271, 275n, 276n, 283, 285
Stephenson, Thomas Bowman, 168
Stephenson, William, 89
Stevens, William, 43n, 107n, 118
Stevenson, Mrs Margaret (Mrs Dall), 125
Stewart, James, 203
Stewart, Matthew, 203, 207, 267, 269-70
Stockton, 137
Stokesley, Yorkshire, 137
Story, George, 51, 76, 83n, 132
Stourport, Worcestershire, 152
Strangers' Friend Society, 416n
Stratton, Cornwall, 134
Strawbridge, Robert, 221, 222, 228, 231, 232-33, 238n, 254
Sueur, Peter le, 190
Sully, Glamorgan, 409

Sunday Service of the Methodists, 249-50, 400
Sunderland, 135, 170
Superintendent, 82
Sutcliffe, Joseph, 75, 91n, 215n, 270, 388
Suter, Alexander, 91, 183, 308, 380
   sons, 114
Suter, Mrs Hannah (née Grills), 91
Suter, Mrs Mary, 380
Swain, Joseph, 444n
Swan, Robert, 183n
Swindells, Robert, 374
Sykes, George, 54, 106, 308

Tadcaster, 139
Taft, Mrs Mary (née Barritt), 35, 104, 112n, 152n, 156, 299, 391, 420
Taft, Zechariah, 104
Tattershall, Thomas, 140
Taylor, Mrs Anne (née Dupuy), 53
Taylor, David, 8, 22, 31, 40, 410
Taylor, Henry, 299
Taylor, Joseph, 168
Taylor, Samuel, 150-51
   family, 118
Taylor, Thomas, 53, 59, 122, 146, 162, 167n, 171, 175, 182, 210n, 223-24, 297n, 300n, 323, 379, 395, 409, 410, 450
   Anne (daughter), 118
Teare, Mrs Mary, 371
Tennant, Thomas, 68, 76
Tennessee, 258
Tentin, Jean, 190
Thirsk, Yorks, 137
Thom, Mrs Hannah (née Spensley), 91
Thom, James, 76, 82, 168, 183n, 298
Thom, William, 76, 91, 183n, 321
Thomas, Barnabas, 91, 298
Thomas, Elizabeth, of Blaen-porth, 34n
Thomas, Mrs Helen (née Clark), wife of Barnabas, 91
Thomas, Philip, of Gelligaer, 409
Thompson, Edgar W, 353
Thompson, Edward, 279n
Thompson, Joseph, 394n

Thompson, Sarah (Mrs Benson), 94
Thompson, Sarah (Mrs Oddie), 100
Thompson, William, 81, 166-67, 199n, 207, 210, 303, 345-46, 380
Thomson, George, 409
Thoresby, Mrs Mary, (née Bickford), 283
Thoresby, William, 282-83, 284, 285, 289
Thorn, Mary, 254
Thornton, Bradford, 317
Thorpe, John, son of, 118
Thwayte, James, 327
Tizard, George, 17
Todmorden, Yorkshire, 78
Todmorden Edge, 16, 129
Tonyloman, Fermanagh, society at, 197
Tooth, Mary, 118
Tooth, Samuel, 328
Toplady, Augustus, 57
Tortola, 279-80
Townsend, John, 359, 360, 380
Trathen, David, 329, 336, 337n
Tregortha, John, 113, 324n, 327
Trembath, John, 324n, 325
Trenton, NJ, 224
Trethewey, Thomas and family, 117
Trevecca College, 319, 354
Trickett, Rebecca (Mrs Gibbon), 345
Trinder, Barrie, 447
Trowbridge, Wiltshire, 346
Truro, Cornwall, 321
Truscott, Francis, 293n
 son, 118
Tunney, William, 324-25
Tunnycliffe, Charles, 51
Tyerman, Luke, 442
Tyrone county, 200-04,

Ulster, 200
Underhill, William, 327
Undrell/Underhill, John, 315 and n
Unthank, John, 316
Urney (Orney), West Tyrone, 202

Valentine, Simon, 408
Valton, John, 28, 52-53, 55, 59, 91n, 102, 156, 158, 161, 168n, 296n, 301
Vasey, Thomas, 49, 54, 248, 250-51, 266, 292n, 355
Vaughan, Admiral, of Trecwn, 175
Vazeille, Mrs. Mary (Molly), (Mrs Wesley) 53, 106, 111, 341
Venn, Henry, 22, 42
Vickers, John, 273, 274-5, 360
Vickery, Amanda, 103
Viney, Richard, 157
Virginia, 229, 233, 238, 258
Voltaire, 2

Wadsworth, George, 211, 346
Wakefield, 42
Wakefield, Gordon, 26
Waldron, Isaac, 292n
Wales, 3, 39, 142, 173-80, 198, 357
 Calvinistic Methodism, 156
 South Wales, 409
 Welsh language, 173, 176-80, 193
Walker, Francis, 293, 315
Walker, Samuel, 22
Walls, Andrew, 265,
Walsh, Ann (Mrs Gilbert), 277n
Walsh, John, 22, 267n, 417n
Walsh, Thomas, 45, 58, 61n, 66, 84, 197, 206, 208, 209n, 210, 338, 343, 385, 410
Walton, Grace, 34
Walvin, James, 278
Warburton, Cheshire, 320
Ward, Joseph, 207
Ward, Reginald, 53, 168, 196, 353, 407
Warren (Pembroke), 175
Warrener, William, 269, 270, 275-76, 276n, 284, 285, 287, 350, 357n
 wife, 124
Warrington, 224-26
Warwick, Thomas, 360
Warwick, Dr Thomas Olivers, 360
Warwickshire, 307
Washington, George, President, 239
Waterhouse family, 241n
Watkins, John, of Llanusk, 177
Watkinson, Richard, of Leeds, 66, 67n
Watson, J. R, 406

General Index 505

Watson, James, 140, 336n
Watson, John jr, 117, 377-78
Watson, John sr, 117
Watson. Matthew, 336, 337n
Watson, Richard, 389
Watters, William, 72n, 231, 232, 240n, 243, 245
Watton, Norfolk, 175
Watts, Michael, 43
Weaver, Richard, 49
Webb, Mrs Grace (née Gilbert), 277
Webb, Thomas (or John), 336, 337n
Webb, Capt. Thomas, 190, 222, 229, 239, 245, 277, 319, 411
Webster, Eleazer, 336n, 337n
Wednesbury, Staffordshire, 333
Wellington, Shropshire, 37
Wells, Samuel, 18, 27-28, 61n, 130
Werrill/Worrell, Thomas, 271, 275n, 276n, 284, 357
Wesley, Charles
  and the Church, 37, 352, 411
  hymnwriter, 406
  in Ireland, 195-96
  marriage and family, 92, 93, 101, 111, 174-5, 447
  and the preachers, 157, 160, 227, 292, 295, 297, 303, 322, 331, 332-3, 335-39, 342-43
  quoted, 1, 57, 65, 108, 135, 244, 335-336, 352, 367, 368, 385
  other refs: 7, 24-5, 99, 212, 348, 358, 396, 398
Wesley, John
  and America 12, 220-24, 228-29 231-33, 235-37, 239, 241n, 248-53, 353-55
  and Conference 153, 155-62, 164, 170-2, 209
  correspondence with preachers, 70-72, 139-40, 144, 198, 208, 210, 236, 249, 253, 269, 274, 300, 308-9, 396
  favouring some preachers, 94, 152, 155, 200, 211, 322-33, 331-48, 358, 376-77
  and finance, 148-9, 157, 165, 378
  in Ireland, 195-7, 204, 206-10, 287
  and lay preaching, 8-9, 19, 21-2, 354, 357-8,
  lodgings, 7, 30, 104-5, 318, 371, 389
  and preachers' wives, 92, 104-5, 112, 120-1, 161
  and overseas missions, 266-7, 269-275, 280, 286, 288-9, 357, 359
  and problems with preachers, 32-3, 67, 76, 102, 109, 227, 229-231, 240, 251, 253, 291-301, 304-6, 308-9, 311-4, 316-7, 320-1, 336, 338-47, 353, 411
  promoting younger preachers, 77-83, 167-8
  in Scotland, 182, 356-7
  and stationing of preachers, 12, 19, 26, 75, 81-2, 84-5, 162-4, 211-2, 215, 222, 443
  travelling with preachers, 32, 67-70, 107, 177
  in Wales, 174-77
  other refs: 101, 106, 110-11, 252, 352-59, 367-68, 385, 398, 413
Wesley, Samuel, jr, 335n
Wesleyan Methodist Association, 416
Wesleyan Methodist Magazine, 417
Wesleyan Reform, 415, 416
Wesleyan Takings, 14
West, John, 206
West, Robert, Sketches of Ministerial Character, 14
West, William, 199n, 206
West Indies, 265, 266, 276-80, 286, 357, 359, 361
  Conference, 287-8
West Tyrone, 200-204, 211
Westell, Jane (Mrs Allen), 102, 104n
Westell, Thomas, 33, 47-48, 51n, 336n, 337n
Whalley, Lancashire, 2, 4
Whatcoat, Richard, 49, 80, 249, 250, 251-52, 255-56, 263, 355, 378, 441
Wheatley, James, 298, 336n, 337n, 408
Whitby, Yorkshire, 137, 151, 303, 305, 320
White, Charles, 247n
White, Judge Thomas, 243, 244, 254

White, Bishop William, 353-54
Whitefield, George, 8, 22, 23, 24, 32, 62, 84, 92, 101, 127, 156, 221, 266, 319, 367, 410, 421
Whitehaven, Cumbria, 50, 187, 305, 323
    circuit, 148, 186, 341
Whitehead, Dr John, 7-8, 55, 324, 344-45, 414
Whitehead, Thomas, 347n
Whitfield, George, 415, 420
Whitford, Mrs Hannah (née Brooke), 317
Whitford, John, 84n, 316-17
Whitley, Francis, 79-80
Whitley, John, of Eldwick, Yorkshire, 79-80, 325
Whitley, John of Monaghan, 79n
Whitworth, Abraham, 233
Wick, Glamorgan, 408
Wicklow circuit, 214
Wigger, John, 256n, 263n
Wilberforce, William, 278, 380
Wild, James, 326
Wilder, James, 15
Wilkinson, Henry, 361n
Wilkinson, John, 329
Wilkinson, Robert, 61n, 85, 142-43
Williams, Enoch, 135n
Williams, Richard, 328
Williams, Robert, 12, 222, 229, 232, 245, 263
Williams, Roger, 303
Williams, Thomas, 135n, 195, 317
Williams family, of Wrexham, 176
Wilmer, Mary, 254
Wilson, Ann (Mrs Lumb), 279n
Wilson, James, 327
Wilson, Bishop Thomas, 4
Wilson, William, 61n
Wiltshaw, John, 107n
Wiltshire South circuit, 322
Winscom, Jasper, 36n, 84, 85, 90, 141n, 326, 341, 347
Wirral, 407
Wogan, Miss (Mrs Roberts), 102

women, 87-108, 144, 277, 283-4, 289
    American, 254
    and childbirth, 111-13, 140
    Irish, 208
    preachers, 33-35, 106-7
Wood, James, 44, 45, 145, 394n, 450
Wood, Thomas, 124
Wood, William, 361n
Woodhouse, Mary ('Polly'), 107
Woodhouse Grove School, 115, 116
Woodley (Derbyshire), 129
Woolf, Francis, 84, 325-26, 329
Worrell, Thomas, *see* Werrill
Wray, James, 266, 269, 275-76, 276, 276n, 280, 281, 359
Wrexham, 176, 177-78
Wride, Thomas, 72, 198, 292n, 308, 340
Wright, Mrs Dorothy (née Gibbon), 100
Wright, Duncan, 52, 68, 83, 85, 90, 100, 104, 183, 392
Wright, Richard, 222, 232, 234n
Wrigley, Francis and Elizabeth, 100
Wynne, John, bishop of St Asaph, 174

Yarm, 137, 226
    circuit, 137-8
Yearbury, Joseph, 222, 232-33, 234n, 305
Yewdall, Mrs Agnes (née Mackrill), 100n
Yewdall, Zachariah, 66, 70, 100n, 136, 146, 147, 408
York, 37, 145, 227, 317
    circuit, 139, 149, 408
Yorkshire, 304, 307
    East Riding, 42
    North Riding, 42, 50
    West Riding, 40-42
Young, Anne (Mrs Moore), 93, 104
Young, Edward, *Night Thoughts*, 400
Young, Isabella (Mrs Rutherford), 93, 112, 119, 207
Young, Samuel, 361n

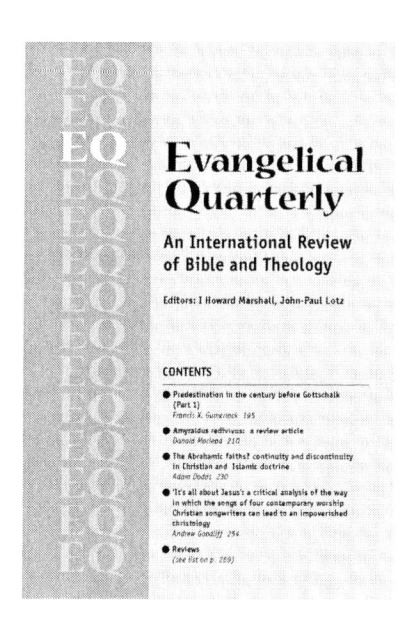

**Edited by I. Howard Marshall
and John-Paul Lotz
EVANGELICAL QUARTERLY**
*96pp., 210x145mm,
ISSN 0014-3367*
This well-established academic journal includes articles on a wide variety of biblical and theological topics. Books of current interest are reviewed in depth by well-known scholars.
Edited in association with the London School of Theology.

**Edited by Denis Alexander
and Rodney Holder
SCIENCE AND CHRISTIAN BELIEF**
*96pp., 243x170mm (April and October),
ISSN 0954-4194*
Science and Christian Belief, sponsored by Christians in Science and the Victoria Institute, offers an important resource to all whose interests extend across the boundary between science and religion. Each issue contains two or three major features in addition to shorter articles, abstracts and book reviews.
Science and Christian Belief is also available in electronic form.

All USA and Canada subscriptions to:
EBSCO Subscription Services, P.O. Box 1943, Birmingham, AL 35201-1943, USA

All UK and other international subscriptions to:
Paternoster Periodicals, c/o AlphaGraphics, 6 Angel Row, Nottingham NG1 6HL, UK
Tel UK: 0800 597 5980 • Fax 0115 852 3601
Tel: Overseas +44 (0)115 852 3614 • Fax: +44 (0)115 852 3601
email: periodicals@alphagraphics.co.uk

Subscriptions can be ordered online at:
www.paternosterperiodicals.co.uk (non USA and Canada subscriptions only)
All orders placed via our website will receive a 5% discount off the total price.
Rates displayed on the website will reflect this discount.

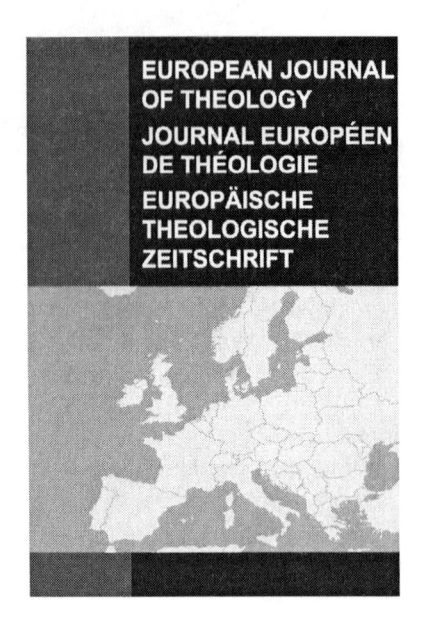

Edited by Pieter Lalleman
THE EUROPEAN JOURNAL OF THEOLOGY
96pp., 245x185mm (April and October), ISSN 0960–2720
This unique journal reflects the new Europe. Founded and edited with the aid of scholars and church leaders from many European countries, it offers to ministers, students and theologians a new European focus for their theology. Publishing articles and reviews in German, English and French, the *Journal* seeks to reflect the diversity of European evangelical theology.

Edited by Justin Thacker
EVANGELICAL REVIEW OF THEOLOGY
96pp., 210x145mm (Quarterly), ISSN 0144–8153
Published on behalf of the Theological Commission of the World Evangelical Fellowship. Some issues contain articles and reviews selected from publications worldwide for an international readership, interpreting the Christian faith for contemporary living, whilst others contain original material with a thematic focus.

All USA and Canada subscriptions to:
EBSCO Subscription Services, P.O. Box 1943, Birmingham, AL 35201-1943, USA

All UK and other international subscriptions to:
Paternoster Periodicals, c/o AlphaGraphics, 6 Angel Row, Nottingham NG1 6HL, UK
Tel UK: 0800 597 5980 • Fax 0115 852 3601
Tel: Overseas +44 (0)115 852 3614 • Fax: +44 (0)115 852 3601
email: periodicals@alphagraphics.co.uk

Subscriptions can be ordered online at:
www.paternosterperiodicals.co.uk (non USA and Canada subscriptions only)
All orders placed via our website will receive a 5% discount off the total price.
Rates displayed on the website will reflect this discount.

Studies in Evangelical History and Thought
(All titles uniform with this volume)
Dates in bold are of projected publication.
Condensed details are given for volumes published before 2004.

Andrew Atherstone
Oxford's Protestant Spy
The Controversial Career of Charles Golightly

Charles Golightly (1807–85) was a notorious Protestant polemicist. His life was dedicated to resisting the spread of ritualism and liberalism within the Church of England and the University of Oxford. For half a century he led many memorable campaigns, such as building a martyrs' memorial and attempting to close a theological college. John Henry Newman, Samuel Wilberforce and Benjamin Jowett were among his adversaries. This is the first study of Golightly's controversial career.

Andrew Atherstone is an Anglican minister and has worked for churches in Islington, Reading and Oxfordshire, UK.

2007 / 978-1-84227-364-7 / xvi + 334pp

John Brencher
Martyn Lloyd-Jones (1899–1981) and Twentieth-Century Evangelicalism
'An evaluation of perhaps the greatest British preacher of the twentieth century', David Bebbington.

2002 / 978-1-84227-051-6 / xvi + 268pp

Donald A. Bullen
A Man of One Book?
John Wesley's Interpretation and Use of the Bible

John Wesley claimed to be 'a man of one book'—the Bible. He was clear in his mind what the Bible meant and taught. Donald Bullen carefully explores the biblical hermeneutic of John Wesley. Using the insights of reader-response criticism we may comprehend better Wesley's understanding and interpretation of the Bible. The so-called 'Quadrilateral', rooted in American Methodism, gives further insight into Wesley's use of tradition, experience, reason, scripture and their inter-relation.

Donald A. Bullen is a Methodist Minister in Liverpool, UK.

2007 / 978-1-84227-513-9 / xxx + 230pp

Jonathan D. Burnham
A Story of Conflict
The Controversial Relationship between Benjamin Wills Newton and John Nelson Darby

Burnham explores the controversial relationship between the two principal leaders of the early Brethren movement. In many ways Newton and Darby were products of their times, and this study of their relationship provides insight not only into the dynamics of early Brethrenism, but also into the progress of nineteenth-century English and Irish evangelicalism.

Jonathan D. Burnham is the University Professor of Church Leadership, Palm Beach Atlantic University and Senior Pastor, Boca Raton Community Church, Florida, USA.

2004 / 978-1-84227-191-9 / xxiv + 268pp

Robert W. Caldwell III
Communion in the Spirit
The Holy Spirit as the Bond of Union in the Theology of Jonathan Edwards
This study explores the central connection Edwards drew between his doctrines of religious experience and the Trinity: the person and work of the Holy Spirit. Edwards envisioned the Spirit's inter-trinitarian work as the affectionate bond of union between the Father and the Son, a work which, he argued, is reduplicated in a finite way in the work of redemption. Salvation is ultimately all about being drawn in love into the trinitarian life of the Godhead. Dr Caldwell takes us through the major regions of Edwards' theology—his trinitarianism, his doctrine of the end for which God created the world, his christology, and his doctrines of justification, sanctification and glorification—to demonstrate the centrality of the Holy Spirit throughout his theology.
Robert W. Caldwell III is Assistant Professor of American Church History, Southwestern Baptist Theological Seminary, Fort Worth, Texas, USA.
2006 / 978-1-84227-422-4 / xvi + 212pp

Richard Carwardine
Transatlantic Revivalism
Popular Evangelicalism in Britain and America, 1790–1865
The focus of this classic text is on British and American evangelicals during the late-eighteenth century to the mid-nineteenth century, examining the effect of aggressive conversion techniques used by American evangelicals upon the revival movement.
Richard Carwardine is Rhodes Professor of American History, St Catherine's College, University of Oxford, UK.
2006 [1978] / 978-1-84227-373-9 / xviii + 250pp

James M. Collins
Exorcism and Deliverance Ministry in the Twentieth Century
An Analysis of the Practice and Theology of Exorcism in Modern Western Christianity
This study seeks to demonstrate that exorcism/deliverance ministry is an innately enthusiastic practice utilising Knox's classic study of Christian enthusiasm. The twentieth century is an ideal arena for such a study since it frames a complete lifecycle for this rite from its infancy during the early decades, through its heyday in the 1970s and 80s on to creeping routinisation by the end of the century. The study provides the foundation for future investigation of the manner in which enthusiastic experience is presented for apologetic purposes, the relationship between exorcism/deliverance ministry and millenarianism and the practice of this rite within non-Western churches.
James M. Collins is Pastor of Redhill Baptist Church, UK.
2009 / 978-1-84227-626-6 / xviii + 236

J.N. Ian Dickson
Beyond Religious Discourse
Sermons, Preaching and Evangelical Protestants in Nineteenth-Century Irish Society
Drawing extensively on primary sources, this pioneer work in modern religious history explores the training of preachers, the construction of sermons and how Irish evangelicalism and the wider movement in Great Britain and the United States shaped the preaching event. Evangelical preaching and politics, sectarianism, denominations, education, class, social reform, gender, and revival are examined to advance the argument that evangelical sermons and preaching went significantly beyond religious discourse. The result is a book for those with interests in Irish history, culture and belief, popular religion and society, evangelicalism, preaching and communication.
J.N. Ian Dickson is Senior Lecturer and Director of Postgraduate Studies at Belfast Bible College, Northern Ireland, UK.
2007 / 978-1-84227-217-6 / xx + 296pp

Neil T.R. Dickson
Brethren in Scotland 1838–2000
A Social Study of an Evangelical Movement
'A pioneering and noteworthy book', Mark A. Noll.
2003 / 978-1-84227-113-1 / xxviii + 510pp

Neil T.R. Dickson and Tim Grass (eds)
The Growth of the Brethren Movement
National and International Experiences
The essays in this book have been contributed in honour of Dr H.H. Rowdon, a teacher of several generations of students at the London Bible College (now London School of Theology) and a historian of the Brethren movement. The book includes reflections on the historiography of the Brethren, but it is their character and growth which form the principal focus.

Neil T.R. Dickson is the Convenor of the Brethren Archivists and Historians Network.

Tim Grass is a Fellow of the Royal Historical Society and Associate Tutor in Church History at Spurgeon's College, London.

2006 / 978-1-84227-427-9 / xiv + 272pp

Daniel W. Draney
When Streams Diverge
The Origins of Protestant Fundamentalism in Los Angeles
The importance of this study is that it examines the complex political and religious currents influencing the modern world. It focuses on the emergence of Protestant fundamentalism in Los Angeles, beginning with late nineteenth-century trends towards religious radicalism and culminating in the splitting of radical and moderate fundamentalist groups at the Bible Institute of Los Angeles in the late 1920s. Highlighted in this study are the complex tensions between mainline Protestants and an emerging sectarian trend among those who would become militant fundamentalists, which continues to shape Protestant religion today.

Daniel W. Draney is Adjunct Instructor in the field of American Religious History at Fuller Theological Seminary, Pasadena, California, USA.

2008 / 978-1-84227-523-8 / xvi + 266pp

James M. Gordon,
James Denney (1856–1917)
An Intellectual and Contextual Biography
James Denney is now best known for his *The Death of Christ*, considered a standard treatment of objective atonement understood in substitutionary terms. However there is a breadth and depth to Denney's thought, a richness and passion in his theological work, an attractive integrity and spiritual immediacy in his writing, that resists any reducing of his legacy to that of being an apologist for one aspect of Christian doctrine. This is the first major study of Denney to use the large corpus of Denney's unpublished theological papers and sermons held in New College, Edinburgh. These, together with Denney's published work, and wider biographical research, form the basis for this intellectual and contextual biography of one of Scotland's most attractive and forceful theological personalities.

James M. Gordon is Principal of the Scottish Baptist College, at the University of Paisley, Scotland, UK.

2006 / 978-1-84227-399-9 / xviii + 286pp

Tim Grass
The Lord's Watchman
Edward Irving

The theology of Edward Irving has been rediscovered in recent decades, and his contributions to our understanding of the person and work of Christ and the work of the Holy Spirit have excited considerable interest among both academics and leaders of the charismatic movement. But what made him tick? Based on extensive research and the use of newly-discovered family letters, this biography portrays Irving as first and foremost a pastor, formed by his upbringing in southern Scotland. Not only was he arguably one of the first modern charismatics, but he was also one of the last Scottish Covenanters.

Tim Grass is a Fellow of the Royal Historical Society and Associate Tutor in Church History at Spurgeon's College, London, UK.

2009 / 978-1-84227-426-2 / approx. 390pp

Crawford Gribben and Timothy C.F. Stunt (eds)
Prisoners of Hope?
Aspects of Evangelical Millennialism in Britain and Ireland, 1800–1880

This volume of essays offers a comprehensive account of the impact of evangelical millennialism in nineteenth-century Britain and Ireland.

Crawford Gribben is Senior Lecturer in Early Modern Print Culture, Long Room Hub, Trinity College, Dublin, Ireland.

Timothy C.F. Stunt has taught in England, Switzerland and the USA.

2004 / 978-1-84227-224-4 / xiv + 208pp

Mathew Guest
Evangelical Identity and Contemporary Culture
A Congregational Study in Innovation

In response to the decline of church attendance in the twentieth century the evangelical movement has, since the 1960s, sought a more profound engagement with its cultural context in an attempt to be more relevant. This volume explores how evangelical congregations have appropriated the values and media of contemporary culture in the propagation of a Christian message, and explores how this process has reconfigured the parameters of evangelical identity. It builds on an ethnographic study of St Michael-le-Belfrey church in York, a recognized leader in charismatic renewal, mission and evangelical innovation since the 1960s, exploring how a persistent tradition of cultural engagement may generate growth, while at the same time bringing about significant changes in the structure and function of the evangelical congregation, and in the social construction of Christian identity itself.

Mathew Guest is Lecturer in Theology and Society, University of Durham, UK.

2007 / 978-1-84227-440-8 / xxvi + 264pp

Khim Harris
Evangelicals and Education
Evangelical Anglicans and Middle-Class Education in Nineteenth-Century England

This groundbreaking study investigates the history of English public schools founded by nineteenth-century Evangelicals. It documents the rise of middle-class education and Evangelical societies such as the influential Church Association, and includes a useful biographical survey of prominent Evangelicals of the period.

Khim Harris was previously a Lecturer at the University of Western Australia, and is now the Manager of Education at Perth Zoo, Western Australia.

2004 / 978-1-84227-250-3 / xviii + 422pp

James Heard
Inside Alpha
Explorations in Evangelism
From small beginnings in the early 1970s, Alpha has grown to become a global success. Churches from across the denominational spectrum have enthusiastically seized upon the course, seeing it as the remedy for declining church attendance. Heard explores such claims through richly grounded qualitative research on six Alpha courses. He assesses Alpha's primary aim of converting non-churchgoers and its longer-term goal of spiritual maturity, and questions whether the Alpha programme is as successful as it claims at uniting evangelism and discipleship, mission and spiritual formation.

James Heard is Curate of All Saints, Fulham, London, UK.

2010 / 978-1-84227-672-3 / *approx. 300pp*

Mark Hopkins
Nonconformity's Romantic Generation
Evangelical and Liberal Theologies in Victorian England
A study of the theological development of key leaders of the Baptist and Congregational denominations at their period of greatest influence, including C.H. Spurgeon and R.W. Dale, and of the controversies in which those among them who embraced and rejected the liberal transformation of their evangelical heritage opposed each other.

Mark Hopkins lectures at the Theological College of Northern Nigeria in Bukuru.

2004 / 978-1-84227-150-6 / xvi + 284pp

Don Horrocks
Laws of the Spiritual Order
Innovation and Reconstruction in the Soteriology of Thomas Erskine of Linlathen
Horrocks argues that Thomas Erskine's unique historical and theological significance as a soteriological innovator has been neglected. This timely reassessment reveals Erskine as a creative, radical theologian of central and enduring importance in Scottish nineteenth-century theology, perhaps equivalent to that of S.T. Coleridge in England.

Don Horrocks is Public Affairs Manager for the Evangelical Alliance and a Research Associate, London School of Theology, UK.

2004 / 978-1-84227-192-6 / xx + 362pp

Kenneth S. Jeffrey
When the Lord Walked the Land
The 1858–62 Revival in the North East of Scotland
'A milestone in the study of religious movements', David Bebbington.

2002 / 978-1-84227-057-8 / xxiv + 304pp

William K. Kay
Apostolic Networks in the United Kingdom
Apostolic networks link congregations together through personal relationships. They centre around apostolic figures who have the ability to mobilise resources, make rapid decisions and utilise charismatic gifts. Networks of churches organised in this way can respond to postmodernity and cultural innovation. This book takes the story of the emergence of apostolic networks in Britain from the visionary work of Arthur Wallis through the charismatic renewal into the full-fledged Restoration Movement of the 1980s. It covers the events of the 1990s, including the Toronto Blessing, and contains fresh information based upon interviews with leading figures and new survey data, as well as re-analysis of historical documents.

William K. Kay is Director of the Centre for Pentecostal and Charismatic Studies at the University of Wales, Bangor, UK.

2007 / 978- 1-84227-409-5 / xxii + 378pp

John Kenneth Lander
Itinerant Temples
Tent Methodism, 1814–1832
'Takes us to the heart of sociological and ecclesiastical questions about Methodist identity', T.S.A. Macquiban.
2003 / 978-1-84227-151-3 / xx + 268pp

Donald M. Lewis
Lighten Their Darkness
The Evangelical Mission to Working-Class London, 1828–1860
'A splendid work', Sheridan Gilley.
2001 [1986] / 978-1-84227-074-5 / xviii + 372pp

R. Todd Mangum
The Dispensational–Covenantal Rift
The Fissuring of American Evangelical Theology from 1936 to 1944
This study explores how the fight between dispensationalists and covenant theologians started and how sociological factors were largely responsible for enflaming it. Surprisingly, most of the original protagonists on both sides were Presbyterians, and soteriology, rather than eschatology, was the original bone of contention between them. Understanding how the feud began may hold the key for rapprochement today.
R. Todd Mangum is Associate Professor of Theology, Biblical Theological Seminary, Hatfield, Pennsylvania, USA.
2007 / 978-1-84227-365-4 / xvi + 320pp

David B. McEwan
Wesley as a Pastoral Theologian
Theological Methodology in John Wesley's Doctrine of Christian Perfection
In this book, Wesley's theological methodology is uncovered from the perspective of his holistic vision of the God–human relationship being centred in love and defined by the qualities of trust and passion, rather than an intellectual comprehension of propositional truths about God. Accordingly, pastoral theology is much more important than academic, systematic theology for Christian experience and spiritual formation. In his theological method Scripture, reason, community ethos and Christian experience are utilised in an interconnected dynamic network, energised by the presence of the Holy Spirit. God is clearly the sole theological authority and the elements of the system are the means he uses for communication with his people. This interconnected system is explored through an investigation of the doctrine and practice of Christian perfection as Wesley offered pastoral guidance to the people called Methodists. This is a valuable contribution to the current interest in pastoral theology and theological methodology.
David B. McEwan is Academic Dean and Lecturer in Theology at Nazarene Theological College, Brisbane, Australia
2010 / 978-1-84227-621-1 / approx. 260pp

Patricia Meldrum
Conscience and Compromise
Forgotten Evangelicals of Nineteenth-Century Scotland
The book explores the history of Evangelical Episcopalians in nineteenth-century Scotland. Doctrinal differences with the Scottish Episcopal Church, particularly concerning evangelism, eucharistic and baptismal thought, are studied in detail against the background of the social history of this important group of churchmen.
Patricia Meldrum has worked for the Medical Research Council, Cambridge, and taught biology at the Cambridgeshire College of Arts and Technology, UK.
2006 / 978-1-84227-421-7 /xxiv + 416pp

Herbert McGonigle
'Sufficient Saving Grace'
John Wesley's Evangelical Arminianism
'A distinguished contribution to Wesley studies', Henry D. Rack.
2001 / 978-1-84227-045-5 / xvi + 350pp

Lisa S. Nolland
A Victorian Feminist Christian
Josephine Butler, the Prostitutes and God
Josephine Butler was an unlikely candidate for taking up the cause of prostitutes. This book explores the particular mix of perspectives and experiences that came together to envision and empower her remarkable achievements. It highlights the vital role of her spirituality and the tragic loss of her daughter.
Lisa S. Nolland is chaplain at an inner-city secondary school in Bristol and gained her doctorate at the University of Bristol, UK.
2004 / 978-1-84227-225-1 / xxiv + 328pp

Don J. Payne
The Theology of the Christian Life in J.I. Packer's Thought
Theological Anthropology, Theological Method, and the Doctrine of Sanctification
J.I. Packer has wielded widespread influence on evangelicalism for more than three decades. This study pursues a nuanced understanding of Packer's theology of sanctification by tracing the development of his thought, showing how he reflects a particular version of Reformed theology, and examining the unique influence of theological anthropology and theological method on this area of his theology.
Don J. Payne is Associate Dean and Assistant Professor of Theology and Ministry at Denver Seminary, Denver, Colorado, USA.
2006 / 978-1-84227-397-5 / xx + 322pp

Ian M. Randall
Evangelical Experiences
A Study in the Spirituality of English Evangelicalism 1918–1939
'A quite exceptional piece of work', Harold Rowdon.
1999 / 978-0-85364-919-9 / xii + 310pp

Ian M. Randall
Spirituality and Social Change
The Contribution of F.B. Meyer (1847–1929)
'A wide-ranging, perceptive, sympathetically critical study', Clyde Binfield.
2003 / 978-1-84227-195-7 / xx + 184pp

Dyfed Wyn Roberts (ed.)
Revival, Renewal, and the Holy Spirit
The revival of 1904–05 had a profound effect not only on Wales, but also on many other nations. This volume of academic papers from the centenary conference in 2004 explores the local and international impact of the revival as well as previous eighteenth- and nineteenth-century Welsh revivals. Contributors include David Bebbington and Mark A. Noll.
Dyfed Wyn Roberts is a Minister of Emmanuel Church, Anglesey, Wales, UK.
2009 / 978-1-84227-374-6 / xx + 286pp

James Robinson
Pentecostal Origins
Early Pentecostalism in Ireland in the Context of the British Isles
Harvey Cox describes Pentecostalism as 'the fascinating spiritual child of our time' that has the potential, at the global scale, to contribute to the 'reshaping of religion in the twenty-first century'. This study grounds such sentiments by examining at the local scale the origin, development and nature of Pentecostalism in Ireland in its first twenty years. Illustrative, in a paradigmatic way, of how Pentecostalism became established within one region of the British Isles, it sets the story within the wider context of formative influences emanating from America, Europe and, in particular, other parts of the British Isles. As a synoptic regional study in Pentecostal history it is the first survey of its kind.

James Robinson is a retired teacher whose doctorate, on which this study is based, was completed at Union Theological College, Belfast, Northern Ireland, UK.
2005 / 978-1-84227-329-6 / xxviii + 378pp

Geoffrey Robson
Dark Satanic Mills?
Religion and Irreligion in Birmingham and the Black Country
'A formidable research achievement', David Hempton.
2002 / 978-1-84227-102-5 / xiv + 294pp

Doreen Rosman
Evangelicals and Culture
In this seminal work, evangelicals' attitudes to music, art, literature and academic study are examined in the period 1790 to 1833.

Doreen Rosman lectured in the School of History, University of Kent, 1974–2001.
2009 / 978-1-84227-576-4 / approx. 250pp

Nigel Scotland
Apostles of the Spirit and Fire
American Revivalists and Victorian Britain
This is a book about American revivalist religion and the ways in which it impacted British Christianity in nineteenth-century England. The term 'revivalist' seems to have first been used in the period after the 'Second Great Awakening' in the United States. It designated those individuals and churches who sought to manufacture or create revival by human endeavour rather than, as in former times, pray and wait for a sovereign move of God's Spirit. Revivalism had a number of marked features which are charted in detail in chapter 1. It was inevitably characterised by emotion, excitement and religious exercises. Particular attention has been given to ways in which the different American revivalists understood revival and the methods by which they sought to achieve it. The book includes a focus on one or two female revivalists whose work has tended to be overlooked in some studies.

Nigel Scotland is a Tutor at Trinity College, Bristol, and an Honorary Research Fellow at the University of Gloucestershire, UK.
2009 / 978-1-84227-366-1 / xxii + 242pp

Roger Shuff
Searching for the True Church
Brethren and Evangelicals in Mid-Twentieth-Century England
Shuff holds that the influence of the Brethren movement on wider evangelical life in England in the twentieth century is often underrated. The peak of their strength occurred when evangelicalism was at it lowest ebb, immediately before World War II. They then moved into decline as evangelicalism regained ground in the post war period. Accompanying this downward trend has been a sharp accentuation of the contrast between Brethren congregations who engage constructively with the non-Brethren scene and the isolationist group commonly referred to as 'Exclusive Brethren'.
Roger Shuff is Pastor of Westerham Evangelical Congregational Church, UK.
2005 / 978-1-84227-254-1 / xviii+ 296pp

Mark Smith (ed.)
British Evangelical Identities Past and Present
Volume 1. Aspects of the History and Sociology of Evangelicalism in Britain and Ireland
Evangelical Christianity has been characterised by a remarkable degree of dynamism and diversity. This volume explores that diversity by investigating the interaction of evangelicalism with national and denominational identities, race and gender, and its expression in spirituality and culture from the evangelical revivals of the eighteenth century to evangelical churches and movements of the present. A second volume will investigate similar issues in relation to evangelical interactions with the Bible and theology.
Mark Smith is University Lecturer in Local and Social History, University of Oxford, UK.
2008 / 978-1-84227-390-6 / xvi + 280pp

James H.S. Steven
Worship in the Spirit
Charismatic Worship in the Church of England
'A pioneering volume', David Martin.
2002 / 978-1-84227-103-2 / xvi + 238pp

Peter K. Stevenson
God in Our Nature
The Incarnational Theology of John McLeod Campbell
This radical reassessment of Campbell's thought arises from a comprehensive study of his preaching and theology. Previous accounts have overlooked both his sermons and his Christology. This study examines the distinctive christology evident in his sermons and shows that it sheds new light on Campbell's much debated views about atonement.
Peter K. Stevenson is Director of Training, Spurgeon's College, London, UK.
2004 / 978-1-84227-218-3 / xxiv + 458pp

Kenneth J. Stewart
Restoring the Reformation
British Evangelicals and the Francophone Réveil 1816–1849
Stewart traces British missionary initiative in post-Revolutionary Francophone Europe from the genesis of the London Missionary Society, the visits of Robert Haldane and Henry Drummond, and the founding of the Continental Society. While British Evangelicals aimed at the reviving of a foreign Protestant cause of momentous legend, they received unforeseen reciprocating emphases from the Continent which forced self-reflection on Evangelicalism's own relationship to the Reformation.
Kenneth J. Stewart is Professor of Theological Studies, Covenant College, Lookout Mountain, Georgia, USA.
2006 / 978-1-84227-392-0 / xvi + 282pp

Rob Warner
Reinventing English Evangelicalism, 1966–2001
A Theological and Sociological Study
Grounded in empirical data and interviews with many senior evangelicals, this study explores the trends within evangelicalism in the latter twentieth century and develops new insights into the increasing diversity, conflicting identities and relative durability of the evangelical tradition. As such, this book provides a detailed theological analysis and a constructive sociological critique for anyone wanting a fuller understanding of the social and religious significance and the evolutionary dynamics of this influential and diversifying religious tradition.
Rob Warner is Lecturer in Sociology of Religion and Practical Theology, University of Wales, Lampeter, UK.
2007 / 978-1-84227-570-2 / xx + 284pp

Martin Wellings
Evangelicals Embattled
Responses of Evangelicals in the Church of England to Ritualism, Darwinism and Theological Liberalism 1890–1930
'Wellings' important book…fills a large hole in the history of modern Anglicanism', John Walsh.
2003 / 978-1-84227-049-3 / xviii + 352pp

James Whisenant
A Fragile Unity
Anti-Ritualism and the Division of Anglican Evangelicalism in the Nineteenth Century
'Enables the reader to emerge with a genuine understanding of the issues', Dale A. Johnson.
2003 / 978-1-84227-105-6 / xvi + 530pp

Paul Richard Wilkinson
For Zion's Sake
Christian Zionism and the Role of John Nelson Darby
This groundbreaking book debunks decades of misrepresentation of Christian Zionism and questionable theology, exploding the myth that J.N. Darby stole the doctrine of the pre-tribulation Rapture from his contemporaries. By revealing the truth behind the man and his message, Paul Wilkinson vindicates Darby and spotlights the imminent return of the Lord Jesus Christ as the centre piece of his theology.
Paul Richard Wilkinson is Assistant Minister at Hazel Grove Full Gospel Church, Stockport, Cheshire, UK.
2007 / 978-1-84227-569-6 / xxii + 308pp

Linda Wilson
Constrained by Zeal
Female Spirituality amongst Nonconformists 1825–1875
'A significant contribution to current debates on women and religion', Sue Morgan.
2000 / 978-0-85364-972-4 / xvi + 294pp

New and unscheduled titles:

Cary Balzer
John Wesley's Developing Soteriology and the Influence of The Caroline Divines
978-1-84227-522-1 / approx. 300pp

Grayson Carter
Anglican Evangelicals
Protestant Secessions from the Via Media, c.1800–1850

This study examines, within a chronological framework, the major themes and personalities which influenced the outbreak of a number of Evangelical clerical and lay secessions from the Church of England and Ireland during the first half of the nineteenth century. Though the number of secessions was relatively small—between a hundred and two hundred of the 'Gospel' clergy abandoned the Church during this period—their influence was considerable, especially in highlighting in embarrassing fashion the tensions between the evangelical conversionist imperative and the principles of a national religious establishment. Moreover, through much of this period there remained, just beneath the surface, the potential threat of a large Evangelical disruption similar to that which occurred in Scotland in 1843. Consequently, these secessions provoked great consternation within the Church and within Evangelicalism itself, they contributed to the outbreak of millennial speculation following the 'constitutional revolution' of 1828–32, they led to the formation of several new denominations, and they sparked off a major Church–State crisis over the legal right of a clergyman to secede and begin a new ministry within Protestant Dissent.

[2001] / 978-1-84227-401-9 / xvi + 470pp

James M. Gordon
Evangelical Spirituality
From the Wesleys to John Stott (Revised Edition)

Through a series of penetrating studies, contrasting the experiences and emphases of contemporary figures, Evangelical spirituality is placed in a living historical and cultural context. The variety of figures include the Wesleys, Edwards, Whitefield, Simeon, Hannah More, Spurgeon, Forsyth and Stott. In the process the study reveals the recurring hallmarks and enriching variety, the changing continuities and openness to growth and development that have characterized Evangelical spiritual tradition. This completely revised edition includes a new essay reflecting on contemporary developments, continuing change, and increasing variety in the expressions of Evangelical spirituality. In addition the core chapters have been revised, and referenced literature completely updated to take into account a growing field of academic study and wider interest.

2nd edn / 978-1-84227-361-2 / approx. 300pp

Joseph P. Gouverneur
The Third Wave
A Case Study of Romantic Narratives within Late Twentieth Century Charismatic Evangelicalism
978-1-84227-514-6 / approx. 300pp

Stephen R. Holmes (ed.)
British Evangelical Identities
Volume 2. Theology and Biblical Studies
978-1-84227-391-3 / approx. 300pp

Hugh Osgood
African Neo-Pentecostal Churches and British Evangelicalism 1985–2005
978-1-84227-633-4 / approx. 300pp

Mark S. Sweetnam
Each Waking Band
Studies in Dispensational Spirituality 1800–2000
Dispensationalism emerged from the ferment of prophetic speculation that stirred the evangelical world at the start of the nineteenth century. From these origins it spread to become one of the most widely diffused and culturally significant modes of biblical interpretation. In spite of its importance, scholarly engagements with dispensationalism have been limited. This volume provides a number of new studies by leading scholars of dispensationalism, which examine the nature of dispensationalist spirituality and dispensationalism's impact as a 'lived theology'.
978-1-84227-529-0 / approx. 300pp

D. Allen Tennison
Logic of the Spirit
The Shape of Pneumatology in the Pentecostal Movement in the United States 1901–1930
978-1-84227-673-0 / approx. 300pp

Barbara Waddington
The Letters, Diary and Journal of Edward Irving
978-1-84227-577-1 / approx. 300pp

Tim Walsh
'To Meet and Satisfy and a Very Hungry People'
The Origins and Fortunes of English Pentecostalism 1907–1925
978-1-84227-624-2 / approx. 300pp

Haddon Willmer
Evangelicalism 1785–1835: An Essay (1962) and Reflections (2004)
Awarded the Hulsean Prize in the University of Cambridge in 1962, this interpretation of a classic period of English Evangelicalism, by a young church historian, is now supplemented by reflections on Evangelicalism from the vantage point of a retired Professor of Theology.
978-1-84227-219-0 / approx. 300pp